MONETARY POLICY AND INFLATION IN SPAIN

Monetary Policy and Inflation in Spain

Edited by

José Luis Malo de Molina

José Viñals

and

Fernando Gutiérrez

for the Research Department
Banco de España

First published in Great Britain 1998 by
MACMILLAN PRESS LTD
Houndmills, Basingstoke, Hampshire RG21 6XS and London
Companies and representatives throughout the world

A catalogue record for this book is available from the British Library.

ISBN 0–333–71788–0

First published in the United States of America 1998 by
ST. MARTIN'S PRESS, INC.,
Scholarly and Reference Division,
175 Fifth Avenue, New York, N.Y. 10010

ISBN 0–312–21295–X

Library of Congress Cataloging-in-Publication Data
Monetary policy and inflation in Spain / edited by José Luis Malo de
Molina, José Viñals, and Fernando Gutiérrez for the Research
Department, Banco de España.
p.   cm.
ISBN 0–312–21295–X (cloth)
1. Monetary policy—Spain.   2. Inflation (Finance)—Spain.
I. Malo de Molina, José Luis.   II. Viñals, José, 1954–   .
III. Gutiérrez, Fernando, 1957–   .   IV. Banco de España. Servicio
de Estudios.
HG1135.M66 1998
332.4'946—dc21   97–38847
                                                       CIP

This book is printed on paper suitable for recycling and made from fully managed and
sustained forest sources.

10   9   8   7   6   5   4   3   2   1
07   06   05   04   03   02   01   00   99   98

Printed and bound in Great Britain by
Antony Rowe Ltd, Chippenham, Wiltshire

Contents

PART III   SPANISH MONETARY POLICY: CURRENT
SITUATION AND OUTLOOK

List of Figures

List of Tables

List of Boxes

Notes on the Contributors

All contributors except the following are affiliated to the Banco de España Research Department:

Alvaro Almeida: Financial Markets Group, London School of Economics, and Faculdade de Economia do Porto.

Matthew B. Canzoneri and **Behzad Diba**:   Georgetown University.

Charles A.E. Goodhart: Financial Markets Group, London School of Economics

Part I
Introduction and Overview

Introduction

José Luis Malo de Molina

AIMS OF THE BOOK

In 1994, the Spanish Parliament adopted the law on the autonomy of the Banco de España, which conferred full independence on the Bank for the conduct of monetary policy, and its primary aim of achieving price stability. In the same year, the Governing Council, elected under the procedures set forth in the new law, resolved to introduce an innovative programme of monetary targets based on the direct monitoring of inflation. These changes completed a long process begun almost 25 years ago of putting in place an active monetary policy aimed at the establishment of a stable financial environment conducive to anti-inflationary discipline, the stability of macro-economic equilibria and, finally, sustained economic growth.

In accordance with the various stages through which the Spanish economy has passed, and the evolving views of economists on the monetary policy transmission mechanism, various changes have been envisaged, analyzed and explained in the many studies published by the Banco de España in recent years. This book endeavours to discuss in depth the latest of such changes and the new design of monetary policy. It is based on a series of papers drafted by the Research Department and a number of external collaborators that encompass an intensive analytical examination of the underpinnings of the new scheme and a detailed description of the various empirical and operational aspects of its application.

The book therefore comprises papers of diverse orientation, both as regards the topics examined and the relevant methodologies. The overall aim, however, is to provide a broad yet detailed picture of the new design of monetary policy and the role it plays in combatting inflation. A general work plan set forth unifying guidelines, and these have been followed to ensure the necessary interaction between the several contributions without, how-ever, sacrificing either methodological consistency or specificity of focus in each of the areas studied.

The book is largely a joint production of the economists in the Research Department who have attempted with some assistance from external con-sultants, to give expression to the new monetary policy adopted for imple-mentation by the Banco de España under its newly granted legal autonomy. Coordination of the work was supervised by Fernando Gutiérrez and José Viñals. External collaboration bore fruit in the form of the chapters which were assigned to Professors Goodhart and Canzoneri. Although a work of this nature recapitulates or expands on some of the basic studies that supported the new monetary policy programme, it does not represent the views of the Banco de España in the broad range of topics covered. Each chapter reflects, as it should, the opinions of its author(s). This Introduction first sets out a number of general observations on the rationale of the anti-inflationary stance of Spanish monetary policy, and then goes on to discuss the design and content of the book.

THE ANTI-INFLATIONARY AIM OF MONETARY POLICY

Monetary policy has evolved rapidly in recent decades and the role of a central bank in a modern economy has become one of the main topics in the economic policy debate. The most controversial issues are not strictly technical matters, as they were in the discussions of the 1970s and 1980s concerning the design and instrumentation of monetary policy, but other more fundamental questions linked to the end targets of such policy and the means of achieving them.

The whole discussion about the ultimate aim of monetary policy in fact turns on the question of whether monetary policy is capable of achieving many-sided and complex targets, or whether it should be focused solely on preserving the value of the currency, i.e. price stability, as its main contribution to the smooth operation of the economy. Although no consensus can be said to exist either on this point or on many other related issues, a view does seem to be emerging that is strongly favored by the majority, and broadly shared in a variety of quarters, which maintains that it is impossible to achieve manifold aims with a single instrument and that monetary policy should give priority to the goal of price stability. This prevailing view is based on the conviction that, in the medium and long term, there is a complementary relationship between price stability and economic growth which makes it inadvisable to use monetary policy for purposes of stimulating activity and employment, as such effects are likely to be temporary and, moreover, prejudicial to long-term macroeconomic stability.

The commitment of monetary policy to price stability is based on the rational conviction that growth is determined by real factors and that inflation, over the long term, is primarily a monetary phenomenon. The development of these attitudes was also fostered by a growing awareness of the high cost of inflation. Systematic price increases create distortions in the decisions of savers and investors, unsettle resource allocation, and have a serious redistributive impact that negatively affects the incomes of the less protected segments of society.

Granting priority to the target of price stability says little about the most appropriate behavior in the various economic situations. The goal of price stability cannot mean, as some seem to have interpreted it, that monetary policy actions can be decided on independently of the economic situation. Attuning the tone of monetary policy to each concrete cyclical phase is a complex problem, the answer to which does not lie in simply invoking principles or final targets. In this area, central banks prefer not to be too explicit, so as not to raise the ghosts of a monetary activism having the potential to generate the same inflationary processes that afflicted the past. When this issue arises, there is a tendency to fall back on the notion that applying the final target of price stability in each instance is something that belongs to the sphere of the central banker's art or craft, without it being possible to make specific, concrete recommendations.

Nevertheless, it seems clear that starting from inflationary conditions, the target of price stability should be pursued with a measure of gradualism, as the inflation target set by monetary policy cannot be independent of the inflation rate at the outset. This is a result of the undeniable costs of the disinflation process, even though the complementary relationship between economic growth and price stability prevails in the long term. This statement concurs reasonably well with the usual practice of central banks facing inflationary processes and also with the philosophy underlying the convergence plans of the European Union (EU) countries. However, excessive gradualism could give rise to major difficulties in the management of monetary policy, with the attendant risk of creating situations in which there is a temporary inconsistency and loss of credibility. It is perhaps for this reason that the relevant empirical evidence does not seem to be highly favorable to excessive gradualism.

For those countries which have reached a stable path, an inflation target of between 1 per cent and 3 per cent seems satisfactory, as there is no clear evidence that a closer approach to zero inflation is necessarily better than the acceptance of moderate rates within this range. There is no reason why inflation, at low rates, should not reflect trends in the variable conditioning factors of supply and demand. It should not be forgotten that the proper functioning of an economic system requires constant change in relative prices and that information costs and uncertainty lead to asymmetric behavior, under which reductions in price levels are more costly than increases. A certain positive rate of inflation, albeit a small one, may be inevitable. This reasoning may explain why no central bank has succeeded in maintaining a pattern of absolute price stability or why in the major monetary unions there are persistent regional disparities in inflation.

However, to return to the thread of our argument, it should be stated that even defining a clear position on the target of monetary policy, though this is important, leaves open a number of questions that are to some degree controversial. One point in the discussion turns on whether or not an express mandate for the conduct of monetary policy is desirable. There is no uniformity in the legal framework of the industrial countries in this respect. Some, like Germany, clearly lay down a specific target for monetary policy, while others, like the United States, list multiple targets for the Federal Reserve, which is required to pursue both price stability and full employment. As is well known, the statutes of the European System of central banks and the reforms being undertaken by the European central banks are patterned on the German model.

There is a growing conviction that an explicit mandate for price stability enhances the functioning of an economy. This conviction is based both on a comparative analysis of the various experiences with specific programmes, and above all on the analytical results of the several theoretical models supporting the optimality of strategies oriented toward the medium and long terms that avoid the problems arising from temporary inconsistency as a result of the desire to achieve complex targets in changing environments. Setting price stability as a monetary policy target – an easily understood target which is, in principle, consistent over time – has the advantage of favoring credibility and the control of monetary policy itself, thereby increasing its efficiency and lowering the possible costs associated with a stabilizing strategy.

Once a mandate with these features has been adopted, the question arises as to whether or not it should be expressed in a programme of monetary policy instrumentation with rules precisely defining the response of the monetary authorities in each particular instance. The theoretical models that attempt to show the superiority of pre-established rules to discretionary action on the part of the authorities have a long tradition in economic monetary theory. Nevertheless, it cannot be said that the results obtained in various attempts to design monetary policy based on the automatic application of rigid rules of conduct have been fully satisfactory. It is common knowledge that many countries have tried, at one time or another, to apply relatively strict rules regarding the growth of monetary or credit aggregates, or exchange rate trends. In neither case, however, has it been possible to conduct affairs using automatic controls to the desired extent. Although monetary or exchange targets have always played an important part in the implementation of monetary polices, their pursuit has always required generous amounts of interpretation and discretionary behavior on the part of the central banks.

Taking into account the many factors of instability or simple volatility existing in today's financial markets, which are highly deregulated, open to full international mobility and rapidly innovating, the application of rigid rules to a given financial variable is virtually impossible, and in any case may generate distortions. An element of interpretation or discretionary action is inevitable. The various types of rules which have been applied have generally proven to be – with the notable exception of countries which have adopted the 'currency board' model – a rule of conduct that, in the view of the markets and agents, links monetary policy actions to the desired final targets, rather than an automatic response mechanism.

If it is not possible to adopt self-activating rules that mechanically reflect the explicit commitment to price stability, other mechanisms must be devised to ensure that the authorities do not deviate from the target when acting within the permitted margin of discretion. The institutional provisions governing the form of the central bank and its decision-making bodies thus become a matter of crucial importance.

AUTONOMY OF THE CENTRAL BANK

Central banks should be clearly separated from government in general, given the inclination of governments faced with the political costs involved in raising taxes or reducing expenditure to resort to the ostensibly less expensive way of paying their bills by printing more money. Coupled with this standard justification is the need to keep monetary policy from direct exposure to the pressures generated by specific sectoral interests, the agreements arising in connection with electoral cycles, or fluctuations in public opinion, which do not always allow sufficiently for longer-term repercussions. Placing the central bank at a certain distance from the political process, and protecting it under the proper institutional provisions, helps its decision-making bodies adhere to criteria based on medium and long-term targets.

This kind of separation from the government is what is generally understood by central bank 'independence' or 'autonomy'. The scope of central bank autonomy as regards economic policy responsibilities involves two different areas. First, central banks should be free from the distortions arising from government financing. This means that government, in the broadest sense, should abstain from any type of central bank financing and from the use of the various special financing mechanisms in the remainder of the financial system. Thus the instruments of monetary policy, such as reserve requirements or interest rates, should be used neither as a collection mechanism nor as a substitute for subsidies that ought to be identified as such in state budgets. Without orthodox financing of the public deficit, it is not possible to profess effective autonomy in the conduct of monetary policy. Second, central banks should have considerable room for manoeuvre in outlining monetary policy, and in setting targets and identifying the various instruments to be used to achieve them. The performance of these broad monetary policy duties is inevitably influenced by the government's economic activities; the assigned tasks do not eliminate the need for a degree of coordination. They also make it necessary for the central bank to act in an advisory capacity *vis-à-vis* the government on economic policy matters.

A proper legal and institutional structure that provides the required degree of autonomy may be extremely useful, but it should not be regarded as the sole solution to all the problems of an efficient anti-inflationary policy, as these problems frequently have their roots in the organization of the economic system and in the habits of economic agents. Over and above legal structure, the autonomy of a central bank depends on its actual room for manoeuvre. This is determined not only by provisions of law, but also, and primarily, by a body of rules of conduct which establish, either tacitly or explicitly, relations with other social bodies and government agencies. In actual fact, although its formal independence may be guaranteed a central bank may act with relative independence only if there is an adequate social consensus regarding the importance of preserving economic stability as a target. It is therefore unwise to encourage the idea that central bank autonomy may, on its own, solve complex problems that are rooted in economic agents' cultural background and in the structural deficiencies of an economy.

THE SPANISH EXPERIENCE

All these ideas have been implicit in the development of Spanish monetary policy in recent decades and have taken shape in the amended programme of monetary targets introduced on the occasion of the legal autonomy of the Banco de España. This book attempts to explain them in comprehensive detail. However, it is not only ideas which have helped bring this new direction to fruition. The conditions under which the Spanish economy developed during these years have also made a fundamental contribution.

The strong arguments in favor of price stability as an essential requirement for sustained growth have been buttressed by the constant problems generated by the traditional inflationary biases of the Spanish economy, i.e. recurrent severe recessions and a tendency to widespread and persistent unemployment. Episodes of runaway inflation have invariably metamorphosed into deep recessions, and these have entailed serious delays in a gradual closing of the prosperity gap with the core European economies, as well as rapid loss of the jobs created during the preceding phase of expansion.

These costs were becoming increasingly apparent as the Spanish economy moved toward integration with an area characterized by more solidly established levels of macroeconomic stability, levels which are among the chief features of its programmed targets. In this sense, Spanish participation in the various stages of the European integration process has been a sharp spur for the adoption of stability guidelines in the orientation of macroeconomic policy, especially in view of the impact of the full liberalization of capital

movements and the influence of the convergence requirements for participation in the Monetary Union, which will involve the adoption of a single
currency in a framework of monetary stability.

Advancement of this project has greatly heightened the sensitivity of
markets and economic agents to price performance in all the economies of
the region, even to the point of causing a change of economic policy regime
in those countries with less well established stability, as markets in this new
context tend to penalize vigorously any divergent impulses they perceive.
Regardless of the final schedule for Monetary Union and the point at which
each country is in a position to join it, the forces unleashed make it necessary
for all the countries concerned to adopt a regime of monetary stability. This
has become a prerequisite for remaining competitive in the single market,
ensuring sustainable, job-creating growth, and for living free from excessive
shocks, with the effects of intense capital mobility.

From this standpoint, it should be borne in mind that central bank
independence is one of the basic requirements for incorporation into the
Monetary Union. It was also one of the fundamental criteria underlying the
law on the autonomy of the Banco de España, the wording of which meets
not only the general requirements of the Treaty, but also the model of the
statutes of the European System of central banks included in the relevant
protocol.

The Government and Parliament of Spain understood that meeting the
pertinent treaty requirements before the prescribed deadline would foster
stability of the economy and its capacity for convergence. The law thus
conferred exclusive competence and responsibility on the Banco de España
for defining and implementing monetary policy, clearly stating that the basic
aim of said monetary policy was to ensure price stability, the ultimate reason
for granting autonomy to the Bank.

This institutional change, the most far-reaching revision since a central
bank was established in Spain, consolidated a number of traits that are
essential to efficient monetary policy, which had been gradually emerging
in measures of diverse scope during recent years. A case in point was the
need to eliminate the distortions caused by inconsistent mechanisms for
public sector financing. The gradual suppression of the various types of
special financing, which entailed so many obstacles to efficient monetary
controls, led to the abolition of any kind of monetary financing for the public
sector, and also to a downward revision of reserve requirements to levels
appropriate to their strictly monetary functions, as they ceased to be used as
a covert tax.

Relinquishing the traditional approach of setting intermediate targets for
a broad monetary aggregate, which the Banco de España had been applying
uninterruptedly since the end of the 1970s, in favor of a new design based on
the direct pursuit of inflation targets, was also an answer to the difficulties

and inadequacies of the formulas used up until then. As discussed at length
in this book, simplifying the extensive literature on the subject, the Spanish
experience sheds considerable light on the problems involved in pursuing a
quantitative target for monetary aggregates, particularly when ongoing
changes in the regulatory and fiscal framework continue to alter the determining factors in agents' portfolio decisions. These difficulties have tended
to increase as innovative financial products have proliferated and further
blurred the forever elusive line of demarcation for liquidity, while the liberalization of capital movements has reduced the relevance of the geographical
location of asset holdings and increased the ambiguity of the very concept of
an economy's liquidity.

This however does not mean that with the sources of information available
today – and coverage in the financial area is particularly complete – we
cannot analyze with relative accuracy the evolution of the various concepts
of liquidity deemed appropriate and their relation to the most important
macroeconomic variables, mainly nominal spending. The Spanish experience
seems to illustrate the difficulty of counting on the future stability of relationships, estimated at any given moment using data based on past experience, between the various definitions of money and the behavior of the
variables it is hoped to influence. This problem has an effect above all on
how agents perceive the real reasons for monetary policy actions, and consequently on monetary policy credibility and effectiveness. When a monetary
target has to be constantly interpreted in light of ongoing financial developments which affect the relationship between monetary aggregates and prices,
and when, moreover, there are structural problems in the economy linked to
a lack of flexibility and competitiveness in some markets – which account for
the presence of deeply rooted inflationary biases – it becomes very difficult
to sustain over time the confidence of agents and markets in the anti-
inflationary stance of monetary policy.

The trajectory of the long held practice in Spain of fixing targets for a
broad monetary aggregate has been one of decreasing efficiency in transmitting the desired monetary policy signals and impetus. This has occurred
despite an ongoing effort to maintain the most appropriate definition of
the monetary aggregates used as an intermediate target and an explanation,
at any time, of the assumptions underlying the anticipated relationship
between the monetary aggregate and the final inflation target. These difficulties became particularly clear in the new setting created by the inclusion
of the peseta in the exchange rate mechanism of the European Monetary
System (EMS). New conflicts and dilemmas arose between monetary targets
and maintaining the newly assumed exchange obligations, and resulted, as is
common knowledge, in a series of traumatic devaluations which finally
produced a serious crisis in the monetary control system in force at the
time. Consequently, it is worthwhile analyzing EMS membership at some

length, and the conclusions drawn from it with regard to restructuring the design of monetary policy targets.

Including the peseta in the EMS was a strong bid to accelerate the convergence effort and to overcome, at the lowest possible cost, the divergent path which marked the recent history of the Spanish economy, in contrast to core European patterns of stability and macroeconomic equilibrium. It was hoped that EMS membership would introduce an element of discipline into the behavior of agents and the conduct of the various aspects of economic policy, and thus help to initiate the changeover to a regime based on respect for economic stability as a prerequisite for achieving other targets, such as economic growth, the redistribution of income, etc. In particular, the decision to maintain the accepted degree of stability would require the application of strict demand policies – mainly of a fiscal nature, as monetary sovereignty was severely limited by the margins of exchange rate fluctuation – which would avoid excessive expansions leading to a systematic real appreciation of the currency through accumulated inflation differentials. In any case, adopting fixed, but adjustable, exchange rate arrangements also offered the possibility of correcting any potential gaps in competitiveness through parity realignments, whose negative effects on credibility would be offset by the adoption of a suitable economic policy mix with which to move toward the convergence of inflation rates. It was likewise assumed that the new framework would offer adequate incentives for carrying out the structural reforms needed to achieve flexibility and efficiency in market functioning and set the stage for the desired change of regime. As a counterpart to the principle requirements arising from this commitment, it was hoped that an increment in credibility and confidence would strengthen the effectiveness of the necessary policies and ease their inevitable costs.

There is no doubt that the exercise had a number of positive consequences for the development of the Spanish economy, and these have been adequately stated by a number of scholars. Nevertheless, the subsequent behavior of the peseta in the successive crises of the exchange rate mechanism showed that fundamental aspects of the commitments and targets formulated as conditions for successful adherence to the System failed to be met. Although the peseta devaluations were prompted in part by external factors linked to general uncertainty about the Monetary Union and the sustainability of the parity grid existing at the time, they reflected above all an inadequate adjustment to the newly accepted arrangements. Expectations regarding the EMS were not met because the benefits provided by the System in terms of credibility were not used to accelerate the shift from a regime of macroeconomic functioning toward one based on price stability and the exchange rate; the necessary adjustments for this change were spun out in the area of wage increases, budget policy adjustment, and the readdressing of the balance of payments.

First of all, in contrast to what would have been necessary in order to remain competitive with the economies to which the exchange rate was now linked, the strength of the currency made it possible to sustain increases in real wages at relatively high rates. Exchange appreciation facilitated containment of the prices of imports comprising part of the working population's basket of consumer goods, while nominal wages and the prices of domestically produced goods and services continued to rise sharply.

Second, exchange rate stability prior to the EMS crisis made it possible to maintain a procyclical budgetary policy during the upward phase of the cycle, leaving most of the responsibility for containing inflation to monetary and exchange rate policy. Applying a globally expansive budgetary policy during the upward phase of the cycle caused public finances to deteriorate in terms of increasing the deficit and the high stock of public debt in proportion to GDP, in an economic situation in which the financial soundness of Member States had become a basic requirement for participation in the proposed Monetary Union and for an enhancement by the financial markets of the real possibilities of convergence among the various national economies.

Third, the sizable inflow of capital, which was sustained not only by the attraction of potential returns from the Spanish economy, but also by the combination of high interest rates and a stable exchange rate, made it easy to finance the balance of payments deficit on current account. Thus, setbacks were accumulating in the level of competitiveness while there were no sufficiently strong inducements to make the appropriate response either in the area of setting wages or in the defining of monetary policy.

From this perspective, the peseta devaluations under the EMS crisis were the logical consequence of a tardy and inadequate adaptation of economic agents' behavior and of decisions in some areas of economic policy to the requirements of a change of regime entailed by adherence to the EMS and the desire to participate in the Monetary Union. In this sense, the devaluations were a penalty imposed by the financial and exchange markets for the continued pursuit of divergent policies and practices.

Successive adjustments of the peseta's central rate in the parity grid of the Exchange Rate Mechanism (ERM) and a broadening of the fluctuation bands introduced as a result of the successive crises, overcame the recurrent episodes of exchange and financial instability of past years, and eliminated conflicts between the domestic and external targets of monetary policy. Nevertheless, the monetary control system remained in a relatively precarious position. The targets set for a monetary aggregate no longer provided a readily understood reference for the markets that could serve as a guide for implementing and explaining monetary policy decisions. The EMS experience had also shown that exchange rate stability depended on a complex set of factors, which the central bank was unable to influence directly, so that it could not serve as a nominal mooring place at which to anchor all decisions of the monetary authorities.

It therefore seemed necessary for the new powers vested in the Banco de España under the law on autonomy to rest on arrangements less vulnerable to the credibility problems that accumulated under the previous approaches. Under the circumstances, introducing a system for the direct pursuit of inflation targets offered clear comparative advantages, above all by lending visibility to the anti-inflationary commitment of the newly independent monetary policy and by making the grounds for decisions more transparent. Yet as will become clear in the course of this book, the new arrangements were not immune to the possibility of problems arising that are similar to those which undermined the previous system.

The chance taken in the change of approach was necessary but risky in view of the inflationary trends perceived at the moment of inception. Fortunately, satisfactory results were achieved during the initial application of the new strategy. The first benchmarks established for the behavior of inflation in the spring of 1996 were comfortably met, and the markets have regained their confidence in the stabilizing efficiency of the new monetary control measures. Nevertheless, the period covered is too short for a final judgement to be made. It must also be borne in mind that in economic policy not only does building a favorable reputation require steady effort and clear proof of consistency, but the capital accumulated at considerable cost over long periods may also quickly go up in smoke unless action is coherent under all circumstances.

The chapters in this volume show plainly the transmission mechanisms which intervene between the variables falling within the scope of monetary controls and the final behavior of prices and, therefore, the difficulty of implementing a system of direct inflation targets. The efficiency of the system depends on the response of an extremely broad set of variables to central bank intervention. These variables include a wide range of financial asset prices which have an impact on the chain of effects, such as substitution, income, wealth, liquidity, financing, and the creation of expectations, on which the effectiveness of monetary policy is based.

It would be inexpedient for the new system to give the impression that inflation is a variable which is effectively under central bank control, and that price stability is the exclusive responsibility of monetary policy so that, once entrusted to an independent central bank, the other components of economic policy need take no part in it. Nothing could be further from the truth. Setting an inflation target establishes only the basic principle of monetary policy actions and their frame of reference; unfortunately, nothing ensures that such actions are enough to achieve the established goals, especially if there is no effective contribution from the other components of economic policy, especially budgetary policy, as is pointedly emphasized in various chapters in this book.

Although this Introduction cannot claim to address, even in a concise manner, all aspects of the new monetary policy, these comments would be incomplete if it were not pointed out that abandoning the system of intermediate targets in favor of the direct pursuit of inflation targets does not mean that the monetary aggregates lose their status as leading indicators of monetary conditions, nor that exchange stability is being underrated as an essential component of the aim pursued by monetary policy. Nevertheless, all these matters are analyzed in depth in this book. They attempt to explain, with rigor, all aspects of the new monetary policy model and the grounds for its adoption.

STRUCTURE AND CONTENT OF THE BOOK

The various contributions are organized in 3 parts. Part I is completed by chapters by José Viñals and by Charles Goodhart and Alvaro Almeida.

Chapter 1 by José Viñals examines various issues that are essential for a proper understanding of the causes and effects of the inflationary process, and for assessing the contribution of monetary policy to price stability. This chapter pays special attention to the costs of inflation, examining their various sources, and the room for manoeuvre available to monetary policy for coping with inflation in both the short and long terms, with special emphasis on the constraints imposed by the economy's lack of flexibility. The chapter ends with a review of the recent experience of central banks in their search for effective anti-inflationary monetary policy strategies. It also sets out the various reasons which, in recent years, have led a growing number of countries to introduce legal reforms which make price stability the main goal of monetary policy and confer considerable autonomy on central banks.

In his chapter 2, Charles Goodhart of the London School of Economics, with the collaboration of Alvaro Almeida, conducted a comparative study of the various monetary policy strategies in an effort to determine the extent to which adoption of an inflation target influenced the conduct of central banks. Based on the experience of all the countries which have applied such a strategy in recent years, they analyzed the pertinent features and methods, noting the capacity of this strategy to maintain an almost unvarying rule of response, compared with the inevitable discretionarity of other approaches, which may permit a gain in efficiency owing to greater transparency and credibility.

For the authors, the key question in assessing the effectiveness of this new approach is whether banks that have adopted it have been able to respond sufficiently in advance, and with the necessary vigor, to the perceived risks of future inflation. In reviewing the various outcomes, they find that while monitoring inflation targets generally reduces the volatility of short-term interest rates and creates somewhat greater stability in the financial markets, the evidence that interest rate movements are able to check potential risks of inflation is inconclusive. This disappointing result, i.e. that monitoring direct inflation targets did not alter the conduct of monetary policy, needs to be qualified by the short period for which data are available, the consequent limited length of the relevant statistical series, and the preliminary nature of the empirical analysis carried out. As the authors of the chapter observe: 'It is still very early to draw robust and statistically significant conclusions about the effects of the new model on macroeconomic performance.'

The 3 parts that follow have been arranged with the intention of showing, first of all, the background to the change of model, reviewing various aspects of the recent course of Spanish monetary policy. Analysis then focuses on the new monetary policy design, discussing in detail all the issues related to the various indicators applied in monitoring inflation and establishing a decision-making rationale. The current situation is also examined, as is the outlook for instrumentation of the operational system. In Part III, several chapters deal with the complex question of the transmission mechanism of monetary impulses, combining a comprehensive review of the mechanism with a detailed analysis of the most relevant transmission channels, together with their most sensitive links.

The Trajectory of Spanish Monetary Policy

Part II of the book dealing with the trajectory of Spanish monetary policy opens with Chapter 3, written by Juan Ayuso and José Luis Escrivá that consists of a descriptive analysis of monetary strategy and control developments in Spain from 1973 to 1995. Although the pace of change has been steady on the whole, the authors decided, in the interest of clarity and simplicity, to break down the period into stages having relatively distinct features. While this approach involved the difficulty of assigning specific dates to changes as they occurred in the design of monetary targets, it had the advantage of permitting a sharper presentation of the type of monetary control strategy implemented at each stage. The period from 1973 to 1983 is defined as one in which the monetary control system was typical of an economy financially isolated from the outside world. The subsequent period, up to the inclusion of the peseta in the EMS exchange rate mechanism, is viewed as a period of transition, in which targets for a monetary aggregate were combined with the use of a reference for exchange rate behavior. Thereafter, the specific problems posed for monetary control by membership in the EMS is examined, with a distinction being made between the 'honeymoon' period, which took place in a context of extreme stability of the parity grid, and the turbulence triggered by the successive crises of the exchange rate mechanism. Finally, an outline is provided of the recent shift toward the new system of direct inflation targets.

In Chapter 4, Juan Luis Vega addresses the major question of the stability of the money demand function, given that, as is well known, the effectiveness of a two-tier system of monetary control, based on pursuit of a target for a monetary aggregate, depends fundamentally on a sufficient degree of stability in the econometric estimates of the demand for the corresponding aggregate to enable it to serve as a reliable reference for achievement of the desired final targets.

This chapter starts from the long trajectory of estimates made by the Banco de España Research Department in a steady and strenuous effort to determine, with sufficient exactness, the degree of stability required to maintain the role of M3 or ALP (liquid assets held by the public) as an intermediate monetary policy target. Although the results were satisfactory in the initial stages, it became increasingly difficult to achieve estimates offering reasonable expectations of future stability that were not contingent on variables beyond the control of the monetary authorities. The most recent estimates by Juan Luis Vega produced good stability properties, but their dependence on external interest rates to maintain stability of the function in a context of total capital mobility, revealed the vulnerability of quantitative targets for a monetary aggregate. This empirical finding was a major factor in the decision to abandon the traditional two-tier monetary control system.

Part II closes with a chapter in which Matthew Canzoneri, in collaboration with Behzad Diba, presents a stylized model that attempts to approach analytically one of the main problems of the new Spanish monetary policy. During his stay at the Banco de España on a year's sabbatical, Canzoneri realized that one of the chief concerns of monetary policy managers as a result of their new duties was the impossibility of achieving the monetary targets of lower inflation without an adequate contribution from fiscal policy. The model developed by Canzoneri and Diba fully covers this issue and shows that, within the limits of a macroeconomic model created using highly restrictive assumptions, only when fiscal policy actions ensure compliance with the solvency restriction on the public sector over the long term–meeting any shock that increases the level of public debt in relation to GDP with measures guaranteeing creation of the surpluses needed to maintain the solvency restriction in equilibrium – is monetary policy able to influence price trends in the desired direction. In other words, only when there are mechanisms ensuring sound public finances is it possible to synchronize successfully a monetary policy oriented toward price stability. Otherwise, it is budgetary policy which determines the inflation rate in contrast to a powerless monetary policy, which finds itself in the compromising position of having to avoid the inflationary effects attendant on a passive attitude to such a situation, while being unable to achieve the aims to which it had committed itself. Certainly this line of argument provides a sound, and relatively original, analytical foundation for both the criterion of public deficit convergence under the Maastricht Treaty – independently of the final figure arbitrarily selected as the limit on excessive deficits – and the stability pact proposed to ensure the success of the Monetary Union.

Spanish Monetary Policy: Current Situation and Outlook

Part III opens with Chapter 6 by Fernando Gutiérrez, describing in detail the new design of Spanish monetary policy. It first discusses the basic features of the law on the autonomy of the Banco de España as the general framework for the conduct of monetary policy. The author then goes on to examine the circumstances underlying the creation, beginning in 1995, of a new monetary policy programme based on dealing directly with inflation, and then gives an account of its most typical features. Finally, he provides a necessarily brief and provisional assessment of the performance of the new strategy since its introduction.

Adopting a system of direct inflation targets confers special importance on the monitoring and analysis of price trends. The following chapters therefore examine in depth the indicators used in diagnosing the inflationary and monetary situation and in providing a basis for decision-making in the new monetary control system. This begins with an introductory chapter (Chapter 7) drafted by Pilar L'Hotellerie-Fallois which investigates the data and instruments available to the Banco de España for the careful monitoring of price trends in the business cycle. This method of observation and interpretation is applied, together with a univariate treatment of price series and a study of the determining inflationary factors within the National Accounts framework. The chapter undertakes a meticulous description of the numerous series of price statistics available, giving special attention to their relevance as an indicator of the various aspects of the inflationary process. An explanation is also given of the selection of the Consumer Price Index (CPI) as a variable to which precise quantitative references are applied which define inflation targets more clearly.

Together with the various price series, other variables are examined that determine inflationary tendencies, including those yielding data on production costs – such as labor costs, import costs, the exchange rate, direct and indirect taxes, social contributions, and subsidies – and those yielding data on demand conditions – such as nominal spending and its distribution between the public and private sectors, the use of productive capacity, the output gap, etc. Finally, mention is made of the indicators available on inflation expectations.

The methods of analysis applied to these data include predictions obtained from various modelling techniques which are discussed in subsequent chapters, and forecasts based on the data in the various series – subject, however, to the accounting consistency requirement laid down in the System of National Accounts. The review of all these data and the methods used for a systematic arrangement of the signals indicating present and future price trends, includes a discussion of the methodological scenario for the regular reports on inflation which are published with a view to making monetary policy more visibly accountable.

From this perspective, the conventional use of the rate of change of a price index may lack the precision needed for a description of inflationary trends and a diagnosis of their tendencies, as the index is affected by changes in relative prices which differ from the generalized and sustained price rises proper to inflationary processes. This problem is examined in Chapter 8 by Luis Julián Álvarez and María de los Llanos Matea, summarizing the results of the extensive research routinely conducted by the Research Department in this area and which has been more strongly emphasized in the new monetary policy scheme. They discuss the various measures developed to capture those changes in the relevant price index which represent a steadier signal regarding the development of the inflation process (latent inflation and underlying inflation). Along the same lines, they examine the 'estimators of limited influence', which calculate the inflation rate on the basis of a weighted median or a truncated mean rather than the usual arithmetical mean. This reduces the weight of the extreme values which, in principle, may be contaminated by the changes in relative prices. The statistical approach is complemented by other measures of inflation obtained as a result of economic estimates that take into account data over and above those of the price series itself and include a number of restrictions originating in the propositions of economic theory, especially as regards the long-term behavior of the different variables. Thus, by including the interrelation between prices and the level of activity, the component of inflation that is independent of transitory fluctuations in the level of economic activity (latent inflation) or the component that arises from the disturbances that influence the inflation rate over the long term (permanent inflation) may be obtained. Both concepts are consistent with the view that there is no long-run trade-off between unemployment and the inflation rate.

As mentioned above, the abandonment of a two-tier system based on quantitative targets being set for a monetary aggregate having a stable relationship to the final variable does not mean that monetary aggregates have lost their privileged position in the analysis of a given situation and its adaptation to the aim of reducing inflation. There are two reasons for this. First, because the quantity of money in circulation – or, to put it another way, the economy's degree of liquidity – is a determining factor of the first order in the medium and long-term behavior of prices. Second, because the money stock, although it is not an exogenous variable, is more directly subject to the influence of the central bank than other variables having an effect on inflation.

Far from abandoning monetary aggregates, the new system required an expansion of ongoing analytical efforts in order to obtain whatever information they might yield about future inflationary trends. Chapter 9 by Alberto Cabrero Bravo, Jorge Martínez Pagés, and María Pérez-Jurado summarizes work carried out in this area, describing the results of 3 separate exercises. The first two assess the content of the existing monetary and credit indicators using the methodology of Granger's causal analysis and an analysis of the possible cyclical relation between these indicators and price behavior. The third consists of constructing an alternative monetary aggregate, weighting the individual assets according to their informational content regarding the future trends of nominal spending (Divisia Aggregates). The results seem to indicate that most of the aggregates examined are useful indicators for monetary policy, although not all to the same degree. There would appear to be evidence that the most liquid assets have a relatively greater informational content, as does credit to enterprises and households.

Together with price indicators and in addition to monetary and credit aggregates, application of the new monetary strategy requires the management of concise and well developed data on the conditions prevailing in financial markets and on agents' expectations regarding both the future conduct of monetary policy and inflation rate trends in relation to the identified target. From this standpoint, the progress made in yield curve analysis is extremely useful, as the term structure of interest rates provides information about market expectations regarding future inflation and interest rates. Chapter 10, written by Juan Ayuso and Soledad Núñez is devoted to an in-depth examination of problems related to the use of the yield curve as a monetary policy indicator. Their work shows the difficulty of accurately circumscribing the expectations represented by forward rates. Nevertheless, they indicate that the premia for maturity and inflation risk are small and vary little, and that *ex ante* real interest rates (calculated with estimated expectations of inflation) are relatively stable. Under these conditions, the forward rate curve may serve as a useful monetary policy indicator, as its shifts may generally be regarded as a reflection of changes in expectations, subject always to the prudence required when dealing with the possibility of identifying a variable which is not directly observable and may be exposed to a wide variety of influences.

The analysis of the various indicators for monitoring inflation ends with Chapter 11 by Luis Julián Álvarez, Fernando C. Ballabriga, and Javier Jareño which attempts to evaluate econometrically the forecasting capability of a number of variables that are determining factors in price behavior. The chapter presents an econometric model of multivariate forecasting for the Spanish economy based on a limited number of variables and quarterly intervals. This model was recently developed by the Banco de España using Bayesian methods and specific characteristics of time series analysis, to provide a representative framework for the empirical reality of the Spanish economy and to facilitate the forecasting of inflation, taking into account the interactions between the various variables.

The exercises conducted with this model seem to indicate that multivariate techniques help to predict the future behavior of inflation with greater accuracy than does consideration of only the past course of the series. The predictions obtained with the constraints of this model are more stable when new data is introduced than those obtained without the specific constraints of multivariate modelling. The results achieved seem to authenticate this model as an adequate empirical representation of the Spanish economy and endorse it as a useful additional tool for analyzing and forecasting inflation in Spain. A particularly practical feature of this forecasting model is that is shows the probable distribution of inflation rates forecast for each time horizon. This permits an evaluation of the likelihood of achieving the targets set and their development over time.

Once the various techniques used to monitor the final target have been discussed, it is necessary to supplement the general outline of monetary policy with a review of all the procedures, techniques and instruments used by the Banco de España in its efforts to achieve the desired targets. Eloísa Ortega and Gabriel Quirós have dedicated Chapter 12, the last chapter of Part III, to the current situation of, and the outlook for, the instruments of Spanish monetary policy. In the context of a general overview of the functions which individual instruments should perform, they describe and discuss those used by the Banco de España. In their detailed review of the instruments of Spanish monetary policy, the authors underline the key role of the liberalization of capital movements and EMS membership in the drastic reduction of the reserve requirement and in increasingly strict controls on short-term interest rates. These two issues may be regarded as the most significant recent changes in the operational procedures of monetary control in Spain, and were based primarily on the performance of open market operations, channelled mainly through 10-day repurchase tenders. The type of instrumentation adopted has both supported and favored the free functioning of both market mechanisms and price formation.

The ongoing adjustment of operational procedures to the steady improvements in Spanish markets and payment arrangements has been accompanied by the satisfactory development of the relevant instruments. The only problems of note are those created by the excessive reliance of credit institutions on liquidity lent by the Banco de España. Monetary tensions have occasionally arisen owing to a lack of sufficient collateral. Nevertheless, these problems, rooted in specific features of the course followed in the past, will gradually be solved as the required adjustments are made to the instrumentation procedures planned for the Central European Bank in the future Monetary Union, a description of which completes this chapter. Among the tasks involved in adjusting the array of Spanish instruments, the only significant difficulties arise from the need to include the private sector paper as acceptable guarantees for operations.

The Monetary Policy Transmission Mechanism

The final section of the book addresses various aspects of the infinitely problematic question of monetary policy transmission mechanisms. This issue has constantly occupied the centre of the debate on the part played by money in the overall functioning on an economy. Nevertheless, it has been extremely difficult to obtain empirical estimates sufficiently representative of the complexity of the multiple channels through which the operational instruments of monetary policy manage to influence the target variables. Research in this area has generally been conducted along two complementary lines. In the first instance, there is an in-depth examination of certain parts of, or links in, the transmission process, about which more information is considered crucial and concerning which sufficient data is available, even if such a partial focus means passing over the interactions with other transmission channels or links in the process. The results obtained in this way are always incomplete, and unfortunately, inconclusive, although they are extremely useful in identifying concrete aspects of the dissemination of monetary impulses. In the second case, an attempt is made to summarize the overall effects of monetary policy actions through the estimates of macroeconomic models, which may be regarded as an adequately reliable representation of the main rules and restrictions on the behavior of an economy, even at the cost, in this case, of a significant loss of data on many of the interconnected effects which combine to determine the overall result. Part IV of the book, results are presented from research conducted along both lines. Such presentation involves some gaps and leaves some blanks. Allowing for the difficulty of the topic, however, it offers on the whole valid and enlightening background on the major aspects of the transmission process of Spanish monetary policy. At the very least, it summarizes the best known patterns of conduct using the available statistical data and analytical instruments.

The detailed analysis of some of the most important links shows, first of all, the role played by financial intermediaries in transmitting monetary policy signals, both through their activities in issuing liquid assets, and above all, in connection with the fixing of interest rates for their assets and liabilities, which are extremely important in the spending and financing decisions of private agents. These problems are examined by Teresa Sastre in Chapter 13 on the role of the banking system in the monetary transmission mechanism. Banking institutions are noted as major providers of external financing and instruments for the placement of private sector savings – despite the development of non-intermediate financing markets – which confers on these institutions a leading role among financial transmission mechanisms, especially in view of the strong involvement of bank inter-mediation in all the lending and borrowing activities of the Spanish private sector. The chapter deals specifically with the factors which have influenced interest rate trends in Spanish banking markets since the latter were fully liberalized, in an environment of growing competition among banks. It also discusses the effect this has had on the efficient transmission of interest rate movements resulting from Banco de España intervention. Sufficiently con-clusive empirical evidence shows the influence of financial liberalization in terms of a more rapid and vigorous transmission of monetary impulses to both the cost of bank financing and the remuneration of bank liabilities.

The next link in the chain of monetary effects is the impact of interest rates on private spending in Spain, a matter addressed in Chapter 14 by Ángel Estrada, Ignacio Hernando and Javier Vallés. Two distinct methodo-logies are used. Under the first, in a partial equilibrium exercise which abstracts from the remaining channels of the transmission process, consumer demand and investment functions are estimated, with a distinction being made both between types of goods, and enterprises and families. These estimates, which include restrictions among the variables typical of neoclas-sical models, permit approximations to be made of the direct influence of the relevant interest rates in each spending component under review. The func-tions identified show the effect of interest rates both on household decisions regarding the purchase of housing and consumer durables, and on corporate investment decisions, although the estimated quantification of the direct effects of intertemporal substitution appears to be reduced. However, it should be remembered that this estimate refers only to the lower portion of a part of the total effect, which is also communicated through other transmission channels. The second methodology attempts to reduce the conditioning influences resulting from the explanatory factors of spending being regarded as exogenous variables. To overcome this limitation, estim-ates are used, in application of the methodology of auto-regressive vectors, from a reduced-form model which contemplates the possibility of interest rates being endogenous, and permits an approximation of the overall impact of monetary policy measures.

From the theoretical standpoint, the efficiency of credit as a transmission channel depends on the absence of ideal substitutes for bank financing for enterprises, and on the cost of external financing for enterprises actually being higher than that assigned to the use of funds generated internally.

Under such conditions, the effect conveyed by the supply of credit would strengthen the effect of the traditional channel of monetary policy transmission through the money supply, although with a differential impact on agents, the impact being greater on those who rely more on bank financing or who have more difficulty in providing suitable collateral. Generally speaking, this means consumers with low levels of net wealth and small-scale enterprises. The empirical comparisons made in the case of Spain suggest that monetary policy measures bring about changes in the terms of access to bank credit and generate a reordering of corporate liabilities. This would seem to confirm the effectiveness of the credit channel of transmission.

In Chapter 15, Juan Peñalosa examines the effect of agents' financial position on the transmission of monetary impulses. The underlying assumption of this approach is that the income and wealth effects of interest and exchange rate movements brought about by monetary policy, and the terms of access to credit, which are pivotal links in the transmission process, depend on agents' financial positions. From an analysis of trends in the financial positions of households, enterprises, and general government during the past 10 years, the factors may be assessed that facilitated or obstructed the transmission of monetary policy, bearing in mind such components as the composition and net balance of the financial wealth of each sector, the maturities of their financial balances, lags in the revision of the reference interest rates of the various instruments, reliance on bank intermediation, the possibility of substitution *vis-à-vis* the products offered by the credit system, etc.

The study shows that the financial position of the Spanish non-financial sector tends to favor the transmission of monetary impulses, owing mainly to the relative importance of the banking system in the intermediation of financial flows. However, there are noteworthy differences in the responses of each sector. Household sensitivity to monetary policy stems mainly from reliance on bank credit for the financing of major expenditures, i.e. for housing and consumer durables. These effects abundantly offset those that would arise from a strong credit position, which would tend to obstruct the transmission of monetary policy. Corporate sensitivity originates not only in a reliance on credit, which is lower for enterprises than for households – as their greater flexibility permits them to diversify their sources of financing – but above all in their debtor position and the relatively short maturities of most of their liabilities.

In the final Chapter 16, Javier Andrés, Ricardo Mestre and Javier Vallés analyze the transmission mechanism in a series of simulation exercises using a macroeconomic model estimated with a high degree of aggregation for the Spanish economy. The model contemplates an open and financially integrated economy in which the central bank sets the intervention interest rate in order to reduce the inflation differential with other countries. Using these simulations, inflation rate trends and the rate of growth of GDP in the base scenario are compared with the trends in the various alternative monetary policy scenarios. The compact and stylized nature of the model requires the sacrifice of accuracy in the representation of some of the transmission channels for the sake of an increased capacity for simulating overall effects. It then becomes possible to answer some of the most important questions about the process, particularly the response of demand to changes in interest rates, the importance of competitiveness in monetary transmission, and finally, the speed with which expectations are adjusted.

The model's main problem is that the level of nominal variables remains undetermined when the short-term interest rate is used as the operational variable for achieving inflation targets. This indeterminacy gives rise to a certain ambivalence in the theoretically possible anti-inflationary strategies. However, this ambivalence yields to the non-viability, in practical terms, of the alternative, which consists of trying to balance domestic and foreign inflation through immediate and permanent reductions in the interest rate. Once this alternative has been eliminated, the model permits a description, using various simulations, of the transmission of the effects of a temporary rise in the inflation rate, taking into account its impact on the exchange rate, competitiveness, and the path of growth.

* * *

The chapters comprising this book do not provide a full and systematic picture of all aspects of the new design of Spanish monetary policy. Nor do they ensure total consistency among the approaches adopted for the analysis of the component parts of the monetary control mechanism. Indeed, the complexity of the subject under study made it advisable, at the outset of the project, to abandon such ambitious plans. Nevertheless, the final results represent a broad and orderly review of the work conducted by the Research Department of the Banco de España with a view to establishing, applying, and improving the new monetary policy. They are published with the hope of contributing to a better knowledge and understanding of this policy, while enhancing, even if only indirectly, its transparency and effectiveness.

1 Monetary Policy and Inflation: From Theory to Practice

José Viñals

(Selected E31
countries) E52

INTRODUCTION

Inflation may be defined as a continuing increase in the general price level. As a deeply rooted characteristic of many economies, it receives considerable attention from the public, and is assiduously studied by economists. The experience of recent decades has given rise to the conviction that inflation entails sizable economic and social costs, and that controlling it is one of the prerequisites for achieving sustained growth. As a result, the authorities in a growing number of countries have recently begun to pay increasing attention to price trends and to tailor the conduct of monetary polices more closely to the achievement of lower inflation rates.

In some countries, this trend has crystallized in legal reforms establishing price stability as the primary goal of monetary policy, while at the same time granting extensive independence to central banks for achieving that end. In other countries, even if there have been no specific legal changes, monetary policy has been pursuing direct inflation targets in order to enhance the visibility of the authorities' commitment to price stability. Finally, even in those countries which have maintained their earlier legal norms and monetary policy arrangements, there has been in many cases a strengthening of the anti-inflationary orientation of economic policy, and particularly of monetary policy.

Public awareness of inflation, and the increasingly widespread gearing of national monetary polices to bring inflation rates down to acceptable levels, requires an in-depth analysis of the factors that comprise the inflationary process, and especially of the links between monetary policy and inflation in various time horizons. This chapter examines a number of questions which are essential both for a proper understanding of the causes and effects of the inflationary process, and for assessing the contribution of monetary policy to price stability. These questions are: (1) What are the economic costs of inflation? (2) How does monetary policy affect the course of inflation? (3) What are the most appropriate monetary policy strategies for combating inflation?

In an attempt to answer these questions, the remainder of the chapter has been organized as follows: it first looks at how the public perceives the costs of inflation. Then it examines the various channels through which inflation may generate economic costs, and provides a summary of the available empirical evidence as to their extent. Once it has been confirmed that inflation is economically costly, it analyzes the determining factors of inflation, distinguishing between the short and long term. It then examines the recent experience of central banks in the search for alternative anti-inflationary monetary policy strategies and explains why an increasing number of countries have in recent years adopted inflation targets, and why in many cases there have been legal reforms that enshrine price stability as the primary objective of monetary policy, while conferring considerable independence on central banks. Finally, the chapter summarizes the main conclusions and policy implications.

THE COSTS OF INFLATION

In the Introduction, inflation was defined as a continuing increase in the price level. 'Price stability' was also mentioned on several occasions, although not specifically defined. As price stability is an economic policy goal in most countries – and the primary goal of monetary policy in many – it may be well to begin this section by explaining what is generally meant by this term. It is, after all, precisely in the absence of such stability that an inflationary process begins, bringing economic costs in its wake.

In economic policy discussions, price stability is usually defined in a pragmatic manner. Indeed, far from being regarded as a situation of constancy in the price level, it is rather identified with an inflation rate that is low enough not to distort the decision-making processes of economic agents, either in the areas of production, saving, or investment[1]. In numerical terms, an annual inflation rate of between 1 and 2 or 3 per cent is considered as a reasonably approximate figure for what, in practice, is to be considered price stability (see Fischer, 1994).

There are a number of reasons why price stability should be interpreted in relative, rather than absolute, terms. On the one hand, it is statistically difficult to measure adequately the true evolution of cost of living standards through traditional consumer price indices. The consumer's ability to substitute cheaper goods for those which have become more expensive, the improvements in the quality of many goods, the continuous emergence of new products, and the opportunities to purchase similar goods at lower prices in hypermarkets and department stores tend to cause CPI changes to overstate statistically the increase in the cost of living by a magnitude that has been estimated in various countries at between 0.5 per cent and

1.5 per cent per annum.[2] On the other hand, in economies characterized by the downward rigidity of prices and wages, a positive inflation rate permits the necessary regular changes in relative prices to take place fluidly, resulting in an improvement in the overall efficiency of the economy.[3]

Popular Perception

Once it has been agreed that in practice price stability corresponds to a rate of inflation of between 1 and 2–3 per cent per annum, the next step is to ask how the public perceives the costs of inflation. A detailed survey has recently been carried out in a number of countries (see Schiller, 1996) with a view to answering this question. The survey shows that the public regards inflation as globally harmful inasmuch as it lowers the standard of living. However, the survey results are much less clear with regard to how the public views the specific channels through which inflation entails costs.

The popular perception of the economically costly nature of inflation has frequently been criticized on the grounds that economic agents – on the basis of their experience in stagflationary periods – may wrongly ascribe to inflation those costs which actually come from lower economic growth. If this were true, it would not be inflation as such which is in fact costly but rather the sluggish pace of economic activity. Nevertheless, the validity of this criticism may be disputed. Since the stagflationary periods that occurred in the mid-1970s and early 1980s are now – fortunately – relatively remote in time, it does not seem reasonable to assume that memories of such periods are behind present popular perceptions that inflation undermines standards of living.

From a different standpoint, it has also been argued (Katona, 1976) that the popular view of inflation as deleterious to the standard of living has its roots in the existence of money illusion, which would cause people to regard the increase in nominal wages accompanying the inflationary process not as a result thereof, but rather as an acknowledgement of their professional merits. In contrast, the steady increase in the general level of prices would be ascribed to the inflationary process which, in this way, would end up by undermining purchasing power. While this logic could be a plausible explanation of the popular perception of the costs of inflation in the short term, it does not appear to offer an adequate explanation of such costs in the medium term, a time frame in which money illusion is seriously weakened.

To summarize, although it seems to be true that the perceived costliness of inflation is quite widespread, the surveys conducted to date do not adequately explain what are the actual reasons behind this perception. From a strictly economic standpoint, it is thus essential to provide a theoretically convincing and empirically meaningful explanation of the various ways in which inflation erodes the public's standards of living.

Diversity of Costs and their Actual Importance

In recent decades, particularly as a result of the generalised increase in inflation rates in many countries following the oil shocks of the mid-1970s and early 1980s, a considerable number of theoretical models have been constructed that are able to establish the adverse effect of inflation on people's standard of living and welfare.[4] However, it is only recently that these conceptual advances have been coupled with empirical evidence corroborating that the costs of inflation are indeed significant. Consequently, we shall now describe briefly the main costs associated with inflation, and then summarize the available empirical evidence concerning their magnitude.

In examining the costs of inflation, a distinction should be made between those costs of inflation that are anticipated and those that are not. Anticipated costs of inflation usually arise in the following ways.

Firstly, since in efficient financial markets inflationary expectations are incorporated into interest rates, inflation raises the opportunity costs of maintaining liquid balances and reduces the demand for money. This effect (shoe leather costs), with which the names of Bailey (1956) and Friedman (1969) are associated, makes inflation costly because the demand for money is reduced below what is socially optimal, thus entailing a welfare loss. Nevertheless, the empirical evidence on the magnitude of this cost suggests that, although it may be considerable in economies with high or soaring inflation rates, it is relatively small in economies with moderate or low inflation rates.[5]

Secondly, it is argued that even fully anticipated inflation is socially costly because it obliges firms to revise the prices of their products, and thus incur the corresponding administrative costs (menu costs). Although these costs may be sizable in economies with high or soaring inflation rates, in which firms must frequently revise prices, it is hardly likely that such costs are very important in economies with moderate or low rates of inflation, where most price changes occur only once a year (see Blinder, 1993).

It is clear from the above that if inflation costs were limited solely to those mentioned, it would be extremely difficult to explain the widespread perception that inflation is harmful in countries with low or moderate rates of inflation. Hence it is necessary to consider those costs that arise as a result of the impact of inflation within a legal and contractual framework which is not fully adapted to it, and also the costs linked to the uncertainty which generally is associated with the inflationary process.

One of the most important economic costs entailed by inflation, even if it is fully anticipated, consists of the disincentives and inefficiencies that its interaction with the tax system introduces into the functioning of the economy (Feldstein, 1983). Indeed, the fact that tax systems in most countries are not adapted to offsetting the effects of inflation on effective tax rates has major consequences. As is well known, in progressive systems, the lack of full indexation of personal income taxation causes inflation to push taxpayers steadily toward higher tax brackets, thus raising the tax rate effectively applied to real income. As regards corporate taxation, inflation reduces real after-tax profitability since the tax falls not only on real profits, but also on the additional profits which in principle serve to compensate investors for expected inflation. Lower real after-tax profitability, in turn, discourages investment. As distinct from what happens in the case of other costs, those arising from the interaction between the tax system and inflation have a strong economic impact. Studies which have attempted to approximate such costs in various countries[6] tend to confirm their significance even in economies with moderate or low inflation, as magnitudes are reached which tend to exceed 1 per cent of GDP per year (see Feldstein, 1996).

So far, the costs identified have been those associated with anticipated inflation. In practice, however, inflationary processes are usually accompanied by a notable degree of volatility and uncertainty, both as regards changes in the inflation rate and in the structure of relative prices.[7] The most immediate effect of such uncertainty is the inclusion of an inflation risk premium in interest rates which has a negative influence on investment decisions. The impact of uncertainty on the economy's relative price structure, both at home and abroad, then generates distortions in the functioning of the price system which reduce the efficiency of resource allocation. The reason for these efficiency losses – first shown by Phelps (1970) and Lucas (1973) – stems from the fact that economic agents' uncertainty as to whether the price changes they observe correspond to actual changes in relative prices, or whether they are the result of changes in the general price level, is a factor in these agents' decisions. Taken together, these problems ultimately induce economic agents to earmark more resources for protection against inflation – to the detriment of productive activities. It should also be mentioned that it is difficult to approximate empirically the magnitude of the costs linked to the uncertainty of the inflationary process, even if such costs are assumed to be considerable.

Finally, it should be noted that when inflation is not anticipated or when, if anticipated, it affects the public's economic entitlements and obligations, it entails a significant redistribution of income and wealth which tends to affect adversely those segments of society having fewer resources with which to protect themselves against inflation. Although it is very difficult to obtain estimates of the magnitude of this cost, they are likely to be very significant.

Having identified some of the main theoretical ways in which the economic costs of inflation manifest themselves, we now need to determine the actual size of such costs. As already mentioned, given the considerable difficulty of empirically approximating the magnitude of each of these costs individually and the desirability of conducting a comprehensive analysis, there have recently been attempts to evaluate the overall economic impact of inflation in the medium term. These analyses start from the assumption that regardless of the ways in which inflation adversely affects an economy, it ultimately undermines the growth of *per capita* income – either temporarily or permanently – by reducing the rate of factor accumulation and/or the efficiency with which these factors are applied in productive processes. Thus, for instance, to the extent that inflation reduces the after-tax rate of return on productive capital, there will be a slower capital formation. Moreover, insofar as inflation distorts the functioning of the price system, a less efficient allocation of resources is also to be expected. For these reasons, it seems appropriate to proxy the costs of inflation by their medium term impact on the growth of *per capita* income.

In recent years, numerous empirical studies have been conducted with a view to determining whether inflation is associated with a reduction in either the level or the rate of growth of *per capita* income. These studies are generally based on econometric estimates of equations in which the level of per capita income or its medium-term growth rate depends on the average inflation rate and other macroeconomic variables. However, studies differ notably on their degree of consistency with the basic postulates of growth theory and on the type of macroeconomic variables included.[8]

Given the diversity of approaches, geographical coverage, and time frame of the above mentioned empirical studies, it should come as no surprise that their results differ considerably. Many authors find a negative medium-term relationship between economic growth and inflation for various countries and periods (e.g. Fischer, 1991; De Gregorio, 1996; and Barro, 1995) which leads them to conclude that inflation is harmful for the economy in the medium term. By contrast, other authors (Levine and Renelt, 1992 and Levine and Zervos, 1993) find that the relationship between growth and inflation is not robust to changes in econometric specification. Recently, however, it appears that the available evidence increasingly tends to support the view that, in general, inflationary processes entail significant economic costs in industrial countries (cf. De Gregorio, 1996). Still, differences remain as to the size of such costs and their significance in countries that have achieved moderate rates of inflation (Barro, 1995).

With a view to supplementing and updating the existing empirical evidence on the medium-term relationship between inflation and growth (cf. Figure 1.1), Andrés and Hernando (1996) recently conducted a study which is solidly anchored in growth theory and which covers OECD countries in the period 1960–93. They found that inflation entails significant costs and that these costs exist both in countries with below-and above-average inflation. Specifically, the authors conclude that an average increase in

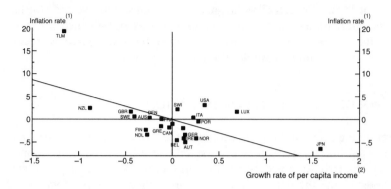

Figure 1.1 Growth of *per capita* income and inflation rates, 1961–93: components not explained by *per capita* income

Notes: 1 Residuals of linear regression of inflation rate on the level of initial *per capita* income.

2 Residuals of linear regression of the growth rate of *per capita* income on the level of initial *per capita* income.

Source: Andrés and Hernando (1996).

inflation of 10 percentage points would have reduced the growth of real *per capita* income in the average OECD country by 0.6 percentage points per annum in the period 1961–93. Furthermore, such annual costs, as explained in Andrés, Hernando, and Krüger (1996), may reach between 0.8 and 1.6 percentage points once the bias resulting from not taking into account the influence of the exchange rate regime is corrected.[9]

To sum up, a sensible reading of the available empirical evidence for industrial countries would seem to be that inflation is in no case beneficial, that it is generally associated with lower economic growth rates over prolonged periods, and that such costs exist in countries with both moderate and low rates of inflation.

Admittedly, most of the existing empirical studies may be criticized owing to the fact that inflation and growth are mutually determined variables in a general equilibrium framework, with the relationship between them finally depending on the macroeconomic policies applied in the countries involved. However, the results generated both by studies having a theoretical framework firmly anchored in growth theory and by those using statistical procedures to take into account the endogeneity of inflation[10] generally validate the assumption that countries which enter into an inflationary process never see an improvement in their growth perspectives and have a high probability of experiencing a deterioration in their economic growth rates over long periods of time. Consequently, it may be argued that the empirical evidence is consistent with the widespread public perception that inflation erodes standards of living. Nevertheless, it must be conceded that we are still far from adequately understanding the complex processes by which inflation manifests itself in modern economies, and from being able to provide precise assessments of the true magnitude of the relevant costs.

THE MAIN DETERMINANTS OF INFLATION

After examining some of the main economic costs of inflation, and reaching the conclusion that the pursuit of price stability is a highly desirable monetary policy objective, it is necessary to identify those factors that play a key role in determining the path of inflation. This section therefore focuses on the study of the determinants of inflation, with a distinction being made between the short and the medium term. This distinction is essential for a proper understanding of the complexity of the inflationary process since in the short term price developments are influenced by a variety of supply and demand factors, whereas in the medium term certain conditions are verified which greatly simplify the analysis of the inflationary process.

Inflation in the Medium Term

Determinants of Inflation

A most firmly established behavioral relationship in monetary theory is that which links, in the medium term, the inflation rate, the growth of output, and the rate of money expansion. This relationship, which emerges necessarily from any well constructed macroeconomic model, is based on the simultaneous equilibrium of money, goods, and factors markets, and serves to reaffirm that, on average, the rate of monetary expansion finances the trend growth of output and the sustained increase in the general price level.

Viewed from a medium-term general equilibrium perspective, this relationship also shows that the inflation rate equals, on average, the rate of monetary expansion which exceeds the needs for financing the potential growth of the economy. This occurs in any economy, regardless of its economic structure, its degree of openness to the outside world, the concrete strategy of monetary or exchange policy followed by the authorities, and the specific features of the monetary policy transmission mechanism.

Having identified the determinants of the inflationary process in the medium term, it is of interest to look at national macroeconomic trends with a view to evaluating how important each of these determinants is in explaining cross-country differences in inflation over extended periods. Doing so definitely confirms that the existing differences among national inflation rates are mainly the result of different rates of expansion of liquidity in the various countries. This fact comes as no surprise if it is borne in mind that, generally speaking, average output growth rates recorded in highly diverse economies fluctuate within a fairly limited range – particularly in the industrial countries – while, by contrast, rates of monetary expansion vary considerably. To illustrate this point, Figure 1.2 shows the various inflation rates which, on average, have been registered in the industrial countries during the last 30 years. Figure 1.3 displays the positive relationship between inflation and the rate of monetary growth in this group of countries during the period under consideration.

It may be inferred from the above that, in practice, the rate of expansion of liquidity is the main determinant of medium-term inflation, and that regardless of the speed with which monetary impulses are transmitted to inflation, those countries which on average have higher rates of monetary expansion will also be those which on average experience higher inflation.[11] This in turn explains the monetary authorities' concern, even in countries which have adopted highly divergent monetary policy arrangements (e.g. intermediate monetary targets and direct inflation targets), with reaching a rate of liquidity creation that on average is compatible with financing potential economic growth under conditions of price stability.

The conclusions reached in the above paragraphs inevitably lead to the following question: If inflation entails significant economic costs for society

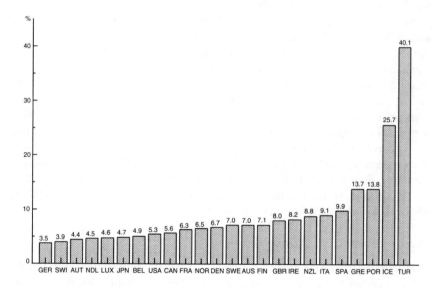

Figure 1.2   Average inflation, 1965–95
Source: OECD.

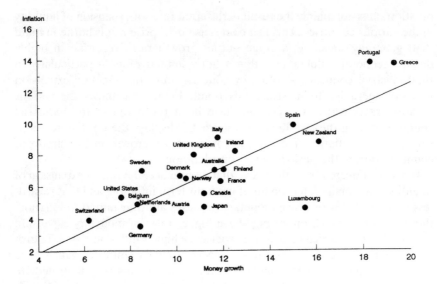

Figure 1.3 Average inflation and money growth, 1965–95
Source: OECD and IMF.

as a whole in the medium term, and if monetary policy is the main determining factor of the path followed by inflation in the medium term, what prevents a rate of monetary expansion from being adopted that is compatible with achieving and maintaining price stability? This question cannot be answered, however, in simple and direct terms. Indeed, far from being a mechanical phenomenon, monetary policy is a highly complex process in which a whole array of factors – economic, political, and social – converge and ultimately determine its course. Moreover, even if it is granted that going to a situation of price stability has a favourable impact on standards of living in the medium term, the fact remains that certain short-term costs are likely to arise in the course of the disinflation process. The existence of such costs – even when they are smaller in magnitude than the above-mentioned benefits – may influence the authorities' decision to postpone or soften (e.g. for electoral reasons) the policy measures aimed to achieving price stability. These issues are discussed in what follows.

Monetary Policy: Conditioning Factors

Having concluded that monetary policy is the main determinant of inflation in the medium term, the next step is to attempt to identify the factors that influence the medium-term stance of monetary policy. To do this, we draw on both economic theory and experience.

Combining some of the main results of monetary theory and the lessons learned from the experience of a number of countries in conducting monetary policy over the years indicates that there are two main reasons which explain why monetary polices may diverge from a path compatible with the achievement of price stability: the difficulties arising from a structurally unbalanced budgetary policy, and the problems of dynamic inconsistency which result from the authorities' temptation to exploit the trade-off between unemployment and inflation in order to step up the pace of economic activity.

In the medium term, an unbalanced budgetary policy may force monetary policy to expand liquidity at a rate in excess of what is needed to finance the sustained growth of the economy under conditions of price stability. The most direct way in which an excessively loose budgetary policy brings about the creation of excessive liquidity occurs when the fiscal deficit is monetized by the central bank. This situation, which is characteristic of non-industrial countries with high budget deficits and poorly developed capital markets, reveals that keeping the fiscal deficit under control is essential for maintaining moderate rates of monetary expansion and inflation.

However, industrial countries may also experience the adverse effects exerted in the medium term by structurally imbalanced budgetary policy on the anti-inflationary stance of monetary policy (see Rojo, 1985). A fiscal deficit financed in an orthodox manner by the issue of debt may have inflationary consequences if the debt has a high degree of liquidity, since it becomes a near substitute for money.[12] In such a case, the shorter the maturity of the debt, the higher its degree of liquidity is likely to be. It may also occur that financial intermediation activities in the private sector lead to the creation of more liquid financial assets based on the debt issued. In both cases, the issue of debt would be inflationary, either directly or indirectly.

Furthermore, as stated by Sargent and Wallace (1981), fiscal deficits which lead to an unsustainable growth of public debt lead to monetary expansions and to higher inflation rates. And although it may be argued that there are fortunately few industrial countries currently facing the problems of financially unsustainable debt, the above reasoning is still relevant if it is borne in mind that in countries with relatively high deficits and levels of debt, pressure may be exerted on the central bank to keep interest rates comparatively low in order to ease and lower the cost of financing the deficit through debt.[13] In such a case, even if the deficit is not directly monetized it is nevertheless monetized indirectly, which also has an adverse effect on inflation.[14]

It may be concluded from the above that, apart from the problems which an excessively loose budgetary policy entails for short-term price developments, persistent budgetary imbalances may undermine the anti-inflationary credibility of monetary policy and, in the medium term, cause the money supply to expand at a rate incompatible with achieving and maintaining price stability.

The growing consensus as to the importance of the macroeconomic problems arising from a structurally imbalanced budgetary policy, both with regard to the impact on monetary policy and inflation and to the adverse effect on potential economic growth, has in recent years led the authorities in many countries to adopt measures to improve their public finances. For example, the introduction by the European Union of fiscal discipline rules to regulate access to the Monetary Union and, after accession, to prevent the emergence of excessive deficits, together with the recent entry into force of legal provisions prohibiting any central bank financing of the public sector, is a significant step toward solving the inflationary problems which, in the medium term, arise from imbalanced budgetary polices.

In addition to the difficulties posed by fiscal policy, monetary policy may find that the pursuit of price stability is also rendered more difficult by dynamic inconsistency problems, stemming from the inclination of the authorities to exploit the short-term trade-off between unemployment and inflation in order to boost economic activity.[15] Most of the theoretical models setting forth this problem reach the conclusion that the proclivity of the authorities to systematically run an expansionary monetary policy to stimulate their economies simply leads to higher inflation without bringing any benefit in terms of higher output or employment. The main reason for this result is that once economic agents become aware of the authorities' policy, they adapt price and wages accordingly. This prevents the authorities from achieving their real targets, and induces them to accept a higher inflation rate.

One of the basic contributions that the literature on dynamic inconsistency has made to monetary theory is to permit identification of a series of factors that influence the size of the inflationary bias (see Appendix, p. 48). These factors, which will be examined below, are the following: the existence of more policy targets than instruments; the extent to which the authorities value price stability relative to other policy goals; structural distortions that limit potential output; and the authorities' ability to engineer short-term movements in economic activity through monetary surprises.[16]

One of the main problems traditionally faced by the authorities is that of having to achieve a variety of monetary policy targets with an insufficient number of instruments. As originally stated by Tinbergen (1952) and as later qualified by Brainard (1967), economic policy dilemmas arise when there are not at least as many instruments as there are policy targets. Thus, when the authorities' goal is to reach a high rate of economic activity under conditions of price stability, and only monetary policy is available for this purpose there is an overburdening of monetary policy. Under such circumstances, the lower the priority given to price stability relative to other goals, and the more pressure there is on the authorities to shortern the horizon of monetary policy decisions (owing, for example, to elections at regular intervals), the greater will be the inflationary bias. The request that monetary policy should satisfy several independent goals is thus a necessary condition for it to adopt a stance which is not compatible with the pursuit of price stability.

In a context of multiple monetary policy targets, the second factor which – in accordance with the models of dynamic inconsistency – influences the medium-term stance of monetary policy is the difference between the level of the economy's potential output and the level of output targeted by the authorities. For instance, if the authorities' target is to achieve the level of potential output that would prevail in a more efficient and competitive framework, while the level of potential output actually attainable is lower, owing to the rigidities and distortions that disturb the smooth functioning of goods and labour markets, this introduces an expansionary and inflationary bias to monetary policy. In less formal terms, the more constrained are the levels of output and employment due to the presence of market rigidities and distortions, the greater are the pressures for monetary policy to stimulate economic activity.

The third factor which according to the theory of dynamic inconsistency causes an inflationary bias in monetary policy is the extent to which the authorities are able to boost the rate of economic activity in the short term through monetary surprises. Hence the stronger the authorities' conviction, right or wrong, that monetary policy can stimulate the economy in the short term, the greater will be the temptation to expand liquidity systematically and thus the greater the departure from price stability.

To sum up, the analysis in this section has shown that monetary policy, far from being exogenous, is a complex process affected by a number of conditioning factors. Indeed, the difficulties in implementing an anti-inflationary monetary policy may result from the persistence of imbalanced budgetary polices, from the relatively low priority attached by the authorities to price stability compared to other policy goals, from the lack of cooperation from non-monetary policies in achieving these goals, from an excessively short horizon of monetary policy decisions, and from the presence of market distortions and rigidities. All this also explains why it is so difficult to reduce inflation on a lasting basis unless: an adequate degree of budgetary discipline and a balanced macroeconomic policy mix are restored; structural reforms are implemented that improve the functioning of goods and labour markets; the economic authorities become convinced that price stability is a highly desirable goal for society as a whole; and there is widespread agreement that the sole task that monetary policy can perform efficiently in the medium term is precisely the achievement of this goal.

The Short Term

An analysis of the factors influencing price developments in the short term is essential for gauging the actual ability of monetary policy to control inflation over limited periods of time, and also for understanding why policies designed to achieve price stability are often postponed or phased in only gradually, even when it is generally recognized that achieving such a target will have a favourable impact on the economy in the medium term.

In practice, there are several factors, in addition to those of a strictly monetary nature, which have a direct impact on the price level in the short-term. Any factor influencing aggregate demand or supply in an economy may in principle induce a change in the inflation rate within that time frame, for example: fiscal policy, the behaviour of economic and social agents in price and wage formation processes, international economic trends, and import prices. Furthermore, experience confirms that, in many cases and for relatively short periods, the above variables frequently exert a stronger influence on prices than does monetary policy, owing to the fact that the effects of monetary policy on nominal magnitudes tend to become fully visible only with the passage of time.

The short-term impact of monetary policy on prices and output has long been one of the most widely discussed issues in macroeconomic theory. It is also of considerable practical importance for the topic in hand. In particular, even where there is a firm belief that price stability is good for a country's economic health, the authorities must also assess what is the magnitude of the short-term output costs of disinflation in order to determine the pace at which inflation should be reduced to reach the established goals.[17]

Although there is abundant theoretical literature and empirical evidence concerning these matters, the differences among the assumptions underlying the various theoretical models and the diversity of national experiences in periods of disinflation make it very difficult to reach definitive conclusions on the short-term impact of monetary policy on inflation. The most we can hope to do is to set out some of the more generally accepted points, while identifying those important issues still open to discussion.

A point on which there is broad consensus is that the more rapidly agents adjust their inflationary expectations, and the more flexibility there is in the setting of prices and wages, the greater the ability of monetary policy to reduce inflation without entailing temporary output or employment costs (sacrifice ratio). On the one hand, the more confident agents are that the authorities will stick to a less inflationary monetary policy, the more intense and rapid will be the adjustment of expectations. On the other hand, when goods markets are highly competitive and the labour market is flexible enough to permit the rapid adjustment of wages to lower expected inflation, disinflation will be faster and entail lower output costs.

Along with this core of agreement, which is fairly well established in the thinking of most central banks, there are a number of factors that may influence the ability of monetary policy to achieve disinflation with low output costs but whose practical significance remains controversial. Among those which have received the most attention are: the initial level of inflation, the economy's degree of openness, and the speed with which the disinflation process takes place.[18]

As regards the first issue, it is often assumed that the lower the initial inflation rate the costlier it is to reduce it further, implying that the short-run Phillips curve becomes flatter at low rates of inflation. While this assumption is broadly supported by the experience of those countries which registered disinflationary processes starting from high or very high inflation rates, it nevertheless remains very controversial as concerns the experience of industrial countries, which started their disinflation processes from significantly lower inflation rates.

Considerable attention has also been given to whether the success of disinflationary policies – as measured by the sacrifice ratio – depends on an economy's degree of openness. As the logic goes, because an open economy expands the number of channels through which monetary policy influences the price level – by adding the exchange rate channel – it can affect inflation more directly and at a lower output cost. However, neither the experience of the United States at the beginning of the 1980s, following the appreciation of the dollar which resulted from the combination of an expansionary fiscal policy and tight monetary policy, nor the empirical evidence available for OECD countries seem to fully validate the null hypothesis. Instead, what the international experience and the available empirical evidence seem to suggest is that while it is true that in disinflationary periods the speed of disinflation is increased by the economy's degree of openness, such openness does not lead to an improvement in sacrifice ratios.

Finally, there is the question of how the sacrifice ratio is influenced by the greater or lesser gradualism with which disinflationary policies are carried out. In accordance with the Keynesian school – which emphasizes the inertia with which prices and wages tend to adjust – a more gradual disinflationary process would be less costly in terms of economic activity since it would give more time for prices and wages to adjust in the direction and magnitude entailed by the disinflationary policy applied. By contrast, the more neoclassical school – which stresses the role of expectations – states that the faster the disinflationary process, the greater its favourable impact on both inflationary expectations and inflation, and the lower its short-term output costs.

Although it may be reasonable to conclude on the basis of the experience of countries with extremely high inflation rates, that in such cases it may be better to implement relatively abrupt disinflationary policies in order to signal the commitment of the authorities and to foster a more rapid adjustment of inflationary expectations, the situation is quite different in countries which want to disinflate starting from more moderate inflation rates. The importance of empirically assessing which of the two viewpoints mentioned fits better the experience of industrial countries has given rise to several recent studies (Andersen, 1992; Ball, 1995) which carefully look at the economic performance of OECD countries during episodes of disinflation. The conclusion reached in these studies is that, in general, the faster disinflation is, the lower the output cost tends to be. However, as the above authors state, this does not necessarily mean that stringent disinflationary policies should be implemented, for although the total output cost is lower, the impact on social welfare is greater as costs are concentrated in a shorter period. Consequently, a resolute but gradual implementation of disinflation policies would seem to be a reasonable alternative.

To summarize, this section has made it clear that while in the long run inflation is basically a monetary phenomenon, in the short term there are many factors which influence the evolution of the price level. In particular, the success of the authorities in moving to a lower rate of inflation relatively quickly and with low output costs critically hinges on the overall anti-inflationary credibility of macroeconomic policy and the degree of downward flexibility of wages and prices. Thus, it may be concluded that policy initiatives aimed towards strengthening budgetary discipline, improving the functioning of goods and labour markets, and adopting mechanisms to reinforce the antiinflationary stance of monetary policy will favourably contribute to the achievement of price stability at a low cost. Since it was pointed out earlier that there are important permanent benefits in achieving price stability, the abovementioned policy initiatives would not only improve the benefit – cost ratio of moving towards price stability but would also make it easier, from a political-economy viewpoint, to achieve this goal.

ALTERNATIVE MONETARY POLICY STRATEGIES FOR FIGHTING INFLATION

Having analyzed in the preceding sections the problems confronted by monetary policy in achieving price stability and concluded that strengthening the anti-inflationary stance of monetary policy is very important for this purpose, I now turn to examining recent trends in national monetary policy strategies so as to discuss their underlying rationale and analyze their practical effectiveness.

As was seen from the analysis of the factors influencing inflation in the medium term, the problems of time inconsistency arising from a discretionary monetary policy introduce an inflationary bias. The initial solution proposed in the theoretical literature to the problem of time inconsistency involved replacing discretionality in the authorities' conduct of monetary policy with rigid or fixed rules of the sort proposed by Milton Friedman (1959). These rules predetermine the time-path of monetary variables to be consistent with the achievement and maintenance of price stability, without taking into account the future course of economic or financial variables. This solution has, nevertheless, serious practical drawbacks. It prevents monetary policy from taking into account and reacting to macroeconomic distur-bances, which are particularly frequent in financial markets. Furthermore, since there is no guarantee that a fixed rule will not be abandoned at some point in time, this undermines its anti-inflationary credibility.

Probably owing to these difficulties, virtually no country is implementing monetary policy with rigid or fixed rules. Those countries which do apply rules of some kind – usually linked to the performance of a monetary aggregate or the exchange rate – in practice tend to manage them with a certain degree of flexibility in order to take into account general economic conditions. However, it should be noted that the application of more flexible rules is not trouble-free (see Rojo, 1988). The attempt to combine the presumed advantages of rules as regards credibility with the ability to react to specific disturbances has led to excessive discretionality in most cases. This in turn has eroded public confidence in the anti-inflationary commit-ment of monetary policy.

Given the well-known inflationary risks associated with an excessively discretionary monetary policy and the problems with fixed or rigid policy rules, the idea has been gaining ground in recent years that a good way to ensure that the necessary flexibility in monetary policy management does not introduce inflationary biases is to assign to the central bank the primary goal of price stability and provide it with the necessary means to achieve it.[19] In some countries (e.g. New Zealand) contracts have recently been entered into under which the central bank undertakes *vis-à-vis* the government to achieve a specific inflation target within a given time by applying the monetary policy it deems appropriate. The central bank authorities are accountable to the government in the event that the target is not reached. The theoretical rationale for this approach is found in the work of Walsh (1993), and Persson and Tabellini (1993) (see Appendix, p. 48).

In contrast to the contractual approach – but with similar objectives – an increasing number of countries have opted in recent years for the more ambitious route of introducing legal reforms that establish price stability as the primary goal of monetary policy in the medium term and endowing the central bank with considerable independence for achieving it. This consider-ably reduces the risks of short-term subordination of price stability to other monetary policy targets, and allows monetary policy decisions to be adopted

with a sufficiently long time horizon and independently from the political
cycle.

Indeed, as highlighted in the work of Goodhart and Viñals (1995) and
Fernández de Lis (1996) among others, the central banks of a fairly large
number of countries – both inside and outside the European Union – nowadays enjoy a high degree of independence in the conduct of monetary policy.
In the specific case of EU countries, the conviction that this is the proper
approach for overcoming inflation on a lasting basis has been enshrined in
the Maastricht Treaty, which contemplates the establishment of a European
System of Central Banks (ESCB) which is fully independent to formulate
and execute monetary policy so as to achieve and maintain price stability in
the European Monetary Union as a whole. The Treaty also makes it man-
datory for national central banks to have, by the establishment of the ESCB,
a legal status that is fully compatible with that of the System. Doubtless, the
provisions of the Treaty are behind the efforts now being made by many
European countries to bolster the independence of their respective central
banks.

In view of the many studies that justify from a theoretical standpoint
granting considerable independence to central banks in conducting a monetary policy that achieves price stability, it is particularly useful to review,
albeit briefly, the empirical evidence on the degree of success which independent central banks have had in combating inflation.

The record would seem to indicate that countries having a well established
tradition of central bank independence perform best as regards price stability. The German example is a case in point. The Bundesbank not only has a
long history of independence, it has also achieved enviable success in maintaining low inflation rates over the past forty years. However, it must be said
that the success of the Bundesbank is not solely the result of its independence *vis-à-vis* the government. It also stems from the strong aversion to
inflation of the German people, which has its roots in the devastating impact
of the hyperinflation experienced in the inter-war period. It is quite likely
that the underlying reason for the independence of the Bundesbank lies
precisely in German society's fear of again having to suffer the terrible
economic and social consequences of the erosion of monetary stability. In
all honesty, however, and by way of exception, it must also be noted that
there is a country, Japan, which despite the relative dependence of its central
bank on the government, has managed to maintain lower inflation rates than
have countries whose central banks enjoy greater independence. Nevertheless, as will be discussed below, the conclusions generally drawn from considering the empirical evidence on international price trends and their
relation to the degree of central bank independence are consistent with
the hypothesis that, other things being equal, greater independence is associated with better inflationary performance in the medium term.

The more rigorous analyses conducted to verify the existence of a stable and robust relationship between inflation and central bank independence are generally based on relatively simple econometric models which rely on numerical indicators that proxy for the degree of political and operational independence of national central banks. In these analyses it is very difficult to synthesize the complexity of the many economic and institutional factors which shape a central bank's degree of independence. But even if the ultimate causes governing the relationship noted between the degree of independence and inflation performance are not sufficiently known, the results available for various groups of countries, for different periods, and using a variety of indices to approximate the degree of independence, generally tend to confirm the existence of a positive and significant relationship between a central bank's degree of independence and its success in fighting inflation (see Figure 1.4).[20]

In line with the above, if it is agreed that introducing an institutional framework that guarantees central bank independence helps to strengthen the credibility and anti-inflationary discipline of monetary policy, it must nevertheless be asked whether this is achieved at the cost of a less favourable performance by real variables, such as the level and variability of output. Fortunately, most of the available empirical evidence suggests that these adverse effects do not occur.[21]

Given the various reasons offered earlier to justify the favourable medium-term economic effects of implementing policies aimed at achieving price stability, it is necessary also to review the reasons why granting more independence to the central bank does not adversely affect the stability of real variables in the short term. In this respect, although it is likely that an independent central bank seeking to achieve price stability will tend to be

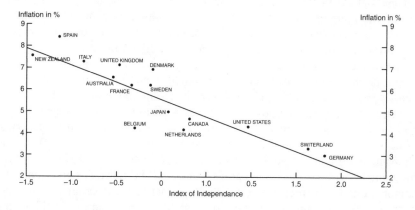

Figure 1.4   Inflation and central bank independence, 1955–90
Source: De Long and Summers (1992).

less accommodating to certain macroeconomic disturbances that affect output, it is also possible that its greater independence will enable it to avoid disturbances of another kind, i.e. those that are political in origin.[22] Moreover, it may be argued that insofar as the monetary policy implemented by an independent central bank enjoys greater anti-inflationary credibility, the monetary authorities will tend to find they have more room for manoeuvre in countering specific macroeconomic disturbances that affect output, without running the risk that the public will incorrectly interpret transient changes in monetary conditions as a change in the monetary policy stance.[23] Finally, the increased credibility of monetary policy may also help economic agents to distinguish between changes in the general price level and changes in relative prices, thus prompting a more rapid adjustment of prices and wages to macroeconomic disturbances. This will reduce the need for monetary policy to play a compensating role in the short term.

From the discussion so far, it may be concluded that endowing the central bank with considerable independence can favourably contribute to the achievement of price stability. Nonetheless, as experience shows, such contribution will be all the more important the wider the support that the final goal of price stability receives from overall economic policy.

The increasing attention paid in recent years to making legislative changes to ensure that monetary policy can be conducted in a medium-term perspective and without government interference has shifted the discussion about which monetary strategy best performs the role of 'nominal anchor' from a relatively technical to an institutional level. In this regard, it can be stated that once price stability has been legally established as the primary goal of monetary policy and the central bank granted an independent status, the resulting strengthening of anti-inflationary credibility provides more room for manoeuvre in the choice of specific monetary strategies (e.g. monetary vs. inflation targets). This may explain why a number of central banks, all of which enjoy considerable independence, nevertheless conduct their monetary policy on the basis of different monetary policy strategies.

Because the experience with inflation targets is reviewed in other chapters of this book,[24] there is no need for a detailed discussion of their nature and characteristics at this point. However, it should be noted that inflation targeting has appealed both to countries with independent central banks and to those whose central banks are under government control. Leaving aside considerations of a technical nature – which are important when choosing a particular monetary strategy – the adoption of inflation targeting by countries with independent central banks may be viewed as an attempt to complement and further develop the independence law in order to make the central bank's commitment to nominal stability more concrete, credible and transparent. In turn – again leaving aside the technical reasons which may have made it advisable to abandon intermediate targets – the adoption of inflation targets by non-independent central banks may be rationalized as an attempt by the central bank to take a clearer stand on inflation and therefore to affirm its *'de facto'* independence *vis-à-vis* the government.

Finally, the recent trend in many countries toward introducing legal reforms that place price stability as the primary goal of monetary policy and provide central banks with a significant degree of independence can be regarded as a useful compromise between rules and discretion which, by strengthening the anti-inflationary credibility of monetary policy, allows greater flexibility in adapting monetary conditions to changing economic and financial circumstances.[25] How to make use of this flexibility on a day-to-day basis is the great challenge facing central banks in the context of what is known as *the art of central banking*.

CONCLUSIONS

This chapter has discussed a number of issues which are relevant to a proper understanding of the causes and effects of the inflationary process, and to an assessment of the contribution that monetary policy may make to achieving price stability. It began by identifying the various channels through which inflation generates economic costs, and provided evidence of the actual empirical magnitude of these costs. It then went on to examine the various factors that influence inflation in the short and the medium term, focusing particularly on the role played by monetary policy. Finally, it reviewed the recent experience of central banks in their efforts to develop successful anti-inflationary monetary policy strategies.

It was concluded above that the popular belief that inflation is costly for society is supported both by economic principles and by the experience of many countries. It was thus determined that the most significant costs of inflation are those resulting from its interaction with a legal and contractual framework which is not fully adapted to coping with it, and those linked to the uncertainty and volatility of the inflationary process itself. The international empirical evidence tends to confirm that countries entering into an even moderate inflationary situation never see an improvement in their growth prospects and, in contrast, have a high probability of experiencing a deterioration in economic growth during prolonged periods of time. It may therefore be said that the evidence is broadly consistent with the popular perception that inflation erodes standards of living, although it must be acknowledged that we are still far from fully understanding the complexity of the inflationary process in modern economies, to say nothing about providing precise estimates of the magnitude of its costs. However, this should not obscure the main conclusion: price stability is a highly desirable economic policy goal.

The analysis conducted of the factors affecting price trends made it clear that as inflation in the medium term is fundamentally a monetary phenomenon, it is monetary policy that is best able to ensure price stability, and it should accordingly assume responsibility for doing so. However, it was also found that as monetary policy is a highly complex process in which a whole series of economic, political, and social factors converge, it is often the case that the rate of monetary expansion diverges from that which would be compatible with maintaining price stability. It was also concluded that the main difficulties in implementing an anti-inflationary monetary policy can be traced to unsustainable budgetary polices, to the relatively low priority that may be assigned by the authorities to price stability relative to other economic policy goals, to the short-sightedness of monetary policy decisions, and to the distortions and rigidities prevailing in goods and factor markets.

In this chapter, we have also examined the factors that influence inflation in the short term in order to gauge the actual capacity of monetary policy to guide price trends in this time frame. At the same time, we have sought to determine why policies aimed at price stability are often postponed or phased in gradually, even when it is generally recognized that achieving such a goal will have a favourable medium-term impact on the economy. Our examination showed that since various and very different factors influence inflation in the short term, the temporary output or employment costs of a monetary policy aimed at reducing inflation become smaller, the greater the anti-inflationary credibility of macroeconomic policy as a whole and the greater the degree of downward price and wage flexibility. It may thus be concluded that strengthening budgetary discipline, implementing structural reforms to improve the functioning of goods and labour markets, and adopting mechanisms to enhance the anti-inflationary orientation of monetary policy, are of fundamental importance for achieving price stability as rapidly as possible and at the lowest cost.

After examining the problems facing monetary policy in achieving price stability and concluding that reinforcement of the anti-inflationary stance of monetary policy is essential for establishing the framework of nominal stability required for sustained economic growth, the chapter reviewed recent changes in national monetary policy strategies, discussed their underlying rationale and analyzed their effectiveness. In accordance with the analysis in this section, the inflationary risks arising from an excessively discretionary monetary policy and the problems linked to rigid or fixed policy rules help to explain why in recent years the idea has been gaining ground that a convenient way to prevent an inflationary bias from emerging without unduly constraining monetary policy is to assign to the central bank the basic objective of achieving and maintaining price stability, and to endow it with the necessary means for doing so. Indeed, as corroborated by experience, this constitutes a useful blend of rules and discretion which, by strengthening the anti-inflationary credibility of monetary policy, allows greater flexibility in adapting monetary conditions to a changing economic and financial environment. However, it was also stressed that, regardless of the chosen institutional framework, anti-inflationary monetary policies will be all the more effective, the greater the support that price stability receives from other economic policies and, ultimately, from society as a whole.

Appendix[26]

This Appendix contains a formal analysis of some of the concepts discussed in the text. Specifically, concepts such as time inconsistency, discretionality, the role of the central bank, and inflation targets are examined within the framework of various strategic interactions between the authorities/central bank and the private sector. In the interest of simplifying formal treatment, the model used is non-stochastic and the sources of uncertainty are omitted.

THE MODEL

The model considered below is static and represents a closed economy. As is usual in the literature, it is assumed that the authorities minimize a quadratic loss function (L) consisting of the deviations of inflation (π) relative to target (π^*) and of the deviations of output relative to the equilibrium level (y) with regard to another objective level (y^*), using the inflation rate as an instrument. That is,

$$\min_{\pi} L = \frac{1}{2}[(\pi - \pi^*)^2 + \lambda(y - y^*)^2], \ \lambda > 0 \tag{1A.1}$$

subject to an aggregate supply function of the Lucas (1972) type

$$y = \alpha(\pi - \pi^e), \ \alpha > 0 \tag{1A.2}$$

in which π^e are private sector inflation expectations. In (1A.1), the parameter λ indicates the relative importance for the authorities of the two objectives included in the loss function, so that if $\lambda = 0 (\lambda = \infty)$, the inflation target (the output target) is the only one that counts. (1A.2) tells us that only unexpected inflation has real effects. Without losing generality, let us assume that $\pi^* = 0$ and $y^* = \alpha\bar{y} > 0$. This latter assumption indicates that owing to the existence of rigidities in the goods and labour markets, the authorities' target in terms of output deviates from $y^* = 0$.

Substituting (1A.2) for (1A.1) therefore gives

$$\min_{\pi} L = \frac{1}{2}[\pi^2 + \lambda\alpha^2(\pi - \pi^e - \bar{y})^2] \tag{1A.3}$$

Time Inconsistency

If the authorities had sufficient credibility to commit themselves to a specific rate of inflation, the private sector would have confidence in this commitment, so that $\pi = \pi^e$ and $y = 0$. As a result, the loss function in this case would be

$$L = \frac{1}{2}[\pi^2 + \lambda\alpha^2\bar{y}^2] \tag{1A.4}$$

so that optimal inflation and the related output, designated in this case as π^c and y^c, would be

$$\pi^c = 0\,, y^c = 0 \tag{1A.5}$$

Nevertheless, in equilibrium the authorities have an incentive for deviating from the optimal inflation rate since

$$(\partial L/\partial\pi)_{\pi=\pi^e=\pi^c} = \pi + \lambda\alpha^2(\pi - \pi^e - \bar{y})|_{\pi=\pi^e=\pi^c} = -\lambda\alpha^2\bar{y} < 0 \tag{1A.6}$$

that is, around π^c, a small increase in inflation reduces the value of the loss function, which is to the advantage of the authorities. Therefore, the prior assumption of credibility no longer holds, and the private sector recognizes this when forming its inflationary expectations. This is the problem popularly known as *time inconsistency*.

Time Consistency and Discretionality

Time consistency without a credible commitment means that the authorities take π^e as given when selecting π and that agents form their expectations rationally, so that π^e equals the optimal value of π. In other words, the authorities are aware that the private sector will internalize any deviation from the optimal inflation rate π^c. Therefore, in minimizing (1A.3), a new optimal inflation rate π^d is obtained which satisfies the first order condition:

$$\pi^d + \lambda\alpha^2(\pi^d - \pi^e - \bar{y})|_{\pi^d=\pi^e} = \pi^d - \lambda\alpha^2\bar{y} = 0 \tag{1A.7}$$

the optimal rate of inflation and the relevant output being represented in this case by

$$\pi^d = \lambda\alpha^2\bar{y} > \pi^c = 0\,, y^d = \alpha(\pi^d - \pi^e) = y^c = 0 \tag{1A.8}$$

It should be noted that there is an inflationary bias, represented by $\lambda \alpha^2 \bar{y}$, without any gain in real terms, compared with the case in which $\pi^e = 0$ is selected. This is the so called *discretionality problem*. In turn, the inflationary bias will be higher: the lower the priority given by the authorities to fighting inflation (greater λ), the greater the short-term impact of inflationary surprises on output (greater α), and the greater the market distortions (greater $\bar{y}$).

THE ROLE OF THE CENTRAL BANK

As a solution to the problem of discretionality described earlier, Rogoff (1985) suggests that the authorities delegate the selection of π to a 'conservative' central banker. This means that if the preferences of the central banker are such that λ is small (i.e. he cares a lot about inflation relative to output) the inflationary bias will tend to be reduced without any real output loss. In fact, at the limit, if $\lambda = 0$, the optimal solution expressed in (1A.5) is obtained.

INFLATION TARGETS

The above result as regards delegation to a 'conservative' central banker is valid only in the absence of uncertainty. If there were uncertainty owing, for example, to the presence of a disturbance in the aggregate supply function (1A.2), it is easy to show the impossibility of implementing the optimal situation. In fact, there would be less variability in inflation than in the case of discretion, but more variability in output. Therefore, there exists an optimum degree of aversion to inflation (λ) which minimizes the sum of both variances, but which in no case achieves the optimal variability associated with a solution of the (1A.5) type in a context of uncertainty.

For this reason, other alternatives have been suggested based on a 'contractual' approach (see Walsh, 1993) under which a linear penalty is applied to the central bank if inflation exceeds the target $\pi^* = 0$. In such a case, the loss function in (1A.3), now referred to the central bank, is converted into

$$\min_{\pi} L^b = L + h\pi = \frac{1}{2}[\pi^2 + \lambda \alpha^2 (\pi - \pi^e - \bar{y})^2] + h\pi \qquad (1A.9)$$

where h is the penalty imposed on the central bank for every point of deviation in inflation. Operating in the same manner as in (1A.7), the first order condition implies

$$\pi^b + \lambda\alpha^2(\pi^b - \pi^e - \bar{y}) + h|_{\pi^b = \pi^e} = \pi^b - \lambda\alpha\bar{y} + h \qquad (1A.10)$$

so that selecting $h = \lambda\alpha\bar{y}^2$ gives $\pi^b = \pi^c = 0$ and $y^b = y^c = 0$; that is, the optimal solution is implemented.

Svensson (1995) has shown that implementing the contract referred to above is equivalent to providing the central bank with a loss function such as that of the authorities, but with a different inflation target ($\tilde{\pi}$). In this case, (1A.9) would be

$$\tilde{L}^b = \frac{1}{2}[(\pi - \tilde{\pi})^2 + \lambda\alpha^2(\pi - \pi^e - \bar{y})^2] =$$

$$= \frac{1}{2}[\pi^2 + \lambda\alpha^2(\pi - \pi^e - \bar{y})^2] - \tilde{\pi}\pi + \text{constant} = \qquad (1A.11)$$

$$= L - \tilde{\pi}\pi + \text{constant}$$

It should be noted that (1A.11) has the same form as (1A.9), in which $\tilde{\pi} = -h = -\lambda\alpha^2\bar{y}$. Therefore, it is necessary that $\tilde{\pi} < 0$, which is equivalent to assuming that the inflation target of the central bank is lower than that of the authorities $\pi^* = 0$. Obviously, the fact that $\tilde{\pi}$ is negative is a consequence of the assumption $\pi^* = 0$; if we had assumed $\pi^* > 0$, it would have resulted that $\tilde{\pi} < \pi^*$.

Notes

1. This pragmatic definition of price stability was coined by Alan Greenspan, Chairman of the Federal Reserve.
2. See, for instance, the article by Edey (1994), which summarizes and gives supporting evidence for the various ways in which actual inflation rates are statistically overestimated.
3. See Akerlof, Dickens and Perry (1996). Although it has also been pointed out by Summers (1991) that a positive rate of inflation is desirable since it allows negative interest rates in severe recessions, this argument would not seem to be applicable to the medium term.
4. See, *inter alia*, the survey articles of Fischer and Modigliani (1978), Driffil, Mizon and Ulph (1990), Edey (1994), and Briault (1995).
5. The costs estimated by Lucas (1994) for the United States are significantly higher, and the costs estimated by Mulligan and Sala-i-Martin (1996) are much lower, than those of Bailey (1956) when the initial rate of inflation is very low.
6. See, among others, Edey (1994), Fischer (1994), Black, Macklem, and Poloz (1993), and Feldstein (1996). For an opposite viewpoint, see Aiyagari (1990).
7. For a critical view of the assumed empirical relationship between inflation and the degree of uncertainty, see Driffil, Mizon, and Ulph (1990).
8. A synthesis of these studies may be found, among others, in Fischer (1994), De Gregorio (1996), and Andrés and Hernando (1996).

9   The studies by Andrés and Hernando (1996), and Andrés, Hernando, and Krüger (1996) referred to are based on a neoclassical growth model expanded with human capital. They find that the effect of inflation on the growth rate lasts for decades, although it is not permanent. In any case, the level of steady-state *per capita* income declines permanently when inflation increases.

10 For example, Cukierman, Webb, and Neyapti (1992).

11 See Lucas (1996). In Canzoneri and Diba (1996), Chapter 5 in this volume, debt plays a fundamental role in the determination of the price level.

12 See Wallace (1981), and Canzoneri and Diba (1996) in Chapter 5 in this volume.

13 This specific example is also linked to the issue of dynamic inconsistency discussed below. See 16 below.

14 Ultimately, efforts to keep nominal interest rates low through faster money supply growth result in greater inflation and higher nominal interest rates, without reducing real interest rates. In this way, the deficit is ultimately financed indirectly by the central bank.

15 The seminal studies are those of Kydland and Prescott (1977), and Barro and Gordon (1983). Englander (1990) and Cukierman (1992) analyze in depth the various factors determining the inflationary bias of monetary policy. See also the Appendix to this chapter, p. 48.

16 There are also problems of time inconsistency linked to the existence of budgetary and balance of payments targets, as pointed out by Cukierman (1992).

17 In those cases where hysteresis effects exist, the costs of disinflation are felt not only in the short term, but also in the medium term.

18 These issues have recently been empirically examined by Ball (1993). The remainder of this sub-section draws heavily on his results.

19 A pioneer study along these lines is that of Rogoff (1985) who notes the advantage of appointing a central banker whose degree of aversion to inflation is relatively greater than that of society as a way to reduce the inflationary bias. Cukierman (1992) presents a theoretically and empirically very complete analysis of the issues related to central bank independence.

20 See, among other empirical studies, those of Grilli, Masciandaro, and Tabellini (1991), Cukierman (1992), Cukierman, Webb, and Neyapti (1992), De Long and Summers (1992), Alesina and Summers (1993), Debelle and Fischer (1995), Eijffinger and De Haan (1995), and De Gregorio (1996). Posen (1993) criticizes most of these studies, noting that the inverse relationship between the degree of central bank independence and inflation does not arise because the former 'causes' the latter. Posen argues rather that societies which are highly averse to inflation tend both to establish independent central banks and to register lower inflation rates. For a reply to criticisms of this kind, see Cukierman, Webb, and Neyapti (1992).

21 An updated summary of this evidence is provided by Cukierman (1995) and De Gregorio (1996). See also Debelle and Fischer (1995), and Walsh (1993) for critical views of the impact of central bank independence on the costs of disinflation, and De Gregorio (1996) for a reply.

22 On this point, see Alesina and Gatti (1995).

23 On this point, see Begg *et al.* (1991).

24 In this volume, the international experience with inflation targets is examined by Almeida and Goodhart (1996), chapter 2, and the Spanish experience by Gutiérrez (1996), chapter 6. See also Melcón (1995).

25 On this point, see Crockett (1993).

26 Juan Dolado contributed to preparing this Appendix.

References

AIYAGARI, S.R. (1990) 'Deflating the case for zero inflation', *Quarterly Review*, Federal Reserve Bank of Minneapolis, Summer, 2–11.

AKERLOF, G, W. DICKENS, and G. PERRY (1996) 'The macroeconomics of low inflation', *Brookings Papers on Economic Activity*, 1, 1–59.

ALESINA, A. and R. GATTI (1995) 'Independent central bank: low inflation at no cost', *American Economic Review*, 85; 106–200.

ALESINA, A. and L.H. SUMMERS (1993) 'Central bank independence and macroeconomic performance: some comparative evidence', *Journal of Money, Credit and Banking*, 25, 157–162.

ALMEIDA, A. and C. GOODHART, (1996) 'Does the adoption of inflation targets affect central bank behaviour?', chapter 2 in this volume.

ANDERSEN, P. (1992) 'OECD country experiences with disinflation', in A. Blundell-Wignall (ed.), *Inflation, Disinflation and Monetary Policy*, Canberra: Reserve Bank of Australia–Ambassador Press.

ANDRÉS, J. and I. HERNANDO (1996) '¿Cómo afecta la inflación al crecimiento económico? Evidencia para los países de la OCDE', *Working Paper*, 9602, Research Department, Banco de España.

ANDRÉS, J., I. HERNANDO, and M. KRÜGER (1996) '¿Cómo incide el régimen cambiario en la medición de los costes de la inflación?', *Boletín Económico*, Banco de España, May.

BALL, L. (1993) 'What determines the sacrifice ratio?', *Working Paper*, 4306, National Bureau of Economic Research.

BAILEY, M.J. (1956) 'The Welfare Cost of Inflationary Finance', *Journal of Political Economy*, 64, 93–110.

BARRO, R. (1995) 'Inflation and Economic Growth', *Bank of England Quarterly Bulletin*, 35, 166–176.

BARRO, R. and D. GORDON (1983) 'A Positive Theory of Monetary Policy in a Natural Rate Model', *Journal of Political Economy*, 91, 589–610.

BEGG, D. *ET AL*. (1991), *Monitoring European Integration: The Making of Monetary Union*, Centre for Economic Policy Research.

BLACK, R., T. MACKLEM and S. POLOZ (1993) 'Non-superneutralities and some benefits of disinflation: a quantative general equilibrium analysis', Bank of Canada, mimeo.

BLINDER, A. (1993) 'Why are prices sticky? Preliminary results from an interview study', in E. Sheshinski, and Y. Weiss (eds) *Optimal Pricing, Inflation and the Cost of Price Adjustment*, Cambridge, MA: MIT Press.

BRAINARD, W. (1967) 'Uncertainty and the effectiveness of policy', *American Economic Review*, May.

BRIAULT, C. (1995) 'The costs of inflation', *Bank of England Quarterly Bulletin*, February, 33–45.

CANZONERI, M. and B. DIBA (1996) 'Fiscal constraints on central bank independence and on price stability', chapter 5 in this volume.

CROCKETT, A. (1993) 'Rules vs. discretion in monetary policy', Bank of England, mimeo.

CUKIERMAN, A. (1992) *Central Bank Behaviour, Credibility and Independence: Theory and Evidence*, Cambridge, MA: MIT Press.

CUKIERMAN, A. (1995) 'The economics of central banking', paper presented at the XI World Congress of the International Economic Association, Tunis.

54   *José Viñals*

CUKIERMAN, A., J. WEBB and B. NEYAPTI (1992) 'Measuring the independence of central banks and its effects on policy outcomes', *World Bank Economic Review*, 6, 353–98.

DEBELLE, G. and S. FISCHER (1995) 'How independent should a central bank be?', in *Goals, Guidelines, and Constraints Facing Monetary Policy-makers*, Federal Reserve Bank of Boston.

DE GREGORIO, J. (1996) 'Inflation, growth and central banks: theory and evidence', *Policy Research Working Paper*, 1575, The World Bank.

DE LONG, B. and L. SUMMERS (1992) 'Macroeconomic policy and long-run growth', in *Policies for Long-Run Economic Growth*, Federal Reserve Bank of Kansas City.

DRIFFIL, J., G. MIZON and A. ULPH (1990) 'Costs of inflation', in B. Friedman, and F. Hahn (eds) *Handbook of Monetary Economics, vol. II*, Amsterdam: North-Holland.

EDEY, M. (1994) 'Costs and benefits of moving from low inflation to price stability', *OECD Economic Studies*, 23, Winter, 109–30.

EIJFFINGER, S. and J. DE HAAN (1995), 'The political economy of central bank independence', University of Tilburg, mimeo.

ENGLANDER, A.S. (1990) 'Optimal monetary policy design: rules versus discretion again', *Research Paper*, 9019, Federal Reserve Bank of New York.

FELDSTEIN, M. (1983) *Inflation, Tax Rules and Capital Formation*, Chicago: University of Chicago Press.

FELDSTEIN, M. (1996) 'The cost and benefits of going from low inflation to price stability', *Working Paper*, 54 69, National Bureau of Economic Research.

FERNÁNDEZ DE LIS, S. (1996) 'Classifications of central banks by autonomy: a comparative analysis', *Working Paper*, 9604, Research Department, Banco de España.

FISCHER, S. (1991) 'Growth, macroeconomics and development', *Working Paper* 3702, National Bureau of Economic Research.

FISCHER, S. (1994), *Modern central banking*, Tercentenary Lecture, central banking Symposium, Bank of England.

FISCHER, S. and F. MODIGLIANI (1978) 'Towards an understanding of the real effects and costs of inflation', *Weltwirtschaftliches Archiv*, 114, 810–32.

FRIEDMAN, M. (1959) *A Program for Monetary Stability*, New York: Fordham University Press.

FRIEDMAN, M. (1969) 'The optimum quantity of money', in M. Friedman, *The Optimum Quantity of Money and Other Essays*, Chicago: Aldine.

GRILLI, V., D. MASCIANDARO, and G. TABELLINI (1991) 'Political and monetary institutions and public financial policies in the industrial countries', *Economic Policy*, 13, 341–92.

GOODHART, C. and J. VIÑALS (1995) 'Strategy and tactics of monetary policy: examples from Europe and the Antipodes', in *Goals, Guidelines and Constraints Facing Monetary Policy-makers*, Federal Reserve Bank of Boston.

GUTIÉRREZ, F. (1996) 'Monetary policy following the law of autonomy of the Banco de España', chapter 6 in this volume.

KATONA, G. (1976) 'The psychology of inflation' in R.T. Cartin (ed.) *Surveys of Consumers*, Institute for Social Research, University of Michigan, 9–19.

KYDLAND, F. and E. PRESCOTT (1977) 'Rules rather than discretion: the inconsistency of optimal plans', *Journal of Political Economy*, 85, 473–92.

LEVINE, R. and D. RENELT (1992) 'A sensitivity analysis of cross-country growth regressions', *American Economic Review*, 82, 942–63.

LEVINE, R. and S. ZERVOS (1993) 'What have we learned about policy and growth from cross-country regressions?', *American Economic Review*, 83, 426–30.

LUCAS, R. (1973) 'Some international evidence on output–inflation trade-offs', *American Economic Review*, 63, 3, 326–34.

LUCAS, R. (1994) 'On the welfare cost of inflation', University of Chicago, mimeo.

LUCAS, R. (1996) 'Nobel Lecture: monetary neutrality', *Journal of Political Economy*, 104(4), 661–82.

MELCÓN, C. (1995) 'Estrategias de política monetaria basadas en el seguimiento de objetivos directos de inflación. Las experiencias de Nueva Zelanda, Canadá, Reino Unido y Suecia', *Working Paper*, 9426, Research Department, Banco de España.

MULLIGAN, C. and X. SALA-I-MARTIN (1996) 'Adoption of financial technologies: implications for money demand and monetary policy', *Discussion Paper*, 1358, Centre for Economic Policy Research.

PERSSON, T. and G. TABELLINI (1993) 'Designing institutions for monetary stability', *Carnegie–Rochester Conference Series on Public Policy*, 39, 53–84.

PHELPS, E. (1970), *Microeconomic foundations of Employment and Inflation Theory*, New York: Norton.

POSEN, A. (1993) 'Why central bank independence does not cause low inflation: there is no institutional fix for politics', in R. O'Brien (ed.), *Finance and the International Economy*: 7 Oxford: Oxford University Press.

ROGOFF, K. (1985) 'The optimal degree of commitment of an intermediate monetary target', *Quarterly Journal of Economics*, 110, 1169–90.

ROJO, L.A. (1985) 'Déficit público y política monetaria', *Cuadernos de Economía*, CSIC, 13, (36), 3–32.

ROJO, L.A. (1988) 'Innovaciones financieras y política monetaria', *Papeles de Economía Española*, 36, 2–24.

SARGENT, N. and N. WALLACE (1981) 'Some unpleasant monetarist arithmetic', *Federal Reserve Bank of Minneapolis Quarterly Review* 5, 1–17.

SCHILLER, R. (1996) 'Why do people dislike inflation?', Yale University, mimeo.

SUMMERS, L. (1991) 'How should long term monetary policy be determined?', *Journal of Money, Credit and Banking* 23, (3), part 2, 625–31.

SVENSSON, L. (1995) 'Optimal inflation targets, "conservative" central banks, and linear inflation contracts', *Discussion Paper*, 1249, Centre for Economic Policy Research.

SVENSSON, L. (1996) 'Inflation forecast targeting: implementing and monitoring inflation targets', paper presented at the European Summer Symposium in Macroeconomics, Centre for Economic Policy Research, Roda de Bará.

TINBERGEN, J. (1952) *On the Theory of Economic Policy*, Amsterdam: North-Holland.

WALLACE, N. (1981) 'A Modigliani–Miller theorem of open-market operations', *American Economic Review*, June, 267–74.

WALSH, C. (1993) 'Optimal contracts for independent central bankers: private information, performance measures and reappointment', *Working Paper*, 9302, Federal Reserve Bank of San Francisco.

WALSH, C. (1994) 'Central bank independence and the costs of disinflation in the EC', *Working Paper*, 9404, Federal Reserve Bank of San Francisco.

2 Does the Adoption of Inflation Targets Affect Central Bank Behaviour?

Alvaro Almeida and Charles A.E. Goodhart

INTRODUCTION

Perhaps both the most difficult, and the most crucial, decision for a study of how those central banks which have adopted inflation targets (ITs) have fared, is to decide which Central Banks to include within the chosen set. Nowadays almost all central banks make price stability their main objective. Price stability is regarded, for this policy purpose, as a low rate of inflation,[1] low enough to prevent agents consciously factoring in expectations of future inflation into their price/wage setting decisions. Consequently virtually *all* central banks have an IT, though this may be unquantified and implicit rather than quantified and explicit. Our objective in this chapter is not to discuss the adoption of price stability as the main objective for monetary policy, but to examine the implications of publicly announcing and making this objective explicit and precise. An explicitly numerically quantified inflation target is one feature that is common to all IT countries, but not unique to this group. Several non-IT countries also publicly report a numerical value for the inflation rate which they are seeking to achieve at some future date (e.g. France, Italy or Portugal).

What does seem to be somewhat more distinct among IT countries is that there is no other specified, numerically quantified, intermediate target,[2] such as a monetary or an exchange rate target, the achievement of which is treated as a means of achieving the inflation target. But any dividing lines between IT and non IT central banks remain fuzzy. For example, as we discuss on p. 000, the distinction between the role of the concurrent rate of monetary expansion on the monetary policy decisions in Spain and Germany is not that large. In both countries, policy decisions are based on a wide set of indicators, with the growth of a money aggregate having a privileged role. The situation is, perhaps, even more indistinct with respect to exchange rates. In all the IT countries, variations in the exchange rate are perceived as having an important influence on future inflation, as we discuss on p. 73, although it is not regarded as a target in its own right. Nevertheless, given the IT comfort zones for the exchange rate can be internally defined, and monetary policy could be based on those 'targets'. By comparison, the Central Banks in Latin America (e.g. Argentina, Brazil, Chile, Colombia, Mexico, Peru) generally combine both an exchange rate operating target and an inflation objective. But in these cases, the key operational decisions are primarily driven by the exchange rate target rather than the attempt to achieve a numerically specified inflation objective.

The most problematical case is that of Israel which combines an intermediate exchange rate objective (a crawling peg) with an explicit numerically quantified IT. In their conference on experiences with inflation targets, which the Bank of England hosted in March 1995, the proceedings of which can be found in Haldane (1995a), Israel was included as an IT country. We believe, however, that Israel should be included, with the Latin American countries, as primarily operating on the basis of an intermediate exchange rate target. Although increased importance has been attached to the targeting of inflation in the last two years, the existence of an announced crawling band may sometimes force the Central Bank to take policy actions which are only triggered by exchange rate developments and are not related to inflation concerns, as it would happen in a pure IT country, but the distinction is fine.[3]

Our set of IT countries is the same as that adopted by the Bank of England, apart from Israel, which we exclude from our group, and the one adopted by the Bank for International Settlements, and includes Australia, Canada, Finland, New Zealand, Spain, Sweden and the UK. What distinguishes this group from other countries where price stability is the sole objective of monetary policy is that there is an *official commitment* from the monetary authorities to achieve a *clearly defined*, numerically quantified, target for inflation,[4] together with the absence of any other intermediate target.[5] In the IT countries policy changes are usually explained and justified as caused by prospective movements in inflation, for which prior monetary or exchange rate movements will often be a prime explanation; whereas in the non-IT countries, policy decisions will normally be explained and justified in terms of the rate of growth of some intermediate monetary target or some change in the exchange rate, unless there are good grounds for believing that these are not giving a reasonable prediction for future inflation.

The existence of an explicit and precise IT, instead of a simple reference to price stability being the objective of policy, provides an anchor for inflation expectations and helps to make the monetary authorities more accountable.[6] Many of the countries in our sample, but not all, have recently been granted greater independence from government for determining interest rates.[7] While there was a move in that direction in the United Kingdom in 1992–3, the formal decision to alter interest rates remains with the Chancellor. Unless there is an operational exchange rate target, (and it is highly dubious whether the wide band ERM in being since August 1993 represents an operational target), or an unusually well behaved demand-for-money (velocity) function, then the grant to Central Banks of greater independence to vary interest rates ('instrument independence' as defined by Fischer, 1994), has usually in the last few years been accompanied by the acceptance by the Central Bank of a more transparent, and numerically quantified, IT. The exception to that may be the prospective European Central Bank, though it is still possible that it may set such a quantified IT for itself. The absence, in the Maastricht Treaty, of any requirement for such transparency and hence accountability has been criticized (Goodhart, 1991, 1992; Kenen, 1992; Cukierman, 1995).

Another difficult choice we had to make regarded the dates of introduction of IT in the countries in our sample. It is hard to assign a specific date to changes in policy frameworks, especially for inflation targeting, given the similarities between inflation targeting and other frameworks where price stability is the objective of policy. This is a problem similar to the choice of countries to include in the IT set, and the reasons behind our choice of dates are the same as for our choice of countries. Our emphasis is on the existence of an official *explicit* commitment from the monetary authorities to achieve a *precisely defined*, numerically quantified, target for inflation. Thus, we took the date of introduction of IT to be the date of the official announcement of the commitment to achieve a precisely defined target. According to this criterion, the dates of the announcements of inflation targets were as follows:

Australia	1993[8]
Canada	1991, 26 February[9]
Finland	1993, 2 February
New Zealand	1990, 2 March[10]
Spain	1995, 1 January[11]
Sweden	1993, 15 January
UK	1992, 8 October

Policy frameworks are not changed in one day, and it is likely that some Central Banks were already behaving as IT, even before the official announcement of the target. Furthermore, giving the usually long policy lags, some of the observed performance of IT countries must reflect monetary policies that were in place before the adoption of IT. These problems should be taken into consideration when analysing the results of our exercises that involve the use of the announcement dates.

Our chosen set of countries is small, and they have only adopted IT for a short period. Since our data period ends in most cases at the end of 1995, it is far too short a period to make any robust claims about the effectiveness of IT, as McCallum (1995) also emphasized in his recent review article on inflation targeting. Nonetheless such is the interest in this subject that we could not resist making such attempts.

One of the major problems is that the last few years have been characterized by a special world-wide set of conditions (themselves no doubt partly reflecting the shift of emphasis in monetary policies in many countries). Among these conditions have been a rapid decline in inflation to low levels, which was generally sharper than forecast either by Central Banks or private sector commentators, and in many, but not all, countries a further increase in unemployment. So, by comparison with their own earlier history, IT countries may be assessed as having been, (a) successful with their prime aim of reducing inflation, (b) congenitally likely to exaggerate the future likelihood of a resurgent inflation, and (c) having only achieved low inflation by higher unemployment. But all these phenomena may result more from the international context, rather than from any special particularities resulting from the adoption of IT itself.

In order to try to guard against such problems we have, in various exercises, tried to compare the results of the IT countries against those from a set of comparable countries. But which countries might be comparable? All our set of IT countries were industrialized OECD countries, so we restricted our comparator group to that set. Most of our IT countries started with middling inflation rates; so we chose as comparator countries those with roughly similar initial inflation rates.[12] Nevertheless, such a choice is always problematical so we chose four, overlapping, non-IT control groups. The first two groups consisted of countries with similar inflation levels in the 1980s (one is composed of five and the other of seven countries), the third consisted of seven countries with similar inflation levels in the period 1987–92, and the fourth is composed by seven countries that we subjectively chose as facing similar economic environments as the IT countries.

But one cannot make a silk purse out of a sow's ear. Our selected set of IT countries is small, and the selection process debatable. So is the selection of a control group. The number of years in which the Central Banks have been applying IT is very small, and these years had some special world-wide characteristics. Given the lack of data, the results are likely to be sensitive to the empirical methods used. It is far too soon to reach any robust, statistically significant conclusions about the effects of that choice on the macroeconomic outcome.

Where it may be somewhat easier, at least in some matters, to establish whether the adoption of IT made a major difference is with respect to its influence on the behaviour of the Central Banks themselves. The adoption of a numerically quantified IT makes the comparative success, or failure, of a central bank more transparent. But the lengthy lags in the effect of interest rates on nominal incomes and on inflation make it necessary to adjust interest rates *now* to *forecast* future inflation, if there is to be much hope of controlling inflation to the desired degree of accuracy. With the Central Bank now also having greater responsibility for adjusting domestic interest rates, the shift to IT is likely to bring with it the need for revised and expanded communications, with both government and public, about both inflation forecasts and current actions. Moreover, there are some instances where the upwards shock to inflation comes from the supply rather than from the demand side.[13] In general the Central Bank should *not* seek to offset the first-round effect of that. How easily, if at all, can the central bank not only follow that precept, but also communicate it to the general public?

Large interest changes (especially if upwards) are not only unpopular but may also be destabilising to the economy and to the financial system. Moreover, any reversals of direction of interest rate changes within any short period (e.g. up, then down) may give an appearance of vacillation in policy and uncertainty in approach. Whether for these, or other, reasons Central Banks have typically smoothed interest rate adjustments, i.e. they tend to make a consecutive series of some six, or so, small adjustments (of about 1/2 per cent each typically) in discount (base) rates over a period lasting several quarters, rather than fewer, larger adjustments (see Rudebusch, 1995; Goodhart, 1996). This syndrome has been criticized as 'too little, too late', and resulting in strong auto-correlation in inflation. Since the objectives of IT have been, as we shall demonstrate, demanding both in terms of level and permitted range of fluctuation (between the bands), has this caused any difference either to Central Banks' operating techniques or reaction functions? In particular, is there any evidence among IT countries that they have varied interest rates earlier or in larger steps than in the past?

Our main focus is, therefore, on whether and how the adoption of IT may have affected the behaviour of those Central Banks. This will, we believe, represent our main contribution. In order to obtain more information and understanding, especially on this aspect of the behaviour of IT central banks, we wrote to them in January 1996, and with one exception we received full, frank and helpful replies. We are particularly grateful to these senior officials for being so patient, courteous and helpful. Much of the body of this chapter could have been undertaken only with their assistance.

EXECUTION OF MONETARY POLICY

Reasons Behind the Adoption of Inflation Targets

The adoption of IT has usually followed the recognition of the failure of the previous monetary policy framework. This is obvious in the cases of the United Kingdom, Sweden and Finland, where IT was adopted just after the collapse of the fixed exchange rate regimes.[14] The adoption of

IT in Spain, although it followed the granting of autonomy to the Central Bank, also reflected some disappointment with the use of both monetary aggregates and the exchange rate as an intermediate target (following the 1992–3 ERM crisis and consequent widening of the fluctuation bands). In Canada, New Zealand and Australia, the adoption of IT followed a period of discretionary monetary policy, where no explicit and quantified target was used, a framework that was generally judged to have been unsatisfactory and was implemented only in the absence of a better alternative.[15]

Given the differences in the monetary policy frameworks previously in place, we should expect the observed effects of the adoption of IT in the behaviour of the Central Banks in our sample to be substantially different for European and non-European Central Banks. The transition from a fixed exchange rate regime to a floating exchange rate regime implies, by itself, substantial changes in the execution of monetary policy. For the European countries in our sample, the adoption of an IT coincided with such a regime switch. Thus, we cannot separate empirically the changes in behaviour caused by the change in exchange rate regime and the adoption of IT. This is not the case for the non-European countries, where the adoption of an IT was not accompanied by any other major change in the monetary policy framework. In the following analysis, such differences between the two groups should be kept in mind.

The adoption of IT can be seen, in all the countries in our sample, as an alternative to discretionary monetary policy, in an environment where the use of exchange rates or money aggregates as intermediate targets is thought to be unsatisfactory. The official statements made at the time of the adoption of IT usually advance two arguments for the abandonment of a discretionary monetary policy: the need to provide an anchor for inflation expectations and the need to make the Central Bank[16] more accountable. The private sector cannot understand fully the stance and the consequences of a discretionary monetary policy, nor can they anticipate correctly the actions of the central bank. In this situation, the formation of inflation expectations becomes a complicated process, and uncertainty about future inflation is much higher than in a framework where a credible IT has been previously set. Also, under a discretionary monetary policy it is difficult to evaluate the performance of the Central Bank, since there are no clear and easy to verify benchmarks against which the performance can be compared. An explicitly and precisely set IT provides such a benchmark, thus making the central bank more publicly accountable.

Where the accountability of the monetary policy decision process was an important reason for the adoption of IT, such targets were set as the outcome of an agreement between the Central Bank and the government (in New Zealand, Canada and the United Kingdom). Where the main concern was to provide an anchor for inflation expectations, the IT was set unilaterally by the Central Bank, although in some cases these targets were later endorsed by the government (as happened in Australia, Finland and Spain). The fact that the IT is announced jointly by the Central Bank and the government may enhance the credibility of the target, as long as the joint announcement implies a commitment by one party, the agent, which is monitored by the other, the principal, especially if the agent deciding on monetary policy suffers an effective penalty if targets are not met.[17]

The first reason why a joint commitment could be credibility-enhancing is that in some countries budgetary measures may be necessary to help control inflation and inflation expectations. Where fiscal problems were one of the main causes of the past inflationary pressures, and high stocks of public debt can raise the spectre of the government eventually forcing a partial monetization of the debt, low inflation can be a credible target only if measures to reduce the budget deficit are put in place. A strong commitment from both the government and the Central Bank to an inflation target reinforces the likelihood that the targets will be achieved, if this joint commitment can be interpreted as a sign of monetary and fiscal policy coordination.

The other reason one could expect higher credibility from a joint commitment is the fact that as long as the right incentives are in place,[18] the external monitoring may play the role of a 'precommitment technology' that could overcome the 'time-inconsistency' problem of monetary policy, as described in Kydland and Prescott (1977) and Barro and Gordon (1983a). For central banks who unilaterally set the IT, there are few effective sanctions. A Central Bank Governor missing a pre-stated target is unlikely to sanction himself, though he might face public obloquy. Even if a government was secretly happy with faster monetary expansion (than the target would imply),[19] the fact of missing a published target to which the government had set its name will give rise to demands for it to respond; sacking, or fining, the Governor will be relatively painless for the government itself (in most cases). Also, a joint announcement is more likely to be realistic: knowing that it may be held accountable for missing it, the Central Bank will not accept the over optimistic targets politicians tend to set.

The only incentive to stick to the target Central Banks who unilaterally set their target have, is the effect on their long-term reputation of missing (or constantly changing) it.[20] If their track record on inflation, before the adoption of IT, is not very good, their current reputation will be low, and losing it would not be a very serious problem. Only after the Central Bank has established a track record by meeting the targets for a reasonably long period will the inflation target become credible, since only then will the damage to the reputation of reneging the announced targets have a significant cost. Rogoff (1985) suggested that if the Central Bank is independent from the government, and the Central Bank Governor is 'conservative' – i.e. places a higher relative weight upon inflation stabilisation – the 'time-inconsistency' problem may disappear. Thus, it could be argued that an IT announced by an independent Central Bank could be as credible as a joint commitment. The adoption of IT in the countries in our sample has been associated with changes to, or attempts to change, the legal framework of the Central Bank to make it more independent. However, even in the case of an independent Central Bank the credibility of the IT will not be as high as in the joint announcement with sanctions case:[21] first, because legal independence does not necessarily mean actual independence; second, because an independent central banker is not necessarily the same as a 'conservative' central banker.[22] Again, only after a reasonably long period of proving that the Central Bank is actually independent and the governor is 'conservative' will the IT become credible. Making the Central Bank independent does not eliminate the need for reputation building. Only the existence of external monitoring associated with the appropriate incentive scheme may have a short term effect on credibility.

The issue discussed in the paragraphs above refers to what Andersson and Berg (1995) call 'operational credibility' of IT, i.e. the likelihood that the IT will effectively be met, given the current institutional framework, which they distinguish from the 'political credibility' of IT, i.e. the likelihood of a regime shift, where the current framework may be replaced by another not favouring price stability. 'Political credibility', *inter alia*, depends on the size of public debt and current budget deficits (as incentives to generate inflation in the future), but it depends above all on the support given to the IT framework by the political opposition. Any legislative framework favouring price stability introduced by one government may be reversed by future governments. If the opposition political parties are against the IT, the long-term credibility of the framework is seriously affected.[23] Only an IT endorsed by the current government and by all the opposition political parties that are likely to become (part of) the government in the medium term may be credible, and varying degrees of support by opposition parties is likely to be reflected in empirically observed varying degrees of credibility.[24]

Choice of Target

An IT must be credible, to provide a good anchor for inflation expectations. This implies that it should be stated in a simple and clear way, and it has to be feasible. It must be flexible, in the sense that it should allow for monetary policy to accommodate some unexpected (supply) shocks and to adjust to changing economic environments. It must be easily verifiable, to

Box 2.1   Design of Inflation Targets

Australia
Index: Underlying CPI (excluding fruit and vegetables, petrol, interest costs, public sector prices and other volatile prices)
Caveats: None
Target: 2%–3% on average
Horizon: Immediate

Canada
Index: CPI (underlying CPI – excluding food, energy, and first round effects of indirect taxes – is used as the base for policy decisions)
Caveats: Large increases in oil prices, natural disasters
Target: 2% ± 1%
Horizon: 1995–8 (new target to be set by 1998)

Finland
Index: Underlying CPI (excluding effects of taxes, subsidies and housing related capital costs)
Caveats: None
Target: Around 2%
Horizon: From 1995

New Zealand
Index: CPI
Caveats: Significant changes in indirect taxes or government charges, significant changes in import or export prices, interest costs, natural disasters (in practice, the target is an underlying CPI index, calculated by the RBNZ as the CPI modified by the caveats)
Target: 0%–2%
Horizon: To the end of Governor's term (currently 31 August 1998)

Spain
Index: CPI
Caveats: Only generic caveats (e.g. role of fiscal policy and wage behaviour)
Target: Less than 3%
Horizon: During 1997

Sweden
Index: CPI
Caveats: None
Target: 2% ± 1%
Horizon: From 1995

UK
Index: RPIX (RPI excluding mortgage interest payments)
Caveats: Effects of indirect taxes and subsidies and interest costs
Target: 1%–2.5%
Horizon: By the end of this Parliament (1997)

make the Central Bank accountable. These desirable characteristics of an optimal IT restrict the choice of each Central Bank, but there is still some scope for differences. Box 2.1 compares the targets adopted by the countries in our sample, and the main trade-offs are briefly discussed below.

When defining an IT, the first choice to be made is which price index is going to be targeted. All Central Banks in our sample target consumer price inflation. The Consumer Price Index (CPI) is the best known and most commonly used (e.g. in wage negotiations) measure of inflation. It also has some technical advantages, like being promptly released and seldom revised. The impact on expectations and credibility of such a measure of inflation should be greater than alternative measures that rely on complex statistical treatment or are released with a considerable lag, like the GDP deflator.

However, the headline CPI is affected by a number of shocks that cannot be controlled by monetary policy, and do not reflect the underlying inflationary pressures the Central Bank should be worrying about. Changes in indirect taxes or subsidies are not usually related to inflationary pressures, but can have a significant (short-run) impact in the CPI. When the CPI includes interest-related costs, it responds perversely to monetary policy changes: a tightening of policy in reaction to rising inflation will imply higher interest costs, and thus even higher CPI. Some supply-side shocks that raise inflation and lower output (like large changes in commodity prices or natural disasters) should be accommodated, to avoid the adverse implications for real activity of a restrictive monetary policy.[25] A flexible monetary policy, able to adjust efficiently to these problems, should be based on a target expressed in terms of some measure of underlying inflation that would exclude the effects of this type of shocks. The problem with the underlying CPI is that usually it does not have similar desirable features of statistical simplicity and general acceptability as the headline CPI. Thus, a target expressed in terms of underlying CPI tends to have a smaller impact on expectations. The alternative is to set the target in terms of headline CPI, but to include some escape clause (or caveats) that would justify missing it, in order to allow for some flexibility in monetary policy.

In both solutions mentioned above, transparency and accountability are affected. The performance of the Central Bank can be easily verified only if the targeted price index is calculated by an independent agency. In our sample, targets based on an underlying CPI are used only by Australia and Finland, and in both countries the underlying CPI targeted is computed by statistics agencies independent of the Central Bank, and thus accountability is not jeopardised. The problem is that in most countries even when the statistics agencies publish some underlying CPI, it seldom excludes all the relevant shocks. In this case, the Central Bank has to choose between calculating its own index (with the corresponding loss in transparency and credibility) or using the less adequate external index. A similar choice must be made regarding the caveats if the target is set in terms of headline CPI. Transparency suggests that the list of caveats must be precise and exhaustive, but this reduces flexibility, since some shocks are unpredictable, even in nature. It should be stressed, however, that in practice the distinction between headline and underlying CPI targets tends to become blurred. In all the countries where the formal target is based on headline CPI, monetary policy decisions are based in some measure of underlying inflation, not headline inflation. Judging from our sample, it seems that there is no effective choice, and IT have to be set in terms of underlying CPI, since this is the price index monetary policy is best able to control.[26] The only real question arises in the long term, if the two measures exhibit persistent differences.[27] Then, if the target is defined in terms of headline CPI, the operational policy targets for underlying CPI have to be changed so that headline CPI comes within the target range. If the target is defined in terms of underlying CPI, no change is needed, and headline CPI will deviate from the target, and this may have an important impact on inflation expectations.

The design of the IT in our sample suggests that Central Banks believe that monetary policy is able to control underlying inflation but not in a precise and accurate way. The targets are either range targets or point targets that are supposed only to hold on average, and in either case this means the inflation rate is not going to be kept constant at some pre-set level. Some (limited) volatility of the inflation rate will be tolerated since some uncontrollable shocks are likely to affect inflation and monetary policy technology is not considered to be accurate enough to forecast, or bring about, finely calibrated changes in the inflation rate. Where the target range is precisely defined,[28] the usual band width is 2 or 3 percentage points.[29] The optimal band width involves a trade-off between the credibility-enhancing effects of choosing a demanding target and achieving it, and the credibility-damaging effects of missing it (Goodhart and Viñals, 1994). This would suggest that Central Banks that need to build a reputation should choose narrow range targets, whilst more credible Central Banks may opt for wider bands. A highly credible Central Bank could even set a soft-edged band, similar to Finland's,[30] where only the mid-point is defined and no explicit deviation ranges are set. The choice of 2 percentage point bands seems to reflect a preference for credibility-enhancing narrow bands. If so, the question is whether monetary policy is precise enough to achieve an inflation level inside such a band. In Section 3 we discuss this issue in the light of the outcomes of monetary policy prior to the adoption of IT and the *ex post* success of the Central Banks in our sample in achieving their targets.

A common feature in our sample is the absence of price level targets. Price level targets reduce the uncertainty about the future price level, but are more restrictive since they imply that high inflation in one period must be compensated by low inflation in the next period. Also, since price levels are permanently affected by supply-side shocks they are less flexible in accommodating those shocks. Central Banks in our sample may have opted for price change (i.e. inflation) targets because they prefer to have more policy flexibility (even at the cost of higher uncertainty), but it could also be that they decided to go one step at a time. The new monetary framework was tried first with the less restrictive version of price change targets, instead of going straight to the stronger version of targeting price levels. If this was the case, we might expect to see some of them adopting price level targets some time in the future. But although there are no price level targets, there are point targets that should hold on average, as in Australia.[31] This kind of target might be interpreted as (moving) price level targets, since both have the same effects in terms of reducing uncertainty about the future price level. Setting an average inflation rate of 2 per cent, strictly means setting the future price level at any point in time, if 'average' means that an inflation rate of 3 per cent in one period implies a rate of 1 per cent the next period.[32] We are unsure, however, whether average targets should be interpreted so strictly.

The adoption of IT reflects the view that price stability should be the only (medium-and long-term) objective of monetary policy. However, price stability does not necessarily mean a zero inflation rate. In fact, for all the countries in our sample, the target is a positive rate of inflation, although small (around 2 per cent). The question of the optimal rate of inflation, and the empirical and theoretical arguments that imply that the optimal rate of inflation is positive, has been extensively discussed.[33] The main theoretical arguments against a zero inflation rate refer to the non-negativity of the real interest rates (the 'Summers effect'),[34] to the existence of downward nominal rigidities in the labour and product markets,[35] to the optimal inflation tax,[36] and to bias in measures of consumer price inflation. Of these, the only argument that one can find in the official statements of (some of) the Central Banks in our sample is the latter.[37] The IT of around 2 per cent is said to reflect the average bias in the CPI caused by the introduction of new goods, the improvement in the quality of existing goods, and changes in consumer demand in response to changes in relative prices for which the measured CPI does not account. Estimates of this bias in different countries, however, suggest that the bias is in the 0.5 per cent–1.5 per cent range.[38] Thus, some (or all) of the other arguments may also be behind the choice of a 2 per cent target, although not explicitly stated.[39] Given the likely differences among countries in this statistical bias, and especially in the effects of the other arguments for a positive inflation rate, we find the similarity of the target levels striking. The mid point of the ranges is between 1 per cent and 2.5 per cent for all countries, with the majority concentrating around 2 per cent.

We are not aware of any studies quantifying the optimal rate of inflation in each country, supporting *ex ante* the choice of a given target. Perhaps, Central Banks just assume that 2 per cent is the small positive number that theoretical arguments suggest the optimal rate of inflation should be, or simply chose to target the same inflation level other countries were targeting.[40]

Given the long lags in monetary policy, the target is usually set initially for some future date, at least two years ahead.[41] Where the current inflation was above the target, the Central Banks in our sample set a downward path for inflation, to reap as soon as possible the benefits of lower inflation expectations the IT is supposed to provide. These 'transition targets' could serve as a benchmark against which the progress towards the ultimate objective could be measured, and meeting the 'transition targets' would help to establish the credibility of the final target,[42] since it is likely that the credibility of the target, and its impact on expectations, will be achieved only by the success in meeting it, and not by its simple announcement. Box 2.2 describes the timing of the targets in our sample. The inflation rate at the time of the announcement was above the final target range in Canada, New Zealand, Spain and the United Kingdom, but the intermediate targets only demanded a strong deflationary effort in Spain, since current inflation was inside the first 'transition target' in the other countries. The impact on expectations of a less ambitious target will tend to be smaller, although a too ambitious target might not be credible. The differences between less and more ambitious targets should be kept in mind when analysing whether inflation outcomes were consistent with the targets (see p. 90) and the impact on expectations of the announcement and subsequent inflation performance (see p. 102).

	Box 2.2	Timing of Targets		
	Date of announcement	*Current inflation*[43] *Target*	*Target date*	*Transition path*
Australia	1993	1.9% 2–3%	1993	none
Canada	Feb 1991	3.9% 1–3%	1995	2–4% Dec 1992; 1.5–3.5% mid 1994
Finland	Feb 1993	2.6% 2%	1995	none
New Zealand	Mar 1990	3.3% 0–2%	1993	3–5% Dec 1990; 2.5–4.5% Dec 1991; 1.5–3.5% Dec 1992[44]
Spain	Jan 1995	4.3% <3%	1997	3.5–4% early 1996
Sweden	Jan 1993	1.8% 1–3%	1995	underlying inflation not increasing
United Kingdom	Oct 1992	4.0% 1–2.5%	1997	1–4%

Reaction Function

Under an IT framework the final objective is targeted directly, and no intermediary targets are used. Given the lags in monetary policy, this means that an (explicit or implicit) forecast of future inflation is the intermediary target.[45] In principle, the monetary policy decision process would start with the computation of a point forecast for inflation X periods ahead, with X being the policy lag. Monetary conditions would then be adjusted according to the relative position of the forecast to the target range: if the forecast is on target, no action is required; if the forecast is above the target, monetary conditions should be tightened; if the forecast is below the target, monetary conditions should be relaxed. Thus, IT would be different from the money or exchange rate targeting frameworks because policy reacts to a quantified inflation forecast, and not to current changes in the *ex post*, actual data for some financial variable. Also, in principle, IT involves a quasi-formalised reaction rule, that distinguishes it from a discretionary monetary policy. However, the actual policy decision processes do not always follow the simple rules outlined above, and the distinction of IT from other policy frameworks is less clear than the process outlined above might suggest.

In principle, IT involves the computation of a quantified inflation forecast that is going to be compared with the target. As we show in Box 2.3, although quantified inflation forecasts are used in all the Central Banks in our sample, policy decisions are not based exclusively on those quantified forecasts, but also on a subjective evaluation of several leading indicators. In some countries (e.g. Australia, Finland), quantified inflation forecasts are just one of the indicators used for policy decisions. Even in the countries where the quantified inflation forecasts are the key input in the policy decision process, much subjective judgement is put into the forecasts, and furthermore the policy-makers also look at other indicators, not only the point forecast. This is usually justified on the grounds that point inflation forecasts are deemed to be unreliable and subjective judgements of the inflationary pressures in the economy are thought to improve the results. Another way of avoiding the limitations of point forecasts is to do some form of 'risk analysis', by computing different forecasts under alternative scenarios,[46] or describing the inflation forecasts as a probability distribution and not a point estimate.[47]

Another of the distinctive features of the IT framework would be the use of several indicators as inputs into the decision process and forecasting procedure, with no indicator having a predominant role, as an intermediary target would have. In practice, this distinction is less clear, since some Central Banks in our sample give a large weight to a particular variable, like the exchange rate in New Zealand or broad money in Spain (see Box 2.3, paragraph **B**). It is difficult to see, for instance, where the behaviour of the Banco de España differs, in this respect, from the behaviour of the

Box 2.3   Inflation Targeting Monetary Policy Framework

A The inflation target is the final objective of monetary policy. Given the usually long policy lags, decisions have to be made in terms of future inflation, not current inflation. Future inflation can be assessed by means of a quantified inflation forecast or a subjective evaluation of future inflationary pressures based on several indicators:

Australia	subjective evaluation of several indicators, including inflation forecasts
Canada	use econometric model (including judgement) to estimate the time path of monetary conditions necessary to keep future inflation (approximately 2 years ahead) near mid-point (monetary aggregates are used as an independent check on the economic projection)
Finland	subjective evaluation of several indicators; since October 1995, also inflation forecast 6 to 8 quarters ahead
New Zealand	inflation forecast 2 to 8 quarters ahead
Spain	use of econometric models and subjective evaluation of several indicators
Sweden	inflation forecast 1–2 years ahead
United Kingdom	inflation forecast 2 years ahead

B The inflation outlook (point forecast or subjective evaluation) is based on several quantitative and qualitative indicators, covering a wide range of financial and non-financial variables, like exchange rates and other asset prices, expansion of money (and other financial) aggregates, inflation expectations, wage settlements and other cost and price increases and excess demand or supply in goods and labour markets. Each Central Bank pays special attention to a subset of indicators, and in some cases one indicator has a predominant role. The importance given to each indicator may change over time. For the Central Banks in our sample, the key indicators are:

Australia	inflation expectations, wage settlements, output gap
Canada	M2+, M1, output gap, wage indicators
Finland	wages, inflation expectations, exchange rate, yield curve, money aggregates
New Zealand	exchange rate
Spain	ALP (liquid assets held by private sector) growth of not more than 8 per cent is used as a reference
Sweden	output gap, inflation expectations, yield curve
United Kingdom	output gap, inflation expectations, observed prices, M0, M4

C Monetary conditions (the operational target) are then adjusted according to the inflation outlook. Monetary conditions are tightened if inflation is forecast to be 'too high' and relaxed if inflation is forecast to be 'too low'. Given that the countries in our sample are medium-size and small open economies, the operational target is usually some combination of a short-term interest rate and the (trade-weighted) exchange rate. This combination can be expressed in terms of a computed 'monetary conditions index' (MCI)[48] or be left to subjective evaluation. The operational targets are:

Australia	money market overnight rate
Canada	MCI, where the 90 day commercial paper rate weighs 75 per cent and the exchange rate index 25 per cent
Finland	evaluation of monetary conditions, where the key interest rate is the one month tender rate
New Zealand	subjective evaluation of monetary conditions, where the emphasis is on the trade weighted exchange rate and the key interest rate is the 90 day bank bill rate
Spain	money market overnight rate
Sweden	MCI, where the money market overnight rate weighs 75 per cent and the exchange rate index 25 per cent
United Kingdom	commercial banks' base rate

D Policy instruments are then adjusted in order to achieve the desired level for the operational target. If policy changes are necessary, these are signalled by announcing new values for the policy instrument. The key variables for signalling policy changes are:

Australia	operating target for the overnight money market rate
Canada	operating band for the overnight money market rate
Finland	tender rate
New Zealand	settlement cash balances at the RBNZ (used to influence the money market overnight rate)
Spain	intervention rate (10-day repo rate)
Sweden	repo rate
United Kingdom	money market dealings rate

Central Banks who use a monetary target framework, like the Bundesbank. In Spain, the growth of the monetary aggregate ALP (liquidity assets held by the private sector) is the main indicator behind policy decisions, although other indicators are also considered, and the liquidity growth targets are not taken as fixed rules, but just as a means of achieving price stability. In money targeting countries, interest rate changes are said to be conditioned on the movement of some monetary aggregate, like the M3 in Germany, but other indicators are also considered, and the money targets are frequently overruled due to other economic factors.[49]

Finally, the IT framework differs from a discretionary policy because a quasi-formalised reaction rule exists. In practice, the straightforward application of the rule raises several problems, whose solution generally involves considerable discretion for the policy-makers.[50]

The first question is whether the target is the range or the mid-point of the range. On the latter case, the bands may be interpreted as confidence intervals indicating where *ex post* inflation might be expected to lie if policy is directed at the mid-point, and the Central Bank should act whenever the forecast differs from the mid-point. In Canada, for example, policy actions are directed at keeping forecast inflation near the mid-point of the band. Where the target is the band, strictly, the rule only demands action when the forecast is outside the target range. However, even in this case a prudent Central Bank might wish to act as long as the forecast is close to the boundaries, to minimise the risk of missing the target given the uncertainty surrounding any inflation forecast. In New Zealand, where the target is the band, the RBNZ initially would not react as long as the forecast was inside the band. More recently, after an unexpected and short-lived surge in the price of fresh vegetables that drove underlying inflation 0.2 per cent above target in the second quarter of 1995, although all the previous forecasts for that quarter were inside the target range, the RBNZ decided to adopt the strategy of acting as long as the forecast is close to the boundaries (Mayes and Riches, 1996).

The second problem is whether any deviation from target, no matter how small, should trigger a reaction, or whether policy should respond only to significant deviations. The credibility and accountability of the IT would suggest reactions to any deviation, to minimise deviations from target, but some Central Banks (e.g. the Bank of England) will react only to significant deviations. The reason is that small deviations imply small adjustments in monetary conditions, and small adjustments might be undesirable (for instance, the Bank of England has only initiated interest rate changes of at least 1/4 per cent). The final question is, if the forecast lies off the target in one period, whether the policy response should be strong, so that inflation quickly returns to the range, or gradual. Again, the credibility and accountability issues would suggest a sharp response, to minimise the number of periods the target is going to be missed. However, some Central Banks (e.g. in Sweden and Spain) prefer a gradual approach, because a radical response could be destabilising and drive inflation through the other end of the range, since forecasts are not precise and the effects of policy are not known exactly.

Instruments and Operational Targets

The IT framework differs from other monetary frameworks in terms of the final objectives (a quantified level for inflation) and intermediary targets (no single intermediary target). There is no apparent reason why the adoption of IT would imply changes in policy instruments or operational targets. In fact, no Central Bank in our sample claimed to have made such changes due to the adoption of IT. Paragraphs **C** and **D** of Box 2.3 describe the policy instruments and operational targets currently in use in the countries in our sample. Changes in policy instruments have occurred in the IT period, for instance in Finland, Sweden and the United Kingdom, but usually for microeconomic reasons. Nevertheless, being a new policy framework, IT should lead to different policy responses, that could be translated into a different usage of the policy instruments and in a different behaviour of the operational targets. In this section, we try to identify any changes the adoption of IT induced in the behaviour of exchange rates and short-term interest rates.

Foreign Exchange Rates

If the sole objective of monetary policy is the control of inflation, then Central Banks must be prepared to accept the level of the exchange rate that is compatible with the inflation target, whatever that level is. This does not mean that IT is necessarily incompatible with some (loosely defined) desired level for the exchange rate. If inflation levels are similar at home and abroad, IT is also a rough mechanism for maintaining the external value of the currency, as long as PPP holds. However, conflicts between external and internal objectives may often arise. Under IT this must be resolved by the abandonment of the external objective, which implies that IT countries must be prepared to accept larger short and medium-term swings in the exchange rate, if necessary.

Obviously, IT is an alternative, and is different from, a regime of exchange rate targets. It could be argued that exchange rates fixed to low inflation currencies and IT are not fundamentally different, since they are just different ways of achieving price stability, and, if inflation is low at home and abroad, exchange rates will tend to be stable even under IT. However, in the presence of significant real shocks, under IT we might observe large swings in the nominal exchange rate, with no changes in inflation levels, as the real exchange rate adjusts to the new economic conditions.[51] This type of adjustment could not occur under exchange rate targeting, at least as long as targets are kept unchanged.

Box 2.4 describes the role and the behaviour of foreign exchange rates under IT. Medium-term control of the exchange rate is attempted only if large changes threaten the IT, and short-term control is abandoned, as we show in paragraph **A** of Box 2.4. No Central Bank in our sample tries to stabilise the exchange rate in the short term, except the Bank of Finland who occasionally does interventions to avoid sharp intra-day movements, and this should imply higher short-term volatility of the exchange rate for the European countries, who had exchange rate targets before the adoption of IT. Evidence that supports this hypothesis is presented in Paragraph **B** of Box 2.4, where it is shown that short-term exchange rate volatility during the IT period is generally higher than during the fixed exchange rate period, for the European countries. On the other hand, exchange rate volatility is lower during IT than during the discretionary period, for almost every country in our sample.

Compared to a discretionary monetary policy, IT seems to be able to provide more stable foreign exchange rates. This could be explained by a reduction in the uncertainty of market participants regarding the future

Box 2.4   Foreign Exchange Rates under Inflation Targeting

A THE ROLE OF THE EXCHANGE RATE IN THE POLICY DECISION PROCESS

In the countries in our sample, exchange rates have, at least, an informative role in the policy decision process. In some cases, exchange rates may act as operational targets, but they are not intermediary targets. In our sample, the role of the exchange rate is as follows:

Australia	exchange rate is only relevant if excessive depreciation threatens future inflation
Canada	exchange rate is a component of the 'monetary conditions index', the operational target
Finland	large changes in exchange rate are allowed, although some of the actions the Bank of Finland in early 1993 were motivated by the threat of the collapse of the markka and it does occasional interventions on both sides to stop sharp intra-day movements (but not affecting the trend)
New Zealand	exchange rate is the key variable in the operation of monetary policy due to its strong and rapid influence on prices, but it is not a target in its own right; given the inflation forecasts, comfort zones for the exchange rate are defined, and adjusted as parameters are revised; movements of the exchange rate within the zone are normally tolerated until the rate approaches the margins; however there is no direct intervention on forex markets
Spain	there is a formal commitment to keep the peseta within the widened bands of the ERM, but only permanent trends (not temporary fluctuations) shape policy decisions and as long as it may endanger the inflation target; forex stability is viewed more as a result that will come about with price stability than an end in itself;
Sweden	return to exchange rate targets only when it is compatible with price stability
United Kingdom	there are no targets for the exchange rate

B SHORT-TERM EXCHANGE RATE BEHAVIOUR

Figure 2.1 plots the absolute value of the daily changes in the exchange rate of the countries in our sample from 3 January 1986 to 27 February 1996.[52] For the Australian, Canadian and New Zealand dollar the exchange rates used are US dollar rates; for the Finnish markka, the Spanish peseta and the Swedish krona, DM rates are used; for the British pound both USD and DM are presented. The vertical dotted lines indicate the date of the adoption of IT. In some of the charts, large outliers were truncated for presentational purposes.

Visual inspection of Figure 2.1 suggests that the adoption of IT was associated with higher short-term exchange rate volatility in Finland and Sweden, and with lower short-term volatility in New Zealand. To test formally for the existence of such changes in volatility we used the ARCH framework, where we allowed the conditional variance to be affected by changes in the monetary policy regime. Following Baillie and Bollerslev (1989) and

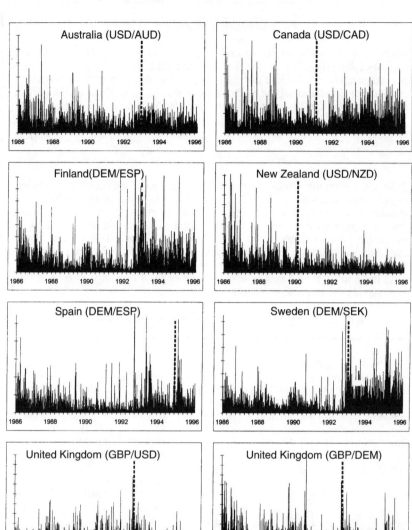

Figure 2.1 Exchange rate daily absolute changes, 1986–96

Hsieh (1989) we assumed exchange rate returns follow a GARCH (1,1) process of the form:

$$r_{i,t} = \mu_i + \varepsilon_{i,t} \qquad (2.1)$$

$$\varepsilon_{i,t} \mid \Psi_{i,t-1} \sim G(0, h_{i,t}) \qquad (2.2)$$

$$h_{i,t} = \gamma_i + \alpha_i \varepsilon_{i,t-1}^2 + \beta_i h_{i,t-1} + \delta_i D_{i,t} \qquad (2.3)$$

where $r_{i,t}$ is the daily return for exchange rate i at period t, $D_{i,t}$ is a dummy variable, taking the value 1 before the adoption of IT, and μ_i, γ_i, α_i, β_i, and δ_i, are parameters. The conditional distribution $G(.)$ was assumed to be normal. The unconditional variance of the model in equations (2.1)–(2.3) for the IT period, σ_{iT}^2, and for the non-IT period, σ_{iN}^2, are given by

$$\sigma_{iT}^2 = \gamma_i/(1 - \alpha_i - \beta_i) \qquad (2.4)$$
$$\sigma_{iN}^2 = (\gamma_i + \delta_i)/(1 - \alpha_i - \beta_i) \qquad (2.5)$$

Table 2.1 reports the results of estimations of this model, for the countries in our sample, over the period 3/1/1986 to 27/2/1996 (t-statistics in parenthesis).[53] A simple comparison of the exchange rate volatility in the IT and non-IT period, reveals significant decreases in the IT period for Australia, the UK, and, in particular, New Zealand, where exchange rate volatility fell more than 75 per cent after the adoption of IT. On the other hand, volatility increased with IT in Finland, Spain and Sweden. For these countries (and to a smaller extent in the UK) the non-IT period was mainly a period of fixed exchange rates, and that may explain the increase in volatility.

Table 2.1 Volatility of daily exchange rates before and after IT

	Dummies definition	γ_i ($\times 10000$)	α_i	β_i	δ_i ($\times 10000$)
Australia	$D : t < 1/1/93$	0.08514 (11.7)	0.1365 (10.1)	0.7269 (46.6)	0.01317 (2.3)
Canada	$D : t < 26/2/91$	0.01587 (15.0)	0.1074 (11.1)	0.7824 (72.2)	−0.00088 (−1.2)
Finland	$D : t < 2/2/93$	0.4236 (16.2)	0.2454 (16.1)	0.6155 (52.1)	−0.2434 (−10.4)
New Zealand	$D : t < 2/3/90$	0.10828 (19.9)	0.1699 (14.6)	0.6407 (44.9)	0.33196 (21.1)
Spain	$D : t < 1/1/95$	219.262 (9.6)	0.3422 (30.8)	0.5635 (68.0)	−55.9597 (−2.6)
Sweden	$D : t < 15/1/93$	3.63103 (15.2)	0.4111 (37.0)	0.3412 (18.3)	−2.9481 (−13.3)
UK	$D : t < 8/10/92$	0.07903 (12.6)	0.1041 (15.7)	0.8519 (152.3)	0.01433 (2.6)

In order to separate the effects of the adoption of IT and the floating of the currency, we estimated a model similar to the one in (2.1)–(2.3), but with equation (2.3) replaced by

$$h_{i,t} = \gamma_i + \alpha_i \varepsilon_{i,t-1}^2 + \beta_i h_{i,t-1} + \omega_i G_{i,t} + \lambda_i F_{i,t} \qquad (2.3')$$

where $G_{i,t}$ is a dummy variable, taking the value 1 during the period of discretionary monetary policy, and $F_{i,t}$ is a dummy variable, taking the value 1 during the fixed exchange rate period. The results of the estimation of this model are reported in Table 2.2.

Table 2.2 Volatility of daily exchange rates during IT and the fixed rate period

	Dummies definition	γ_i ($\times 10000$)	α_i	β_i	ω_i ($\times 10000$)	λ_i ($\times 10000$)
Finland	$G: 8/9/92 < t$ $< 2/2/93$ $F: t <= 8/9/92$	0.5521 (15.9)	0.2334 (14.2)	0.5554 (36.7)	0.44895 (3.3)	−0.32521 (−11.2)
Spain	$G: t < 19/7/89$ or $15/9/92 < t$ $< 1/1/95$ $F: 19/7/89 < t$ $< 15/9/92$	503.284 (11.4)	0.4048 (26.4)	0.3063 (18.6)	−28.680 (−0.7)	−355.617 (−8.5)
Sweden	$G: 18/11/92 < t$ $< 15/1/93$ $F: t <= 18/11/92$	4.2447 (15.4)	0.3018 (15.2)	0.3044 (11.8)	13.0131 (8.7)	−3.474 (−13.7)
United Kingdom	$G: t < 5/10/90$ or $15/9/92 < t$ $< 8/10/92$ $F: 5/10/90 < t$ $< 15/9/92$	0.11439 (13.0)	0.0932 (13.7)	0.8318 (115.9)	0.07458 (7.9)	−0.05258 (−6.8)

When we control for the existence of a fixed exchange rate period, then we observe that exchange rate volatility in the IT period is significantly higher than in the fixed exchange rate period in the four countries where such a regime existed, but significantly lower than in the discretionary regime for five of the seven countries in our sample (Australia, Finland, New Zealand, Sweden and the United Kingdom).[54]

monetary policy, that the existence of a clear target for monetary policy could provide. Compared to exchange rate targets, the adoption of IT leads to a cost in the form of an increase in short- and medium-term exchange rate uncertainty, as would be expected, but allows for easier adjustments to real shocks and reduces the probability of speculative crises in the forex market.

Short-term interest rates

Given that a different policy framework should imply different policy responses, we investigated whether the adoption of IT implied a change in the use of the interest rate instrument. Our first hypothesis was that Central Banks would raise interest rates earlier than before, relative to observed inflationary pressures. The argument is that under IT, Central Banks can resist pressures not to raise them more easily, since interest rate changes can be justified with reference to the inflation forecast and the target. Although there is some evidence that could indicate a more forward-looking behaviour in the non-European countries, we could not find evidence of a systematic change in behaviour in the data available so far: the timing of interest rate changes, after the adoption of IT, was not unusually early relative to observed inflation, especially for the European countries. However, a general change to a more forward-looking attitude might have occurred, but the tests performed, presented in Box 2.5, were not powerful enough to detect it, given the relatively short data series available.

The argument that Central Banks can justify their actions more easily under IT, would also suggest that we would observe less interest rate smoothing, at least in the non-European countries. Supported by their inflation forecasts, a Central Bank could compute the necessary interest rate change to achieve the desired level of inflation, and do the change in one move, instead of doing it in a series of small changes of the same sign.[55] Again, we could not find such a change in behaviour in the data for our sample, although for some countries (e.g. Australia and Canada) there are some indications that the adoption of IT might lead to a more vigorous use of the interest rate instrument, as we describe in Box 2.6. For the European countries, who previously had exchange rate targets, it is likely that before IT interest rates would be changed more frequently and in larger amounts. When the target is the exchange rate, the effects of the policy change are almost immediately observed, and policy must be continuously adjusted. Exchange rate targets demand monitoring and policy reactions almost to the minute, and it is possible that some of those reactions might have to be quick and vigorous, particularly during speculative attacks to the exchange rate. No such emergency policy reactions are needed under IT, and interest rate adjustments can be made more gradually, if interest rate smoothing is seen as desirable. The lack of accuracy of inflation forecasts and the uncertainty about the nature of shocks and the effects of monetary policy might recommend such gradual actions.[62]

The evidence so far does not allow us to conclude that the adoption of IT has significantly changed the behaviour of the Central Banks regarding the use of the interest rate instrument, although for the non-European countries there are some indications that such a change in behaviour might be found in the future. Where we did find some differences is on short-term volatility of money market interest rates, analysed in Box 2.7. For analogous reasons as those outlined in the previous paragraph, we would expect to find a lower short-term interest rate volatility after IT in the European countries, and indeed we found it. But we also found a lower short-term interest rate volatility in Australia and New Zealand, that cannot be explained by the transition from a fixed to a floating exchange rate. It seems under IT interest rates might be less volatile than in either

Box 2.5   Inflation and Interest Rate Changes

The hypothesis tested in Box 2.5 is whether the adoption of IT changed the timing of interest rate changes relative to observed inflation (see argument in main text). In order to test for Granger-causality between quarterly inflation and Central Bank controlled interest rates,[56] the following bivariate VAR was used

$$p_t = \alpha_1 + A(L)p_{t-1} + B(L)r_{t-1} + \varepsilon_t$$
$$r_t = \alpha_2 + C(L)p_{t-1} + D(L)r_{t-1} + \mu_t$$

where p_t and r_t are first differences[57] of inflation and short-term interest rates, respectively, and $A(L), B(L), C(L)$ and $D(L)$ are polynomials in the lag operator L, with four lags. F-tests on the parameters of $B(L)$ and $C(L)$ provide tests of Granger-causality from interest rates to inflation and from inflation to interest rates, respectively.

If the parameters in $C(L)$ are jointly significant, then inflation Granger-causes interest rates, which may be interpreted as meaning that Central Banks react to past inflation, increasing interest rates only when the inflationary pressures are evident. The interpretation of joint significance for the parameters in $B(L)$, that is interest rates Granger-causing inflation, is less straightforward. The monetary policy transmission mechanism provides the theoretical economic causation from interest rates to inflation, with higher interest rates today causing lower inflation in the future. However, if Central Banks react to expected future inflation, increasing interest rates when expected future inflation is higher, then the data would also show Granger-causation from interest rates to inflation, not related to the transmission mechanism.[58] Our choice of lags in this exercise, makes the latter more likely to be the legitimate interpretation. The monetary policy lag is usually considered to be longer than four quarters, but it is likely that Central Banks react to expected inflation four quarters ahead, given the difficulties in forecasting. Also, the two interpretations have different implications for the signs of the coefficients, since the transmission mechanism interpretation suggests a negative relationship between interest rates and inflation, but the second interpretation implies a positive relationship. Thus, the signs of the coefficients in $B(L)$ could provide some clue to which is the legitimate interpretation. If the hypothesis tested here is true, then before IT inflation would Granger-cause interest rates, but after IT interest rates would Granger-cause inflation. An additional problem of interpretation arises in the countries where the headline CPI includes interest rate related costs; there, interest rates could Granger-cause inflation just because they are one of the components of the CPI. To avoid this problem we used indices of underlying inflation where available, but since the underlying inflation series usually do not cover the period before IT, we report the results with the headline CPI also.

Table 2.3 summarises[59] the significance levels of the Granger-causality tests performed, for the null hypothesis of non-causality. The tests were performed over two subsamples of the period 1982:1 to 1996:1: the first subsample, corresponding to the period before IT, ran from 1982:1 to the quarter of the adoption of IT; the second subsample, corresponding to the period after IT, ran from the quarter following the adoption of IT to 1996:1. Note that the number of degrees of freedom involved in the estimation of the VAR is small, especially for the 'after IT' model, and that tends to increase the significance levels of the tests. Thus, a high significance level should be interpreted as a signal that the data is not rich enough to allow for any conclusions, and *not* as a rejection of the causality hypothesis. On the other hand, a low significance level may be interpreted as a rejection of non-causality, i.e. one may accept the causality hypothesis.

Table 2.3 Granger-causality between interest rates and inflation

Granger causality		From inflation to interest rates		From interest rates to inflation	
		Before IT (%)	After IT (%)	Before IT (%)	After IT (%)
Australia	Headline	35	15	5	9
	Underlying		80		0
Canada	Headline	44	10	76	0
	Underlying		83		6
Finland	Headline	99	99	73	85
	Underlying		92		35
New Zealand	Headline	1	23	41	37
	Underlying		53		8
Spain[60]		18	74	47	31
Sweden		81	65	30	85
United Kingdom	Headline	21	67	6	27
	Underlying	50	46	28	41

Using the traditional significance levels, the results of the test suggest that after IT the Central Banks in the non-European countries have a forward-looking behaviour, although the available information does not allow one to rule out that this behaviour existed even before IT. In Canada, the headline inflation data suggests that this was not the case: Granger-causality from interest rates to inflation is evident in both indices after IT, and it did not exist in headline inflation before IT. In Australia, the opposite occurs: Granger-causality from interest rates to inflation is evident in both indices before and after IT, suggesting that no change in behaviour occurred. Finally, in New Zealand there is no apparent change in the only index that is available for both periods, in terms of Granger-causality from interest rates to inflation, although it seems that before IT the RBNZ had a backward-looking interest rate setting behaviour, that might have been abandoned.[61] For the European countries there is no significant evidence of Granger-causality from interest rates to inflation or vice versa.

discretionary or exchange rate targeting monetary policy frameworks. The reason for the difference with the former could be that, as we already mentioned for the exchange rate, the adoption of IT provides market agents with a guideline that reduces uncertainty about future monetary policy.

Box 2.6   Aggressiveness of Interest Rate Increases

Using monthly data on short-term interest rates[64] from *International Financial Statistics*, we tried to assess whether after the adoption of IT the Central Banks in our sample raised interest rates more aggressively than before. Since under IT the argument for not smoothing interest rates seems to be stronger (see main text), one could expect that after the adoption of IT increases in interest

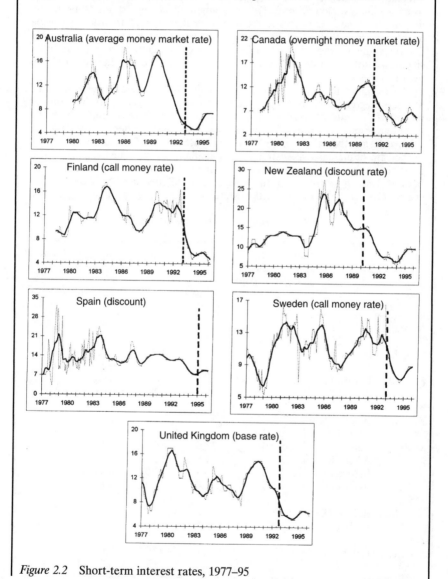

Figure 2.2   Short-term interest rates, 1977–95

rates would be larger and quicker than before. Figure 2.2 plots selected short-term interest rates for the countries in our sample. The vertical dashed lines indicate the date of the adoption of IT, the dotted lines the monthly rates, and the solid line is a 'centred' 12-month average, used to capture the 'trend' in interest rates.

Visually one cannot detect significant changes in the aggressiveness of interest rate increases after the adoption of IT. If interest rate changes were quicker, the interest rate curves would be steeper, but the slope of the curves does not seem to have changed significantly. The only apparent change seems to be in the magnitude of the changes, which seem to be smaller after IT. In order to provide quantified data that supports these visual conclusions, the following table describes the average monthly rate of change, magnitude and duration of significant interest rate increase episodes[65] in the period January 1977 to February 1996.

The evidence in Table 2.4 suggests that the interest rate increase after IT was less aggressive than previous interest rate increases, either in terms of magnitude or rate of increase. For all the countries in our sample, both the magnitude and the rate of increase were smaller, either in absolute or relative terms, than the average of the increases before IT, with the exception of the rate of increase in Australia and Canada. However, the evidence in this table should not be interpreted as suggesting the Central Banks in our sample became less aggressive after the adoption of IT, because the data are too scarce. One of the reasons why the interest rate increases were less aggressive

Table 2.4   Episodes of interest rate increases

		Number of episodes	Av. duration (months)	Av. magnitude		Av. monthly rate of increase	
				Absolute (pp)	Relative	Absolute (pp)	Relative
Australia	Before IT	3	24	9.4	117%	0.39	4.8%
	After IT	1	6	2.8	60%	0.46	10.0%
Canada	Before IT	3	31	9.0	132%	0.32	4.6%
	After IT	1	13	4.4	121%	0.34	9.3%
Finland	Before IT	4	12	6.1	63%	0.60	6.4%
	After IT	1	16	1.3	28%	0.08	1.7%
New Zealand	Before IT	3	11	11.9	126%	1.17	10.6%
	After IT	1	19	5.2	97%	0.27	5.1%
Spain	Before IT	5	15	13.0	164%	1.12	14.6%
	After IT	1	6	1.9	25%	0.31	4.2%
Sweden	Before IT	4	24	8.4	122%	0.38	5.3%
	After IT	1	13	2.0	28%	0.15	2.1%
United Kingdom	Before IT	3	17	8.0	116%	0.50	6.8%
	After IT	1	6	1.5	29%	0.25	4.8%
All IT countries	Before IT	25	19	9.5	121%	0.66	8.0%
	After IT	7	11	2.7	55%	0.27	5.3%

was because the shocks they were counteracting were milder. The only episode of interest rate increases after IT was in 1994–5, when the inflationary shock and the interest rate increases world-wide were relatively mild by historical standards. If the 1994–5 inflationary shock is assumed to be mild, then the rates of increase in Australia and Canada could be seen as more aggressive, since they are higher than the historical average.

The main apparent changes in the behaviour of the instruments or operational targets are related to the short-term volatility of financial market prices, interest and exchange rates.[63] Some of the changes are probably associated with the change from fixed to floating exchange rates, and not to the adoption of IT directly, although it is questionable whether we should consider these two events as completely distinct. The differences, in this respect, between the discretionary and the IT frameworks suggest that IT could be a key factor in providing stability to financial markets. Markets need a transparent monetary policy, one they can anticipate and understand, and this increase in transparency is one of the main reasons behind the adoption of IT. If this is true, then IT may be the only feasible floating exchange rate framework in some situations. In an economy where money demand is not sufficiently predictable to allow for money targeting and the credibility of a discretionary monetary policy is not high enough to satisfy financial markets, then the only options available are between an exchange rate target or floating exchange rates with IT. The timing of the adoption of IT in the UK, Sweden and Finland, right after the abandonment of fixed exchange rates, suggests that this was probably the case in these countries.

Box 2.7 Short-term Interest Rate Volatility

To assess if the adoption of IT affects the behaviour of market short-term interest rates we analysed 3-month interest rates of the countries in our sample from 3 January 1986 to 21 February 1996.[66] The rates are Treasury bill rates for Australia, Canada, Sweden and the United Kingdom and interbank rates for Finland, New Zealand and Spain. Figure 2.3 plots the absolute value of the daily changes in the 3-month interest rate. The vertical dotted lines indicate the date of the adoption of IT. In order to keep the scale the same in all charts, large outliers were truncated for presentational purposes in some of the charts.

   The visual inspection of Figure 2.3 suggests the adoption of IT is associated with lower daily volatility of short-term interest rates. This pattern can be seen in all the countries in our sample, except for Canada, where sufficient data for the period before IT was not available. To test formally for the existence of such changes in volatility we used the ARCH framework, where we allowed the conditional variance to be affected by changes in the monetary policy regime. Given that interest rate changes tend to be autocorrelated, we used the following model:

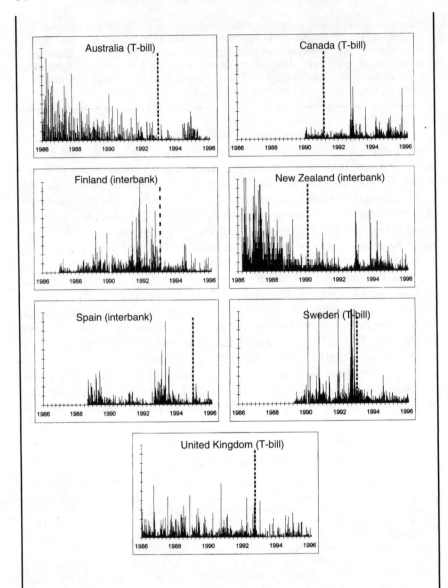

Figure 2.3   3-month interest rate daily absolute changes, 1986–96

$$c_{i,t} = \mu_i + \rho_i c_{i,t-1} + \varepsilon_{i,t} \qquad (2.6)$$

$$\varepsilon_{i,t} | \Psi_{i,t-1} \sim G(0, h_{i,t}) \qquad (2.7)$$

$$h_{i,t} = \gamma_i + \alpha_i \varepsilon_{i,t-1}^2 + \beta_i h_{i,t-1} + \delta_i D_{i,t} \qquad (2.8)$$

where $c_{i,t}$ is the weekly[67] change for interest rate i at period t, $D_{i,t}$ is a dummy variable, taking the value 1 before the adoption of IT, and μ_i, ρ_i, α_i, γ_i, α_i, β_i, and δ_i are parameters. The conditional distribution $G(\cdot)$ was assumed to be normal. Table 2.5 reports the results of estimations of this model, for the countries in our sample, over the period 3 January 1986 to 27 February 1996 (t-statistics in parenthesis).

Table 2.5   Volatility of weekly interest rates before and after IT

	Dummies definition	γ_1 ($\times 1000$)	α_i	β_i	δ_1 ($\times 1000$)
Australia[68]	$D : t < 1/1/93$	0.6944 (9.0)	0.1933 (9.3)	0.7458 (42.1)	7.989 (7.5)
Finland	$D : t < 2/2/93$	1.314 (4.4)	0.1732 (8.9)	0.8244 (81.9)	4.405 (4.8)
New Zealand	$D : t < 2/3/90$	7.2393 (6.2)	0.4176 (7.7)	0.5731 (21.7)	18.172 (3.2)
Spain[69]	$D : t < 1/1/95$	304.14 (9.1)	0.9046 (9.6)		4.773 (0.1)
Sweden	$D : t < 15/1/93$	4.288 (2.2)	0.6866 (10.9)	0.5711 (14.7)	38.70 (8.1)
United Kingdom	$D : t < 8/10/92$	0.7789 (6.8)	0.0132 (2.3)	0.9008 (71.2)	5.083 (9.2)

A simple comparison of the interest rate volatility in the IT and non-IT period, reveals significant decreases in the IT period for most of the countries in our sample where the model used was appropriate (Australia, Finland, New Zealand and the United Kingdom),[70] that confirm the inferences from the visual inspection of the charts.

Communication with Public and Government

One major area of change initiated by the adoption of IT is the communication of Central Banks with the public and government. Under IT, the effects of the Central Bank's policy actions can be observed only after a long time, since monetary policy takes several quarters to influence inflation. Under other frameworks, the existence of intermediate targets that reflect policy actions more quickly makes monitoring of Central Banks easier, but no such intermediate targets exist with IT. We claimed above that credibility and accountability concerns were the main forces driving the adoption of IT. For these reasons, IT demands that Central Banks develop new forms of communication, to transmit clearly and precisely and to explain their policy actions to other agents. Box 2.8 describes the main changes in communication channels introduced by the Central Banks

Box 2.8 Communication with Public and Government

A NEW COMMUNICATION CHANNELS

All the Central Banks in our sample improved the communication channels with the public and government, in recent years. Although some of the changes were not contemporary with the adoption of IT, they are all part of the same trend towards increased transparency and accountability. The main changes introduced by each Central Bank regarding communication are:

Australia
- *Quarterly Report* includes a large section on inflation and extensive discussion of monetary policy changes
- press releases announcing changes in policy, explaining in detail the reasons for the change

Canada
- *Monetary Policy Report* introduced in May 1995, published twice a year
- publication of the Governor's comments to the Board of Directors on *Economic and Financial Conditions and Monetary Policy* (after the following Board meeting)
- press releases announcing changes in policy
- regular meetings of the Governor and Minister of Finance
- appearances of the Government before committees of the House and Senate
- more frequent public speeches of the Governor and other senior staff

Finland
- quarterly article on policy with focus on inflation outlook in the monthly *Bank of Finland Bulletin* (in English) and in the quarterly *Markka & Talous* (in Finnish)
- press statement after policy changes
- more use of public speeches by the Governor to inform on monetary policy and inflation outlook

New Zealand
- *Monetary Policy Statement* introduced in April 1990, published twice a year
- inflation forecasts and expository articles regarding monetary policy included in RBNZ's *Quarterly Bulletin*
- occasional statements on unexpected developments that affect monetary policy
- public scrutiny of the Governor by Parliament's Finance and Expenditure Committee
- extensive programme of private and public speaking engagements by the Governor to inform on and explain policy developments

Spain
- *Inflation Report* introduced in March 1995
- press releases to explain some policy changes
- Banco de España *Annual Report* and monthly *Economic Bulletin* improved to include more information on monetary policy
- appearances by the Governor before the Parliamentary Committee for Economic Affairs

Sweden
- *Inflation and Inflation Expectations in Sweden* introduced in October 1993, published quarterly
- public hearings before the Finance Committee of the Parliament
- more regular and public reviews of Central Bank actions, in speeches and lectures by the Governor and staff

UK
- *Inflation Report* introduced in February 1993, published quarterly
- formalisation of the regular monthly meetings between Governor and Chancellor
- publication of the minutes of the meeting (2 weeks after following one), since April 1994
- press notice after each policy change explaining the reasons for the change
- Governor appearances before the Treasury Select Committee
- more use of public speeches by Governor and Directors

B INFLATION AND MONETARY POLICY REPORTS
Five of the seven Central Banks in our sample introduced special publications after the adoption of IT, to inform the public on inflation and monetary policy issues. In spite of the (slight) differences in the titles – some are called 'inflation' and other 'monetary policy' reports – the structure of these publications is very similar, and includes the following points:

- a discussion of recent monetary policy decisions, and their justification in the light of the inflation targets[71]
- an overview of recent developments in inflation
- a review of the trends for real and financial variables relevant to future inflation
- an inflation outlook, and its implications for monetary policy
- 'technical boxes', where specific questions related to the implementation of policy or the analysis of economic indicators are discussed

Given that the reports are usually directed to the general public, discussions in the main text are generally kept at a non-technical level, and almost all data is presented in charts, with very few tables.[72] Deeper and more technical analyses are confined to the 'technical boxes'. Only the RBNZ's and the Bank of England's reports include quantified inflation forecasts; for the others the inflation outlook includes only the discussion of future trends.

in our sample in recent years. Some of the changes were not directly related to the adoption of IT, but we include them in our analysis since they are all part of the same trend towards increased transparency and accountability.

The public must know what policy actions the Central Bank is taking in order to have an impact on credibility, and they need to understand and believe those actions to be the appropriate ones to achieve the target. In order to achieve these goals, a Central Bank may use a set of different communication channels. First, a Central Bank can immediately and fully disclose policy changes, and the reasons for the change, through press releases issued at the precise moment the measures are taken. This is particularly important in those countries where there is no administratively set interest rate, and the Central Bank acts mainly through intervention in money markets. For instance, the Reserve Bank of Australia immediately announces, through press releases, any change in its operational target range for the money market rate, instead of just signalling it through market interventions, as happened previously. The disclosure of this information reduces uncertainty about current policy, and may contribute to reduce instability in financial markets, besides allowing agents to form a more informed view of future inflation prospects. Even in the countries where the nature of the policy instrument implies an immediate disclosure of the change, the accompanying press release has an important role in explaining the reasons for the move. For instance, in the United Kingdom, changes in the main instrument, the money market dealings rate, have to be immediately disclosed, since it is an administratively set rate. Nevertheless, the press release is important because it explains in detail the reason for the change, and this justification may contribute to persuade the agents that the move is consistent with the inflation target, thus strengthening the credibility of the monetary policy.

Another channel Central Banks may use to improve the credibility of their policy is regular monetary policy and inflation reports. These reports could take the form of a separate publication or they could be included in regular Central Bank bulletins. Most Central Banks in our sample (five out of seven) preferred to introduce a separate publication, probably thinking that it would have a stronger impact on agents' expectations, because a separate publication will receive more attention from the media than a bulletin article. The structure of these reports is also described in Box 2.8. Through these reports, the public can monitor and evaluate monetary policy with an inflation target. In some countries (e.g. Spain) the report is sent to Parliament, increasing the transparency and political accountability of the Central Bank activities. The main role of the Reports is to make public the Central Bank's inflation outlook and explain how this outlook was formed. The reports may also be used to provide a detailed justification of current monetary policy actions, and explain why these actions are consistent with the inflation target. Finally, the reports may be used to educate the public on the problems involved in the execution of monetary policy, and the importance of price stability.

We would expect, in a situation where the public believe the Central Bank's implicit objectives coincide with the inflation target, believe the model the Central Bank is using is adequate and believe all available information is being used by the Central Bank, that the report would have a major impact on expectations. In fact, in the ideal situation described above, there is no reason why agents would not take official forecasts as their own inflation expectations. However, that is not what we observe, as we will see below, when we discuss the quality of official forecasts and their impact on expectations, which suggests that the public suspects that the Central Bank's 'secret' objectives are different from the IT, or is sceptic about the technical abilities of the Central Bank's staff, or believes that the Central Bank has some private information that they are not disclosing.

The information disclosed in press releases and inflation reports may be complemented by regular speeches by the Governor and other senior officials. These speeches may play an important role in explaining policy decisions, or the importance of price stability, specially because they can address the particular concerns of specific audiences. For instance, the Governor of the RBNZ explained the implications of the New Zealand's new policy framework to exchange rate developments in a speech delivered to the Auckland Manufacturers' Association, whose members had been expressing some concern about the need to have a 'favourable' exchange rate (Brash, 1992). This strategy has been pursued by some Central Banks in our sample (especially the RBNZ), who have increased significantly the number of contacts of Central Bank senior officials with the public, since the adoption of IT.

All this information disclosure improves, by itself, the accountability of the Central Bank. But democratic accountability could be enhanced by regular contacts with Parliament and government. Being forced to explain their policies to democratically elected powers is an additional source of pressure that forces Central Banks to stick to targets, especially if penalties can be imposed on the Central Bank's Governor if the policy is not consistent with the IT. This is the case in New Zealand, where the Governor can be dismissed if targets are not met, and inflation outcomes are closely monitored. When in June 1995 underlying inflation overshot the target by 0.2 percentage points (and again in March 1996, when the target was overshot by 0.1 percentage points), the Minister of Finance immediately called for an official report on the performance of the Governor from the nonexecutive Directors at the RBNZ Board.

Finally, communication channels can be powerful policy instruments. In certain cases the communication of future developments in inflation is an instrument of monetary policy in itself. In New Zealand, for example, the financial markets almost invariably deliver the necessary monetary conditions as a reaction to Central Bank comments on inflation outlook. These comments are the instrument the RBNZ has used most frequently; the settlement cash instrument was used only three times since 1991.[73] In the United Kingdom, the Bank of England comments on the inflation outlook may have the effect of putting pressure on the Chancellor, who has to decide on interest rate changes.[74] In general, if communication succeeds in shaping agents' expectations it will give an important contribution to the final objective of controlling inflation, since inflation expectations play a key role in inflation developments. But agents will only be convinced if the quality of the information is high, and the Central Bank is credible. The quality of Central Bank forecasts and the credibility of monetary policy are the topics of the following sections.

INFLATION FORECASTING AND CONTROLLABILITY

The IT framework implies that an (explicit or implicit) inflation forecast is the intermediate target of policy. Svensson (1996, pp. 14–15) argues that the inflation forecast is an ideal intermediate target because it possesses a number of desirable characteristics:

- the inflation forecast is the variable that has the *highest correlation* with the policy objective (future inflation);
- the inflation forecast is *controllable* through changes in monetary conditions (and it is even more controllable than future inflation itself);
- the inflation forecast is *easy to observe* (and easier to observe than future inflation).

Inflation forecasts have these characteristics virtually by definition, and we are not going to discuss whether inflation forecasts are better intermediate targets than other possible alternative intermediate targets. In this section, we investigate whether inflation forecasts are intermediate targets good enough to deliver the policy outcomes implicit in the design of the IT. The fact that inflation forecasts have the highest correlation with future inflation, certainly does not imply that this correlation is 1, and not even that it is high enough to be consistent with staying within the target range. Inflation forecasts are not precise, and we discuss whether they are sufficiently accurate as a guide to future outcomes to serve as an intermediate target in a policy directed at keeping inflation inside a narrow range. Not only are inflation forecasts inaccurate, but uncertainties about the timing and strength of monetary policy actions, together with other limitations on their unfettered use, imply that such actions cannot generally be taken to bring such forecasts back to their desired central level wisely and quickly, i.e. that inflation *forecasts*, as well as current inflation, cannot be precisely controlled. These facts, as well as late shocks affecting inflation after it is too late for monetary policy to be sensibly used to offset them, given the lengthy lags in their normal operation, will cause inflation outcomes to deviate from any pre-set target, and we discuss whether monetary policy may be expected to keep inflation inside a 2–3 p.p. a wide band. Finally, we compare the inflation performance of IT countries with non-IT countries, to assess whether the IT framework has delivered superior outcomes.

Forecasting Record

Inflation forecasts are central to the IT framework: as described on p. 000, the policy rule is defined in terms of an inflation forecast. Thus, an efficient IT policy framework demands good inflation forecasts, i.e. forecasts implying low forecast errors. In Box 2.9, the quality of the forecasts made by some of the Central Banks in our sample is analysed. The results suggest that in the past forecast errors were large, relative to the width of IT bands. The average MSE for forecasts four quarters ahead is almost as large as the target ranges. This suggests that the probability of the targets being missed is quite high, even if the forecast is kept always at the mid-point of the band, if the forecasting accuracy does not improve. Also, Central Banks tended to overestimate or underestimate inflation for quite long periods. Nevertheless, there are some encouraging signs. The quality of the forecasts seems to be improving over time, which could suggest that the initial errors were the result of a period of learning how to operate in a new framework, and that in time forecasts may achieve an improved level of accuracy.

Forecasting inflation several quarters in advance is difficult. Central Banks recognise that, either in their words (e.g. King 1996, p. 5) or their actions, since they do not apply the inflation target rule blindly and mechanically. As we have seen above, in practice there is not always a clear distinction between a discretionary policy and IT, since policy decisions are not based exclusively on inflation forecasts. The forecasting record of some of the Central Banks so far suggests that it is prudent to do so.

Inflation Controllability

Before the adoption of IT, the general opinion was that inflation could not be controlled easily or precisely, and the initial comments on the adoption of IT reflected this view. This was also the view among the Central Banks that adopted this framework, and this was reflected on the adoption of ranges, instead of point targets, and on some clauses that determine the targets should not be met at every moment but should only hold on average. Past behaviour of inflation and simulation studies justified such caution and suggested that even 2 percentage points bands might well be too narrow.[75]

Box 2.10 describes our efforts at assessing Central Banks' experiences with setting and achieving such targets. It is still too early to make any

Box 2.9   Inflation Forecasts and Inflation Outcomes

The only data regarding the Central Bank's forecasts available are for Australia, New Zealand and the United Kingdom. Table 2.6 describes the forecast mean error and mean absolute error (MAE) for these three countries, over different periods of time, of the forecasts of inflation made 1 year before.

Table 2.6   Inflation forecast errors, 1981/88–95

	Australia		New Zealand		United Kingdom	
	Mean	MAE	Mean	MAE	Mean	MAE
1981/88*	−0.3	1.7	−0.6	2.1		
1988/92	0.2	1.1	0.3	1.6		
1993/95	0.0	0.3	−0.4	0.5	0.6	0.8
1994	0.5	0.5	−0.2	0.3	1.0	1.0
1995	−0.1	0.1	−0.9	0.9	0.3	0.6

Note: * 1974/88 for New Zealand.

Evidence from Table 2.6 suggests that the RBA and the RBNZ tended to underpredict inflation during the high inflation period of the 1980s, and to overpredict it during the disinflationary period of the early 1990s. More recently, there has been no systematic bias in the predictions of the RBA, but there has seemed to be a slightly regular underestimation of the inflationary pressures in New Zealand.

The mean absolute forecast error tends to be relatively large, even in the period of low and less volatile inflation, compared to the width of the target bands. Even if these Central Banks manage to keep forecast inflation exactly at the mid-point of the band, the error margins implicit in the target ranges (0.5, 1 and 1.5 percentage points, respectively in Australia, New Zealand and the United Kingdom) are not much larger than the MAE, which suggests that the probability of missing the target must be high.

Early in our sample period forecasts tended to be less accurate. This is probably due to the higher levels of inflation, but it could also be the result of an improvement in the quality of forecasts, because of a learning process inherent in any period of transition between regimes.

The forecasts on Table 2.6 were prepared under the technical assumption of unchanged monetary policy. It could be argued then that the differences between the outcomes and the forecasts could be explained by the policy actions taken on the basis of these forecasts, and are not a consequence of forecasting inaccuracy. Although we accept this could explain part of the divergence, we believe that this problem has a small influence, and most of the divergence reflects forecasting inaccuracy. First, because monetary policy is supposed to act on inflation with a lag of at least 6 quarters, policy changes made after the forecast should not have a significant effect in the 4 quarters ahead forecasting period. In a study of inflation forecasts in Australia, over the period 1985–94, Stevens and Debelle (1995, p. 89) adjust the inflation outcomes for the effects of policy changes; using their data, and comparing them with official forecasts, one still gets MAE of around 1.3 p.p., versus 1.8 p.p. before the adjustment. Second, evidence provided in the February 1996 Bank of England's *Inflation Report* suggests that private forecasts tend to be no better or even worse than the Bank's forecasts. Data from the RBNZ also suggest that in New Zealand forecasts from the private sector are no better than the Bank's. Stevens and Debelle data provide similar evidence: the official forecasts in Australia have MAE that are roughly equal to the ones of private forecasts (around 1.8 p.p.). Private forecasts should not have the drawback of assuming unchanged policies, and the errors in their forecasts may be taken as evidence of the limitations of current forecasting technology.

definitive judgements, given the short experience in most of the countries, but the results so far suggest that the target ranges have been set too narrowly. Of the four countries where the targets have been in force for more than two years, only the United Kingdom has a 100 per cent success[76] (see Table 2.7 in Box 2.10). In New Zealand and Canada, the countries where IT was first introduced, headline CPI (the formal target) was outside the set target range for more than 50 per cent of the quarters. In Canada, all the target misses consisted of undershooting the transition path, and do not relate to the 'final' target. In New Zealand, all (except two) of the deviations from target can be explained by the exemption caveats or an unexpectedly early success in reducing inflation, that caused inflation to undershoot the 'transition' targets. Still, even if the Bank of Canada and RBNZ can claim that they were successful in reducing inflation even faster than expected, these results raise two questions. First, although the results for New Zealand improve if we use underlying inflation, i.e. a measure of inflation that controls for all the caveats in the PTA, it is questionable whether we should use this measure when analysing the controllability of the IT. After all, the target is set in terms of headline CPI, and that measure of inflation was significantly outside the target for several quarters. If underlying inflation is the target, *de facto*,[77] then it would probably be better, from the point of view of credibility, to set the formal target in terms of the underlying inflation index. Second, while it can reasonably be argued that given the prior history of high inflation in the countries in our sample, an undershooting of the transition path was a good outcome, not a bad one, from the point of view of *controllability*, this is still a sign that inflation was not accurately forecast, and hence easily controllable. If the Central Banks could have accurately forecast inflation, then they would have set a steeper transition path, compatible with what they thought was the desirable outcome for inflation.[78]

The results for the other countries were more encouraging, since (with the possible exception of Finland) the targets were met so far (see Box 2.10).[83] The fact that the targets in Australia and the United Kingdom were less ambitious (wider bands or average inflation) might have helped

Box 2.10 Inflation Targets and Inflation Outcomes

In Box 2.10 we try to assess, from the experience of the Central Banks in our sample, how controllable inflation is, by comparing the targets that they had set with the inflation outcomes. The purpose of this exercise is to measure how easy it is for a Central Bank to set a target and achieve it, and *not* to measure the success of monetary policy. This is for several reasons; first, because in some

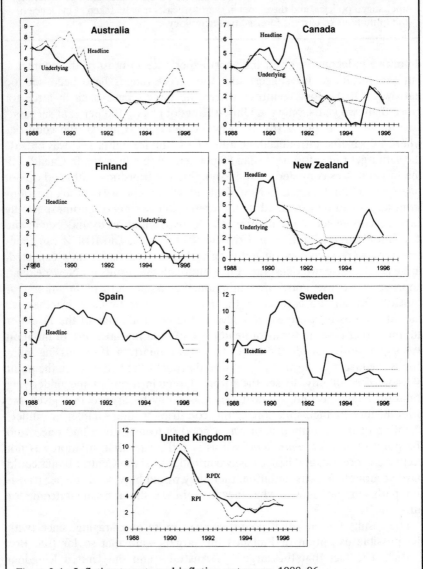

Figure 2.4 Inflation targets and inflation outcomes, 1988–96

countries the design of the IT does not require inflation to be inside the target range all the time, and thus missing the target in one quarter does not constitute a failure.[79] Second, because some targets are not precise enough to determine objectively if a given outcome is a success, we had to make some assumptions that may be questioned.[80] Finally, because some of the results include 'transition targets' that may have a secondary status relative to the 'final targets'.

The exercise in Box 2.10 uses quarterly data, from the first quarter of 1988 to the first quarter of 1996, for the headline and underlying (where available) CPI.[81] Figure 2.4 plots these data as well as the inflation targets adopted by each Central Bank. The thick solid line represents inflation measured by the index officially targeted, the thin dashed line represents the other measure of inflation, and the horizontal dotted lines represent the target limits.

The charts in Figure 2.4 show that in Spain, Sweden and the United Kingdom the targets were met in every quarter. In Australia, Canada and New Zealand inflation was outside the target range for several quarters. Finland also missed the target, although our definition of what 'around 2 per cent' means may be questioned. Table 2.7 quantifies the number of quarters the targets have been in force up to 1996: Q1, and in how many of those the targets have been missed.

We interpret the results in Table 2.7 as evidence that the uncertainty surrounding inflation forecasting and the effects of monetary policy makes it difficult to set a 2 p.p. target range and achieve it. This was possible in Sweden and Spain, but the data period is small. More data are available for the United Kingdom, where the targets have always been met, but there the width of the band is 3 p.p. In Australia, Canada and New Zealand the band seems to be too narrow, since inflation was outside the range about half of the quarters.

Table 2.7   Official targets and inflation outcomes

Official target	Quarters with target	Quarters outside target range	
		Number	Percentage
Australia	13	5	38
Canada	17	10	59
Finland	5	5	100
New Zealand	22	12	55
Spain	1	0	0
Sweden	5	0	0
United Kingdom	14	0	0

When analysing Table 2.7, it must be taken into consideration that in Australia the targets are supposed to hold on average. The average underlying inflation for the period 1993:Q1 to 1996:Q1 in Australia was 2.3 per cent, which means that so far the Reserve Bank of Australia has been meeting their target. Also, the Bank of Finland does not have an explicit band. Although the inflation outcomes would be outside a 3 p.p. band, it is a matter of judgement whether inflation outcomes in Finland were 'around 2 per cent'. Anyhow, the mean absolute deviation from the 2 per cent target, for the period 1995:Q1 to 1996:Q1 was 2.2 percentage points, which we interpret as evidence supporting our claim that 2 p.p. bands are too narrow.

In New Zealand and in Canada, the inflation target is defined in terms of the headline CPI, but with some caveats, so that in practice the target is considered to be a measure of underlying inflation that extracts the influence of the caveats from headline inflation. Using these indices of underlying inflation, the likelihood of meeting the pre-set targets increases, as described in Table 2.8

Table 2.8   Inflation targets and underlying inflation

Underlying inflation	Quarters with target	Number	Percentage
Canada	17	7	41
New Zealand	22	8	36

Even if we consider the exceptions in Table 2.8, the likelihood of Central Banks meeting their targets is still relatively low. The countries with the longest record of targets, Canada and New Zealand, have missed them for a significant number of quarters. The only promising feature of the evidence in Box 2.10 is that most of the misses occurred in the transition period. If we consider only the 'final' targets, then the only misses are in New Zealand, in 1995:Q2 and 1996:Q1. However, in terms of 'final' targets the evidence is even more scarce,[82] and no strong conclusions can be drawn.

their better performance. Anyhow, even if the data are not rich enough to allow for definitive judgements two conclusions may already be drawn. First, headline CPI is not as easily controllable as underlying CPI, a fact that puts into question the credibility of narrow targets set in terms of this index. The impact on expectations of establishing a target and missing it half of the time, even if you can justify the deviations using the caveats, is probably less than the impact of a target set in terms of a less transparent but more controllable index of underlying inflation. Second, as is obvious, even underlying inflation cannot be controlled perfectly, and some of the Central Banks in our sample have already missed the target for some quarters.

Inflation Performance in IT and Non-IT Countries

If we accept the view that, given the prior history of high inflation in most of our sample, for many of the Central Banks it was more important to reduce inflation than to keep it inside a narrow range, the performance of the Central Banks in our sample could then be described as good. Average inflation after the adoption of IT was 2.7 per cent, against 6.0 per cent in the period between 1987 and the adoption of IT (see Box 2.11). The average standard deviation was also lower (1.1 per cent against 2.4 per cent), although the decrease in variability of inflation is due to the lower levels of inflation (the coefficient of variation has increased from 0.37 to 0.47).

Box 2.11   Inflation Outcomes in Selected Countries

Quarterly consumer price inflation data from *International Financial Statistics* for the OECD countries were used to compare the inflation performance of IT and non-IT countries. In order to assess the impact on inflation performance of the adoption of IT, we compared our IT countries with a control group of similar non-IT countries. When making this type of comparison, two main problems arise. The first problem is the choice of the period over which the exercise is going to be made. Somewhat subjectively, we decided to make the comparison over two sets of periods, 1980/89 versus 1990/95 and before IT (since 1987) versus after IT. Since the first IT was introduced in 1990, the first periodicity compares the 1980s, a decade when the world did not know IT, with the 1990s, the decade of IT. The second periodicity tries to compare the inflation performance of each country (in a shorter period) before and after IT. Since four of the countries in our sample introduced IT near the end of 1992, for the non-IT countries the period before IT was taken to be 1987/92 and the period after IT, 1993/95.

The second question, the choice of a comparable group, is always problematical. In order to obtain more robust results, we chose to select four (overlapping) control groups, according to different criteria, as follows:

Group 1 the countries where average inflation for the period 1980/89 was within the range of average inflation in the IT countries (6.5–11.9 per cent): Denmark, France, Ireland, Italy and Norway; this is a group of countries of similar inflation experiences in the 1980s;

Group 2 group 1 plus USA and Portugal, the two countries where average inflation in the period 1980/89 was, respectively, immediately below and above group 1; this group was chosen to give group 1 the same number of countries as in the IT group (7);

Group 3 a group of countries chosen to have the same average inflation in the period 1987/92 as the IT countries before IT (6.0 per cent): Italy, Norway, Portugal, Switzerland and the United States; the reason for the choice of this group is the same as in group 1, but according to the before IT versus after IT periodicity;

Group 4 a group of seven countries that face similar economic environments as IT countries; this group is composed of Japan, the United States Norway and Denmark, France and Portugal, and Italy, that we subjectively chose to be the closest match to Australia, Canada, Finland and Sweden, Spain and New Zealand and the United Kingdom.

Table 2.9 reports the average inflation level in each of the periods considered, for these four groups as well as for our sample of IT countries. Also reported are *t*-statistics for two types of test. Test 1 compares the IT group with each control group, where the null hypothesis is that the control group and the IT group have the same average inflation. Test 2 compares the group average in both periods, for a given group, and the null hypothesis is that the group average is the same in both periods.[84]

Table 2.9　Average inflation in selected OECD countries, 1980s–1990s

	Group average inflation				Test 1				Test 2	
	1980s	1990s	Before	After	1980s	1990s	Before	After	1990s	After
IT	8.5	3.8	6.0	2.7					−5.6	−4.8
G1	8.6	3.0	4.0	2.5	−0.1	1.0	2.4	0.3	−5.7	−2.0
G2	9.5	3.8	5.0	2.9	−0.6	0.0	0.8	−0.4	−3.3	−1.8
G3	9.2	4.6	5.9	3.3	−0.3	−0.9	0.1	−0.9	−1.7	−1.7
G4	8.5	3.7	4.9	2.7	0.0	0.1	0.9	0.0	−2.4	−1.7

The data in Table 2.9 show that average inflation has fallen significantly in the IT countries, but it also fell in the non-IT countries. The results for Test 1 show that average inflation in IT countries is not significantly different from any of the control groups, either before or after the adoption of IT. The inflation experience of the IT countries seems to be shared by all our control groups, and it is not a specificity of the adoption of IT. The only data that might suggest IT countries are different refers to Test 2. The significance level of the fall in inflation is generally higher than for the control groups, but this is probably a consequence of the fact that the IT group is more homogeneous than the control groups.[85] After realising that IT did not have any significant impact in the level of inflation, we tested for differences in inflation uncertainty, measured by the standard deviation of quarterly inflation. Table 2.10 reports the results of those tests.

Table 2.10　Inflation uncertainty in selected OECD countries, 1980s–1990s

	Average standard deviation				Test 1				Test 2	
	1980s	1990s	Before	After	1980s	1990s	Before	After	1990s	After
IT	3.6	2.2	2.4	1.1					−2.9	−2.0
G1	4.7	0.8	1.1	0.5	−1.4	3.6	1.7	2.3	−5.2	−1.7
G2	4.9	1.2	1.2	0.6	−1.7	1.9	1.8	2.2	−4.7	−2.2
G3	4.3	1.7	1.5	0.8	−0.8	0.9	1.1	1.2	−2.3	−2.2
G4	4.2	1.3	1.3	0.6	−0.8	1.8	1.7	2.2	−3.8	−2.5

Again there is no evidence the adoption of IT had a significant impact in inflation uncertainty. Inflation uncertainty decreased significantly in IT countries, but it also decreased in non-IT countries. Inflation uncertainty after IT is higher in IT countries than in the control groups (and significantly higher in three of the groups), but it was also higher before the adoption of IT (although less significantly). Finally, we tried to assess whether or not the lower standard deviation was a consequence of the lower levels of inflation, by looking at the coefficient of variation, reported in Table 2.11.

Here the results are completely different for IT and non-IT countries: the coefficient of variation increased in the IT countries, but decreased in all the control groups. Although inflation variability fell in absolute terms in all

Table 2.11   Relative inflation variability in selected OECD countries, 1980s–1990s

	Average coefficient of variation				Test 1				Test 2	
	1980s	1990s	Before	After	1980s	1990s	Before	After	1990s	After
IT	0.43	0.61	0.37	0.47					2.2	0.9
G1	0.54	0.28	0.27	0.23	−1.6	3.6	1.1	2.1	−3.7	−0.6
G2	0.53	0.31	0.25	0.21	−1.7	3.8	1.6	2.6	−3.9	−0.8
G3	0.50	0.36	0.29	0.26	−1.2	2.4	0.8	1.6	−1.7	−0.3
G4	0.56	0.38	0.31	0.31	−1.7	2.3	0.6	1.0	−1.8	0.0

groups, it increased in relative terms only in the IT countries. This different behaviour in the two sets of countries could be a direct consequence of the adoption of IT: since IT Central Banks are trying to keep inflation inside a narrow range, they will tend to force it up and down more frequently than the non-IT countries, that are content to let inflation drift and only react to large swings. However, this could also be a small sample result, not related to IT adoption. One sign in this direction is the fact that these results are statistically significant for the '80/90' comparison, but not for the 'before/after' comparison which is more closely related to the adoption of IT.[86]

However, inflation performance in IT countries benefited from favourable international conditions. Box 2.11 reports the inflation outcomes in selected OECD countries compared to the outcomes in our sample. The results are very similar for IT and non-IT countries. The fall in the levels and variability of inflation can be observed in all control groups. The only difference relates to the coefficient of variation, that was roughly unchanged or even decreased in the non-IT countries, but increased in the IT countries. The fact that relative variability increased in the IT but not in the non-IT countries could mean that IT causes inflation to become more unstable in the short term. In order to keep inflation inside a narrow range, IT Central Banks may have to seek constantly to pull it up and down, whether non-IT Central Banks may let inflation drift. Perhaps, the target instability that was observed in money and exchange rate targets may also apply to IT.

Even if the final results in terms of the fall in inflation were similar in the IT and non-IT countries, this does not mean that the adoption of IT did not make a difference for the disinflation processes. Because the adoption of IT may generate expectations of lower future inflation, it might have facilitated the disinflation process, inducing faster and/or less costly (in terms of increased unemployment or output lost) disinflations. In Box 2.12 we examine the disinflation episodes in IT and some non-IT countries, since 1980, and measure the rate of disinflation and sacrifice ratios in each episode.

The adoption of IT was associated with faster disinflation, at least relatively to disinflations in non-IT countries in the same period. It also seems that under IT the disinflation process is less costly, especially in terms of output lost, although the evidence is less conclusive in this issue. Thus, although the OECD countries with high inflation in the 1980s managed to reduce it in the 1990s, whether they adopted IT or not, how they did it seems to depend on the monetary policy strategy. The adoption of IT might have helped the disinflation process.

To conclude this section, we must ask whether inflation is controllable to the point that we can expect inflation targets, with a 2–3 p.p. range, to be

---

Box 2.12 Inflation, Growth and Unemployment in Selected Countries

The adoption of an IT may facilitate the process of disinflation, by immediately creating expectations of lower inflation. In Box 2.12, we analyse the disinflation episodes, in the period 1981:Q1–1995:Q4, in IT and non-IT countries, and try to assess whether disinflation under IT was easier than before, and/or easier than in other non-IT countries, by measuring the speed of disinflation, and the costs in terms of unemployment and output growth in each episode. Apart from the countries in our sample, we analysed disinflations in the four control groups considered in Box 2.11, and the quarterly data for these countries were obtained from *International Financial Statistics OECD Main Economic Indicators* and *Quarterly National Accounts*.[88] Disinflation episodes were identified using a methodology similar to Ball (1994): each disinflation episode is a period when 'trend' inflation falls substantially.[89] In each inflation episode we examined the disinflation rate and the cost in terms of unemployment and output.

The rate of disinflation was computed as the average fall in inflation per quarter, measured in percentage points, between the quarters with the highest and the lowest inflation in each episode. Table 2.12 summarises the results for each IT country and for each of the four control groups considered, for the whole 1981/95 sample and for three subsamples, for the periods 1981/89 (1980s), 1990/95 (1990s) and after the adoption of IT (IT).[90]

With few exceptions, one episode in the 1980s and another in the 1990s were identified. The speed of disinflation in the 1990s' episode is lower than in the 1980s' episode across all countries (except for Sweden) and groups. In the 1980s' episode, the average speed of disinflation was similar in the IT and non-IT countries, but in the 1990s it was significantly higher in IT countries, whatever the control group used. If we assume the 1990s correspond to the period of IT, then it would seem that IT was associated with a higher rate of disinflation. However, this conclusion needs two qualifications: first, for some of the IT countries, the 1990s episode occurred (or at least started) before the adoption of IT (although when we take only the period under IT the results are not significantly affected); second, the results are largely (but not fundamentally) influenced by the results for Sweden, and could be just a small sample result.

Table 2.12   Rate of disinflation in IT and non-IT countries, 1980s–1990s

	Numbers of episodes			Rate of disinflation $(p.p./q^{tr})$			
	1980s	1990s	IT	1980s	1990s	IT	1981–95
Australia	1	1	0	1.1	0.8	*0.4*	0.9
Canada	1	1	1	0.6	0.5	0.5	0.6
Finland	1	1	#	0.4	0.3	*0.2*	0.4
New Zealand	2	1	1	2.0	1.0	1.0	1.7
Spain	1	1	0	0.6	0.2	*0.3*	0.4
Sweden	1	2	1	0.4	1.2	0.8	0.7
United Kingdom	2	1	#	1.0	0.9	*0.8*	1.0
IT	1.3	1.1		0.9	0.7	0.7	0.8
G1	1	1		0.7	0.2		0.5
G2	1.1	1		0.9	0.3		0.6
G3	1.2	1		0.9	0.3		0.5
G4	1.1	1		0.8	0.3		0.5

Disinflation processes are usually associated with increases in unemployment and lower output growth. By contributing to create lower inflation expectations, the adoption of IT could help to reduce the unemployment and growth costs of disinflation. For each of the inflation episodes identified using the methodology above, we computed sacrifice ratios in terms of unemployment and output. The ratio for unemployment was computed as the increase in unemployment (Δu) over the decrease in inflation $(-\Delta\pi)$, between the quarters with the highest and lowest inflation in each episode. Output lost due to a disinflation episode (λ) was computed as the difference between potential and actual output growth over the same period, with potential output growth assumed to correspond to an yearly rate of growth equal to the average over the 1981–94 period, for each country. The sacrifice ratio in terms of output growth is the ratio between the output lost (λ) and the decrease in inflation

Table 2.13   Sacrifice ratios in IT and non-IT countries, 1980s–1990s

	Unemployment $(\Delta u/-\Delta\pi)$				Output growth $(\lambda/-\Delta\pi)$			
	1980s	1990s	IT	1981–95	1980s	1990s	IT	1981–95
Australia	0.1	0.6	−0.5	0.3	−0.3	1.0	−1.5	0.3
Canada	0.4	0.0	0.0	0.2	0.1	0.1	0.1	0.1
Finland	0.1	1.9	0.6	0.8	−1.0	2.1	−2.3	0.3
New Zealand	0.1	0.5	0.5	0.3	−0.9	0.6	0.6	−0.2
Spain	0.4	1.3	−0.4	0.6	−0.3	1.0	−0.3	0.0
Sweden	0.0	0.4	0.5	0.3	−0.8	0.2	0.0	−0.2
United Kingdom	0.3	0.4	0.1	0.3	−0.1	0.7	0.0	0.2
IT	0.2	0.7	0.3	0.4	−0.5	0.8	−0.3	0.1
G1	0.2	0.7		0.2	−0.1	1.2		0.1
G2	0.1	0.5		0.2	−0.1	1.0		0.1
G3	0.1	0.3		0.2	−0.2	1.0		0.2
G4	0.1	0.5		0.2	−0.1	1.6		0.3

$(-\Delta\pi)$. Table 2.13 summarises the results for the sacrifice ratios in terms of unemployment and output, for the same countries, groups, and periods used in the previous table.

In all countries (with the exception of Canada) and groups the sacrifice ratios are higher for the 1990s episode. In terms of unemployment, the IT countries have ratios similar to group 1, and above the other groups, either in the 1980s or in the 1990s. In terms of output, the sacrifice ratio is lower in the IT countries, but again this happens in both periods. If one takes only the period under IT instead of the 1990s the performance of the IT countries improves; both ratios are lower than for any other group. Significance tests for the difference between the averages of the IT and the other groups (not presented here) show that the sacrifice ratio in terms of output (but not in terms of unemployment) is significantly lower under IT than in any other group. However, these results rely substantially on the data for Finland and the United Kingdom where the episode under IT is just part of a larger episode that started in early 1990. If one takes only the countries with a complete episode under IT, then the sacrifice ratios are not significantly different for the IT and other groups, although they are still lower. Even if one takes all the qualifications into account, the results in Table 2.13, although not conclusive, still suggest that the adoption of IT may have made the disinflation processes somewhat less costly, especially in terms of output growth lost.

met if the Central Bank follows a sensible policy? It is too early to reach a conclusion, but it seems that it is not possible to control headline inflation, precisely or quickly. It is probably possible to control, on average and over a period of time, some measure of underlying inflation[87] within a reasonable range, but this might come at the cost of an increase in the short term variability of inflation. If this lack of controllability is confirmed by future evidence, then the positive effects on the credibility of monetary policy that IT is hoped to have, could even turn out to be of the opposite sign.

CREDIBILITY OF THE INFLATION TARGET

One of the major (if not the major) objectives of the adoption of IT was to provide an anchor for inflation expectations. In this section we try to evaluate if this objective was achieved, based on data from household and business surveys, financial markets and wage settlements. Again the lack of data prevents us from reaching definitive conclusions, but some tentative results can be extracted from the available information, although one must not forget that expectations are affected by an array of factors of which the monetary policy framework is just one; at the specific moment when IT was adopted, other factors (e.g. fiscal policy concerns or political instability) might have been affecting expectations in a way that would conceal any (eventual) impact of the IT adoption. Also, in some countries (e.g. Canada and New Zealand) price stability was seen as being the objective of monetary policy even before the Central Bank announced an explicit IT, and this might have reduced the impact of the announcement. Nevertheless, in this latter case, since the aim of this chapter is to discuss the effect of publicly announcing an explicit IT, the lack of an announcement effect is still a sign that IT, as such, does not have an impact on credibility, at least not more than doing what many countries not included in our sample have done, that is adopting price stability as the objective for monetary policy.

Household and Businesses Surveys

Results from different consumer and business surveys that covered inflation expectations in the countries in our sample are reported in Box 2.13. We could not identify any relation between the announcement of IT and inflation expectations. This suggests that the *announcement* of IT does not provide a credible anchor for inflation expectations: words without actions are not enough, as one would expect; it would be surprising to find that a Central Bank may earn credibility simply by setting a target. However, one would expect that words with actions should have an impact, and that the ability to follow a policy consistent with the target would build credibility: after some years of low inflation and some track record of meeting the targets, these should become credible, and expected inflation should be inside the target range. The evidence in Box 2.13 suggests that credibility was not (yet) fully achieved, although in some countries some measures of inflation expectations are consistent with the targets.

Financial Markets

The evidence that long-term government bond yields were affected by the announcement of an IT is scarce. Either in absolute terms or relative to the yield in Germany or the United States, there was no significant change in long term government bond yields, as can be seen in Box 2.14, paragraphs **A** and **B**. There are only some signs that the adoption of IT may have contributed to the credibility of monetary policy in Finland, New Zealand, Sweden and the United Kingdom, but these are not very strong. The evidence in the three European countries is probably related to the exchange rate regime change, and in New Zealand the change was not contemporaneous with the adoption of IT, although it might be argued it was helped by the achievement of the IT targets.

Data for bond market inflation expectations in Australia, Canada, Sweden and the United Kingdom (also in Box 2.14, paragraph **C**) also reveal the relatively low credibility of the announcements: long-term expected inflation

Box 2.13   Households' and Businesses' Inflation Expectations

Figure 2.5 plots data of different surveys of inflation expectations. The surveys are of two types. In the first, used for the non-European countries and Sweden,

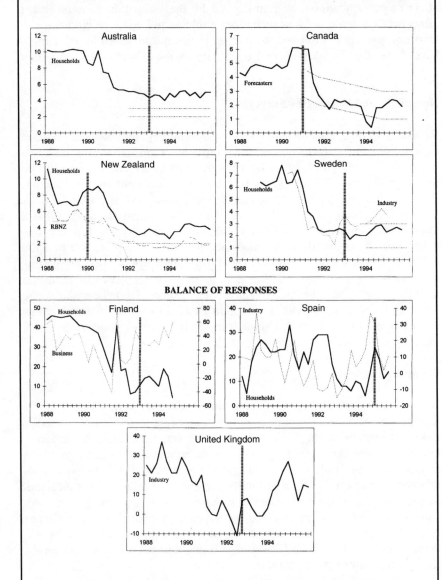

Figure 2.5   Households' and businesses' inflation expectations, 1988–94: expected changes in the CPI in the next 12 months

individuals are asked which is the inflation rate they expect in the next 12 months. In the second, used for Finland, Spain and the United Kingdom, individuals are asked if they expect future inflation[91] to be higher or lower than current inflation, and the results presented correspond to the difference between the number of the two responses.[92] The vertical dashed line marks the moment of the adoption of IT and the horizontal dotted lines the inflation targets.[93]

The main conclusions that may be drawn from Figure 2.5 are that the *announcement* of IT does not seem to affect inflation expectations and that households and businesses do not find the targets fully credible. In Australia expectations were practically unchanged since 1991 (before the adoption of IT), and they are well above the 2–3 per cent target. In Canada, the data correspond to the expectations of professional forecasters, not to the expectations of the common non-expert household or business. These have been inside the target range most of the time, and might have been affected by the announcement. However, one cannot tell whether this is a consequence of the adoption of IT or just a good forecast of the actual inflation performance.[94] In New Zealand, household expectations are still well above the 0–2 per cent target. The RBNZ survey, which covers households and businesses, tends to show lower inflation expectations, but even those lie outside the target range for some periods. Only in Sweden do households seem to find the IT credible: since the target was adopted, household inflation expectations were always inside the 1–3 per cent target range (but had been at those levels even before IT). However, the target is not fully credible for industrial agents, whose expectations tended to lie outside the target range. Finally, although the data for Finland, Spain and the United Kingdom is more difficult to interpret, it shows that inflation expectations were not significantly affected by the IT announcement. In the United Kingdom (and to a smaller extent in Finland) there was even an increase in inflation expectations, which suggests that also in these countries the target announcements were not fully credible.

is above the target ranges, and even in the shorter horizons of 2–5 years expected inflation has not always been inside the target ranges.

Whatever the measure of expectations used, a common feature among the countries in our sample is that inflation expectations were not significantly affected by the IT announcement, and the IT's credibility remained low during the early stages of the adoption of the framework. At least in some countries, there are some signs (e.g. medium-term expectations in Canada or bond yield differential in New Zealand) that early successes in meeting targets improved the credibility of monetary policy. However, the evidence is also consistent with a scenario where expectations formation is adaptive, and lower expected inflation is a consequence of the lower observed inflation, the adoption of IT having no effect whatsoever. Since inflation expectations are generally (still) above the targets, a sign that these are not fully credible, the latter explanation cannot be ruled out.

Box 2.14   IT Credibility and Bond Yields

A   LONG-TERM GOVERNMENT BOND YIELDS

Figure 2.6 plots the redemption yield on long-term government bonds,[95] daily from 1 January 1988 to 20 February 1996. The vertical line marks the date of the IT announcement. From the charts, we cannot find any significant impact of

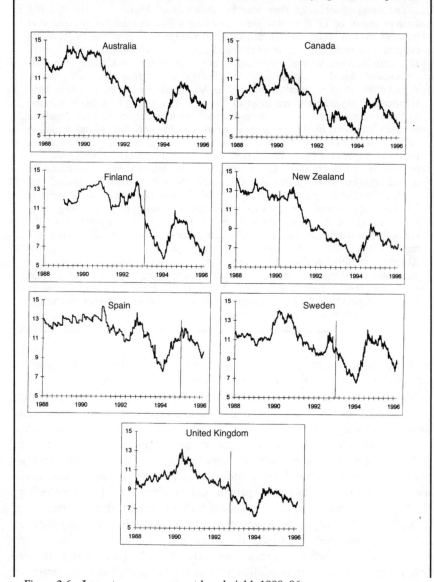

Figure 2.6   Long-term government bond yield, 1988–96

the IT announcement. In Finland, Sweden and the United Kingdom the announcement is associated with a fall in bond yields, but these were already falling before the announcement, and were subsequently reversed. The change in bond yields for these three countries is most likely associated with the adoption of a floating exchange rate (and subsequent depreciation of the currency) than with IT.

Figure 2.7 plots the same data, but only for a few months around the date of IT announcement,[96] so the specific effects of the announcement of IT may be easily identified. Finland, Sweden and the United Kingdom have similar patterns: a fall in bond yields on the day of the floating (particularly large in Sweden),[97] followed by subsequent falls for several weeks that extend beyond the IT announcement. The only effect the IT announcement appears to have in these countries is to reinforce the decreasing trend in yields. In the weeks immediately before the announcement, yields seem to have stabilised (in Finland) or slightly increased (in Sweden and the United Kingdom), but start falling again immediately after the announcement. If this pattern is really a consequence of IT, this would mean that IT helped to provide

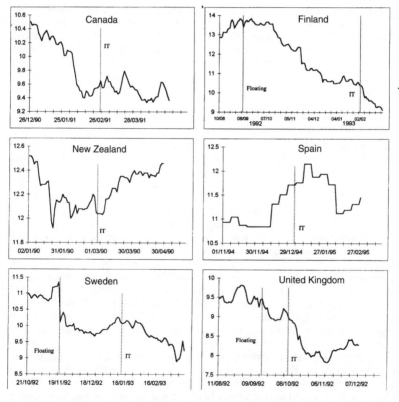

Figure 2.7 Long-term government bond yield around IT announcement, selected periods

credibility to the monetary policy of countries where it had been questioned by the abandonment of the previous monetary framework. However, this effect is exclusive of these countries, since it cannot be found in Canada, New Zealand or Spain.

B LONG BOND YIELD DIFFERENTIAL TO SELECTED NON-IT COUNTRIES
Government bond markets are global markets, thus changes in bond yields might not be caused by domestic factors, but be related to international events. In order to eliminate the effect of international conditions on bond yields, we computed the differential in bond yields between the countries in our sample and some reference country, which we took to be the United States for the non-European countries and Germany for the European countries.[98] Figure 2.8 plots the monthly long bond yield differential. Apart from the fall in yields in Finland, Sweden and the United Kingdom, we had already identified (and had associated more with the floating exchange rate regime than with the adoption of IT), the remarkable feature of Figure 2.8 is the fall in the average yield differential in New Zealand from about 400 b.p. until the end of 1990, to about 150 b.p. from mid 1991 onwards. This dramatic change is not associated with the *announcement* of IT, since it occurred approximately one year after it, but it is contemporaneous with a large fall in inflation and the achievement of the first targets. Although it can be claimed that bond yields were only reacting to the fall in inflation, the size and the speed of the adjustment were probably increased by the achievement of the first inflation targets and its impact on monetary policy credibility.

C INFLATION EXPECTATIONS IN BOND MARKETS
Changes in inflation expectations are just one of the many factors that determine bond yield changes. Comparing the yields in fixed rate and index-linked bonds allows a better measure of financial markets expectations about inflation to be computed. In some of the countries in our sample such measures of long term inflation expectations are available. Figure 2.9 plots quarterly data for the bond market implied inflation rates for Australia, Canada, Sweden and the United Kingdom.[99] The vertical dashed line marks the moment of the adoption of IT and the horizontal dotted lines the (medium term) inflation targets. The common pattern of Figure 2.9 is the lack of full long-term credibility of the IT, although the results improve on shorter horizons. In Australia, Canada and the United Kingdom longer-term inflation expectations are (slightly) above the upper limits of the target ranges, and well above the range mid-point these Central Banks are targeting. Expectations over the 2–5 year horizon, in Canada, Sweden and the United Kingdom, have been outside or in the upper half of the target range, suggesting that even in the shorter horizons the targets are not fully credible.

The implied inflation data could also be used to analyse the impact on expectations of the announcement of IT. Figure 2.10 plots 2 and 10 years implied inflation in the United Kingdom daily from 17 June 1992 to 31 December 1992, a period that covers both the change in exchange rate regime and the adoption of IT. The implied inflation data for the United Kingdom reinforces the pattern we observed in the previous charts. Expectations were affected by the floating of the British pound, but not by the announce-ment of IT, although the announcement is associated with the stabilisation of the inflation expectations that had been increasing since the floating of the pound. This evidence supports our previous claim that IT helped to provide credibility to the monetary policy of countries where it had been ques-tioned by the abandonment of the previous monetary framework.

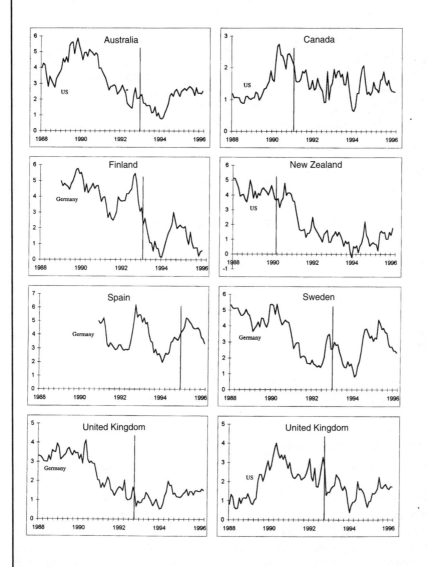

Figure 2.8 Long-term government bond yield, differential to Germany or the United States, 1988–96

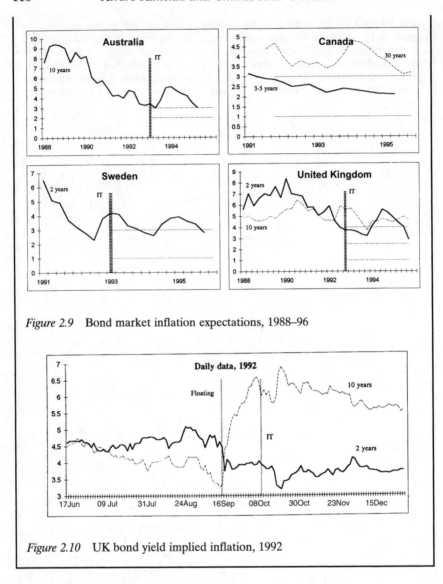

Figure 2.9   Bond market inflation expectations, 1988–96

Figure 2.10   UK bond yield implied inflation, 1992

Some measures of short-and medium-term expectations are consistent with the targets, but the long-term measures are not. This could be a consequence of the IT having 'operational credibility' but not 'political credibility': agents may believe (although not fully) that under the current framework the targets may be achieved, but they do not believe that the framework is going to be maintained, and fear that future policy frameworks will be more inflationary. 'Operational credibility' may be improved by redesigning the policy framework, and strengthening the incentives to achieve price stability. However, since any framework created by a government or Central Bank may always be changed in the future, no monetary policy framework can provide 'political credibility' in countries where high budget deficits and high levels of public debt provide the incentives to generate inflation, or a large part of the population (and of the political parties) do not regard price stability as a fundamental value to be maintained at all costs.

Wage Settlements

One of the major channels through which inflation expectations are supposed to affect actual inflation are wage settlements. Box 2.15 describes some anecdotal evidence that suggests the IT may have had some effect in centralized wage bargaining, and that in some countries wage increases have been relatively low. These are encouraging signs, given the importance of wage cost increases in inflationary processes. However, it is still too early to tell whether these changes in wage settlements are a result of the credibility of the target, or just a consequence of the unfavourable conditions workers faced in labour markets in this period. The relatively high levels of unemployment experienced in the early 1990s in all the countries in our sample are likely to have weakened the bargaining power of the workers in general, and the unions in particular. A definitive conclusion can be drawn only after we have observed some wage settlements reached under excess demand conditions in labour markets, although the evidence from New Zealand suggests that the IT might provide a good anchor for inflation expectations even under conditions more favourable to workers.

Box 2.15   Wage Settlements

We have no hard evidence of changes in the wage setting behaviour, especially because it is still to soon to have a sufficient long time series of wage agreements to make any form of quantified statement. We only have anecdotal evidence from several sources, including the Central Banks in the answer to our letter. Some of this evidence is reported below:

Australia	'Accord' between unions and Government refers to the IT;
Canada	some anecdotal evidence that negotiators pay more attention to IT;
Finland	a 2-year centralised wage agreement (for 1996–8) provided very moderate pay increases with a reference to the inflation target; after IT, initially there were no nominal wage increases because of 'crisis consciousness' but comparatively high wage increases were negotiated at branch level for 1995;

New Zealand	unions recognized the implications of the IT; wage settlements have been remarkably low in recent years (most in the 0–3 per cent range, except for small categories of skilled staff), and that despite the fact that unemployment fell from 10.9 per cent in 1991 to 6.1 per cent in December 1995;
Spain	wages have been bargained taking the IT as reference and wage settlements in 1994–5 were in line with the IT (before 1994 wage increases were regularly above official inflation projections);
Sweden	wage formation remains troublesome; despite the increased unemployment, wage increases have been higher than in the rest of the world; the centralised bargaining process is presently turning out a 5–6 per cent annual increase in nominal wages, even at a rate of unemployment of 10 per cent;
United Kingdom	wage settlements have been consistent with IT; wage growth has undershot current inflation.

Households and businesses probably do not understand the implications of the adoption of an IT, and it is even likely that they were not immediately aware of such a change. It was not surprising, then, that we did not find any impact on survey data expectations of the announcement of an IT. But asset prices are supposed to reflect the actions of well informed agents, who should be able to assess the true meaning of changes like the adoption of an IT, and we have not been able to find any significant impact of the announcement of an IT on financial markets data. It seems that contrary to some Central Bankers and economists, market agents have so far believed that IT is not a different monetary policy framework, or at least, that in practice nothing has really changed yet with the adoption of IT. The evidence we presented in this chapter seems to indicate that once again markets may have been right.

CONCLUSIONS

In Scottish law, criminal cases do not have to be adjudged either guilty, or not guilty. There is a third category, unproven. Mainly because we have too few data on which to base our judgement, that, we believe, is for the time being the appropriate judgement. One needs a longer experience with IT for any significant differences in Central Bank behaviour to emerge, if they exist. There are some signs that IT might have had a positive impact, especially in the countries where it has been in force for a longer period (New Zealand and Canada), but most of these are country-specific. Systematic patterns across all IT countries are hard to find.

The IT countries have been more successful than their Central Banks, or outside commentators, had initially expected in lowering, and then holding their inflation rates to the low desired mean levels. But then so equally were our various control groups. Both groups were helped in this by the international context, although the IT countries may have achieved low inflation faster and at a lower cost in terms of output growth. On the other hand, IT countries have missed their own targets on several occasions, which suggests that in order that IT be successful the target ranges should be wider than the usual 2 percentage point bands.[100]

Many of the apparent changes in operational characteristics among IT countries were the natural and self-evident results of shifting from an exchange rate target (Finland, Spain, Sweden and the United Kingdom) to an inflation target (i.e. the exchange rate becomes more volatile, the interest rate less so). Apart from those changes, there is little sign of any significant shift in operational behaviour. It is possible that the adoption of IT is instrumental in achieving stability in financial markets, but the evidence is not strong. In particular we looked hard to see if there was any evidence of interest rates being adjusted earlier or in larger jumps (more aggressively) in response to prospective inflationary pressures. There are a few straws in the wind (notably in Canada) and several of the Central Banks concerned are aware that such a change in behaviour might be needed, if the demanding targets are to continue to be kept. But the bulk of the evidence, so far, makes it impossible to dismiss the null hypothesis of no significant change in operational behaviour.

We have, at several places in this chapter, drawn a distinction between those IT Central Banks whose target is jointly set with the government, and those where it is unilaterally set by the Central Bank itself. *Pace* the Roll Report, we believe that the former, joint setting is likely to prove a far firmer bulwark against resurgent inflation. Consequently, we do see a greater likelihood of success in Canada and New Zealand than in the European cases.[101] Perhaps because of this differentiation, it is in Canada and New Zealand that there are some signs of a credibility effect. For the rest (including the United Kingdom) it is not, once more, possible at the moment to dismiss the null hypothesis of no maintained effect.

If expectations and inflation outcomes are not significantly affected, is there anything really new in the IT framework? The differences with an exchange rate target framework are the obvious differences between operating in a fixed or in a floating exchange rate regime. There is no fundamental difference between monetary targeting and IT; money targeting is just IT when inflation forecasts are exclusively based on money aggregates. When money aggregates are not good predictors of future inflation, IT is a clearly superior framework, and money targeting is not really an option. Where there is an option is between IT and a purely discretionary framework, compared to which IT has two main (positive) differences: the adoption of a quasi-formalized rule, that explicit states price stability as the only objective for monetary policy, and increased transparency and accountability. The evidence we gather suggests that the impact on credibility of the adoption of a policy rule is small, and limited to the short term.

The main difference is probably on the transparency and accountability side. The one field where there is clear evidence of a change in behaviour is in the nature of communications with both the public in general and government in particular. As documented earlier, such communication has generally become quicker, fuller and franker. In some instances (e.g. in Australia) some part of this shift towards greater transparency pre-dated the move to IT. Moreover this trend, towards more open communication, has been world-wide. Nevertheless we believe, (though such a qualitative issue is hard to test statistically) that such greater openness has gone further, faster in IT countries than in non-IT countries. This is one patent benefit of the regime change, even if elsewhere much remains unproven.

Notes

The authors wish to thank Avraham Ben-Bassat, Donald Brash, Clive Briault, Kevin Clinton, Charles Freedman, Andrew Haldane, Lars Heikensten, David Longworth, Ian Macfarlane, José Luis Malo de Molina, Michael Reddell, Pierre Siklos, Antii Suvanto and José Viñals for helpful comments and suggestions. Any errors or omissions remain our own responsibility.

1   The alternative, of adopting a target for the *price level*, has been discussed by economists in several theoretical contributions – e.g. Fischer (1994), Goodhart (1994), McCallum (1995) – but has not yet been considered a serious practical possibility by Central Banks. See p. 63 on this issue.
2   The United States has no other intermediate targets either, but it is not regarded as an IT country. It has no explicitly quantified, numerical target for inflation, and is currently required (by Act of Congress) to take into consideration several other objectives besides price stability.
3   Israel will probably become an IT country, even according to our strict definition, since the relative importance of the inflation target and the exchange rate target has been changing in favour of the former. Since mid-1995 the width of the crawling band was enlarged and the exchange rate has been allowed to move more freely within the band, thus reducing the role of short-term exchange rate concerns in shaping monetary policy. The role of the exchange rate targets and inflation targets in the monetary policy of Israel is discussed, for example, in Ben-Bassat (1995).
4   Although we chose this sample in part because we thought that these countries had clearly defined targets, after investigation we realised that, at least in some of them, the targets are somewhat less precise than we had initially believed. Still, the definition of the targets in the sample countries is more precise than in

non-IT countries, where the policy objective is defined as 'price stability' with few details of what is meant by that.

5   After completion of the first draft, we came across a paper by Svensson (1996) where the set of countries described as having an IT framework is the same as ours, and where the description of the characteristics of the IT framework is similar to our own.

6   The argument for adopting an explicit IT is discussed on p. 60.

7   Briault, Haldane and King (1996) discuss why there has been a general move towards more Central Bank independence in recent years.

8   It is difficult to determine precisely the date of the announcement of IT in Australia. Initially the Central Bank unilaterally adopted a quantified numerical IT without the involvement or blessing of the Government. Subsequently, however, Ministers came to speak approvingly of this initiative, and with a Labour Government having thus consented to it, and the new Liberal Government also in favour, IT in Australia can be viewed as firmly established. For the exercises that require the use of the announcement date, we assumed it to be 1/1/1993.

9   This is the date of the joint announcement of the inflation-reduction targets by the Government, as part of its annual budget presentation, and the Bank of Canada, through a press release. Although the Governor of the Bank of Canada, John Crow, had been publicly stressing for some time (at least since his Hansen Lecture of 1988) that price stability was the monetary policy objective, we believe these statements do not represent the sort of official commitment to a precisely defined target that we take to be the characteristic of IT countries.

10   This is the date the first Policy Targets Agreement (PTA) between the Reserve Bank of New Zealand and the Government was signed. Since April 1988, the Minister of Finance, Roger Douglas, and the Associate Minister of Finance, Peter Nelson (the Ministry of Finance was then responsible for monetary policy), had been making several statements stressing the Government's intention of bringing inflation down to very low levels. Again, as in the case of Canada, we believe that these statements do not fulfil the characteristics of an IT as we define it, and that only after the signing of the first PTA New Zealand had an official commitment to achieve a precisely defined target.

11   In Spain, the IT was announced in December 1994, but was formally adopted as of 1 January 1995.

12   We regard this as an important criterion. Countries that had low inflation at the outset (e.g. Germany) may find it hard to improve on their performance; while the experience of initially high inflation countries may be startlingly good, or bad, and in either case bias the conclusions.

13   The existence of continuing supply-side shocks is taken as axiomatic in much of the literature on Central Bank independence. With the important exception of the various oil shocks, it is less clear how large or frequent such supply-side shocks have been in practice.

14   The Finnish markka and the British pound were floated in September 1992, and the Swedish krona in November 1992, and IT was adopted in October 1992, January 1993 and February 1993, respectively in the United Kingdom, Sweden and Finland.

15   New Zealand had abandoned exchange rate targets in 1985. Monetary targets were used in Australia (from 1976 to 1985) and Canada (from 1975 to 1982),

but were abandoned because they were not considered to be reliable indicators of policy.

16   Or, in the UK case, the Chancellor, who is responsible for monetary policy.

17   Walsh (1995) and Persson and Tabellini (1993) show that an adequate incentive contract for Central Bankers may eliminate any inflationary bias they may have. The monitoring and associated penalties could be seen as such an incentive contract.

18   In New Zealand, the Central Bank Governor may be dismissed if the inflation targets defined in the Policy Targets Agreement, signed between the Central Bank and the government, are not met. Here the incentives to achieve the target are apparently high, since there are explicit sanctions for failures. In Canada and the United Kingdom there are no pre-set sanctions, but the fact that one party publicly monitors the performance of the other may constitute a sufficient incentive. In the United Kingdom the Chancellor is responsible for monetary policy, and the Bank of England monitors the inflation performance: if targets are not met, the Bank of England publicly announces it, and this could harm the government politically. In Canada, the fact that an explicit target set by the government is missed may be used as a political argument not to reappoint a Central Bank Governor the government dislikes; if the targets are met, the non reappointment of a Governor that achieved the targets the government itself has set might be politically difficult to explain. The incentives to stick to the target exist in the three countries, although it may be argued that they are not strong enough to make the IT fully credible.

19   The inflationary bias of politicians was one of the main arguments the Roll Committee Report (1993, Sections 2.5 and 3.3) advanced against joint targets.

20   Reputational solutions for the time-inconsistency problem may be found, for example, in Barro and Gordon (1983b).

21   Note that the argument for joint announcements only holds if the Central Bank is effectively independent from the government. If this is not the case, government and Central Bank are the same entity in terms of decision power, and in this case a joint announcement is in fact an unilateral announcement.

22   Mexico provides an example of a Central Bank to which formal independence has been granted, but is perceived to be not completely independent from the government. Russia provides an example of an independent Central Bank that was less 'conservative' than the Government: under Governor Gerashchenko, the monetary policy in Russia was highly inflationary, much more than the Yeltsin government desired.

23   Svensson (1995) and Andersson and Berg (1995) argue that in the case of Sweden the main problem was of 'political credibility', especially before the elections of September 1994. The opposition social-democrats were against the IT, and they were expected to change the Riksbank board (and adopt inflationary policies) if they won the elections, as they eventually did. After the election the social-democrats surprised observers by appointing an independent chairman to the board, who reinforced the IT as the monetary policy objective. Ammer and Freeman (1994) refer to similar doubts about the medium-term permanence of the IT before the 1993 elections in Canada. The 'political credibility' of the New Zealand IT has also been recently affected by calls to abandon the PTA framework by two opposition parties.

24   Evidence regarding the credibility of IT is presented below on p. 102.

25   Usual references to supply side shocks are to those increasing inflation, such as the oil price increases of the 1970s, but there is no reason to rule out supply-

side shocks of the opposite sign. The disinflation process of the 1990s might be partially explained by such shocks, e.g. the increased retail competition in the United Kingdom or the decline in food prices as a result of Finland's EU membership.

26   See p. 000 on the controllability of inflation.
27   Underlying inflation is supposed to capture the fundamental trends in headline inflation, and deviations between the two indices are usually assumed to be temporary, but this is not necessarily true. Yates (1995) presents some evidence (although not conclusive) that different price indices in the United Kingdom are not directly substitutable even in the long term (although they cointegrate).
28   In Finland and Spain the target ranges are not precisely defined. In Spain the upper bound of the range is defined (3 per cent), but not the lower bound. In Finland, the 2 per cent target should be interpreted as the mid-point of a soft-edged band; the Bank of Finland explicitly stated that deviations on both sides will be allowed, but no explicit toleration ranges were specified.
29   The target for Australia should be interpreted as a 'thick' point rather than a range.
30   It is arguable, however, whether its high credibility was the reason behind the Bank of Finland's choice, given the country's inflation history and substantial depreciation of the markka at the time of the adoption of their point target. The single figure was preferred since it was considered that it would provide a better guide for the formation of inflation expectations (Brunila and Lahdenperä, 1995, p. 129).
31   Economists at the Bank of England (e.g. King, 1996) also interpret the UK target as a point target that should hold on average, together with an indication of the range within which *ex post* inflation might be expected to lie if policy is directed at this point.
32   Note that a price level target is not necessarily a constant level target. One may set a target for the price level that is higher than the current price level. In the short run (over one period), there is no fundamental difference between an inflation and a price level target: if the current price level is 100, it is equivalent to set an inflation target of 0–2 per cent or a price level target of 100–102. This is not the case over several periods, since inflation targets allow for base drift, but price level targets do not. If inflation is higher than the inflation target in one period, the price level is permanently affected, since the future ITs will refer to the current (higher) price level. This is not the case under a price level target, since too high inflation in one period must be compensated by lower inflation in the following periods. A similar result arises if we use an IT that must hold on average, since for the average to hold, high inflation in one period must be compensated by low inflation in the following periods. For example, assume the current price level is 100, and price stability is defined as an inflation rate of 2 per cent per period. If the targets are continuously met, it is (roughly) equivalent to set the targets as (i) an inflation target that should hold every period, (ii) an inflation target that should hold on average, or (iii) a price level target. The price level on the second period will be (approximately) 104 in every case. But assume that inflation in the first period is 3 per cent, i.e. the price level is 103. Meeting the targets in the second period implies for target (i) an inflation rate of 2 per cent, i.e. a price level of 105; for target (ii) a price level of 104, i.e. an inflation rate of 1 per cent; for target (iii) an inflation rate of 1 per cent (so that the average is 2 per cent), i.e. a price level of 104. The outcome is the same for targets (ii) and (iii), but not for target (i).

33   Yates (1995) provides a good review of the discussion.

34   Summers (1991) pointed out that since nominal interest rates are always non-negative, a zero inflation rate implies that real interest rates must also be non-negative. Summers' argument for a positive inflation rate is that in some circumstances (like in a deep recession), negative real rates of interest might be appropriate. Even if the need for negative real interest rates may be infrequent, they could be very important in those rare cases and should not be ruled out by the adoption of a zero inflation rate.

35   If there is some downward nominal rigidity in the labour market, short-run decreases in the real wage cannot be achieved under zero inflation. In countries where the labour market structure is such that nominal wage cuts are rare (or ruled out by law), a positive rate of inflation may be the less costly way of generating short run real wage decreases.

36   An inflation tax may be part of the optimal mix of revenue-raising methods a government can use, and thus should not be ruled out by adopting a zero inflation target.

37   For example, this was the argument used by the Bank of England (1992).

38   Brunila and Lahdenperä (1995) claim that the bias in the CPI might be as high as 1.5–2 per cent in the United States, but is likely to be smaller in the UK and in Canada (of the order of 0.5–1 per cent).

39   For New Zealand, which has a mid-point target of 1 per cent, might one argue that the statistical bias was the only reason behind the choice of a positive inflation target. However, since it is likely that in New Zealand the bias in the CPI is smaller than elsewhere (Archer, 1995), i.e. smaller than 0.5 per cent, even for this country some of the other arguments were probably (implicitly) behind the choice of target.

40   In Finland and Sweden the 2 per cent target was chosen because this was the level of inflation other European countries were seen to be targeting.

41   Note that usually an initial date for the application of targets is set, but not a final date. At first, a planned path for a reduction in inflation may be set, but once inflation reaches the final target it should stay there indefinitely. The exceptions are Canada and New Zealand, where current targets hold only until 1998, and new targets must be set before that date to hold in subsequent periods.

42   The 'transition targets' could also be useful as a guideline for policy decisions. Nicholl and Archer (1992) claim that was the case in New Zealand, where the 'transition target' has given the RBNZ 'a clear framework for policy decisions, and has provided the motivation to take policy actions that might be politically difficult' (p. 322).

43   'Current inflation' refers to the formal target index on the quarter before the time of the announcement, except for Canada and New Zealand where it refers to the underlying inflation index used for policy decisions.

44   The targets in New Zealand were changed twice. The first Policy Targets Agreement (PTA), signed in March 1990 set the final target of 0–2 per cent by the end of 1992, and in April the RBNZ announced the 'transition targets' of 3–5 per cent in December 1990 and 1.5–3.5 per cent in December 1991. A new PTA was signed in December 1990 extending the final target for the end of 1993, and following this the RBNZ announced in February 1991 the new 'transition targets' of 2.5–4.5 per cent in December 1991 and 1.5–3.5 per cent in December 1992. Finally, a third PTA was signed in December 1992 where the target was set to hold from that moment until the end of the Governor's term in

1998. We took the targets to be the ones set more recently at each point in time, that is, the 'transition targets' to be 3–5 per cent in December 1990, 2.5–4.5 per cent in December 1991, 1.5–3.5 per cent in December 1992, and the final target of 0–2 per cent to hold from the first quarter of 1993.

45   Svensson (1996) provides a formal analysis of the inflation forecast role in an IT framework.

46   For example, at the Bank of Canada the staff prepares a base forecast and several alternative forecasts according to different scenarios for the exogenous variables; the management then will treat the different alternatives according to their view of the likelihood of such scenarios (Longworth and Freedman, 1995).

47   For example, the Bank of England stresses that the uncertainty surrounding inflation forecasting will make the inflation outcome 'always' different from the forecast. For this reason, since February 1996, the inflation forecasts in the *Inflation Report* are presented as confidence intervals, and not as point forecasts

48   The role of a 'monetary conditions index' in the conduct of monetary policy has been given considerable attention in recent research, in particular at the Bank of Canada (see, for example, Freedman, 1995b).

49   Clarida and Gertler (1996) claim that in Germany, the money targets are meant as guidelines and in no sense do they define a strict policy rule (p. 2), that the Bundesbank has tolerated deviations from the targets as a reaction to the development of economic activity (p. 7), and that moderating market interest rate fluctuations takes precedence over monetary targeting (p. 11). Helmut Schlesinger, former President of the Bundesbank, quoted in von Hagen (1995, p. 108) said that the Bundesbank has never conducted a rigid policy geared at the money supply alone, and all available information about financial markets and the economy is analysed regularly.

50   The degree of ongoing discretion may be reduced by describing thoroughly all the details of the operation of the targets the moment they are announced. Many Central Banks have described in some detail how they interpret the targets, and this implies that many of the choices discussed in this and the following paragraphs were made *ex ante*. However, this was not always the case, and some Central Banks still have some degree of discretion in some of the issues discussed.

51   An example of such an adjustment, is the Finnish experience of 1992–4.

52   The exchange rate data are US dollar Bankers' Trust mid-quotes at 3.00 pm, New York time, available from *Datastream*. The DM rates were computed from the USD rates.

53   The results reported for Finland were obtained from a model that included two dummies taking the value of 1 in 14 November 1991 and 9 September 1992, respectively, when major devaluations occurred. Without the inclusion of these dummies the variance would not be stationary.

54   The difference in exchange rate volatility between the IT and discretionary frameworks might be less important than these results suggest, since the 'discretionary period' for Finland and Sweden was only a short period (5 and 2 months respectively) after the abandonment of the fixed exchange rate regime in the end of 1992, and that was a period of abnormal instability in forex markets. For the UK, the discretionary period also includes this period, but it is not restricted to it.

55   It could be argued that with free international capital movements, any interest rate changes are conditioned on the interest range changes in the core currency countries. If these countries smooth interest rates, then other countries have to

smooth them too, and thus we should not expect a significant change in behaviour in that respect just due to the adoption of IT.

56   The headline inflation and interest rates data are from *International Financial Statistics*. The headline inflation series are the quarterly average of year-on-year consumer price inflation. The interest rates used were the average of the overnight money market rate for Australia, Canada, Finland and Sweden, the end of period discount rate for New Zealand (although New Zealand does not have a discount rate, this is the name the *IFS* uses for the bank rate they provide) and Spain, and the end of period London clearing banks base rate, for the UK. The data for Sweden exclude the abnormally high interest rates of September 1992. The common assumption for all these rates is that they are determined by the Central Banks, and thus reflect accurately the monetary policy stance. We would prefer to use money market data in all countries, but sufficiently long series were not available. Tests over the sample periods for which data for both bank and market rates were available indicated the conclusions of this and other exercises in the chapter would be similar whatever the interest rate used. The underlying inflation series for Australia, Canada and New Zealand were provided by the respective Central Banks. The 'RPIX' series for the UK was obtained from *Datastream*, and for Finland underlying inflation is the series 'Indicator of underlying inflation (1990 = 100)', published in the *Bank of Finland Bulletin* (data for 1996:Q1 refers to February only).

57   First differences were used because pre-testing of the data indicated that for all countries in our sample, the quarterly inflation and interest rate series are $I(1)$. The use of error-correction models was ruled out because pretesting also indicated that inflation and interest rates are *not* cointegrated. Details of these tests can be obtained from the authors.

58   In general, time series that reflect forward-looking behaviour, such as financial asset prices, tend to Granger-cause many key economic time series. This does not mean that those series *cause* inflation or GNP to move up or down. Instead, the value of those series reflects the anticipated future movements in inflation or GNP. Granger-causality tests for such series may be useful for investigating whether markets (or Central Banks) are concerned with future inflation, but should not be used to infer a direction of economic causation. On the use of Granger-causality tests to assess forward-looking behaviour, see Hamilton (1994), chapter 11.

59   Details of the estimation and the tests may be obtained from the authors.

60   In the case of Spain, the tests were performed using 2 lags, instead of 4, so that the model could be estimated over the 'after IT' period.

61   In all the cases interest rates were found to Granger-cause inflation, the significant coefficients in the $B(L)$ polynomial were positive, supporting the view that this Granger-causality should be interpreted as Central Banks reacting to future expected inflation, and not as a consequence of the transmission mechanism.

62   For a detailed analysis on why Central Banks might prefer to smooth interest rates, see Goodhart (1996).

63   We also looked at the behaviour of narrow and broad money aggregates, before and after the adoption of IT. Again, we could not find any significant change. These tests are not reported here, but may be obtained from the authors.

64   The interest rates used were the same as in Box 2.5, just the frequency was changed from quarterly to monthly (see Box 12.5 for details). We have reasons to believe that the data for Australia and New Zealand in late 1983 early 1984 is

inaccurate, but used them in the absence of a better alternative. None of the results is significantly affected by this.

65   Interest rate increase episodes were selected using a methodology similar to Ball (1994). First, 'trend' interest rate (the 12-month moving average) is used to identify 'peaks' and 'troughs'. A peak is a month in which 'trend' interest rate is higher than in the previous 6 and the following 6 months; a trough is defined by an analogous comparison. An interest rate increase episode is any period that starts at an interest rate trough and ends at an interest rate peak, with the 'trend' rate more than 1 point higher than the trough. Then, the lowest and the highest monthly rates in each episode were used to compute the statistics in the table. The 'duration' is the number of months between the month with the lowest and the month with the highest rates, the 'magnitude' is the difference between the rates in these months, and the 'monthly rate of increase' is the ratio of the 'magnitude' over the 'duration'. Statistics for each episode are not provided here, but may be obtained from the authors.

Absolute and relative changes are both used to describe interest rate increases because there are large differences in the level of interest rates across the sample period, ranging in some cases from 5 per cent to 35 per cent. The problem this large difference causes when comparing the size of different rate increases is whether we should consider an 3 p.p. increase from 5 to 8 per cent or from 32 to 35 per cent as being similar changes. The alternative is to consider as similar two 50 per cent increases, be they from 5 to 7.5 per cent or from 20 to 30 per cent. The impact on real interest rates suggests we use the former criterion, but we also present the latter to provide a measure of the relative change.

66   For some countries, restrictions in data availability reduced the sample period.

67   In our sample, the variance of daily interest rate changes tends to be integrated. Using weekly data, the likelihood of finding integrated variances is reduced.

68   The model used for Australia was modified by replacing (2.6) by: $c_{i,t} = \mu_i + \rho_i c_{i,t-1} + \phi_i c_{i,t-2} + \varepsilon_{i,t}$

69   The model used for Spain was modified by replacing equation (2.6) and (2.8) by:

$$c_{i,t} = \mu_i + \rho_i c_{i,t-1} + \phi_i \sqrt{h_{i,t-1}} + \varepsilon_{i,t} \tag{2.6$'$}$$

$$h_{i,t} = \gamma_i + \alpha_i \varepsilon_{i,t-1}^2 + \delta_i D_{i,t} \tag{2.8$'$}$$

70   Inference cannot be made for Canada, due to lack of data, and for Sweden, where the estimated parameters are not consistent with the stationarity of the variance.

71   The Bank of England's report does not include any discussion on monetary policy decisions, because in the UK the Chancellor is responsible for monetary policy, not the Bank.

72   The only exception is the Banco de España's report, that includes a statistical annex.

73   Mayes and Riches (1996, p. 8).

74   It has been argued by some commentators (for example, Svensson 1996), that this is why the Bank of England's *Inflation Report* is, by far, the more detailed of all the Reports. Although all the Reports have similar structures, the detail of information provided varies significantly, with some (e.g. Canada and New Zealand) relying more on non-technical text and charts (with very few tables), and others (e.g. the United Kingdom) providing a more technical analysis and

large amount of data. It could be argued this is a consequence of the incentives for writing the report, with the former being directed at influencing the expectations of the non-expert general public and the latter being directed at influencing the Chancellor.

75   Freedman (1995a, p. 27) refers that empirical work undertaken at the Bank of Canada at the time of the IT adoption suggested bands wider than 2 p.p. should be used. Simulations for Australia (Stevens and Debelle, 1995) and the United Kingdom (Haldane and Salmon, 1995) also suggest that the optimal band width should be higher than the width adopted.

76   Note that the United Kingdom has also the widest bands, at least in this transition period (3 p.p.).

77   As officials in the RBNZ claim it to be, and as it seems to be accepted by the public in New Zealand.

78   A related question is whether reactions to a breach in a final target range should be symmetrical. Will governments and public tend to accept undershooting, but not overshooting, of the target? In terms of final targets we have no evidence so far, but the reaction to the undershooting of the transition paths suggest that this is a possibility.

79   For example, the Bank of Canada recognizes that the role of monetary policy is not to keep inflation permanently inside the target range, but to ensure that inflation returns to the range if some shock pushes it outside. Other targets (e.g. New Zealand) are meant to hold at all times.

80   The first assumption refers to the definition of the Bank of Finland's IT: it is not obvious what should be considered as 'around 2 per cent'. Given that the point of Box 2.10 is to assess how easy it is to meet a range target of the usual 2–3 per cent width, for Table 2.7 we assumed the Bank of Finland had a $2\% \pm 1.5\%$ target. The Banco de España set a 'transition target' for 'early 1996', which we took to mean the first quarter average. Finally, the RBNZ set 'transition targets' that were changed twice, and only refer to inflation in 1990:Q4, 1991 and 1992. The assumptions regarding the change of targets are described in footnote 44, and the targets for the 1991:Q1–3 and 1992:Q1–3.

81   The headline inflation data corresponds to the series 'Annual changes for consumer prices' from *International Financial Statistics*. The underlying inflation series for Australia, Canada and New Zealand were provided by the respective Central Banks. The 'RPIX' series for the UK was obtained from *Datastream*, and for Finland underlying inflation is the series 'Indicator of underlying inflation (1990=100)', published in the *Bank of Finland Bulletin* (data for 1996: Q1 refers to February only). Except for Australia and New Zealand, where the inflation data is released quarterly, the quarterly inflation was computed as the average of the monthly inflation rates.

82   'Final' targets are the ones which correspond to the definition of 'a low and stable level of inflation' for each Central Bank. 'Final' targets are defined in opposition to 'transition' targets, which set a downward path for inflation. This does not mean that 'final' targets cannot be changed; in New Zealand and Canada, the current 'final' targets only apply until 1998. These 'final' targets have been in force in New Zealand, since the first quarter of 1993 (13 data points available), in Finland and Sweden, since the first quarter of 1995 (5 data points available), and in Canada since the fourth quarter of 1995 (2 data points available). The Australian target is in force since 1993 (13 quarters), but if we take the target to be the average inflation, then only 1 data point is available.

83   In Australia the target does not have to hold at all quarters, only on average, so formally there was not a failure to meet the target, although inflation was outside the target range for more than a third of the quarters. In Finland, the target does not define explicit bands, so one cannot claim it was missed, although the deviations from the 2 per cent target are larger than would be compatible with a band 3 p.p. wide.

84   The 1990s' are compared with the 1980s' and the 'after' with the 'before' IT.

85   The standard deviation of inflation levels in the IT group is lower than in the control groups. The lower standard deviation implies that any test to the average inflation in the group will tend to have higher significance levels.

86   The behaviour of the coefficient of variation in the individual countries also suggests the small sample result. The coefficient of variation increased after the adoption of IT in four (Australia, Canada, Finland and New Zealand) out of the seven IT countries, which is not very different from the eight out of 17 increases we observe in non-IT OECD countries.

87   This is something of a tautology, because the measure of underlying inflation is designed to include only the inflationary pressures monetary policy can control.

88   The inflation data are the yearly changes in consumer prices from *International Financial Statistics*, the unemployment data are OECD standardised unemployment rates, and the GDP data are OECD standardised GDP volume indices (except for New Zealand, which were obtained from *Datastream*).

89   'Trend' inflation is defined as a centred, 9-quarter moving average of actual inflation. To identify disinflation episodes, we identify 'peaks' and 'troughs' in trend inflation: a 'peak' is a quarter in which trend inflation is higher than in the previous four and the following four quarters, and a 'trough' is defined by an analogous comparison. A disinflation episode is any period that starts at an inflation peak and ends at a trough with an yearly rate of inflation at least 2 percentage points lower than the peak. See Ball (1994) for a justification of the procedure.

90   Results for each individual episode and country are not presented here but may be obtained from the authors. The episodes under IT are included in the 1990s' group. Only for Canada, New Zealand and Sweden can we identify a complete disinflation episode after IT. For Finland and the United Kingdom the 1990s' episode ended under IT, but started before; in these cases, marked '#', the data for the 1990s' is for the whole episode, but the data for IT is just for the period after IT. For Australia and Spain no disinflation episode was identified under IT; the data for IT (not included in the 1990s data) corresponds to a period when inflation fell, but does not qualify as an episode according to the methodology adopted; the average for the IT group for the IT period does not include these data for Australia and Spain.

91   In the next 3 months, for the business surveys, and in the next 12 months in the household surveys.

92   The data sources and expectations series for Figure M.1 are:

Australia	Westpac/IAESR inflation expectations survey (provided by *Datastream*);
Canada	Conference Board of Canada quarterly Survey of Forecasters (provided by the Bank of Canada);
Finland	Consumer survey of Statistics Finland, Business survey of the Confederation of Finnish Industry and Employers (published in Kuismanen and Spolander, 1995);

> **New Zealand**   *Marketscope* survey of inflation expectations (house-
> holds), Reserve Bank survey of expectations of senior
> business leaders and other key opinion leaders (pro-
> vided by the Reserve Bank of New Zealand);
> **Spain**   European Economy – Consumer opinion on economic
> and financial conditions, Ministerio de Industria e
> Energia – Survey of manufacturing industry (provided
> by Banco de España);
> **Sweden**   Statistics Sweden, National Institute of Economic
> Research (published in *Inflation and Inflation Expecta-
> tions in Sweden*, Sveriges Riksbank, June 1995)
> **United Kingdom** Confederation of British Industry monthly inquiry –
> expected prices of domestic orders (provided by *Data-
> stream*).

93 The dates in the charts correspond to the moment the surveys were made. The
targets were shifted back 12 months so they refer to the same period as the
expectations do.

94 The Bank of Canada's *Monetary Policy Report* of May 1996 mentioned that
83 per cent of respondents to the Conference Board business confidence
survey expected inflation to be 2 per cent or less, which suggests that also
among the business community the IT has (at least now) gained substantial
credibility.

95 The data in Figure 2.7 and 2.8 are indices of long-term government bonds
computed by *Datastream*. The maturities of the bonds used on these indices
differ slightly across countries: 10 years for New Zealand, 7 to 10 years for
Australia, Sweden and the United Kingdom, 3 to 5 years for Canada, all
maturities for Finland and 'long-term' for Spain.

96 Figure 2.8 does not include Australia, because we are not aware of a specific IT
announcement date for this country.

97 In the day of the floating, bond yields fell 123, 34 and 17 basis points respectively in Sweden, Finland and the United Kingdom.

98 The differential was computed using *Datastream* long-term government bond
indices. Given the strong links between the UK and US economies, we also
computed the differential in bond yields in these two countries.

99 The data for Sweden and for the 3–5 years, horizon in Canada are not computed from market yields, but are based on surveys of bond market investors.
The data sources and expectations series for Figure 2.9 are:

> **Australia**   difference between nominal and indexed 10-year bond
> yields, adjusted for an 8-month indexation lag (provided
> by the Reserve Bank of Australia);
> **Canada**   differential between conventional and real return 30-year
> bond yields (calculated using the appropriate compound
> interest formula), *Consensus Economics Inc.*'s 'Consen-
> sus Forecasts 3 and 5 years ahead (average)' (published
> in the Bank of Canada's *Monetary Policy Report*, May
> 1996);
> **Sweden**   Aragon Fondkommission – Survey of bond investors'
> inflation expectations (published in *Inflation and Infla-
> tion Expectations in Sweden*, Sveriges Riksbank);
> **United Kingdom** Bank of England's estimated market expectations of
> inflation, based on 2-and 10-year bond yields.

100   This point has recently received a lot of attention in New Zealand, the country
      with a longer experience in IT, for example. The *Financial Times* of 28 June
      1996 reported that in New Zealand there is a widespread criticism of the
      current 2 p.p. bands, and several critics (including opposition parties) have
      called for wider bands.
101   In Finland, Spain and Sweden because it is not clear how much the govern-
      ment is committed to the target; in the United Kingdom because the Bank of
      England does not have independent control of the interest rate.

References

ÅKERHOLM, J. (1994) 'Finland's experience with a floating exchange rate', *Bank of Finland Bulletin*, 3, 9–13.

ÅKERHOLM, J. and A. BRUNILA (1995) 'Inflation targeting: the Finnish experience', in L. Leiderman and L.E.O. Svensson (eds), *Inflation Targets*, London:
Centre for Economic Policy Research, 90–106.

AMMER, J. and R.T. FREEMAN (1994) 'Inflation targeting in the 1990s: the
experiences of New Zealand, Canada and the United Kingdom', Board of Governors of the Federal Reserve System, *International Finance Discussion Paper*, 473,
June.

ANDERSSON, K. and C. BERG (1995) 'The inflation target in Sweden', in A.G.
Haldane (ed.), *Targeting Inflation*, London: Bank of England, 207–25.

ARCHER, D. (1995) 'Some reflections on inflation targets', in A.G. Haldane (ed.),
Targeting Inflation, London: Bank of England, 246–64.

BÄCKSTRÖM, U. (1994) 'Monetary policy and the inflation target', Sveriges Riksbank, address at SOX Day, Stockholm Stock Exchange, Stockholm, 9 December
1994.

BÄCKSTRÖM, U. (1995) 'Swedish monetary policy in a European perspective',
Sveriges Riksbank, address at the Euromoney International Bond Congress, London, 13 December 1995.

BAILLIE, R.T. and T. BOLLERSLEV (1989) 'The message in daily exchange rates: a
conditional-variance tale', *Journal of Business and Economic Statistics*, 7(3), 297–
305.

BALL, L. (1994) 'What determines the sacrifice ratio?', in N.G. Mankiw (ed.),
Monetary Policy, Chicago: University of Chicago Press, 155–82.

BANCO DE ESPAÑA, *Economic bulletin*, 1993–6, Madrid.

BANCO DE ESPAÑA, *Inflation report*, 1995–6, Madrid.

BANK OF CANADA, *Monetary policy report*, 1995–6, Ottawa.

BANK OF CANADA, *Bank of canada review*, 1991–6, Ottawa.

BANK OF ENGLAND, *Inflation report*, 1993–6, London.

BANK OF ENGLAND, *Bank of England Quarterly Bulletin*, 1992–6, London.

BANK OF ENGLAND (1992) 'The case for price stability', *Bank of England Quarterly Bulletin*, November, 441–8.

BANK OF FINLAND, *Bank of Finland Bulletin*, 1992–5, Helsinki.

BARRO, R.J. and D.B. GORDON (1983a) 'A positive theory of monetary policy in a
natural rate model', *Journal of Political Economy*, 91(4), 589–610.

BARRO, R.J. and D.B. GORDON (1983b) 'Rules, discretion and reputation in a
model of monetary policy', *Journal of Monetary Economics*, 12(1), 101–22.

BEN-BASSAT, A. (1995) 'The inflation target in Israel: policy and development', in A.G. Haldane (ed.), *Targeting Inflation*, London: Bank of England, 15–48.
BOWEN, A. (1995a) 'British experience with inflation targetry', in L. Leiderman and L.E.O. Svensson (eds), *Inflation Targets*, London: Centre for Economic Policy Research, 53–68.
BOWEN, A. (1995b) 'Inflation targetry in the United Kingdom', in A.G. Haldane (ed.), *Targeting Inflation*, London: Bank of England, 59–74.
BRASH, D. (1992) 'The exchange rate and monetary policy', *Reserve Bank of New Zealand Bulletin*, 55(4), 324–33.
BRIAULT, C.B., A.G. HALDANE and M.A. KING (1996) 'Independence and accountability', Bank of England, *Working Paper Series*, 49, April.
BRUNILA, A. and H. LAHDENPERÄ (1995) 'Inflation targets: principal issues and practical implementation', in Andrew G. Haldane (ed.), *Targeting Inflation*, London: Bank of England, 119–34.
CLARIDA, R. and M. GERTLER (1996) 'How the Bundesbank conducts monetary policy', Cambridge, MA: NBER, mimeo.
CUKIERMAN, A. (1995) 'Targeting monetary aggregates and inflation in Europe', presented at the Association for the Monetary Union of Europe's International Conference on Future European Monetary Policy, Kronberg, Germany, 30 November-1 December.
FISCHER, A. (1995) 'New Zealand's experience with inflation targets', in L. Leiderman and L.E.O. Svensson (eds), *Inflation Targets*, London: Centre for Economic Policy Research, 32–52.
FISCHER, S. (1994) 'Modern central banking', in F. Capie, S. Fischer, C. Goodhart and N. Schnadt (eds), *The Future of central banking*, Cambridge: Cambridge University Press.
FREEDMAN, C. (1995a) 'The Canadian experience with targets for reducing and controlling inflation', in L. Leiderman and L.E.O. Svensson (eds), *Inflation Targets*, London: Centre for Economic Policy Research, 19–31.
FREEDMAN, C. (1995b) 'The role of monetary conditions and the monetary conditions index in the conduct of policy', *Bank of Canada Review*, Autumn, 53–9.
GOODHART, C.A.E. (1991) 'The draft statute of the European System of Central Banks: a commentary', LSE Financial Markets Group, *Special Paper*, 37.
GOODHART, C.A.E. (1992) 'The ESCB after Maastricht', in C.A.E. Goodhart (ed.), *EMU and ESCB after Maastricht*, London: LSE Financial Markets Group, 180–215.
GOODHART, C.A.E. (1994) 'What should Central Banks do? What should be their macroeconomic objectives and operations?', *Economic Journal*, 104, November, 1424–36.
GOODHART, C.A.E. (1996) 'Why do the monetary authorities smooth interest rates?', LSE Financial Markets Group, *Special Paper*, 81, February.
GOODHART, C.A.E. and JOSÉ VIÑALS (1994) 'Strategy and tactics of monetary policy: examples from Europe and the Antipodes', LSE Financial Markets Group, *Special Paper*, 61, August.
HALDANE, A.G. (ed.) (1995a), *Targeting Inflation*, London: Bank of England.
HALDANE, A.G. (1995b) 'Rules, discretion and the United Kingdom's new monetary framework', Bank of England, *Working Paper Series*, 40, November.
HALDANE, A.G. and C.K. SALMON (1995) 'Three issues on inflation targets', in A.G. Haldane (ed.), *Targeting Inflation*, London: Bank of England, 170–201.
HÄMÄLÄINEN, S. (1994) 'National economic policy and its credibility', *Bank of Finland Bulletin*, 11, 3–7.

HAMILTON, J.D. (1994) *Time Series Analysis*, Princeton: Princeton University Press.
HEIKENSTEN, L. (1996) 'The interest rate and the Swedish krona', Sveriges Riksbank, conference arranged by the Stockholm Chamber of Commerce and Veckans Affärer, Stockholm, 30 January 1996.
HSIEH, D.A. (1989) 'Modeling heteroscedasticity in daily foreign-exchange rates', *Journal of Business and Economic Statistics*, 7(3), 307–17.
HUERTAS, J.A. (1996) 'Is there a trade-off between exchange rate risk and interest rate risk?', Banco de España–Servicio de Estudios, *Documento de Trabajo*, 9529.
KENEN, P. (1992) 'EMU after Maastricht', in C.A.E. Goodhart (ed.), *EMU and ESCB after Maastricht*, London: LSE Financial Markets Group, 7–179.
KING, M. (1994) 'Monetary policy in the UK', *Fiscal Studies*, 15(3), August, 109–28.
KING, M. (1996) 'Do inflation targets work?', *CEPR Bulletin*, 65, Winter 1995/96, 4–6.
KUISMANEN, M. and M. SPOLANDER (1995) 'Inflation expectations in Finnish survey data', *Bank of Finland Bulletin*, 6–7, 3–7.
KUOSMANEN, H. (1993) 'Instruments of Central Bank policy in Finland', *Bank of Finland Bulletin*, 5, 3–7.
KYDLAND, F.E. and E.C. PRESCOTT (1977) 'Rules rather that discretion: the inconsistency of optimal plans', *Journal of Political Economy*, 85(3), 473–91.
LLOYD, M. (1992) 'The New Zealand approach to Central Bank autonomy', *Reserve Bank of New Zealand Bulletin*, 55(3), 203–20.
LONGWORTH, D. and C. FREEDMAN (1995) 'The role of the staff economic projection in conducting Canadian monetary policy', in A.G. Haldane (ed.), *Targeting Inflation*, London: Bank of England, 101–12.
MCCALLUM, B.T. (1995) 'Inflation targeting in Canada, New Zealand, Sweden, the United Kingdom and in general', presented at the Bank of Japan's VII International Conference, Tokyo, 26–27, October.
MAYES, D. and B. CHAPPLE (1995) 'Defining an inflation target', in A.G. Haldane (ed.), *Targeting Inflation*, London: Bank of England, 226–45.
MAYES, D. and B. RICHES (1996) 'The effectiveness of monetary policy in New Zealand', *Reserve Bank of New Zealand Bulletin*, 59(1), 5–20.
NICHOLL, P. (1994) 'Intervention techniques under a deregulated financial environment', *Reserve Bank of New Zealand Bulletin*, 57(2), 130–43.
NICHOLL, P. and D. ARCHER (1992) 'An announced downward path for inflation', *Reserve Bank of New Zealand Bulletin*, 55(4), 315–23.
NOËL, T.E. (1995) 'Bank of Canada operations in financial markets', Bank of Canada, notes for remarks to the Toronto Association for Business and Economics and the Treasury Management Association of Toronto, Toronto, 25 October 1995.
ORTEGA, E. and J.M. BONILLA (1995) 'Reasons for adopting an inflation target', in A.G. Haldane (ed.), *Targeting Inflation*, London: Bank of England, 49–58.
PERSSON, T. and G. TABELLINI (1993) 'Designing institutions for monetary stability', *Carnegie–Rochester Conference Series on Public Policy*, 39, 53–84.
PIKKARAINEN, P. and A. RIPATTI (1995) 'The role of monetary indicators in the design of monetary policy', *Bank of Finland Bulletin*, 8, 3–7.
PIKKARAINEN, P. and T. TYRVÄINEN (1993) 'The Bank of Finland's inflation target and the outlook for inflation over the next few years', *Bank of Finland Bulletin*, 6–7, 8–12.
RESERVE BANK OF NEW ZEALAND, *Monetary Policy Statement*, 1990–5, Wellington.
RESERVE BANK OF NEW ZEALAND, *Reserve Bank Bulletin*, 1990–6, Wellington.

ROGOFF, K. (1985) 'The optimal degree of commitment to an intermediate monetary target', *Quarterly Journal of Economics*, 100(4), 1169–89.
ROLL COMMITTEE REPORT (1993) 'Independent and accountable: a new mandate for the Bank of England', London: Centre for Economic Policy Research.
RUDEBUSCH, G.D. (1995) 'Federal Reserve interest rate targeting, rational expectations and the term structure', *Journal of Monetary Economics*, 35(2), 245–74.
SCHOEFISCH, U. (1993) 'The Reserve Bank's approach to inflation forecasting', *Reserve Bank of New Zealand Bulletin*, 57(2), June, 130–43.
SHAPIRO, M.D. (1994) 'Federal Reserve policy: cause and effect', in N.G. Mankiw (ed.), *Monetary Policy*, Chicago: University of Chicago Press, 307–32.
STEVENS, G. and G. DEBELLE (1995) 'Monetary policy goals for inflation in Australia', in A.G. Haldane (ed.), *Targeting Inflation*, London: Bank of England, 81–100.
SUMMERS, L. (1991) 'How should long term monetary policy be determined?', *Journal of Money, Credit, and Banking*, 23(3), part 2, 625–31.
SVENSSON, L.E.O. (1995) 'The Swedish experience of an inflation target', in L. Leiderman and L.E.O. Svensson (eds), *Inflation Targets*, London: Centre for Economic Policy Research, 69–89.
SVENSSON, L.E.O. (1996) 'Inflation forecast targeting: implementing and monitoring inflation targets', presented at the CEPR European Summer Symposium in Macroeconomics, Roda de Bara, Spain, 29, May.
SVERIGES RIKSBANK, *Quarterly review sveriges riksbank*, 1991–5, Stockholm.
SVERIGES RIKSBANK, *Inflation and inflation expectations in Sweden*, 1993–5, Stockholm.
THIESSEN, G.G. (1995) 'Uncertainty and the transmission of monetary policy in Canada', *Bank of Canada Review*, Summer, 41–58.
VON HAGEN, J. (1995) 'Inflation and monetary targeting in Germany', in L. Leiderman and L.E.O. Svensson (eds), *Inflation Targets*, London: Centre for Economic Policy Research, 107–21.
WALSH, C.E. (1995) 'Optimal contracts for central bankers', *American Economic Review*, 85(1), 150–67.
YATES, A. (1995) 'On the design of inflation targets', in A.G. Haldane (ed.), *Targeting Inflation*, London: Bank of England, 135–69.

Part II
The Trajectory of Spanish Monetary Policy

3 Trends in the Monetary Policy Strategy in Spain

Juan Ayuso and José Luis Escrivá

INTRODUCTION

During the last two decades, the Spanish economy has undergone substantial changes. These have consisted mainly of its transformation from a mostly closed economy with a strictly regulated financial system to its present status as an economy widely open to international markets with a fully liberalized financial system. In tandem with these developments, the Banco de España has been introducing significant changes in its monetary strategy and in the instruments used in the conduct of monetary policy.

In this chapter we shall discuss the salient features of the ongoing changes in the design of monetary policy that have resulted from the reshaping of the Spanish economy in the 1980s and early 1990s. Although these changes follow a continuous line of development over time, we have decided to break them down into stages. This approach has meant selecting somewhat artificial dates for the beginning and end of each phase. At the same time, however, it permits the key features of each phase to be thrown into greater relief.

The chapter outline is as follows: we first describe the monetary framework in operation between 1973 and 1983 as being typical of an economy barely open in financial terms, and easily able to isolate itself from the outside world. It had a classic implementation on two levels and a broad monetary aggregate as the intermediate target of monetary policy. We then discuss the gradual transformation of this plan to the end of the 1980s, a transformation highlighted by growing flexibility of the two-level framework, the relatively diminished significance of strict control of the monetary aggregate, and the occurrence of several episodes in which the Banco de España was faced with serious dilemmas in both the internal and external facets of monetary policy.

The transformation culminated in the inclusion of the peseta in the European Monetary System (EMS), with its fixed but adjustable exchange rates. This opened a new phase in monetary policy strategy in which the relationship between monetary targets and the exchange rate commitment provided the framework for official action. The resulting changes in the

131

Banco de España's monetary framework are analyzed, and we then briefly discuss the shift in monetary strategy that took place in January 1995. The final section contains a concise summary of the main findings.

1973–83: STANDARD MONETARY POLICY STRATEGY IN A CLOSED ECONOMY

The collapse of the fixed exchange rate system that characterised the International Monetary System (IMS) stemming from the 1945 Bretton Woods agreement, occurred against a backdrop of economies out of kilter, marked inflationary strains, and sizable current account imbalances. Such circumstances enhanced the appeal of an active monetary policy with its goals of controlling the money stock and curbing inflation. Moreover, the free-floating exchange rates that followed the collapse of the IMS ensured the degree of autonomy required for applying such a policy.

This was the setting in which the Banco de España in 1973 began to design a two-level strategy for monetary policy.[1] On the first level, final targets were decided for the growth of price levels and (real) gross domestic product. These were to be pursued through control of a broad liquidity aggregate which would perform the role of intermediate target and provide advance information on trends in the final targets. On the second level, the target of aggregate monetary growth was pursued through the control of an instrumental variable, closely related to the former.

Broad money (M3) was the monetary aggregate selected as the intermediate target, while the bank reserves (bank deposits and liquid assets, with the Banco de España) acted as the instrumental variable. This twofold selection involved allowing interest and exchange rates to fluctuate as needed to ensure that both aggregates would proceed along the programmed path. In any case, as already mentioned, floating exchange rates were seen at the time as a key positive factor that guaranteed the degree of autonomy monetary policy needed to tackle vigorously the domestic targets of the country's economic policy. Tight controls on capital limited the integration of Spanish money and capital markets into those of the rest of the world, and thus reinforced the autonomy of monetary policy.

In 1978, the Banco de España publicly announced its intermediate target in the form of minimum and maximum limits on the growth of M3. The announcement was made following a sizable devaluation in the spring of the previous year and a major advance in the area of incomes policy with the signing of the 'Moncloa Agreements'. The Banco de España's public statement of its monetary targets was intended to help shape a new scenario, a centrepiece of which would be the restoration of the process of forming expectations about future prices.

Table 3.1 Monetary aggregate growth (%), 1978–94

Year	Target band	Effective growth
1978	14.5–19.5	20.3
1979	15.5–19.5	19.4
1980	16.0–20.0	16.1
1981	14.5–18.5	15.7
1982	13.5–17.5	15.3
1983	11.0–15.0	12.8
1984	10.5–14.5	13.9
1985	11.5–14.5	13.2
1986	9.5–12.5	11.4
1987	6.5–9.5	14.3
1988	8.0–11.0	11.0
1989	6.5–9.5	11.0
1989	6.5–9.5	11.0
1991	7.0–11.0	10.8
1992	8.0–11.0	5.2
1993	4.5–7.5	8.6
1994	3.0–7.0	8.2

Note: M3 until 1983, ALP thereafter.

This monetary policy approach made notable progress in terms of achieving the intermediate target, as may be seen in Table 3.1. However, not only did the growth of M3 perform consistently with projections – only in 1978 was the upper limit of the band slightly exceeded – exceptional reductions in the inflation rate were achieved as well. As Figure 3.1 shows, inflation went from levels above 15 per cent in the late 1970s to below 10 per cent in the mid-1980s.

Nevertheless, in the course of the 1980s, significant changes occurred in the context in which the classic framework had operated. Difficulties were followed by doubts about whether the framework should be maintained. First of all, financial innovations began to proliferate which, from the framework's standpoint caused a loss of stability in the relationship between M3 and the final targets. From 1984, this loss of stability finally resulted in a change in the intermediate target of monetary policy.

Mention should also be made of the Banco de España's increased concern with the stability of the financial system. The orderly development of financial markets contributes, along with other positive externalities, to improving the transmission mechanisms of monetary policy. In this respect, interest rate stability acquired greater relevance, especially as the high levels of interest rate variability, which had to be accepted as a result of strict controls on bank reserves, began to generate increasing costs. It must be borne in mind that the process of liberalizing bank lending and

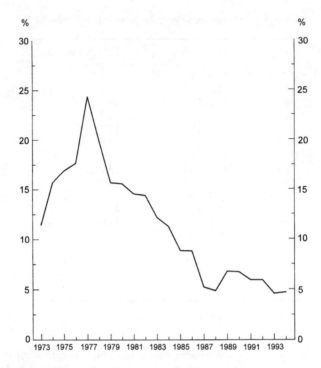

Figure 3.1   Average annual inflation rate, 1973–93
Source: Banco de España.

borrowing interest rates – that spread over the years 1978 to 1987 – the emergence of intense government borrowing requirements financed by the issue of negotiable instruments and the gradual integration of peseta-denominated financial assets into international capital markets, meant that the sudden fluctuations in interbank interest rates further to monetary control decisions were ceasing to be simply manifestations of local financial instability, and were spreading increasingly to banking operations as a whole, to foreign exchange markets, and to the government debt market. There was thus a gradual increase in the number of economic agents who found themselves exposed to high rates of risk, and this had a negative effect on their investment and financing decisions.

Finally, the isolating aspects of free-floating rates began to be challenged as awareness grew of the negative influence of fluctuating exchange rates on economic activity, particularly on trade flows, productive sector specialization, and above all on the climate of stability in which the process of forming medium-and long-term expectations ought to take place.[2] These developments took on special relevance in view of the impetus of the integrating currents on the international scene.

1984–9 (JUNE): THE TRANSITION TO A NEW STRATEGY

The loss of stability in the relationship between M3 and the final targets of monetary policy, growing concern with the stability of financial markets and mounting doubts about the merits of fully flexible exchange rate systems inspired the changes in monetary strategy introduced by the Banco de España from 1984.

Thus, in 1984, the intermediate target of monetary policy became a broader aggregate which, together with the assets included in M3, expanded to embrace a wide range of highly liquid financial assets, which had proliferated in the shadow of financial innovation, and which were identified as private sector liquidity (ALP by their Spanish name).[3] As might be expected, with this expansion, the targeted monetary aggregate – which now included bank liabilities not subject to reserve requirements and short-term government debt issued by the state – became more difficult to control. This, along with other factors, meant that the pursuit of growth targets for the money stock and the correction of any deviations that might have occurred in them, tended increasingly to be achieved through a gradual adjustment of ALP toward the desired path of nominal expenditure expansion.

This monetary strategy is consistent with the empirical evidence available on the nature of the links between ALP and the final variables (level of prices and real GDP). Such linkage, understood as a trend or long-term relationship, remained highly reliable in the 1980s, even during periods of intense financial innovation.[4]

Moreover, the Banco de España began to ease the control over bank reserves in favor of interest rates as the instrumental variable – specifically, a very short-term interest rate. The idea was that interest rate control would result, via expectations, in greater stability of the remaining interest rates throughout their intertemporal structure.[5] Figure 3.2 shows how the Banco permitted ever-increasing deviations in the development of its bank reserves target, and how central bank actions had considerably reduced short-term interest rate fluctuations.[6]

Finally, the Banco de España became concerned about the course of the exchange rate and thus, in 1984, began to monitor a concrete indicator: the index of the nominal effective position against developed countries. In accordance with the various levels of trade, this index weighed exchange rates against a group of countries with which active trading relationships were maintained. Naturally, in a system of growing international integration, the monetary and exchange rate targets must be compatible, so that the more narrowly the one is controlled, the more flexible must be the control of the other. This greater concern with the exchange rate is a factor to be added to those mentioned above for an understanding of why, through-

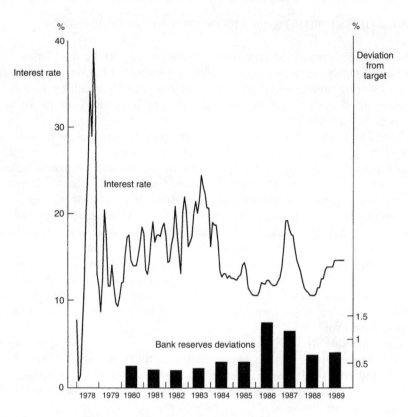

Figure 3.2　Intervention interest rate of the Banco de España and deviations from 10-day targets for Bank reserves,[2] 1978–89

Notes: 1　Until April 1990, daily monetary regulation loan tenders.
　　　　2　Annual standard deviation of log-differences between the 10-day average of observed daily bank reserves data and the corresponding targets.
Source: Banco de España.

out the 1980s, ALP growth targets were interpreted with increasing flexibility.[7]

In any case, it should be pointed out that in the first 2 years of this period, the exchange rate indicator does not seem to have played a significant role in the monetary policy decisions of the Banco de España. However, the exchange rate was becoming increasingly important in the monetary framework. Indeed, following Spain's accession to the European Community (EC) in 1986, the index of nominal effective position against developed countries was replaced by an index of nominal effective position against EC countries, excluding Greece and Portugal. In 1988, this index was in turn replaced by a bilateral nominal exchange rate against the

D-Mark. Parallel to these changes, as shown in Escrivá and Santos (1991), the exchange rate was also gaining significance in the Banco de España's reaction function. Lastly, Spain's entry into the EC meant its involvement in the process of European integration, for the success of which exchange rate stability seemed virtually indispensable. This explains why the movements of the reference exchange rate then became a key variable in the Banco de España's monetary policy decision-making. It also explains, as an immediate consequence, the growing clarity of the constraints being imposed by the external sector on the autonomous exercise of Spanish monetary policy.[8]

Indeed, the Spanish inflation rate was markedly above that of the core Community countries, an imbalance the Banco de España endeavoured to correct. However, as a result of its efforts, interest rate levels remained higher than those of the countries in question. Set against the gradual integration of financial markets, this encouraged massive capital inflows. Admittedly, the favourable outlook for returns offered by the Spanish economy owing to its integration into a much broader market accounted for the arrival of long-term capital seeking to benefit from the various investment opportunities available. In addition to these funds, however, capital of a more speculative nature also entered the country with a view to taking advantage of the interest differential entailed by a tighter monetary policy, and which was not offset by expectations of more or less immediate devaluations. Moreover, these short-term capital inflows were mostly channelled through the banking system (see Ariztegui and Fernández de Lis, 1989) which further complicated the application of a two-level monetary strategy.

This situation made it difficult to harmonize the domestic and external strands of monetary policy. A critical point was reached in the first half of 1987. Symptoms of an overheating of the Spanish economy made it advisable to keep monetary policy tight. However, strict adherence to monetary targets required a considerable increase in the level of interest rates which, given the growing international mobility of capital, exerted strong upward pressure on the peseta. The extent of intervention needed to contain this appreciation virtually ruled out any thought of sterilizing it completely. A vicious circle had been entered in which interventions in the foreign exchange market to contain the upward trend of the peseta touched off deviations in the monetary targets. Correcting the latter required new rate hikes and these generated further inflows of capital which again put pressure on the exchange rate. The outcome of this process may be seen in Figure 3.3, which shows the trend both of the nominal exchange rate of the peseta against the D-Mark[9] and changes in Banco de España foreign reserves. It is clear that during the first half of 1987, the peseta appreciated almost continuously while Banco de España reserves grew uninterruptedly.

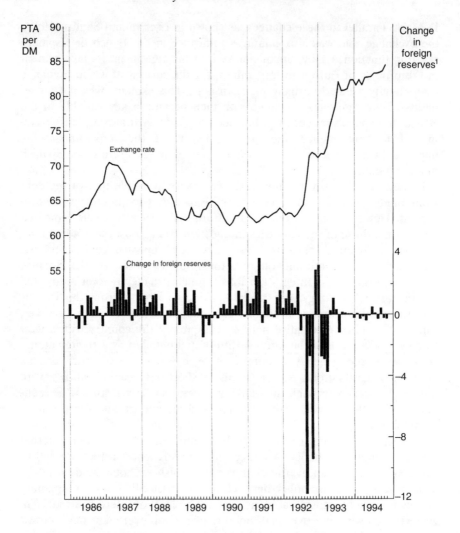

Figure 3.3   PTA/DM exchange rate and changes in foreign reserves, 1986–94

Note: 1   Changes in reserves in billion dollars.
Source: Banco de España.

   Given the exceptional nature of the situation, an attempt was made to break the circle by temporarily introducing capital controls. Early in 1987, restrictions were imposed on the acceptance of peseta deposits from non-residents and on foreign currency borrowing by banks; government debt repo operations with non-residents were banned, and maturities for private sector borrowing abroad were limited to less than 3 years. These limits were subsequently expanded to all maturities. However, restrictions on capital movements failed to ease in any significant or lasting way either the upward pressures on the peseta or the build-up in foreign reserves. What did ensure was the proliferation of mechanisms for evading the restrictions themselves.

In an environment of growing financial innovation in international capital markets, restrictive measures of this kind serve only to curb speculative flows temporarily, i.e. for as long as it takes the financial markets to develop alternative instruments. The various products denominated in pesetas with various terms may be transformed and converted into close substitutes. Thus, for instance, the restrictions on payment of interest on non-residents' pesetas led to the development of debt repos and swap operations with non-residents. The limits on the latter in turn generated an increase in outright firm purchases of government instruments, with private agreements being concluded for resale or reverse repo transactions. Limits on the acceptance of external credits by resident enterprises shifted the demand for credit toward domestic credit markets, which finally produced an excessive demand for credit, while rates were pushed upward by capital inflows through other channels.

Although the controls may have been effective for a while, the conviction that they were virtually useless in the medium and long terms, together with the persistence of inflationary strains, meant that the Banco de España basically had two choices. First, it could maintain strict controls on liquidity and accept the appreciation of the peseta. Doing so would have had a clearly negative effect, not only on domestic demand but also on its components; investment and exports would have been adversely affected, and this was incompatible with the targets of stable growth in the medium and long term.

The second alternative, and the one for which the Banco de España opted, was to accept deviations from the monetary target. The short-term interest rate was modified to relieve, at least partly, exchange rate strains. A position was adopted which may be seen as a compromise between the clearly divergent requirements of the internal and external strands of monetary policy. In this way, faced with an ALP growth target in 1987 of between 6.5 per cent and 9.5 per cent, effective growth was 14.3 per cent, while the peseta appreciated over the year as a whole by about 3 per cent against the D-Mark.

These strains did not subside altogether and returned with particular severity in the first quarter of 1989. Despite the vigorous expansion of the Spanish economy after entry into the EC, in overall terms, major headway had not been made in correcting the basic imbalances of the economy, and this complicated convergence with the more stable countries in the Community.

Monetary policy difficulties encountered in the late 1980s are a concrete example of how the economic integration process in an environment of intense capital mobility may at length severely curtail the degree of autonomy available for conducting a monetary policy differentiated from that of the other countries in the area. In view of this, concentrating on exchange rate stability, in addition to being an essential requirement for such integration, appeared as an attractive alternative in the search for monetary discipline.

In this context, external constraints exert a dual influence. Maintaining exchange rate stability provides an element of discipline and credibility which may help to curb inflationary expectations, thus promoting a clearly anti-inflationary economic policy stance. However, it also imposes glaring limits on monetary policy autonomy as compared with that of other countries, inasmuch as the existence of inflation levels higher than those of such countries would make it necessary to adopt a more restrictive monetary approach.

Nevertheless, this was not quite the state of affairs in Spain in 1989. Although the central bank had entered into various exchange rate commitments, these had not been formalized. As a result, economic agents were not fully aware of them. This was a clearly unfavorable situation in which the Banco de España faced all the costs entailed by external constraints but did not fully enjoy the attendant benefits in terms of discipline and credibility.

Thus, in the first half of 1989, when conflicts between monetary targets and the desired exchange rate behavior again flared, the Spanish authorities opted for an express formalization of exchange rate commitments, resolving in June 1989 to bring the peseta into the Exchange Rate Mechanism (ERM) of the EMS. Considerations of timeliness also contributed to this decision. At the time, the project for European economic integration had received a boost from the approval of the European Council at its Madrid summit, in June 1989, of the report on Economic and Monetary Union in the European Community, prepared by a committee of experts under the presidency of Jacques Delors. This climate doubtless fostered adoption of an express commitment to stability of the peseta *vis-à-vis* the currencies of the central countries of the Community, as part of the ERM.

Entry of the peseta into the EMS was accompanied by stabilization of its exchange rate,[10] in marked contrast to the difficulties previously encountered in containing its tendency to appreciate. One of the most immediate effects of stabilization was an easing of the constraints that had hitherto weighed on monetary policy. This enabled domestic liquidity controls to be implemented that were more in accord with targeted inflation rates.

MONETARY POLICY STRATEGY WITHIN THE ERM FRAMEWORK

June 1989–Summer of 1992: ERM Stability

The peseta joined the European Monetary System on June 19, 1989 with a fluctuation band of ±6%. While membership was intended to formalize a situation that, to some extent, already existed '*de facto*', the importance of this step should not be underestimated. Completing the formalities was also intended to make the exchange rate commitment part of the body of information handled by agents in forming their expectations. Spanish monetary policy would thus benefit from the credibility effect anticipated from increased exchange rate firmness.

As is well known, monetary policy effectiveness increases in proportion to the credibility of monetary policy targets for the various agents of an economy. However, there are at least two sources of uncertainty which hamper the perfect credibility of such targets. The first springs from the possibility of a time inconsistency in the monetary authorities' decisions, if monetary policy includes both inflation and output or employment targets.[11] Despite their announcement of a specific inflation target, the monetary authorities may be led to move away from this target in order to induce a certain level of inflation, not anticipated by agents, in order to increase the output level (while reducing the level of unemployment). However, if agents are rational, they will anticipate such conduct and act accordingly. The end result is an improvement in neither output nor unemployment, but on the contrary, a higher-than-optimal inflation rate (inflationary bias).

The second source of uncertainty stems from the fact that the monetary authorities control only a part of economic policy, so that they do not have sole power to influence price trends. Put another way: the price target should be compatible with the other economic policy targets, particularly fiscal policy targets. Policy incompatibility will raise doubts as to the ultimate outcome of the conflict, that is, whether the monetary authorities will have sufficient autonomy to maintain their targets regardless of the attendant costs.

These two problems are quite distinct from each other. While the first depends on agents' perception of the monetary authorities' real target (anti-inflationary reputation), the solution to the second requires participation by the other economic policy decision-makers concerned, namely the fiscal authorities. Admittedly, joining the EMS was an attempt to come to grips with the problem of reputation at a time when the Spanish economy again faced rising inflation amidst strong growth in domestic demand and a loss of confidence in the ability of monetary policy, focused on achieving an intermediate ALP target, to cope with it. By fixing the exchange rate against the currencies of countries with solid anti-inflationary credentials (particularly Germany) the authorities tried to infuse as much of this credibility as possible into the conduct of their own monetary policy.

Fixing the exchange rate did not do away with the problem, but rather changed its nature. Agents' degree of confidence in the maintenance of the exchange rate commitment now became the relevant variable.[12] The inference was drawn that confidence in the maintenance of the exchange rate policy depended on the growth of liquidity in the economy being compatible with an inflation rate close to that of the core countries to whose currencies the exchange rate had been pegged. Immediately abandoning the pursuit of growth targets for liquidity did not seem advisable at a time when – regardless of the margin of uncertainty involved in interpreting liquidity trends – liquidity was growing at a rate clearly incompatible with the inflation rate of the EMS core countries.[13]

It was thus essential to convince agents as quickly as possible of the firmness of the new monetary policy stance, and this meant curbing the headlong growth rates at which the monetary (14 per cent) and credit (20 per cent) aggregates were running in mid-1989. The entry of the peseta into the ERM was therefore accompanied by a package of economic policy measures, of a primarily monetary nature: the minimum reserve requirement was raised, and the Banco de España intervention interest rate was increased by 1 point.

However, these measures were not considered sufficient to break the expansive surge of domestic demand. Budgetary policy had contributed but little to the task, and raising interest rates had made it difficult to keep the exchange rate within the maximum limit of appreciation. Under these exceptional circumstances, the authorities decided to introduce emergency measures consisting of temporary restrictions on the expansion of bank credit to firms and households. The effectiveness of these measures also required exchange control measures to counter circumvention of the restrictions through recourse to external credit.

The purpose of these steps was to bring the rate of liquidity growth rapidly back to a pace compatible with the new exchange rate target, without resorting to interest rate increases, which would have endangered maintenance of the target. In this way, additional room was obtained for other economic policy measures to take over in connection with macroeconomic stabilization (particularly in the areas of budget and income) and help strengthen the credibility of the new framework. Thus, shortly after entry of the peseta into the ERM, a fiscal consolidation plan was unveiled which would balance the budget by end-1992, and efforts were made in 1990 and 1991 to reach as industrial relations agreement on wage restraint.

The administrative controls introduced were designed with awareness of its necessary short-lived nature. Thus, the limits on the growth of bank credit to firms and households took the form of Banco de España recommendations (agreements by moral suasion) to financial intermediaries. In this way, any formal regulation was avoided which might raise doubts as to whether the measure actually was temporary. In an environment of sophisticated financial markets, the authorities knew that sooner rather than later, mechanisms would be developed with which to circumvent these restrictions.[14]

During the first months the controls were applied, a marked decline was noted in the financing received by enterprises and households. ALP growth also slowed, and domestic demand and expenditure rates fell notably. Nevertheless, to what extent these slowdowns were an effect of credit curbs, completion of the expansionary economic cycle, or the impact over time of the high real interest rates prevailing since 1987, is open to doubt. In any case, as credit ceilings lost their effectiveness – and costs mounted from an inefficient allocation of resources – they were revoked in January 1991. A few months later, the restrictions on borrowing capital abroad were also lifted.

Once administrative credit ceilings had been dropped, the new monetary framework came into full swing. Although ALP growth targets have been maintained, for purposes of evaluating liquidity expansions which could pose problems for the medium-term sustainability of the exchange rate commitment (see Cabrero, Escrivá and Sastre, 1992), the commitment itself rules out the possibility of any systematic reaction to deviations from target. On the contrary, the trend is toward a more flexible one-level framework, where changes in the intervention interest rate are decided upon – within the room for manoeuvre permitted by the relevant position of the peseta within the EMS – after taking into account a broad and complex body of information from both the monetary sector (in which deviations from the ALP targets continue to play an important part) and the real sector. Table 3.1 shows ALP developments during this period, compared with the targets set at the beginning of each year.

During the first 3 years of ERM membership, the peseta remained (for almost all the period under consideration) in the upper range of its band against the other ERM currencies, after coming close to the maximum permitted appreciation ceiling. Figure 3.4 shows the effective margins of appreciation and depreciation available to the peseta during these first 3 years of EMS membership. As can be seen, from the mid-1990s the available margin of appreciation did not exceed 3 percentage points, while at all times the margin of depreciation was located at considerably higher levels.

The movements in the peseta reflected the attitude of the authorities, who used the leeway available to set a monetary stance that was both

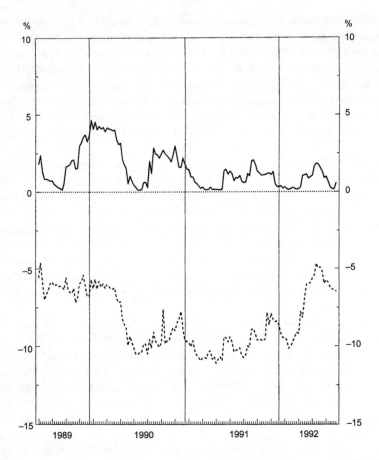

Figure 3.4   Effective appreciation/depreciation margins of the peseta in the EMS, 1989–92

Note: The solid line denotes the maximum possible appreciation of the peseta at any time, in accordance with the relative position of the other EMS currencies. The broken line depicts, with a negative sign, the maximum possible depreciation.
Source: Banco de España.

consistent with combating inflation and compatible with the exchange rate commitment. This strategy availed itself of the stabilizing effect of the upper limit of appreciation in the peseta's band. Indeed, although the peseta rate approached this limit, intense exchange rate strains did not generally occur, nor did speculative attacks seeking to push the peseta beyond the limit. On the contrary, even without intervention by the Banco de España being required, market pressure abated as the peseta rate reached the maximum point of appreciation against another ERM currency. Such a situation contrasts with the above-mentioned difficulties that the Spanish authorities faced prior to entry into the ERM in seeking to limit market pressures that were driving up the peseta. ERM membership thus enabled the monetary authorities to maintain high interest rates, thereby contributing to combating inflation.

The exchange rate strategy pursued by the Spanish authorities in the EMS seems to have benefited from the asymmetry of the stabilizing effects of maximum and minimum band limits. This asymmetry tends to emerge in the case of countries, such as Spain, the trajectories of whose nominal magnitudes do not converge sufficiently with the levels prevailing in the area as a whole.

However, this positive assessment from the standpoint of short-term monetary control of the first 3 years of ERM membership should not conceal the fact that the medium-term sustainability of this monetary policy framework faces difficulties and challenges. Two problems deserve special attention.

First, as the inflation differential with the central ERM countries was narrowing more slowly than had been hoped (see Figure 3.5), an upward movement of interest rates would have been desirable, at least in principle. However, as mentioned above, the position of the peseta within the EMS left no room for manoeuvre in this direction. Clearly, in the coming stage, a leading role would have to be played by the right mix of economic polices. Specifically, all responsibility for the struggle against inflation and the creation of conditions conductive to sustained and stable growth could not be assigned to monetary policy. Collaboration from budgetary policy and from more flexible supply-side policies were essential to correct the basic imbalances in the Spanish economy.

However, there has been little contribution from fiscal policy in recent years. Figure 3.6 shows how, in contrast to the expectations created by entry into the ERM, the government deficit continued to grow, while fiscal policy continued to be essentially procyclical.[15] The resulting monetary and fiscal policy mix was of little help in correcting the basic imbalances in the Spanish economy. Similarly, wage negotiation made no contribution to anti-inflation efforts. Between 1990 and 1992, wage settlements remained somewhat more than 2 points above the inflation targets announced by the government, despite which, ample progress was made toward achieving the targets, in contrast with the experience of 1977 and 1989.

Second, mention should be made of the difficulty of coordinating the economic polices of the various countries in the System. Some of these countries enjoyed considerable macroeconomic stability, while others have yet to achieve such levels. During the early years of the ERM, the most stable country (Germany) set, with virtual independence, a growth rate for liquidity compatible with the German inflation target; the others imported this target by maintaining the exchange rate. This asymmetrical

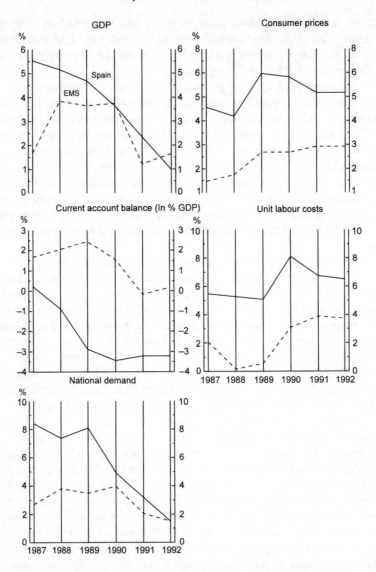

Figure 3.5 Economic indicators: Spain–EMS narrow band, 1987–92

Note: EMS data correspond to the weighted average of the countries participating in the
ERM that maintained bands of ±2.25 per cent; Italy is not included.
Source: Banco de España.

arrangement, which at the time contributed significantly to the success of
the system, was less suited to the 1990s.

A number of countries had already reached notable levels of price stability and reasonable levels of anti-inflationary credibility. Beginning in

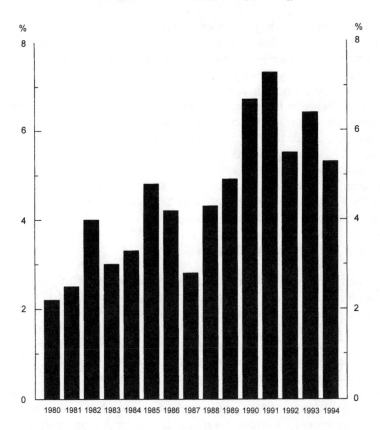

Figure 3.6   Government structural deficit as a percentage of GDP, 1980–94
Source: European Commission.

1990, unification brought the German economy into a difficult period. This complex process involved the introduction of a strongly expansionary fiscal policy that had to be counterbalanced by severe monetary tightening. The other countries had trouble coming to grips with this economic policy mix, as their economies were in low cyclical positions and enjoyed a high degree of macroeconomic stability.

In contrast to these countries, other ERM members had not yet reached this level of stability, but were making serious efforts to do so. The episode involving the peseta and the French franc in March 1991 may serve to illustrate the problems arising from this situation. On the latter date, as the peseta reached its maximum limit of appreciation against the French franc, the Spanish inflation rate was resisting efforts to bring it down, and the shadow of recession hung over France. Their exchange rate positions

obliged both countries to move their interest rates in a direction contrary
to that required by their domestic circumstances. The asymmetrical
arrangement provided no clear rule of action under such circumstances, as
neither of the two countries performed the role of anchor in the system.
Nevertheless, under a framework that provided for more coordination and
cooperation between the member countries, rules could be established to
determine for each of the countries involved (and even of those not
involved) how much their interest rates should move, in accordance with
their actual economic positions.

The difficulty in designing both the general thrust of monetary policy for
the system as a whole and the specific stance of each of the national
polices in a coordinated and harmonious manner may help explain why the
system went into crisis as from the spring of 1992.

Summer of 1992–December 1994: ERM Crises

In the final quarter of 1992, the ERM was beset by the most serious crisis
in its history: the lira and sterling dropped out of the ERM (the former
after a devaluation of its central parity) while two other currencies saw
central parities devalued (the escudo and the peseta, the latter on two
occasions). Early in 1993, the Irish pound was also devalued, and in May
1993, the peseta and the escudo were again devalued. Finally, on 2 August,
1993 the fluctuation bands were widened to ±15 per cent.[16]

The crisis was system-wide. As extensively discussed by Ayuso, Pérez
Jurado and Restoy (1994), the standard approach to an analysis of
exchange rate crises could not provide an adequate explanation of the
ERM crisis at that time. A more useful frame of reference in this respect
is one which distinguishes between essential factors in the crisis, which
explain the potential return on a 'bet' on a given currency, and contributing
factors, which determine the perceived probability of success of the wager
and the attendant risk. Among the essential factors which may help understanding the ERM crisis are first of all the losses of competitiveness of
countries with greater inflationary inertia, largely owing to insufficient fiscal discipline and the rigidities of their goods, services and labor markets.
Second among these factors are the economic policy dilemmas that arose
in countries which were obliged by the exchange rate commitment to maintain interest rates at levels deemed hard to sustain by the markets, given
that such levels were excessive in relation to the low levels of economic
activity posted by the countries in question. Factors that contributed to
economic policy dilemmas were the asynchronism of the economic cycles
of Germany (in the process of absorbing the inflationary effects of unification) and most of the other member countries (with low rates of activity),
in an environment of coexisting but poorly adapted national policy mixes.

Moreover, medium-term coordination of monetary polices within the ERM was inadequate.

The contributing factors were closely related to the inadequacy of the system's defence mechanisms. Thus, the perceived probability of successful bets was increased by the inability of the monetary authorities to head off, in time and in cooperation, the strains arising from heightened uncertainty about the process of Monetary Union as a result of the Danish and French referenda. The subsequent exit by sterling and the lira from the ERM and the ensuing series of linked devaluations eroded confidence in the ERM still further. Other similar factors were the difficulty of raising interest rates that were already high in the weak-currency countries, and the inability of official intervention to ease strains in the foreign exchange markets. Together with the scant margins still available within their bands for most of these currencies, these factors helped increase market perception of the Nyborg–Basle instruments as being largely ineffective. Finally, the narrowness of the bands and the perfect credibility of the limits of maximum appreciation created a low-risk situation for bets against the currencies deemed weak.

The combined effect of these contributing factors in an environment of high capital mobility was to bring about a clearly unstable state of affairs. Potentially profitable bets could now be identified that had a high probability of success and a low degree of risk. As these bets were made, however, they gave rise to exchange rate turbulence which finally caused the bands that had been a feature of the ERM since it was set up in 1979 to be abandoned. The broader bands meant an increased equilibrium between possible losses and gains as a result of bets against a currency, not only because they increased the range of depreciation available prior to an eventual devaluation, but also because they increased the probability that, even if an attack on a currency managed to force its devaluation, the new band and the old would overlap to a considerable extent. Overlapping of the bands not only prevented devaluation from automatically involving a depreciation of the market exchange rate, it even permitted the rate to appreciate following a devaluation. Thus, broadening the bands created a situation in which successful attacks on a currency could ultimately rebound as losses to those conducting them.[17]

As to the effects of this monetary storm on the Spanish monetary framework, Figure 3.7 shows the peseta's position against the D-Mark as from January 1992. As may be seen, the Danish referendum on ratification of the Treaty on Economic Union (the outcome of which has been considered the immediate cause of the storm) marks the beginning of the peseta's gradual loss of its position in the margin of appreciation against its central parity, and its steady depreciation against the D-Mark. There was little the Banco de España could do about such pressure as, at the same time, the

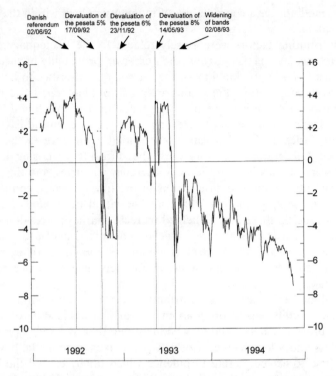

Figure 3.7 Position of the PTA against the DM, 1992–4[1]

Note: 1 Appreciation (+) and depreciation (−) of the nominal exchange rate of the PTA against its central parity with the DM.
Source: Banco de España.

peseta was coming dangerously close to its limit of maximum appreciation against sterling. In any case, the Banco intervened fairly frequently in the exchange market to defend the peseta and pushed short-term interest rates upwards (Figure 3.8).

As September unfolded, this position became increasingly difficult to maintain. On 17 September, the British and Italian governments decided to withdraw sterling and the lira from the ERM. The Spanish authorities then proceeded to devalue the peseta's central parity by 5 per cent in order to recover some room for manoeuvre in anticipation of the more general realignment expected to follow reinsertion of the Italian lira, whose departure from the ERM had been presented as a short-term emergency measure. It was generally felt that the system offered an adequate framework for a speedy recovery of exchange rate stability, whereas abandoning it could seriously erode the conditions for economic stability. Amidst fears of creating greater instability on the eve of the French refer-

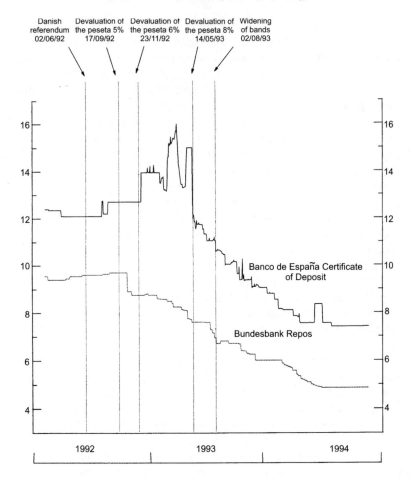

Figure 3.8 Intervention interest rate, 1992–4
Source: Banco de España.

endum on Monetary Union, a general realignment was postponed. When it was subsequently decided to devalue the peseta's central parity, this move was coupled with the introduction of exceptional, temporary measures[18] aimed at raising the price of the borrowing by non-residents of pesetas in the very short-term, thus boosting the price of speculation against the peseta.

As may be seen from Figure 3.7, devaluation did not succeed in breaking the trend of depreciation against the D-Mark set in train after the Danish referendum. It also failed to check the increasing loss of confidence in the durability of the exchange rate commitment. These developments have generally been interpreted as signifying that the markets deemed the devaluation insufficient to absorb the Spanish economy's losses of competitiveness since June 1989. In any case, it should be noted that the exceptional measures did avert the need to raise domestic interest rates; without them there would probably have been far more interventions in the foreign exchange markets.

In any case, widespread expectations of a peseta devaluation made renewed and increased intervention necessary to defend the currency. Finally, on 21 November, it was decided to devalue again, this time by 6 per cent. A rise in the intervention interest rate accompanied this second devaluation, while the exceptional and temporary administrative measures adopted after the previous devaluation were rescinded.

Despite the lifting of controls, the new devaluation seemed to check the peseta's tendency to depreciate against the D-Mark. However, amidst ongoing uncertainty as to both the domestic macroeconomic situation and the future of the Monetary Union, early general elections were called in April 1993. This added a new element of instability, exacerbated by various voter poll reports which indicated there would be considerable difficulty in forming a government with adequate guarantees of stability.

Naturally, this was faithfully reflected in the financial markets. The peseta again began to show a slow but steady tendency to depreciate, which neither tighter interest rates nor frequent Banco de España interventions in the foreign exchange markets managed to change. The persistent drain of reserves, the difficulty of maintaining a measure of monetary rigour in a domestic economic context that was becoming increasingly frayed and, particularly, the growing uncertainty over the election results, culminated in a new 8 per cent devaluation of the peseta on 14 May (accompanied this time by an additional devaluation of the escudo). This move coincided with the release of new negative data on the domestic macroeconomic situation in connection with the inflation rate and, above all, on the level of unemployment. With the new devaluation, short-term interest rates could be cut substantially without causing strains on the foreign exchange market. Nevertheless, strains reappeared in the summer of 1993, and finally, on 2 August 1993, the peseta's permitted margin of exchange rate fluctuation against the other EMS currencies in the exchange rate mechanism was broadened, as were those of the other ERM currencies, to the ±15% currently in force.

None of the EMS countries with currencies in the ERM used the increased room for monetary policy manoeuvre under the new band to introduce less firm policies for inflation control. The Banco de España was no exception to the rule and maintained relatively tight monetary conditions both in the last quarter of 1993 and throughout 1994 (see Table 3.1 and Figure 3.8). The broader band did indeed permit a more flexible adjustment of monetary conditions to the Spanish economy's cyclical position. In fact, the peseta's exchange rate showed greater variability in the course of this period.[19]

Finally, this period of turbulence suggests that in an economy such as that of Spain – given its dimension, degree of external openness, and structural characteristics – adopting a strategy for exchange rate stability and maintaining it over a fairly long period does not in itself ensure the achievement of sufficient discipline for converging the domestic inflation rate with that prevailing in the relevant area.[20] The Spanish experience shows how such a strategy tends to peter out if not seconded by a budgetary policy resolutely oriented toward regulating domestic demand and appropriate wage behavior. In the absence of such coordination, the real costs generated by maintaining the exchange rate commitment finally become too high, and a devaluation becomes necessary. Although the economic authorities may be reluctant to take such a step, the logic of the foreign exchange market as it functions in an environment of unrestricted capital movements, and the perception that a particular medium-term policy cannot be sustained, eventually forces a devaluation. Although a devaluation is inevitable once this stage has been reached, such a development should not hide the fact that a policy of fairly regular devaluations is by no means an adequate strategy from the monetary policy standpoint. After all, a policy of periodic nominal devaluations implicitly assumes a target for the real exchange rate which would have trouble playing the role of nominal anchor for the economy.

FROM 1995: THE NEW ONE-LEVEL MONETARY POLICY STRATEGY

The reform of the EMS by broadening the bands of its ERM to 15 per cent posed a serious dilemma for monetary policy. First, it eliminated the possibility of using exchange rate stability as an instrument for the nominal anchoring of the economy. Second, the downward plunge of the depreciating peseta beginning in the summer of 1992 could have triggered an inflationary spiral. Only the extreme sluggishness of demand during these years prevented this danger from materializing in a moderately intense upsurge of inflation in 1993–4. Under the circumstances, and with the prospects of a cyclical recovery of the economy, it was necessary to restore the confidence of both the financial markets and economic agents in general in the ability of monetary policy both to moderate the growth of nominal expenditure and contribute to macroeconomic stability. To do so, it was absolutely essential to avoid giving the impression that monetary policy was to a large extent discretionary. It was therefore advisable to redefine the monetary framework in order to restore the necessary degree of credibility.

One possibility was to strengthen the traditional two-level framework, based on intermediate money stock targets. However, as Vega (1996) explains at some length (chapter 4 in this volume), such a strategy did not offer sufficient reliability, given the distortions noted in the most recent monetary aggregate trends and the growing complexity and stability problems revealed by their demand functions. In fact, the formulation of monetary targets for 1994 confirmed the growing difficulty of maintaining the existing monetary strategy and set out some of the basic principles of the new monetary control strategy – which were introduced a year later.[21] Thus, it was affirmed at the time that it is essential for monetary policy conduct to be based more on the *monitoring of inflation and the assessment of its medium-term trajectory in relation to the guidelines followed in the core EMS countries*, with the aim of achieving price stability.

These general ideas, already outlined in 1994, were fully developed in a new one-level monetary policy strategy introduced in 1995 that featured explicit inflation rate targets. Adoption of this plan had been greatly fostered by both the passing in June 1994 of the Law on the Autonomy of the Banco de España, which enshrined price stability as the main target of monetary policy (see Ortega and Bonilla, 1995), and the first-rate performance of a strategy of this type applied in recent years in countries such as Canada, Australia, and the United Kingdom. In any case, as Gutiérrez (1996) amply demonstrates (chapter 6 in this volume) the characteristics of the new framework and the results of its first year of operation, there is no need here to expand on this new monetary policy strategy in Spain.

SUMMARY

The contents of the chapter are summarized by a table (Table 3.2) that provides a conspectus of the trends over time in the weight of a number of variables – inflation, money stock, exchange rate, short-term interest rates and Bank reserves – in Spain's monetary policy strategy. As can be seen, this is a double entry table, in which the rows represent the various stages identified in the chapter, while the columns show the relevant variables. A brief explanation is given in the table cells of the part played by the individual variables in each respective stage, thus summarizing the more detailed exposition appearing in the previous sections.

Table 3.2 The role played by specific variables in monetary policy decisions, 1973–95

	Inflation	Money stock	Exchange rate	Short-term interest rates	Bank reserves
1973–83	General target of economic policy, in accordance with government directives set forth in State Budget	Strictly pursued intermediate target	Endogenous behavior	Endogenous behavior	Single instrumental variable, strictly controlled
1984–89		Flexibly pursued intermediate target	Main indicator applied in decision-making	Split instrumental variable, in combined rate and quantity control	Split instrumental variable, in combined rate and quantity control
1989–92		Intermediate target pursued either through direct controls (1989–90), or through indirect mechanisms	Formal commitment to stability in the EMS		
1992–4					
1995–	Primary and direct target of monetary policy, set independently and specifically by the Banco de España (< 3% in the medium term)	Supplementary medium-term reference	Formal commitment to stability in an EMS with frequent realignments, first (7: 92–7: 93), and widened bands since (8: 93–)	Single instrumental variable, strictly controlled	Endogenous behavior

Notes

1   A detailed description of this strategy and the rationale for its introduction may be found in Rojo and Pérez (1977) and Aríztegui (1990).
2   See Williamson and Miller (1987).
3   A detailed account of this substitution process may be found in Sanz (1988).
4   See, among other papers, those of Vega (1991) and Cabrero, Escrivá and Sastre (1992).
5   Escrivá and Santos (1991) evaluate each of the reaction functions of the Banco de España regarding monetary policy instrumentation in terms of quantities and interest rates which, empirically, have provided support since bank reserves lost their importance as an instrumental variable in the mid-1980s.
6   It should be mentioned in connection with Figure 3.2 that, as from 1987, the design of the specific reference (rather than target) path for bank reserves included the loss of importance of the latter as an instrumental variable, and reflected not so much the nature of the money supply as the demand for base liquidity that was constantly anticipated by the monetary authorities. The deviations in 1988 and 1989 are thus not strictly comparable with those in the years immediately prior to these.
7   Escrivá and Peñalosa (1989) construct an indicator of the intensity of ALP control in the short term. The indicator has a clear downward trajectory from 1983.
8   These complications are described in detail in Malo de Molina and Pérez (1990) and Escrivá and Malo de Molina (1991).
9   This rate may be taken as a good indicator of the nominal effective exchange rate against the EC prior to 1988.
10 See Ayuso (1991).
11 This problem gave rise to the well known controversy over rules versus discretion in the exercise of monetary policy (see Kydland and Prescott, 1977) and has been widely discussed in the literature (see Blackburn and Christensen, 1989, for an overview).
12 The development of exchange rate credibility is dealt with at length in Pérez-Jurado (1996).
13 This line of reasoning is developed in greater detail in Malo de Molina and Pérez (1990).
14 Indeed, it was not long before such mechanisms made their appearance. The demand for financing, which the banks were prevented from meeting, tended to move toward the commercial paper market, which experienced an extraordinary expansion in 1990, or toward non-bank financial entities exempt from the restriction. At the same time, limits on external borrowing prompted the development of direct loans from foreign parent companies to resident subsidiaries, which are regarded as direct investments rather than loans.
15 See Marín and Peñalosa (1996).
16 With the exception of the band for the guilder–D-Mark rate which remained at ±2.25 per cent.
17 See Ayuso, Pérez-Jurado, and Restoy (1994) for a more detailed description of the reasoning behind, and the advantages of, broadening the EMS bands.
18 Banco de España Circulars 16/92 and 17/92.
19 However, as shown by Ayuso, Pérez-Jurado and Restoy (1995), this did not involve an increase in the level of exchange risk, owing to the greater credibility agents assigned to the new commitment.

20   This argument is developed at greater length by Pérez-Jurado (1996).
21   See Banco de España (1993).

References

ARÍZTEGUI, J. (1990), 'La política monetaria, un período crucial', in J.L. García Delgado (ed.), *Economía española de la transición y la democracia*, Madrid: CIS.
ARÍZTEGUI, J. and S. FERNÁNDEZ DE LIS (1989), 'Foreign interest rates and monetary policy in Spain', in *International Interest Rate Linkages and Monetary Policy*, BIS.
AYUSO, J. (1991), 'Los efectos de la entrada de la peseta en el SME sobre la volatilidad de las variables financieras españolas', *Moneda y Crédito*, 193.
AYUSO, J., M. PÉREZ-JURADO, and F. RESTOY (1994), 'El SME: causas y consecuencias de la ampliación de bandas', *Banco de España, Boletín Económico*, July–August.
AYUSO, J., M. PÉREZ JURADO, and F. RESTOY (1995), 'Exchange rate risk under a peso problem: the case of the peseta in the ERM', in C. Bordes, E. Girardin, and J. Melitz (eds), *European Currency Crisis and After*, Manchester: Manchester University Press.
BANCO DE ESPAÑA (1993), 'La política monetaria en 1994', *Banco de España, Boletín Económico*, December.
BLACKBURN, K. and M. CHRISTENSEN (1989), 'Monetary policy and policy credibility', *Journal of Economic Literature*, 27 (1).
CABRERO, A., J.L. ESCRIVÁ and T. SASTRE (1992), *Demand equations of the new monetary aggregates*, Banco de España, *Estudios Económicos*, 52.
ESCRIVÁ, J.L. and J.L. MALO DE MOLINA (1991), 'Implementation of Spanish monetary policy in the framework of European integration', Banco de España, *Working Paper*, 9104.
ESCRIVÁ, J.L. and J. PEÑALOSA (1989), 'Indicadores sobre la intensidad del control de la cantidad de dinero por parte del Banco de España', *Banco de España, Boletín Económico*, March.
ESCRIVÁ, J.L. and R. SANTOS (1991), 'A study of the change in the instrumental variable of the monetary control outline in Spain', Banco de España, *Economic Bulletin*, October.
GUTIÉRREZ, F. (1996), 'Monetary Policy and Inflation in Spain', Chapter 6 in this volume.
KYDLAND, F.E. and E.C. PRESCOTT (1977), 'Rules rather than discretion: the inconsistency of optimal plans', *Journal of Political Economy*, 85.
MALO DE MOLINA, J.L. and J. PÉREZ (1990), 'La política monetaria española en la transición hacia la unión monetaria europea', *Papeles de Economía*, 43.
MARÍN, J. AND J. PEÑALOSA (1996), 'Implicaciones del marco institucional y de la política presupuestaria para la política monetaria en España', in *La política monetaria y la inflación en España*, Servicio de Estudios del Banco de España, Alianza Editorial.
ORTEGA, E. and J.M. BONILLA (1995), 'Reasons for adopting an inflation target', in A.G. Haldane (ed.), *Targeting Inflation*, London: Bank of England.
PÉREZ-JURADO, M. (1996), 'El SME y la convergencia en inflación: el papel de la credibilidad', in *La política monetaria y la inflación en España*, Servicio de Estudios del Banco de España, Alianza Editorial.

ROJO, L.A. and J. PÉREZ (1977), *La política monetaria en España*, Banco de España, *Estudios Económicos*, 10.

SANZ, B. (1988), 'Los agregados monetarios y su calidad como objetivos intermedios', Banco de España, *Boletín Económico*, December.

VEGA, J.L. (1991), 'Tests de raíces unitarias: aplicación a series de la economía española y al análisis de la velocidad de circulación del dinero (1964–1990)', Banco de España, *Documento de Trabajo*, 9117.

VEGA, J.L. (1996), Chapter 4 in this volume.

WILLIAMSON, J.M. and M. MILLER (1987), 'Targets and Indicators: A Blueprint for International Coordination of Economic Policy', New York: Institute for International Economics.

4 The ALP Long-run Demand Function

Juan Luis Vega

(Spain)   E41
                 E52

INTRODUCTION

Ever since the article by Poole (1970), a stable and predictable relationship between the demand for money and its determinants has been considered essential for the formulation of monetary policy strategies based on intermediate monetary targeting. As shown by Goldfeld and Sichel (1990), it is precisely these monetary policy requirements that have given rise to the numerous econometric studies, many of them conducted by national central banks, which have described the properties of the empirical functions of the demand for money.

Spain is no exception in this respect. Since the mid-1970s, when efforts were first made to design an active monetary policy for the country, the estimation of the demand functions of various monetary aggregates and inquiries into the properties of the estimated functions has been an area of ongoing investigation in the Banco de España's Research Department. Many relevant papers have been published as a result: Pérez (1975); Rojo and Pérez (1977); Dolado (1982, 1983, 1985, 1988); Mauleón (1987a, 1987b); Dolado and Escrivá (1992); Cabrero Escrivá and Sastre (1992); Vega (1992); Ayuso and Vega (1994); Vega (1994); Sánchez (1995).

However, it is beyond the scope of this chapter to review the extensive literature on the demand for money in Spain. On the contrary: the second section of this chapter summarizes only the most recent results on the stability of ALP long-run demand as published in Vega (1994). However, it is only fitting that mention be made of the indebtedness of this study to all its predecessors in this line of research.

The remainder of this section is concerned with placing Vega's paper in the framework of the needs experienced by monetary policy in 1993–4 and of the various studies conducted at the time in the Banco de España's Research Department to evaluate the strategic alternatives available. These activities culminated in 1995 with the abandonment of intermediate ALP targets and the adoption of an inflation target.

As outlined in chapter 3 by Ayuso and Escrivá (1996), developments in the late 1980s had shown that a monetary policy strategy based on intermediate monetary targeting and the short-term control of the money supply had become an extremely complex matter in an environment of developed and integrated financial markets. During these years, as it became difficult to maintain strict short-term controls on liquidity, the weight of the peseta exchange rate increased in the Banco de España's reaction function, and monetary control strategy shifted toward a more gradualist approach; short-term deviations in the targets were regarded as conveying little information, and the monetary authorities needed to analyze a wide range of indicators for the evaluation of monetary trends.

Inclusion of the peseta in the EMS Exchange Rate Mechanism (ERM) in June 1989 confirmed the pre-eminence of the exchange rate commitment. Although annual targets for ALP growth continued to be published, the exchange rate constraint limited the authorities' ability to respond to undesirable trends in the monetary aggregates. ALP became less a target in itself than an economic policy reference that served to warn of possible medium-to long-term conflicts between domestic and external targets.

The idea underlying these considerations was the possibility of reconciling major short-run instabilities of the demand for money with a stable long-run demand. From the econometric standpoint, the concept of cointegration seemed capable of merging both aspects, as became apparent from the empirical research conducted by the Banco de España's Research Department: Dolado (1988), Dolado and Escrivá (1992) and Cabrero, Escrivá and Sastre (1992).

However, the economic environment changed substantially toward the end of 1993. Broadening the fluctuation bands of the currencies participating in the EMS ERM in August 1993 ended the period of exchange rate turbulence that began in mid-1992. However, the monetary authorities now had to take major decisions regarding the most appropriate monetary policy strategy for the emerging situation.[1] The new context presented a twofold challenge: first, that of resolving the credibility problems resulting from the successive devaluations of the peseta; and second, that of fashioning a framework which would minimize the monetary policy dilemmas attendant on the peseta's inclusion in the ERM – owing to the simultaneous existence of intermediate exchange rate and ALP targets. Specifically, the possibility emerged that the reduced nominal anchor provided by the exchange rate after the broadening of the bands would be offset by closer attention to the performance of various domestic indicators.

A broad monetary aggregate such as ALP was an obvious candidate for a central role in this context. Not only had ALP been a standard monetary policy reference since the mid-1980s, but the accumulated empirical evidence also seemed to advise against any of the other theoretical alternatives available. Conclusions along these lines were reached in several papers published by the Banco de España's Research Department: in Cabrero, Escrivá and Sastre (1992) for the narrower monetary aggregates (M1 and

M2); Vega (1989, 1992) for domestic credit granted by the credit system and the money markets to the non-financial households and firms sectors; and Ayuso and Vega (1994) for various weighted monetary aggregates (divisia indices and liquid equivalents).

However, it was also widely perceived that the historical relationships which had supported selection of ALP as the intermediate target of monetary policy had markedly deteriorated in recent years. Not only the signals seen in the aggregate's movements in the shorter term, but also its trend over time seemed to be involved, and this suggested a significant structural change in ALP long-run demand.

Thus, the Banco de España's *Annual Report* for 1992 explained the deviation between the targets (8 per cent–11 per cent) and the actual growth of ALP that year (5.2 per cent) by 'the convergence of a number of factors that caused shifts in the public's holdings far beyond expectations and which ultimately resulted in lower ALP demand'. Cited among these factors were: the process of tax regularization begun in 1991, the growth of medium-and long-term government debt held by mutual funds, and the full liberalization of capital movements which, starting in February, allowed bank deposits to be made with non-resident institutions. It was concluded that ALP growth in 1992 was below the long-run path of demand for this aggregate.

The 1993 *Annual Report* noted that the rapid growth of ALP in 1993 could be explained only in part by its determinant variables. Reference was made to the need for further explanations regarding the context in which Spanish financial markets had developed in recent years, a context characterized by a growing interconnection with international financial markets, diversification of financial instruments, a marked reduction of the reserve requirement ratio, and heightened competition among institutions and markets.

More generally, the analyses of monetary developments and short-term economic reports regularly produced by the Research Department began to suggest various hypotheses as to the economic causes behind the apparent instabilities noted in ALP demand. Some proposed the higher savings rate and the financial wealth of the resident private sector as one of the underlying factors. Others argued in favor of the increase in the sensitivity of the monetary aggregate to fluctuations in the interest rates of both the financial assets included in the definition of ALP and the alternative assets. In turn, this phenomenon was related to the extraordinary expansion of mutual funds and the growing competition for deposits among financial institutions.

Finally, the gradual lifting of administrative obstacles to the free circulation of capital was an additional source of 'financial disturbances'. The opening up of the Spanish financial system to international markets saw a marked expansion of investment and financing opportunities for the resident private sector, which increased the array of financial assets that could be substituted for those included in ALP.

In this context, the Research Department undertook a number of econometric studies aimed at (1) rigorously analyzing the available empirical evidence for a structural change in the ALP long-run demand function which would refute the relationships formerly estimated, and (2) testing the various hypotheses about the nature of such a structural change. The next section of this chapter summarizes the relevant results as published in Vega (1994) and updates some of the estimations included therein. In the paper, a number of test studies are used to test for structural stability in regressions with first order integrated variables and for the existence of cointegration in the presence of structural change. An attempt is then made to draw some relevant conclusions from the monetary policy standpoint.

ALP LONG-RUN DEMAND: COINTEGRATION AND STABILITY

Since the paper by Dolado (1988), empirical studies on the estimation of money demand functions in Spain have stressed – consistently with the relevant international evidence – the existence of a long-run equilibrium relationship between integrated variables (cointegration) which may be interpreted as a real balances demand function. Such studies have further highlighted the estimation of error correction mechanism (ECM) models to describe the dynamics of adjustment to this long-run equilibrium.

Thus, in Cabrero, Escrivá and Sastre (1992) – the immediate predecessor of Vega (1994) in the related papers published by the Banco de España Research Department – demand equations are calculated for various monetary aggregates as follows:

$$\Delta(m-p)_t = k - \alpha\left[(m-p) - (m-p)^d(.)\right]_{t-1} + \delta_0(L)\Delta(m-p)_{t-1}$$
$$+ \delta_1(L)\Delta Y_t + \delta_2(L)\Delta r_t^p + \delta_3(L)\Delta r_t^a + \delta_4(L)\Delta^2 p_t + \in_t \quad (4.1)$$

$$(m-p)_t^d(.) = \alpha_0 + \alpha_1 Y_t + \alpha_2 r_t^p + \alpha_3 r_t^a + \alpha_4 \Delta_4 p_t \quad (4.2)$$

in which: m_t, y_t, p_t, r_t^p, r_t^a and $\Delta_4 p_t$ stand for,[2] respectively, the nominal monetary balances, Gross Domestic Product in real terms (GDP), the consumer price index (CPI), the average weighted interest rate net of taxes of the assets included in the monetary aggregate, a representative interest rate for the alternative assets (internal rate of return net of taxes on government debt) and the inflation rate in terms of the CPI;[3] Δ and Δ_4 are, respectively, the regular and seasonal first difference operators and $\delta_i(L)$

are finite order polynomials in the lag operator. All the variables (except the interest and inflation rates) are measured in logarithms. (4.1) represents the dynamic form of the demand for money, whose equilibrium specification, in terms of desired demand for real balances (m_t^d), is given by (4.2).

In the case of the ALP monetary aggregate enlarged with commercial paper (ALP2), the paper concludes that cointegration existed in the period 1979:QI–1989:QII, and also affirms that specific short-run instabilities in the equations estimated coexisted with a high degree of stability in the long-run relationship, although no formal tests were conducted in this respect. Other authors – Escrivá and Malo de Molina (1991) and Dolado and Escrivá (1992) – arrived at similar conclusions.

Starting from this emphasis on the long-run properties of the monetary aggregate, Vega (1994) focuses on the long-run demand for real balances relationship given by (4.2), attempting to determine whether the passage of time had made it necessary to modify any of the above conclusions, and if so, in what way. The parameters in (4.1) describing the short-run dynamics are treated as nuisance parameters and not examined. The paper also aims at applying estimation methods that, beyond the traditional superconsistency results (Stock, 1987), permit the use of standard inference (asymptotic) procedures on the long-run parameters.

Table 4.1 is taken from Vega (1994) and shows the estimation for the period 1979:QI – 1993:QIV in equation 2, along with various residual-based tests that help evaluate the empirical evidence on the existence or not of cointegration during the period under study.[4]

Table 4.1 ALP long-run demand, 1979Q I – 1993Q IV

$$(m-p)_t = -\ \underset{(32.38)}{9.09}\ +\ \underset{(55.55)}{1.67}\ y_t\ +\ \underset{(7.75)}{3.43}\ rp_t\ -\ \underset{(6.66)}{1.43}\ ra_t\ -\ \underset{(0.81)}{0.09}\ \Delta_4 p_t$$

ADF $= -0.26$	PP $= -1.10$	DHS $= 46.00$	$h_k = 1.11^{***}$
ADF $-$ LS $= -1.89$	$(\hat{\tau} = 91/\text{QIII})$	PP $-$ LS $= -2.28$	$(\hat{\tau} = 91/\text{QIII})$
ADF $-$ RS $= -\ 6.74^*$	$(\hat{\tau} = 89/\text{QIII})$	PP $-$ RS $= -\ 6.19$	$(\hat{\tau} = 89/\text{QII})$
(0.10)		(0.23)	
ADF $-$ RS$^{\alpha 1} = -\ 4.78$	$(\hat{\tau} = 91/\text{QII})$	PP $-$ RS$^{\alpha 1} = -\ 5.24$	$(\hat{\tau} = 91/\text{QII})$
(0.58)		(0.34)	
ADF $-$ RS$^{\alpha 2,\alpha 3} = -5.48$	$(\hat{\tau} = 89/\text{QIII})$	PP $-$ RS$^{\alpha 2,\alpha 3} = -5.62$	$(\hat{\tau} = 89/\text{QII})$

Notes: Method of estimation: FME (fully modified estimation). *t*-ratios in parentheses.
***, ** and * indicate rejection of the null hypothesis at 1 per cent, 5 per cent and 10 per cent, respectively.
Under some tests, the levels of significance are given in parentheses.
Source: Vega (1994).

The ADF and PP tests shown in the table are the augmented Dickey–Fuller test and the Phillips–Perron test, respectively. DHS is a Durbin–Hausman test, proposed by Choi (1994). These 3 statistics test for the null hypothesis of non-cointegration, that is, the existence of a unit root in the residual of the regression. Conversely, the h_k statistic (Leybourne and MacCabe, 1993) directly tests for the null of cointegration.[5] The reason for including the latter is to provide a degree of cover against the traditional criticism that unit root tests offer scant power in finite samples for rejecting the null. Although it is not certain that this lack of power is a differential characteristic of these tests,[6] it is argued that when it is the alternative hypothesis (cointegration) which is of interest, the statistical tests will usually tend not to reject the null (non-cointegration) unless there is substantial evidence to the contrary. Thus, test h_k may be a useful supplementary tool to the foregoing ones, so that if both types of test produce the same inference as to the existence or not of cointegration, we may be relatively confident on the robustness of the result.

When the equation is estimated for the whole period, none of the first 3 tests – ADF, PP, and DHS – permit rejection at standard confidence levels of the null of non-cointegration. Likewise the h_k test rejects the hypothesis of cointegration at extremely high confidence levels. This result differs from those obtained in the above-mentioned papers and is affected, as will be seen later, by the inclusion of the most recent years in the sample period.

The remaining tests in Table 4.1 belong to the group proposed by Gregory and Hansen (1996). Starting from the idea of structural change, these authors broaden the standard ADF and PP tests in order to permit, under the alternative hypothesis, the cointegration relationship to change at an unknown point in the sample period, either the intercept (*LS*), or the entire vector of coefficients (*RS*)[7] including the intercept. In a context of structural change, in which the power of ADF or PP drops substantially, the tests may detect cointegration and, at the same time, they provide an estimate of the date ($\hat{\tau}$) at which the potential structural change occurs. By contrast, when there actually is no structural change, the traditional tests will have greater power.

Based on the results of Table 4.1, it is found that only with the ADF–RS test does some marginal evidence appear in favor of the existence of cointegration when the entire vector of parameters is allowed to change. This evidence becomes even weaker if it is noted that the breaking point ($\hat{\tau}$) is located very much toward the end of the sample – around: 1979:Q3 or 1989:Q4 – implying that changes in the long-run parameters are estimated with limited degrees of freedom. In any case, the results do indeed seem to suggest that there is a cointegration relationship for the first part of the sample.

The latter evaluation is corroborated by the evidence reported in Table 4.2. In this table, the same ALP2 demand equation is estimated for the period between the first quarter of 1979 and the last quarter of 1988. The augmented Dickey–Fuller test (ADF), and those of Phillips and Perron (PP) and Choi (DHS) strongly reject the noncointegration hypothesis for the period under study. Likewise, the Leybourne and MacCabe h_k test provides the same inference, without rejecting the null hypothesis of cointegration. The remaining tests in Table 4.2 (*F*-mean, *Lc* and *F*-sup) are those proposed by Hansen (1992) and they attempt to evaluate explicitly the constancy of the long-run relationship. None of them point to rejection at standard confidence levels of the hypothesis of the existence of a long-run demand for money which is stable in the period 1979:QI–1988:QIV.

Thus, a combined reading of both tables indicates the existence of an ALP2 long-run demand function which is stable until 1988. However, there is scant evidence in favor of the hypothesis of cointegration if the sample period is extended until end-1993. This suggests a structural change in the ALP2 long-run demand function. It is estimated that this structural change occurred about 1989. Moreover, it is seen how the solution of allowing all the parameters to change proves unsatisfactory in that the RS tests provide little evidence in favor of the hypothesis of two cointegration regimes.

A further possibility examined by Vega (1994) is that of restricting the type of structural change which would have affected ALP2 demand under the alternative hypothesis in the Gregory and Hansen RS tests. This permits both an increase in the power of the tests, and an analysis of more precise hypotheses as to the nature of the possible structural change. Specifically, the other tests in Table 4.1 analyze the 3 related lines of argument discussed in the introduction to the chapter.

First, it was stated that the recent increase in the resident private sector savings rate and wealth may be one of the underlying factors in the instabilities identified in ALP demand. From this perspective, the high long-run income elasticity estimated for this aggregate (1.51 in the equation in Table 4.2) would capture wealth effects not explicitly included in (4.2). As a result, changes in the income–wealth ratio would cause instability in

Table 4.2　ALP long-run demand, 1979:QI – 1988:QIV

$$(m - p)_t = -\ 7.64\ +\ 1.51\ y_t +\ 3.01\ rp_t -\ 1.10\ ra_t -\ 0.41\ \Delta_4 p_t$$
$$(12.61)\quad(23.03)\quad(9.89)\quad(7.81)\quad(2.87)$$

ADF $= -4.89^{**}$	PP $= -5.20^{**}$	DHS $= 1119.7^{***}$	$h_k = 0.061$
$F - \text{mean} = 5.89$	$Lc = 0.38$	$F - \text{sup} = 16.30$	$(\tau^* = 81/QI)$

Notes: See notes for Table 4.1.

the estimated equation and, more specifically, in the parameter which measures long-run income elasticity (α_1).

To test the role played by factors of this type, the $\text{ADF} - \text{RS}^{\alpha 1}$ and $\text{PP} - \text{RS}^{\alpha 1}$ tests in Table 4.1 limit the possibilities of structural change under the alternative hypothesis to the intercept and the parameter of income in (4.2).[8] The results of the tests shown in the table continue not to allow rejection of the null hypothesis of non-cointegration.[9]

Second, it was also argued that another possible factor underlying the apparent instability of ALP demand was the increased sensitivity of the aggregate to interest rate fluctuations. In principle, this idea does not challenge the evidence presented for 1989 as the approximate date for the structural change affecting ALP2. Indeed, at end-1989, ahead of the Banco de España's thoroughgoing reform of the reserve requirement ratio early in 1990, the first incidents occurred in what was termed the 'war of super accounts' (high-yield deposit accounts). This episode ultimately became part of a broader process of growing competition among financial institutions to raise deposits. The extraordinary growth of mutual funds, especially stock investment funds, early in the 1990s likewise played a major role in this respect.

The $\text{ADF}-\text{RS}^{\alpha 2,\alpha 3}$ and $\text{PP}-\text{RS}^{\alpha 2,\alpha 3}$ tests reported in Table 4.1 restrict the change of regime to the intercept and to the parameters of the own and alternative interest rates in (4.2). On the basis of these tests as well, the evidence does not permit a rejection of the null hypothesis of non-cointegration when the alternative permits the change described in the parameters affecting both interest rates in the ALP2 long-run demand equation.

Finally, it has also been argued that the gradual elimination of administrative obstacles to free capital movements and the resulting opening up of the Spanish financial system to international markets greatly increased the opportunities for resident private sector investment and financing. As a result, the array of substitute assets for those included in ALP had also increased, which created a source of potential instabilities in the estimated historical relationships.

From this standpoint, although the major liberalizing breakthrough took place in 1987,[10] the year 1989 was also important as it saw the abolition of quantitative limits on investments in securities issued in external markets.[11] This process was subsequently consolidated by successive liberalizations: of ECU deposits in September 1989; of the purchase of foreign money market securities in April 1990; and of resident holding of bank accounts in pesetas and foreign currency in non-resident banks in February 1992. Likewise, the lowering of the foreign exchange risk resulting from the peseta's entry into the ERM on 19 June 1989 was a key development in the opening up of the Spanish financial system.

Table 4.3   ALP long-run demand, 1979:QI – 1993:QIV

$$(m-p)_t = - \underset{(28.25)}{9.08} + \underset{(48.12)}{1.67} \ y_t + \underset{(7.03)}{3.34} \ rp_t - \underset{(5.78)}{1.41} \ ra_t - \underset{(0.67)}{0.10} \ \Delta_4 p_t + \underset{(0.009)}{0.001} \ rx_t$$

ADF $= -0.25$	PP $= -1.07$	DHS $= 40.26$	$h_k = 1.32^{***}$
ADF $- RS^{\alpha5} = - 6.48^*$	($\hat{\tau} = 89/QIII$)	PP $- RS^{\alpha5} = - 6.07$	($\hat{\tau} = 89/QII$)
(0.07)		(0.15)	

Notes: See notes for Table 4.1.

In accordance with the above, an interest rate on external assets was added to the variables grouped in (4.2). More specifically, Table 4.3 estimates include the simple average of 3-month interest rates for the D-Mark and the dollar in the Euromarket (rx_t).[12] As Table 4.3 shows, the influence of this variable is nil when the equation is estimated for the entire period 1979:QI–1993:QIV. Moreover, the ADF, PP, DHS and h_k tests continue not to allow any change to the earlier conclusions about the absence of cointegration. By contrast, the results of the ADF$-RS^{\alpha5}$ and PP$-RS^{\alpha5}$ tests do produce some evidence suggesting the existence of cointegration when the possibility is envisaged of a change in ALP2 sensitivity to changes in the foreign interest rate, with the first and the second tests rejecting, at levels of confidence of 93 per cent and 85 per cent, respectively, the unit root hypothesis in the estimated residuals (non cointegration). The change-of-regime date $(\hat{\tau})$ continues to be estimated as around 1989, while the foreign interest rate turned out not to be significant in the previous period.

In accordance with the latter assessment, Table 4.4 shows an updated ALP2 long-run demand equation estimated by Vega (1994) in which, starting in 1989, the real balances demand of the monetary aggregate is allowed to be sensitive to changes in 3-month Euromarket interest rates for the dollar (r_t) and the D-Mark (r_t^{DM}). For practical estimation purposes, the rx_t variable was replaced by two variables that had zero values before 1989; as from that date, they capture the course of both interest rates. At the same time, a *dummy* step is included that offsets the discontinuity arising in the

Table 4.4   ALP long-run demand, 1979:QI – 1995:QIV

$$(m-p)_t = - \underset{(13.56)}{7.82} + \underset{(24.77)}{1.54} \ y_t + \underset{(3.63)}{2.47} \ rp_t - \underset{(2.47)}{0.83} \ ra_t - \underset{(2.42)}{0.37} \ \Delta_4 p_t$$
$$- \underset{(7.56)}{0.77} \ r_t^{\$} - \underset{(4.55)}{1.14} \ r_t^{DM} + \underset{(7.96)}{0.172} \ S89/I$$

Notes: See notes for Table 4.1. Variables S89/I, $r_t^{\$}$ and r_t^{DM} take zero values before 1989.

first quarter of 1989. The results basically confirm those obtained in Vega (1994): foreign interest rates appear as highly significant when they are included as from 1989 and no significant changes occur in the remaining coefficients with regard to the estimate to 1998:QIV as shown in Table 4.2. The long-run semi-elasticities of ALP2 to changes in $r_t^\$$ and r_t^{DM} are estimated at about −0.77 and −1.14, respectively.

Figure 4.1 sheds some light on the importance of foreign interest rates, showing the deviations of ALP2 from the long-run paths calculated with the equations estimated in Tables 4.2 (broken line) and 4.4 (solid line). Prior to 1989, both lines have very similar profiles. However, as from that year, the monetary aggregate shows a clear tendency to grow at rates above those compatible with the demand equation estimated in Table 4.2. As a result, the deviations from the long-run path steadily increase and become persistent. On the other hand, by including both foreign interest rate as from 1989 among the determinants of ALP2 demand – that is, if foreign assets denominated in foreign currency are considered as substitutes for those included in ALP – more stationary deviations are obtained. From this standpoint, the high interest rate differentials during these years would be a basic factor in the high growth of ALP2 during the period. This in turn would be consistent with the small-scale size of resident portfolio investment abroad and with the increasing weight of the external sector in the financing of households and non-financial firms.

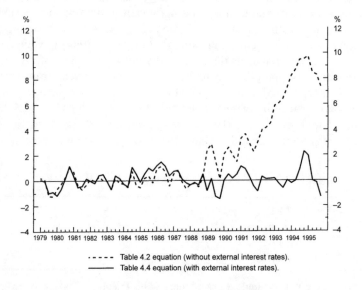

Figure 4.1 ALP deviations from its long-run demand, 1979–95

To sum up, it would appear necessary to modify the conclusions drawn by other authors on the ALP demand equation, particularly those concerning the existence of cointegration and the stability of the coefficients which define the long-run relationship. The empirical evidence analyzed in this section indicates that the shifts in ALP demand in recent years, far from being transitory episodes limited to the short run, have substantially changed the long-run properties of the aggregate.

As to the meaning of this structural change, 3 hypotheses have been examined: the increase in the private sector savings rate, the heightened sensitivity of ALP to changes in its own and alternative interest rates, and the growing openness of the Spanish financial system to international markets. It is the third hypothesis that seems to play a pivotal role in explaining the apparent instability of the traditional ALP demand equations. Thus, only when the returns alternative to those included in ALP are expanded to include, as from 1989, foreign interest rates is it possible to recover an ALP long-run demand equation reasonably stable in recent years.

CONCLUSIONS

The stability of the demand for money function is a key factor in assessing the viability of monetary policy strategies based on intermediate monetary targeting. However, the stability hypothesis is far from being uncontroversial. Since the mid-1970s, many researchers have abundantly documented a number of episodes of both *missing money* and *great velocity decline* in various countries. These episodes have often been related to portfolio adjustments against a background of intense financial innovation and market deregulation.

As regards Spain, the evidence for the stability of money demand is mixed. On the one hand, the equations estimated have been invariant against the changes made since 1978 in the basic monetary policy framework. Adopting an instrumental variable of interest rates, rather than bank reserves, or the greater weight of the exchange rate in the monetary authorities' reaction function, does not appear to have caused significant shifts in the estimated empirical relationships. This has reinforced the structural interpretation of such relationships, as opposed to an alternative reduced form interpretation. In this respect, the Lucas critique does not appear to have been empirically relevant in the case of the demand for money in Spain.[13]

By contrast, the changes in the financial environment of the Spanish economy in recent decades seem to have had a powerful impact on the estimates in question. During the 1980s, major portfolio adjustments by the public as a result of financial innovation and market deregulation led the Banco de España to broaden the definition of its intermediate target, which became ALP as from 1984. In response to such financial innovation which increased the degree of asset substitutability, successive changes were made in ALP to include financial assets regarded as close substitutes for those already covered by the definition of money.

Early in the 1990s, with the liberalization of capital movements and the definitive opening up of the Spanish financial system to international markets, instability was again noted in the estimated relationships. Indeed, the empirical evidence analyzed in the previous section indicates that the recent shifts in the demand for this aggregate – far from representing transitory, short-run episodes – had substantially changed its long-run properties.

Econometrically, in both cases it has been possible to re-specify the money demand equations so that they become stable again. This is done either by re-defining the monetary aggregate, or by including new variables among its determinants. However, there are also other factors which cast doubt on whether monetary aggregates can provide a sufficiently solid basis for monetary policy design. Such considerations, and others of a more institutional nature, led the Banco de España in 1995 to announce a change in monetary policy strategy,[14] the terms of which are amply discussed in the previous chapters.

First of all, the evidence provided in the previous section focused solely on the parameters that define the ALP long-run demand equation. Yet this should not obscure the fact that the description of the process of dynamic adjustment to the long-run path may often be of fundamental importance (e.g. when a forecasting equation is needed). In the context of annual monetary planning, factors which are difficult to gauge and which have not been taken into account, notably expectations of exchange rate depreciation, may be crucial in interpreting short-run ALP developments. This was the case with the significant, if temporary, cross-border deposit shifts in the quarters of 1992 prior to the successive devaluations of the peseta. More generally, the broadness of the ALP aggregate, which includes financial assets that differ widely in the liquidity services they provide, greatly complicates interpretation of the aggregate's behaviour, as demand combines strictly transactional motives with savings or portfolio motives.

Second, the inclusion of foreign variables, and more specifically foreign interest rates, among the determinants of ALP demand reduces the central bank's ability to influence the money stock through the control of an instrumental variable, namely the short-term interest rate.

Finally, a monetary policy strategy which gives priority to medium-to long-run considerations in response to frequent short-run instabilities in the demand for money is not problem-free. The reason for this is the extraordinarily complicated process of discriminating empirically between one-off instabilities in the estimated equations and shifts in the long-run demand function. From the econometric stand point, this problem becomes more acute at the end of the relevant sample period, precisely the time when the central bank has to explain publicly the changes in monetary conditions and the prospects of meeting targets. The monetary authorities are thus involved in an ongoing and increasingly complex task of interpreting developments in monetary aggregates on a case-by-case basis, which may ultimately erode the credibility of its commitment. An additional factor in this respect is the existence of a considerable lag between when the effects on the demand for money of a given change in the financial environment are first perceived and – once agents have fully adapted to the new context – when these effects may be estimated econometrically and included in new specifications. During these intermediate periods, monetary policy consequently operates with a markedly increased degree of uncertainty.

In short, as uncertainty increases about the course of the monetary aggregate and it becomes less amenable to control, all these factors combine to erode the role ALP performed as an intermediate monetary target. However, the persistence of a long-run relationship between ALP and nominal expenditure continues to warrant its use as a privileged indicator in the analysis of monetary conditions.

Appendix: Econometric Tests Used

1 Null hypothesis tests of non-cointegration
 – ADF = augmented Dickey – Fuller test
 – PP = Phillips – Perron test
 – DHS = Durbin – Hausman type test proposed by Choi (1994).

2 Null hypothesis tests of cointegration
 – h_k = test proposed by Leybourne and McCabe (1993).

3 Tests of the null hypothesis of noncointegration which allow for the existence of structural change under the alternative hypothesis of cointegration:
 – ADF – LS and PP – LS = extensions of augmented Dickey – Fuller and Phillips – Perron tests, respectively, which allow the intercept of the long-run relationship to change at an unknown point (τ, to be estimated) in the sample period (Gregory and Hansen, 1996).
 – ADF – RS and PP – RS = extensions of the augmented Dickey – Fuller and Phillips – Perron tests, respectively, which permit change in both the intercept and the remaining coefficients of the long-run relationship (Gregory and Hansen, 1996).
 – ADF – $RS^{\alpha i}$ and PP – $RS^{\alpha i}$ = extensions of the augmented Dickey – Fuller and Phillips – Perron tests, respectively, which permit the intercept and the coefficient of the variable X_i to change.

4 Tests of the stability of the cointegration relationship
 – F-mean, Lc, and F-sup = tests proposed by Hansen (1992).

Notes

1   See Ortega and Bonilla (1995).
2   See Cabrero, Escrivá and Sastre (1992) for an exact definition of the variables and their sources.
3   The order of integration of the variables appearing in (4.2) has been examined in numerous papers: Cabrero, Escrivá and Sastre (1992), Ayuso and Vega (1994), etc., Generally speaking, it holds that monetary aggregates and prices behave like second order integrated variables $I(2)$, while monetary aggregates in real terms, income, inflation and interest rates are $I(1)$ during the sample period under study.

4   The method of estimation used is that proposed by Phillips and Hansen (1990): *fully modified estimation* (FME), in which the suggestions of Andrews (1991) and Andrews and Monahan (1992) have been incorporated for estimating the long-run variance–covariance matrix. This procedure is asymptotically equivalent to maximum likelihood, and makes it possible to (1) alleviate the second order biases which, in finite samples, are found in estimates of cointegrating vectors based on static regressions; and (2) use standard inference (asymptotic) procedures.

5   None of these tests has a standard distribution. Critical values for ADF and PP may be found in MacKinnon (1991); the asymptotic critical values for DHS and h_k are tabulated in the references cited.

6   See Gonzalo and Lee (1996).

7   The asymptotic critical values of both tests have been tabulated in the reference cited.

8   Obviously, this is an indirect test, limited by the lack of an historical quarterly series for private sector wealth in the Spanish economy.

9   The critical values in finite samples for these tests are given in Vega (1994).

10 Ministerial Order of 5/25/87 which implemented Royal Decree 2374/1986.

11 Ministerial Order of 19/12/88.

12 Strictly speaking, these interest rates should be corrected for expectations of exchange rate depreciation. This problem has been eliminated here arguing that this component would be $I(0)$, and not affect (asymptotically) the estimation of the long-run parameters.

13 See Dolado (1988) for a detailed discussion.

14 The January 1995 *Economic Bulletin* contains a transcription of the address by the Governor of the Banco de España to the Spanish Parliamentary Committee on Economic Affairs on the monetary policy targets for 1995.

References

ANDREWS, D.W.K. (1991) 'Heteroscedasticity and autocorrelation consistent covariance matrix estimation', *Econometrica*, 59, 817–58.

ANDREWS, D.W.K. and J.C. MONAHAN (1992) 'An improved heteroscedasticity and autocorrelation consistent covariance matrix estimator', *Econometrica*, 60, 953–66.

AYUSO, J. and J.L. ESCRIVÁ (1996) 'The development of the monetary control strategy in Spain', Chapter 3 in this volume.

AYUSO, J. and J.L. VEGA (1994) 'Agregados monetarios ponderados', *Revista Española de Economia*, 11(1), 161–89.

CABRERO, A., J.L. ESCRIVÁ and T. SASTRE (1992) 'Ecuaciones de demanda para los nuevos agregados monetarios', *Estudios Económicos*, 52, Servicio de Estudios, Banco de España.

CHOI, I. (1994) 'Durbin – Hausman tests for cointegration', *Journal of Economic Dynamics and Control*, 18, 467–480.

DOLADO, J.J. (1982) 'Procedimientos de búsqueda de especificación dinámica: el caso de la demanda de M3 en España, *Estudios Económicos*, 24, Servicio de Estudios, Banco de España.

DOLADO, J.J. (1983) 'Contrastación de hipótesis no anidadas en el caso de la demanda de dinero en España', *Cuadernos Económicos de ICE*, 24, 119–39.

DOLADO, J.J. (1985) 'La estabilidad de la demanda de dinero en España (1974–84)', *Boletín Económico*, Banco de España, September, 13–21.

DOLADO, J.J. (1988) 'Innovación financiera, inflación y estabilidad de la Demanda de ALP', *Boletin Económico*, Banco de España, April, 19–35.

DOLADO, J.J and J.L. ESCRIVÁ (1992): 'La demanda de dinero en España: definiciones amplias de liquidez', *Moneda y Crédito*, 195, 111–34.

ESCRIVÁ, J.L. and J.L. MALO DE MOLINA (1991) 'La instrumentación de la política monetaria en el marco de la integración Europea', *Documento de Trabajo*, 9104, Servicio de Estudios, Banco de España.

GOLDFELD, S.M. and D.E. SICHEL (1990) 'The demand for money', in *Handbook of Monetary Economics* B. Friedman and F. H. Hahn (eds), New York: Elsevier Science Publishers.

GONZALO, J. and T. LEE (1996) 'Relative power of t-type tests for stationary and unit root processes', *Journal of Time Series Analysis*, 17(1), 37–48.

GREGORY, A.W and B.E. HANSEN (1996) 'Residual-based tests for cointegration in models with regime shifts', *Journal of Econometrics*, 70, 99–126.

GREGORY, A.W., NASON, J.M. and D.G. WATT (1996) 'Testing for structural breaks in cointegrated relationships', *Journal of Econometrics*, 71 (1, 2), 321–41.

HANSEN, B.E. (1992) 'Tests for parameter instability in regressions with $I(1)$ processes', *Journal of Business and Economics Statistics*, 10, 321–35.

LEYBOURNE, S.J. and B.P.M. MCCABE (1993) 'A simple test for cointegration', *Oxford Bulletin of Economics and Statistics*, 55, 97–103.

MACKINNON, J.G. (1991) 'Critical values for cointegration tests', in R. Engle and C.W.J. Granger (eds), *Long Run Economic Relationships*, Oxford: Oxford University Press, 267–76.

MAULEÓN, I. (1987a) 'La demanda de ALP: una estimación provisional', *Boletín Económico*, Banco de España, October, 43–52.

MAULEÓN, I. (1987b): 'La demanda de dinero reconsiderada', *Documento de Trabajo*, 8709, Servicio de Estudios, Banco de España.

ORTEGA, E. and J.M. BONILLA (1995) 'Reasons for adopting an inflation target', in A.G. Haldane (ed). *Targeting Inflation*, London: Bank of England, 49–58.

PÉREZ, J. (1975) 'Un modelo para el sector financiero de la economia Española', *Estudios Económicos*, 6, Servicio de Estudios, Banco de España.

PHILLIPS, P.C.B. and E. HANSEN (1990) 'Statistical inference in instrumental variable regression with $I(1)$ processes', *Review of Economic Studies*, 57, 99–125.

PHILLIPS, P.C.B. and C.E. QUINTOS (1993) 'Parameter constancy in cointegrating regressions', *Empirical Economics*, 18, 675–706.

POOLE, W. (1970) 'Optimal choice of monetary policy instruments in a simple stochastic macro model', *Quarterly Journal of Economics*, 74, 197–216.

ROJO, L.A. and J. PÉREZ (1977) 'La politica monetaria en España: objectivos e Instrumentos', *Estudios Económicos*, 10, Servicio de Estudios, Banco de España.

SÁNCHEZ, C. (1995) 'Ecuación de demanda de ALP: propiedades de corto plazo y utilización en el análisis monetario', *Boletín Económico*, Banco de España, July–August, 57–67.

STOCK, J.H. (1987) 'Asymptotic properties of least-squares estimators of co-integrating vectors', *Econometrica*, 55, 1035–56.

VEGA, J.L. (1989) 'Las variables de crédito en el mecanismo de transmisión monetaria: el Caso Español', *Documento de Trabajo*, 8902, Centro de Estudios Monetarios y Financieros.

VEGA, J.L. (1992) 'El papel del crédito en el mecanismo de transmisión monetaria', *Estudios Económicos*, 48, Servicio de Estudios, Banco de España.

VEGA, J.L. (1994) 'Es estable la función de demanda a largo plazo de ALP?', *Documento de Trabajo*, 9422, Servicio de Estudios, Banco de España.

(Europe)

5 Fiscal Constraints on Central Bank Independence and Price Stability*

Matthew B. Canzoneri and Behzad Diba

E58
E31

INTRODUCTION

The fiscal convergence criteria in the Maastricht Treaty reflect the rather widely held view that an overextended fiscal policy can jeopardize central bank independence and price stability. The Treaty established reference values for the deficit to GDP ratio (0.03) and the debt to GDP ratio (0.60) to help in determining whether a country's deficits are 'excessive'; if a country's deficits are deemed excessive, it will not be allowed to participate in EMU.

The debt criterion's inclusion in the Treaty is thought to be necessary for the 'political independence' of the central bank. The worry is that a government trying to cope with large debt payments might be tempted to pressure the central bank for low interest rates. In this chapter, we will argue that the deficit criterion's inclusion in the Treaty (or something like it) is necessary for the 'functional independence' of the central bank. Without it, the central bank would not be capable of controlling the price level, even if it had political independence and a mandate for price stability.

Figure 5.1 plots the debt to GDP ratios of four countries – Belgium, Italy, Spain and Germany – for the period of the EMS.[1] Belgium and Italy are high-debt countries, while Germany and Spain are low-debt countries.[2] These plots may seem paradoxical. Both Spain (a low-debt country) and Italy (a high-debt country) have experienced inflationary episodes, and both have had difficulties in maintaining their exchange rates; Belgium (the highest-debt country) has generally been able to maintain a credible peg. Clearly, the level of government debt is not the only determinant of price stability.

Monetary policy is related to fiscal policy by an intertemporal budget constraint, which says that the present value of future surpluses (including

* We would like to thank the Banco de España its encouragement and support. We would also like to thank (without implicating) Juan José Dolado, José Luis Malo de Molina, José Viñals, Georg Winckler and Michael Woodford for their helpful comments, and Francisco de Castro for patiently collecting the data. The views expressed here are solely those of the authors.

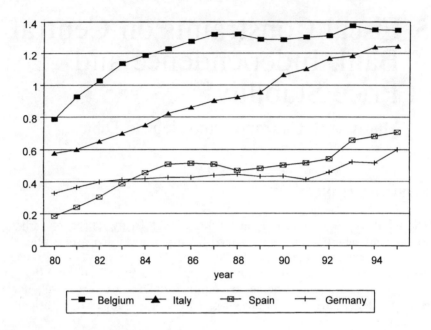

Figure 5.1   Gross debt/GDP ratios, 1980–95

central bank transfers) has to be able to pay off the current government debt. (If financial markets do not believe that the government is solvent, then the government will not be able to place its debt.) This present value budget constraint is at the heart of some recent research – by Auernheimer and Contreras (1990); Leeper (1991); Sims (1994, 1995); and Woodford (1994, 1995) – on the theory of price determination; Woodford (1996) and Bergin (undated) use the theory to analyze fiscal policy and price stability in a European context. We will use this new theory to characterize the functional independence of a central bank and to discuss the implications of fiscal policy for price stability.

The new theory of price determination asserts that if primary surpluses do not respond to the level of government debt in a systematic way, the price level will be determined by the present value government budget constraint (and not by the supply and demand for money, as in conventional analyses). Basically, the price level has to adjust to make the real value of the existing debt equal to the present value of future primary surpluses.[3] We call this a fiscal-dominant (FD) regime, because the price level is determined by the dictates of fiscal solvency. The central bank can affect the price level, but only by changing the amount of transfers to the treasury. And since seigniorage revenue is so small (when compared to the level of government debt), we will see that policy changes of the usual magnitude have almost no effect on the price level. However, we will also see that shocks to the primary surplus or changes in the long-run inflation target can have big effects on the price level. Price stability may well be beyond the control of the central bank. If on the other hand primary surpluses tend to rise when government debt is growing too quickly, then it turns out that the present value budget constraint is automatically satisfied for any real value of the existing debt. The price level is determined in the familiar way by money supply and demand. We will call this a monetary dominant (MD) regime, because the price level is determined independently of the present value budget constraint, and the central bank can control it directly and without regard (if it so chooses) to the dictates of fiscal solvency.

We would argue that a central bank is 'functionally independent' if it is operating in a MD regime. In this regime, the central bank can control the price level directly, and it can be held responsible for price stability if that is the central bank mandate. In a FD regime, the central bank may be justified in asserting that it has lost control of the price level to the vacillations of fiscal policy, and that it should not be held responsible for price stability. We might also note at this point that there may not be a close relationship between 'functional independence' and 'legal independence.' The difference between a MD regime and a FD regime is whether financial markets believe that primary surpluses tend to rise when the government debt is growing too quickly.

The rest of the chapter is organized as follows: we review the new theory of price determination, and define the MD and FD regimes. It turns out that this theory of price determination sheds light on two related areas: (1) the dynamics of debt reduction, and (2) the old question of whether the price level is determined when the central bank is using the nominal interest rate to target money supply growth or inflation. We will discuss these issues in passing, even though they are only indirectly related to our central theme: the constraints of fiscal policy on central bank independence and price stability. The basic theory we present in this section is not new; it was worked out in the papers referred to above. However, our exposition and our interpretation of the theory are different from what is available elsewhere. In particular, we present the theory in a way that is more amenable to policy discussions and empirical testing and we give the MD regime more emphasis. Indeed, it is the regime that the Maastricht Treaty (implicitly) envisions, and may be quite efficient in achieving. Those who are already familiar with the theory (or are willing to accept our assertions about price determination) may wish to skip to the third section.

There, we assess the quantitative importance for price stability of being in the MD regime rather than the FD regime. We ask how fiscal shocks (such as meeting the Maastricht convergence criteria) and monetary shocks (such as lowering the inflation target) affect the price level in the two regimes. We also assess the importance of the level of government debt, sometimes with surprising results.

We then discuss ways to test for which regime is operative, and we suggest ways to change the regime. In particular, we discuss legislation that would ensure the MD regime, and we show that the Maastricht Treaty's deficit criterion is an example. The debt criterion may be necessary for the 'political independence' of the central bank, while the deficit criterion (or something like it) is necessary for the 'functional independence' of the central bank. A final section concludes.

MONETARY-DOMINANT (MD) AND FISCAL-DOMINANT (FD) REGIMES

First, we review some recent research on price determination, and show how it can be used to define regimes in which the central bank is functionally independent, and regimes in which fiscal policy is the primary determinant of price stability (or instability). Then, we extend the discussion to ask which central bank operating procedures serve as nominal anchors and how the regime affects debt dynamics. These extensions are tangential to what follows; they can be skipped by readers who are not interested in such matters.

The discussion in this section is based on certain simplifying assumptions. Our purpose here is to give an intuitive exposition of some recent work on price determination, and to motivate our definition of the MD and FD regimes. The general insights we obtain will also be relevant when the simplifying assumptions are relaxed.

Price Determination and Policy Regimes

The new research on price determination centres around two equations:

$$M_{t+1}V = P_t y_t \tag{5.1}$$

$$W_t/P_t y_t = \sum_{j=t}^{\infty} \beta^{j-t}(s_j + \tau_j) \tag{5.2}$$

where $W_t = B_t + M_t$, $\tau_t = (1/V)[i_t/(1+i_t)]$ and $\beta = (1+n_t)/(1+r_t) < 1$. M is the monetary base, and B is the stock of net interest bearing liabilities of the public sector (including the central bank). Money and debt are measured at the beginning of each period. So, M_{t+1} is the money that is used in period t, and the stock that is available at the beginning of period $t+1$, before new injections are made. y_t is real GDP, which for simplicity is assumed to be exogenous, and growing at the rate n_t. $B_t/P_t y_t$ is the ratio of debt to GDP; s_t is the ratio of the primary surplus to GDP; and τ_t is the ratio of central bank transfers (to the Treasury) to GDP. $s_t + \tau_t$ will be referred to as the surplus inclusive of central bank transfers.

(5.1) is a Cambridge Equation; V is base velocity, which is assumed to be constant. (5.2) is the present value government budget constraint. It is derived formally in the appendix, but basically it just says that current and (expected) future surpluses (inclusive of transfers) must be able to pay off the existing debt; it is the government's solvency condition. The discount factor, β, is equal to $(1+n_t)/(1+r_t)$, where r_t is the real interest rate; the GDP growth factor, n_t, gets into β because everything is expressed as a ratio of GDP. For simplicity, we assume that β is constant over time, and less than 1. We interpret the term τ_t as central bank transfers (relative to GDP); more precisely, it should be called the present value of transfers that the Treasury will receive next period. Our interpretation of τ_t is best understood as follows: the central bank makes profits by issuing liabilities that do not pay interest – the money base – in exchange for assets that do pay interest. Its profits (relative to GDP) at the end of the period will be $(1/V)i_t$, and the present value of these profits is $(1/V)i_t/(1+i_t)$.

It should be noted here that our W refers to the net liabilities of the public sector, including the central bank. This concept is very closely related to the OECD's 'general government net financial liabilities'.[4] In what follows, we will refer to $W_t/P_t y_t$ as the debt to GDP ratio. The debt concept used in the Maastricht Treaty is closely related to the OECD's 'general government gross financial liabilities', which are not adjusted for the government holdings of financial assets. The difference between the gross and net liabilities of the government can be significant. Figure 5.2 plots the OECD's net debt to GDP ratios, while Figure 5.1 showed the gross debt to GDP ratios.[5]

The present value budget constraint (5.2) comes from a period by period constraint:

$$W_t/P_t y_t = \beta(W_{t+1}/P_{t+1}y_{t+1}) + s_t + \tau_t \qquad (5.3)$$

(5.3) is derived formally in the Appendix (p. 000), but basically it says that the current debt has to be financed by borrowing (here the present value of next period's debt) and the primary surplus inclusive of central bank transfers.

Suppose now that the primary surplus (inclusive of central bank transfers) is following some arbitrary path, independent of the level of debt. The only way (5.2) can be satisfied is if P_t adjusts to make the real value of

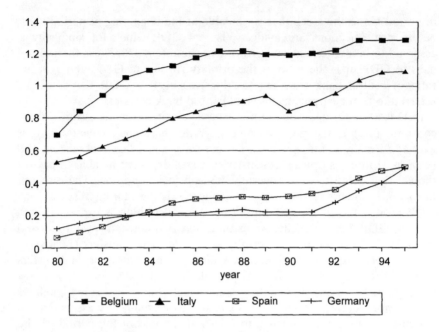

Figure 5.2   Net debt/GDP ratios, 1980–95

the existing debt equal to the present value of current and (expected) future surpluses. Perhaps the best way to understand this is to make an analogy with coupon bonds. Think of the existing government debt as a bond, and think of the primary surpluses (inclusive of central bank transfers) as coupon payments. The price level's adjustment is just the market's evaluation of this bond, and its (expected) coupon payments. The coupon bond analogy is quite close, given the simplifying assumptions we have made. However, we should note that, in a more realistic setting, the adjustment process might also affect some of the coupon payments. For example, if base velocity responded to interest rate movements and if wages were sticky (so that GDP responded to the price level changes), then the current period's adjustment of prices, interest rates and GDP might also be expected to affect the current period's primary surplus (inclusive of central bank transfers). In any case, we will find the analogy useful.

The volatility of the price level depends on the volatility of present and (expected) future primary surpluses. For example, 'news' that the market takes as a signal of increased future deficits will cause an immediate increase in the price level. Price stability also depends on the level of the existing public debt. Somewhat paradoxically, a large public debt can actually be stabilizing. With a large debt, the price level does not have to adjust very much to offset a given decrease in expected future surpluses.

The central bank does have some leverage on the price level, but it has to work through fiscal policy to exert it. By raising the nominal interest rate, the central bank can raise its transfers to the Treasury; this increases the (transfers inclusive) surplus and lowers the price level. However, as we will see in the next section, the scope for this is rather limited (since velocity is small relative to the debt to GDP ratio in all EU countries). The central bank might worry that it has lost control of the price level (and the exchange rate) to the vacillations of fiscal policy. In any case, when primary surpluses are not perceived to be related to the level of government debt, the price level is determined by the present value budget constraint. We call this a *fiscal-dominant (FD) regime*, because the price level is determined solely by the dictates of fiscal solvency.

Suppose instead that primary surpluses (inclusive of central bank transfers) tend to increase when the debt is rising too quickly. For example, suppose fiscal policy makes the debt to GDP ratio converge on a specific target, θ, as is implied by the Maastricht Treaty's convergence criteria:

$$w_{j+1} - \theta = \lambda(w_j - \theta) \tag{5.4}$$

where $w_j = W_t/P_t y_t$ and $\lambda < 1$. (In the Appendix, we show that convergence to a fixed target is much stronger than necessary for what follows.[6]) The path for primary surpluses that accomplishes this is:[7]

$$s_j + \tau_j = (1 - \beta\lambda)(w_j - \theta) + (1 - \beta)\theta \tag{5.5}$$

Using (5.3), (5.4), and (5.5) in (5.2), it is easy to show that the present value budget constraint will be satisfied for any real value of the existing debt. The price level, P_t, can be any number in (5.2), because primary surpluses are limiting the growth in the debt to GDP ratio in a way that automatically guarantees solvency, for any initial real debt.

With fiscal policy guaranteeing solvency, the price level is determined elsewhere in the model. In our model, the price level is determined by (5.1). The central bank has complete control of the price level, and fiscal shocks have no effect on price stability. The strength of this result is however due to the simplicity of our model; more generally P_t will be determined simultaneously by a number of equations. The point is that the present value constraint (5.2) will not be involved in price determination. This equation is automatically satisfied by an endogenous fiscal policy, no matter what variables – prices, interest rates, or outputs – are being fed into it from elsewhere in the model. We call this a *monetary-dominant (MD) regime*. Price determination is independent of fiscal solvency, and the central bank can control the price level without working through the present value budget constraint.

At this point, we should emphasize the generality of the view we are presenting here. In particular, we do not need to assume that prices are 'flexible'. Woodford (1995, 1996) has for example extended the analysis to a model in which the current price level is partially or completely predetermined; he obtains results that are consistent with what we report here.

To summarize, then, when primary surpluses are determined in an arbitrary way (that is, independent of the level of public debt), the price level is determined by the present value budget constraint, to assure solvency of the government. Price stability is subject to the vacillations of fiscal policy. The central bank is not functionally independent of the government's fiscal policy; it has to work through its transfers the Treasury to control the price level, and (we will argue in the next section) this may not be feasible in practice. We call this a FD regime. If on the other hand primary surpluses (inclusive of central bank transfers) have a tendency to increase when public debt is rising too fast, then the present value budget constraint is automatically satisfied, and the price level is determined elsewhere. The central bank is functionally independent of the government's fiscal policy; it does not have to work through seigniorage to achieve price stability. We call this a MD regime.

Implications for Debt Reduction

The present chapter is primarily concerned with fiscal constraints on monetary policy, and developing a definition of 'functional' central bank independence. However, it turns out that the FD and MD regimes have surprising different implications for debt reduction. Since debt reduction plays an important role in the Maastricht Treaty, and therefore the future of monetary policy in Europe, we pause to draw these implications out.

In a MD regime, primary surpluses are controlling the growth in the debt to GDP ratio. An increase in this period's primary surplus means that future debt to GDP ratios will be smaller. This is not true in a FD regime. An increase in this period's primary surplus means an increase in this period's debt to GDP ratio, and no change in future debt to GDP ratios. This rather paradoxical result follows immediately from the present value constraint (5.2). Suppose this period's surplus, s_t, is increased, while all future surpluses are expected to stay the same as before. This period, the right-hand side of (5.2) increases, and the left-hand side has to increase in response (through a fall, or a less rapid rise, in the price level). On the other hand, starting in period $t+1$, the surpluses (and their present value) are the same as before; so, the real value of future debt to GDP ratios will not be affected by this period's fiscal contraction. The analogy to coupon bonds may be helpful here. Suppose we have two bonds whose coupons differ only in the current period; their market value will be identical from the next period on.

This suggests that countries operating in a FD regime will have a very difficult time meeting the Treaty's debt criteria. Clearly, the framers of the Treaty envisioned the debt dynamics of a MD regime.

Operating Procedures and Nominal Anchors

Many central banks set short-term nominal interest rates in an attempt to control either inflation or money growth. Canzoneri (1994) reviews an old literature that questions whether such a procedure can serve as a nominal anchor; that literature asserts that the price level is not determined under such a monetary policy. This price indeterminacy may or may not be a problem in reality, but it does raise methodological problems for central bank staff members when they formulate models for policy evaluation. The new research on price determination sheds some light on this controversy.

A traditional discussion of the price indeterminacy problem would proceed as follows: In a Keynesian model, the real interest rate is determined by an *IS* curve (in conjunction with an output supply curve); in a more neoclassical model it is determined by an Euler equation describing the intertemporal substitution of consumption. In any case, we have just been assuming that the real interest rate is a constant:

$$i_t - (P_{t+1} - P_t)/P_t = r \tag{5.6}$$

If the central bank is setting the money base M_{t+1} (in an attempt to control either inflation or, say, M2 growth), then (5.1) and (5.6) have to simultaneously determine P_t and i_t. Here, there is no problem.[8] On the other hand, if the central bank is setting i_t (in an attempt to control inflation or money growth), then there is a problem. Here, (5.1) and (5.6) have to determine P_t and M_{t+1}. (5.6) determines the rate of inflation, but not the level P_t; and (5.1) cannot determine M_{t+1} unless P_t is known. (The same would be true even if velocity depended on the nominal interest rate.) Real variables are determined, but there is no nominal anchor.

The traditional discussion of this problem makes no mention of the government budget constraint, and this is where the new research on price determination makes a contribution. In a FD regime, the present value budget constraint, (5.2), can determine the price level. If the central bank is setting the nominal interest rate, then central bank transfers, τ_t, are determined, and the right-hand side of (5.2) is fixed. P_t has to adjust to make the real value of the existing debt equal to the present value of current and (expected) future surpluses. With P_t determined by (5.2), (5.1) can determine the money base, M_{t+1}. Everything is pinned down. The need for fiscal solvency provides a nominal anchor, even when the central bank sets the nominal interest rate instead of the money base. This fundamental point was made in most of the papers referenced in the introduction.

There are, however, two additional points that tend to get lost. First, in a FD regime, the central bank loses control of base money if, as in (5.1), base velocity is insensitive to the interest rate. If the central bank tried to set base money, M_{t+1}, instead of the nominal interest rate, then the price level would be overdetermined. Second, in a MD regime, the present value budget constraint is always satisfied; it is of no use in determining the price level. In this case, we are back to where we started. (5.1) and (5.6) have to simultaneously determine P_t and i_t if the central bank sets M_{t+1}, and they have to determine P_t and M_{t+1} if the central bank sets i_t.

Summarizing, the question of whether a given operating procedure provides a nominal anchor depends on the policy regime that is in place. In a FD regime, the price level is determined when the central bank sets the nominal interest rate, but may be overdetermined if the central bank tries to set the monetary base. In a MD regime, the price level is determined when the central bank sets the monetary base, but not when it sets the nominal interest rate; in this case, the traditional view of the indeterminacy problem remains.

SOME PRACTICAL EXERCISES: CHANGES IN FISCAL AND MONETARY TARGETS

In this section we analyze the interactions between fiscal and monetary targets (and shocks) in alternative policy regimes. To illustrate the quantitative magnitudes of the effects involved, we assume that the Belgian and German economies can be characterized as MD regimes; we use Italy and Spain to illustrate our results for FD regimes. We pick two countries in each regime because some of our quantitative results depend on the size of the debt to GDP ratio. Belgium and Italy are high-debt countries, while Germany and Spain are low-debt countries.

Our assignment of countries to regimes is, of course, impressionistic and used mainly for the purpose of exposition. The calculations presented below can be easily performed for any country assumed to be in a particular regime, using the data in Table 5.1. Also, all of our calculations are linear; multiplying the size of the change in the primary surplus or inflation target by a constant would multiply the magnitude of all the effects by the same constant.

To quantify our results, we use the relevant figures for 1995 reported in Table 5.1. The figures for total and primary budget balances as percentages of GDP are the OECD figures for 'General Government Financial

Table 5.1 Fiscal and monetary variables as percentages of GDP, 1995

Country	Monetary base*	Net public-sector liabilities	Primary budget balance	Total budget balance
Belgium	6.1	128.4	+4.2	−4.4
France	3.4	35.0	−1.8	−5.0
Germany	9.0	49.0	+0.2	−3.1
Italy	13.0	109.2	+2.9	−7.4
Spain	12.8	49.9	−1.1	−6.0
United Kingdom	4.0	38.8	−2.1	−5.0
United States	6.4	51.5	+0.5	−1.6

Note: * The monetary base figure for Belgium is for 1992, the Italian figure is for 1993. The 1995 figures were not available.
Sources: The monetary base and GDP figures were taken from *International Financial Statistics*. The fiscal data were taken from the OECD's *Economic Outlook*.

Balances' and 'General Government Primary Balances'. Our figures for the debt to GDP ratio are the OECD figures for 'General Government Net Financial Liabilities'. In some of our thought experiments, we also use the OECD projections (as of December 1995) for fiscal balances and debt to GDP ratios in 1996 and 1997. Our monetary base and GDP figures are from *International Financial Statistics*.

Fiscal and Monetary Targets in the MD Regime

The interdependence of fiscal and monetary policies (and targets) in the MD regime is essentially the same as their interdependence in a model with *real* bonds, discussed in the literature following Sargent and Wallace (1981). We briefly review the relevant effects and magnitudes below, mainly to set the stage for contrasting them with the interactions of fiscal and monetary policies under the FD regime.

Consider first the fiscal consequences of a decrease in the central bank's inflation target. Lower inflation leads to a loss of revenues from seigniorage or, equivalently, to a decrease in central bank transfers. In a MD regime, the fiscal authority must increase current and/or future primary surpluses to offset this loss of revenue. The particular fiscal adjustment rule we used in the last section − (5.5) − implies that s_j is adjusted each period to offset any change in τ_j. The questions here are: how much does the surplus have to be increased to accommodate a given reduction in the inflation target? Will the monetary tightening cause a severe fiscal problem?

Viewed from the perspective of central bank transfers, changing the interest rate by Δi_t changes transfers by approximately:

$$\Delta\tau_t = (1/V)\Delta[i_t/(1+i_t)] \approx (1/V)\Delta i_t = (1/V)\Delta\pi_t \qquad (5.7)$$

where we are ignoring the effect of changes in interest rates (or inflation) on velocity (V). The last equality in (5.7) reflects the fact that in our model, monetary policy has no effect on the real interest rate; changes in the nominal interest rate, i_t, are synonymous with changes in (expected) inflation, π_t, between dates t and $t+1$.

The ratio of the monetary base to GDP (which equals $1/V$) was 9 per cent for Germany in 1995, and 6.1 per cent for Belgium in 1992 (the latest figure available). Thus, reducing the inflation rate (or the nominal interest rate) by 1 percentage point would reduce the ratio of central bank transfers to GDP by 0.09 percentage points for Germany, and by 0.06 percentage points for Belgium.[9] These are the revenue losses that would have to be offset by an equal increase in the ratio of the primary surplus to GDP, s_t, and they seem quite small.

The main point here is that, in a MD regime, the fiscal consequences of changing the nominal interest rate or the inflation target are small. The reason is that most EU countries no longer rely very heavily on the inflation tax. An independent monetary policy should not put heavy burdens on fiscal policy.[10]

Turning to the effects of changes in fiscal policy, we temporarily suspend our particular fiscal rule in (5.5) above because this rule does not allow us to entertain the possibility of an exogenous increase in the primary surplus. Instead of using (5.4) or (5.5), we think of a MD regime as one in which monetary policy sets the path of the price level, and fiscal policy adjusts to satisfy the present value budget constraint (5.2). By definition, in such a regime, changes in fiscal policy have no implication for the inflation rate.

The fiscal trade-offs associated with increasing the primary surplus by Δs_t are the familiar ones. One possibility is that the primary surplus is allowed to decrease at some future date. For example, s_{t+1} may be changed to satisfy $\Delta s_t + \beta\Delta s_{t+1} = 0$. More to the point in the EC context, some countries (in particular, Belgium) may use an increase in the current primary surplus to reduce their debt to GDP ratio. This trade-off is given by $\Delta s_t + \beta\Delta(W_{t+1}/P_{t+1}y_{t+1}) = 0$. If, for example, the ratio of the primary surplus to GDP is increased by 1 percentage point, next period's debt to GDP ratio drops by slightly more than one percentage point, due to interest savings on current debt.

The above decrease in future debt to GDP ratios would move the country closer to meeting the fiscal convergence criteria of the Maastricht treaty, both in terms of the 60 per cent target for the ratio of debt to GDP and in terms of the 3 per cent target for the ratio of the total deficit (inclusive of interest payments) to GDP. In Belgium, for example, the ratio of the total deficit to GDP was 4.4 per cent in 1995, despite a primary surplus amounting to 4.2 per cent of GDP. If the primary surplus had been increased to 6.2 per cent, the debt to GDP ratio of 1996 would drop by slightly more than 2 per cent – from 126.5 per cent (according to the OECD projection) to 124.5, in terms of net public sector debt. At a nominal interest rate of 7 per cent the associate reduction in interest payments would be 0.14 per cent of GDP.

The above figures illustrate the well known point that a country like Belgium would need very large primary surpluses for many years before the ratio of debt to GDP was adjusted to an 'acceptable level' according to the Maastricht treaty. The adjustment process, however, as painful and slow as it may be, does move the debt to GDP ratio in the right direction in the long run. As such, our results for the MD regime are consistent with the conventional wisdom on how primary surpluses affect future debt. By contrast, as we will see in the following subsection, the dynamics of debt are quite different (and intuitively less obvious) in a FD regime.

Fiscal and Monetary Targets in the FD Regime

In a FD regime, changes in fiscal and monetary targets affect the equilibrium value of the debt to GDP ratio, and thereby the current price level, via the present value government budget constraint (5.2). Consider first a change in s_t. Holding the other terms on the right-hand side of (5.2) constant, this change is matched by an equal change in the debt to GDP ratio:

$$\Delta\{W_t/P_t y_t\} = \Delta s_t \qquad (5.8)$$

That is, if s_t were higher by 1 percentage point, the price level would be sufficiently lower to increase the debt to GDP ratio by 1 percentage point.

The above increase in net liabilities would be offset by the effect of the primary surplus on next period's debt, leaving the debt to GDP ratio of period $t+1$ equal to what it would have been in the absence of the increase in s_t; that is, $\Delta\{W_{t+1}/P_{t+1}y_{t+1}\} = 0$. This surprising result can be understood better by considering the analogue of (5.2) for date $t+1$. The ratio of debt to GDP at date $t+1$ must equal the present value of primary surpluses and central bank transfers from date $t+1$ onwards $(s_j + \tau_j,$ for $j = t+1, t+2, \ldots)$. If these future surpluses and transfers do not change, the debt to GDP ratio of date $t+1$ does not change either. Thus, for a country that is caught in a FD regime, a one-period increase in the primary surplus to GDP ratio just increases the current debt to GDP ratio, without reducing the long-run debt to GDP ratio at all. A country with a large debt to GDP ratio would have difficulty in meeting the Maastricht Treaty's debt criterion, and if the country was not admitted to the monetary union in the first round, its problems would be compounded. Suppose, say, Italy is required to reduce its deficit to GDP ratio for n years in order to qualify, and suppose that once the new criterion is met, primary balances are expected to go back to their original levels. Then, by the same line of reasoning, we would get:

$$\Delta\{W_t/P_t y_t\} = \Delta s_t + \beta\Delta s_{t+1} + \ldots + \beta^{n-1}\Delta s_{t+n-1} \tag{5.9}$$

and $\Delta\{W_{t+n}/P_{t+n} y_{t+n}\} = 0$. Note that the longer the increase in the primary surplus is required to last (i.e. the larger is n) the bigger is the effect on the current debt to GDP ratio.

Since the nominal value of the debt, W_t, is predetermined, the ratio of the debt to GDP adjusts to its equilibrium value via changes in nominal GDP, which in our model reflect changes in the price level. The implied price level changes can be calculated from:

$$\Delta\{W_t/P_t y_t\} = -(\Delta P_t/P_t)\{W_t/P_t y_t\} \tag{5.10}$$

where $\Delta P_t/P_t$ measures the disinflationary impact of the hypothetical fiscal contraction we are contemplating. Note that for a fixed value of the left-hand side change, the disinflationary effect is inversely related to the debt to GDP ratio. That is, the same fiscal contraction is more disinflationary in a low-debt country like Spain than in a high-debt country like Italy.

Consider next a change in the nominal interest rate, i_t, or (equivalently) in the expected central bank target, π_t, for inflation between dates t and $t + 1$. The impact on central bank transfers is given by (5.7) above. The associated change in the debt to GDP ratio, implied by (5.2), is:

$$\Delta\{W_t/P_t y_t\} = \Delta\tau_t == (1/V)i_t = (1/V)\Delta\pi_t \tag{5.11}$$

This equation is analogous to (5.8) and has the same interpretation. The only difference is that (5.8) deals with changes in the primary surplus, while (5.11) deals with central bank transfers. The analogy highlights the fact that, in a FD regime, only fiscal aspects of monetary policy affect the current price level. Again, the price changes associated with the implied changes in the left-hand side of (5.11) can be calculated from (5.10).

Before attempting to quantify the above effects, we should emphasize that our calculations for changes in the current price level are based on a model with no price rigidities. In our neoclassical model, the current price level jumps immediately in response to inflationary or deflationary pressures. In reality, of course, the price level adjusts to such pressures slowly in the short run. Thus, the inflationary (deflationary) effects calculated below would correspond to the Keynesian concepts of an inflationary (recessionary) gap, which would impinge on output as well as the price level in the short run.

Consider now a 1 percentage point increase in the ratio of the current primary surplus to GDP ($\Delta s_t = 0.01$), leaving all the other terms on the right-hand side of (5.2) unchanged. As noted above, this change will raise the equilibrium value of the debt to GDP ratio by 1 percentage point: $\Delta\{W_t/P_t y_t\} = 0.01$. The associated effect on the current price level depends on debt to GDP ratio.

For Italy, net public debt was about 109 per cent of GDP in 1995. So, (5.10) implies $0.01 = -1.09(\Delta P_t/P_t)$, which yields $\Delta P_t/P_t = -0.009$. That is, the current price level would have to be 0.9 percentage points lower than what it would have been in the absence of the fiscal contraction. A fiscal change of the same magnitude ($\Delta s_t = 0.01$) would have a larger disinflationary effect in Spain, where net public debt is about 50 per cent of GDP. To reduce the debt to GDP ratio by 1 percentage point, the inflation rate would have to drop by 2 percentage points.

Could the central bank easily offset deflationary pressures of the above magnitudes? Not likely! In a FD regime, to offset the deflationary effect of a fiscal contraction, the central bank would have to hold the debt to GDP ratio constant; it would have to set $\Delta\tau_t = -\Delta s_t = -0.01$ in (5.2). From (5.7), we can calculate the requisite change in the current interest rate: $\Delta i_t = V\Delta\tau_t = -0.01$. The monetary base was 13.0 per cent of GDP for Italy in 1993 (the latest figure available), and 12.8 per cent of GDP for Spain in 1995; so, we can set $V = 1/0.13 = 7.7$ for both countries. In either country, the nominal interest rate would have to be lowered by 7.7 percentage points to offset the deflationary effect of a one percentage point increase in the ratio of the primary surplus to GDP! A policy change of this magnitude is not plausible.

The preceding exercise was cast in terms of the disinflationary effects of further fiscal contractions. A more topical thought experiment for some EC countries is to calculate the inflationary effects that would result from an announcement that planned fiscal contractions would be delayed or not materialize at all. According to the 1995 OECD projections, Italy's primary surplus will increase from 2.9 per cent of GDP in 1995 to 3.8 per cent in 1996 and to 4.3 per cent in 1997. The projected fiscal contraction for Spain is from a 1.1 per cent primary deficit in 1995 to a 0.4 per cent surplus in 1996 and a 1.3 per cent surplus in 1997. These projections represent sizable fiscal contractions, and one may ask what would happen if they had to be revised.

Suppose for example that 'bad news' leads to the expectation that Spain will only be able to attain a primary budget balance in 1996 and 1997, rather than the more ambitious OECD projections. This change of expectations corresponds to setting $n = 2$, $\Delta s_t = -0.004$ and $\Delta s_{t+1} = -0.013$ in

(5.9). Suppose we set $\beta = 0.98$;[11] then (5.9) implies $\Delta\{W_t/P_t y_t\} = -0.004 - 0.98(0.013) = -0.017$. With a net public debt amounting to 50 per cent of GDP, (5.10) implies $\Delta P_t/P_t = 0.034$. That is, the current inflation rate would have to rise by 3.4 percentage points. And as in the preceding example, this inflationary pressure could not be offset by an interest rate change of plausible magnitude.

Consider next a more direct thought experiment on the trade-off between the interest rate and the current price level. Suppose the central bank has announced a 1 per cent decrease in its inflation target π_t (for the change in prices between date t and date $t + 1$), and suppose no change in the primary surplus to GDP ratio is contemplated. We saw earlier that reducing the nominal interest rate (or the inflation target, π_t) by 1 percentage point in either Spain or Italy would reduce the current debt to GDP ratio by $\Delta\tau_t = 1/V = 0.13$ per cent. The implied change in the current price level can be calculated by setting the debt to GDP ratio equal to 0.50 for Spain, and 1.09 for Italy. For Italy, $\Delta P_t/P_t = 0.0013/1.09 = 0.0012$, a 0.12 per cent increase. For Spain, $\Delta P_t/P_t = 0.0013/0.50 = 0.0026$, a 0.26 per cent increase.

Two aspects of the above calculation are noteworthy. First, although the central bank has some leverage in affecting the current price level in the FD regime, the trade-off between the nominal interest rate and the current price level is quite steep: large changes in interest rates are required to move the price level by small amounts. This point was implicit in our earlier experiment setting $\Delta s_t + \Delta\tau_t = 0$.

Second, the sign of the trade-off between the nominal interest rate and the price level does not accord with our usual (Keynesian) intuition. To see this point, note that in our Neoclassical model, a lower nominal interest rate requires a monetary contraction – that is, a lower (expected) growth rate of the monetary base. So, in the FD regime, increasing the current price level requires an expected monetary contraction. Perhaps, a more transparent way of stating the result is that a *decrease* in expected future inflation *raises* the current price level.

This last observation motivates a final thought experiment. To meet the Maastricht convergence criterion, countries like Italy and Spain need to reduce their inflation rates and increase their primary surpluses. What would happen to the price level if the requisite monetary adjustment is expected to occur but the fiscal contraction is not? The answer, in a FD regime, is that the economy would face short-run inflationary pressures despite a credible commitment to long-run disinflation. This might lead the central bank, and the private sector, to believe that (in the short run anyway) the price level is beyond the central bank's control.

To get a sense of the magnitudes involved, suppose the expected path of the primary surplus does not change in Italy but the inflation target (the nominal interest rate) is reduced by 1 percentage point for all future dates. From (5.7), we get

$$\Delta\tau_j = (1/V)\Delta\pi_j = 0.13(-0.01) = -0.0013, \text{ for all } j = t, t+1, \ldots \quad (5.12)$$

From (5.2), we know that the present value of these foregone central bank transfers must be matched by the change in the debt to GDP ratio:

$$\Delta\{W_t/P_t y_t\} = (1 - \beta)^{-1}\Delta\tau = -0.0013/0.02 = -0.065 \quad (5.13)$$

a 6.5 per cent decrease. From (5.10), the increase in the price level for Italy would be $\Delta P_t/P_t = 0.065/1.09 = 0.06$; the current price level would have to increase by 6 percentage points. Conducting the same thought experiment for Spain would yield the same (6.5 per cent) decrease in the debt to GDP ratio (because Italy and Spain have roughly the same base velocity). But since the ratio of debt to GDP is only 50 per cent in Spain, the requisite change in the price level would be much larger: $\Delta P_t/P_t = 0.065/0.50 = 0.13$, a 13 per cent increase.

The numerical implications of the above thought experiment, unlike those of our earlier experiments, are sensitive to the value of β, because we are calculating the present value of forgone central bank transfers. The numerical values would be twice as large if we set $\beta = 0.99$; setting $\beta = 0.96$ would cut the numerical values in half. Nevertheless, for all plausible values of β, the short-run inflationary pressures associated with long-run disinflation are sizable. This is in sharp contrast with the MD regime, where a change in monetary policy was immediately successful. The bottom line here is that in a FD regime, a credible commitment to a lower inflation target requires an auxiliary fiscal commitment to larger primary surpluses, to offset the short run inflationary pressures.

WHICH REGIME IS OPERATIVE? CAN THE MD REGIME BE ASSURED?

In the last section, we assumed for illustrative purposes that Germany and Belgium were in the MD regime while Spain and Italy were in the FD regime. We gave no justification for making those assignments, and indeed we had none to offer. It is quite possible, for example, that the Banco de España – with its new 'legal independence' and its recent emphasis on inflation targeting – is now operating in a MD regime. In this section, we discuss the possibility of testing for which regime is operative, and we will discuss legislative ways of ensuring the MD regime, which we have equated with 'functional independence' of the central bank.

Testing for which Regime is Operative

There would seem to be two approaches to determining which regime is operative. First, one might use time series data to test whether primary surpluses tend to increase when the debt to GDP ratio is rising too rapidly; this would be evidence of the MD regime. In particular, one could look for a relationship like (5.5) in the data. Second, one might ask how recent monetary and fiscal shocks have affected price levels or exchange rates; the last section suggests that a given shock should have different effects in the two regimes. We have not tried either approach yet. The most we can do here is discuss the strengths and weaknesses of each approach.

There are two potential difficulties with the time series approach. The Maastricht Treaty has given some governments an incentive to be more fiscally conservative, and fiscal policy formation may be different now from what it was just a few years ago. The Treaty also requires member countries to make their central banks legislatively independent, and there has been some movement in this direction in a number of countries. Moreover, the currency crises of 1992–3 made some central banks change their operating procedures. Given all this institutional change, one might worry that the regimes have shifted, and that there is not yet enough data to test which regime is currently operative in most EU countries.

The second difficulty with the time series approach is that (5.5) is an overly stringent characterization of what is needed to ensure the FD regime. In the Appendix, we show that the debt to GDP target, θ, can actually be growing without bound (so long as it is not growing too fast). There may be econometric difficulties in testing for the more general formulation presented in the appendix. But, we will not pursue these issues here.

The second approach – documenting the effects of recent shocks – may be more promising. If, for example, prices and exchange rates are extremely sensitive to news about current and future deficits, then this would be evidence in favor of the FD regime. In any case, this too is left to future research.

Legislating 'Functional Independence'

We have argued that a central bank is 'functionally independent' if it is operating within a MD regime. Only then is it free to set the price level independently of the present value government budget constraint and (if it so chooses) without regard to the needs of fiscal solvency. The Maastricht Treaty tries to legislate independence by assuring that the central bank's decision-makers are free from political influence, and this may well be important in and of itself. But, as we have seen, a MD regime places restrictions on fiscal decision-making, and not political influence on the central bank. Legislation that assures functional independence must make primary surpluses (inclusive of central bank transfers) increase when the debt to GDP ratio is growing too rapidly. Here, we explore the types of legislated rules that would result in a MD regime.

Interestingly, the Maastricht Treaty's deficit criterion is just such a rule. It says that the primary deficit (inclusive of central bank transfers, which are included in government receipts) plus interest payments on the debt may not exceed 3 per cent of GDP; in our notation:

$$-s_j - \tau_j + i_j w_j \leqslant 0.03 \tag{5.14}$$

When this constraint is binding, the deficit criterion can be rewritten as:

$$s_j + \tau_j = i_j w_j - 0.03 \tag{5.15}$$

Since nominal interest rates are always positive, this is just the sort of fiscal response that guarantees a MD regime.

Some might argue that the Maastricht Treaty's deficit criteria is unrealistic for some countries, and therefore not credible. Italy, for example, is already running large primary surpluses, but will probably not be able to meet the 3 per cent limit in 1997 because of the huge interest payments on its debt. If (5.15) lacks credibility, then it can not ensure a MD regime.

It is interesting to ask therefore if the deficit criterion could be modified for some countries, while still assuring a MD regime. It might seem reasonable for example to put a lower limit on the primary surplus to GDP ratio for a high-debt country. But, this would not suffice. A MD regime requires that the primary surplus respond in a systematic way to the level of the debt.

There are simple modifications of the Maastricht Treaty's deficit criterion that would ease the burden on high-debt countries and still assure a MD regime. For example, the 'deficit' could be redefined to be the primary deficit plus, say, half of the interest payments on the debt. (5.15) would become:

$$s_j + \tau_j = 1/2 i_j w_j - 0.03 \tag{5.16}$$

The fraction could be chosen to make the deficit criterion feasible, and therefore credible. (5.16) ensures a MD regime just as well as (5.15), if it is believed by the financial markets.

A further modification of the deficit criterion could eliminate a perverse incentive that exists with either (5.15) or (5.16). In particular, the government of a high-debt country has incentive to put pressure on its central bank to lower interest rates just to make it easier to qualify for EMU. To eliminate this incentive, the term $1/2i_t$ could be replaced with a constant fraction α. (5.15) would become:

$$s_j + \tau_j = \alpha w_j - 0.03 \qquad (5.17)$$

This rule would ensure a MD regime, and the government could not blame the central bank if it did not qualify for EMU because of the deficit criterion.

In any case, the Maastricht Treaty's fiscal convergence criterion is not likely to be revised. There is, however, a question as to how strictly it should be interpreted. Our analysis supports the view that the deficit criterion (perhaps in a modified form) should be interpreted quite strictly. Strict adherence to the deficit criterion would ensure a MD regime, and a central bank that is 'functionally independent'. The debt criterion is less closely related to functional independence and could, from this point of view anyway, be interpreted more liberally.

CONCLUSION

Standard textbook discussions of the interactions between fiscal and monetary policies are usually cast in terms of theoretical models in which the government issues real (indexed) bonds. Our conventional wisdom, based on these models, has recently been challenged by a new theory of price determination which recognizes that governments issue nominal debt. In a model with nominal bonds, the determination of the price level and the interactions between fiscal and monetary targets critically depend on whether the path of future primary surpluses is expected to respond to the debt to GDP ratio.

If an increase in the debt to GDP ratio is expected to generate a fiscal policy response, increasing the ratio of the primary surplus to GDP, the economy operates in a monetary-dominant (MD) regime. In this case, our conventional wisdom (based on models with real government debt) essentially applies. First, monetary policy can control the current price level; changes in the primary surplus and in the long-run inflation target do not pose a threat to short-run price stability. Second, the fiscal consequences of long-run disinflation are not very significant for European countries; the primary surplus increases within each period to offset the small loss of revenues from central bank transfers. Third, a transitory increase in the primary surplus reduces the long-run debt to GDP ratio.

By contrast, if the path of the primary surplus is expected to be independent of the debt to GDP ratio, the economy operates in a fiscal-dominant (FD) regime. In this regime, the current price level is determined by the government's present value budget constraint. Decreases in current and (expected) future surpluses create short-run inflationary pressures. These pressures are likely to be too severe to be offset by changes in monetary policy (the requisite changes in the interest rate are too large). Moreover, a credible commitment to long-run disinflation leads to short-run inflationary pressures, unless it is accompanied by a credible commitment to larger primary surpluses. Finally, a transitory increase in the ratio of the primary surplus to GDP does not affect the debt to GDP ratio in the long run.

A central bank is 'functionally independent' when it is operating in a MD regime. Only then can the central bank be given a mandate of price stability, and held accountable for the results. It turns out that the Maastricht treaty's deficit criterion provides sufficient fiscal discipline to put the economy in a MD regime. Less stringent fiscal rules assuring a MD regime could also be legislated. A simple example would be a cap on the sum of the primary deficit to GDP ratio and a small fraction of the debt to GDP ratio. In any case, the present analysis provides support for a strict interpretation of the deficit criterion. The debt criterion is less closely related to functional independence and could thus be interpreted more liberally. However, as we have already noted, some would argue that the debt criterion is necessary for 'political independence', another matter entirely.

Appendix

In this technical appendix, we do three things. First, we show how to derive the period by period budget constraint (5.3). Second, we show how to derive the present value budget constraint (5.2). And finally, we prove an assertion that was made about the MD regime; in particular, we show that if primary surpluses (inclusive of central bank transfers) tend to increase when the debt to GDP ratio rises too rapidly, then the present value budget constraint is satisfied for any real value of the existing debt.

DERIVING (3), THE PERIOD BY PERIOD GOVERNMENT BUDGET CONSTRAINT

In nominal terms, the period j constraint is:

$$B_j = (T_j - G_j) + (M_{j+1} - M_j) + B_{j+1}/(1 + i_j) \qquad (5.A1)$$

(5.A1) says that the existing debt has to be financed by the primary surplus $(T_j - G_j)$, base money creation (via the central bank's acquisition of public debt), or borrowing from the private sector. The first step is to divide by nominal GDP, $P_j y_j$, to express the variables as ratios to GDP:

$$B_j/P_j y_j = (T_j - G_j)/P_j y_j + (M_{j+1} - M_j)/P_j y_j \\ + (P_{j+1} y_{j+1}/P_j y_j)(B_{j+1}/P_{j+1} y_{j+1})/(1 + i_j) \qquad (5.A2)$$

Defining growth and inflation rates by:

$$y_{j+1} = (1 + n_j)y_j \text{ and } P_{j+1} = (1 + \pi_j)P_j \qquad (5.A3)$$

and the real interest rate, r_j, by:

$$(1 + r_j) = (1 + i_j)/(1 + \pi_j) \qquad (5.A4)$$

(5.A2) becomes:

$$B_j/P_j y_j = s_j + (M_{j+1} - M_j)/P_j y_j + \left[(1 + n_j)(1 + \pi_j)/(1 + i_j)\right](B_{j+1}/P_{j+1} y_{j+1}) \\ = s_j + (M_{j+1} - M_j)/P_j y_j + \left[(1 + n_j)/(1 + r_j)\right](B_{j+1}/P_{j+1} y_{j+1}) \qquad (5.A5)$$

The next step is to convert this constraint into a constraint in $W(=B+M)$. Taking $M_j/P_j y_j$ to the left-hand side of (5.A5), and using (5.A3) and (5.A4):

$$
\begin{aligned}
(B_j + M_j)/P_j y_j &= s_j + M_{j+1}/P_j y_j + [(1+n_j)/(1+r_j)](B_{j+1}/P_{j+1} y_{j+1}) \\
&= s_j + (M_{j+1}/P_j y_j)\{1 - [(1+n_j)/(1+r_j)](P_j y_j/P_{j+1} y_{j+1})\} \\
&\quad + [(1+n_j)/(1+r_j)](B_{j+1} + M_{j+1})/P_{j+1} y_{j+1} \\
&= s_j + (M_{j+1}/P_j y_j)\{1 - [(1+n_j)/(1+r_j)]/[(1+n_j)(1+\pi_j)]\} \\
&\quad + [(1+n_j)/(1+r_j)](B_{j+1} + M_{j+1})/P_{j+1} y_{j+1} \\
&= s_j + (M_{j+1}/P_j y_j)[i_j/(1+i_j)] \\
&\quad + [(1+n_j)/(1+r_j)](B_{j+1} + M_{j+1})/P_{j+1} y_{j+1} \\
&= s_j + \tau_j + \beta[(B_{j+1} + M_{j+1})/P_{j+1} y_{j+1}]
\end{aligned}
$$

$$(5.A6)$$

This is (5.3) in the text.

DERIVING (5.2) THE PRESENT VALUE GOVERNMENT BUDGET CONSTRAINT

Iterating (5.A6) forward from the current period (that is, period t):

$$
(B_t + M_t)/P_t y_t = \sum_{j=t}^{\infty} \beta^{j-t}(s_j + \tau_j) + \lim_{T \to \infty} [\beta^T (B_{t+T} + M_{t+T})/P_t + T^y_{t+T}]
$$

$$(5.A7)$$

The consumer's transversality condition implies that the last term vanishes. So, (5.A7) reduces to (5.2) in the text.

PROVING THE ASSERTION ABOUT MD REGIMES

First, we generalize (5.4) to:

$$
w_{j+1} - \theta_{j+1} = \lambda(w_j - \theta_j) \tag{5.A8}
$$

where $w_j = (B_j + M_j)/P_j y_j$, $\theta_{j+1} = \gamma\theta_j$, $\gamma < 1/\beta$, and $\lambda < 1/\beta$. The debt to GDP target, θ_j, need not be a fixed number, as in the text. Indeed, it can grow without bound, but it can not be growing at a rate faster than $1/\beta = (1+r)/(1+n)$. Moreover, the actual debt to GDP ratio does not even have to converge on the target, but the deviation, $w_j - \theta_j$, cannot grow at a rate faster than $1/\beta = (1+r)/(1+n)$.

The surplus policy that results in (5.A8) can be found by substituting (5.A8) into (5.A6):

$$
\begin{aligned}
s_j + \tau_j &= -\beta w_{j+1} + w_j = -\beta(w_{j+1} - \theta_{j+1}) + (w_j - \theta_j) - \beta\theta_{j+1} + \theta_j \\
&= (1 - \beta\lambda)(w_j - \theta_j) + (1 - \beta\gamma)\theta_j
\end{aligned}
\tag{5.A9}
$$

Note that the restriction on λ implies that the coefficient $(1 - \beta\lambda)$ is positive. (5.A9) says that the surplus (inclusive of central bank transfers) must increase when the debt to GDP ratio is rising too quickly.

We want to prove the following lemma.

Lemma: If fiscal policy is guided by the rule (5.A9), then the present value constraint (5.2) is satisfied for any real value of the existing debt, $(B_t + M_t)/P_t y_t$.

The proof is straightforward. Using (5.A9) and (5.A8),

$$
\begin{aligned}
\sum_{j=t}^{\infty} \beta^{j-t}(s_j + \tau_j) &= \sum_{j=t}^{\infty} \beta^{j-t}[(1 - \beta\lambda)(w_j - \theta_j) + (1 - \beta\gamma)\theta_j] \\
&= \sum_{j=t}^{\infty} \beta^{j-t}[(1 - \beta\lambda)\lambda^{j-t}(w_j - \theta_j) + (1 - \beta\gamma)\gamma^{j-t}\theta_j] \\
&= [(1 - \beta\lambda)/(1 - \beta\lambda)](w_t - \theta_t) + [(1 - \beta\gamma)/(1 - \beta\gamma)]\theta_t \\
&= w_t
\end{aligned}
$$

$$
\tag{5.A13}
$$

This completes the proof of the lemma.

Notes

1   The debt to GDP ratios in Figure 5.1 come from the OECD's *Economic Outlook*. The OECD's definition of 'General Government Gross Financial Liabilities' differs slightly from the Maastricht Treaty's definition of gross debt.
2   Spain's debt is however rising rapidly.
3   Woodford (1996) extends the analysis to a model in which the current price level is predetermined. He comes to much the same conclusions as we do.
4   To arrive at our definition from the OECD figures, we should subtract central bank assets denominated in domestic currency and add the monetary base.

Quantitatively, however, the size of this adjustment (which equals the difference between net international reserves and the central bank's net worth) is a
negligible fraction of GDP.

5   The debt to GDP ratios in Figure 5.2 are for 'General Government Net
     Financial Liabilities'. They are taken from the OECD's *Economic Outlook*.

6   The target, θ, can actually be growing, and at a rate that is explosive, so long
     as it is not growing faster than the discount factor; that is, we can let
     $\theta_{j+1} = \gamma\theta_j$ where $\gamma \leqslant 1/\beta$. This more general case is treated in the Appendix.

7   This follows from substituting (5.4) into the period by period equation for the
     evolution of government debt.

8   That is, $P_t = (V/y_t)M_{t+1}$ from (1), and $i_t \approx r + (\mu - n)$ from (5.2), where μ is
     the growth rate of base money and n is the growth rate of GDP.

9   These calculations pertain to an anticipated change in inflation. An unantici-
     pated change in the current price level would affect the real value of out-
     standing government debt. We won't attempt to quantify this effect because
     our model with one-period bonds is not likely to yield reliable figures, which
     would require data on the maturity structure of outstanding government debt.

10   A monetary tightening would of course have further budgetary consequences
     if it were to cause a decline in GDP. Our discussion generally abstracts from
     'Keynesian' problems.

11   To estimate β, we calculated the average values of $(1 + n)/(1 + r)$ across var-
     ious years and countries. The results were typically between 0.97 and 0.99.

References

AUERNHEIMER, L. and B. CONTRERAS (1990) 'Control of the interest rate
    with a government budget constraint: determinacy of the price level, and other
    results', mimeo.
BERGIN, P. R. (n.d.) 'Fiscal restrictions in a currency union: further lessons on the
    interaction of monetary and fiscal policies', mimeo.
CANZONERI, M. (1994) 'Inflation targeting and nominal anchors', September,
    mimeo.
LEEPER, E. (1991) 'Equilibria under "active" and "passive" monetary policies',
    Journal of Monetary Economics, 27, 129–47.
SARGENT, T., and N. WALLACE (1981) 'Some unpleasant monetarist arithmetic',
    Federal Reserve Bank of Minneapolis, *Quarterly Review*, Fall, 1–17.
SIMS, C. (1994) 'A simple model of study of the price level and the interaction of
    monetary and fiscal policy', *Economic Theory*, 4, 381–99.
SIMS, C. (1995) 'Econometric implications of the government budget constraint',
    October, mimeo.
WOODFORD, M. (1994) 'Monetary policy and price level determinacy in a cash-
    in-advance economy', *Economic Theory*, 4, 345–80.
WOODFORD, M. (1995) 'Price level determinacy without control of a monetary
    aggregate', *Carnegie–Rochester Conference Series on Public Policy*, 1995.
WOODFORD, M. (1996) 'Control of the public debt: a requirement for price sta-
    bility?', February, mimeo.

Part III
Spanish Monetary Policy:
Current Situation and Outlook

Part III

6 Monetary Policy Following the Law on the Autonomy of the Banco de España

Fernando Gutiérrez

(Spain) E52
E58

INTRODUCTION

In 1995 the Banco de España substantially altered its monetary policy strategy, discarding a two-stage scheme based on intermediate targets in the form of a monetary aggregate, and adopting an approach in which inflation, the final target, was directly monitored. This move was considerably influenced by the increasing inefficiency of the earlier model: in Chapter 3 of this book, Ayuso and Escrivá describe the conduct of Spanish monetary policy from the 1970s, and the factors that gradually undermined the efficiency of traditional policy. In Chapter 4, Vega discusses the problems of instability that arose in the late 1980s in the relationship between ALP (liquid assets held by the public) – i.e. the monetary aggregate used as the intermediate target – and nominal expenditure, problems which played a significant role in the change in monetary strategy.

However, these were not the only factors behind the revision of monetary policy strategy. In fact, the balance was tipped by institutional considerations. Adoption of the Law on the Autonomy of the Banco de España in June 1994 meant a complete departure from the context in which Spanish monetary policy had previously evolved. Positing price stability as the overriding target of monetary policy, and endowing the Banco de España with full autonomy for pursuit of this target, created the framework for the revised scope and tenor of monetary policy strategy and provided the foundation for many of its specific features. In particular, it was decided that in the new legal environment a clear and precisely quantified linking of monetary policy targets to the Banco de España's legally assigned task could consolidate credibility, thereby increasing efficiency and reducing the costs of the deflationary process indicated for the Spanish economy. Special attention is therefore given below to the relationship between the relevant legal changes and those introduced in the area of monetary policy design.

Drawing on the extensive literature generated in recent years on the setting of inflation targets and the best mechanisms for enhancing their efficiency, the basic features of Spanish monetary policy design are explained and clarified, and compared with those of other countries which have adopted similar strategies. This review naturally includes the indicators – of key importance to monetary policy decisions – used by the Banco de España in analyzing the inflationary picture. Subsequent chapters (7–11) describe these indicators in greater detail and give an account of recent Banco de España research in this area. The examination of Spanish monetary policy is completed by an analysis of its implementation procedures in Chapter 12 by Ortega and Quirós.

As the new monetary policy approach has been operational for only a short period, no definitive assessment can be made at this point of its contribution to the disinflation of the Spanish economy or to the reduction of the costs of this process. These difficulties are clearly noted in Chapter 2 by Almeida and Goodhart, who compare the results observed in countries which have introduced programmes of direct monitoring of inflation with those recorded by countries pursuing other strategies. The present chapter includes a review of the monetary policy recently implemented in Spain and some reflections on the causes of the decline in the inflation rate as from the summer of 1995. It also examines the impact of the measures adopted under the new strategy on the behavior of agents and on the shaping of expectations of greater stability. This leads to a number of observations on the recent functioning of the monetary policy transmission mechanism, which is discussed in greater detail in Part IV of the book, Chapters 13–16.

The contents of the chapter are organized as follows: we examine the legal framework of monetary policy on the basis of the Law on the Autonomy of the Banco de España, and outline the rationale for conferring independent status on the Banco de España. We then discuss the reasons for replacing the previous monetary policy approach and selecting an inflation target as compared with other available options. We then outline the new monetary policy strategy from the standpoint of target definition, indicators, and the institutional framework for communication with agents. The final section covers monetary policy performance in 1995 and the first half of 1996.

THE NEW LEGAL FRAMEWORK OF MONETARY POLICY: AUTONOMY OF THE BANCO DE ESPAÑA

Legal Independence and Effective Independence

The concept of central bank independence (or autonomy) can be contemplated from several angles. It generally means a situation in which the central bank is protected from political decisions, with a view to ensuring that its duties are performed with greater objectivity and impartiality. As noted by Fernández de Lis (1996), theoretical or legal autonomy may differ considerably from practical autonomy. Both notions can be further defined from many standpoints, from those covered by the expression 'functional autonomy' (which usually refers to monetary policy, although the relationship between monetary policy and other central bank functions should not be forgotten) to those used to define 'organic autonomy' (mainly in connection with the independence of the bank's decision-making bodies), or those involved in 'financial autonomy', which generally refers to the management of income and expenditure.

The various components of central bank regulation and their inter-relationships, the influence of a wider legal and institutional framework, and the impact of historical factors and inherited practices make it difficult to determine the exact extent of a given central bank's independence (or autonomy). Even two central banks having laws with identical provisions may differ considerably in the degree of their autonomy. In view of these complications, we shall not attempt in this chapter to evaluate the many factors influencing the independence of the Banco de España. Focusing more closely on the purely legal side, we shall examine those aspects of the Law on Autonomy directly related to monetary policy design and implementation, in order to show how these legal considerations fostered the structural change in monetary strategy and its basic characteristics.

Why Independence for the Banco de España?

The Law on the Autonomy of the Banco de España was directly motivated by Article 108 of the Treaty of Maastricht on European Monetary Union (EMU) which requires the statutes of the Member States' Central Banks, specifically the provisions on independence and the primary objective of promoting price stability, to be adapted to those of the European System of Central Banks (ESCB) no later than the date on which the agency is established. This will happen when it is decided which countries will go on to the third stage of EMU. The practical importance of this requirement, often referred to as the 'other' convergence criterion, is clear: the failure to adapt, or inadequate adaptation, will disqualify the Member State from full participation in EMU.

This Treaty requirement and the fact that Spain fulfilled it comfortably in advance of what was initially expected to be the deadline for implementation refer back to more general issues of monetary policy effectiveness, which have arisen both at the theoretical level and in practice. As mentioned in Chapter 1 by Viñals, the widely held belief that the advantages and costs of inflation are negative on balance continues to gain hold in both areas. Steady increases in real output and income cannot be achieved at the expense of higher inflation rates. Indeed, increasingly significant empirical findings indicate that higher rates of price growth lead to lower economic growth in the long term.[1] The Banco de España, in particular, has repeatedly expressed this view (see, *inter alia*, Banco de España, 1995b). Given the priority of price stability, the rationale for central bank independence is supported by theoretical papers which, in the main, start from observed problems of time inconsistency among economic policy targets.[2] The theoretical literature is in turn corroborated by empirically oriented studies which attempt to demonstrate the existence of an inverse relationship between central bank independence and the inflation rate (or its variability).[3] Despite the practical difficulties encountered by such studies, e.g. the problems involved in 'measuring' central bank independence, and above all in isolating this factor from others in the general economic context which may affect the inflation rate, the literature indicates a certain expert consensus. More important still, this consensus has spread to official economic circles and is also widely reflected in public opinion. The upshot has been a trend, even in countries which are not necessarily candidates for EMU membership, towards institutional arrangements under which the central bank is assigned by law the task of achieving and maintaining price stability, and is provided with the means of doing so – including greater independence *vis-à-vis* the government – (see Table 6.1). This is the general trend under which the Law on the Autonomy of the Banco de España was adopted.

Situation Prior to the Law on Autonomy

The shaping of the Banco de España into an independent agency on the basis of the Law on Autonomy represents the end of a long process (see Trujillo, 1995). In the Decree Law on the Nationalization of the Banco de España in 1962, the Bank was conceived as an appendage of the government, to which it answered directly through the Ministry of Finance. Under Article 9, monetary authority rested with the government, which issued directives to be implemented by the Banco de España. However, it was also stated that, even as an instrument of the government, the Banco de España would be autonomously organized on the technical side. Moreover, the preamble of the law noted that to achieve the stipulated purposes of the Bank, it was deemed necessary to confer greater managerial autonomy on the Bank by designing its Executive Council in a way that 'permitted a flexible corporate spirit to exist amidst the independence of views resulting from the full commitment of each of its members'.

In the years following the Nationalization Law, new powers were delegated to the Banco de España by the Ministry of Finance. Of particular relevance to monetary policy were the powers relating to foreign currency

Table 6.1   Recent changes in central bank regulations

	Date	Final target of monetary policy	Revised under the new regulations?	Increase in central bank autonomy
EMU countries				
Belgium	1993	Not explicit	–	Yes
Spain	1994	Price stability	Yes	Yes
Finland	Pending			
France	1993	Price stability	Yes	Yes
Greece	Pending			
Netherlands	1993	Safeguard currency value	–	Yes
Luxembourg	Pending			
Portugal	1995	Price stability	Yes	Yes
Sweden	Pending			
Rest of the world				
Chile	1990	Foreign/domestic stability of currency	Yes	Yes
Hungary				
	1991	Safeguard foreign/domestic value of currency		
Mexico		Price stability	Yes	Yes
New Zealand	1993	Price stability	Yes	Yes
Czech Republic	1989	Currency stability	Yes	Yes
	1992		Yes	Yes

Sources: EMI (European Monetary Institute), *Annual Report*, 1994; EMI, *Report on Convergence*, 1995, and Goodhart and Viñals (1994).

and external payments issuing from the Spanish Foreign Currency Institute (IEME).

The next basic law was that on the governing bodies of the Banco de España of 1980 (LORBE). This was not a law on functions in the strict sense, but it did set them out and, in the absence of the anticipated complementary legislation outlining the terms under which these functions were to be exercised, it became the basic law governing the Banco de España. As it was incomplete and inevitably somewhat ambiguous, it permitted more actual autonomy than was provided for in the legislation. The LORBE stated that the Banco de España was a public law entity with legal personality, having full public and private capacity to act independently of the State administration, within the limits set forth in the law, in order to achieve the purposes set forth in Article 3. The law exempted the Banco de España from state laws on contracts, budgets, and asset management, and from the regulations governing autonomous entities. The Banco de España was thus given a special legal structure, the basic features of which were not changed by the Law on Autonomy, as it already had sufficient flexibility for the pursuit of its specific activities.

As set out in Article 3, the functions of the Banco de España included those relating to the circulation of notes and coin; state treasury services; the functions of bankers' bank and banking supervision; and the centralization of reserves and external collections and payments. As regards monetary policy, it was provided that the Banco de España would conduct both the domestic and external aspects of monetary policy, in accordance with the general targets set by the government, implementing them in the way it deemed most appropriate for achieving the appointed ends, particularly that of safeguarding the value of the currency. The Banco de España was also to inform and advise the government in connection with these matters. It was likewise empowered to take the initiative in preparing such reports as it deemed relevant, and to report to Parliament whenever the latter so requested.

The wording of the LORBE represented a broader acknowledgement of monetary policy autonomy, as the Banco de España was given extensive decision-making powers with respect to the general targets outlined by the government. This increased autonomy was enhanced by the power to draft reports on its own initiative, a power which subsequently became important as a means of increasing Banco de España input into decisions on matters of interest to the Bank (chief among which, naturally, was monetary policy). However, under the general scheme, monetary authority remained with the government at the political level, while the Banco de España operated as a technical or operational authority.

The Law added no particularly significant features to the other functions of the Banco de España, although mention should be made of its enhanced 'organic' autonomy: a minimum period was set for the terms of office of the members of its governing bodies, considerably increasing both security of tenure and the professional qualifications required for these posts, the latter now being ensured by a specific list of incompatibilities; the role of joint governing bodies was also strengthened.

In sum, the LORBE represented marked progress towards the practical independence of the Banco de España, and was in many respects an important legislative precursor of the Law on Autonomy, even though the latter introduced far-reaching qualitative changes, particularly as regards monetary policy.

The Law on the Autonomy of the Banco de España

Under the Law on Autonomy, adopted in June 1994, the general legal framework of the Banco de España remains much as it was before. The Bank is organized as a public law entity, with full public and private capacity, and subject to the code of private law, except in the exercise of its administrative powers. The laws governing the budgetary, financial, and contractual arrangements of State public sector entities are not applicable. As indicated, this regime not only provides the Bank with sufficient flexibility for the performance of its particular functions, e.g. monetary supervision, but also fosters its organic autonomy. However, organic autonomy is reflected primarily in the degree of independence of its governing bodies. The law includes in this respect a number of provisions designed to ensure that the decisions of governing bodies are adopted objectively and in conformity with the targets set forth in the law. These provisions include:

1　those that strengthen security of tenure by fixing minimum terms of office and clearly specifying the reasons for termination
2　The joint structure of the Governing Council and the Executive Commission
3　Professional qualifications to be met by the members of governing bodies, a strict regime of incompatibilities and limits on other activities
4　A confidentiality requirement applicable to members of governing bodies.

In connection with financial autonomy, it is provided that Parliament – not the government – approve the budget of the Banco de España. In a broader context, but also related to functional autonomy, provisions are included that tie in with Articles 104 and 104A of the Treaty on Monetary Union. These bar the government from receiving any type of financing from the Banco de España, either through credits or by direct Bank purchase of public debt (except such secondary market acquisitions as the Bank needs for the fulfillment of its duties).

As to the independent performance of its functions, the law provides that, while the Banco de España is answerable to the government in a general way, it will enjoy full autonomy in the area of monetary policy to help achieve the price stability objective. The first consequence resulting from this formulation is a dichotomy in the arrangements governing the Banco de España depending on the functions assigned to it. In functions other than monetary policy, the Bank's functional autonomy is limited by government guidance. Under Article 7, these functions are: to hold and manage foreign currency reserves and implement exchange rate policy; to further the smooth functioning and stability of both the financial system and the payments system; provide Treasury services to the State and such autonomous communities as may request them; and supervise financial institutions and markets falling within its purview. With regard to these tasks, the Banco de España's autonomy does not differ substantially from that provided for in earlier legislation. The close link between monetary policy and exchange rate policy raises various questions which will be dealt with further on.

The Bank is fully autonomous as regards monetary policy. This is clearly set out in Article 10.2 which provides that neither the government nor any other agency can give the Banco de España instructions regarding the targets or implementation of monetary policy. Under Article 8, in formulating this policy, the Banco de España may set intermediate growth targets for monetary aggregates or interest rates, or apply such other procedures as it deems appropriate.

Together with these autonomous powers regarding the design and implementation of monetary policy, the Law also confers more independence on the Bank in another area closely related to the above, that is, the issue and control of banknotes and coin that are legal tender. Under the new Law, the Bank retains decision-making powers regarding the circulation of banknotes and is now also responsible for setting the annual limit on the issue of coin, a power formerly held by the government.

Other provisions of the Law strengthen independent action in areas related to monetary policy, and are designed to allow the Bank to act without interference from other political agencies. Thus, those who are members of the Governing Council by the nature of their office (the Director-General of the Treasury and the deputy Chairman of the National Securities Market Commission) are unable to vote when the Council acts on monetary policy related matters; no government authority may revoke an act or ruling which emanates from the Banco de España in connection with the performance of these functions; finally, the Bank may issue precise rules regarding monetary policy in the form of Monetary Circulars.

Exchange rate policy deserves special attention. The Law on Autonomy makes the government, after consultation with the Banco de España, responsible for adopting the exchange rate regime and the parity of the peseta with other currencies. The Banco de España is in charge of managing external reserves and implementing exchange rate policy, in the course of which it may carry out such operations as it deems relevant. The difficulty of clearly separating monetary policy from exchange rate policy introduces an element of ambiguity to be found in nearly all countries in which the central bank is independent where responsibility for the exchange rate is usually assigned to the government. Under such circumstances, and excluding countries which maintain a floating exchange rate in the strict sense, the effective autonomy of monetary policy depends to a large extent on the practical solution to this division of responsibilities worked out between the government and the central bank.

In this connection, experience shows that the optimum solution is co-operation between the government and the central bank, whereby:

1   the central bank is consulted, and shares the view of the government as to the appropriate regime and parity, essentially ensuring that both regime and parity are appropriate to achieving and maintaining price stability
2   the government issues sufficiently broad exchange rate guidelines, leaving adequate room for manoeuvre as regards monetary policy
3   government decisions regarding changes in parity or the exchange rate regime are coupled in a coordinated manner with other corrective measures (in the fiscal area, or in other areas falling under government purview), if it is perceived that they may adversely affect price trends.

The Law on Autonomy explicitly provides some of the elements referred to: the exchange rate regime and currency parity are to be established after consultation with the Banco de España, and should be compatible with the price stability target. On the other hand, the Bank has broad decision-making powers within the area of exchange policy implementation, which permits better coordination with monetary policy. It should also be noted that the current exchange rate regime enables the Banco de España to act with considerable latitude. However, permanent coordination based on analyses of the situation at any given time remains clearly essential.

Transparency and Credibility

As indicated, the legal independence of the Banco de España is important in improving the effectiveness of monetary policy, but this is possible only if the Bank's aims and actions are perceived as being more credible than they were under the previous conditions. Therefore the Law, in addition to dealing with those aspects designed to ensure effective independence – discussed in detail above – also includes provisions that both promote transparency in Banco de España activities and permit economic agents to judge and evaluate them. These provisions, dealing with matters that can be summarised in the concept of *accountability*, are an absolutely essential component of the legal framework of the Bank's independence.

Particularly relevant provisions in the Law on Autonomy are the following: first, the explicit identification of price stability as the overriding target of monetary policy. This provides straightforward guidelines for the Bank in shaping its activities and for the public in judging them. The Bank is also required to announce its general monetary policy targets and implementation procedures at least once a year, and whenever significant changes occur. Moreover, the Governor must report regularly to Parliament on the monetary policy pursued, and to appear before the Congress, the Senate, or the Fiscal and Financial Policy Council of the Autonomous Communities, whenever summoned by them. To keep open channels of coordination with the government, it is also provided that the Governor may be required to attend meetings of the Council of Ministers or the Alternate Committee on Economic Affairs. Moreover, the Minister of Economy and Finance or the Secretary of State for Economy can attend meetings of the Governing Council of the Banco de España, in which they can participate but not vote.

To sum up, the Law on the Autonomy of the Banco de España forms a legal framework that carefully complies with the requirements of the Treaty of Maastricht for access to EMU and empowers the Banco de España to take decisions in all areas of monetary policy, even on highly strategic issues (such as the fixing of targets), without receiving instructions from any other government agency. It is this empowerment that has enabled the Banco de España to effect a qualitative change in monetary policy design, while also providing the framework conductive to greater credibility and, by extension, more effective monetary policy.

WHY A DIRECT INFLATION TARGET?

International Experience

The revision of the monetary policy framework is by no means unique to Spain. Many industrial countries have introduced changes of varying depth in the formulation, design, and implementation of monetary policy. Such changes have frequently been linked to modifications in the legal frame-work of monetary policy, of the type described above in connection with Spain, which increase central bank autonomy and/or clearly identify the final target of monetary policy – price stability or safeguarding the value of the currency.

In many – but not all – countries, monetary policy strategy changes have been broadly similar to those carried out in Spain, involving a shift from an arrangement based on intermediate targets to the direct monitoring of inflation targets. The reasons for these changes are both institutional and technical. Among the former, mention may be made of the growing perception in society as a whole of the advantages of price stability, and, in many cases, the attribution of greater independence to central banks. Both elements reduce the risk that a strategy such as the monitoring of inflation as a final target (which permits somewhat more discretionality, at least in the short term) will lead to an undue easing of monetary policy. Moreover, once a central bank has been assigned the task of ensuring price stability as its basic target, and this target becomes measurable (although not without some difficulty, as will be seen further on) the direct monitoring of inflation fosters the transparency of monetary policy. Agents are in a much better position to assess the Bank's actions and the achievement of its targets. Increased transparency, provided the policy applied is consistent, is a powerful means of enhancing central bank credibility. This increases the impact of monetary policy on agents' expenditure decisions and reduces the costs of checking inflation, or of keeping it within limits compatible with price stability.

Other significant reasons for the growing number of countries that set direct inflation targets are to be found in the problems linked to other more traditional strategies, namely two-stage strategies. Among the latter, the most widespread are those that set intermediate growth targets for a monetary aggregate (or, less often, a credit aggregate), and those that set exchange rate targets for a currency (or, in some cases, a basket of major currencies) which acts as an anchor.

As regards monetary aggregates, financial innovations and the outward opening of economies, and above all of financial markets, have tended to upset the traditional relations between the money stock and nominal expenditure, making it difficult (more so in some cases than in others) to use these variables as basic guidelines for monetary policy.

The internationalization of economies has increased the attractiveness of exchange rate strategy, particularly in small countries with strong exposure to foreign trade, and those such as West European countries which not only fit the above description but also aspire to integration in a common monetary area. However, this cannot be considered a generally valid formula. In most countries, the exchange rate has become an increasingly important factor in the formulation of monetary policy. But, in fairly large countries, or those in which international trade does not represent such a high percentage of economic activity, the nominal exchange rate may not be a satisfactory anchoring mechanism. On the other hand, setting a strict target for the nominal exchange rate may or may not be desirable depending on what type of shock is predominant and the flexibility of nominal wages and prices in a given economy. Specifically, if nominal wages and prices are relatively rigid, some exchange rate flexibility is required. In more practical terms, recent experience has shown that, partly as a result of the internationalization of financial markets, currency prices have tended to undergo strong fluctuations, in some cases unrelated to the economy's fundamentals, and in others magnifying the changes in these fundamentals. Under such conditions, maintaining strict parities with the anchor currencies may prove extremely difficult. As a result, in some situations, the monetary policy implemented to meet the exchange rate target has became unsustainable, or at any rate no longer appropriate to the domestic economic situation. The outcome of such developments has often been a breakdown of the system, causing serious losses of monetary policy credibility and adverse effects on macroeconomic stability.

This does not mean that direct inflation targets should be interpreted as a recent problem-free discovery. This strategy had already been examined in the 1970s when many industrial countries set growth targets for monetary aggregates. Two basic considerations kept it from being adopted. First, the limited ability of the central bank to control inflation in both the short and medium terms. Second, even though a long-term relationship can be established between monetary policy measures and inflation, the lags involved and the intensity of that relation have not been accurately determined.

These problems have not disappeared in recent years, but the above-mentioned arguments concerning the advantages of the direct monitoring of inflation have begun to carry more weight. Moreover, the difficulties referred to have been eased by progress made on two fronts. First, the techniques for price analysis and forecasting have improved, largely through the use of indicators other than the monetary aggregates. Second, the mechanism for transmitting intervention interest rates to expenditure decisions is currently better known and generally faster than it was: more open trade and liberalization measures have tended to strengthen the exchange rate channel, while the reaction of interest rates that are important to agents has become quicker and more intense, mainly as a result of increased competition on financial markets.[4]

As a result of such considerations, a certain number of countries, including the United Kingdom, Sweden and Finland in Europe, and Canada and New Zealand in other areas (see Table 6.2), have recently decided to eliminate intermediate targets and introduce the setting and direct monitoring of inflation targets (ITs). Allowing for some national differences, these strategies have a number of points in common, which are discussed below.[5]

- *Aims*

To further spell out the central bank (or in some cases, government) commitment to price stability in order to increase its credibility.

At the same time, medium-term goals are communicated to agents to help them avoid wrong reactions about temporary price shocks.

- *General principles*

The main ways in which these strategies differ from conventional approaches based on intermediate targets are:

1 that priority is more explicitly given to price stability
2 the medium-to long-term time frame of the targets: as against the usually annual monetary aggregate targets, or the immediate nature of

exchange rate targets, ITs are generally defined with a time frame of
two years or more
3 a publicly announced, precise and quantified definition of the final targets, expressed by an inflation rate or band.

Note that, in defining medium-and long-term ITs, matters involving the
authorities' responses in the shorter term tend to be less explicitly outlined
than they are in other strategies, particularly exchange rate strategies. This
means there is somewhat more discretionality involved in short-term decisions, and thus the pursuit of greater credibility and monetary policy transparency must be guided by a number of principles and precautionary
measures. These include legal measures, such as those included in the Law
on the Autonomy of the Banco de España, strengthening the central
bank's independence, its commitment to price stability, and its accountability to the public. In addition, and frequently without such a legal requirement, the monetary authorities usually agree to:

1 announce explicitly the measure of inflation selected as a target and the
time frame for this target, if medium-term achievement is aimed at, an
indicative reference is often given for the appropriate path of inflation
during the projected time frame for achievement of the target
2 define and publish the indicators to be used in assessing the course of
inflation
3 respond to deviations of inflation from the targets and, in some cases,
give advance notice of circumstances under which deviations may occur
without triggering corrective measures (e.g. changes in indirect taxation, natural disasters, etc.)
4 introduce mechanisms for the publication of targets that explicitly
reflect the above considerations
5 maintain channels of communication, of known periodicity, enabling
the central bank to convey to the public its assessment of the inflationary situation and an explanation of monetary policy actions.

The Spanish Experience

The Spanish experience in this area is by no means atypical. It too shows
acute manifestations of the traditional problems linked to intermediate targets. This book (see Chapter 3 by Ayuso and Escrivá) describes how the
Banco de España developed a framework based on monetary aggregate
targets, in which exchange rate considerations became increasingly important. As from June 1989, the exchange rate commitment was specific and
public: the peseta was to be maintained within a band of ±6 per cent *vis-à-
vis* its central parity with the other currencies in the EMS exchange rate

Table 6.2 Countries with direct inflation targets (ITs): technical aspects

	New Zealand	Canada	United Kingdom	Sweden	Finland
Date of first announcement of inflation targets and implementation schedule	March 1990 December 1992: 0%–2% (in December 1990, target extended to December 1993). Thereafter, same range	February 1991 • End-1992: 2%–4% • Mid-1994: 1.5%–3.5% • End-1995: 1%–3% Same range to 1998	October 1992 1996–7, at end of current legislative session: 1%–4% (targeted position: lower half of range)	January 1993. As of 1995: 1%–3%	February 1993 1995: about 2%
Target price index	Consumer Price Index	Consumer Price Index	Consumer Price Index excluding mortgage costs	Consumer Price Index	Consumer Price Index, excluding mortgage costs, housing prices, indirect taxes and subsidies
Operational internal indices	CPI excluding oil prices, credit costs, and indirect taxes	CPI excluding food and energy prices	CPI excluding mortgage costs, indirect taxes, and local government taxes	CPI excluding indirect taxes and subsidies	CPI excluding indirect taxes and subsidies
Permitted deviations from target: disturbances of significant magnitude, that – if stipulated *a priori* – justify deviations.	• Changes in VAT and other taxes • Changes in mortgage costs through interest rates • Changes in real terms of trade • Natural disasters	• Changes in indirect taxes • Changes – owing to oil price fluctuations – in real terms of trade and natural disasters may even justify a target adjustment	Not determined *a priori*	• Changes in indirect taxes and subsidies • Sudden and intense changes in real terms of trade	• Disturbances which, in other countries, normally justify deviations, by definition do not affect the target index
			Institutional aspects		
Central Bank Legal objective	Price stability	Regulate credit and money, protect the external value of the currency, and alleviate swings in employment, output, and prices	No explicit references	No explicit references	Maintain a secure and stable monetary system, and facilitate circulation of money

	Formal independence, subject to meeting inflation targets; the government has certain prerogatives, economic dependence on government	Effective, not legislated, independence, subject to certain prerogatives of the Ministry of Finance	Answerable to Ministry of Finance	Legislated independence and answerable to Parliament	Legally and economically independent of the government, answerable to Parliament
Autonomy	Formal independence, subject to meeting inflation targets; the government has certain prerogatives, economic dependence on government	Effective, not legislated, independence, subject to certain prerogatives of the Ministry of Finance	Answerable to Ministry of Finance	Legislated independence and answerable to Parliament	Legally and economically independent of the government, answerable to Parliament
Inter-institutional assignment of functions					
Exchange rate policy:					
• selection of exchange rate regime	• Government	• Government	• Government, with prior consultation of central bank	• Central bank, with prior consultation of government	• Government, on a proposal from central bank.
• implementation	• Central bank and government	• Central bank, agent and advisor of Ministry of Finance	• Central bank	• Central bank	• Central bank.
Monetary policy	• Government: setting of targets (in discussions with governor of central bank) • Ministry of Finance: authorized to issue instructions to governor (valid for 1 year) • Central bank: implementation	• Central bank: governor ultimately responsible for monetary policy • Ministry of Finance: authorized to issue instructions to governor (in writing). Not used. • Central bank: implementation	• Government: setting of inflation target and reference ranges of monetary aggregates • Government and central bank: official interest rates • Ministry of Finance: authorized to issue instructions to governor, under exceptional circumstances • Central bank: implementation within guidelines agreed with government	• Central bank: formulation, with prior consultation of government, and implementation	• Central bank: – Board: setting of inflation targets and reference ranges of monetary aggregates – Parliamentary Supervisory Board: official interest rates
Bank supervision	Central Bank	Independent agency	Central Bank	Independent agency	Independent agency

Source: C. Melcón (1994).

mechanism (ERM). This does not mean that no great significance was assigned to the exchange rate before 1989, but references were not made public and monitoring was less rigorous.

As regards domestic references, during this period targets were set in terms of a growth range for the broad monetary aggregate ALP. ALP demand functions, periodically revised, were used to set the annual range. Drawing on forecasts for the performance of real output and prices (based on those in the state budget, and usually including a strong normative element), and an array of interest rate forecasts for the instruments included in ALP and alternative financial instruments, these equations provided a basic reference for setting the target range. Also taken into account were the possible risks of deviation from the forecasts and the possible financial shifts caused by fiscal or other developments not included in the demand equations.

With the peseta's entry into the ERM, the exchange rate became the chief factor in the practical conduct of monetary policy; as long as the peseta's limits of fluctuation provided room for manoeuvre, interest rates could be managed in accordance with monetary targets. As the peseta frequently approached its maximum appreciation limit in the period 1982–92, ALP monitoring inevitably became less strict than it had been earlier.

Beginning in 1992, these parameters underwent significant changes. The ERM crisis affected the capacity of the exchange rate commitment to serve as a guide to monetary policy measures because, for most of the ERM countries, maintaining it meant accepting strong interest rate variability and interest rate levels inappropriate to the recession and the levelling-off of inflation rates prevailing in most of Europe. The unstable exchange rate situation further complicated efforts to strictly control exchange rates. As already mentioned, the traditional instruments proved inadequate: national foreign currency reserves were not sufficient to permit effective intervention against an overwhelming volume of operations against specific currencies in the exchange markets. Moreover, the normally stabilizing effect attributed to fluctuation limits proved to be much weaker than expected, sometimes even showing a contrary sign. Instances of 'vertigo effect' frequently occurred: as a currency was approaching its maximum limit of depreciation, speculative attacks, rather than relenting, gained force, making use of the range within the band ineffective or counterproductive. Finally, the orthodox relationship between interest and exchange rates began to unravel. The market frequently 'punished' interest rate increases, while, by contrast, specific currencies were strengthened when interest rates fell.

This situation affected the various currencies in the ERM in different ways. Some had to leave the system; others, including the peseta, devalued repeatedly. Only the broadening of the bands in the summer of 1993, combined with several other factors, restored some stability to the currency markets. The events of the crisis period highlighted the difficulties involved in using the exchange rate as the single intermediate target variable for guiding monetary policy. Furthermore, it had already been observed in 1992 that ALP grew at rates which could not be satisfactorily explained by the current demand equations. It appeared that the stability of the relationship between ALP and nominal expenditure was deteriorating, and this considerably reduced the reliability of monetary aggregates as intermediate monetary policy targets.

These problems were dealt with in the monetary programming for 1994. Faced with exchange rate uncertainty and the lack of solid findings as regards the disturbances that might be affecting ALP, a mixed approach was used in the setting of targets that blended various aspects of monetary target formulation, without making radical changes. Inflation trends were underlined as being of major importance for monetary policy conduct, although no precise target was fixed, while keeping the peseta in the ERM remained a high priority. At the same time, ALP was given a broader band than it had in the past, with a function that was not strictly that of a target, but rather of a reference as to whether or not monetary conditions were appropriate for continuing the planned advance toward price stability. In view of the problems affecting ALP, a number of complementary indicators were identified, which would also be used in assessing the monetary situation: domestic credit to the private sector, the narrower monetary aggregates, and the yield curve.[6]

Thus, a fairly complex framework was drawn up, useful under highly uncertain conditions, but also reflecting serious shortcomings, particularly as regards transparency. For the future, developing a more precise scheme of references for monetary policy became essential, mainly because the entry into force of the Law on the Autonomy of the Banco de España, still pending at the time, required a strong emphasis on transparency and rigor to strengthen the credibility of the institution which was going to become legally responsible for monetary policy. Moreover, it was assumed that progress would be made in clarifying the nature and scope of the exchange rate and monetary aggregate problems that had arisen in the previous period.

Options Available for Monetary Policy Targets

In the course of planning monetary policy for 1995, which took place in the summer and autumn of 1994, with the Law on the Autonomy of the Banco de España already in place, the variables were examined which could be used in setting monetary targets.

The exchange rate regime is always a major factor in any monetary policy strategy. The starting point in Spain was the priority assigned to keeping the peseta in the ERM, owing both to the inflationary relevance of maintaining exchange rate stability with the main trading and commercial partner countries, and to the need, from a broader perspective, to take on the commitments regarding convergence toward EMU. However, basing monetary policy on the strict and automatic monitoring of the exchange rate, as practiced in other European countries, was discarded as an option. The arguments for doing so are well known: a relatively large and closed economy – by Western European standards – still having sizable structural rigidities and real incomes below the European average, would require, during its convergence period, some room for manoeuvre in the short term. Only in this way can an adequate response be implemented to various shocks which may differ in the nature and the timing of their effects, compared to other more homogeneous economies with closer links to each other.

This was true when the ERM was firmly in place and the peseta was showing marked stability within a ±6 per cent band. It was even more so under the circumstances prevailing at the time of the reform in monetary planning, with a weakened ERM and flagging confidence in its stabilizing capacity, the possibility of fluctuations of up to ±15 per cent, and the peseta's recent history of devaluations, which weakened the credibility of any excessively rigid commitment.

As a result, it was decided that exchange rate stability should be maintained over the medium and long terms, with strict and immediate monitoring being ruled out, while no other quantitative references should be used than the ±15 per cent bands in effect. On this basis, exchange rate stability could be included in a monetary policy approach based on domestic variables.

Among the latter, consideration was given to the alternative of redesigning a strategy based on the use of monetary aggregates as intermediate targets, which made it necessary to solve the problem of ALP demand stability. The results obtained at the time (see Vega's Chapter 4 in this volume) showed that around 1989 a structural change had taken place in the demand for money which had affected its long-term properties. The main factor in this breakdown seemed to be the outward opening of the economy and the financial system. Indeed, if external interest rates were included in the equation, it became possible to reconstitute a statistically satisfactory relationship between ALP and nominal expenditure. However, the new demand equation also showed some minor changes regarding the impact of domestic interest rates on ALP, possibly as a result of the higher degree of competition in the liberalized Spanish financial system (see Figure 6.1).

Despite these results, the option of using a monetary aggregate as an intermediate target was ruled out for a number of reasons. First, there was no assurance that the empirical relationships derived from this revision of ALP demand would remain stable in the future; there was no guarantee

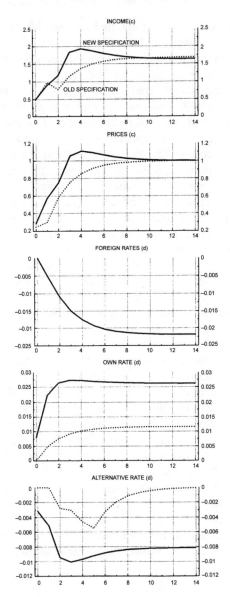

Figure 6.1   Accumulated response function (a) and ALP demand (b)
Notes:
a   The reference time period is quarterly.
b   Includes commercial paper and special debt, to avoid breaks in series owing to restrictions in 1989 and 1990 and the fiscal regularization process from end-1991 to early 1992.
c   Elasticities.
d   Semi-elasticities.
Source: Banco de España.

that the process of structural change had reached its term. Moreover, several years of financial shifts and adjustments had considerably weakened the credibility of monetary aggregates as intermediate targets, making it difficult to use them as supports for the reputation of monetary policy. Finally, the newly calculated equations were more complex and included variables such as foreign interest rates, which are beyond the control of the Banco de España. Apart from implications regarding the controllability of ALP, this complicated the interpretation of the factors underlying given monetary aggregate trends, and therefore reduced the transparency of the relevant monetary policy decisions. However, the properties of ALP demand in its new specification made it an extremely useful aggregate for assessing the monetary situation and the inflationary outlook.

Other variables (credit aggregates, real interest rates, and above all, nominal GDP) suggested as intermediate targets in the theoretical literature[7] or envisaged in other countries, involved a number of serious problems which discouraged their use. The soundest approach therefore seemed to be the direct monitoring of inflation, which some countries were already applying, as mentioned above.

This option involved some risks from the Spanish standpoint. These included the need to accept some uncertainty about agents' response, after several decades of fairly high inflation, to targets being set that would significantly lower the growth rate of prices. Moreover, the financial disequilibrium in the public sector posed significant obstacles for implementing a monetary policy committed to achieving a precise inflation target by a fixed deadline (see Marín and Peñalosa, 1997, and Canzoneri and Diba, Chapter 5 in this volume). However, there were also considerations of a markedly more auspicious nature. First, the widespread support for nominal convergence with Europe as a priority goal. Second, the Law on the Autonomy of the Banco de España established the powers needed to enhance the credibility of monetary policy, provided the proper framework was designed for developing these capacities. For these reasons, setting direct inflation targets was regarded as replacing an older approach whose credibility had worn thin with a new one clearly and directly linked to the fundamental mission of the Banco de España, the achievement of price stability.

THE NEW SPANISH MONETARY POLICY STRATEGY

This section describes in detail the monetary policy approach currently applied in Spain. It chief features are summarized and compared with those of the previous system in Figure 6.2. Some debatable aspects of the choices are clarified, while mention is made of the similarities and

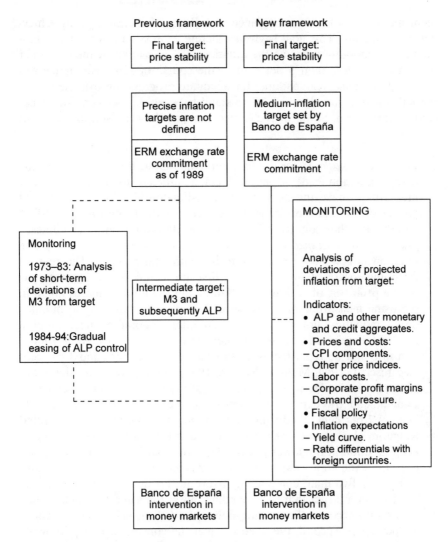

Figure 6.2   The new monetary policy framework
Source: Banco de España.

differences found in the arrangements of other countries applying strategies of the same type.

The Target

The target arises directly from the Law on the Autonomy of the Banco de España, which provides that the Banco de España is to define and imple-

ment monetary policy in accordance with the fundamental goal of achieving price stability. This goal is given concrete expression in the aim of gradually and smoothly reducing the inflation rate, measured by the consumer
price index, to less than 3 per cent in the course of 1997. Reference was
also made to a shorter deadline: for adequate progress towards the target,
the CPI growth rate should have to stand between 3.5 per cent and 4 per
cent in early 1996. Some of the implications of these prescriptions are as
follows:

1 *The target is outlined for the medium term* (about three years from the
   date it is announced), a period deemed sufficient for monetary policy
   measures to have the desired effect. Estimated lags for the near-total
   impact of monetary policy measures are usually in the range of 18–24
   months. In other countries, 2–5 years are allowed for target deadlines.
2 *The target is quantified as a growth rate of less than 3 per cent.* Setting
   inflation targets above a zero rate is a universal practice. The reasons
   for doing so are of two kinds: the first are technical and focus mainly
   on the problems of measuring inflation and the upward biases noted in
   the usual measurements.[8] The second involve the best way to monitor
   direct monetary policy targets in an intertemporal context. From a
   practical standpoint, this means that the optimal (most credible) inflation rate may be regarded as a value between 1 per cent and 3 per cent
   (see Fischer, 1994, Malo de Molina, 1995). As regards rigor, the Spanish target is similar to those set by Australia (2 per cent–3 per cent),
   Canada and Sweden (1 per cent–3 per cent) and Finland (approximately 2 per cent), and somewhat stricter than the rate in the United
   Kingdom (1 per cent–4 per cent), although the latter is endeavoring to
   keep inflation in the lower part of the band, that is, at a limit of 2.5 per
   cent. Only the New Zealand rate (0 per cent–2 per cent) is clearly more
   ambitious. Two main components figure in this quantification: first, the
   need to set a target that is demanding but at the same time achievable,
   taking into account the starting point (the CPI at end-1994 was about
   4.5 per cent). Second, the need to meet the convergence requirements
   of the Treaty of Maastricht. Although the inflation rate stipulated for
   advancing to the third stage could not be known, it was estimated that
   if Spanish inflation were below 3 per cent, there would be a very good
   chance of meeting the requirement of not exceeding 1.5 percentage
   points of the rate of the 3 countries with lowest inflation.
3 *The target is defined in terms of the CPI.* Unlike other countries (e.g. the
   United Kingdom and Finland), the index used does not exclude certain
   components, such as mortgage loan rates, indirect taxes, etc., nor are
   the factors that could justify deviations explicitly identified (as in the
   case of several of the countries referred to).

The Spanish approach arose from the fact that using the CPI enhanced the simplicity and transparency of the target. The CPI is the measure of inflation, calculated by an autonomous institution (the National Statistics Office), most familiar to the public, which tracks its progress, and it also influences a broad range of contracts and agreements. By contrast, any alteration of the CPI, even if based on sound economic reasons, would lack these strengths. Specifically, it was felt that it would not be appropriate to monitor an index prepared on the basis of CPI, but using criteria defined by the Banco de España, because of a possible reduction in target credibility.

Similar criteria of simplicity and transparency discouraged preparation of a specific list of grounds for deviations from the target. First of all, it would be difficult to draw up an exhaustive list. On the other hand, if only those grounds deemed most important or probable were listed, in the event that any of the less likely developments arose, the Banco de España's position would be even more awkward. However, when monetary policy targets were being determined, significant factors did arise that were unrelated to monetary policy decisions, but which could have a major effect on inflation: an increase in VAT and other special taxes was planned for early 1995. It was felt that the impact would be temporary and have subsided by 1997. However, considerable allowance was made for it during preparation of the reference for price trends in the short term. As it was assumed that the effect of a tax increase on the year-on-year CPI rate would disappear in early 1996, the reference was established for the beginning of the year. Signals or specific price references of this type, with varying degrees of rigor and dissemination, have been used in countries applying such strategies (New Zealand, for instance) when the inflationary starting point was clearly above the designated target.

Monetary Policy: Technical Framework and Indicators

As noted above, among the commitments accepted under the ERM, exchange rate stability is a key factor in the new monetary policy approach. Under present circumstances, the sole quantitative reference is that provided by the current fluctuation band (± 15 per cent) on either side of the peseta's central parity.

These bands are doubtless not a particularly strict reference, and the systematic use of their width does not seem to be consistent with macroeconomic stability. However, achieving increased exchange rate stability within the bands is not interpreted as the definitive guideline for monetary policy measures. It is seen rather as the result of a coherent package of economic policies, aimed at convergence with the most stable economies in Europe.

As a result, only those exchange rate trends regarded as permanent and significant, capable of affecting price stability, should play a role in shaping monetary policy decisions.

In this respect, the Spanish strategy differs from that of other countries with direct inflation targets and which usually apply a floating regime. However, there is less of a difference than might at first appear. In European countries (Sweden, and the United Kingdom), the authorities' room for manoeuvre is strongly conditioned by the performance of the D-Mark. Canada's links to the US economy means that monetary policy is tightly controlled by the exchange rate of its currency against the US dollar.

Over and above the exchange rate and its particular characteristics, all countries assess inflationary trends using a relatively complex group of indicators. In some cases, notably the United Kingdom, data are summarized as inflation forecasts that are made public and in practice become a kind of intermediate target that shapes monetary policy implementation and interpretation. Other countries, including Spain, prepare such forecasts but do not publish them. The differences in this respect are explained by individual assessments of the advantages and drawbacks involved in such a practice, and these in turn largely depend on institutional factors.

First of all, it should be pointed out that publishing inflation forecasts is a matter of secondary importance. It may be appropriate insofar as it provides clearer and more transparent information about monetary policy measures. However, in the short term, inflation forecasts may be highly sensitive to monthly changes in the CPI, and it is difficult to determine the extent to which they represent either a temporary or permanent change in inflation trends. In view of which, a central bank that publishes them may come under strong pressure to take specific decisions without being convinced of their appropriateness. Added to this problem is the general uncertainty usually involved in medium-term inflation forecasts, as these are obtained from a very broad range of quantitative and qualitative indicators. Under certain conditions, publishing them may result in the wrong signals being sent to agents.

Owing to these problems, the publication of inflation forecasts is generally seen as being more appropriate to non-independent central banks. In such cases, inflation forecasts may serve as a useful means of warning about inflationary risks and help persuade the decision-making bodies (usually the government) to take the requisite steps. By contrast, independent central banks explicitly committed to price stability and empowered to define monetary policy in accordance with said commitment do not benefit from these advantages, and may prefer to present their assessment of inflation in a more qualified manner, underlining those inflationary risks which lie beyond their own field of action in order to influence the relevant authorities in those areas.

It is interesting to note that awareness of the problems involved in publishing inflation forecasts has led a number of institutions (for instance, the Bank of England) to alter their forecast format in such a way that emphasis of any specific forecast is avoided, while a range is introduced within which inflation may evolve with various degrees of probability. By contrast, countries which do not publish these forecasts use a number of mechanisms to limit the amount of discretionality allowed to monetary policy: these include the publication of references for inflation in shorter horizons, as well as regular appraisals and reports on inflation. In these cases, precise identification of the indicators deemed relevant by the monetary authorities is particularly important.

In most cases, this set of indicators is very similar. They include all the main measures of prices and costs, other than the target. In Spain they comprise the various components of the CPI, other price indices (wholesale and farm prices, and the foreign trade unit prices), wages and unit labor costs, corporate profit margins, and other standard indicators of demand pressure and the thrust of fiscal policy.

In addition to these real indicators, financial indicators are also used. With regard to Spain, particular mention should be made of monetary and credit aggregates, which have traditionally played a key role in monetary policy. It was explained above why ALP is still considered a relevant indicator of monetary conditions and the future trends of nominal expenditure and prices, even though it has ceased to be an intermediate target. Under the new monetary policy approach, ALP remains a leading indicator which is provided with a specific reference: a medium-term growth rate below 8 per cent, which would be consistent with the final target of inflation of less than 3 per cent. Even though higher short-term growth of ALP does not necessarily indicate undesirable performance of expenditure and prices, the lack of convergence towards the specified rate over an extended period would be carefully examined. The information yielded by ALP has to be supplemented by data obtained from other monetary aggregates, both broader and narrower (M2, in particular, according to empirical evidence presented later in this book), which signal possible financial shifts and their impact on ALP, and by the analysis of the supply-side factors that explain the growth of liquidity (the ALP counterparts: domestic credit to the public and private sectors, and net external assets).

The combined indicators used are supplemented by other financial variables from which information may be obtained concerning agents' expectations about inflation and/or the exchange rate. In the published monetary targets for 1995 (Banco de España, 1995a, 1995b) specific mention is made of the interest rate differentials with other countries and the yield curve pattern. Analysis of these indicators is also useful in studying the credibility of monetary policy measures.

Subsequent chapters discuss the principal tools used by the Banco de España to evaluate the inflationary situation and monetary conditions. A number of recent papers on the improvement and development of these tools are also examined. It should be pointed out that Banco de España policy is eclectic and aims at maximizing the usefulness of all relevant information. The techniques for exploiting such information are constantly evolving, and draw on the results of ongoing empirical research.

The Communications Framework

As mentioned above, the strategies for the direct monitoring of prices inevitably involve some margin of discretionality in the short term. The abundance of pertinent indicators and the steady development of useful analytical tools also contribute to the considerable store set by a clearly presented diagnosis of the inflationary situation and the monetary conditions prevailing at a given time (particularly whether such conditions are deemed satisfactory or otherwise). This places a certain obligation on the monetary authorities to keep elected representatives and public opinion abreast of developments. As already noted, the need to do so is often reflected in legal texts, an essential aspect of a central bank's responsibility and independence. The monetary authorities may also take steps that are not strictly required by the regulations, but which help create a transparent environment for monetary policy.

In Spain, communication mechanisms are similar to those of other countries that apply the same strategy; many of them are set out in the Law on the Autonomy of the Banco de España and have been discussed in detail on pages 211–12 above. In addition to these legal provisions, which broadly establish the obligation to publish targets and report regularly to parliament and the government on the design and implementation of monetary policy, the Banco de España has other communication channels:

– monetary policy targets and the Governor's introductory speech are published annually in the *Economic Bulletin*
– regular quarterly reports on the Spanish economy, and monthly monetary memoranda, both also published in the *Bulletin*, are important channels for the transmission of information and opinions
– in line with the revised monetary policy approach and the widespread practice in countries that pursue direct inflation targets, the Banco de España publishes, on a semi-annual basis, a specific report on inflation trends and prospects, which also contains analyses of monetary policy actions in connection with target achievement.

RECENT SPANISH MONETARY POLICY: ASSESSMENT AND OUTLOOK

Monetary Policy in 1995 and 1996

A year and a half is doubtless a very short period on which to base an evaluation of the new monetary policy strategy, given the need for a medium-term perspective. Even over a longer period, it will not be easy to distinguish the contribution of the new strategy to price stability from that of other economic policies, or from the impact of exogenous shocks on monetary policy. Such difficulties are shown clearly in the Chapter 2 by Almeida and Goodhart in this book.

However, some impressions may be formed of monetary policy performance in 1995 and early 1996. In doing so, it should be noted that the stated inflation target is a challenging goal, appropriate to the need to guide the Spanish economy onto a path of stability within a period and under conditions that permit fulfillment of the Maastricht terms for access to the third stage of EMU. Moreover, the new monetary policy approach was launched under particularly difficult circumstances: inflation was showing a tendency to stagnate at about 4.5 per cent, after declining in early 1994. Furthermore, unlike other countries which had adopted similar strategies at an earlier date, the new approach was initiated during a period of cyclical recovery. This made it more difficult to obtain immediate results which would have a favorable impact on inflation expectations, thus increasing the effectiveness of future monetary policy measures (Banco de España, 1995b) (see Figure 6.3).

At the time the new strategy was launched, other factors added to the uncertainty as to whether the Spanish economy would be able to converge toward Europe's more stable economies. These included the depreciation of the peseta in the immediate past and the persistent risk of exchange rate volatility, despite the broadening of the EMS bands in the summer of 1993. Furthermore, indirect tax increases in early 1995 created doubts about current price trends and apprehensions about renewed inflationary strains. From a broader perspective, the political situation gave rise to fears about the future orientation of other economic policies, particularly fiscal policy, that are key factors in price trends. These considerations, together with developments on the international scene, increased uncertainty and affected the behaviour of financial and foreign exchange markets: the peseta exchange rate, which had been easing downward throughout 1994, showed signs of weakening even further toward year-end, and long-term interest rates had risen sharply (four points) in the course of the year. Even though international markets were generally moving in the same direction, the effect was more pronounced in Spain, where the

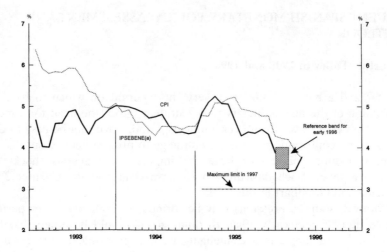

Figure 6.3   Year-on-year inflation, targets and reference, 1993–6

Note: (a)   IPSEBENE = Index of services and non-energy processed goods.
Source: Banco de España.

10-year differential with Germany had widened by about two points. ALP growth was also accelerating, up to a rate of about 11 per cent, owing to a marked expansion of credit to general government. Over and above these difficulties were those generated as agents began the necessary process of adapting to a new monetary policy context.

At the beginning of 1995, the Banco de España raised the intervention rate from 7.35 per cent to 8 per cent, mainly with a view to limiting the impact of the indirect tax increase and preventing it from spreading to price formation processes and thence to future inflation (see the *Report on Inflation*, March 1995). However, at a time of exchange rate instability in the ERM – largely attributable to international factors such as the depreciation of the dollar – this action was incorrectly interpreted as a short-term measure intended to defend the peseta exchange rate. The result was an additional weakening of the peseta and an erosion of agents' expectations, as reflected in the fact that long-term interest rates remained high. The conjunction of all these problems led to a fresh devaluation of the peseta in early March, which was immediately followed by a further increase of half a point in official interest rates. The primary reason for this step was to prevent a further slide in the peseta exchange rate, like that which could have occurred after the devaluation, from fuelling price strains. This measure had a beneficial effect on the exchange rate, which began to recover a few days after the devaluation. Despite occasional fluctuations, short-term interest rates gradually began to decline (see Figure 6.4).

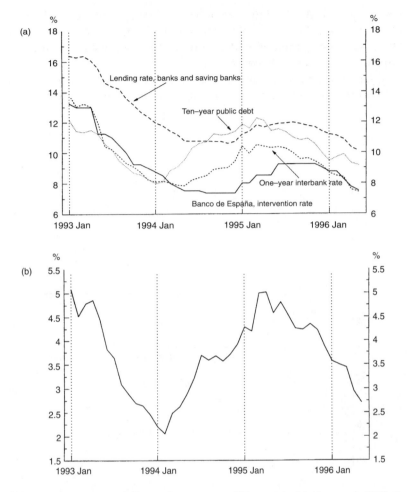

Figure 6.4 Interest rates and 10-year interest rate differential with Germany, 1993–6
a   Interest rates
b   10-year interest rate differential with Germany
Source: Banco de España.

During the second quarter of 1995, a significant deterioration of the inflation indicators was noted. Early in July, this led to a fresh tightening of monetary policy, with an increase of 0.75 points in the official intervention rate. It was followed by a marked strengthening of the peseta and a downward trend in long-term interest rates. In a context of persistent political problems, these developments received a boost from events on the international scene (appreciation of the dollar, a downward trend in German rates). They also indicated agents' growing familiarity with the operating procedures of the new monetary policy approach and awareness of the preventive nature of the monetary policy measures adopted early in 1995. As a result, there was an improvement in agents' expectations about inflation in Spain (see Figure 6.5).

In fact, during the summer months, price trends took a decided turn for the better. The September report on inflation announced a considerable

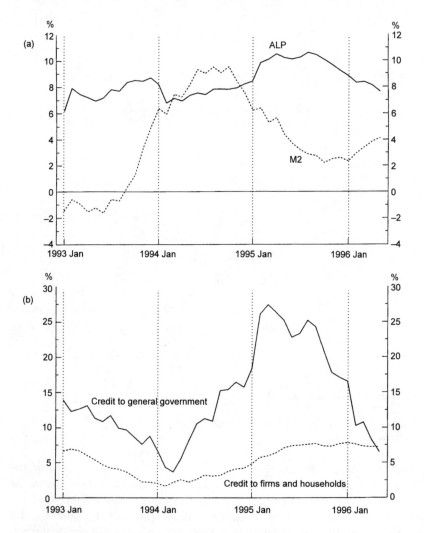

Figure 6.5　Monetary and credit aggregates, 1993–6

a　Monetary aggregates, annual growth rates
b　Credit aggregates, annual growth rates
Source: Banco de España.

increase in the probabilities of inflation falling within the forecast reference range, i.e. between 3.5 per cent and 4 per cent, early in 1996. Subsequently compiled data confirmed this assessment: in December 1995, the year-on-year growth rate of the CPI was about 4.4 per cent, virtually the same as the year before and lower by almost one percentage point than the peak rate reached in April 1995. The available indicators seemed to signify a pattern of expectations of a more stable economic framework. Furthermore, a strong downturn was noted in the major European economies and in Spain itself, albeit with less intensity. In accordance with this situation, and with an easing of inflationary strains in most European countries, official interest rates were lowered towards the end of the year, initially in Germany and then in a large number of European countries.

This was the general framework for the formulation of monetary policy for 1996, with generally favorable prospects for a continued decline in inflation. In announcing its 1996 targets, the Banco de España limited itself to affirming its commitment to the medium-term target, that is, lowering the year-on-year growth rate of the CPI to less than 3 per cent in 1997. As stated at the time, this implied that in early 1997 inflation would already be close to that figure. The group of indicators likewise remained unchanged, and the medium-term reference for ALP growth – below 8 per cent – remained consistent with progress towards achieving the inflation target (Banco de España, 1996a, 1996b).

In the autumn of 1995, the Banco de España had followed a strict monetary policy line. Despite lower current CPI growth rates and the promising performance of the relevant indicators, it kept the intervention interest rate at the level reached in July 1995. Only in December did it begin to ease the rate downwards, stepping up the process in early 1996 as earlier positive signs were confirmed. In the March 1996 report on inflation, a relatively optimistic assessment was made of price trends and the various monetary and financial indicators, which supported the interest rate adjustments: between December 1995 and June 1996, interest rates fell 2 points before levelling off at 7.25 per cent, slightly below the level reached in December 1994, when the last round of rate increases began. This trend has been reinforced by a decline in the CPI; in March, the year-on-year rate reached a low of 3.4 per cent. Although an upward trend was noted in subsequent months, it was prompted by the prices of unprocessed foods, which are subject to sharp (doubtless temporary) increases, while the underlying price index (which excludes energy and unprocessed food prices, and is assumed to provide data on more medium-term trends) continued to fall before levelling out in May at 3.7 per cent, one-tenth below the CPI (see Figure 6.6).

Lower official rates have had a salutary impact on financial variables: the exchange rate has remained above its central parity *vis-à-vis* the D-Mark,

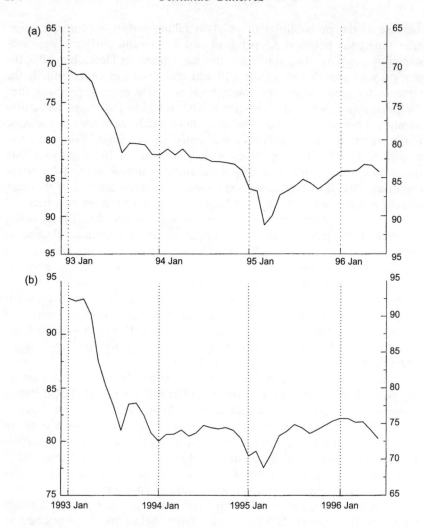

Figure 6.6 PTA/DM exchange rate and index of effective nominal exchange rate *vis-à-vis* industrial countries, 1993–6

a   PTA/DM exchange rate
b   Index of effective nominal exchange rate of PTA *vis- à-vis* industrial countries
Source: Banco de España.

with the peseta frequently emerging as the most highly valued currency in the EMS ERM, while steadily maintaining a level even somewhat above that reached late in 1994, prior to the process that led to the devaluation of March 1995. Medium-and long-term interest rates have significantly declined, and by a greater amount than have short-term rates. From a peak of more than 12 per cent in early 1995, the 10-year rate had fallen below 9 per cent by end-June 1996. This meant a reduction of nearly 3 points in the differential with Germany for this rate, which at the end of the first half of 1996 was less than 2.5 points. Finally, there was a notable easing in monetary growth beginning in the second half of 1995, which finally stabilized below the 8 per cent reference figure. Taken together, these data confirm a marked improvement in the inflation expectations for the Spanish economy and encourage the hope that the target will be reached in 1997 (see Figure 6.7).

Some Reflections on the Transmission of Monetary Policy

Inflation recently seems to have reacted rapidly and sharply to increases in official interest rates. The possible reasons for this behavior are discussed below.

An initial examination indicates that a number of factors, largely unrelated to monetary policy, fostered this development: in the international environment, the slump in the prices of raw materials in 1995, following price surges the year before, and the absence of inflationary strains in most of the industrial economies were transmitted to the Spanish economy through the prices of imports, which play an increasingly greater role in the domestic market. In the national sphere, it bears noting that the recovery of demand, which peaked in the first half of 1995, was based on investment and exports and thus helped ease inflationary strains. Subsequently, economic activity began to fall off gradually, which no doubt affected agents' expectations and contributed to a further easing of inflationary strains. Partly related to this development was the continued moderation in wage settlements, which combined with the reduction in social security contributions in early 1995 to temper the growth of unit labor costs. Finally, the improvement in public sector accounts, albeit modest, helped allay the occasional fears of budgetary overruns and may have contributed to shaping expectations of the Spanish economy's greater stability in the future.

Taking these factors into account, it is nevertheless important to see whether there are indications in the monetary policy transmission mechanism of any change that may throw light on the recent path of inflation.[9]

First of all, it is worth mentioning that significant structural modifications have taken place in recent years: the increased openness of the Spanish economy to competition has caused major changes in the financial markets as well as the labor and goods markets. As regards the labor market, these changes may partly explain recent wage behavior, which seems to have lost some of its traditional rigidity, and thus labor costs appear to be responding more rapidly and with less stress to monetary policy. However, changes have been particularly apparent in the financial markets,

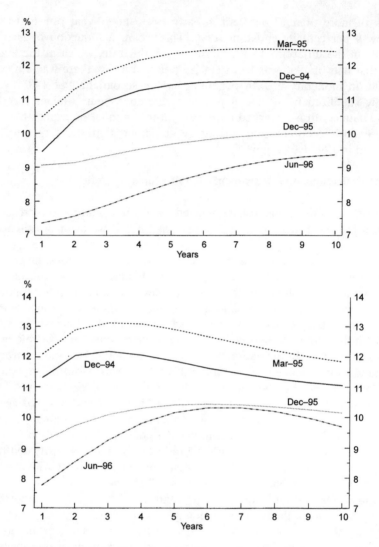

Figure 6.7   Term structure of spot rates and forward rates at 1 year

a   Term structure of spot rates
b   Term structure of forward rates at 1 year
Source: Banco de España.

where the liberalization process took place earlier and in greater depth. As a result, monetary policy impulses are promptly and efficiently translated by the Spanish financial system; in this respect, banking rates – specifically credit rates – are particularly significant. Evidence is presented elsewhere in this book of an acceleration in recent years in the transmission of money market rates to credit markets. This development, confirmed by the data in Figure 6.4, was a factor in the recent decline in the rate of inflation, and may have been strengthened by a financing structure that generally fosters the transmission of monetary policy, and by the credit channel, which would tend to enhance the efficiency of monetary policy.

Nevertheless, the empirical evidence indicates that the impact of these interest rates on private expenditure is more subdued and dilatory. This is partly due to the nature of the markets involved, where agents' access to information is not as swift, and to the possible persistence of certain rigidities in price formation. This makes it difficult to affirm that the direct interest rate channels were a determining factor in the price deceleration which began in the spring of 1995.

Since April 1995, the exchange rate has followed an upward trend that is consistent with the gradual easing of inflationary strains. Among the factors that would tend to increase the efficiency of the exchange rate channel are the growing openness of the Spanish economy and the increasing importance of the exchange rate in shaping inflation expectations. Nevertheless, it will later be seen in this book how the direct short-term relationship – via import prices – between the exchange rate and inflation seems, despite its historical intensity, to have weakened since 1992. Although, taken as a whole, the impact of the exchange rate on inflation appears to have intensified, in no case could such a rapid effect on the CPI be attributed to the recent rise in the exchange rate.

It may therefore be concluded that the recent favorable price trends may be due to a combination of factors – some of which are unrelated to monetary policy – whose impact may have been increased through a direct effect on agents' inflation expectations. This effect is generally difficult to quantify, but some confirmation of its existence may be deduced from the above-mentioned trends in financial indicators, and perhaps from the conduct of wage negotiations. We may venture to say that the new monetary policy strategy has made a positive contribution to expectations, at least from the time agents became more familiar with how it works. Most likely the setting of a price target – strict, but attainable – by an independent institution and the publication of detailed explanations of the inflationary situation and outlook, together with the reasons for monetary policy measures, have helped to enhance the credibility of the central bank's commitment to curbing inflation. By extension, these factors also increased the effectiveness of the tightening of monetary policy in early 1995, which permitted a subsequent adjustment of interest rates, as expectations seemed to emerge of a gradual reduction of inflation toward levels unprecedented in the last thirty years.

However, the apparent increase in the credibility of monetary policy and the impact thereof on agents' expectations, do not mean that these trends have been established once and for all. Even excluding the possibility of unfavorable shocks, further progress is required if the Spanish economy is to achieve a stable inflation rate below 3 per cent in 1997. But this progress is subject to certain risks derived from the fundamental problems of the Spanish economy, which are reflected both in an excessively high general government deficit and in numerous rigidities in the goods, services, and factors markets. To a large extent, these conditions explain why the recent decline in inflation in Spain was not enough to reduce significantly the differential with more stable European countries. They also feed agents' remaining doubts about the future course of prices, which are reflected in high, albeit declining, medium and long-term interest rates, and sizable differentials with these same countries.

It is thus clear that monetary policy alone cannot steer the Spanish economy towards a path of stability without the help of other economic policies. Indeed, only if these policies take the appropriate course will monetary policy be able to increase its credibility and effectiveness in the medium term and make a stronger contribution to sustained, i.e. non-inflationary, growth.

Notes

1   See, for instance, Fischer (1993), Rudebusch and Wilcox (1994), and Andrés and Hernando (1996). A general survey of the arguments put forth in this discussion can be found in Escrivá and López-Salido (1996).
2   See, among many others, Barro and Gordon (1983), Rogoff (1985), Alesina (1989), and Cukierman (1992). The gain in credibility of an independent institution, which concludes a contract with either the government or the Parliament, has been argued by Walsh (1995) and Persson and Tabellini (1993).
3   For instance, Grilli, Masciandaro and Tabellini (1991), Cukierman, Webb and Neyapti (1992), Alesina and Summers (1993) and De Gregorio (1996).
4   The bearing of these developments on the Spanish case will be examined in greater detail further on in the chapter. Chapters 13–16 discuss recent studies by the Banco de España in these areas.
5   A broad and detailed survey of these details can be found in Melcón (1994). For discussions of cases by country, see Haldane (1995), Bank of England (1994; 1995), Bank of Canada (1991), Lloyd (1992), Sveriges Riksbank (1994 and 1995) and Friedman (1994).
6   See Banco de España (1994).
7   In particular, since the end of the 1970s, a number of well known authors have suggested setting intermediate income or nominal expenditure targets, for instance, Meade (1978), Tobin (1980) and Gordon (1985).
8   See the Interim Report to the Senate Finance Committee (1995).
9   Many of these observations are based on the conclusions reached in Chapters 13–16 of this book, which outline the available evidence and discuss research work done on the monetary policy transmission mechanism in Spain.

References

ALESINA, A. (1989) 'Politics and business cycles in industrial democracies', *Economic Policy*, 8, Spring.

ALESINA, A. and SUMMERS (1993) 'Central bank independence and macroeconomic performance: some comparative evidence', *Journal of Money, Credit and Banking*, 25, May, p. 151–162.

ALMEIDA, A. and C. GOODHART (1996) 'Does the adoption of direct inflation targets influence the behavior of central banks?', Chapter 2 in this volume.

ANDRÉS, J. and I. HERNANDO (1996): 'Cómo afecta la inflación al crecimiento económico? Evidencia para los países de la OCDE', *Working Paper*, 9602, Research Department, Banco de España.

AYUSO, J. and J.L. ESCRIVÁ (1996): 'The evolution of monetary control strategy in Spain', Chapter 3 in this volume.

BANK OF CANADA (1991) 'Targets for reducing inflation', *Bank of Canada Review*, March.

BANK OF ENGLAND (1994, 1995) *Inflation report*, various issues.

BANCO DE ESPAÑA (1994) 'Monetary policy in 1994', *Economic Bulletin*, January.

BANCO DE ESPAÑA (1995a) 'Monetary policy objectives in 1995: address by the Governor of the Banco de España to the Spanish Parliamentary Committee on Economic Affairs', *Economic Bulletin*, January.

BANCO DE ESPAÑA (1995b) 'Monetary policy objectives and implementation in 1995', *Economic Bulletin*, January.

BANCO DE ESPAÑA (1995c) *Inflation report*, March.

BANCO DE ESPAÑA (1995d) 'Discurso de presentación del informe anual de 1994, pronunciado por el Gobernador ante el Consejo de Gobierno del Banco de España', June.

BANCO DE ESPAÑA (1995e) *Inflation report*, September.

BANCO DE ESPAÑA (1996a) 'Monetary policy objectives in 1996: Address by the Governor of the Banco de España to the Spanish Parliamentary Committee on Economic Affairs', *Economic Bulletin*, January.

BANCO DE ESPAÑA (1996b) 'Monetary policy objectives and implementation in 1996'. *Economic Bulletin*, January.

BANCO DE ESPAÑA (1996c) *Inflation report*, March.

BARRO, R. and D. GORDON (1983) 'Rules, discretion and reputation in a model of monetary policy', *Journal of Political Economics*, 12.

CANZONERI, M. and B. DIBA 'Fiscal constraints on the independence of central banks and on price stability', Chapter 5 in this volume.

CUKIERMAN, A. (1992) 'Central bank behaviour, credibility and independence: theory and evidence', Cambridge, MA: MIT Press.

CUKIERMAN, A., J. WEBB and B. NEYAPTI (1992) 'Measuring the independence of central banks and its effects on policy outcomes', *World Bank Economic Review*, 6.

DE GREGORIO, J. (1996) 'Inflation, growth and central banks: theory and evidence', *Policy Research Working Paper*, 1575, Washington, DC: The World Bank.

EMI (1995) *Progress towards convergence*.

EMI (1996) *1995 Annual Report*.

ESCRIVÁ, J.L. and J.D. LÓPEZ-SALIDO (1996) 'La política monetaria y la especificación de objectivos de inflación', Banco de España, Mimeo.

FERNÁNDEZ DE LIS, S. (1996) 'Classifications of central banks by autonomy: a comparative analysis', *Working Paper*, 9604, Research Department, Banco de España.

FISCHER, S. (1993) 'The role of macroeconomic factors on growth', *Journal of Monetary Economics*, 32(3), December.

FISCHER, S. (1994) 'The costs and benefits of disinflation', in J. Onno de Beaufort Wijnholds, S.C.W. Eijffinger and L.H. Hoogdwin (eds), *A Framework for Monetary Stability*, CEPR Financial and Monetary Policy Studies, 27, Boston: Kluwer Academic Publishers.

FRIEDMAN, C. (1994) 'Formal targets for inflation reduction: the Canadian experience', in J. Onno de Beaufort Wijnholds, S.C.W. Eijffinger and L.H. Hogdwin (eds), *A Framework for Monetary Stability*, CEPR Financial and Monetary Policy Studies, 27, Boston: Kluwer Academic Publishers.

GOODHART, C. and J. VIÑALS (1994) 'Strategy and tactics of monetary policy: examples from europe and the Antipodes', in Jeffrey C. Fuhrer (ed.) *Goals, Guidelines and Constraints Facing Monetary Policy-makers*, Conference Series Boston: Federal Reserve Bank of Boston.

GORDON, R.J. (1985) 'The conduct of domestic monetary policy', in A. Ando *et al.* (eds), *Monetary Policy in Our Times*, Cambridge, MA: MIT Press.

GRILLI, V., D. MASCIANDARO and G. TABELLINI (1991) 'Political and monetary institutions and public financial policies in the industrial countries', *Economic Policy*, 13.

HALDANE, A.G. (ed.) (1995) *Targeting Inflation*, London: Bank of England.

Interim report to the Senate Finance Committee (1995) 'Towards a more accurate measure of the cost of living'.

LLOYD, M. (1992) 'The New Zealand approach to the central bank autonomy', *R B Bulletin*, 55(3), Auckland: Reserve Bank of New Zealand.

MALO DE MOLINA, J.L. (1995) 'Comment on Stanley Fisher *The costs and benefits of disinflation*', in J. Onno de Beaufort Wijnholds, S.C.W. Eijffinger and L.H. Hoogduin (eds), *A Framework for Monetary Stability*, CEPR Financial and Monetary Policy Studies, 27, Boston: Kluwer Academic Publishers.

MARÍN, J. and J. PEÑALOSA (1997) 'Implicaciones del marco institucional y de la política presupuestaria para la política monetaria en España', in *La política monetaria y la inflación en España*, Servicio de Estudios del Banco de España, Alianza Editorial.

MEADE, J.E. (1978) 'The meaning of internal balance', *Economic Journal*, 88.

MELCÓN, C. (1994): 'Estrategias de política monetaria basadas en el seguimiento directo de objetivos de inflación', *Working Paper*, 9426, Research Department, Banco de España.

ORTEGA, E. and G. QUIRÓS (1996) 'The implementation of monetary policy current situation and outlook', Chapter 12 in this volume.

PÉREZ-JURADO, M. (1997) 'El SME y la convergencia en inflación: el papel de la credibilidad cambiaria', in *La política monetaria y la inflación en España*, Servicio de Estudios del Banco de España, Alianza Editorial.

PERSSON, T. and G. TABELLINI (1993) 'Designing institutions for monetary stability', *Carnegie Rochester Conference Series on Public Policy*, 39, December.

ROGOFF, K. (1985) 'The optimal degree of commitment to an intermediate monetary target', *Quarterly Journal of Economics*, November.

RUDEBUSCH, G.D. and D. WILCOX (1994) 'Productivity and inflation: evidence and interpretation', Washington, DC Federal Reserve Bank, April.

SVERIGES RIKSBANK (1994, 1995) 'Inflation and Inflation Expectations in Sweden', Economics Department.

TOBIN, J. (1980) 'Stabilization policy 10 years after', *Brookings Papers on Economic Activity*, 1.

TRUJILLO, M.J. (1995) *'La potestad normativa del Banco de España. E1 régimen actual establecido en la Ley de Autonomía'*, Legal Department, Banco de España.

SVERIGES RIKSBANK (various issues) *Inflation and inflation expectations in Sweden*.

VEGA, J.L. (1996) 'The ALP long-term demand function', Chapter 4 in this volume.

VIÑALS, J. (1996) 'Monetary policy and inflation: from theory to practice', Chapter 1 in this volume.

WALSH, C. (1995) 'Optimal contracts for central bankers', *American Economic Review*, 85.

7 Analysis of Inflation from the Monetary Policy Standpoint

Pilar L'Hotellerie-Fallois

INTRODUCTION

Price stability, the fundamental objective of monetary policy, is not synonymous with the firmness of each and every price in an economy, but is rather a concept related to the rate of average price variation (or rate of inflation) and consistent with the adjustments in relative prices necessary for proper resource allocation. Of course, both the concept of price stability and the method of measuring it must be validated in practice but, be that as it may, the monitoring of prices and the analysis of their determinants are essential components of the information that the monetary authorities must collect in order to make decisions.

In Spain, moreover, the current monetary policy strategy is based on the attainment of a direct inflation objective. In this context – wherein the ultimate objective of price stability is identified with a numeric inflation rate value – analysis of the inflationary phenomenon is important; not only must its trend be monitored, but the degree of attainment of the direct objective must also be continually assessed. The change in monetary policy strategy has not substantially altered the Banco de España's approach to the analysis of aggregate price developments, which is centred essentially on estimating trend or underlying movements in inflation and explaining these movements by studying their determinants. Nevertheless, there has been a shift in emphasis, so that forecasting price movements in the relevant target period has become important in making monetary policy decisions (in the short and, most importantly, the medium term). Moreover, special attention is also given to the indicators of inflationary expectations, which provide information about the price movements expected by economic agents and which are, therefore, one of the keys to their future trend.

The purpose of this chapter is to describe the information and tools available for monitoring inflation in Spain and for obtaining an *ex ante* view of the inflationary situation, upon which to base monetary policy decisions. Thus, no attempt is made to analyze the effects of the measures adopted, through the channels of monetary policy transmission, or the information necessary for doing so, although, obviously, both types of analysis have points in common. The Banco de España's concern with observing and interpreting price movements has been constant and, as a result, it has developed an array of analytical techniques based on the statistical treatment of the price series and on studying the determinants of inflation within the framework of the national accounts. However, with the change in monetary policy strategy, a number of efforts have been undertaken to improve inflation monitoring and forecasting in the short and medium terms. Consequently, in the following sections, in addition to the traditional analytical techniques, mention will be made of research in progress and tentative conclusions concerning the use of certain indicators. Before embarking upon a detailed description of the information available for analyzing prices in Spain, a few general comments are given, as well as a brief summary of the experiences of other countries. A final section contains some concluding comments.

INFLATION AND VARIABLES PROVIDING INFORMATION ON THE TREND OF PRICES: THE EXPERIENCE OF OTHER COUNTRIES

Overview

The concept of both inflation and price stability are generic and must be specifically defined in order to be of any use. In practice, the trend of prices is measured by a variety of indices, and a determination must be made as to which one or which ones are considered the most appropriate for representing all of the prices in an economy. This very variety implies that there is no one measure of inflation – defined as the rate of general price growth – but as many as there are price indices accepted as representative.[1] The consumer price index (CPI) and the GDP and aggregate expenditure deflators are price indicators widely used to monitor prices and overall inflation. Normally, they refer to the prices of final goods and services in the economy. The specific characteristics of indices that measure prices are such that the concept of stability is frequently associated with slightly positive inflation rates, although it is not the purpose of this chapter to enter into that discussion.[2]

In countries where the monetary policy is aimed at attaining a direct inflation objective-and, therefore, where the concept of price stability is associated with a specific numeric value, a decision must be made as to which price index will be used to define the objective. Most countries with this type of strategy use the corresponding general consumer price index (or the equivalent price index) or some of its components to define their monetary policy objectives. Once this decision has been made, all of the information necessary to properly monitor attainment of the objective must be identified. Given that the instrumental variables used by central banks (normally, the intervention interest rates) can affect prices after a considerable lapse of time (the lags are usually estimated at about 2 years), analyzing the contemporaneous pressures on prices is insufficient. Available information must be collected on the future behavior of prices and the channels through which potential inflationary pressures may develop. This means that it is necessary not only to monitor the price index used to define the objective, but also a potentially wide range of indicators that can provide clues as to the possible course of prices in the short and medium terms. In any case, monitoring and extracting information from a broad spectrum of indicators is not an exclusive characteristic of central banks that pursue direct inflation objectives. In countries where two-stage strategies are pursued, and although logically the intermediate variable (generally, the exchange rate or a monetary aggregate) is a determining factor in the decisions of the monetary authority, it is increasingly common for other indicators to be carefully monitored, especially those that signal possible inflationary pressures, to supplement the information provided by the intermediate variable.

Owing to the variety of indicators that contain information about an economy's inflationary situation and the numerous methods of extracting this information, price monitoring assumes different characteristics in each central bank. Nevertheless, it is worth trying to give a general (although probably incomplete) description of this series of indicators and methods, in order to comment subsequently on experiences in certain specific cases. Regarding the *type of indicators* that can provide valuable information for the analysis of inflation, mention should first be made of the price series themselves, not only consumer prices or the index taken as the main point of reference, but also deflators, producer prices, etc. Secondly, there is another set of variables that provides information on price determinants. The most important are costs (wages, import prices and exchange rate, and fiscal variables such as contributions and indirect taxes) and the pressure of demand (output gap, capacity utilization, public expenditure). Variables that provide information on the trend of nominal expenditure, such as monetary aggregates, can also be included. A third set of relevant variables consists of indicators of inflationary expectations. Some of the variables mentioned, such as the exchange rate and inflationary expectations, not only provide clues about the probable course of prices, but are also channels for the transmission of monetary policy, so that monitoring them enables the monetary authorities to check the possible effects of the measures adopted.

Various methods can be used to analyze the indicators selected and to extract information from them concerning present and future price trends. These methods include the univariate modeling of the series as well as the estimation of structural models, the preparation of composite indicators, and the use of accounting figures to estimate macroeconomic aggregates. Obviously, a given indicator can be used in different ways; thus, wage indicators can be used to construct various types of models, develop composite indicators, or estimate macroeconomic aggregates.

The information obtained using various methods to analyze the indicators will relate to the actual or projected trend of prices in different target periods. For example, some of the information will be indicative of contemporaneous inflationary pressures: thus, the univariate modeling of the price series, forecasts of which essentially incorporate the past trend of the series and therefore presuppose future behavior similar to that of the recent past, will facilitate a useful characterization of current inflation through the calculation of centred rates, in addition to providing accurate short-term forecasts that can be improved via transfer functions. Multivariate models (such as VARs) and structural models, to the extent that they incorporate variables representative of inflationary pressures in the coming months or quarters (for example, wage increases approved for the period, trend of import prices and of the exchange rate) will provide more precise information on inflationary pressures within the time frame of a few quarters. When only known information is used in these models, the resulting forecasts will be conditional upon keeping policies within hitherto known parameters; nevertheless, simulations can also be used, under various assumptions concerning the trend of exogenous variables and the implementation of economic policy.

Moreover, the estimation and forecasting of macroeconomic aggregates with the simple requirement that they be consistent from an accounting standpoint, but also confirmed by the analyst's economic knowledge, are an alternative method of introducing known information on inflationary pressures in the near future and of making the forecasts conditional upon a given trend in the exogenous variables and in economic policies. The main difference between the projections obtained using structural econometric models and the forecasts arrived at with the simple requirement of accounting consistency is that in the latter, the relationships between variables are not predetermined by econometric estimates, but depend instead on the analyst's opinion, which is influenced by data of a very different sort, including the estimated elasticities in the econometric models themselves. The composite inflation indicators constitute another method of extracting information on the future trend of prices, which is increasingly used in many central banks, but without discarding other kinds of tools.

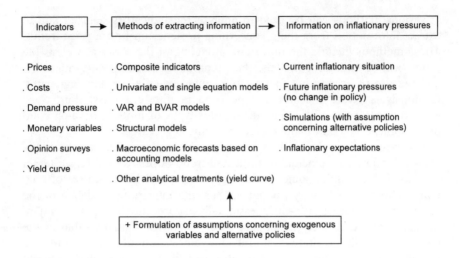

Figure 7.1 Analysis of inflation through the various available indicators

Figure 7.1 summarizes the ideas expressed in the preceding paragraphs. The basic information on prices comes in the form of indicators. These are processed, individually or collectively, using various methodologies and, when necessary, adding assumptions about exogenous variables and alternative policies to obtain information on inflationary pressures in various periods and on inflationary expectations. Of course, the methodology used in each case is not dissociated from the information sought nor from the available indicators. Moreover, given the broad spectrum of usable indicators and methodologies, the information obtained in each case must be prioritized in order to arrive at a single diagnosis of the inflationary situation. Each central bank prioritizes this information in a different way and places more emphasis on one or other method of inflation analysis. In the following section, the experiences of other central banks are briefly reviewed.

The Experiences of Other Central Banks

Naturally, not all central banks ascribe the same importance to the various indicators analyzed, nor do they use the various methodological approximations mentioned in the preceding section with the same degree of intensity. Following is a review, by way of example, of the procedures used in the central banks of the United Kingdom, Sweden, Canada, and New Zealand. All are characterized by the fact that they pursue direct inflation objectives.

In the *Bank of England*, the information obtained from the series of real and monetary indicators analyzed is synthesized in a medium-term (2 years) inflation forecast (measured using the retail price index),[3] presented in the form of a probability distribution. This forecast is considered a *summary statistic* and has a role similar to that of an intermediate variable in a two-stage monetary policy strategy, in the sense that if this forecast is inconsistent with the price objective, the Bank recommends an appropriate adjustment of the official interest rate. To arrive at this medium-term forecast, the results of a quarterly, small-scale (20 equations) structural econometric model are taken as a basis. This initial projection is modified with expert opinions and information not included in the model, so that the final forecast is a synthesis of all the information received. The Bank of England also prepares a short-term forecast (3 months), using univariate methods.

Sveriges Riksbank, the Swedish central bank, has taken a more eclectic approach than the Bank of England, as its inflation analysis does not revolve crucially around the initial projection obtained using an econometric model, but is based instead on estimates of structural equations as well as leading indicators, an index of monetary conditions, etc. which provide information on inflationary pressures in different periods.

To make inflation forecasts, the *Bank of Canada* uses projections taken from a quarterly structural model, the QPM, which is calibrated on the basis of existing empirical evidence. In this case as well, the initial projection is modified to reflect the experts' opinions, and a number of iterations are performed before arriving at the final projection. Said projection, which is a conditional forecast, includes paths for the two variables that make up the indicator of monetary conditions, the short-term interest rate and the exchange rate. These paths serve as a highly useful reference for the monetary authority, as they indicate the degree of monetary tightness compatible with the price objective, under the assumptions incorporated into the projection. However, they cannot be used as a mechanical gauge for adjusting the monetary conditions. In fact, alternative projections are also made, under different conditions from those in the base scenario, which, at any given moment, can be considered more probable than the base scenario itself.

Lastly, the *Bank of New Zealand* (RBNZ) uses a standard mark-up pricing model as a point of departure for its projections. As with the Bank of Canada, special emphasis is placed on the structural trend of interest rates and the exchange rate, as these variables promptly reflect inflationary expectations and are an integral part of the transmission mechanism. In particular, the RBNZ estimates a tolerance range for the exchange rate, which is the main determinant of the inflation forecasts. A range is also estimated for nominal interest rates, although deviations in these ranges do not elicit reactions from the Bank automatically. The inflation forecasts are published, making them explicitly conditional upon the exchange rate path.

INFLATION MONITORING AND ANALYSIS IN SPAIN

Characteristics of the Information Available for the Analysis of Inflation

In Spain, the preferred price index for measuring inflation and defining monetary objectives is the CPI, owing to its wide dissemination and its use in the pricing of all types of contracts. Moreover, the fact that it is pre-pared outside the Banco de España and is not subject to change by the Bank itself promotes the transparency of monetary policy. The Banco de España defines its objectives in terms of the year-on-year rate of the CPI (the rate of variation between a given month and the same month of the preceding year). Therefore, a significant part of the effort to monitor infla-tion is focused on the analysis of this index and its immediate determ-inants. However, as with the other central banks mentioned in the preceding section, the Banco de España also monitors a large number of indicators to formulate its opinion on the inflationary pressures developing in the Spanish economy and on the inflationary expectations of economic agents. The Banco de España's focus is rather eclectic, like that of the Swedish *Riksbank*, without relying explicitly on the predictions of a struc-tural model to prepare a quantified diagnosis of inflation.

As indicated in Figure 7.1, the first group of indicators available for the analysis of inflation consists of the various price indices prepared for the Spanish economy. These indices can be used to approximate the contem-poraneous growth of prices in various stages of the price formation pro-cess, through the estimation of trends, and to assess to what extent accelerations and decelerations are temporary or incorporate more permanent elements.

A second group of extremely varied indicators provides information on the determinants of prices and the price formation process. It has already been pointed out that in the Banco de España, this information is analyzed from a number of perspectives, ranging from the individual analysis of indicators to their collective use in models, composite indicators, and macroeconomic estimates. Although a quarterly model – small in size and structural in nature – is being prepared, it is not used at present as the basic starting point for medium-term inflation forecasts, but mostly in simulation exercises for alternative monetary policy measures, as explained in Andrés, Vallés and Mestre (1996), Chapter 16 in this volume. A BVAR multivariate model is also used, which relates the CPI to several of its basic determinants and the activity in question. Moreover, the preparation of quarterly macroeconomic estimates and forecasts in the context of national accounting makes it possible to check the consistency of price forecasts (measured with deflators) with the expected movements in their determinants, on both the demand and cost sides, making these forecasts conditional upon a given macroeconomic policy action and a given external context and exchange rate.

In order to explore all possible methods of forecasting the future course of prices, a composite leading indicator of prices has also been constructed, which is now in the testing phase. Variables representative of prices, income, and the real sector have been incorporated into this indicator, as well as monetary variables. The latter are also used in other ways (through expert analysis, the estimation of demand for money equations, or the construction of weighted monetary aggregates) to extract the information they contain on the future course of prices.

Lastly, a third group of indicators monitored by the Banco de España are those related to inflationary expectations. The most important of these are interest rates and their relationships through the yield curve, as well as the information gleaned from opinion surveys.

The diversity of the information that can be used to analyze inflation underscores, on the one hand, the importance of the quantitative and econometric techniques used to extract, as efficiently as possible, the information contained in the various indicators and sets of variables; and, on the other, the necessity of prioritizing this information, which, on occasion, can give contradictory signals. This is the basic task of the analyst, who must arrive at the most accurate diagnosis possible of the situation and of the trend of inflation, using a wide variety of information.

The following section contains a more thorough discussion of the major tools used in the Banco de España to evaluate the behavior of prices in the short and medium terms. Although the list is not exhaustive, an effort is made to cover the basic sources of information used for this purpose. Some of the procedures mentioned have long been used to analyze inflation; others are lines of research embarked upon more recently to improve the results of the analysis. Mention is made first of the direct price indicators, followed by their determinants on both the cost and demand sides. Then the monetary indicators are discussed, setting the stage for the introduction of the composite inflation indicator. Next, the available information on the inflationary expectations of economic agents is presented, ending with the quarterly BVAR model. Although the structural model is not among the analytical tools mentioned in this chapter, it can also be used to evaluate price movements. The following sections will also help introduce and provide a context for the next four chapters of this volume, which provide a detailed description of some of the most important work in the Banco de España in recent years to improve the analysis of prices.

Indicators for Inflation Monitoring and Forecasting

Direct Price Indicators

There is a type of indicator that provides price data directly and that normally takes the form of an index number. As mentioned above, the most
important of these is the CPI, the purpose of which is 'to measure movements over time in the level of prices of consumer goods and services
acquired or purchased by households'.[4] This index has been adopted as a
reference for defining the price objectives of monetary policy.

   The CPI is a monthly Laspeyres index, i.e. it is calculated on the basis of
a fixed basket of goods in the base year, which remains constant throughout the life of the index. At present, the base year is 1992 and the basket
of goods comes from the 1990–1 Household Expenditure Survey. The 471
items that make up the index are grouped according to the PROCOME
classification, whose highest level of aggregation corresponds to the eight
consumption functions (food, clothing, housing, household goods, medical
services, transportation, recreation and others). Alternatively, the items in
the CPI are grouped into five components (unprocessed food, processed
food, non-energy industrial goods, energy, and services), which is the
breakdown used for CPI analysis in the Banco de España. The processed
food, non-energy industrial goods, and services components reappear in
the index of prices of services and non-energy manufactured goods (*indice
de precios de servicios y bienes elaborados no energéticos – IPSEBENE*). The
construction of a subaggregate of consumer prices excluding the prices of
energy and unprocessed foods, which are considered especially volatile, is
a widespread international practice.

   Because it is a Laspeyres index, the CPI is subject to the so-called 'substitution bias,' owing to the fixed nature of the basket of goods and the
weights, which makes it necessary to re-base the index every so many
years. The expenditure and added value deflators, on the other hand, are
Paasche indices and are therefore subject to another type of bias, although
not the substitution bias, since a contemporaneous basket is used for their
weights. The deflators are estimated in the context of the national accounts
and are annual and quarterly. Although the GDP deflator and the private
consumption deflator could, in principle, serve as more appropriate measurements of aggregate inflation than the CPI itself, as they are quarterly
rather than monthly, the more imprecise nature of their estimates (being
implicit deflators), the successive revisions to which they are subject and
the longer delay in the availability of their data make the CPI a better
choice. In any case, the deflators provide an additional measurement of
price variations and are particularly useful for analyzing inflation from the
standpoint of its determinants, as they are consistently estimated using
other national accounting variables.

In addition to the CPI and the deflators, which capture the trend of final prices in the economy, there are other indices that show the behavior of the producer prices of certain productive activities: the industrial price index (IPRI) and the prices for agricultural products index. Both exclude VAT, but the IPRI includes other production taxes net of subsidies. Lastly, to highlight only the most important price statistics, mention should be made of the foreign trade unit value indices (UVI). Although the UVIs are not price indices strictly speaking, but are instead constructed on the basis of data concerning the amount and value of traded goods listed in customs declarations or Intrastat[5] documents, they provide the best approximation of the trend of foreign trade prices currently available.

Of course, the first problem to be solved in analyzing inflation is that of obtaining an accurate measurement of the subject of analysis. Price indices in general, and the CPI in particular, reflect changes in relative prices as well as changes in the general level of prices, i.e. the inflation rate. The latter can also be associated with more permanent or persistent movements of price indices, as changes in relative prices give rise to transitory movements. Moreover, regardless of whether they reflect changes in relative prices, price index movements can be erratic and therefore difficult to interpret. In the study by Álvarez and Matea (1996) Chapter 8 in this volume, various methods are described which are applied specifically to the CPI to obtain a permanent signal of the trend of prices, in order to eliminate general index movements resulting from adjustments in relative prices and not reflective of changes in the overall level of prices, and, in general, to obtain a stable signal of the trend of inflation. One of the most common methods of doing this is to eliminate those components of the CPI which, owing to the type of goods they include, are considered more likely to reflect erratic or relative price movements, and to approximate inflation by means of the rate of variation in the components that make up the so-called 'inflationary core'. The components excluded from the measurement of this core (which coincides with the IPSEBENE) are the prices of unprocessed foods and consumer energy products. Nevertheless, there is a good deal of disagreement over whether the exclusion of these prices is justified, on the basis that they are more likely to be affected by supply shocks.

One method of avoiding the *a priori* exclusion of certain prices while attempting to eliminate price movements not indicative of changes in the general level of prices is to use limited-influence estimators – such as the trimmed mean and the weighted median – the calculation of which excludes extreme price variations, on the assumption that the effects of changes in relative prices are concentrated in the tails of the distribution.

Another method of obtaining a streamlined measurement of inflation is by estimating a trend price signal: the trend, free of seasonal and irregular

elements, can be used to define the more stable and permanent elements
of price movements, and, therefore, provides a more suitable basis for calculating the economy's inflation rate. Underlying inflation is defined precisely as the rate of duly centred, year-on-year variation, calculated on the
basis of the price trend. It can be shown that the centred, year-on-year rate
of the original series' 3-month moving average provides a reliable approximation of underlying inflation in the case of the CPI. It should be noted
that the estimation of this rate for the most recent period requires the use
of predictions.

The concept of underlying inflation, as defined above (the centred, year-
on-year rate of the price trend), applies to price indices other than the
CPI, for which it is also possible to find approximations of underlying inflation in terms of centred rates, calculated on the basis of moving averages
(with more or fewer terms, depending on the case) of the original series.

Lastly, another method of using price indices to obtain trend measurements of the inflation rate is based on the use of VAR-type autoregressive
models, which differs from the above methods in that information from
outside the price index itself is used (multivariate measurements of inflation). In the Banco de España, two measurements of this type have been
estimated – permanent inflation and latent inflation – using a VAR model
with two variables (CPI and GDP), in which the condition of a vertical,
long-run Phillips curve is satisfied. The first of these measurements captures the influence of those disturbances which affect the long-term inflation rate, while latent inflation captures the impact on prices of those
disturbances which do not affect long-term production. In practice, the two
are very similar to each other and to the observed rate of inflation, which
indicates the predominance of nominal-type, permanent disturbances in
determining inflation in Spain.

Price predictions are necessary for more reasons than calculating a trend
signal. The availability of predictions is useful in and of itself as a quantitative expression of the prospective trend of prices implicit in the information series used to obtain these predictions; they therefore facilitate a more
accurate appraisal of the new price data that appear. There are numerous
methods of predicting prices, whether on a conditional or non-conditional
basis, ranging from univariate models to multivariate models and including
structural econometric models. A balance must therefore be struck
between simplicity and economy of means, on the one hand, and volume
of information and the analytical capacity of the resulting predictions, on
the other, which must be resolved in accordance with the purposes of the
analysis. In this chapter, which focuses on the means available for evaluating the inflationary situation in the short and medium term – and not so
much on assessments of the interaction of macroeconomic variables – the
formulation of monthly or quarterly forecasts is of special interest. For the

CPI, single equation models – described briefly below – and the BVAR model – summarized in a subsequent section and the subject Chapter 11 in this volume – are available.

The use of single-equation models (ARIMA and transfer functions) for short-term price predictions is particularly useful because these models very efficiently capture the monthly dynamics of these series and are a very powerful tool for evaluating new data. ARIMA models can be used to extrapolate a series using its own past as the sole source of information, whereas transfer function models include information from other variables that anticipate the behavior of the series analyzed, in order to improve the results of the projection. Matea (1993) provides a detailed analysis of the problems associated with predicting prices using models of this type. In any case, because the predictions they yield are highly inertial, they are inappropriate for medium-and long-term predictions. They can be used in the short term, however, to appraise the processes of price acceleration or deceleration, based on the systematic deviations of the new data from predictions thereof. Figure 7.2 illustrates this point in the case of the CPI: each new datum contributes new information, which is incorporated in the forecasts for the following months, and, therefore, modifies the estimate of underlying (trend) inflation in the preceding months, demonstrating the effects of the information contained in the new datum on the trend of prices.

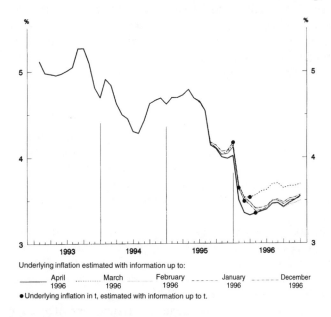

Figure 7.2   Underlying inflation in the CPI

Sources: INE and Banco de España.

In the case of the CPI, modelling and prediction are via models estimated for its basic components (except the energy component), since both its dynamics and its determinants – and, therefore, its potential indicators – are different. Thus, it has been shown that the prices for agricultural products contribute valuable information for predicting the unprocessed foods price component by means of a transfer function. For the prices of processed food and of non-energy industrial goods, the corresponding producer price indices (components, in turn, of the IPRI) are appropriate indicators. Moreover, tests are under way to include other variables – which, *a priori*, seem appropriate – in the models for predicting the components of the CPI.

Matea and Regil (1996), in fact, explore the possibilities of improving the analysis and short-term prediction of the CPI and the IPSEBENE using other variables from the real sector (prices, demand, activity) and the monetary sector that could anticipate their behavior. As the focus of the analysis is the short term, work has been done on stationary transformations of the potentially useful series, initially considering a total of 25 possible real sector and monetary sector quarterly indicators. In the iterative selection process, the following were identified as CPI indicators: prices received by farmers, the IPRI of capital goods, the projected trend of prices from the Monthly Business Survey (*Encuesta de Coyuntura Industrial*), the employed population, and the peseta/dollar exchange rate. The indicators identified for the IPSEBENE were, in the following order: the IPRI of capital goods, the employed population, the peseta/dollar exchange rate, and capacity utilization. Nevertheless, predictions utilizing component models are, for the present, superior to those derived from the use of CPI or IPSEBENE models, even if expanded with prior variables.

The Price Formation Process: Costs

From a macroeconomic standpoint, analysis of the price formation process is essential for explaining the past and present behavior of inflation and for making short-and medium-term conditional forecasts. With this analysis, it is possible to determine the contribution of the various cost components, as well as that of decisions concerning margins (i.e. supply factors), to the trend of prices.

The price formation process can be analyzed by means of direct cost and price indicators (using wage, output, employment, and price statistics), which are also useful for properly monitoring cost pressures disaggregated by productive activity.[6] The National Accounts also provide precise information for studying the formation of prices, in a context where the various cost and margin measurements acquire internal consistency, although the disaggregated analysis is complicated in this case by the delay in publishing the information and the revisions made to it. In any case, at the aggregate level, National Accounts data provide an overall view of price formation in the economy and are the most appropriate framework for making conditional forecasts of medium-term cost pressures.

The price formation process, at the aggregate level and in the context of the National Accounts, is approximated by breaking down the final demand deflator.[7] The annex to this chapter shows how the expression of the final demand deflator as a function of costs can be arrived at, based on National Accounts figures and the relationships established between the various account aggregates. The expression obtained for the deflator is:

$$\Delta Pdf \simeq \omega_y[\Delta P_y + \Delta\lambda_y] + \omega_m[\Delta P_m + \Delta\lambda_m] \qquad (7.1)$$

where

$$\Delta P_y = \omega_r \Delta CLU + \omega_e \Delta\left(\frac{EB^*}{y}\right) + \omega_t \Delta\left(\frac{TN}{y}\right) \qquad (7.2)$$

P_{df}, P_y and P_m are the deflators for final demand, GDP and imports, respectively; λ_y and λ_m the share of GDP and imports in final demand, in real terms, respectively; and ω_i the weights of the various components of final demand and GDP, as defined in the annex. In (7.2), *CLU* are labor costs, EB^* is the adjusted gross operating surplus, as explained in the Appendix (p. 271), and *TN* indirect taxes net of subsidies, all at current prices; lastly y is GDP in real terms.

(7.1) and (7.2) summarize the price formation process at the aggregate level by making explicit the contribution of domestic costs (labor) and external costs (imports), as well as the impact of net indirect taxes and the behavior of unit margins. As these expressions demonstrate, the contribution of the domestic factors – summarized in the GDP deflator – and of the cost of imports to the variation of the deflator depends not only on the movement of the corresponding GDP and import deflators, but also on how their 'market shares' have evolved, i.e. the extent to which final demand, in real terms, is satisfied with domestic production or with imported goods and services. Despite this being merely an accounting breakdown, the two expressions together have a high interpretative content if analyzed in light of a mark-up pricing model, wherein the component (EB^*/y) reflects the extent to which entrepreneurs do or do not pass on to prices the full impact of costs and indirect taxes.

As for the factors behind the external component of final prices, the trend of import prices will be explained by the behavior of international prices and the exchange rate. Of course, this is not the only way that movements in these variables can affect the process of inflation in an economy (although it is the most direct and quantifiable). The prices of domestic goods that compete with imported goods will also have to move in line with import prices, expressed in pesetas. Furthermore, the movements of external prices and the exchange rate take a certain amount of time to show up in import prices and in domestic prices, so that monitoring the corresponding indicators is very important for evaluating the inflationary situation, for, as mentioned below, they may serve as leading indicators of inflation. In short, there is more to analyzing the external sources of inflation than studying the import deflator and its direct contribution to the formation of final prices in the economy.

The domestic price components in the expression for the GDP deflator, (7.2), summarize the principal means by which inflationary pressures are generated on the supply side of the economy. Thus, unit labor costs reflect the pressure from wages and other labor costs, and the effect of public sector decisions (through taxes and contributions) on these costs. Likewise, through productivity, they reflect the technological and cyclical circumstances of the economy. The impact of indirect taxation on the price formation process also stems from public sector decisions. Lastly, unit margins are the result of a variety of factors, ranging from the degree of competition in product markets to the level of demand pressure, which is not a supply issue, as prices are not the result of supply factors but rather of the confluence of the latter with demand. Any information concerning the probable behavior of the components of short-and medium-term costs will be useful for pinpointing potential cost pressures in that span of time.

By way of illustration, Table 7.1 presents the weights, rates of variation, and contributions of the various cost and margin components to the growth of the GDP and final demand deflators for 1992–5. Similarly, Figure 7.3 shows the growth rates and contributions of these same components for a more extended period (1987–95). As for the contributions of domestic and import costs to the growth of the final demand deflator, what stands out most throughout the period is that the share of imports has systematically expanded in the Spanish market, except in 1993. Until that year, import prices posted substantially lower rates of variation than those of GDP, spurred by the appreciation of the peseta during the period, so that their growing weight in final demand was a moderating factor in final prices. In more recent years, however, import prices have accelerated markedly, reflecting the depreciation of the peseta since the summer of 1992.

Unlike import prices, the GDP deflator slowed in 1993, owing to the appreciable moderation of labor costs. One of the components of the GDP deflator that stands out is the strong growth of the surplus per unit of output throughout the period, which signals a sustained process of expanding margins in the economy as a whole. The lack of competition in a significant segment of the goods and services markets and, in general, the existence of rigidities in the functioning of the markets are reflected quantitatively and in summary fashion by the continued growth of the unit surplus. The

Table 7.1 Composition of the gross domestic product (GDP) and final demand (DF) deflators, 1992–5

	Weights				Rates of variation				Contributions to growth			
	1992	1993	1994	1995	1992	1993	1994	1995	1992	1993	1994	1995
Unit labor cost (CLU)	58.3	58.3	57.8	56.1	6.8	3.3	1.0	2.2	4.0	2.0	0.6	1.2
Compensation per employee	–	–	–	–	9.2	6.1	3.6	2.5	–	–	–	–
Output per employee	–	–	–	–	2.2	2.6	2.7	0.3	–	–	–	–
– Real GDP	–	–	–	–	0.7	–1.2	2.1	3.0	–	–	–	–
– Total employment	–	–	–	–	–1.5	–3.7	–0.6	2.6	–	–	–	–
Net indirect taxes	8.1	8.7	7.3	7.8	15.3	–12.5	10.5	6.9	1.2	–1.1	0.8	0.5
Gross operating surplus (EBE)	33.6	33.0	34.9	36.1	4.9	10.4	7.4	8.5	1.6	3.4	2.6	3.1
GDP DEFLATOR	100.0	100.0	100.0	100.0	6.8	4.3	3.9	4.8	6.8	4.3	3.9	4.8
Domestic costs	83.1	83.1	83.3	81.9	5.5	5.2	2.1	3.2	4.5	4.4	1.7	2.7
GDP per unit of final demand	–	–	–	–	–1.3	0.9	–1.7	–1.5	–1.1	0.7	–1.5	–1.2
GDP deflator	–	–	–	–	6.8	4.3	3.9	4.8	5.7	3.6	3.3	3.9
Import costs	16.9	16.9	16.7	18.1	6.1	3.3	12.6	10.1	1.0	0.6	2.1	1.8
Imports per unit of final demand	–	–	–	–	4.8	–3.1	6.3	5.0	0.8	–0.5	1.0	0.9
Import deflator	–	–	–	–	1.3	6.6	6.0	4.9	0.2	1.1	1.0	0.9
FINAL DEMAND DEFLATOR	100.0	100.0	100.0	100.0	5.6	4.9	3.9	4.5	5.6	4.9	3.9	4.5

Source: INE and Banco de España.

moderation of unit labor costs in the most recent period and the persistent pressure of business margins are clearly illustrated in Figure 7.3.

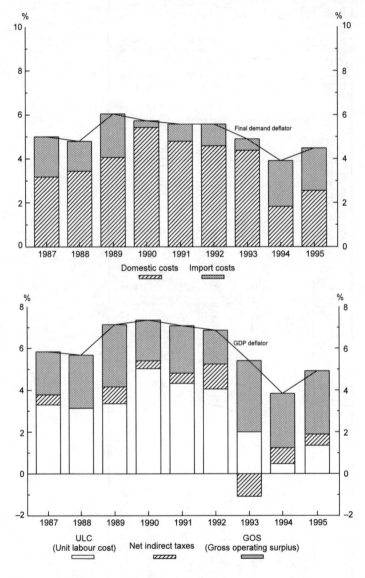

Figure 7.3 Composition of the final demand deflator: contributions to its growth and growth of the GDP deflator, 1987–95

a   Contributions to growth of the final demand deflator
b   Contributions to growth of the GDP deflator
Sources: INE and Banco de España.

The Pressure of Demand on Capacity and Prices

In addition to the various measurements of cost pressure analyzed above, the other important group of indicators and variables that must be taken into account in studying the determinants of short- and medium-term prices comprises those which approximate the pressure of demand. In some cases, the purpose of these indicators is to measure the existing gap between real expenditure and a measurement of trend or potential output, either directly, such as the output gap, or indirectly, such as capacity utilization (CU). In other cases, they represent approximations of nominal expenditure, either of a particular sector (public or private sector, for example) or of the economy as a whole (such as certain monetary aggregates, which are analyzed in the following section). Some measurements of the pressure of expenditure rely on conditional estimates and forecasts made in the context of the National Accounts, such as the output gap, although there are exceptions, such as CU or the monetary aggregates.

The pressure of demand on capacity is an important factor in explaining possible price accelerations (surges in inflation) in a mark-up type pricing model. The indicators available for these purposes range from measurements such as the output gap, which attempts to measure the cyclical component of GDP, to others such as the non-accelerating inflation rate of unemployment (NAIRU) or CU, both of which provide information on the degree of input utilization.

There are several methods of measuring the output gap – i.e. the gap between trend or potential output and that actually observed – which depend on how trend or potential output is calculated. In general terms, two types of calculation methods can be distinguished: those that are based on statistical procedures and those that take a more analytical approach, attempting to apply the concepts of economic theory. The statistical methods employ the observed values of the GDP series to obtain the trend component of this variable. Initially, linear trends were used, which could vary from one cycle to another. Later, Hodrick and Prescott (1980) proposed smoothing the GDP series with a linear filter, which allows the user to select the desired degree of smoothing. The latter method is the one most widely used, at least among those with a statistical focus, given its ease of use, although it does have some disadvantages, including the fact that it is not based on the criteria of economic theory and that estimating the trend at the extreme ends of the sample period is sensitive to the receipt of new information and varies with it.

Among the methods with an analytical focus, that most widely used is based on the estimation of an output function that permits the approximation of potential output using existing quantities of inputs. This is the approach taken in the OECD (see Giorno *et al.*, 1995), where potential output is calculated subject to the requirement that it should not lead to price accelerations (i.e. potential employment is measured in terms of the NAWRU, or non-accelerating wages rate of unemployment). One of the advantages of these methods is that they have a clear economic interpretation, although they are more difficult to use than the purely statistical procedures and the results depend on the structural assumptions that must necessarily be made. Moreover, the VAR model estimated by Álvarez and Sebastián (1995) for the CPI and GDP, in addition to providing estimates of latent and permanent inflation, can also be used to measure trend output. Given that there is no general criterion accepted as superior, the ideal method would be to obtain various measurements of the output gap, if possible, in order to compare them. In the Banco de España, the output gap is generally estimated using the Hodrick–Prescott filter and the above-mentioned VAR model, although attention is also paid to the statistical measurements published by other institutions.

For indicators that attempt to approximate the pressure of demand through the degree of input utilization, quarterly information on the degree of capacity utilization in the industrial sector can be obtained from the opinion surveys of entrepreneurs in that sector. Urtasun (1994) has assessed the goodness of fit of this indicator for signalling inflationary pressures in the 1972–93 period, and it has been shown that there is a level of utilization beyond which prices are driven up; for the period under consideration, it is estimated that this level is situated slightly above 80 per cent. The estimate was obtained using various measurements of inflation in the industrial sector (IPRI, industrial VA deflator), as well as more general measurements (CPI). The use of this estimate is similar to that of the NAIRU.

On the subject of the pressure of demand, one of the most relevant aspects to be analyzed is to what extent general government activity may be curbing or encouraging the excessive growth of nominal demand. It should be noted, first, that not all general government activity related to the determination of prices at the macroeconomic level is reflected in its impact on aggregate demand. Some of this activity has a direct impact on costs and prices (indirect taxes, operating subsidies, contributions) and is captured by the fiscal variables[8] included in the equation for breaking down the final demand deflator described above.

The simplest method of assessing the contribution of public spending to the growth of demand is to compare the rates of nominal variation of both variables. Taking a somewhat more sophisticated approach, Martí and Argimón (1996) propose monitoring two quarterly indicators, designed specifically to approximate the impact of general government activity on prices, through aggregate demand. The first captures the trend of general government final demand (government consumption plus public investment). An indicator of direct demand can also be defined that excludes civil service wages from government consumption, i.e. which includes only general government purchases of goods and services and public investment. In any case, the series are deflated to obtain an indicator of real demand. The purpose of the second indicator is to measure the indirect effect of fiscal policy on demand, transmitted through household disposable income and, therefore, through private consumption. The indicator is constructed as the sum of social security benefits minus income and wealth taxes and minus workers' social contributions, all of which are deflated. These indicators are prepared using annual nominal series derived from estimates and forecasts made in the context of the national accounts, interpolated with government and social security budget outturn data to obtain quarterly periodicity. In any case, these indicators are of recent construction and will have to be enhanced as they are progressively used.

One very prevalent method of analysing general government activity is to construct fiscal impulse indicators (see Gómez Jiménez (1993) and Gómez and Roldán (1995)). Indicators of this type, widely used by international organizations, attempt to assess in summary fashion the expansive or contractive nature of the fiscal policy implemented from a macroeconomic perspective, whereby the cyclical movements of the deficit must be eliminated. These indicators are not, therefore, designed to measure public sector pressure on demand, although they do provide valuable information about the relationship between fiscal policy and inflation, since, insofar as the impulse is countercyclical, it will help moderate inflation movements throughout the cycle. It should be remembered that their construction involves estimating a cyclical component of the general government balance, which is derived from the automatic stabilisers incorporated into public revenue and expenditure, and a structural component of the deficit, associated with the discretionary action of the fiscal authorities. The fiscal impulse indicators should be interpreted with caution, because their synthesizing function poses problems, stemming from the difficulties of making an accurate temporal allocation of the discretionary fiscal measures and the assessment of the cyclical component itself. In some cases, the expansive or contractive nature of this discretionary action is related to comparison with a base year (as in the IMF indicator, for example), which qualifies any conclusions derived therefrom. Generally, these indicators do not aim to provide precise information on the level of the various components of the public deficit (as a percentage of GDP), but rather on the change in that level, so as thus to assess whether a given year's fiscal policy stance is expansive or contractive.

Fiscal policy stance indicators distinguishing between cyclical and structural components are open to criticism because, by calculating one of the components as a residual, they incorporate into it, along with genuinely structural or cyclical (according to the case) elements, transitory effects. An alternative approach for extracting the various components of the fiscal balance is to make a distinction between a trend component that would capture the more permanent elements of the deficit, a cyclical component correlated with the fluctuations in output, and a third residual component that would capture the impact of discretionary measures and non-cyclical factors, with transitory effects, all measured in terms of budgetary variables expressed as a percentage of GDP. This approach has two advantages: separation of the transitory elements from the definition of structural deficit, and the direct estimation of the stabilising effects of fiscal policy on variables as a percentage of GDP, which is a way of deflating the variables so that the results can be interpreted in real terms. This line of research is currently being pursued in the Banco de España.

Monetary Variables and Nominal Expenditure

The monetary aggregates are, in principle, leading indicators of nominal expenditure; thus, they can anticipate inflationary pressures stemming from an excessive increase in demand. In fact, this relationship between monetary aggregates and nominal expenditure is the basis of two-stage monetary policy strategies that take one of these aggregates as an intermediate objective. In Spain, the switch from a two-stage strategy based on the use of the ALP aggregate as an intermediate objective to the direct monitoring of a price objective was largely prompted by stability problems in the relationship between ALP and expenditure, as explained in another chapter of this book. Despite this, interest in analyzing monetary aggregates remains strong, and aggregates are still considered excellent indicators for making monetary policy decisions.

The study of Cabrero Bravo, Martínez Pagés and Pérez-Jurado (1996), chapter 9 in this volume, re-examines the short-term relationship between aggregates, nominal expenditure, and prices. As demonstrated in this study, the informational content of the various aggregates is high and various methodologies are used to extract information on prices and nominal expenditure. The first method of extracting information from monetary and credit variables is centred on the capacity of these variables to anticipate the turning points of inflation, as measured by the CPI (which task is linked to the procedure followed for the summary indicator, discussed in the following section). First, a test is performed for causality between the various monetary and credit aggregates (taken separately) and prices, from which an initial conclusion is drawn concerning the predictive capacity of the various aggregates. Regarding the lead of the turning points of inflation, a decision was made to use the rate of variation of inflation, corrected for deterministic effects, as a reference variable in the study. The results indicate asymmetries among the various indicators in capturing the turning points. Moreover, the peaks – indicative of the start of a period of slower inflationary growth – are captured with less dispersion than the troughs; the lead period is longer in the peaks than in the troughs. Using various criteria for the goodness of fit of the lead, the most consistent aggregate and the one that best satisfies said criteria is domestic credit to businesses and households, broadly defined. The best monetary aggregates are ALP and M2.

The second line of research described in the above-mentioned study is the construction of weighted monetary aggregates, in which the weights of each asset included in the definition reflect its distinct degree of liquidity (as not all assets are perfect substitutes from this standpoint). To calculate the weights, and, given the difficulties of doing so using interest rate differentials in respect of an alternative, illiquid asset, a procedure was used consisting of estimating, by means of a leading indicator model, those weights which, when applied to the various components of a given aggregate, yield a liquidity growth that anticipates the trend of nominal expenditure in a more stable manner. In the case of ALP2 and its disaggregation into 3 sub-aggregates (APL2–M3, M3–M2 and M2), a weighted aggregate is obtained that anticipates the movements of nominal GDP and the GDP deflator in a stable manner. The weight structure obtained makes it possible to analyze both the relative liquidity of the various groups of assets making up the aggregate and their long-term trend, demonstrating that they are not perfect substitutes for one another, owing to their varying degrees of liquidity.

On the whole, the various exercises performed in the study show that the monetary and credit aggregates provide relevant information for the analysis of short-term inflation, as they tend to anticipate movements in the target monetary policy variable. Nevertheless, there is no one aggregate, weighted or unweighted, which is clearly superior to the others in this anticipatory function, so that the best strategy would be to combine all of the information they provide.

Composite Inflation Indicators[9]

As pointed out above, inflation is a phenomenon characterized by a general rise in prices and costs, but, obviously, not all prices or their determinants vary simultaneously. This points to a possible method of predicting inflation – and, specifically, the rate of CPI variation – as the chronological order of cyclical variations in a set of indicators potentially related to final prices can serve as the basis for anticipating the critical points at which the trend of the phenomenon being monitored – i.e. inflation – will change direction. The information contained in this set of leading indicators of inflation can be combined in a composite index, the purpose of which is to qualitatively anticipate the points marking the transition from one phase to another, rather than quantitatively predicting variables.

The methodology of composite leading indicators is rooted in tasks related to the preparation of composite indices to anticipate the turning points in the general index of economic activity, which mark the changes between the expansive and recessive phases of the economy. Conceptually, a composite leading indicator is a time series that summarizes the information contained in a set of partial indicators representative of an economic phenomenon, for purposes of anticipating as precisely as possible the cyclical consistencies of that phenomenon. Insofar as the inflation rate exhibits cyclical behavior, the methodology based on the determination of turning points can play a clear role in the analysis of inflation, by exploiting the predictive capacity of those indicators that anticipate the turning points on the inflationary path.[10]

The preparation of composite indicators capable of anticipating movements in the rate of inflation is complicated in Spain by the shortness of the macroeconomic series which, together with the large trend component of inflation, results in few turning points in the price variation series. Nevertheless, some studies have attempted to construct leading indicators of inflation, e.g. Fernández and Virto (1994). Another more recent study employing a similar methodology is that of Cabrero and Delrieu (1996). What sets this study apart from the previous ones are, first, the use of inflation rate variation (measured by the CPI) as a reference indicator, corrected for deterministic phenomena, instead of the trend component of the IPSEBENE; and, second, the effort to adapt the composite index to the dynamic trend of inflation, in order not only to anticipate the turning points, but also to predict the trend component of medium-term inflation.

In this study, after establishing the reference chronology with the aforementioned indicator, an analysis is performed of a large sample of real, monetary and financial indicators that approximate the pressure of demand on the factor, commodity, and capital markets, to determine their lead capacity *vis-à-vis* the reference chronology. Part of the analysis (i.e. the part related to monetary and credit indicators) was mentioned in the preceding section, in the discussion of these aggregates as indicators of nominal expenditure. The analysis as a whole indicates, as a general concept, that the peaks of the reference indicator are anticipated with greater precision than the troughs.

Based on the individual analyses performed with each indicator, the authors selected those that best anticipate the turning points of the reference indicator, taking as selection criteria the mean and the median lead, the standard deviation, and the number of points in the reference chronology actually anticipated, these criteria being supplemented with a number of tests for causality to determine the possible existence of a dynamic lag–lead relationship between the previously selected variables and the CPI. The synthesis between the set of indicators with the capacity to anticipate turning points in the reference series and those with significant predictive power allows for the selection of a total of 10 indicators to form the composite index. Of these, four are price indicators (the consumer goods industrial price index, the capital goods index, the capital goods unit value index, and prices of agricultural products), two approximate the pressure of demand (merchandise imports and government current expenditure and capital expenditure), one is a cost variable (wage settlements under collective bargaining agreements), and 3 are monetary and financial variables (M2, expanded credit to businesses and households, and the peseta/D-Mark exchange rate).

To combine the selected components in the composite index, the statistical technique of principal components is used to simplify the structure of the data and explain most of the information contained in the indicators through the optimum linear combination thereof. The composite indicator ultimately obtained detects the critical points of the reference indicator with a relatively stable lead, which, on average, can be quantified at around nine months (see Figure 7.4). The goodness of fit of this indicator is reaffirmed by its ability to predict the trend of prices in a continuous and non-discrete environment, which can be verified by estimating and testing a statistical prediction model.

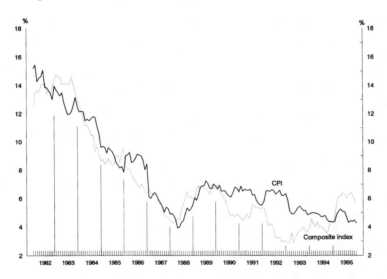

Figure 7.4   Year-on-year growth of the composite index and the CPI, 1982–95
Sources: INE and Banco de España.

Certainly, the results obtained so far in this line of research are encouraging, although they will have to be tested by actually using the indicator and confirming that it provides information additional to that obtained with other prediction models.

Indicators of Inflationary Expectations

A very important channel for the transmission of monetary policy in the current system, which is based on a direct price objective, is the influence on economic agents' inflationary expectations. The importance of this transmission channel is determined by how swiftly and pervasively monetary policy can produce effects through it, and by the weight of the expectations in determining the basic price trend variables. This section contains a few comments on the most representative indicators of expectations.

The financial markets are among those most affected by the trend of inflationary expectations. The swiftness and efficiency of operations in these markets are such that changes in expectations promptly affect equilibrium prices. In certain circumstances, the term structure of interest rates – i.e. the relationship between interest rates and maturities – can provide information on the expectations of economic agents concerning the future trend of inflation and interest rates themselves. In chapter 10 in this book, Ayuso and Núñez (1996) analyze the conditions in which information concerning expectations can be extracted from the term structure of interest rates.

To obtain this information, the first task is to estimate the term structure of interest rates and of the corresponding implicit forward rates. This structure is not directly observable, as the rates observed, which are not available for all terms, contain credit and liquidity risk premia, the effects of taxation, etc. Public debt interest rates, which are not affected by credit risk and which are usually sufficiently liquid, are used for the estimate, which is made under the assumption that the forward rates converge toward a given level and at a certain velocity, which will have to be estimated.

Once the yield curve has been estimated – and, therefore, the structure of implicit forward rates – and given the theoretical relationship between forward rates and the interest rates expected by economic agents, the latter can be derived from the former, provided an estimate of risk premia by term is available. Although this latter condition is not easily satisfied, it appears that these premia are very small in Spain. There is also a theoretical relationship between forward rates and the expected inflation rate, although deriving the latter from the former requires knowledge not only of the premia by term, but also of the inflation premia and the real interest rates expected by economic agents. Again, these latter elements of the forward rates are difficult to disentangle, but there are indications that in our case they are relatively stable; therefore, given the smallness of the premia by term, shifts in the forward rates curve will be indicative of changes in inflationary expectations.

In summary, given the not unrealistic assumption that *ex ante* real interest rates as well as premia by term and inflation premia remain relatively stable, the forward rates curve can be used as a monetary policy indicator, since shifts in it can be associated with changes in two key variables, such as interest rates and expected inflation rates. Thus, shifts in the forward rates curve for the medium term (1 year, for example) can be associated with changes in inflationary expectations, while shifts in the forward rates curve for shorter periods (1 month, for example) can be more easily interpreted as changes in nominal interest rates expected by economic agents in that term, which, in so short a period, will be associated with the expected changes in Banco de España intervention rates.

Apart from the yield curve, there are other indicators of inflationary expectations which are related to nonfinancial markets. Prominent among these are opinion surveys, which provide information on the price expectations of various economic agents, these expectations being, in turn, of a different nature. Thus, the *Monthly Business Survey* (*Encuesta de Coyuntura Industrial – ECI*) provides information on the trend of industrial prices projected by entrepreneurs themselves, who are the ones who will ultimately set these prices. Consumer opinion surveys, on the other hand, also include information on consumer price rises expected by these agents, wherein the variable with the most immediate effect is wages.

The relationship between opinions on the projected price trend (ppt), as captured in the business survey (ECI), and the inflation rate measured by the industrial price index (IPRI) has been discussed in various Banco de España studies. Specifically, Matea (1994) estimated a transfer function using the ppt as an explanatory variable of IPRI variations, arriving at the conclusion that the former actually led the latter. Urtasun (1995) analyzes this relationship by estimating a structural equation derived from an augmented Phillips curve including expectations, whose explanatory variables also include orders on hand and the expected trend in orders on hand as approximations of output gap pressure. The results, still highly provisional, also show the potential of the ppt as a leading indicator of inflation in the industrial sector.

Multi-equation Forecasting Models

As already pointed out, the analysis of more or less varied information on the inflationary situation should lead to the estimation of a projected path of price movements, together with a measurement, if possible, of the uncertainty associated with this forecast. One method of achieving this synthesis of information may be to prepare macroeconomic forecasts, with the sole requirement of accounting consistency. In this case, the expert is entirely free to incorporate his own opinions into the forecast, although the procedure has the disadvantage of not being particularly transparent, and a quantified measurement of the uncertainty associated with the forecasts is not easily obtained. The construction of structural macroeconomic models is another method of synthesizing information on the economy as a whole to obtain forecasts of the principal macroeconomic variables, including prices. Although, in the past, models of this type assumed considerable proportions, they have since tended to shrink, so that the amount of information they contain is, in principle, insufficient for the expert's purposes. However, they are more transparent since the relationships between the variables are explicit and make it possible to quantify the uncertainty surrounding the forecasts. In the case of both expert forecasts and those generated by a structural model, the forecasts will generally be conditional, as they will be subject to the assumptions made concerning the behavior of the exogenous and economic policy variables throughout the forecasting period.

A third method of synthesizing the information is to use a multivariate forecasting model, which, unlike structural methods, uses only the statistical properties of the series selected to estimate the interrelationships between the several variables and obtain forecasts, whether nonconditional, i.e. based solely on the past values of these series, or conditional. This is the type of model that will be described in this section. Before doing so, however, it should be remembered that the various methods of synthesizing information mentioned above are not alternative methods of forecasting inflation, but rather can and should be complementary, so that the results obtained from the models enrich the expert's forecasts, or, alternatively, the latter modifies the results of the models, which in fact happens in some central banks, as mentioned on pages 246–8.

The multivariate model is presented in the study by Álvarez, Ballabriga and Jareño (1996), chapter 11 in this volume. It is a small macroeconometric model, estimated according to the methodology of Bayesian vectors of autoregression (BVAR), the econometric principles of which are explained in the study. Briefly, the BVAR methodology involves estimating the interrelationships within the vector of variables selected on the basis of information provided by the past values of the series and certain *a priori* information on the probability distribution of the model's parameters, which makes their estimation possible without running the risk of overadjusting the model. The distinguishing characteristic of BVAR models is that the *a priori* information does not consist of exclusion conditions imposed on the parameters of the model by economic theory, but is rather of a purely instrumental character and has an empirical origin divorced from theory. The resulting predictions in turn incorporate as basic information the past values of the variables selected and the estimated interrelationships between them.

The BVAR model of the Spanish economy is quarterly and includes nine variables, representative of the four sectors into which the economy has been divided for purposes of the model: the external sector (exchange rate, representative of the competitiveness of the economy and the channel for the transmission of monetary policy, and level of world economic activity); the monetary sector, which includes the monetary authority and the financial institutions (interest rate, channel for the transmission of monetary policy through its effect on spending decisions, and money stock); the public sector (net government financing); and the domestic sector, which includes the domestic economic agents who make decisions concerning production, investment, labor supply and demand, and consumption (prices, approximated by the CPI, wages, employment, and GDP).

The *a priori* information introduced in the model assumes that all of the variables are endogenous, except world economic activity, which is exogenous. Likewise, it is assumed that the interest rate follows an autoregressive process, exogenous to the rest of the variables in the system. Moreover, tests of the predictive capacity of the model – generally, and in relation to inflation – have been satisfactory, especially in medium-term target periods, so that consideration of the interrelationships between variables in forecasting the future behavior of inflation is useful. In short, the BVAR model is a useful, complementary tool for predicting inflation in Spain, the main advantages of which are its transparency and the possibility of supplementing the forecasts with a quantitative measurement of their probability of fulfilment. The structural model, which is discussed in another chapter, can also be used to make forecasts of this type. Its inclusion in the part of the book that examines the transmission mechanism is intended to emphasize its usefulness in analyzing alternative policies.

FINAL CONSIDERATIONS

The Banco de España's current monetary policy strategy, which is characterized by the lack of an intermediate variable and the direct monitoring of a price objective, is based essentially on analysis of the inflationary situation and the diagnosis of price trends. This necessitates the processing and analysis of a wide variety of information, to ensure that the diagnosis is as accurate as possible. As this chapter has endeavored to make clear, the Banco de España takes an eclectic approach to the use of information, as there is not enough confidence in any one technique to make it stand out from the others. This also reduces the likelihood of making major errors. In this context, the Bank's efforts are focused on developing powerful analytical tools, although the analyst's opinion is essential in formulating a diagnosis on inflation.

To ensure the credibility of actions taken by the Banco de España on the basis of this information, it is essential that the information be analyzed with sufficient transparency, hence the importance of the various reports published by the Bank analyzing the inflationary situation, particularly the semi-annual *Inflation Report*. Moreover, the method of analyzing inflation and processing the related data is constantly evolving. The use of increasingly efficient techniques and the incorporation of new information capable of providing a greater understanding of price behavior indicate that the analytical process is constantly being developed and perfected.

Appendix: Breakdown of the GDP and Final Demand Deflators

In the context of the national accounts, one direct method of arriving at an expression of final prices as a function of costs, based on the relationships established between the various account aggregates, is to consider the balance between uses and resources described in the goods and services account:

$$Q + M = CI + DF$$

where Q is total output, M imports, CI intermediate consumption and DF final demand, and the use of capital letters indicates that the variables are valued at the current prices of year t (omitting the t subscript for purposes of simplicity). Given that gross domestic product (Y) equals total output less intermediate consumption in the productive process, it is holds that:

$$Y + M = DF$$

i.e. final demand is satisfied with domestic output or imports. As the deflators are implicit variables, resulting from the division of variables at current prices and at base year prices, the following expression can be derived from the preceding identity:

$$P_{df} = \frac{DF}{df} = \lambda_y P_y + \lambda_m P_m$$

where the use of small letters indicates that the variables are valued at constant base year prices, $\lambda_y = \frac{y}{df}$, $\lambda_m = \frac{m}{df}$ and P_x is generally the deflator of variable X.

The final demand deflator represents the index of aggregate prices of all goods and services in the economy to be used for final consumption and investment purposes, and the preceding expression can be interpreted as the summarized form of the supply curve of these goods and services. However, more than the expression of the final demand deflator in levels, the interesting aspect here is the change in the level. Taking the preceding expression (and disregarding the second order terms), the following is obtained:

$$\Delta P_{df} \simeq \omega_y[\Delta P_y + \Delta \lambda_y] + \omega_m[\Delta P_m + \Delta \lambda_m] \qquad (7A.1)$$

where $\qquad \Delta X = \dfrac{X - X_{-1}}{X_{-1}}, \omega_y = \dfrac{Y_{-1}}{DF_{-1}}$ and $\omega_m = \dfrac{M_{-1}}{DF_{-1}}$

(7A.1) summarizes the contribution of internal and external factors to the growth of the final demand deflator, from the viewpoint of supply, i.e. of resources available to satisfy that demand. As for inflation of domestic origin, the economy's operating account can be used to perform a more detailed analysis. According to this account:

$$Y = RA + EB + TN$$

where RA is the compensation of wage earners, EB is the gross operating surplus, and TN indirect taxes net of subsidies, including VAT and net import taxes. The GDP deflator can therefore be expressed as:

$$P_y = \frac{RA}{y} + \frac{EB}{y} + \frac{TN}{y}$$

so that the variation of this deflator will be:

$$\Delta P_y = \omega_r \Delta \left(\frac{RA}{y}\right) + \omega_e \Delta \left(\frac{EB}{y}\right) + \omega_t \Delta \left(\frac{TN}{y}\right)$$

where $\qquad \omega_r = \dfrac{RA_{-1}}{y_{-1}}, \omega_e = \dfrac{EB_{-1}}{y_{-1}}$ and $\omega_t = \dfrac{TN_{-1}}{y_{-1}},$

The components

$$\frac{EB}{y} \text{ and } \frac{TN}{y}$$

capture the surplus and indirect taxes net of subsidies per unit of real output. As there is no deflator for any of these variables, their contribution to the change in the GDP deflator is obtained directly by multiplying their nominal variation per unit of GDP by the corresponding weight.

Moreover, the expression

$$\frac{RA}{y}$$

Inflation from the Monetary Policy Standpoint 273

is equivalent to the unit labor cost, since dividing by the number of wage earners (A) would yield:

$$\frac{RA/A}{y/A} = \frac{\text{compensation per wage earner}}{\text{productivity per wage earner}}$$

However, productivity is usually measured in terms of total employment (including non-wage earners), since this facilitates comparisons between time periods (productivity per employee is more stable than per wage earner), between sectors, and between countries (to mitigate the effects of different hiring rates). Moreover, the cost of labor would also have to take into account the compensation of non-wage earners. As no information is available concerning the latter, it is assumed that compensation per non-wage earner is equal to compensation per wage earner. Labelling the compensation of employees RE:

$$RE = \frac{RA}{A}E = RA + \frac{RA}{A}(E - A)$$

where E is the total number employed, yields the usual expression of unit labor cost, or cost of labor per unit of output, CLU:

$$CLU = \frac{RE}{y} = \frac{RE/E}{y/E} = \frac{\text{compensation per employee}}{\text{productivity per employee}}$$

The insertion of this variable into the expression of the GDP deflator necessitates redefining the gross surplus to exclude the part allocated to the compensation of employees under the heading of compensation of non-wage earners: So that the variation of the GDP deflator can be reformulated as:

$$EB^* = EB - \frac{RA}{A}(E - A)$$

$$\Delta P_y = \omega_r \Delta CLU + \omega_e \frac{\Delta EB^*}{\Delta y} + \omega_t \frac{\Delta TN}{\Delta y} \qquad (7A.2)$$

where ω_r has also been redefined as

$$\omega_r = \frac{RE_{-1}}{y_{-1}}$$

and ω_e as

Table 7A.1 Composition of the gross domestic product (GDP) and final demand (DF) deflators, 1987–95

	Rates of variation								
	1987	1988	1989	1990	1991	1992	1993	1994	1995
Unit labor cost	5.6	5.3	5.8	8.6	7.4	6.8	3.3	1.0	2.2
Compensation per employee	*6.8*	*7.1*	*7.1*	*8.8*	*8.8*	*9.2*	*6.1*	*3.6*	*2.5*
Output per employee	*1.1*	*1.7*	*1.3*	*0.1*	*1.3*	*2.2*	*2.6*	*2.7*	*0.3*
–Real GDP	*5.6*	*5.2*	*4.7*	*3.7*	*2.3*	*0.7*	*−1.2*	*2.1*	*3.0*
–Total employment	*4.5*	*3.4*	*3.4*	*3.6*	*1.0*	*−1.5*	*−3.7*	*−0.6*	*2.6*
Net indirect taxes	5.2	−0.3	9.4	4.7	6.1	15.3	−12.5	10.5	6.9
Gross operating surplus	6.4	7.8	8.8	5.7	6.9	4.9	10.4	7.4	8.5
GDP DEFLATOR	5.8	5.7	7.1	7.3	7.1	6.8	4.3	3.9	4.8
Domestic costs	3.7	4.1	4.8	6.5	5.7	5.5	5.2	2.1	3.2
GDP per unit of final demand	*−2.0*	*−1.5*	*−2.1*	*−0.8*	*−1.3*	*−1.3*	*0.9*	*−1.7*	*−1.5*
GDP deflator	*5.8*	*5.7*	*7.1*	*7.3*	*7.1*	*6.8*	*4.3*	*3.9*	*4.8*
Imports costs	12.3	8.4	12.1	1.9	4.8	6.1	3.3	12.6	10.1
Imports per unit of final demand	*11.4*	*7.2*	*9.6*	*3.1*	*5.2*	*4.8*	*−3.1*	*6.3*	*5.0*
Import deflator	*0.8*	*1.1*	*2.3*	*−1.2*	*−0.3*	*1.3*	*6.6*	*6.0*	*4.9*
FINAL DEMAND DEFLATOR	5.0	4.8	6.0	5.7	5.5	5.6	4.9	3.9	4.5

	Contributions to growth								
	1987	1988	1989	1990	1991	1992	1993	1994	1995
Unit labor cost	3.3	3.1	3.4	5.0	4.3	4.0	2.0	0.6	1.2
Compensation per employee	–	–	–	–	–	–	–	–	–
Output per employee	–	–	–	–	–	–	–	–	–
– Real GDP	–	–	–	–	–	–	–	–	–
–Total employment	–	–	–	–	–	–	–	–	–
Net indirect taxes	0.5	0.0	0.8	0.4	0.5	1.2	−1.1	0.8	0.5
Gross operating surplus	2.1	2.6	3.0	2.0	2.3	1.6	3.4	2.6	3.1
GDP DEFLATOR	5.8	5.7	7.1	7.3	7.1	6.8	4.3	3.9	4.8
Domestic costs	3.1	3.5	4.0	5.3	4.7	4.5	4.4	1.7	2.7
GDP per unit of final demand	*−1.7*	*−1.2*	*−1.8*	*−0.6*	*−1.1*	*−1.1*	*0.7*	*−1.5*	*−1.2*
GDP deflator	*5.0*	*4.7*	*5.9*	*6.0*	*5.9*	*5.7*	*3.6*	*3.3*	*3.9*
Imports costs	1.8	1.4	2.0	0.3	0.8	1.0	0.6	2.1	1.8
Imports per unit of final demand	*1.7*	*1.2*	*1.6*	*0.5*	*0.9*	*0.8*	*−0.5*	*1.0*	*0.9*
Import deflator	*0.1*	*0.2*	*0.4*	*−0.2*	*−0.1*	*0.2*	*1.1*	*1.0*	*0.9*
FINAL DEMAND DEFLATOR	5.0	4.8	6.0	5.7	5.5	5.6	4.9	3.9	4.5

Source: INE and Banco de España.

$$w_e = \frac{EB^*_{-1}}{y_{-1}}$$

Substituting the expression of the GDP deflator in the expression of the final demand deflator yields:

$$\Delta P_{df} \simeq w_p\left(\left(w_r\Delta CLU + w_e\Delta\left(\frac{EB^*}{y}\right) + w_t\Delta\left(\frac{TN}{y}\right)\right) + \Delta\lambda_y\right)$$
$$+ w_m(\Delta P_m + \Delta\lambda_m)$$

This expression is a breakdown of the final demand deflator that synthesizes the process of final price formation in the economy, as it captures the contributions of the various cost components (labor, imported goods) to the growth of prices, the impact of net indirect taxes and the behavior of unit margins. Table 7A.1 shows the breakdown of the GDP and final demand deflators for 1987–95.

Notes

1   The annual rates of variation in the price index selected, i.e. rates of change in one period (month, quarter) relative to the same period of the preceding year, are normally used to measure inflation. For example, for a monthly index, which is what consumer price indices usually are, it is common practice to use monthly year-on-year rates (one month relative to the same month of the preceding year) and the annual average rates (average for the 12 months of a year, relative to the preceding year's average). This does not preclude the use of other rates, such as month-on-month rates (month relative to the preceding month), which are also widely used. A detailed discussion of rates of variation and their application to economic phenomena can be found in Chapter 5 of Espasa and Cancelo (1993).
2   Price indices are vulnerable to a number of measuring biases, which depend on their characteristics and which can result in a certain overestimation of inflation. See Viñals (1996), chapter 1 in this volume.
3   In the United Kingdom, the equivalent of the consumer price index is the so-called retail price index (RPI). This index includes mortgage interest payments, which can lead to increased RPI growth in response to a hardening of monetary policy; consequently, the Bank of England defines its objectives in terms of the RPIX: the RPI excluding mortgage interest payments.
4   See INE (1994).
5   Intrastat is the system for collecting statistical data on trade in goods with Community countries. It has been in use since the disappearance of intra-Community boundaries in January 1993.
6   This is one of the lines of research currently being pursued in the Banco de España. It should be pointed out, in any case, that to ensure consistency,

276 *Pilar L'Hotellerie-Fallois*

analyses performed with indicators must be based on the structure of the input–output tables.
7   See Banco de España (1991).
8   These variables represent the economy as a whole and therefore include general government and EU taxes and subsidies.
9   Juan Carlos Delrieu assisted in the preparation of this section.
10 See, for example, the seminal study of Burns and Mitchell (1946) and, more recently, Lahiri and Moore (1992).
11 See, *inter alia*, the studies of Klein (1986) and Quinn and Mawdsley (1996).

References

ANDRÉS, J., J. VALLÉS and R. MESTRE (1996) 'Un modelo estructural para el análisis del mecanismo de transmisión de la política monetaria', chapter 16 in this volume.
ÁLVAREZ, L.J. and M. SEBASTIÁN (1995) 'La inflación latente en la economía española', *Boletín Económico*, Banco de España.
ÁLVAREZ, L.J., F.C. BALLABRIGA and J. JAREÑO (1996) 'Un modelo BVAR de previsión para la economía española', chapter 11 in this volume.
ÁLVAREZ, L.J. and M DE. LOS LLANOS MATEA (1996) 'Medidas del proceso inflacionista', chapter 8 in this volume.
AYUSO, J. and S. NÚÑEZ (1996) 'La curva de rendimientos como indicador para la política monetaria', chapter 10 in this volume.
BANK OF SPAIN (1991) 'Indicadores macroeconómicos de costes y precios', *Boletín Económico*, December.
BURNS, A. and W.C. MITCHELL (1946) *Measuring business cycles*, New York: National Bureau of Economic Research.
CABRERO, A. and J.C. DELRIEU (1996) 'Elaboración de un índice sintético para adelantar cambios en los perfiles de crecimiento de la inflación', *Documento de Trabajo*, 9619, Banco de España.
CABRERO BRAVO, A., J. MARTÍNEZ PÁGES and M. PÉREZ-JURADO (1996) 'Los agregados monetarios y crediticios', chapter 9 in this volume.
CANO, M.D. and A. KANUTIN (1995) 'Estimation of structural deficits in EU countries', EMI, mimeo.
ESPASA, A. and J.R. CANCELO (eds) (1993) *Métodos cuantitativos para el análisis de la coyuntura económica*, Madrid: Alianza Editorial.
FERNÁNDEZ, J. and J. VIRTO (1994) *Un indicador adelantado de la inflación en España*, Instituto de Economía Pública, Universidad del País Vasco.
GIORNO, C., P. RICHARDSON, D. ROSEVENE and P. NOORD (1995) 'Estimating potential output, output gaps and structural budget balances', Economics Department, *Working Papers*, 152, Paris: OECD.
GÓMEZ JIMÉNEZ, A.L. (1993) 'Indicadores de política fiscal: una aplicación al caso español', *Documento de Trabajo*, 9304, Banco de España.
GÓMEZ JIMÉNEZ, A.L. and J.M. ROLDÁN (1995) 'Analysis of fiscal policy in Spain: a macroeconomic perspective (1988–1994)', *Estudios Económicos*, 53, Banco de España.
HALDANE, A.G. (1995) 'Inflation targets', *Quarterly Bulletin*, Bank of England, August.
HALDANE, A.G. (ed.) (1995) *Targeting inflation*, London: Bank of England.
HODRICK, R. and E. PRESCOTT (1980) 'Post-war US business cycles: an empirical investigation', Carnegie Mellon University, mimeo.

INSTITUTO NACIONAL DE ESTADÍSTICA (INE) (1994) *Índice de precios de consumo. Base 1992. Metodología*.

KLEIN, P.A. (1986) 'Leading indicators of inflation in market economies', *International Journal of Forecasting*, 2, 403–12.

LAHIRI, K. and G.H. MOORE (1992) *Leading economic indicators: new approach and forecasting records*, Cambridge: Cambridge University Press.

LINDH, I. (1993) 'Monetary policy indicators', *Quarterly Review*, Sveriges Riksbank.

LONGWORTH D. and C. FREEDMAN (1995) 'The role of the staff economic projection in conducting Canadian monetary policy', in A. Haldane (ed.), *Targeting inflation*, London: Bank of England.

MARTÍ, F. and I. ARGIMÓN (1996) 'Indicadores de impacto sobre los precios de la actividad de las Administraciones Públicas', Banco de España, mimeo.

MATEA, MDE LLANOS (1993) 'Análisis de la inflación en España', in A. Espasa and J.R. Cancelo (eds), *Métodos cuantitativos para el análisis de la coyuntura en España*, *Métodos cuantitativos para el análisis de la coyuntura económica* .

MATEA, MDE LLANOS (1994) 'Explotación de la tendencia prevista de los precios como indicador adelantado del índice de precios industriales', Banco de España, mimeo.

MATEA, MDE. LLANOS and A. V. REGIL (1996) 'Indicadores de corto plazo para la inflación', *Documento de Trabajo*, 9621, Banco de España.

MELCÓN, C. (1994) 'Estrategias de política monetaria basadas en el seguimiento directo del objetivo de inflación', *Documento de Trabajo*, 9426, Banco de España.

QUINN, T. and A. MAWDSLEY (1996) 'Forecasting Irish inflation: a composite leading index', Bank of Ireland, mimeo.

ROTH, H.L. (1991) 'Leading indicators of inflation', in K. Lahiri, and G. H. Moore (eds), *Leading economic indicators: new approach and forecasting records*, Cambridge: Cambridge University Press.

SVERIGES RIKSBANK (1993) *Monetary policy indicators*, June.

URTASUN, A. (1994) 'La utilización de la capacidad productiva y su relación con la inflación', Banco de España, mimeo.

URTASUN, A. (1995) 'Precios en las encuestas de opinión. Aportan información relevante?', Banco de España, mimeo.

VIÑALS, J. (1996) 'Política monetaria e inflación: de la teoría a la práctica', chapter 1 in this volume.

8 Measures of the Inflation Process

Luis Julián Álvarez and
María de los Llanos Matea

INTRODUCTION

The entry into force of the Law on the Autonomy of the Banco de España
has made price stability the Bank's primary goal. The adequate measurement of inflation is a complex undertaking and no single variable covers it
fully. The Banco de España therefore uses a relatively complex analytical
approach based on the examination of various indicators, with the consumer price index (CPI) serving as the basic variable. The measures analyzed
in this chapter were constructed on the basis of the CPI, although this does
not prevent their being applied to other indicators.

Although the relevant data is contained in the CPI, a procedure must be
applied that captures the more constant signals of the inflation process.
Thus, for example, the index is influenced by changes in relative prices that
are distinct from the sustained overall price rises that define an inflationary
situation. In other words, the rate of change in the CPI may be contaminated by disturbances in relative prices, which have real effects and may
distort understanding of the true state of the inflation process.

The aim of this chapter is to examine various approaches to the analysis
of inflation trends from a unifying standpoint that stresses their complementary nature. As distinct from earlier papers, in which a specific
approach is developed, this chapter attempts to provide a comprehensive
picture that shows both the positive aspects and the limitations of the various approaches.

Following this introduction, the chapter breaks down into several sections. We analyze the traditional definitions of core inflation and underlying inflation. Core inflation is used to minimize the distortions attendant
on relative price changes by excluding the most volatile components from
the general index. Underlying inflation consists of calculating the rate of
change of a measure of the price index trend, and is therefore simply a
statistical procedure. We then discuss methods based on limited-influence
estimators, which are warranted by the fact that enterprises must deal with
menu costs, and which consist of the trimmed mean and the weighted
median. We then describe the measures of permanent inflation and latent

278

inflation. These approaches are consistent with the existence of a vertical long-term Phillips curve and are multivariate in nature. The final section presents the main conclusions drawn in the chapter.

CORE INFLATION AND UNDERLYING INFLATION

From the monetary policy standpoint, the drawback to direct use of the CPI is that this index is contaminated by passing or fluctuating price movements which hamper the description of lasting and more important price trends. Measures of two kinds were initially proposed in the literature for circumventing or at least reducing this problem. The first involved in excluding highly variable prices from the CPI, while the second focused on using statistical techniques for estimating the trend of the CPI.

These two alternatives have given rise to the terms:[1] (a) core inflation, with reference to the CPI, after its two most variable components have been excluded (unprocessed food and energy)[2] or, alternatively, the index of services and non-energy manufactured goods (*indice de precios de servicios y bienes elaborados no energéticos – IPSEBENE*) and (b) underlying inflation, by which is meant the centred,[3] year-on-year[4] rate of change in the trend of a price index.

It should be stressed that the term 'core inflation' is not meant to be the equivalent of the hard core of inflation, but only to eliminate the most erratic movements in the CPI. In the literature, the terms 'underlying inflation' and 'core inflation' have been qualified in many different ways, including those under review. In the interest of remaining consistent with Banco de España usage, it is the latter which will be used in this book. However, it should be pointed out that some authors have identified what is termed core inflation in this chapter with underlying inflation[5] or with some other index, as the result of excluding various items from the general CPI.[6]

In connection with the change in the CPI base, Matea (1994a) surveys these two traditional concepts of inflation[7] endeavoring in particular to determine whether their characteristics remain unaltered. The author's finding are updated in the following sections.

Core Inflation

The simplest of all the procedures reviewed in this chapter is that which consists of eliminating the most variable components of the CPI. This is done by breaking down the index into its five basic components, i.e.: unprocessed food, processed food, non-energy manufactured goods, services, and energy. This section focuses on whether unprocessed food and energy should be excluded or not.

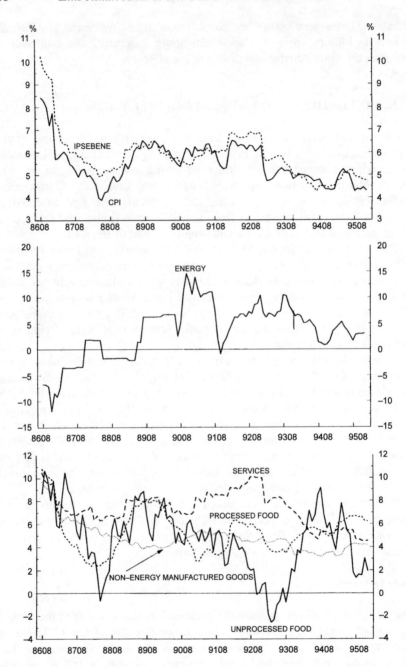

Figure 8.1   Year-on-year rates
Source: INE.

As can be seen in Figure 8.1 – which shows, in addition to the year-on-year CPI and IPSEBENE rates, those for the five basic components – the two components whose year-on-year rates fluctuate most are the energy index and the unprocessed food index. Among the non-energy components, for which ARIMA models are available, the unprocessed food index is the one which has, by far, the greatest residual standard deviation (see Table 8.1).

Because the unprocessed food index is extremely vulnerable to the weather, supply is the main determinant of this greater variability. A further factor is the lower degree of price elasticity in its demand compared with that of other goods and services. If we add to this the ambiguity which arises when its data[8] are being interpreted from an economic perspective, it appears advisable to omit unprocessed food from the index when analyzing the core inflation of the CPI. Otherwise, its inclusion may create some confusion as to the status of inflation.

However, leaving out unprocessed food does not mean neglecting all the data it provides. As can be seen from Figure 8.1, there is some similarity between the year-on-year growth rates of the food indices in that, with the exception of the greater changes in level and more intense fluctuation in the unprocessed food index, there seems to be a certain parallel between both growth rates. This may be owing to the fact that the two share various agricultural products as inputs. It is therefore not surprising that some of the unprocessed food price fluctuations having a permanent impact ultimately transmit themselves to processed foods.

A number of authors make a case for omission of the food index as a whole. As regards the Spanish CPI, the intense impact of the 1995 drought on various processed foods (e.g. olive oil and wine) has indeed caused some to wonder whether the entire food component should not be eliminated, instead of simply unprocessed food. However, processed food prices should be retained, as it would be going too far to omit all of them, given

Table 8.1 Measure of volatility

Component	Measure of volatility*
Unprocessed food	1.07
Processed food	0.20
Non-energy manufactured goods	0.13
Services	0.17

Note: *Residual standard deviation (multiplied by 100) in ARIMA models with intervention analysis, built on the logarithmic transformation.
Source: Authors' calculations.

that other factors are involved in determining these prices which are equally if not more important than the simple trend of at-source prices of agricultural products.

The variability of the energy index was not a problem linked to the frequency of changes of level but to the suddenness and size of such changes. The root of such behavior was to be found in the fact that the index showed only controlled prices. However, currently about 70 per cent of the prices included in the index are on a schedule with maximum prices, and only the index for electricity has a fully controlled price.

On the basis of fuel schedule performance – fuel being the component with the highest impact on the CPI – it may be stated that maximum prices have in practice matched the prices of sales to the public.[9] At any rate, the changes remain significant, even though their frequency has increased and their size has contracted somewhat. Moreover, taxes are a major component of these prices, with the result that the most substantial changes noted each year are owing to changes in indirect taxes. By way of example, since 1992 more than 50 per cent of the increase in the inflation rate for fuels as a whole in the intervening years was the result of tax increases.

Consequently, as the energy index continues to record a fairly considerable portion of controlled prices, while major changes in the prices of maximum price products are the result of indirect taxes – which may be considered as the controlled part of the price – it is not surprising that this index remains highly variable. It may therefore be well to let the IPSE-BENE continue to represent core inflation for the time being.

The main criticism of this type of measure is that prior rejection of specific prices entails the risk that significant inflation information will not be taken into account, and the possibility that excessive weight may be given to outlying, large-scale changes recorded by other non-excluded indices in the measurement of inflation. In other words, the basic problem lies in determining in advance what prices are to be excluded. On the other hand, it offers the advantage of simplicity and, consequently, greater transparency and accessibility for a broad range of users. In any case, it should be stressed that a careful analysis of the inflation process may not be obtained directly from core inflation, which requires supplementary treatment.

Underlying Inflation

One of the procedures used by economic analysts to examine the basic features of an economic phenomenon is the application of statistical signal extraction techniques, in order to break down the variables into the sum of non-observable components. For monetary policy, it is important to know whether price changes reflect temporary behavior or, more importantly, whether they represent long-term behavior. Consequently, it is the trend component which is crucial in the examination of inflation. Through a trend, it is hoped to obtain a signal without movements that are canceled out in the short term, i.e. movements related to the seasonal component, which cease in the course of a year, or those of an irregular nature which sometimes disappear even sooner.

Matea and Regil (1994) applied various procedures for obtaining signals – X11ARIMA, reduced form models and structural models – as regards the CPI with base year 1983, the CPI with base year 1976, and the cost of living index, obtaining highly similar trend components[10] with all of them. However, taking into account the remaining non-observable components, the reduced form models[11] have comparative advantages. As a result, this is the type of model used for trend estimates.

In connection with price indices, there are many occasions when the rate of change in price levels is more relevant than price level trends. As in other papers, underlying inflation is defined as the centred year-on-year growth rate of the pertinent price index trend. Centring this rate is necessary to synchronize it with month-on-month growth.[12]

If an ARIMA model with intervention analysis is available for the series under study, such a model may be regarded as the sum of a stochastic component, shown by the ARIMA contents, and a determinist component, identified through intervention analysis. All the non-observable components may also be disaggregated into stochastic and determinist components, with the final component being the aggregation of the two. To calculate underlying inflation, the year-on-year rate is applied to both components. However, the rate applied to the determinist component is not centred, since if it were the exceptional events shown through the intervention analysis would begin to be noted before they had occurred. Specifically, to obtain underlying inflation,[13] the following equation is used.[14]

$$\text{Underlying inflation} = T^1_{12} (\text{Stochastic trend})^c +$$
$$+ \left[\frac{1}{100} T^1_{12} (\text{Stochastic trend})^c + 1 \right] T^1_{12} (\text{Determinist trend})^{NC}$$

in which the superscript indices C and NC indicate, respectively, whether the rate is centred or not.

In the past, calculation of underlying inflation was simplified by approximating it using a rate of growth. The intuitive idea behind this approximation is based on the fact that the procedure for estimating the trend applies centred weighted moving average, for which a growth rate from the original series which averages a sufficient number of observations is a reasonable approximation. While the base year for the CPI was 1983, the centred T^{12}_{12} [15] of the corrected original series of the intervention analysis was a

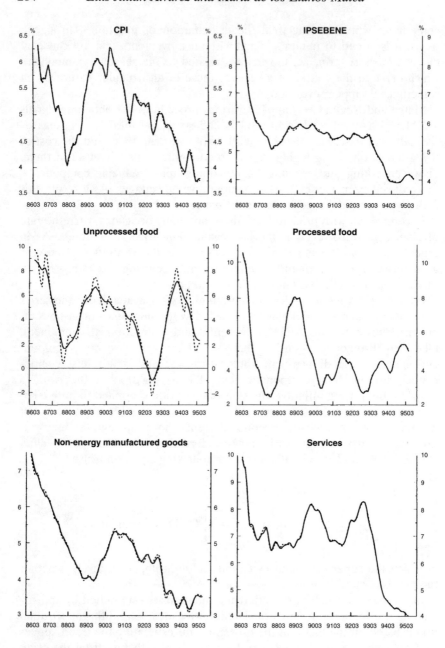

Figure 8.2   Centred growth rates

Note: The solid line is T_{12}^{1} of the stochastic trend. The broken line is T_{12}^{3} of the adjusted original series.

Sources: Authors' calculations and INE.

good approximation of the centred T_{12}^1 of the stochastic trend and considerably simplified calculation of the underlying inflation. Matea (1994a) examined whether this approximation remained valid for the CPI with base year 1992. In general, the centred T_{12}^{12} outlined the basic features of the evolution of the stochastic trend's centred year-on-year growth rate, although the latter fluctuated somewhat more. Even so, at given times there were noticeable differences between the levels of the two rates.[16] By contrast, the centred T_{12}^3[17] would appear to be the most relevant.

Figure 8.2 compares the year-on-year rates of the stochastic trends and centred T_{12}^3 of the series adjusted for intervention analysis. As may be seen, it remains certain that for all indices, with the exception of unprocessed food, centred T_{12}^3 is an excellent approximation. Given the greater variability of the unprocessed food component, longer moving averages are required for estimating its trend component. However, rather than adopt, on the basis of the relevant CPI component, various rates for estimating underlying inflation, the interests of simplicity may be better served if a single rate is adopted. Choosing the centred T_{12}^3 of the corresponding index as the approximation for the year-on-year rate of its stochastic trend would seem to make sense. Moreover, the centred T_{12}^3 has the advantage of requiring only six predictions in order to make calculations for a given month using CPI data up to that month. Other rates with broader moving averages also require more forecasts, so that more checking would be needed as well at the end of the sample.

As a result, the year-on-year growth rate of the final trend, or underlying inflation, is calculated by the following equation:

$$\text{Underlying inflation} \simeq T_{12}^3 \left(\text{Original series adjusted for interventions}\right)^c +$$

$$+ \left[\frac{1}{100} T_{12}^3 \left(\text{Original series adjusted for interventions}\right)^c + 1\right]$$

$$T_{12}^1 \left(\text{Interventions}\right)^{NC}$$

in which superscript indices C and NC indicate, respectively, whether the rate is centred or not.

Figure 8.3 shows the underlying inflation of the CPI, the IPSEBENE, and the components of the latter, which are obtained using the approximation described above.

Although the procedure outlined above is suitable for non-energy components, a complication attendant on indices comprising controlled prices stems from the fact that such prices do not change much, often only once a year, and sometimes – under certain circumstances – at intervals that exceed a year. Rather than evolving smoothly, these indices therefore change suddenly at specific times. In view of this peculiarity, which was

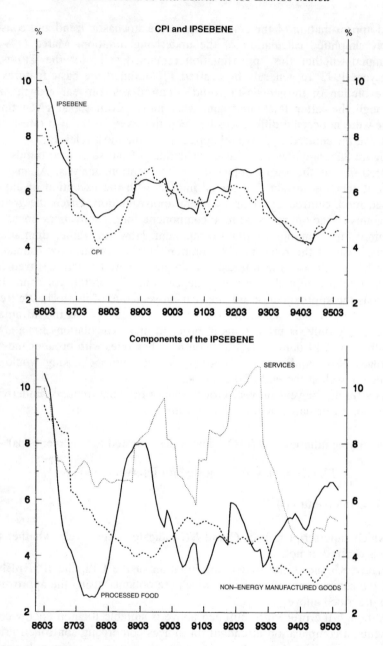

Figure 8.3   Underlying inflation
Sources: Authors' calculations and INE.

especially notable in the energy index, a case has been made for estimating their underlying inflation using the uncentred year-on-year rate of the original series. Currently, although such behavior persists, introduction of the maximum price schedule for fuels has moderated it considerably, and it is likely that in the future, when the sector has been fully liberalized and sufficiently long stochastic series are available, the energy index may be analyzed stochastically. In the meantime, uncentred T^1_{12} may be used provisionally to calculate the underlying inflation of energy prices.

To conclude, it should be noted that underlying inflation is more complicated than the core inflation measure. It also has a drawback in that different authors are able to reach different estimates of underlying inflation either by breaking down the stochastic and determinist aspect of the CPI in different ways, or by using different procedures to estimate the trend. On the other hand, underlying inflation furnishes a more precise measure for assessing the status of inflation.

MEASURES OF INFLATION WITH LIMITED-INFLUENCE ESTIMATORS

The CPI is influenced by changes in relative prices. In order to eliminate them, Bryan and Cecchetti (1994), drawing on a previous paper by Ball and Mankiw (1995) propose using limited-influence estimators[18] of the mid-point of the cross-section distribution (that is, the distribution at all times of the prices comprising the CPI) for calculating the measure of inflation. Specifically, they argue that the weighted median and the trimmed mean[19] should be used rather than the traditional mean. By reducing the weight of the extreme values and therefore the influence of relative price changes, which tend to be concentrated in the tails of the cross-section distribution, these two statistics provide a clearer signal of price level changes. Although in practice it may occur that with these two statistics, the prices of the articles themselves are ultimately omitted, this type of measure nevertheless, has the advantage of not requiring, as does core inflation, prior determination of the origin of shocks to relative prices. As regards the trimmed mean, the greater the area of the tails that is left out, the greater the probability that specific prices will always be excluded. This probability is extremely high in the case of weighted medians.

Theoretical Model

In general terms, Ball and Mankiw's single period model (1995) focuses on the problem of setting enterprise prices for enterprises that incur costs from changes in said prices, so that, facing a disturbance in supply, with a zero mean, that affects all enterprises, only those enterprises will change their prices for which the cost of changing the price of their products is less than the loss entailed by not doing so. By construction, the disturbance affects relative prices, and, depending on its distribution, either will or will not have an impact on the aggregate price level. Specifically, if distribution is symmetric, the effect will be zero, as the price increases of some enterprises will be offset by price cuts made by others. By contrast, if distribution of the disturbance is asymmetric, the aggregate price level will increase or decrease depending on whether the enterprises raising prices or those lowering them are the predominant factor.

A somewhat more formal presentation is made by Bryan and Cecchetti (1994). The model is based on a series of assumptions, the first of which is that it takes place in a single period. There is also a large number of enterprises which, if their prices change once the period has begun, must incur certain costs which are the same for all. On the other hand, the money supply is a known exogenous variable, the velocity of circulation is constant, and the growth rate of trend output is zero. Under these circumstances, at the outset of the period, each enterprise decides to increase its prices by the same proportion as changes take place in the money stock. As a result, aggregate inflation will correspond to the change in the money supply. In other words, if π is the rate of aggregate inflation and $\dot{m}$ is the growth of the money supply, then:

$$\pi = \dot{m}$$

It is assumed that there is a disturbance in the enterprises' production costs and/or demand which may be designated by ϵ_i, in which the subscript i refers to enterprise i. When the disturbance is noted, only enterprises for which ϵ_i, in absolute value, is greater than the cost they must incur to change their prices will carry out this change. For these enterprises, the growth rate of prices π_i will be:

$$\pi_i = \dot{m} + \epsilon_i$$

If it is also assumed that the level, $\bar{\epsilon}$, at which the enterprises decide to change their prices, whether upwards or downwards, is the same, the rate of inflation observed in the economy as a whole, π^o, will be:

$$\pi^o = \pi + \sum_{i=1}^{n} \left[\frac{\epsilon_i}{|\epsilon_i| - \epsilon} \max(|\epsilon_i| - \bar{\epsilon}, 0) \right]$$

in which n is the number of enterprises in the economy. If the distribution of the disturbances ϵ_i is symmetric, the second member of the above equation is canceled, but if it is asymmetric, actual inflation does not match inflation having monetary origins. As the differences between $\pi°$ and π arise from the tails of the distribution of the ϵ_i, one way to reduce their influence is to use limited-influence estimators.

The reason for this is that the distribution of the disturbance is averaged out among the enterprises. It is well known that, with the arithmetic mean, a small change in distribution tails may entail a sizable change in this statistic, while this effect is relativized in a weighted median or a trimmed mean. These two statistics of limited-influence are those recommended by Bryan and Cecchetti as a means of eliminating or at least reducing the effects on the price change rate of the changes in relative prices which are concentrated in distribution tails.

Calculation of Measures of Inflation with Limited-influence Estimators

The subclasses of the CPI, using 156 indices,[20] were taken as the starting point for calculating the weighted median and the trimmed mean. To eliminate the seasonal effect on the position of each index in the cross-sectional distribution, Matea (1994a) used year-on-year rates to reconcile said effect. The results of her paper are updated in this section.

As each of the subclasses comprises the prices of various goods and services, it was assumed that the weighting[21] assigned to each subclass in the CPI basket is equivalent to the number of prices it includes. To calculate the weighted median at any time, the year-on-year rates of the indices are arranged from small to large, multiplying them by their weighting, and the mid-point is selected on the histogram formed by all of them together. For the trimmed mean, the mean of the centre of distribution of the weighted year-on-year rates is calculated. If any subclass is found within the area of the tails that is being discarded and the central area, it is not passed over, but its weighting is changed, and it receives only the part that corresponds to the central area.

To determine whether or not the cross-sectional distribution of the CPI's year-on-year rate is symmetric, and therefore whether low-impact measures should be used, the skewness coefficient was computed. As can be seen in Figure 8.4, skewness has changed considerably over time, and distribution may be considered skewed only in a few cases.[22] As a result, it is reasonable in principle to take into account measures of limited-influence.

Before examining the inflation series obtained with limited-influence estimators, we should mention a number of drawbacks attendant on them as a result of the methodology of the Spanish CPI. Specifically, the presence of goods and services, the prices of which are recorded less often than on a monthly basis (once a quarter or once a year) – largely in the case of prices that do not change often – and not always in the same

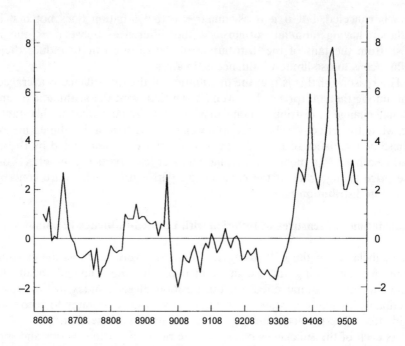

Figure 8.4 Skewness coefficient of the cross-sectional year-on-year CPI rates distribution

Sources: Authors' calculations.

month of the year, causes the rate of change of these prices to be zero in some months, and quite high in others. It is therefore not surprising that they are found in the distribution tails and, in practice, are commonly not taken into account in these measures of inflation. An example of this constraint is found at the beginning of the period examined, as a sizable portion of energy products are usually excluded by a trimmed mean.

It is also debatable whether disturbances have a zero mean at the time they occur; consider, for instance, an across-the board increase in indirect taxes. Another weakness of the model, this time when it is shifted over to construct a time series, lies in the leap into space that occurs when passing from a static model to a dynamic reality. It is reasonable to believe that in practice, and depending on the economic situation, it would be appropriate to change the excluded area of the trimmed mean. Similarly, it may be highly limiting to assume that adjustments to disturbances occur instantaneously. Finally, Zeldes (1994) also criticizes measures of this type by raising doubts as to whether changes in relative prices have to be transmitted to aggregate inflation, in which case there is no reason to eliminate the extreme values. He also notes that there may be permanent shocks to the inflation rate which are combined with changes in relative prices, so that it would be a mistake to eliminate them from the measure of inflation.

To select the size of the central area of the trimmed mean, various options were considered with trim percentages of 5 per cent, 10 per cent, and 15 per cent. Finally, a trimmed mean at 5 per cent was settled on as the resulting series showed less variance over time, a result which is sustained even if a trimmed mean of 0 per cent is included among the various measures. This result differs from that of Bryan and Cecchetti for the CPI of the United States, as they obtain a series with minimum variance with a trimmed mean at 15 per cent.[23] In any case, of the three alternatives considered, very similar series were obtained, with discrepancies appearing of only about half a point in 1986.

In analyzing the trimmed mean at 5 per cent, no subclass fails to be covered in the whole of the period under consideration (from August 1986 to December 1995), although the subclass "potatoes", owing to its more erratic prices, is noteworthy for its appearance 68 per cent of the time in the distribution tails, although without expanding into any particular tail. If, instead of examining the whole area excluded by the trimmed mean, only the lower tail is taken into account, it is "personal computers, typewriters, etc.", at 58 per cent of the time, which are the first to be eliminated by this measure of inflation. At the other extreme are "medical costs", with 45 per cent exclusions, which stand out as recording substantial price increases.

On the basis of these results, there should be no prior exclusion of any subclass, to say nothing of any of the five basic components of the CPI. Even so, an examination of the subclasses grouped under the basic components shows that all those comprising the unprocessed food index were at some time in the tails of the distribution (see Table 8.2), which is similar to what happens with the energy index. By contrast, in the period under consideration, 19 per cent of the subclasses of the processed food index, 36 per cent

Table 8.2 Proportion of basic components always used in calculating the trimmed mean at 5 per cent

Component	Weight within basic components of the subclasses always included in the trimmed mean at 5%
Unprocessed food	0
Processed food	18.79
Non-energy manufactured goods	42.27
Energy	0
Services	35.85

Note: Period covered: August 1986 to December 1995.
Source: Authors' calculations.

of the services index, and 42 per cent of the non-energy manufactured goods index have always been found in the trimmed mean. This result tallies with the description of the IPSEBENE as core inflation.

The five basic components of the CPI are captured in the series constructed with the weighted median. The latter conveys a different message from that of the CPI or the IPSEBENE (see Figure 8.5). It may be seen how, in the initial years, it bears a closer resemblance to the IPSEBENE but separates from this index in 1989 and is thereafter regularly found below the IPSEBENE year-on-year rate, except at end-1990 and in early 1993. Excluding early 1993 as well, beginning in 1989 markedly lower inflation rate levels are obtained with the weighted median than with the CPI, which clearly shows how substantial price increases, which may be termed atypical, have strongly affected the most recent period, not only as regards the CPI but also the IPSEBENE. Moreover, the profile of the weighted median differs from that of the CPI and the IPSEBENE, and in some cases the distinction between the two latter and the former series is about one and a half percentage points. The weighted median thus shows far greater changes in the inflation rate, with pronounced zigzags, which may complicate a description of the status of inflation. By contrast, the trimmed mean does not differ greatly from the year-on-year rate of the CPI, so that it is of no particular interest and need not be used. This outcome is shored up by the fact that between the trimmed mean and the median, first of all, the latter is recommended from the standpoint of soundness; and second, Oosterhoff (1994) shows that with contaminated distributions and large samples, the median is preferable.

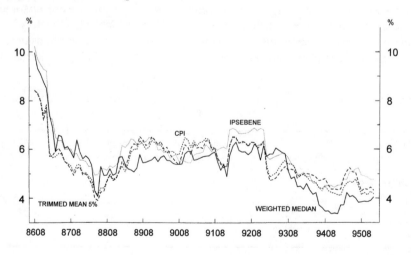

Figure 8.5 Alternative measures of inflation, using uncentred year-on-year rates
Sources: Authors' calculations and INE.

To sum up, of the measures examined so far (core inflation, underlying inflation, and limited-influence estimators), underlying inflation, which may be applied both to the general CPI and some of its components, may be a useful tool for describing the state of inflation. However, for adjusting the index of the more erratic movements, core inflation or the IPSEBENE would seem to be more suitable than the general index. Likewise, in the case of substantial price movements, above all if they belong to the IPSE-BENE, using the measures of limited influence may be effective. Nevertheless, as the trimmed mean does not differ particularly from the year-on-year rate of the CPI, the weighted median alone may be used.

PERMANENT INFLATION AND LATENT INFLATION

As outlined above, we have been using various measures of inflation, either by excluding specific index components, as in the case of measures of core inflation (see p. 279) and limited-influence estimators (see p. 287) or by smoothing as in the case of underlying inflation (see p. 282). The common denominator of these approaches is their univariate nature, that is, they are constructed using only the price series.

Recently, however, some authors (see Table 8.3) have proposed using supplementary measures obtained from structural vector autoregressive (VAR) models. These procedures are characterized by the use of restrictions, based on propositions set forth in economic theory, with regard to both the long-term behavior of several variables, and their multivariate nature. This means that in determining the measures of inflation, they take into account data that supplements price series data (e.g. that contained in the level of activity, or in a given monetary aggregate).

Specifically, two procedures are examined in this section which, even though they are not without limitations, supplement the data obtained by the methods discussed above. These approaches are consistent with a monetary view of inflation in the long term and meet the generally accepted condition that the long-term Phillips curve is vertical, i.e. that there is no long-term trade-off between real output (or the unemployment rate) and the inflation rate, so that changes in nominal magnitudes do not have real effects in the long term. However, these approaches also permit an economy to record disturbances in the short term which – depending on their origins and duration – may affect both the cyclical component and the trend of real activity and inflation. Thus, two alternative measures of the inflation trend are obtained: permanent inflation and latent inflation based on a structural dynamic model of real output and inflation.

The first measure (permanent inflation) shows the impact of disturbances which affect the inflation rate in the long term. Assuming

Table 8.3 Previous papers proposing multivariate measures for long-term inflation

Paper	Country covered	Variables used	Measure of inflation trend
Álvarez and Sebastián (1995)	Spain	Consumer prices GDP	1 Inflation with all disturbances having a temporary effect eliminated (permanent inflation) 2 Inflation with all disturbances having a permanent effect on output eliminated (latent inflation)
Fisher, Fackler and Orden (1995)	New Zealand	Consumer prices GDP, Money	'Monetary' inflation
Quah and Vahey (1995)	United Kingdom	Consumer prices Industrial output	Inflation with all disturbances having a permanent effect on output eliminated
Roberts (1993)	United States	GDP deflator Unemployment rate, Velocity of circulation	'Monetary' inflation

Source: Authors' calculations.

rationality, these disturbances are finally included in the process whereby agents form their expectations, and are therefore the driving force that determines the rate of growth of the nominal variables.

The second measure[24] shows the impact on inflation of those disturbances which do not have a long-term affect on output. Although, unlike the first procedure, no long-term inflation rate[25] can be obtained directly using this second technique, a highly relevant by product is produced in the form of an estimate of the economy's potential output, and by way of difference, of the output gap.[26]

It should be pointed out that the structural interpretation of the disturbances that permit identification of long-term inflation in each instance is not immediate. Specifically, it is not possible to distinguish directly between supply shocks and demand shocks. The permanent inflation procedure distinguishes between disturbances according to their long-term effect on inflation. However, disturbances that affect the inflation process in the long term may arise from both aggregate demand (e.g. changes in the growth rate of the money stock) and the supply side (e.g. changes in the potential growth of the economy). By contrast, the latent inflation procedure distinguishes among disturbances on the basis of their long-term impact on output. However, shocks which do not have a long-term impact on the output level may arise from both the demand (e.g. monetary disturbances) and the supply side (e.g. temporary technological shocks). A comparison of the two measures of latent and permanent inflation with each other and with observed inflation nevertheless facilitates an interpretation of the type of disturbance present in the economy.

In any case, these measures, like any others seeking to approximate a phenomenon as complex as the inflation process, must be assessed and interpreted with due prudence and caution. It should also be pointed out that neither of the two measures of inflation claims to be either a leading indicator or forecaster[27] of the inflation rate. For two reasons. First, because disturbances which temporarily affect the inflation rate (in the case of permanent inflation) and disturbances which permanently affect real output (in the case of latent inflation) have an impact on the actual rate of inflation, although they do not change the respective measures of the trend of inflation. Second, because neither of them is able to take into account possible future changes[28] in the price- and wage-forming mechanisms and in economic policies, and these affect the trend of inflation. The approaches discussed in this section are also limited by their initial assumption that there are only two types of disturbances that affect actual inflation and output. Actually, it seems likely that there are many sources of disturbance and that some of them have differential effects on the economy. Therefore interpretation must a priori be made in terms of groups of disturbances, although a hypothesis may be developed as to the nature of the preponderant disturbances on the basis of an examination of the relevant transmission mechanisms. Moreover, these measures are constructed on the basis of changes in inflation, so that an additional hypothesis is needed to recover its level.

Permanent Inflation

The unrestricted VAR model, common to both latent and permanent estimates, uses a sample period that begins in the first quarter of 1970 and ends in the last quarter of 1995.[29] Four lags are used for each of the variables in the two model equations.[30] As determinist elements, in addition to a constant term, it must be borne in mind that the GDP growth rate series shows different means in the subsamples. Thus, breaks are noted in the mean during the first quarter of 1976 and the last quarters of 1984 and 1991.

To obtain the various types of disturbances and transmission mechanisms that provide the basis for these measures of the inflation trend, the identification procedure first proposed by Blanchard and Quah (1989) is used. The method[31] involves, in this case, the application of long-term identification restrictions in a VAR model which shows the main interactions between the inflation rate and output.

It should be pointed out that the procedure of identification with long-term restrictions used in studies of this kind involves no specific assumption with regard to the short-term transmission mechanism. However, in order to interpret the disturbances in economic terms, not only must the transmission mechanisms be examined, it must also be determined whether the time signs and patterns of the responses match the interpretation being made.

Two types of disturbances are identified for permanent inflation (see Table 8.4) and defined on the basis of their long-term effect on the inflation rate. These disturbances and their transmission mechanisms may be obtained using the procedure outlined in the Appendix (p. 303). Once these are known, the actual inflation rate (π_t) may be broken down into the sum of two components: the first represents the portion of inflation determined by disturbances having a permanent effect (πp_t), while the second is the portion of inflation accounted for by disturbances having a temporary effect (πt_t):

$$\pi_t = \pi p_t + \pi t_t$$

Analysis of the transmission mechanism of the disturbances linked to permanent changes in the inflation rate (those that determine the trend of πp_t), shows that they have a positive but relatively slight impact on output. Such an effect is significant in the short term, but not in the long term. This would be consistent with nominal disturbances having an expansionary

Table 8.4 Identification schemes used to obtain the measures of permanent and latent inflation

Scheme 1	Inflation	Output
Disturbances *not* having a long-term effect on inflation (Identification restriction)		
Disturbances *having* a long-term effect on inflation	Permanent inflation	
Scheme 2		
Disturbances *not* having a long-term effect on output (Identification restriction)	Latent inflation	Economic cycle
Disturbances *having* a long-term effect on output		Trend or potential output

Source: Authors' calculations.

effect on activity in the short term, but which do not have the capacity to change potential output. The effect on output of disturbances having no long-term effect on inflation (those that determine the trend of πt_t) is also positive, but much greater. These disturbances may be linked to technological shocks by their positive and permanent effect on output. Such shocks should not affect the rate of potential growth as they have only a temporary effect on inflation.

By contrast, when the inflation rate is examined, disturbances that permanently affect it are more significant than those having a temporary effect. The latter may be linked to temporary technological shocks to the rate of potential growth, as they have a negative and temporary effect on the inflation rate.

Using the methodology outlined in the Appendix, it is also possible to obtain an estimate of permanent inflation. Two separate considerations must be borne in mind when analyzing this series. First, the difference at all times between actual inflation and permanent inflation, and second, the trend of permanent inflation. The first factor may be disputed as the level of the path of permanent inflation requires an additional hypothesis.[32] However, the second is independent of such an assumption. In the economic assessment of this measure, prime consideration should be given to whether permanent inflation is actually speeding up or slowing down, and not whether it is above or below actual inflation.[33]

As may be seen in Figure 8.6, except for very specific periods, the profile of permanent inflation is generally similar to that of actual inflation. This

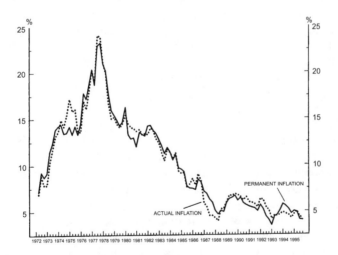

Figure 8.6 Actual and permanent inflation
Sources: Authors' calculations and INE.

result squares with the fact that, in relative terms, temporary disturbances have less effect on inflation, so that the inflation process is dominated by the trend component.

In turn, the evolution over time of the estimated permanent inflation series shows the effect of permanent disturbances in both demand (e.g. monetary disturbances) and supply, which are reflected in changes in the long-term inflation rate. It also bears noting that the rate of permanent inflation and actual inflation, even when not very great, is procyclical and lagged, which indicates the presence of demand disturbances having temporary effects on inflation and activity.

Latent Inflation

For latent inflation, the two types of structural disturbances are defined according to their long-term effect on real output. The first type does not have a long-term effect on product, although it affects actual inflation. The second type affects the long-term output trend, but not latent inflation. Using the method outlined in the Appendix, actual inflation may be broken down into the sum of latent inflation (πl_t) and a residual term (πr_t). Latent inflation is defined as the contribution to inflation of disturbances which have no long-term effect on the level of output:

$$\pi_t = \pi l_t + \pi r_t$$

An analysis of the transmission mechanisms shows that disturbances which do not affect the level of output in the long term (those which determine the trend of πl_t) do have an impact on the latter which is significant in the short term, although slight and fluctuating. The temporary nature of the effect of these disturbances on output, and the path resulting from its contribution to the output series make it possible to link these disturbances to the economic cycle. However, the impact of disturbances having a long-term effect on output (those which determine the trend of πr_t) is considerably larger, even though it too fluctuates. The permanent effect of these disturbances is explained by the fact that output is a nonstationary series and because the other disturbances have a temporary effect on output. The considerable explanatory power of these disturbances of output is such that they may be linked to technological changes which permanently affect factor productivity.

Temporary disturbances of output (which are those that determine the trend of πl_t) have a powerful effect on inflation. Ninety-two per cent of the variance of inflation at the end of a year and a half may be explained by these disturbances, which suggests that the latter are ultimately responsible for changes in the inflation rate. This result is consistent with its characterization of the trend in inflation; it also tallies with those discussed on p. 295. On the other hand, disturbances with permanent effects on real activity also have permanent effects on inflation, perhaps because relative prices do not fully adjust. Nevertheless, their explanatory capacity is considerably lower.

A further application of the Appendix methodology yields[34] a latent inflation series similar to that shown in Figure 8.7. Just as before in the case of permanent inflation, latent inflation represents at all times the major portion of the actual inflation rate during this period. The similarity of changes in latent inflation to those of actual inflation indicates that the dynamic of inflation in Spain has shown an inertial behavior minimally determined by disturbances having a permanent effect on the level of output.

As indicated above, latent inflation reflects the impact of disturbances that do not have a long-term effect on the level of output. In other words, this is the component of inflation which covers the contribution of permanent disturbances of both demand and the cyclical component.[35]

The trend difference between actual inflation and latent inflation shows the size of the disturbances which are not captured by the latter, that is, disturbances which have permanent effects on the level of output. These may be of the technological type, or involve relative energy prices, or changes in public or private investment which affect the production function through the capital stock.

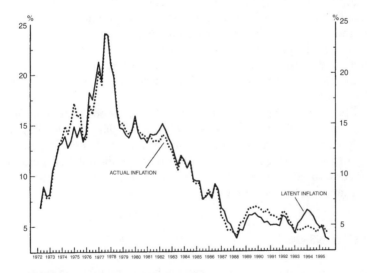

Figure 8.7   Actual and latent inflation

Sources: Authors' calculations and INE.

Comparison of Results: The Determinants of Inflation

Starting from the above results, the determinants of inflations may be interpreted on the basis of two elements: first, a comparison of the permanent and latent inflation rates; and second, a comparison of the trend of these measures of inflations with that of actual inflation.

As mentioned above, permanent inflations is caused by changes, having a permanent effect, in the growth rate of the monetary aggregates, the growth rate of nominal wages, factors that cause permanent shifts in the demand for money (e.g. changes in income elasticity) or technological factors which change the growth potential. Furthermore, latent inflation develops on the basis of shocks to the growth rate of the monetary aggregates, nominal wages, and cyclical disturbances, of both supply and demand, which do not have a long-term effect on the level of output.

Therefore, if changes in the rate of latent inflations resemble those of actual inflation, the inflations process is dominated by the disturbances mentioned that have no long-term effect on real activity. In turn, if changes in the rate of permanent inflation resemble those of actual inflation, said rate may be roughly described as a trend or long-term measure.

Moreover, if both measures of inflation trends are similar, it seems reasonable to believe that, on average, the sample period under consideration was dominated by those disturbances that characteristically have a permanent effect on inflation and do not affect long-term output. By these are meant permanent disturbances of a monetary nature or those involving long-term changes in nominal wages. On the other hand, the difference between the two measures provides data on the disturbances specific to each of the concepts of inflation: i.e. as regards latent inflation, temporary technological disturbances or changes in relative prices, and, as regards permanent inflation, disturbances having a permanent effect on the rate of potential growth.

As can be seen in Figures 8.6, 8.7 and 8.8, the trends over time of permanent inflation and latent inflation are quite similar; nor do they differ excessively from the trend of actual inflation, except at specific times. The similarity of the two measures of inflation trends indicates that permanent disturbances of a nominal nature have played a key role in determining the path of inflation in our economy.

CONCLUSIONS

Direct use of the actual inflation rate in analyzing the inflation process may be problematic, owing to the fact that the rate is contaminated by changes in relative prices, which obscure the true state of inflation. With a view to

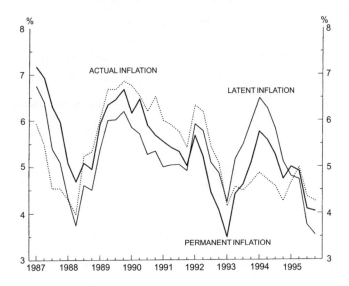

Figure 8.8   Inflation in Spain
Sources: Authors' calculations and INE.

overcoming, or at least reducing, this shortcoming, the literature has developed various measures for capturing the most permanent signals of the inflation process. In this chapter, we have examined various procedures in their application to the Spanish economy.

First of all, we discussed the standard definitions of core inflation and underlying inflation. The former is the result of eliminating the two most variable components from the general CPI: the unprocessed food and energy indices. Underlying inflation, on the other hand, comprises the rate of change in a measure of price level trends. Alternative measures have recently appeared that attempt to overcome some of the inadequacies of the core inflation measure. Thus, rather than always excluding the prices of the same articles, prices are eliminated at all times when they represent an extreme. These measures are the trimmed mean and the weighted median. Of all these univariate measures, underlying inflation is a useful tool for analyzing inflation and showing its behavioral trend. However, it may be better to calculate it on the basis of a subaggregate of the CPI, rather than on the CPI itself. Specifically, its calculation on the basis of the IPSE-BENE may be informative. However, under conditions in which sweeping price changes are observed, it may be better to use measures of limited-influence, and more specifically, the weighted median, if the trimmed mean resembles the CPI too closely. Finally, we have also proposed, from a multivariate perspective, and subject to the presence of a vertical

Table 8.5   Main advantages and drawbacks of the various measures of inflation

Measure of inflation	Advantages	Drawbacks
Core inflation	• Readily understandable and easy to compute	• A prior decision must be made as to articles whose prices are not relevant
Underlying inflation	• Gives a clear signal of the trend of inflation	• Potential differences in the assessment of unusual occurrences and in trend estimate
Trimmed mean	• No need for a prior decision as to articles whose prices are not relevant	• In practice, does not differ greatly from the CPI • A trim percentage must be decided upon
Weighted median	• No need for a prior decision as to articles whose prices are not relevant	• Fluctuates excessively in practice
Permanent inflation	• Consistent with a widely accepted economic theory (vertical long-term Phillips curve) • Multivariate nature	• Available quarterly • An additional hypothesis required to determine level
Latent inflation	• Consistent with a widely accepted economic theory (vertical long-term Phillips curve) • Multivariate nature	• Available quarterly • An additional hypothesis required to determine level

Source: Authors' calculations.

long-term Phillips curve, the permanent inflation measure, which shows the impact of disturbances having a long-term effect on inflation, and the latent inflation measure, which is determined by the effect on inflation of disturbances that do not have a long-term effect on output. Using these two measures permits a reading of the determinants of inflation.

In any case, as all these measures have advantages and disadvantages (see Table 8.5) and none of them takes priority over the others, it is well to examine them all in order to obtain a more reliable description of the state of inflation. While the circumstances at any given time may make it advisable to focus on one of them in particular, it is nevertheless true that diagnosis of the inflation process gains in solidity insofar as they all convey the same message.

Appendix

THE ECONOMETRIC METHODOLOGY OF THE ECONOMIC MEASURES OF INFLATION

To obtain the various types of disturbance on which the economic measures of inflation trends will be based, a model is used that shows logarithmic changes in the gross national product at market prices in real terms and absolute changes in the rate of inflation, using for this the logarithmic year-on-year rate.[36] We denote by X_t the vector $(\Delta\pi_t, \Delta y_t)'$ in which Δ indicates the first difference, π_t the inflation rate and y_t output; we assume that X_t has a structural interpretation.[37]

$$X_t = A(0)e_t + A(1)e_{t-1} + \ldots = \sum_{j=0}^{\infty} A(j)e_{t-j} \qquad (8A.1)$$

with e_t being the vector of structural disturbances in the system $(e_{1t}, e_{2t})'$. This vector shows no serial correlation and has a standardized variance matrix, so that the matrix is identity. (8A.1) shows the transmission mechanism through which structural disturbances affect the economy.

Nevertheless, these structural disturbances e_t are not observed directly, but must be recovered on the basis of the moving average representation of the estimated VAR model:

$$X_t = v_t + C(1)v_{t-1} + \ldots = \sum_{j=0}^{\infty} C(j)v_{t-j} \qquad (8A.2)$$

with the first matrix of the polynomial $C(j)$ being the identity matrix and Ω the covariance matrix of v_t, the vector of reduced form innovations.

Comparison of (8A.1) and (8A.2) shows the presence of a linear relationship between the structural disturbances and those of the reduced form

$$v_t = A(0)e_t \qquad (8A.3)$$

and, moreover, the transmission mechanisms are linked through $A(j) = C(j) \cdot A(0)$ for any j. As v_t is calculated on the basis of residuals of the VAR model, knowing $A(0)$ permits recovery of the structural disturbances. The matrices $A(j)$ that establish the transmission mechanism may also be recovered. Once the structural disturbances and their transmission mechanisms have been recovered, actual inflation may be broken down into two terms. Depending on which identification hypothesis is used, the measures of permanent and latent inflation may be obtained. To do so, it is therefore necessary to identify the four elements of the matrix $A(0)$.

Starting from (8A.3), the relationship

$$\Omega = A(0).A(0)' \tag{8A.4}$$

is obtained, from which 3 restrictions are derived. The fourth restriction required is obtained from the long-term restriction applied.

Thus, with regard to permanent inflation, the two types of disturbance are defined according to their long-term effect on the inflation rate: the first group has a temporary effect, while the impact of the second is permanent. To identify the first group of disturbances, which does not have a long-term effect on inflation, the long-term restriction $\sum_{j=0}^{\infty} a_{11}(j) = 0$ must be met, with $a_{11}(j)$ being the element $(1,1)$ of matrix $A(j)$. To grasp this restriction, it should be noted that $a_{11}(j)$ shows how π_t is affected after j periods following a unit innovation of e_{1t}. Therefore, $\sum_{j=0}^{k} a_{11}(j)$ is the effect on inflation after k periods, so that in order for e_{1t} not to have a long-term impact on inflation, it must be that $\sum_{j=0}^{\infty} a_{11}(j) = 0$.

Once the structural disturbances and their transmission mechanisms have been established, we may obtain the desired breakdown of the change in the inflation rate into two components:

$$\Delta\pi_t = \sum_{j=0}^{\infty} a_{11}(j)e_{1t-j} + \sum_{j=0}^{\infty} a_{12}(j)e_{2t-j} \tag{8A.5}$$

The first term of the second member shows the effect on the change in the temporary component of inflation. The second term of the second member shows the effect on the change in the permanent component of inflation.[38]

With regard to latent inflation, the two types of structural disturbances are defined on the basis of their long-term effect on real output. The first type does not have a long-term effect on output, although it affects actual inflation. The second type has a long-term effect on output, but does not affect latent inflation. Latent inflation is described as the contribution of the first type of disturbance on actual inflation.

In formal terms, to obtain latent inflation, the long-term restriction $\sum a_{11}(j) = 0$ must be replaced by $\sum \tilde{a}_{22}(j) = 0$,[39] so that the disturbance we now denote as $\tilde{e}_{2t}$ does not have a long-term effect on output.

Similar to (8A.5), the inflation rate breaks down[40] as:

$$\Delta\pi_t = \sum_{j=0}^{\infty} \tilde{a}_{11}(j)\tilde{e}_{1t-j} + \sum_{j=0}^{\infty} \tilde{a}_{12}(j)\tilde{e}_{2t-j} \tag{8A.6}$$

The first term of the second member shows the effect on the change in latent inflation and the second shows the effect on the difference between the changes in actual inflation and latent inflation.

Notes

1   See, for example, Espasa *et al.* (1987) and Matea (1993).
2   These are the two components which are most commonly eliminated in Spain. They are not necessarily the indices eliminated by other countries in dealing with the characteristics of their CPI.
3   The year-on-year rate, which is denoted as T_{12}^1, calculates the growth that takes place in a given month compared with the same month in the previous year.
4   A rate of change calculates growth between two periods. Centering consists in assigning said growth to the intermediate point in the period of time under consideration.
5   This is commonly the case in Spain.
6   From this standpoint, and for the European Union, Erichsen and Riet (1995) have compiled the prices which member countries' central banks usually exclude.
7   In that paper, and in the monthly series presented in this chapter, re-worked series are used which take into account the major methodological changes introduced into CPI, base year 1992: the exclusion of the cost of owner-occupied housing and the use of weighted, non-centred, moving averages for the prices of fresh fruit and fresh vegetables, together with the new weightings assigned by the new CPI basket to goods and services. Owing to data constraints, the reconstructed series begins in August 1985, when the first detailed data were published using the old base year 1983, while the last value considered is that for December 1995.
8   When including weighted moving averages of 12 terms in its fresh fruit and vegetable components.
9   Even the differences that did exist between maximum prices and public sale prices shrank considerably when, in January 1993 – in contrast to the previous practice of having prices set by CAMPSA – the refineries were allowed to determine sales prices. This situation would currently seem to be changing.
10   As a trend is a non-observable component, it has no single definition. Indeed, the concept used in this section differs from those used on p. 293.
11   In general terms, this procedure starts from an ARIMA model of the series under study and subsequently assigns each of the roots of the model to the most appropriate non-observable component. Readers interested in this method may consult, for example, Maravall (1987).
12   In other words, so that the maxima and minima of the year-on-year rate match those of month-on-month growth.
13   If a measure free from relative price changes is desired, it may not be appropriate to add the determinist trend, as this may be capturing relative price changes.
14   For the development of this formula, Espasa and Cancelo (1993) may be consulted.

15   T_{12}^{12} is the average growth rate of 12 consecutive months *vis-à-vis* the average of the 12 months immediately preceding, while T_{12}^1 is the year-on-year rate.

16   However, the T_{12}^{12} of the original series virtually matched the T_{12}^{12} of the price level trend.

17   T_{12}^3 represents the growth of the average of three consecutive months *vis-à-vis* the average of the same three months in the previous year.

18   That is, estimators in which the influence of the tails of distribution is reduced.

19   The weighted median reflects the point of distribution which has half of probability on both sides, once the indices have been multiplied by their weightings. As to the trimmed mean, it is equivalent to the mean, except only that the indices with the highest and lowest values are left out of its calculation in equal proportion.

20   These indices resulted from crossing the two types of classification developed by the INE (National Statistics Institute) for subclasses. Thus, in each case, the classification was used that produces most disaggregation.

21   In working with year-on-year rates, these procedures have the drawback of not complying with CPI levels. The problem may be seen more easily if we go to the extreme of calculating the trimmed mean at 0 per cent. In this case, the values obtained do not match the year-on-year rate of the CPI, as the weighted average of year-on-year rates does not match the year-on-year rate of a weighted average. As, in principle, the trimmed mean at 0 per cent and the T_{12}^1 of the CPI should be identical, the weightings of the subclasses have been replaced at all times by the portion of the CPI level of 12 months ago accounted for by each subclass; this is equivalent to correcting the year-on-year rates of the subclasses by a factor on a variable scale.

22   A distribution is symmetric when this ratio is zero, whereas if it has a positive (negative) value, the area on the right-hand (left-hand) side of the distribution is greater than that on the left-hand (right-hand) side.

23   The central banks of both the United Kingdom and Sweden apply this percentage. The Bank of New Zealand calculates the trimmed mean at 10 per cent.

24   This measure was first proposed by Quah and Vahey (1995).

25   From the theoretical standpoint, latent inflation cannot strictly be interpreted as long-term inflation, as not all temporary disturbances of real output are necessarily transmitted to the inflation process. Strictly speaking, this measure covers not only permanent shocks to demand, but also shoks to linked to cyclical changes in output. However, as is shown further on, latent and permanent inflation closely resemble each other in the Spanish economy. As a result, it would seem proper in practice to interpret latent inflation as long-term inflation.

26   This measure is discussed by Álvarez and Sebastián (1995).

27   See also Quah (1993).

28   This limitation is also present in most of the quantitative methods. It is generally assumed that the relationships identified in the estimation stage carry over into the forecasting period.

29   In Álvarez and Sebastián (1995) the sample period ends in the final quarter of 1993. However, there are no appreciable differences between the results discussed here and those obtained in that paper.

30   Four lags adequately cover the dynamics of the process. Using five lags does not produce appreciable differences.

31 This method is outlined in the Appendix (p. 303).
32 The number of possible hypotheses is unlimited. In this chapter, the hypothesis used is that the sum of deviations between both rates of inflation is zero. The logic of using this hypothesis is that, by definition, deviations by the actual inflation rate from permanent inflation can only be temporary.
33 This line of reasoning is also valid for latent inflation.
34 The assumption used in determining the level in this case is more controversial inasmuch as, a priori, the fact that latent inflation deviations and actual inflation must be temporary is not explained.
35 It is obviously not correct to interpret this measure as a cyclically adjusted measure of inflation.
36 These transformations are used, in accordance with the results of the unit root tests of (augmented) Dickey and Fuller and Phillips and Perron, to ensure that we are working with a stationary process. It should be pointed out that the inflation process in the Spanish economy is nonstationary. Moreover, use of the year-on-year rate reflects a nonstationary stochastic seasonality of the CPI, as suggested by Matea's findings (1994b). On the other hand, it is assumed, on the basis of the hypothesis of a vertical long-term Phillips curve and the results of the cointegration tests of Johansen, and Dickey and Fuller, that there is no long-term relationship between the inflation rate and output.
37 To simplify notation, the determinist elements of the model are not included.
38 It should be noted that in assuming that inflation follows a nonstationary process, the change in permanent inflation is obtained, but not its level. To obtain this level, it is necessary to make a further assumption regarding its initial value. The same applies to latent inflation.
39 It should be noted that the coefficients and structural disturbances changes as the identification scheme changes. In this second scheme, we denote structural disturbances and coefficients with a tilde.
40 In an analogous way, the output equation enables us to break down the latter into one term linked to the economic cycle and another linked to trend or potential output.

References

ÁLVAREZ, L.J. and M. SEBASTIÁN (1995) 'La inflación latente en España: Una perspectiva macroeconómica', *Documento de Trabajo*, 9521, Servicio de Estudios, Banco de España.

BALL, L. and N.G. MANKIW (1995) 'Relative-price changes as aggregate supply shocks', *Quarterly Journal of Economics*, 110, 161–93.

BLANCHARD, O.J. and D. QUAH (1989) 'The dynamic effects of aggregate demand and supply disturbances', *American Economic Review*, 79, 655–73.

BRYAN, M.F. and S.G. CECCHETTI (1994) 'Measuring core inflation', in N.G. Mankiw (ed.), 'Monetary Policy', *Studies in Business Cycles*, 29, Chicago: University of Chicago Press, 195–215.

ESPASA, A. and J.R. CANCELO (1993) 'Tasas de crecimiento y la velocidad subyacente en la evolución de un fenómeno económico', in A. Espasa, and J.R. Cancelo (eds), *Métodos cuantitativos para el análisis de la coyuntura económica*, Madrid: Alianza Editorial, 325–99.

ESPASA, A., M.C. MANZANO, M. Ll. MATEA and V. CATASUS (1987) 'La inflación subyacente en la economía española: estimación y metodología', *Boletín Económico*, Banco de España, March, 32–51.

ERICHSEN, S.R. and A.G. RIET (1995) 'The role of underlying inflation in the framework for monetary policy in EU countries', European Monetary Institute, November, mimeo.

FISHER, L.A., P.L. FACKLER and D. ORDEN (1995) 'Long-run identifying restrictions for an error-correction model of New Zealand money, prices and output', *Journal of International Money and Finance*, 14, 127–47.

MARAVALL, A. (1987) 'Descomposición de series temporales: especificación, estimación e inferencia. (Con una aplicación a la oferta monetaria en España)', *Documento de Trabajo*, 8702, Servicio de Estudios, Banco de España.

MATEA, M. Ll. (1993) 'Análisis de la inflación en España', in A. Espasa and J.R. Cancelo (eds), *Métodos cuantitativos para el análisis de la coyuntura económica*', Madrid: Alianza Editorial, 555–604.

MATEA, M. Ll. (1994a) 'Algunas medidas para analizar la inflación', Banco de España, internal document, EC/1994/42.

MATEA, M. Ll. (1994b) 'Contrastes de raíces unitarias para series mensuales: una aplicación al IPC', *Revista Española de Economía*, 11, 7–25.

MATEA, M. Ll. and A.V. REGIL (1994) 'Métodos para la extracción de señales y para la trimestralización. Una aplicación: trimestralización del deflactor del consumo privado nacional', *Documento de Trabajo*, 9415, Servicio de Estudios, Banco de España.

OOSTERHOFF, J. (1994) 'Trimmed mean or sample median?', *Statistics and Probability Letters*, 20, 401–9.

QUAH, D. (1993) 'Forecasting inflation with flexible interpreted VARs', London School of Economics, *Working Paper*.

QUAH, D. and S. VAHEY (1995) 'Measuring core inflation', *Economic Journal*, 105, 1130–44.

ROBERTS, J.M. (1993) 'The sources of business cycles: a monetarist interpretation', *International Economic Review*, 34, 923–34.

ROGER, S. (1995) 'Measures of underlying inflation in New Zealand, 1981–95', *Discussion Paper Series*, G95/5, Reserve Bank of New Zealand.

ZELDES, S.P. (1994) 'Comment to measuring core inflation', in N.G. Mankiw (ed.), 'Monetary Policy', *Studies in Business Cycles*, 29, Chicago: University of Chicago Press, 216–19.

9 Monetary and Credit Aggregates as Indicators of Inflation

Alberto Cabrero Bravo, Jorge Martínez Pagés and María Pérez-Jurado

E31 E51 (Spain)
E32

INTRODUCTION

Toward the end of the 1980s, a rupture occurred in the long-term relationship between ALP (liquid assets held by the public) and nominal expenditure. Although it was possible subsequently to reconstruct an ALP demand equation with satisfactory statistical properties, its greater complexity and its dependence on variables beyond the control of the Banco de España, as well as the recurrence of disturbances affecting the short-term behavior of ALP, were among the reasons prompting abandonment of the monetary policy strategy pursued until 1994. This strategy, based on the establishment of an intermediate objective for said aggregate, was replaced by another consisting of the definition of explicit inflation targets. Yet, the results of the estimated equation justified the establishment of a medium-term benchmark for the growth of ALP, although this had to be supplemented with the monitoring of other monetary and credit aggregates, which helped determine its trend at a given point in time.

At the same time, the precise quantification of a target inflation rate requires the optimal use of all those indicators that help forecast its future trend. Despite the variability in the behavior of the monetary and credit aggregates, there are important theoretical reasons and abundant empirical evidence supporting the hypothesis that these aggregates contain relevant information on the short-term behavior of nominal expenditure and prices.

As for the monetary aggregates, the theoretical relationship between monetary growth and future inflation is based on the use of money as a means of payment. However, the process of financial innovation initiated in Spain in the early 1980s has broadened the range of highly liquid assets demanded (in unknown proportions) as a means of payment and for the deposit of financial wealth. Consequently, it is becoming increasingly difficult to determine exactly which measurement of liquidity is most closely

309

related to nominal expenditure, as the possible candidates include a wide variety of aggregations of financial assets.

The narrower monetary aggregates have the advantage of including assets incorporating liquidity facilities in large, relatively uniform proportions, but they also have the disadvantage of excluding other assets which, albeit in smaller proportions, also incorporate said facilities. The broader aggregates theoretically avoid this disadvantage by taking account of all those assets that can be considered liquid to some extent. However, the usual method of aggregating these indicators (the simple sum of the asset balances included) entails assumptions of perfect substitutability that become less plausible as the aggregate broadens. The observation of this problem has given rise to a large body of literature aimed at constructing monetary variables with different aggregation criteria.

In view of the above considerations, to use the information provided by trends in liquidity, it does not seem advisable to focus on a single aggregate, but rather to analyze the behavior of various alternative indicators. This analysis should be supplemented with the use of the so-called liquidity counterparts: credit to the private sector, credit to general government, and net claims on the rest of the world.

Not all of these monetary and credit aggregates point in the same direction in the short term, and they can even give conflicting signals concerning the foreseeable course of the final variables. Consequently, it is very important to consider the best way of combining the information provided by these indicators.

The purpose of this chapter is to illustrate the informative content of the various aggregates mentioned – both monetary and credit – as leading indicators of nominal expenditure and, above all, of inflation. To accomplish this, 3 different approaches are taken. First, based on the specification of a *trivariate VAR* model, with the rates of change of real income, of prices, and of various monetary and credit aggregates as endogenous variables, a causality analysis is performed using the Granger criterion. However, even though this criterion demonstrates that all of the aggregates generally provide information on future inflation, it does not seem selective enough to help determine which aggregates should be given more weight in the event of conflicting signals.

The second methodology attempts to go further by identifying the so-called *turning points* in the cyclical behavior of both inflation and the aggregates. The informative content of the various monetary and credit aggregates depends on their capacity to anticipate the turning points of inflation. Some results of this analysis have already been presented in this book (see Chapter 7), as they were used to select a monetary aggregate and a credit aggregate for use in constructing – along with other indicators – a composite indicator capable of anticipating the turning points of inflation.

Lastly, the third approach focuses on the monetary aggregates and attempts to shed some light on how they should be combined, or – which amounts to the same thing – how to weight the information provided by the various, mutually exclusive, components of the broader aggregate, so that the resulting *weighted aggregate* is the one with the most informative content concerning future nominal expenditure. Thus, in contrast to simple aggregates that ascribe the same importance to their various components (i.e. consider them equally liquid), in the weighted aggregate, constructed according to the methodology proposed by Feldstein and Stock (1994), the informative content concerning the future course of nominal expenditure determines the liquidity facilities provided by each asset, i.e. the importance that should be given to each asset as an indicator of the final variables.

The rest of the chapter is structured as follows. The composition of the various monetary and credit aggregates is described and the Banco de España's method of processing the corresponding information is explained. After presenting the results of the aforementioned causality tests, we analyze the capacity of the various aggregates to anticipate the turning points that signal a cyclical change in the growth of inflation. We then focus on the construction of a weighted aggregate and assesses its informative content concerning the future course of the final variables. The main conclusions are then presented in the final section.

COMPOSITION AND TREATMENT OF MONETARY AND CREDIT AGGREGATES

In analyzing the monetary situation, the Banco de España takes into account not only ALP but also other monetary aggregates that provide information on the possible existence and intensity of financial shifts that could affect ALP. It is also considered relevant to analyze the factors responsible for the growth of liquidity on the supply side, i.e. the counterparts of ALP. These counterparts are the credit aggregates (credit to the private sector, credit to general government, and net claims on the rest of the world).

To clarify the content and characteristics of each of these indicators, a brief description of their composition and of the information they contain is necessary.

Monetary Aggregates

The current composition of the monetary aggregates was determined by the reform introduced in 1992,[1] the aim of which was to adapt the aggregates to the changes that had occurred in the Spanish financial sys-

Table 9.1 Composition of the monetary aggregates

Financial Assets	Issuer	Eligibility[1]	Source	Periodicity	Lag	% of GDP 1984	1987	1992	1995
Currency held by the public	Treasury and Banco de España	No	COCA and Banco de España	Daily	Ten-day and daily	6.6	6.8	9.6	10.2
Sight deposits	Banco de España Banking system	Yes	Cred. syst. balance sheets[2]	Monthly	1.5 months	13.5	14.0	16.5	14.0
Savings deposits	Banking system	Yes	Cred. syst. balance sheets[2]	Monthly	1.5 months	17.4	16.7	16.4	15.8
Time deposits	Banking system ECAOL	Yes	Cred. syst. balance sheets[2]	Monthly	1.5 months	40.0	29.4	28.4	34.1
Deposits in foreign currency	Banking system	Yes	COCA	Daily	10-day	0.1	0.1	0.4	0.9
Repos of short-term public securities	Banking system ICO ECAOL	No	COCA and Book-Entry Office	Daily	10-day	0.8	8.6	7.4	6.8
Repos of medium-and long-term public securities	Banking system ICO ECAOL	No	COCA and Book-Entry Office	Daily	10-day	–	1.1	5.3	8.2
Repos of other assets	Banking system ECAOL	Yes	COCA	Daily	10-day	0.3	0.9	0.0	0.1
Asset participations	Banking system	Yes	COCA	Daily	10-day	–	0.1	0.1	0.0
Short-term securities of credit institutions	Banking system	Yes	COCA	Daily	10-day	-0.2	2.6	1.3	
Long-term securities of deposit money institutions	Banking system	Yes	COCA	Daily	10-day	3.4	4.8	1.8	2.5
Long-term securities of the ICO and ECAOL	ICO ECAOL	ECAOL, Yes ICO, No	COCA and Cred. syst. balance sheets	Monthly	1-1/2 months	0.3	0.6	0.8	0.7
Insurance operations	Banking system	No	[3]	[3]	[3]	0.6	2.6	0.5	–
Non-interbank private assets transfers	Banking system ECAOL	No	Cred. syst. balance sheets	Monthly	1.5 months	–	0.6	0.3	0.4
Endorsed bills and commercial paper guarantees	Banking system	Yes	COCA	Daily	10-day	0.4	0.0	–	–

Aggregate groupings: M1, M2, M3, ALP, ALP2, ALP2+

Item	Issuer/sector	Recording entity [3]	Recording frequency [3]	Availability lag [3]	Reserve requirement				
Treasury notes held by the public	State		Daily		No	1.6	2.1	0.3	–
Treasury bills held by the public	State	COCA and Book-Entry Office	Daily	10-day	No	–	0.2	4.9	8.2
Short-term securities of other governments	Other general government	CNMV and Book-Entry Office	Monthly	1.5 months	No	–	0.1	0.5	0.1
Commercial paper	Private sector	Cred. syst. balance sheets	Monthly	1.5 months	No	–	1.8	3.2	1.4
Medium-and long-term government debt plus special debt	State	Book-Entry Office	Daily	Daily	No	1.7	2.6	4.7	7.1
Memorandum Items: Cross-border deposits	Non-resident credit sector	Bank for International Settlements	Quarterly		No	2.2	1.6	3.0	4.7
Mutual funds	IIC	CNMV	Monthly	Monthly	No	0.3	1.3	10.0	15.9

Notes:
1 All entities comply with the 10-day reserve requirement (COCA) – as an average of daily data –, except ECAOLs, which do so on a monthly basis, as well as certain credit cooperatives. The ICO (Official Credit Institute) is not required to comply with the reserve requirement.
2 Daily information is obtained through the COCA with a 10-day lag for all bank deposits.
3 The balance of these assets at present is zero, as the issuance of this type of instrument has vanished.
4 Time elapsed until the information is available.
Source: Banco de España.

tem up to that point and to achieve a higher degree of homogeneity with the aggregates of the other EU countries.

Logically, in determining the criteria that the most appropriate definitions of liquidity should satisfy, it was acknowledged that the development of money markets and the characteristics of the financial instruments available to the public make it difficult to choose among the various forces tradition-ally associated with the demand for money. Thus, the rankings established within the aggregates are based both on these more traditional criteria and on others related to the sector holding or issuing liquid financial assets.

The current monetary aggregates are essentially a product of this reform. Table 9.1 summarizes the various assets that make up each of the aggregates, as well as the type of issuer and the information available con-cerning each of them. It also includes a quantified indication of how the relative importance of the various aggregates has evolved in terms of GDP. This table shows that the Banco de España has highly disaggregated and swiftly available monetary statistics; consequently, very reliable advance data on the behavior of the monetary aggregates and their main compon-ents can be obtained before the monitoring period (usually one month) comes to an end.

The data compilation and processing system draws on the reserve requirement figures (COCA in its Spanish acronym) that banking institu-tions must present 3 times a month. This information is supplemented with data on the behavior of markets for state and other general govern-ment debt, obtained from the Public Debt Book-Entry Office. This Office provides daily information that can be used to monitor the preformance of the portfolios of institutions and of the resident and non-resident public. On the basis of daily information covering about 95 per cent of ALP, the Banco de España is able – using quantitative techniques based on very short-term, single equation prediction models – to analyze monetary devel-opments several times a month.[2] This analysis is used, among other things, to monitor short-term portfolio activity, with a view to assessing the possi-ble impact of such activity on the trend performance of the aggregate.

Table 9.1 indicates changes that have occurred in the relative importance of the various components of the aggregates over time. It is thus possible to identify the intensive substitution processes at work among the various components of ALP, which have complicated the task of interpreting its behavior. Some of these processes are:

– Substitution involving deposits (basically time deposits) and other instruments. Phenomena of this type have been occurring continuously since 1984, in an environment of financial innovation associated with taxes, the complete deregulation of interest rates in 1987, and, in recent years, the liberalization of capital movements.

- Increase in cash holdings by the public since 1986, essentially for reasons of tax opacity. This process intensified in the early 1990s as cash became virtually the only financial asset affording a tax haven for those who decided not to avail themselves of the tax regularization process that culminated in 1992.[3]
- Growth of mutual funds in recent years. As the attached table shows, assets of this type have increased significantly, attaining a relative weight in 1995 close to 16 per cent of GDP. This phenomenon would, in principle, tend to affect the monetary aggregates insofar as a shift in assets occurs in the public's portfolio from typical banking instruments to mutual funds, which are not presently classified as financial sector instruments. However, given the most of the funds' investments are in instruments included in ALP, this substitution process is partially internalized. An aggregate that includes outright holdings of medium-and long-term government debt by the public (APL2+) almost wholly incorporates these shifts.

Credit Aggregates

In recent years, the Banco de España has paid increasing attention to credit indicators, insofar as they reflect decisions about indebtedness, which are in turn determined by spending decisions.

The analysis of *credit to non-financial firms and households* (CEEFF in its Spanish acronym) as an indicator of the level of activity seems justified. This indicator is considered pro-cyclical, although there may be a certain lag in the growth of credit *vis-à-vis* aggregate expenditure, explained by the fact that, after a recessive phase, economic agents initially rely on self-financing, and only after economic recovery seems more certain are they willing to incur debt.[4]

Care should be exercised in interpreting the quality of credit to firms and households as an indicator of price pressures. Moreover, it seems necessary to make a distinction as to what type of activity the credit will finance. The inflationary impact of an increase in consumer credit may be different from that of credit granted to finance other components of demand. Thus, monitoring based on a breakdown of credit to the private sector by purpose is especially relevant.

The informative content of *credit to general government* (CAAP in its Spanish acronym) is difficult to assess, given the ways in which it differs from private sector financing, in terms of both objectives and constraints.[5] In any case, this indicator should be monitored in the short term to determine its contribution to the growth of liquidity and the overall financing of the economy.

Table 9.2 Composition of the credit aggregates

	Financial assets	Issuer	Source	Periodicity	Lag	% of GDP			
						1984	1987	1992	1995
CEEFF	Loans	Credit system and money markets	Cred. syst. balance sheets and summary balance sheets of the banking system and ICO	Monthly	1.5 months and 10 days	65.5	63.3	75.8	73.7
	Securities	Other resident sectors	Cred. syst. balance sheets	Monthly	1–1/2 months	7.3	5.7	4.4	4.6
CEEFF+	Commercial paper	Other resident sectors	Summary balance sheets of the banking system and ICO AIAF	Monthly	10 days	–	1.8	3.2	1.4
	Foreign direct loans	External sector	Balance of payments	Monthly	3 months	5.7	1.3	4.7	6.7
FINTOT	State's net position vis-à-vis the Banco de España[1]	Banco de España	Banco de España	Daily	–	4.7	3.9	2.9	0.1
CAAPP	Loans[2]	Credit system	Cred. syst. balance sheets and summary balance sheets of the banking system and ICO	Monthly	1.5 months 10 days	2.9	2.6	5.5	6.6
	Securities	General government	Cred. syst. balance sheet and Book-Entry Office	Monthly Daily	1.5 months	20.5	29.4	24.1	33.1
CAAPP+	Medium- and long-term debt portfolio held by the public	General government	Cred. syst. balance sheets and Book-Entry Office	Monthly Daily	1.5 months	1.7	2.6	5	7.4
	Foreign direct financing	External sector	Banco de España Book-Entry Office	Daily	–	–	0.6	5.4	7.8

Notes:
1 Calculated as the difference between credit outstanding and the Treasury's current account with the Banco de España.
2 Includes grants and loans to official credit institutions.
Source: Banco de España.

Table 9.2 summarizes the composition of the credit aggregates by issuing agent and instrument, as well as by statistical source and periodicity. The percentage that each component represents relative to GDP is also shown for various periods. As indicated in the table, in the credit to firms and households sector (CEEFF), the weight of the loans component – still the largest – has increased over time to approximately 75 per cent of GDP, to the detriment of securities financing. Additionally, the upward trend of foreign direct loans should be noted.

Of the components of credit to general government, financing with securities issued by the state or by local governments is the one with the largest relative weight. The behavior of the state's net position *vis-à-vis* the Banco de España reflects the change in the structure of State financing brought about by Law 21/93 on the State Budget for 1994, which prohibits the state from resorting to the Banco de España for financing. Lastly, as in the private sector, the trends in foreign direct financing reveal the growing reliance of the public sector on this type of credit.

MONETARY AND CREDIT AGGREGATES AS LEADING INDICATORS OF INFLATION

An initial approach to assessing the informative content of the monetary and credit aggregates as leading indicators of inflation is to estimate an econometric relationship between a definition of inflation and each of the aggregates, with a view to checking the predictive capacity assessed by means of a causality test.

Causality Analysis

This methodological approach was based on the specification of a trivariate VAR model in which income, prices, and liquidity are regressed upon lags in the dependent variables themselves, the error correction mechanism, and a set of deterministic variables.[6] In specifying these models, the existing cointegration relationships tested in the recent literature were taken into account.

The causality relationship was checked using the Granger joint significance test, applied to the various aggregates in the corresponding price equation.

Table 9.3 shows the relationships estimated, using this specification, for various definitions of liquidity and credit and with two inflation proxies: the consumer price index (CPI) and the so-called inflationary core, or index of prices of services and non-energy processed goods (IPSEBENE).

Table 9.3 Causality test of various monetary and credit aggregates relative to inflation

Regression of: $\Delta\Delta_4 p$

On: $\Delta\Delta_4 p_{t-j}, \Delta\Delta_4 m_{t-j}, \Delta_4(m-p)_{t-1}$, constant, S844, Δ I801, Δ_4 I861 $j = 1 \ldots k$

Sample period: 1979QII–1994QIV

	CPI		IPSEBENE	
	Lag (k)	Granger test	Lag (k)	Granger test
M1	4	$F(5,46)=2.90$** [0.0232]	5	$F(5,46) = 6.46$** [0.0001]
	5	$F(6,43)=3.28$* [0.0533]	8	$F(9,34)=3.25$*** [0.006]
M2	4	$F(5,46) = 3.31$** [0.0124]	4	$F(5,46) = 6.14$*** [0.0002]
	5	$F(6,43) = 2.93$** [0.0173]	8	$F(9,34) = 3.16$*** [0.007]
M3	4	$F(5,46) = 1.63$ [0.1707]	4	$F(5,46) = 3.25$** [0.013]
ALP	4	$F(5,46) = 4.37$** [0.0024]		
			4	$F(5,46) = 5.85$*** [0.0003]
	5	$F(6,43) = 3.20$** [0.0109]		
ALP2+	4	$F(5,46) = 2.71$** [0.0316]	4	$F(5,46) = 4.56$*** [0.002]
	5	$F(6,43) = 1.46$ [0.2139]	8	$F(9,34) = 1.40$ [0.228]
			4	$F(5,46) = 5.02$*** [0.0009]
CEEFF	5	$F(6,43) = 1.96$* [0.0923]		
			5	$F(6,43) = 3.85$*** [0.004]
			4	$F(5,46) = 4.80$*** [0.001]
CEEFF+	5	$F(6,43) = 2.43$** [0.0413]		
			5	$F(6,43) = 3.79$*** [0.004]
			4	$F(5,46) = 5.65$*** [0.0004]
FINTOT	5	$F(6,43) = 1.86$ [0.1094]	5	$F(6,43) = 4.36$*** [0.002]
			6	$F(7,40) = 3.77$*** [0.003]

Notes: The asterisks indicate the level of significance of the tests:

(***) $P \leq 1$: H_0 not accepted at 1% (causality accepted).

(**) $1 < P \leq 5$: H_0 not accepted at 5% and accepted at 1%.

(*) $5 < P \leq 10$: H_0 not accepted at 10% and accepted at 5%.

$\quad$ $10 < P$: H_0 accepted (causality rejected).

Source: Banco de España.

The results confirm that the monetary aggregates have informative content concerning prices (CPI or IPSEBENE). Specifically, a certain predictive capacity is accepted for ALP2+, ALP, M2, and M1. Regarding the credit aggregates, at a given level of significance, the predictive capacity of domestic credit to the private sector relative to the CPI cannot be rejected. As for the IPSEBENE, all of the monetary and credit aggregates would be accepted as leading indicators.

These results show that the informative content of the monetary and credit aggregates as potential predictors of inflation is not rejected. However, this criterion is not selective enough to determine which aggregates contribute to the best prediction of inflation. To shed more light on this latter point, alternative approaches were taken to the causality analysis. One of these approaches consists of analyzing the correlations between the turning points of these indicators and the turning points of a reference indicator of prices.

Monetary and Credit Aggregates and the Inflation Cycle

A relevant aspect in examining the informative quality of an economic variable relative to a given phenomenon is that of assessing its capacity to anticipate those critical moments at which the trend of the phenomenon being monitored reaches a turning point. Specifically, this section analyzes the capacity of the monetary and credit aggregates to predict discrete changes in the cyclical profile of inflation, i.e. their turning points.

The identification of these points, which is known as the cyclical reference chronology, has resulted in recent years in numerous contributions to the analysis of the main economic variables, as indicated in Boldin (1994). This methodology is derived from studies on the construction of composite indices to assist in forecasting the most relevant changes in the general activity index.[7]

Regarding the analysis of prices, insofar as the inflation rate also behaves cyclically (Zarnowitz and Braun, 1993; Chadka and Prasad, 1994), the methodology based on the determination of turning points can also be used to provide information on which economic indicators are capable of anticipating turning points in the inflationary path. These points would signal the transition from a phase of rising inflation to one of decline, or vice versa.[8]

The following paragraphs describe the results of using this methodology to analyze the informative content of the monetary and credit aggregates in terms of their capacity to lead the turning points of the inflation rate in Spain.[9] The reference indicator for this exercise is a measurement of inflation growth, approximated by the stationary transformation of the consumer price index series corrected for deterministic effects.[10] The turning points of the monetary and credit indicators were identified using the same criterion that was used to identify these points in the reference indicator. In other words, stationary transformation was also considered in the analysis of the various monetary indicators.[11]

Reference Chronology

To determine the points marking the transition from a growth phase to one of contraction or vice versa, and hoc techniques are usually applied, based on the fit of very long moving averages. In this way, the trend of a variable can be approximated for purposes of analyzing deviations from the trend. Thus, a local peak will be considered as having been reached when the rate of growth at a given point in time is relatively greater than the long-term trend of the variable in question, and a local trough when the rate of growth is relatively lower than trend. However, in this paper, a dating programme based on the concept of spectral smoothing was used, because of the advantage of precisely determining the cyclical period which is to be the focus of the analysis. In this case, a function is chosen for which the data are filtered, in order to provide a cyclical characterization covering 18–24 months.[12]

In this way, a reference chronology is obtained which records the peak accelerations and decelerations of the consumer price index, as well as of the corresponding monetary and credit aggregates.

In the sample period, which runs from 1977QI to 1995QIV, five peak turning points are identified in quarterly periods (1980QIV, 1983QI, 1986QIII, 1989QII, 1993QIII) and six troughs (1979QII, 1982QIII, 1985QI, 1987QII, 1991QIV, 1993QIV), which define the reference chronology. Figure 9.1 represents the growth of inflation and the year-on-year rate of the consumer price index, along with the critical points. The reference chronology identifies five cycles in the sample period, four of which have an amplitude of 2–3 years. However, a longer cycle of 5 years is identified, which, starting from a trough in 1987:II, marks the beginning of a process of inflation growth that continues until 1989:II. A turning point is recorded in that quarter, and a new trough is identified in 1991:IV. It can be seen that this cycle more or less coincides with the period of strong growth in the Spanish economy in the late 1980s and the subsequent recession, which lasted until mid-1992.

Determination of the Turning Points of the Monetary and Credit Indicators Relative to the Reference Cycle

Proceeding in the same manner as in the case of the reference indicator, the turning points of the various monetary and credit aggregates are obtained and placed in relationship to the reference chronology. Table 9.4

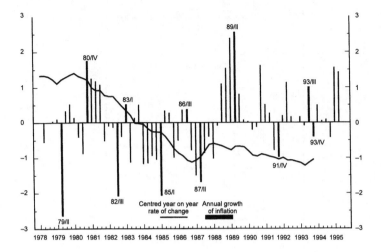

Figure 9.1   Cyclical reference chronology, 1978–95

Notes: 1   Reference variable: CPI series corrected for deterministic effects.
     2   Standardized chart.
Source: Banco de España.

summarizes this relationship by recording the number of quarters that the turning points of each indicator lead or lag the nearest one, identified on the basis of the rate of change of inflation. The table also presents various statistical measurements (mean, median, and standard deviation) to aid in assessing each indicator's lead *vis-à-vis* the various turning points identified for the reference series.

Examination of this table suggests several general comments:

– A certain asymmetry is detected in most of the nine indicators: the mean lead of the peaks tends to be greater than that of the troughs. No general conclusion is reached concerning which mean lead is the strongest, but it can be seen that the most frequent mean lead period for both peaks and troughs exceeds 3 quarters.
– As for dispersion, all of the indicators tend to capture leads for peaks better than leads for troughs. The dispersion around the mean lead at points indicating the end of a period of rising inflation (peaks) is appreciably smaller than those signalling the end of a period of falling inflation (troughs).

Turning to a more detailed analysis, the results can be analyzed in terms of a breakdown by component. Concerning the monetary aggregates:

Table 9.4 Lead, lag or coincidence of monetary indicators *vis-à-vis* the reference indicator[1] (CPI), 1980:IV: 1993:IV

	Peaks								Troughs								
	Reference chronology					Mean lead	Median lead	σ	Reference chronology						Mean lead	Median lead	σ
	1980 QIV	1983 QI	1986 QIII	1989 QII	1993 QIII				1979 QII	1982 QII	1985 QI	1987 QII	1991 QIV	1993 QIV			
ALP2+	...	4	2	2	-1	1.75	2	1.8	-3	...	7	1	-1	...	1	0	3.7
ALP	...	3	2	7	10	7	7.5	2.5	-3	...	7	3	8	5	4	5	3.9
M3	...	4	10	1	-1	3.5	2.5	4.1	-3	...	7	...	-1	...	1	-1	4.3
M2	4	2	4	...	-1	2.3	2	2	...	...	7	1	9	6	5.8	6.5	3
M1	4	-1	4	...	-2	1.3	-1	2.8	-3	...	5	1	10	6	3.8	4	4.5
CEEFF+	4	4	2	6	7	4.6	4.7	1.7	...	5	3	2	5	-1	2.8	2.5	2.3
CEEFF	4	...	...	5	5	4.7	4.7	0.5	...	...	3	...	8	-1	3.3	3	3.7
CAAPP	...	-1	...	...	0	-0.5	-0.5	-0.5	...	6	-3	...	8	3	3.5	3	4.1
FINTOT	1	4	0	-1	5	1.8	1.7	2.3	3	6	0	3	5	-1	2.7	3.7	2.5

Note: The reference indicator is the stationary transformation of the consumer price index corrected for deterministic effects.
Source: Banco de España.

– The various monetary aggregates behave differently, although no clear distinction can be made between broad and narrow aggregates.
– In general, the ALP and M2 aggregates have the longest lead over the turning points. Specifically, ALP leads both the peaks and troughs by more than a year. M2 exhibits greater asymmetry, with a mean lead for the peaks of less than a year (approximately 3 quarters), while the mean lead for the troughs is about a year and a half. However, the dispersion of the M2 values around the mean lead is less than that observed for ALP.
– M1 and M3 exhibit more dispersion. Moreover, in the case of M1, in characterizing the peaks, the lead points are not consistently identified, as demonstrated by the resulting negative median lead.
– The ALP2+ aggregate yields no consistent results relative to other close aggregates such as ALP or M3; its chronology of turning points exhibits highly differentiated behavior, in terms of the lead for both peaks and troughs.

As for the credit aggregates, the most relevant aspects are the following:

– Credit to households and firms, whether broadly or narrowly defined (total credit or loans alone), tends to be better at anticipating leads in both peaks and troughs. These indicators capture turning points indicating the end of a process of rising inflation much sooner (leads of over a year) than the start of a process of accelerating inflation (lead of 3 quarters). Both indicators are also fairly well dispersed around the mean, with broadly defined credit being less so than the narrower definition of credit to the private sector.
– Credit to general government exhibits clearly asymmetrical behavior between the peaks and troughs. In fact, at the peaks, it appears as a non-leading indicator. In any case, this behavior is conditioned by the small number of turning points identified in this indicator relative to the reference indicator, which would *a priori* disqualify it as a leading indicator of inflation growth.
– The identification of the turning points in the total financing aggregate is probably affected by the uneven cyclical trend of credit to the private sector *vis-à-vis* credit to general government. The dating of the turning points is characterized by a mean lead of less than 3 quarters in both the peaks and troughs. The dispersion, however, is similar to or greater than that of the mean leads, which is a sign of undesirable variability in a leading indicator.

As these comments suggest, the problem of asymmetry and the differing behavior of the various aggregates hamper categorical assessments of the quality of the monetary and credit aggregates as leading indicators of inflation. Nonetheless, based on the information in the table, it can be stated that, among the monetary aggregates, ALP and M2 exhibit more satisfactory properties as leading indicators of the turning points of inflation growth, the lead being approximately 1 year.

Among the credit aggregates, domestic credit to the private sector, both broadly and narrowly defined, stands out as the most appropriate leading indicator of the turning points of inflation.

Criteria for Classifying the Monetary and Credit Indicators

As mentioned above, this methodology was used as a point of departure for selecting – from among a very broad set of indicators obviously including the monetary and credit aggregates – those that best anticipate changes in the pattern of inflation growth.

The criteria for this classification were based on the stipulation that potential leading indicators of inflation should exhibit minimum variance around the lead points, so as to be able to guarantee satisfactory predictive quality. In this case, the necessary condition for working with a leading indicator (according to the turning point methodology) is that its dispersion be equal to or less than 3 quarters, and, at the same time, less than the mean and median lead of the turning points.[13]

Table 9.5, which summarizes the results of the classification criteria, shows that, by applying a strict criterion that considers the best leading indicators to be those which satisfy the condition of minimum variance separately for the peak turning points and the trough turning points, the only indicators selected will be domestic credit to households and firms and the M2 monetary aggregate.

However, the number of critical points identified in the various indicators should also be taken into account, as well as the percentage of these points that are actually considered leading with respect to the turning points of the reference indicator. In other words, when the indicator signals an immediate relative peak or trough and it is not subsequently confirmed, a problem of *false signals* arises that should be penalized, as in the case of those points which, instead of reflecting a lead, give a *lag signal*. In this way, weights are constructed which will give greater weight to those indicators with less dispersion and the largest number of turning points, provided that they are related to the reference cycle. Said weights are constructed as follows:

$$\sigma_i^* = \frac{1}{\sigma_i}\left[\frac{T}{N}\frac{1}{H/T}\right] = \frac{1}{\sigma_i}\frac{T^2}{NH}$$

Table 9.5 Criteria for classifying monetary indicators in terms of their capacity to lead the reference indicator[1] (CPI)

	Peak leads				Trough leads				Total leads					
	Turning points	Lead points	σ^*	Satisfies criterion	Turning points	Lead points	σ^*	Satisfies criterion	Turning points	Lead points	Mean lead	σ	Satisfies criterion	σ^*
ALP2+	4	3	0.11	NO	4	2	0.02	NO	8	5	1.4	3	NO	0.09
ALP	4	4	0.15	YES	5	4	0.12	NO	9	8	5.3	3.7	NO	0.17
M3	4	3	0.05	NO	5	1	0.00	NO	9	4	2.4	4.4	NO	0.04
M2	5	3	0.08	YES	5	4	0.15	YES	10	7	4	3	YES	0.15
M1	5	2	0.03	NO	5	4	0.06	NO	10	6	2.7	4	NO	0.08
CEEFF+	6	5	0.22	YES	6	4	0.10	YES	12	9	3.7	2.2	YES	0.28
CEEFF	3	3	0.55	YES	3	2	0.03	NO	6	5	4	2.7	YES	0.14
CAAPP	4	1	0.05	NO	5	3	0.04	NO	9	4	2.1	3.9	NO	0.04
FINTOT	7	4	0.09	NO	8	5	0.11	NO	15	9	2.3	2.5	NO	0.20

Note: [1] The reference indicator is the stationary transformation of the consumer price index corrected for deterministic effects.
Source: Banco de España.

where:

N = Number of turning points identified in the reference indicator.

H = Number of turning points identified in each indicator.

T = Number of points at which the indicator "leads" the nearest turning point in the reference indicator.

Under this criterion, the σ^* ratio serves as a means of ranking the various indicators analyzed and reflects, from the highest to the lowest, the distinct quality of each indicator in terms of anticipating the turning points of inflation. As indicated, the credit aggregates (except for credit to general government) generally have higher ratios than the monetary aggregates. Of the latter, ALP has the greatest weight. This again illustrates the difficulty of selecting a monetary indicator as the best predictor of inflation, since M2 fulfils the conditions imposed in terms of minimum variance, whereas ALP exhibits slightly better qualifications, in terms of σ^*, for anticipating the turning points of the reference indicator.

In sum, the two preceding sections assessed the informative capacity of the set of monetary and credit aggregates used by the Banco de España. In respect of the Granger causality criterion, it is seen that most monetary aggregates exhibit adequate predictive behavior. As for the credit aggregates, the Granger test does not reject domestic credit to households and firms as a cause of inflation.

However, this methodology is somewhat inadequate in terms of clearly distinguishing which indicators are best at anticipating inflationary pressures. The methodological approach consisting of assessing the capacity of the indicators to anticipate the turning points of inflation growth would allow for more tightly focused results, underscoring the superior capacity of the credit aggregates as predictors of inflationary movements. The best predictors of inflation among the credit aggregates appear to be the two definitions examined (broader and narrower) of credit to the private sector. Analysis of the monetary aggregates, however, does not yield such conclusive results. ALP and, more particularly, M2 are the aggregates best qualified to lead the turning points of the reference indicator; however, the classification criteria used make it difficult to distinguish between M2 and ALP.

One possible explanation for these results is that the informative content of the monetary aggregates is dominated by components present in the definitions of both ALP and M2. This necessitates a segmented analysis of the informative content of the various components of the monetary aggregates. Along with other relevant aspects, this method of analysis is discussed in the following section, which concerns the construction of weighted monetary aggregates.

WEIGHTED MONETARY AGGREGATES

The results presented in the preceding section illustrate the difficulties of finding a simple monetary aggregate that captures all of the information on the final objectives of monetary policy provided by the behavior of liquidity in an economy. These difficulties may stem from the unrealistic assumption of the perfect substitutability of assets implicit in said aggregates. The monetary aggregates normally used measure liquidity as the simple sum of the balances of the various assets considered liquid. This method of aggregation implies that all of the assets included in the definition are equally liquid (perfect substitutes). However, it seems more reasonable to assume that the various assets are generally imperfect substitutes for one another. Moreover, it is likely that the conditions of substitutability among assets change over time, as a result, for example, of financial innovation processes.

In response to this problem, a strand of literature has emerged aimed at finding other measurements of the money stock that can be used to weight the various assets precisely according to their degree of liquidity,[14] and that also take account of the changes over time in the degree of liquidity. The monetary aggregates so constructed are known as weighted aggregates, as opposed to the traditional, simple-sum aggregates. The crucial element in this literature is the criterion used to select the weights. The standard approach is to use interest rate differentials *vis-à-vis* an alternative asset that affords no liquidity facility. Because they approximate the opportunity cost of holding liquid assets instead of an alternative asset that differs from the former only by virtue of its total lack of liquidity, these differentials are a measurement of the liquidity facilities included.

However, although the theoretical advantages of weighted monetary aggregates constructed in this manner are clear, significant problems arise in practice, two of which should be pointed out. First, it is very difficult to select an asset that can be considered absolutely illiquid, and, second, the interest rate differentials associated with this reference asset will only reflect changes in the degree of liquidity when the other characteristics (risk, maturity, tax advantages, etc.) are identical.[15]

To avoid these problems in constructing weighted aggregates, an alternative method recently proposed by Feldstein and Stock (1994)[16] is used in this section. It is based on the assumption of the existence of a stable relationship between the growth of liquidity in an economy and the growth of nominal expenditure. Consequently, if increases in the balance of a given component of the aggregate are not generally followed by increases in nominal expenditure, it is concluded that increases in the component do not contribute significantly to a more liquid economy, but, rather, reflect decisions concerning the redistribution of wealth; they are therefore assigned a smaller weight or none at all. Specifically, those weights are estimated which, when applied to the various components of a broad aggregate, yield a measurement of liquidity growth that maintains a stable relationship with nominal expenditure and functions as a leading indicator thereof.

If the basic assumption is true and the relative degree of liquidity of the various components varies significantly over the sample period, the resulting weighted aggregate should capture these differences. To the extent that this is so, said weighted aggregate could be a better leading indicator of nominal expenditure than the corresponding simple-sum aggregate, and, ideally, a better approximation of the liquidity of the economy. Therefore, after describing the estimation procedure, a possible interpretation (in terms of liquidity) of the trend of the weighted estimates is presented, and the informative capacity of the aggregate *vis-à-vis* future variations in nominal expenditure and prices is discussed.

Construction of the Weighted Aggregate

The first decision to be made in constructing a monetary aggregate is selecting the set of assets to be considered. The advantage of weighted aggregates is that they facilitate consideration of a wide range of assets, taking into account their varying informative content with respect to liquidity. Based on said content, the estimation procedure itself will reveal in what proportion (variable over time) the assets should be aggregated. Therefore, the group of assets included is the largest of all those taken into account by the Spanish monetary authority during the period in question (1970–95), as related to nominal expenditure, i.e. ALP2.[17] The level of disaggregation to be considered should theoretically be the highest possible, and it should reveal *a posteriori* whether certain assets can be considered together, owing to their high degree of substitutability. Unfortunately, the complexity of the estimation procedure makes this impractical. Therefore, a typical disaggregation was chosen, so that the mutually exclusive subaggregates considered are: M2, M3–M2, and ALP2–M3. The resulting weighted aggregate will be designated KM2.[18]

In specifying the model, account is taken of the statistical properties of the series considered (see Cabrero, Escrivá and Sastre, 1992, and Ayuso and Vega, 1994). Thus, the rates of variation of nominal expenditure and of the monetary aggregates are $I(1)$, and the difference between the two is $I(0)$. On this basis, a leading indicator model in second differences is specified for nominal expenditure, with an error correction mechanism in first differences:

$$\Delta^2 y_t = \alpha_0 + \delta_t + \alpha(L)\Delta^2 y_{t-1} + \gamma(L)\Delta^2 m_{t-1}^p + \phi(\Delta y_{t-1} - \Delta m_{t-1}^p) + \epsilon_t \quad (9.1)$$

$$\epsilon_t \text{ iid } N(0, \sigma_\epsilon^2)$$

$$\Delta m_t^p = \sum_{i=1}^{n} \beta_{i,t+1} \Delta z_{i,t} \tag{9.2}$$

$$\beta_t = \beta_{t-1} + \eta_t, \quad \eta_t \text{ iid } N(0, \sigma_\eta^2 I) \tag{9.3}$$

$$\text{s.a. } \sum_{i=1}^{n} \beta_{i,t} = 1$$

with ϵ_t and η_t independent of one another, and where y_t is the logarithm of nominal GDP, Δm_t^p the rate of change of the weighted monetary aggregate, approximated by the first difference of the logarithm, $\Delta z_{i,t}$ the first difference of the logarithm of the ith excluding subaggregate, α_0 is a constant deterministic term, and $\alpha(L)$ and $\gamma(L)$ are polynomials in the lag operator of the form:

$$\alpha(L) = \sum_{i=1}^{k} \alpha_i L^{i-1} \ y \ \gamma(L) = \sum_{i=1}^{j} \gamma_i L^{i-1}$$

The time varying parameters are the stochastic seasonal component δ_t and the vector of weights β_t. The weights varied over time in accordance with (9.3). Note that the elasticities of the growth of expenditure relative to variations in the growth of the weighted aggregate are considered constant, while the weights with which the latter incorporates the subaggregates included varied over time. The weights are estimated together with the rest of the model's parameters and, as seen in (9.2), are weights on the rates of change and not on the levels of the components.

System (9.1)–(9.3) is estimated via a maximum likelihood procedure based on the Kalman filter.[19] The estimate is made using quarterly data for the sample period 1970QI–1995QIII. Original, non-seasonally adjusted series are used, excluding the national accounting variables (nominal and real GDP and the GDP deflator) which are already constructed directly in seasonally adjusted form. This justifies the inclusion of the stochastic seasonal component δ_t which is estimated directly in the equation, as proposed by Harvey and Scott (1994).[20] The results are summarized in the following equation:[21]

$$\Delta^2 y_t = - \underset{(0,057)}{0.377} \ I7580_t + \underset{(0,102)}{0.285} \ S86_t + \delta_t + \underset{(0,087)}{0.625} \ \Delta^2 y_{t-1} - \underset{(0,088)}{0.258} \ \Delta^2 y_{t-2}$$

$$- \underset{(0,043)}{0.078} \ \Delta^2 m_{t-1}^p - \underset{(0,038)}{0.103} \ \Delta^2 m_{t-2}^p - \underset{(0,041)}{0.172} \ (\Delta y_{t-1} - \Delta m_{t-1}^p) + \epsilon_t$$

$$\sigma_\epsilon(\%) = 0.266; \ \sigma_\eta(\%) = 0.034; \ \sigma_w(\%) = 0.016$$
$$\log L/\text{no. obs.} = 4.310; \ Q(4) = 6.05$$

As can be seen, both the lags of the second difference of the weighted aggregate and the error correction mechanism are significant. As for the dynamic response, the major impact of variations in the weighted aggregate on the rate of change of nominal GDP occurs with a lag of 3 and 4 quarters. This means that 60 per cent of the long-term response (imposed as unitary) occurs in the first year, and 90 per cent in two years. The imposition of unitary long-term elasticity for the growth rates is justified both by the basic theoretical assumption (relationship between liquidity and nominal expenditure) and by the empirical evidence for the various existing monetary aggregates.

The following section analyzes a possible interpretation (in terms of liquidity) of how the estimated weights change over time. This analysis, as well as the prediction exercises that follow it, is considered useful for assessing the results of the procedure.

The Weights

The estimated weights are shown in Figure 9.2a. Their reasonableness can be analyzed by comparing them with the weights implicit in the simple-sum aggregate comprising the same assets, i.e. ALP2 (see Figure 9.2b). Note that the rate of change of a simple-sum aggregate can also be expressed as the weighted sum of the rates of change of its components. In this case, the weights are the shares of each component in the total aggregate, and the varying degree of liquidity of each component is not taken into account. Conversely, in the case of the weighted aggregate, the weights should reflect changes in said share and the degree of liquidity of the component in question. Thus, the extent to which the weights of the weighted aggregate differ from those implicit in ALP2 can be interpreted as a sign of deviation from the assumption of perfect substitutability among assets.

To facilitate the comparison, the estimated weights are divided among those implicit in the simple-sum aggregate (see Figure 9.2c), with the resulting values being interpreted as indicators of relative liquidity. Given that these indicators are inferred from the explanatory power of nominal expenditure, we will refer to them indiscriminately in terms of relative explanatory power or as indicators of relative liquidity. Note that the procedure used allows for capturing the variation both among assets and over time.

As Figure 9.2c illustrates, the results obtained in constructing the weighted aggregate are consistent with the expected ranking in terms of

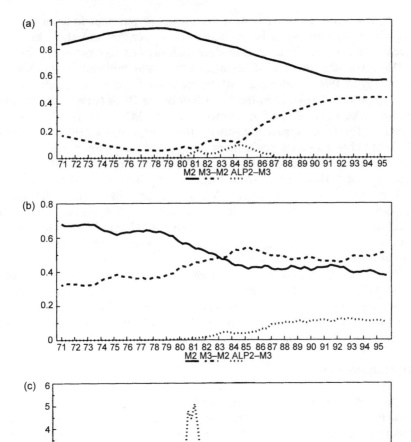

Figure 9.2   Comparison of KM2 and ALP2, 1971–95

a   Weights in the KM2 weighted average.
b   Relative weights implicit in ALP2
c   Relative explanatory power of KM2
Note: 1   The relative explanatory power, for each sub-aggregate, is calculated as the coefficient between its weight in KM2 and its share in ALP2.
Source: Banco de España.

liquidity: excluding the period of intensive financial innovation in the early 1980s, M2 is more liquid than M3–M2, and the latter is in turn more liquid than ALP2–M3. In other words, the means of payment function is more significant among assets in the narrower aggregates and they thus have greater informative content as leading indicators of nominal expenditure.

However, the process of financial innovation initiated in the Spanish economy in 1980 is reflected both in the rising trend of the relative explanatory power of M3–M2 in the latter half of the 1980s (development of the repo market) and in the importance of ALP2–M3 in the first half of that decade. The latter apparently reflects the emergence of new assets, whose liquidity characteristics made them partial substitutes for previously existing liquid assets, with additional attractions in terms of profitability, tax opacity, etc.[22] However, as from 1985, despite the continued steady rise in this component's share of total ALP2 (implicit weight in ALP2), its relative explanatory power *vis-à-vis* the future course of nominal expenditure declined (see Figure 9.2c). As a result, ALP2–M3 vanishes in the last part of the sample as a leading indicator of nominal expenditure, i.e. its weight is nullified (see Figure 9.2a).[23]

In any case, M2 always has a greater relative weight in the weighted aggregate than in ALP2. This seems to suggest that M2 should be given more importance as a leading indicator of nominal GDP than that already implicit in monitoring the trend of ALP2, which is consistent with the results described in the preceding section.

Informative Content

It seems clear from the very process of constructing the weighted aggregate that its power to explain the trend of nominal expenditure should be considerable. In this section, it will be seen to what extent this result is actually obtained, taking the degree of fit provided by the simple-sum aggregates as a reference. In particular, it is interesting to compare the results of KM2 with those of ALP2, which is the simple-sum aggregate that includes the same assets as KM2. Nevertheless, the results for M2 and M3 are also analyzed. Next, evidence is given concerning the extent to which explanatory power *vis-à-vis* the growth of nominal expenditure translates into explanatory power *vis-à-vis* inflation, measured by the GDP deflator.

Figure 9.3 shows the growth rates of nominal GDP, ALP2, and KM2. As can be seen, the growth rates of both aggregates (simple and weighted) evolve, over the long run, in line with the growth in nominal expenditure. However, the weighted aggregate is more variable and adjusts more to transitory variations in nominal GDP. The main differences are recorded in periods of declining GDP. It should be pointed out, moreover, that two relatively prolonged periods are observed in which the growth of nominal expenditure differs from monetary growth, measured by either of the two indicators. Thus, while in 1976 and 1977 the growth of nominal expendi-

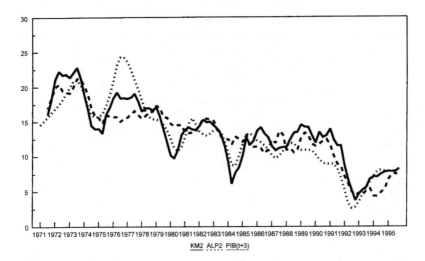

Figure 9.3 Nominal expenditure and monetary aggregates, 1971–95, year-on-year growth rates in percentages

Notes: 1 To facilitate interpretation, nominal GDP was advanced 3 periods, as the effects of the aggregates seem to occur mainly with a lag of 3 quarters.
   2 Owing to the existence of a significant constant in the long-term relationship between the rates change of nominal GDP and ALP2, the latter series was shifted by the size of that constant.
Sources: Instituto Nacional de Estadística and Banco de España.

ture is consistently greater than that of the monetary aggregates, in 1989–92 precisely the opposite occurs. This latter period of divergence may be associated with the process of heavy capital inflows from abroad and the strength of the peseta in the months preceding the inclusion of the peseta in the EMS and up to the 1992 crisis.

However, an examination of Figure 9.3 should be supplemented with a more detailed analysis to aid in assessing the informative content of the weighted aggregate. This analysis is presented below, using the prediction errors (both within-sample and post-sample) for nominal GDP and for the GDP deflator.

The first criterion taken into account is whether the model including the weighted aggregate achieves a high degree of within-sample fit for nominal expenditure. The within-sample fit that models such as (9.1) provide with simple-sum aggregates is taken as a point of reference. Table 6 presents the standard deviations of the residuals of the equations for each aggregate.

This analysis is supplemented with a post-sample prediction exercise. Thus, starting with a sample ending in 1992QIII, the aforementioned equations are estimated both for KM2 and for the simple-sum aggregates.

Table 9.6   Nominal GDP prediction

| Aggregates | Within-sample fit | | | |
	M2	M3	ALP2	KM2
σ_ϵ	0.274	0.284	0.287	0.266
Aggregates	Post-sample fit (with 8 periods)			
	M2	M3	ALP2	KM2
RMSE (1)	0.269	0.224	0.274	0.205
RMSE (2)	0.398	0.379	0.512	0.305
Aggregates	Post-sample fit (with 12 periods)			
	M2	M3	ALP2	KM2
RMSE (1)	0.274	0.222	0.270	0.240
RMSE (2)	0.471	0.363	0.472	0.390
RMSE (3)	0.587	0.383	0.521	0.394
RMSE (4)	0.665	0.443	0.599	0.474
RMSE (5)	0.793	0.530	0.659	0.583
RMSE (6)	0.936	0.625	0.629	0.715

Notes: 1. All data in rates of per cent change.
2. RMSE (n): Root of mean-squared error of prediction at n quarters ahead.
3. For more than 2 periods ahead, predictions of simple-sum aggregates obtained with univariate models are used.
4. As the prediction horizon increases, the number of observations for calculation of the RMSE decreases.
Source: Banco de España.

These estimates were repeated, successively incorporating the information for each additional quarter up to 1995QII and, using the various aggregates, predicting in each case the growth rate of nominal GDP for the next quarter and for various quarters ahead.[24] Note that in the case of KM2, the estimate of the weighted aggregate obtained with the corresponding sub-sample is used at all times, not the aggregate estimated with the complete sample. To complete the process, the predictions obtained in each instance are compared with the observed data and the root of the mean-squared error is calculated as a measurement of post-sample fit (see Table 9.6).

The selection of 1992QIII as the starting point for the post-sample predictions was determined by the above-mentioned irregularity observed in the period 1989–92. This places a constraint on the interpretation of the results, as they relate to a relatively short prediction period (12 quarters). Given that with said period an atypical prediction could significantly affect the overall results, it was deemed useful to present the results of the same exercise for the last 8 quarters of the sample as well.

To begin with, it should be pointed out that according to the results obtained for ALP2 and KM2, it appears that the time trend of the latter and of the weights applied to each component can add useful information when the trend of ALP2 is interpreted in terms of the future course of nominal expenditure. Moreover, the narrowest simple-sum aggregates, M2 and M3, also obtain smaller within-sample and post-sample errors than ALP2, except for the post-sample prediction of the last 12 periods with M2. Nevertheless, even taking these simple-sum aggregates as a reference, the informative content of KM2 with respect to the future course of nominal expenditure seems high. Results are obtained similar to those of the aggregate with the smallest prediction error, or even better in the case of the within-sample fit or the post-sample fit in the last eight quarters of the sample.

To assess the informative content of KM2 with respect to the future course of the GDP deflator, this aggregate is taken as given and is used to specify a leading indicator model such as (9.1) for the deflator. This model predicts changes in the rate of change of the deflator, incorporating an error correction term that takes account of the fact that the growth of real monetary balances is $I(0)$. Again, this is done for KM2 as well as M2, M3, and ALP2. Although the short-term relationship seems weaker than with nominal GDP, all of the aggregates tend to anticipate changes in the inflation rate: M2 and KM2 with a lead of 3 quarters, while M3 and ALP2 also lead by 3, but, more importantly, by 6 quarters.

Note, however, that the KM2 variable is constructed with information on nominal GDP for the entire sample – and, therefore, the deflator – so that estimation of the model with KM2 is subject to endogeneity problems. The results on the within-sample fit should therefore be interpreted with caution, although it is valid to use the model for predictive purposes.[25] This is what occurs in the post-sample prediction exercise, in which, as mentioned previously, as additional quarters are included in the sample, the KM2 aggregate used to estimate the corresponding explanatory equation for the deflator – and to predict it – is not the KM2 aggregate estimated for the entire sample but, rather, the estimate for the corresponding subsample.[26]

Table 9.7 shows the results of the predictions for the GDP deflator with M2, M3, ALP2, and KM2. As can be seen, the results concerning informative content on nominal GDP generally extend to inflation as well, except in the case of the M2 within-sample fit, which is comparatively worse.

CONCLUSIONS

The initial objective of this chapter was to assess the informative content of the monetary and credit aggregates, used by the Banco de España, as leading indicators. As a result of the new strategy formulated in 1995,

Table 9.7   Prediction of the GDP deflator

Aggregates	Within-sample fit M2	M3	ALP2	KM2
σ_ϵ	0.294	0.286	0.285	0.281
Aggregates	Post-sample fit (with 8 periods) M2	M3	ALP2	KM2
RMSE (1)	0.105	0.158	0.183	0.092
RMSE (2)	0.283	0.309	0.387	0.180
Aggregates	Post-sample fit (with 12 periods) M2	M3	ALP2	KM2
RMSE (1)	0.102	0.157	0.178	0.141
RMSE (2)	0.264	0.277	0.322	0.292
RMSE (3)	0.276	0.326	0.397	0.345
RMSE (4)	0.290	0.386	0.476	0.297
RMSE (5)	0.328	0.442	0.503	0.280
RMSE (6)	0.414	0.492	0.554	0.350

Notes: 1. All data in rates of per cent change.
2. RMSE (n): Root of mean-squared error of prediction at n quarters ahead.
3. For more than 2 periods ahead, predictions of simple-sum aggregates obtained with univariate models are used.
4. As the prediction horizon increases, the number of observations for calculation of the RMSE decreases.
Source: Banco de España.

monetary policy decisions are based on the comparison of inflationary prospects at a given point in time with the explicit inflation target established. In assessing said prospects, the monetary nature of the long-term inflationary process leads immediately to the consideration of monetary aggregates and their counterparts in the Banks' balance sheets as possible indicators. However, whereas many studies have been conducted at the Banco de España on the demand functions of the various monetary and credit aggregates, the same wealth of analysis does not exist with respect to the capacity of these aggregates to anticipate changes in the variables that constitute final objectives of monetary policy. An effort has been made in this chapter to provide empirical evidence of that capacity, using various methodological approaches and considering a wide range of aggregates.

Before commenting on the results, a cautionary note is in order. All leading indicator analyses of the type carried out in this chapter are based on the search for predictive power within the sample. However, as Woodford (1994) points out, using a variable related to the monetary policy objective to control that objective tends to obscure the empirical relationship between the two. This fact may, to some extent, skew the results obtained in this chapter regarding the broad aggregates, which were an intermediate monetary policy objective in the sample period.

The first analysis performed in this chapter was a Granger-causality analysis of a trivariate VAR specification (with real income, prices, and various aggregates considered in turn). The results indicate that domestic credit to households and firms as well as both narrow and broad monetary aggregates aid in predicting the future course of prices. Although this is a positive result, it is not possible – although it would be desirable – to select a smaller set of indicators with greater information content than the rest.

The analysis of the capacity of the various aggregates to predict turning points in the cyclical profile of inflation is then introduced as an additional criterion for selecting inflation indicators. Thus, a statistical procedure is used to determine peaks and troughs in the time trend of the rates of change of inflation and of the various aggregates considered. Thus, an analysis is performed of the extent to which – and with what lead – cyclical changes in the aggregates anticipate cyclical changes in inflation.

Mean leads of more than 3 quarters are generally observed, although with significant asymmetries between the various indicators and in the identification of peak and trough turning points for each. In fact, differences are observed in the dispersion with which these points are identified (the leads in the peaks exhibiting less variability than those in the troughs). With all of the caution that the above-mentioned results require, it can be stated that of all the monetary aggregates, the results of ALP and M2 are comparatively superior to the rest and similar to one another. Moreover, of particular note is the positive performance of domestic credit to households and firms (particularly in its broad definition), which is superior to that of any of the monetary aggregates, according to this criterion.

Although this latter focus allows for a bit more selectiveness, the difficulty remains of distinguishing between broad and narrow monetary aggregates. One possible explanation is the existence of components that are common to one or more aggregates, i.e. the informative content of the broad aggregates may be due precisely to the fact that the narrow aggregates are included in their definition. The third exercise performed may shed some light on this subject. The exercise consists of constructing a broad monetary aggregate, with different weights assigned to its components, unlike the simple-sum aggregates that ascribe the same importance to all of the components. According to the methodology proposed by Feldstein and Stock (1994), those weights are estimated which yield a measurement of liquidity growth that maintains a more stable relationship with nominal expenditure and functions as a leading indicator thereof.

The results seem to show that the various components of a broad monetary aggregate have different informative content concerning the future course of nominal expenditure. In particular, the more liquid assets (M2) seem to have a relatively larger informative content. However, it appears that financial innovation in the 1980s partly reduced the difference *vis-à-vis* less liquid assets such as those included in the M3–M2 subaggregate. In contrast, the assets included in ALP2–M3 do not seem to be providing any information at present, although they did so significantly in the first half of the 1980s. In terms of the future course of nominal expenditure and prices (measured by the GDP deflator), the weighted aggregate constructed exhibits a high degree of informative content.

In sum, the behavior over time of the liquidity in an economy is likely to be helpful in anticipating price trends, but the correct measurement of such liquidity in a highly evolved financial environment is complicated. Therefore, it is difficult to select an aggregate that condenses informative content concerning prices. The results of this paper suggest that it is not advisable to consider only the simple-sum aggregate, which weights all of the components equally (broad simple-sum aggregate), to ignore totally the less liquid components (narrow simple-sum aggregate), or to ignore the information provided by the trend of credit to households and firms. On the contrary, the best strategy from the viewpoint of analyzing monetary variables would be to combine all of this information and summarize it as efficiently as possible.

In any case, with due regard for the limitations that any empirical study involves, this chapter provides evidence – apart from the recognized importance of the monetary aggregates in explaining long-term inflation – that the monetary and credit aggregates can contribute, in the short term, to the process of making monetary policy decisions. This is because the behavior of these aggregates tends to anticipate movements in the target variables of monetary policy, although this relationship is far from being sufficiently stable and precise to justify establishing intermediate objectives on monetary and credit variables. According to the evidence presented, these aggregates are necessary – but not entirely sufficient – indicators, which should be supplemented with other variables and models such as those presented in other chapters of this book.

Notes

1   A detailed description of the reform of the monetary aggregates, from both the institutional and empirical perspectives, can be found in separate articles in the Banco de España's November 1991 *Boletín Económico*: '*La reforma de los agregados monetarios*' and '*Criterios empíricos que sustentan la selección de los nuevos agregados monetarios*'.
2   For a detailed description of the techniques used for short-term predictions of the monetary aggregates, see Cabrero and Sánchez (1993).

3   A detailed analysis of this phenomenon can be found in Quirós (1990), Delrieu and Jareño (1993), and, more recently, in Manrique (1996).

4   On this point, see the *Quarterly Report* for the third quarter of 1995 in the Banco de España's October 1995 *Boletín Económico*.

5   These aspects are discussed in greater detail in Chapter 7 of this book.

6   See Sánchez and Vega (1996).

7   See, for example, the pioneering work of Burns and Mitchell (1946), and, more recently, Lahiri and Moore (1991), and Zarnowitz (1992). For Spain, the most relevant references are Rodríguez (1977), Sanz (1984), Fernández (1991), García (1991), and Abad and Quilis (1992).

8   See Garner (1995), Klein (1986), and Roth (1991). For Spain, see, for example, Fernández and Virto (1994).

9   The results presented here are part of a research project which, starting with the identification of the cyclical chronology of a wide range of both real and monetary indicators, attempts to rank these indicators based on their capacity to anticipate the turning points of the indicator of inflation growth. The ultimate objective is to select those indicators which have more informative content, with a view to preparing a composite index for use in anticipating the inflationary profile (see Cabrero and Delrieu, 1996).

10 The original series, corrected for deterministic effects, reasonably approximates the trend performance of prices. To the extent possible, this approximation of the trend avoids the econometric problems stemming from the establishment of quantitative relationships between non-observable components (see, *inter alia*, Maravall, 1994), as well as the problems involved in estimating and revising these components as new information is received.

11 Thus, a differentiation order $\Delta\Delta_{12}$ appears to be the most appropriate both for the CPI series and for the monetary and credit aggregates, inasmuch as the regular component of all these variables is considered $I(2)$ and they evince the existence of non-stationary seasonal behavior.

12 The procedure used is taken from Fernández (1991).

13 The criterion for assuming that the standard deviation is less than 3 quarters is arbitrary, although reasonable insofar as the indicators tend to exhibit mean leads greater than 3 quarters.

14 A basic reference on the problems of defining money and liquidity, as well as the various reasons for demanding money and the implications for the relationship between money stock and nominal expenditure, is Hicks (1967).

15 Ayuso and Vega (1994) estimate some of these weighted aggregates for Spain and comment on these problems in greater detail.

16 A more detailed account of the methodology and the results presented below can be found in Alonso, Martínez, and Pérez, Jurado (1996).

17 This aggregate also includes the special debt issued in early 1992 in exchange for Treasury notes. Ignoring it would entail a break in the series on that date.

18 It has been shown that disaggregating M2 into M2–M1, M1–M0, and M0 does not improve explanatory power with respect to nominal expenditure. However, it is possible that alternative groupings of the assets will yield better results.

19 See Chapter 3 in Harvey (1989). Given a number of initial values for the time-invariate parameters $\theta = \{\alpha_0, \alpha(L), \gamma(L), \phi, \sigma_\epsilon^2, \sigma_\eta^2\}$, the model is rewritten in state-space form to estimate the changing parameters and the likeli-

hood associated with these initial conditions. By means of a numeric optimization procedure, new values of θ are calculated by iterating until reaching a maximum in the likelihood function.

20   The specification of the seasonal component is a trigonometric method that changes stochastically over time (see Harvey, 1989). Note that this involves a treatment of the seasonality of the variables different from that used in the trivariate VAR. This does not necessarily imply inconsistency, however, since the price variables considered are different in each case.

21   Between parentheses, standard deviation of the parameters' estimators. $Q(4)$ is the value of the Ljung–Box test of order 4, and S86 and 17580 are deterministic variables that capture, respectively, a step effect in 1986:I and a double impulse in 1975:I and 1980:I. σ_w is the standard deviation estimated for the seasonal component.

22   In fact, the Banco de España included these assets in its intermediate target variable in 1984. See Sanz (1988) and Ayuso and Escrivá (Chapter 3 in this book).

23   Actually, the weight of ALP2–M3 was negative, although insignificant, as from 1987, which led to imposition of the restriction that this weight be zero as of that date.

24   Predictions several periods ahead in turn require predictions of the growth of the various monetary aggregates, which were obtained with univariate models. Various lags in the publication of data on GDP and the monetary aggregates were taken into account.

25   An alternative would be to estimate the weights of the components of the aggregates, based on the relationship of the latter to the rate of change of the GDP deflator. However, to define the money stock, nominal expenditure should be used instead of prices. In any case, some of the tests performed showed that the weak short-term relationship between monetary growth and inflation (much weaker than the relationship between monetary growth and the growth of GDP) prevents making an adequate distinction between the various explanatory powers of the various sub-aggregates.

26   The variations are small, since the weights estimated with various sub-samples are sufficiently stable.

References

ABAD, A.M. and E.M. QUILIS (1992) 'Elección de una cronología de referencia cíclica para la economía española mediante análisis factorial', Ministry of Economy, *Boletín Trimestral de Coyuntura*, 46, 49–75.

ALONSO, F., J. MARTÍNEZ, and M. PÉREZ-JURADO (1996) 'Weighted monetary aggregates: an empirical approach,' *Working Paper*, 9611, Research Department, Banco de España.

AYUSO, J. and J.L. VEGA (1994) 'Agregados monetarios ponderados: el caso español', *Revista Española de Economia*, 11(1), 161–89.

BOLDIN, M. (1994) 'Dating turning points in the business cycles', *Journal of Business*, 67, 97–131.

BURNS, A. and W.C. MITCHELL (1946) *Measuring business cycles*, New York: National Bureau of Economic Research.

CABRERO, A. and I. SÁNCHEZ (1993) 'Métodos de predicción de los agregados monetarios', *Working Paper*, 9326, Research Department, Banco de España.

CABRERO, A. and J.C. DELRIEU (1996) 'Construction of a composite indicator for predicting inflation in Spain', *Working Paper*, 9619, Research Department, Banco de España.

CABRERO, A., J.L. ESCRIVÁ and T. SASTRE (1992) 'Demand equations of the new monetary aggregates', Banco de España, *Economic Studies*, 52.

CHADKA, B. and E. PRASAD (1994) 'Are prices countercyclical? Evidence from G-7', *Journal of Monetary Economics*, 34, 239–57.

DELRIEU, J.C. and J. JAREÑO (1993) 'Opacidad fiscal, renta y dinero. Una aproximación a la demanda de efectivo en España', *Moneda y Crédito*, 197, 63–90.

FELDSTEIN, M. and J.H. STOCK (1994) 'Measuring money growth when financial markets are changing', NBER, *Working Paper*, 4888.

FERNÁNDEZ, F.J. (1991) 'Indicadores sintéticos de aceleraciones y desaceleraciones en la actividad económica', *Revista Española de Economía*, 8, 125–56.

FERNÁNDEZ, F.J. and J. VIRTO (1994) 'Un indicador adelantado de la inflación en España', Instituto de Economía Pública, Universidad del País Vasco.

GARCÍA, M. (1991) 'Un sistema de indicadores cíclicos para la economía española', Ministry of Economy, *Boletín Trimestral de Coyuntura*, 43, 32–60.

GARNER, A. (1995) 'How useful are leading indicators of inflation?', Federal Reserve Bank of Kansas, *Economic Review*, 80 (2), 5–18.

HARVEY, A.C. (1989) *Forecasting, structural time series models and the Kalman filter*, Cambridge: Cambridge University Press.

HARVEY, A.C. and A. SCOTT (1994) 'Seasonality in dynamic regression models', *Economic Journal*, 104, (427), November, 1324–45.

HICKS, J. (1967) 'The two triads', in J. Hicks, *Critical Essays in Monetary Theory*, Oxford : Clarendon Press.

KLEIN, P.A. (1986) 'Leading indicator of inflation in market economies,' *International Journal of Forecasting*, 2, 403–12.

LAHIRI, K. and G. H. MOORE (1991) *Leading economic indicators: new approach and forecasting records*, Cambridge: Cambridge University Press.

MANRIQUE, M. (1996) 'Determinantes de la demanda de efectivo en España', Banco de España, *Boletín Económico*, March.

MARAVALL, A. (1994) 'Use and misuse of unobserved components in economic forecasting', *Journal of Forecasting*, 13, 157–78.

QUIRÓS, G. (1990) 'La evolución del efectivo en manos del público', *Papeles de economía española*, 43.

RODRÍGUEZ, J. (1977) 'Una aproximación al ciclo de referencia de la economía española: 1965–1975,' Banco de España, Internal Document EC/1977/34, Research Department, mimeo.

ROTH, H.L. (1991) 'Leading indicators of inflation', in K. Lahiri and G.H. Moore (eds), *Leading economic indicator: new approach and forecasting records* Cambridge: Cambridge University Press.

SÁNCHEZ, C. and J.L. VEGA (1996) 'Algunas propiedades de distintos agregados monetarios y crediticios como indicadores adelantados de la inflación', Banco de España, mimeo.

SANZ, R. (1984) 'Análisis cíclico y su aplicación al ciclo industrial español,' *Economía Industrial*, 239, 87–103.

SANZ, B. (1988) 'Los agregados monetarios en España y su calidad como objetivos intermedios', Banco de España, *Boletín Económico*, December, 25–49.

WOODFORD, M. (1994) 'Nonstandard indicators for monetary policy: can their usefulness be judged from forecasting regressions?', in N.G. Mankiw (ed.), 'Monetary Policy', NBER, *Studies in Business Cycles*, 29.

ZARNOWITZ, V. (1992) *Business cycles: theories, history, indicators and forecasting*, Chicago: University of Chicago Press.

ZARNOWITZ, V. and P. BRAUN (1993) 'Twenty-two years of the NBER–ASA quarterly economic outlook surveys: aspects and comparisons of forecasting performance', in J.H. Stock and M.W. Watson (eds), *Business cycles, indicators and forecasting*, NBER, *Studies in Business Cycles*, vol. 28.

10 The Yield Curve as a Monetary Policy Indicator

Juan Ayuso and Soledad Núñez

E52
E43

INTRODUCTION

The monetary control strategy of the Banco de España changed in 1995, when, instead of monitoring an intermediate target, a final direct target in terms of the inflation rate was defined. Within the framework of this new strategy, several indicators have gained a more prominent role, since they provide relevant and timely information on the conditions that affect the development of monetary policy, the extent to which the current course of inflation coincides with the final target, and agents' expectations regarding both the likelihood that this target will be met and the future conduct of monetary policy itself.

Under certain conditions, the term structure – or, which is the same, the relationship between riskless interest rates and their corresponding maturities – provides information on agents' expectations about the future course of interest rates themselves and the rate of inflation. Our objective in this chapter is to analyse the usefulness of the term structure of interest rates, as an indicator for monetary policy in the Spanish case.

In line with this objective, the paper is organised in the following way. We discuss how to estimate the term structure, in that it is composed of interest rates that are not observed. We then analyse both the informative content of the term structure and the conditions in which this content can be used as a relevant indicator for the implementation of monetary policy. We give a series of examples to illustrate the indicator's usefulness, and the final section summarises the main conclusions.

MEASURING THE TERM STRUCTURE OF INTEREST RATES

Definitions

The term structure of interest rates is the relationship, at a moment in time, between interest rates, free of taxes and credit risk, and their maturity. Thus, the term structure is the set of values $i_{t,t+1}, i_{t,t+2}, i_{t,t+3}, \ldots, i_{t,t+M}$; where $i_{t,t+k}$ is the *interest rate*[1] per unit of time that the market applies, at moment t, to evaluate a riskless payment, which is received at moment[2] $t + k$:

$$d_t(k) = e^{-ir_{t,t+k}} \quad \text{or} \quad i_{t,t+k} = -\frac{1}{k}\ln(d_t(k)) \tag{10.1}$$

where $d_t(k)$ is the value of the *discount function* and expresses the value that the market assigns in t to a peseta which is received at moment $t + k$.

From the term structure of spot interest rates, the so-called *implicit forward rates* for different horizons can be obtained. The k-period implicit forward rate at t for h-period horizon $(f_{t+h,t+h+k})$ is the interest rate at which a futures contract involving the purchase (or sale) at $t + h$ of an asset with k periods to maturity will be traded at t. In the absence of arbitrage opportunities, this forward rate would be:

$$f_{t+h,t+h+k} = \frac{1}{k}[(h + k)i_{t,t+h+k} - hi_{t,t+h}] \tag{10.2}$$

Denominating the *instantaneous forward rate* for horizon h $(f_{t,t+h})$ the limit of (10.2) when k tends to 0, and applying a bit of algebra, we obtain:

$$i_{t,t+k} = \frac{1}{k} \int_0^k f_{t,t+\mu}d\mu \tag{10.3}$$

In other words, the k-period spot interest rate is the average of the instantaneous forward rates for horizons from 0 to k.

Starting from (10.2) and (10.3), we find that, by knowing $(i_{t,t+1}, i_{t,t+2}, i_{t,t+3}, \ldots, i_{t,t+M})$, we can know the values of the discount function for different maturities and the forward rates for diverse horizons and maturities. In sum, when calculating the term structure of interest rates, it makes no difference which set of values is used, because each one contains the same information presented in a different form, and, if one of these sets is known, the rest can be easily obtained.

The Term Structure

The spot interest rates that make up the term structure are not observed, because the rates traded on financial markets generally contain credit risk premia, liquidity premia, tax effects, etc. and, moreover, they may not exist for many of the maturities. Therefore, the term structure must be estimated, either to isolate the observed rates from the effects different to maturity or to obtain interest rates for those maturities that are unavailable. For this estimation, the prices of public debt instruments are generally used, since these instruments have certain advantages over other alternatives, given their lack of credit risk and the existence of sufficiently liquid secondary markets for a large set of maturities. Thus, the premia for credit and liquidity risk need not be taken into account.

The term structure estimates must satisfy a series of requirements. First, it must span a large set of maturities – preferably a continuum capable of providing implicit forward rates for diverse horizons. Additionally, it must be capable of reflecting the many forms that the true term structure can take (rising, falling, flat, rising–falling, falling–rising, etc.). Lastly, the estimated term structure must be smooth, especially for the longer maturities.[3]

If the debt instruments were assets involving a single payment (zero-coupon bonds or assets issued at a discount, such as Treasury bills), it would be relatively easy to obtain the term structure, since the percentage price of an asset issued at a discount and with a life of k periods, (P_t), would be:

$$P_t = 100 d_t(k) = 100 e^{-k i_{t,t+k}} \qquad (10.4)$$

However, most debt instruments (medium- and long-term government bonds, in the Spanish case) do not entail only one payment, since they provide a periodic income called coupon. Using the standard assumptions regarding the workings of financial markets, a bond that periodically pays a coupon and which has k periods of life until its maturity is the equivalent of a portfolio comprising k zero-coupon bonds, each with a maturity coinciding with one of the coupon payment dates and principal equal to the coupon (except for the bond with a life of k periods whose principal would be that of the bond itself plus its coupon). The price of this bond will be the same as the sum of the prices of the zero-coupon bonds that it comprises, and, therefore, it is not only a function of $i_{t,t+k}$ but also of $i_{t,t+1}, i_{t,t+2}, \ldots i_{t,t+k-1}$.[4]

In short, if the prices of N debt instruments (Treasury bills and coupon bonds) are observed, then the problem of obtaining the term structure is solved by extracting the $i_{t,t+k}$ from the following system of equations:

$$P_{t,b} + cc_{t,b} = C_b \sum_{i=1}^{i=v} e^{-m_{bi} i_{t,t+m_{bi}}} + 100 e^{-m_{bv} i_{t,t+m_{bv}}}$$

$$= C_b \sum_{i=1}^{i=v} d_t(m_{bi}) + 100 d_t(m_{bv}) \qquad (10.5)$$

$$b = 1,2,3,\ldots, N$$

where:
$b = 1, 2, \ldots, N$ denotes the bond, being $b = 1$ the bond with the shortest maturity and $b = N$ the one with the longest

t = date of observation
$P_{t,b}$ = percentage price excluding accrued interest of bond b at t
$cc_{t,b}$ = accrued interest of bond b at t
C_b = coupon of bond b (in percentage)
m_{bi} = periods in years from t to the payment date of coupon i of bond
        b, in which m_{b1} is periods to the nearest coupon and m_{bv} per-
        iods to the furthest coupon
$i_{r,t+m_{bi}}$ = m_{bi} periods interest rate
$d_t(m_{b,i})$ = value of the discount function for m_{bi} periods

In the system of equations (10.5) there are as many unknowns as there are different payment dates of the N bonds. If the number of unknown factors is the same as the number of equations (N), then the $i_{t,t+m_{bi}}$ and the $d_t(m_{bi})$ can be obtained by simply solving a system of equations.[5]

If the number of unknown factors is less than N, the interest rates for different maturities can be obtained by performing a regression under least squares with the system (10.5) to which an error term is added.[6] In this case, the coefficients to be estimated would be the $d(m_{bi})$, the variable to be regressed would be the price, and the regressors would be the coupons and the principal.

Most of the time, however, there are fewer observations available than unknowns. This is the Spanish case, where some 30 observations and some 60 unknowns are available each day. Drawing on the seminal work of McCulloch (1971, 1975) and in order to reduce the number of parameters to be estimated, the solution proposed in the economic literature is to estimate the discount function by constraining it to a certain functional form characterised by only a few parameters. These methods estimate the discount function for a continuum of maturities, such that, once this function is obtained, the $i_{t,t+k}$ and forward rates are calculated for the required maturities.

The Nelson–Siegel–Svensson Method

Among the methods for estimating the discount function,[7] the one proposed by Nelson and Siegel (1987) and its extension in Svensson (1994) arrive at satisfactory results in that they provide continuous, smooth and, in general, sufficiently flexible term structures, with a globally acceptable goodness of fit (sum of squared price errors, average of the absolute value of the price errors, average of the absolute value of the yield to maturity errors). Several central banks (those of England, Sweden, France and Spain) currently use one or the other for estimating term structures.

The method proposed by Nelson and Siegel assumes that the forward rates converge at a certain level. In other words, forward rates are assumed to be nearly identical as from a given moment in time. Both the level at which forward rates converge and the velocity of convergence are parameters to be estimated. This condition holds if the instantaneous forward rate $(f_{t,t+k})$ is the solution to a second order differential equation, with two equal real roots:

$$f_{t,t+k} = \beta_0 + \beta_1 e^{-k/\tau} + \beta_2 \frac{k}{\tau} e^{-k/\tau} \qquad (10.6)$$

Integrating (10.6) between 0 and k and dividing by k gives the corresponding spot rate, and substituting this for the different maturities in (10.5) gives the equation to be estimated:

$$P_{b,t} + cc_{b,t} = C_b \sum_{i=1}^{v} d(m_{bi}, \beta_0, \beta_1, \beta_2, \tau) + 100 d(m_{bv}, \beta_0, \beta_1, \beta_2, \tau) \qquad (10.9)$$

where $(\beta_0, \beta_1, \beta_2, \tau)$ is the vector of parameters to be estimated.

Parameters $(\beta_0, \beta_1, \beta_2$ and $\tau)$ have the following interpretation: parameter β_0 is the asymptotic value of the *forward* (and spot) rate $(\beta_0 = f_{t,t+\infty} = r_{t,t+\infty})$. The sum of β_0 and β_1 is the instantaneous forward and spot rates $(\beta_0 + \beta_1 = f_{t,t+0} = r_{t,t+0})$. The parameter τ depicts the rate at which the instantaneous forward rate moves towards its asymptomatic level (β_0): given β_1 and β_2 the smaller τ is, the smaller will be the value of m for which the forward rate is nearly identical to β_0. Lastly, the sign of the parameter β_2 determines the existence of a maximum $(\beta_2 > 0)$, a minimum $(\beta_2 < 0)$, or monotocity $(\beta_2 = 0)$ in the structure of forward rates.

The functional form of equation (10.6) allows the term structure to have a minimum or a maximum but not both. This flexibility is usually enough, though some situations may call for a more flexible term structure. To this end, Svensson (1994) proposes adding to (10.6) the term: $\beta_3 (k/\tau_1) e^{-k/\tau_1}$ such that the estimated term structure allows for the existence of a maximum and a minimum, for example, even though two additional parameters must then be calculated. Nonetheless, the methods of Nelson and Siegel and of Svensson give very similar results in most cases, and the curves estimated under the two methods are practically indistinguishable.

In addition to choosing an estimation model (Nelson and Siegel or Svensson), an optimization criterion must be selected. Here, there are two options: to minimise the sum of squared errors in price (observed price minus estimated price), or to minimise the sum of squared errors in yields to maturity (observed yield to maturity minus the estimated yield to maturity).[8] The choice of one criterion over another will depend on the purpose for which the curve is to be used, because the criterion of minimising price errors gives a worse fit, in terms of yields, for the very short maturities, whereas the criterion of minimising yield to maturity errors gives a worse fit in price for the longer maturities.[9] In any event, the estimation under the criterion of minimising yield errors is considerably more complex (especially in a case such as the Spanish one, where the number of observations is relatively small) and the estimated term structure obtained is very similar, for maturities of more than 6 months. Thus, to estimate the daily term structure for the Spanish case in the period 1991–5, we chose the method proposed by Nelson and Siegel, i.e. minimising the sum of the squared errors in price.[10]

TERM STRUCTURE AS AN INDICATOR OF EXPECTATIONS ABOUT INFLATION AND INTEREST RATES

As noted above, the yield curve, the discount factor $d_t(k)$ and forward interest rates are 3 alternative ways of representing the same information set. In this section, we examine the informative content of forward rates, both for the expected course of future monetary policy and for agents' expectations about inflation.

Theoretical Relationship between Forward Rates, Expected Interest Rates and Expectations about Inflation

The theoretical relationship between forward interest rates and expectations regarding the future course of nominal interest rates and the future rate of inflation can be derived from a standard model of intertemporal financial asset valuation.

Thus, suppose that agents choose the composition of their portfolios that maximises the expected utility of the infinite path of future contingent consumption and that their only source of wealth is, precisely, the return on this portfolio. Under these conditions, at each moment t, the agents solve the following problem

$$\max E_t \sum_{i=0}^{\infty} \beta^i U(C_{t+i})$$

subject to the following set of restrictions

$$P_s \left(C_s + \sum_{\tau=1}^{T} W_{s,\tau} \right) = \sum_{\tau=1}^{T} P_{s-\tau} W_{s-\tau,\tau} R_{s-\tau,s}^{\tau}; \quad s \geq t$$

where β is a parameter of term preference; C_s, the real consumption of the representative agent at moment s; $W_{s,\tau}$, the real quantity invested in the period s in a financial asset that matures within τ periods, whose nominal return (including the principal returned) per period is $R_{s,s+\tau}$; and, lastly, P_s is the general level of prices at moment s.

A bit of algebra shows that the first order conditions of the above problem take the form:

$$E_t\left(RMS_{t,t+k}\frac{P_t}{P_{t+k}}R_{t,t+k}^k\right) = 1, \forall t, k \tag{10.10}$$

where $RMS_{t,t\mid k}$ is the marginal rate of substitution between future and current consumption.

Starting from the first order conditions corresponding to zero-coupon bonds at different maturities, the equilibrium relationship between forward interest rates and the expected future nominal interest rates of these bonds can be obtained. Thus, if $rms_{t,t+k}$, $\pi_{t,t+k}$ and $i_{t,t+k}$ represent, respectively, the logarithm of the marginal rate of substitution, the (logarithmic) rate of inflation and the (logarithm of one plus the) nominal interest rate,[11] in the Appendix it is shown that this relationship takes the form:

$$(k-q)f_{t+q,t+k} \equiv ki_{t,t+k} - qi_{t,t+q} = (k-q)E_t(i_{t+q,t+k}) + PP_{t+q,t+k} \tag{10.11}$$

where $f_{t+q,t+k}$ is the forward interest rate – per period – between $t+q$ y $t+k$, implicit in the yield curve prevailing at t, and

$$PP_{t+q,t+k} \equiv \frac{(k-q)^2}{2}V_t(i_{t+q,t+k}) + (k-q)\text{cov}_t(rms_{t,t+k}, i_{t+q,t+k}) \\ - (k-q)\text{cov}_t(\pi_{t,t+k}, i_{t+q,t+k}) \tag{10.12}$$

is the difference between the forward interest rate and the current expectations about the interest rate that will prevail within q periods for a zero-coupon bond whose maturity is $(k-q)$ periods. Therefore, $PP_{t+q,t+k}$ is interpreted as a risk premium, because it measures the difference between the return on a k-maturity risk-free bond and the expected return of an alternative investment strategy between t and $t+k$ that combines a zero-coupon bond maturing at $t+q$ with another bond issued in $t+q$ and redeemed in $t+k$ (and whose return will not be known until $t+q$). Thus, this premium is known as a term premium.[12]

In any event, (10.12) shows how implicit forward interest rates contain information on the nominal interest rates for different maturities that agents expect in the future. To extract this information, however, an estimate of the corresponding term premia must be available.

In addition, to obtain the relationship between forward rates and expectations about inflation, financial assets with returns expressed in real terms must be introduced in the analysis. Thus, if $r_{t,t+k}$ is used to represent the (logarithm of the) real return per period of a k-period zero-coupon bond issued at t and perfectly indexed, in the Appendix it is shown that:

$$ki_{t,t+k} = kr_{t,t+k} + E_t(\pi_{t,t+k}) + PI_{t,t+k} \qquad (10.13)$$

where

$$PI_{t,t+k} \equiv -\frac{1}{2}V_t(\pi_{t,t+k}) + \text{cov}_t(rms_{t,t+k}, \pi_{t,t+k}) \qquad (10.14)$$

measures the difference between the risk-free real rate of return for k-period maturity, and the expected real return for that maturity for an investment in assets whose rate of return is known in nominal terms, but is risky in real terms, since the future rate of inflation is not known. Consequently, this difference can be interpreted as an inflation premium.[13] Note that this inflation premium differentiates (10.13) from the well known Fisher equation.

As to the relationship between forward interest rates and the expected rate of inflation, it is easily shown (see Appendix) that it takes the form:

$$(k-q)f_{t+q,t+k} = E_t(\pi_{t+q,t+k}) + (k-q)E_t(r_{t+q,t+k}) + PP_{t+q,t+k} + E_t(PI_{t+q,t+k})$$
$$(10.15)$$

Therefore, the implicit forward interest rates contain information on inflation expectations. However, obtaining this information requires not only an estimate of the term and the inflation premia but also a knowledge of agents' expectations about future real interest rates.

(10.11) and (10.15) are clearly useful for the monetary authority. For instance, in the Spanish case, there is a monetary policy target set in terms of a year-on-year rate of inflation and the instrumental variable is a very short-term interest. Thus, the choice of the pairs of values (k,q) in (10.11) that maintain a constant and small difference between them (one month, for example) allows us to obtain information on the course of monetary policy expected by agents at different horizons. Likewise, the pairs (k,q) that maintain a constant difference of 12 months between them allow us to estimate, on the basis of (10.15), the year-on-year inflation rate that agents expect in the months or years ahead. All this, however, requires estimating the related risk premia and the expected real interest rates.

Term Premia

There are at least 3 alternative methods in the literature for estimating term premia. The first makes direct use of (10.11), with the additional assumption of rational expectations. If the agents are rational when forming their expectations, the difference between the observed interest rates and the expected interest rates should be, on average, equal to zero. Therefore, the average value of the difference between the forward rates in t and the observed interest rates in $t + q$ provides an estimate of the average historical values of the term premia. This is the approach implicit in the traditional tests of the expectations hypothesis of term structure.[14]

The main weakness of this approach lies in the possibility that the agents may commit forecasting errors which, though tending to cancel out on average, can reach significant values over more or less long periods of time. Furthermore, even though this method provides an estimate of the average premia, it does not inform on the variability of the term premia. Lastly, note that, in the Spanish case, the absence of data on zero-coupon bonds before January 1991 implies that estimates of long-term premia cannot be obtained under this method. However, these drawbacks notwithstanding, this approximation has the advantage of being very simple.

Table 10.1 presents the estimates, provided by this method, of the term premia corresponding to future 1-month interest rates (to obtain an

Table 10.1 (Average) term premia: estimates under the hypothesis of null (average) forecasting error

Within	Term premium corresponding to		1 month forward rate	1 year forward rate
	1 month interest rate	1 year interest rate		
1 month	−0.011	−0.076	10.54	10.98
3 months	−0.408	−0.212	10.84	11.01
1 year	−0.259	−0.490	10.43	10.99
3 years	−2.82	−2.60	11.30	11.84

Notes:
1 Premia estimated from (10.11) by substituting actual rates for expected rates.
2 Annualised premia and rates, measured in percentage points (log approximations).
3 Period analysed: January 1991–December 1995. However, since actual rates are used instead of expected rates, the sample for each premium and each forward rate is reduced by a number of observations equal to the horizon analysed. For example, 3-year premia are calculated from a sample that only covers the period 1991–2.
4 The forward rates are the averages of the rates estimated under the Nelson–Siegel method, for the corresponding periods.

indicator of the expected course of monetary policy) and future 1-year interest rates (to obtain the expected year-on-year inflation). As can be seen, these estimates point towards the existence of quite small term premia in comparison with the level of forward rates (with the exception of those corresponding to the 3-year horizon, for which a very small sample interval is available).

In Backus and Zin (1994), a second method of estimating term premia is given. The set of (10.10) can be viewed as a particular case of a more general condition of absence of arbitrage in financial markets.[15] This more general condition can be expressed as:

$$E_t\left(m_{t,t+k}\,R_{t,t+k}^k\right) = 1, \forall t, k$$

where $m_{t,t+k}$ is an unobservable positive discount factor, which should exist if there are no arbitrage opportunities (see, for example, Huang and Litzenberger, 1988). Backus and Zin (1994) propose a method for estimating term premia starting from different orders for the ARMA process followed by the discount factor.

Their proposal can be briefly summarised in the following steps. First, after characterising the ARMA process for $m_{t,t+k}$, the parameters of this process can be used to characterise not only the current interest rates but also the implicit forward rates and the term premia. Thus, even though the non-observability of the discount factor precludes the direct estimation of its univariate model, once its autoregressive and moving average orders are set, its parameters can be estimated by using as a starting point the relationship between these parameters and the sample moments in the time series of the spot and forward interest rates. Different AR and MA orders give rise to different estimates. Once the model is chosen that best fits the data, the parameters thus estimated can be used to calculate the term premia.

As noted in Restoy (1995), this approach is especially attractive in a case such as the Spanish one, because, unlike the preceding method, it does not require comparing spot interest rates and past forward interest rates, thus reducing the problems associated with the short time span for which zero-coupon bond prices are available. In its current version, however, the method also has several drawbacks. First, it requires that the spot interest rates be stationary series, which, in the Spanish case, runs counter to most of the available evidence. Second, the method is derived in a context of conditional homoscedasticity of the discount factor. As a result, even though the average value of the term premia can be calculated, their degree of variability cannot be estimated.

Restoy (1995) uses this method to estimate term premia for the Spanish case. His results, presented in Table 10.2 together with the average values

Table 10.2   (Average) term premia: Backus–Zin method

Within	Term premium corresponding to		1 month forward rate	1 year forward rate
	1 month interest rate	1 year interest rate		
1 month	0.010	0.009	10.63	10.49
3 months	0.031	0.029	10.89	10.47
1 year	0.119	0.113	10.45	10.48
3 years	0.381	0.301	10.60	10.60
5 years	0.470	0.443	10.56	10.53
10 years	0.698	0.548	10.22	10.20

Notes:
1 Premia taken from Restoy (1995).
2 Annualised premia and rates, measured in percentage points (log approximations).
3 Period analysed: January 1991–July 1995.
4 The forward rates are the averages of the rates estimated under the Nelson–Siegel method for the corresponding periods.

of the 1-month and 1-year forward interest rates, coincide with those in Table 10.1 in that the term premia tend to be small. The signs, however, are different in each case, although it should be borne in mind that the estimates in Table 10.1 include an estimate of the average forecasting error which, as noted, might not necessarily be zero if the period considered is not sufficiently long. In any event, both approaches coincide in pointing towards the scant quantitative importance of the term premia in (10.11).

Lastly, another alternative approach to estimating term premia involves particularising a given utility function in the valuation model described in the above subsection and then directly estimating the conditional variances and covariances which, under (10.12), define these premia. This method also requires estimating the parameters which, given the utility function, characterise the marginal rate of substitution $rms_{t,t+k}$. An example of this approach can be found in the exchange rate risk premium estimates in Ayuso and Restoy (1996).

The main problem of this method of calculating term premia lies in the fact that, to estimate both the conditional variance of the interest rates and their conditional covariances with the marginal rate of substitution and the rate of inflation, an estimate of their conditional mean is needed. But this conditional mean is precisely the type of information that is sought in (10.11), and, therefore, the coherence of both estimates must be guaranteed. Notably, in any event, this approach has a potential advantage over the others in that it would not only allow us to estimate the premia's average values but also to analyse their variability. Unfortunately, there are no estimates of the term premia in the Spanish case obtained under this method.

To summarise, from the estimates in Tables 10.1 and 10.2, it can be concluded that, in the Spanish case, the term premia are negligible when evaluating the informative content in (10.11) and (10.15).

Inflation Premia and Real Interest Rates

Estimating inflation premia and expected real interest rates is greatly complicated by the general lack of financial assets whose yields are expressed in real terms. Indexed bonds are, of course, traded in some countries (in the United Kingdom, for example). But, even in these cases, such markets tend to be relatively illiquid, and the indexing procedure involves delays between the moment of payment and the period for which the price increase is computed. In any event, this type of bond is not traded in Spain, and, as discussed below, this makes it very difficult to break down nominal interest rates into real interest rates, inflation expectations and inflation premia (see (10.13)).

It must be noted, first, that the lack of data on *ex ante* real interest rates – i.e. directly traded at moment t – precludes obtaining an estimate of the average value of the inflation premium on the basis of (10.13), even by imposing the rational-expectations hypothesis. Replacing in this equation the expected inflation rate with the actual inflation rate, it is easy to check that the average value of the difference between nominal interest rates for different maturities and the corresponding *ex post* observed inflation rates provides information on the average value of the sum of the *ex ante* real interest rates and the inflation premia, even though the two components cannot be separated.

In this case, it should be also pointed out that *ex post* real rates cannot be used in place of *ex ante* rates (a common practice in the literature), because, according to (10.13), the inflation risk premium would then be equal to the forecasting error of the future rate of inflation, thus imposing a null average value for this premium. Note, however, that if an unbiased estimate of the *ex ante* real interest rates were available, then an estimate of the average value of the term premia could be derived from (10.13) under the assumption of rational expectations.

As to the possibility of resorting to the other two approaches discussed in the preceding subsection, it should be noted that the Backus–Zin methodology is designed for nominal interest rates and their extension to real rates is difficult, and thus it is not altogether clear that it can be used to estimate inflation premia. Naturally, the inflation risk premia could still be estimated directly from (10.14), but here again the difficulty arises of making the inflation expectations thus obtained compatible with the model for the conditional mean of the inflation rate, necessary for estimating their second order conditional moments.

In Ayuso (1996) the *ex ante* real interest rates are estimated from a valuation model like the one described on p. 34]8. Table 10.3 shows the basic statistics thus obtained for the 1-, 3-, 5- and 10-year real interest rates. As can be seen, the *ex ante* real interest rates estimated are quite stable, and they form a practically flat real yield curve, near the 4.5 per cent level.

Table 10.4 shows the average inflation premia at one year obtained from (10.13), assuming rational expectations and using the *ex ante* real interest rates estimated in Ayuso (1996). Compared with the results in Tables 10.1 and 10.2, the average premia estimated are somewhat higher (0.72 percentage points), although, on average, they still account for a small percentage (less than 7 per cent) of nominal interest rates. Even though this method does not allow for a direct estimation of the variability of inflation premia (recall that they include the expectations error whose average is null but whose variance can be considerable), a 2-sub a period analysis offers quite similar results, possibly indicating the scant variability of term premia.

The available results on the relative weight of the inflation premia in nominal interest rates can be compared with the corresponding evidence

Table 10.3   Basic statistics of *ex ante* real interest rates obtained in Ayuso (1996)

		Minimum	Maximum	Average	Standard deviation
	At 1 year	3.92	5.67	4.88	0.28
$\beta = 0.996$	At 3 years	4.42	5.21	4.85	0.13
$\gamma = 0.22$	At 5 years	4.57	5.06	4.84	0.08
	At 10 years	4.70	4.94	4.83	0.04

Notes:
1 Rates measured in annual percentage points (log approximations).
2 Data are monthly and cover the period 1985:2–1994:12.
3 γ is the estimated coefficient of agents' relative risk aversion.

Table 10.4   (Average) inflation premia: from the estimates in Table 10.3 and the hypothesis of null average (inflation) forecasting error in (10.13)

Period	1-year inflation premium	1-year nominal interest rate
1988:1–1991:6	0.71	12.08
1991:7–1994:12	0.74	10.02
1988:1–1994:12	0.72	11.05

Note
1 Average values, in annual percentage points (log approximations).

available for the case of the United Kingdom, where an indexed bond market exists. Levin and Copeland (1993) analyse the relative weight of real interest rates and the inflation premium in 6-month nominal interest rates over the period 1982–91. According to their estimates, the average real rate was 3.04 per cent and the average inflation premium was −0.16%, whereas the average nominal rate was 9.28 per cent. In addition, both the variability of the real rate and that of the inflation premium were notably lower, and, as a result, the principal source of change in the nominal rate were the changes in the inflation expectations. Meanwhile, Barr and Pesaran (1995) conclude that, throughout the period 1983–93, the predominant factor in the changes in long-term bond prices were revisions in expectations about future inflation rates. Likewise, Mishkin (1992) analyses the Fisher effect in the United States, and concludes that the expectations in the medium and long run (but not in the short term) about future real interest rates are quite stable over time.

Briefly stated, the relative stability of *ex ante* real interest rates, coupled with the (scant) evidence on the volume and variability of inflation premia, counsel a strategy of exploiting the informative content of forward rates in a slightly different way from that suggested in (10.15). If, in addition to low term premia, the inflation risk premia are low, or at least not very variable (as appears to be the case in Spain), and real medium- and long-term interest rates are relatively stable, then differences can be taken in (10.15) and *changes* in the forward rates can be exploited to obtain information on *changes* in inflation expectations:

$$(k - q)(f_{t+q,t+k} - f_{t+1+q,t+1+k}) \simeq E_t(\pi_{t+q,t+k}) - E_{t+1}(\pi_{t+1+q,t+1+k}) \quad (10.16)$$

The next section offers several examples of how the informative content of (10.11) and (10.16) can be exploited.

EXAMPLES

This section presents several examples of how the informative content of the yield curve (concretely, the yield curves of one month and one year forward rates) is exploited to analyse the impact of several economic policy measures on agents' expectations. Also included is an example of the use of the curve to examine the average trends in expectations over a longer period of time. In line with the results in the preceding section, this analysis considers that both real interest rates and term and inflation premia remain relatively stable over time, such that movements in the one month forward rate curve can be associated with changes in expectations about the Banco de España's intervention rate, while changes in the one year forward rate curve reflect changes in expectations about future rates of inflation.

We should bear in mind, however, that movements in the forward rate curves can be produced by factors other than monetary policy measures. Moreover, in some cases such measures can be anticipated to some extent thus moving the forward rate curve before the monetary policy measure is effectively implemented. Even with this caveats in mind, the following examples illustrate the potential usefulness of the yield curve as an expectation indicator.

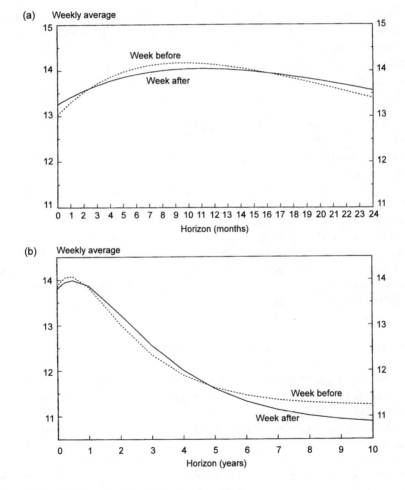

Figure 10.1   PTA devaluation, 17 September 1992

a   1-month forward rates
b   1-year forward rates

The Peseta's Devaluation on 17 September 1992

In the days following the devaluation, the level of the one month forward rate curve declined very slightly for very short horizons (to two months), but moved upwards horizons of up to 18 months (see Figure 10.1a). This pattern could indicate expectations of an easing in the pressures on the peseta in the weeks following the devaluation and the perception that the devaluation was not enough to provide a permanent solution to the weakening in the peseta's position, which would require raising interest rates in the future.

Meanwhile, the 1-year forward rate curve (see Figure 10.1b) shifted slightly upwards for horizons of up to 1 year, suggesting a small increase in inflationary tensions in the months following the devaluation. There was also an upward shift for more distant horizons, reflecting greater uncertainty about the ability of economic policy to maintain sufficiently strict policies in the long run, with the resulting negative impact on inflation.

The Widening of the ERM bands on 2 August 1993

In the days after the widening of the ERM bands, there was a significant downward movement in one month forward rate curve for all relevant horizons (see Figure 10.2a). This could indicate that the markets interpreted the measure to mean that the easing in the pressures on the peseta would allow a reduction in the intervention rate.

The downward shift in the 1-year forward rate curve was also considerable except for horizons longer than 6 years (see Figure 10.2b). Thus, the widening of the bands also heightened the confidence in the effectiveness of monetary policy for achieving lower inflation rates in the medium term. However, there are no signs that this greater confidence actually hold with respect to longer horizons.

The Rise in the Intervention rate on 2 June 1995

As a result of the increase in the Banco de España's intervention rate, the 1-month forward rate curve moved upwards for very short horizons (see Figure 10.3a), which could indicate that the market did not entirely anticipate the increase. For horizons of two or more months, however, there was a downward shift, possibly suggesting that the rise was expected to have a favourable impact on the inflation target after a few months, thus allowing for lower intervention rates than were expected before the measure was taken.

The favourable impact of the increase in the intervention rate on inflation expectations is clearly reflected in the 1-year forward rate curve (see

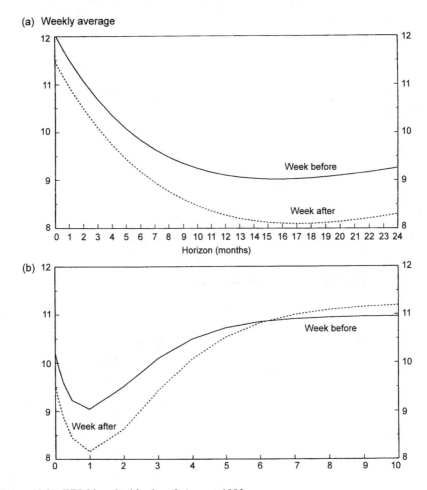

Figure 10.2 ERM band widening, 2 August 1993

a   1-month forward rates
b   1-year forward rates

Figure 10.3b), which moved downwards, especially for medium terms. Nonetheless, the insignificant movement in the more distant horizons suggests that the rise did not improve the expectations regarding the convergence of the Spanish economy.

General Trends in the Curve of Forward Rates during 1995

At the close of 1995, both the 1-month and the 1-year forward rate curve for horizons longer than 2 months reflected considerably lower levels than

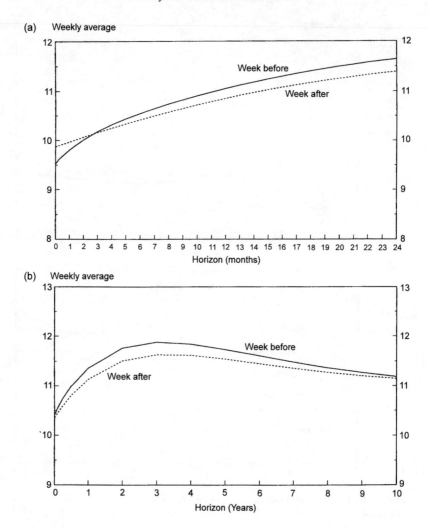

Figure 10.3 Increase in Banco de España intervention rates, 2 June 1995

a 1-month forward rates
b 1-year forward rates

those observed at the beginning of the year (see Figure 10.4). The behaviour of the forward rate structure during 1995 is summarised in the following points.

The first quarter of the year was marked by a foreign exchange crisis that had a pronounced impact on the peseta, leading to its devaluation on 6 March. In addition, inflationary pressures surfaced that led the Banco de

(a) Monthly average of estimated rates

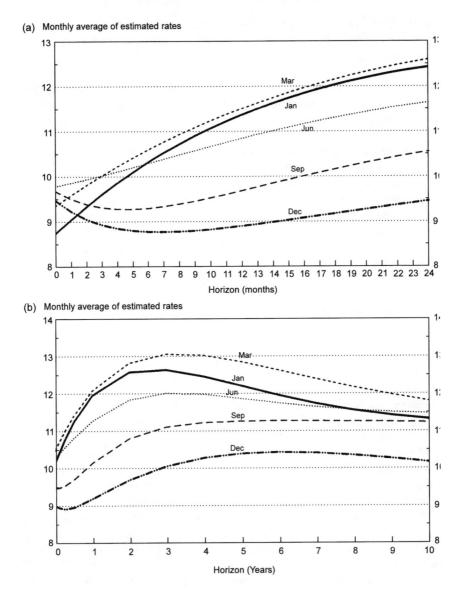

Figure 10.4 1995 evolution
a 1-month forward rates
b 1-year forward rates

España to increase its intervention rate on two occasions (4 January and 6 March). Throughout this period, forward curves moved upwards. Whereas the increase in 1-month forward rates was possibly linked to the rises in the Banco de España's intervention rate, the increase in the 1-year forward rates most likely reflected fears of greater difficulties in meeting the medium-term inflation targets.

During the second quarter, international foreign exchange and debt markets returned to a more stable situation, and forward rate curves slid substantially. However, domestic economic factors, in particular inflationary strains, gained increasing importance and were reflected in upward swings in the curve of 1-month forward rates.

As from the beginning of the third quarter, the favourable international setting (gradual easing in intervention interest rates, lower inflation rates, and coordinated intervention by central banks), together with equally favourable factors in the domestic economy (lower inflationary tensions and a certain containment in the budget deficit), led to a steady improvement in expectations about future inflation rates even – in the final months of the year – for longer horizons, which were accompanied by expectations of lower intervention rates.

SUMMARY AND CONCLUSIONS

The term structure of interest rates contains information on the market's expectations about future inflation rates and also about future interest rates themselves. As a result, this structure is one of the indicators that the monetary authority can use to analyse the conditions surrounding the development of policy measures, to decide whether their implementation is on the right path for achieving the targets set, and to assess agents' perception of its policy stance.

However, since the interest rates that make up the term structure are not observed, this chapter's first task was to estimate the term structure, using a method that draws on the prices of financial assets traded on the market to obtain interest rate structures that span a broad set of maturities and whose form is sufficiently flexible. For this estimation, the prices of public debt instruments were taken as a starting point, because they involve no credit risk and secondary markets usually exist for a broad set of maturities.

Among the methods used to estimate the term structure, those of Nelson–Siegel and Svensson achieve satisfactory results. Many European central banks, including the Banco de España, use one of these two methods in their daily estimates of the term structure. Both methods assume that forward rates converge at a certain level and both the level of convergence and its velocity are parameters estimated in the model.

After estimating the term structure, the information which it contains on expectations of future interest rates and inflation cannot be immediately extracted. To use the term structure as an indicator for monetary policy, term and inflation risk premia must be estimated, and agents' expectations about future real interest rates must also be known. In this work, we also present a series of findings that give an idea of the size of the premia and the variability of real interest rates.

First, the average term premia, estimated as the difference between current nominal rates and past forward rates, as well as the available term premia estimated under the methodology proposed by Backus and Zin, were found to be relatively low. Second, available estimates of *ex ante* real medium-and long-term interest rates point towards considerably stable real rates over the period analysed, around an average level of 4.5 per cent. Lastly, by using these real rates estimates and imposing the rational expectations hypothesis, we can obtain the inflation risk premia, estimated as the difference between the nominal and real rates plus the observed rate of inflation. Here, too, the premia obtained are low – albeit somewhat higher than in the case of term premia – and vary little from one subperiod to another.

In conclusion, the evidence now available does not allow us to distinguish exactly what portion of the forward rates corresponds to expectations about future inflation rates or future levels of interest rates. However, the findings do indicate the relative stability of *ex ante* real interest rates, as well as low and not very variable term and inflation premia. Thus, as shown in several examples, the forward rate curve can be a useful indicator for monetary policy, because its movements between two moments in time that are not too distant can be associated with changes in agents' expectations about the course of the variables in question, namely, inflation and interest rates. This means, for example, that we can analyse the behaviour of agents' expectations over a given period and how their expectations are affected by relevant events such as devaluations and changes in the intervention rate.

Appendix

As noted in the text, the first order conditions of the maximisation problem solved by agents take the form:

$$E_t\left(RMS_{t,t+k}\frac{P_t}{P_{t+k}}R_{t,t+k}^k\right) = 1, \forall t, k \qquad (10A.1)$$

where

$$RMS_{t,t+k} = \frac{\beta^k U'(C_{t+k})}{U'(C_t)}$$

If the 3 factors that appear in the conditional expectation in (10A.1) follow log normal distributions, it is possible to linearise the first order conditions to:

$$E_t(rms_{t,t+k}) + \frac{1}{2}V_t(rms_{t,t+k}) - E_t(\pi_{t,t+k}) + \frac{1}{2}V_t(\pi_{t,t+k}) + kE_t(i_{t,t+k})$$

$$+ \frac{k^2}{2}V_t(i_{t,t+k}) - \text{cov}_t(rms_{t,t+k}, \pi_{t,t+k}) + k\text{cov}_t(rms_{t,t+k}, i_{t,t+k})$$

$$- k\text{cov}_t(\pi_{t,t+k}, i_{t,t+k}) = 0$$

where

$$rms_{t,t+k} = \log(RMS_{t,t+k}), \pi_{t,t+k} = \log(P_{t+k}/P_t), \quad \text{and} \quad i_{t,t+k} = \log(R_{t,t+k})$$

Among the assets included in the above first order conditions, we can now select zero-coupon bonds for different maturities, whose returns are known in t. For these assets, the above equations can be re-written as:

$$E_t(rms_{t,t+k}) + \frac{1}{2}V_t(rms_{t,t+k}) - E_t(\pi_{t,t+k}) + \frac{1}{2}V_t(\pi_{t,t+k}) + ki_{t,t+k}$$

$$- \text{cov}_t(rms_{t,t+k}, \pi_{t,t+k}) = 0 \qquad (10A.2)$$

Analogously, we can consider an investment strategy that consists of acquiring a zero-coupon bond with maturity $q(q < k)$ and later re-investing the profit obtained in zero-coupon bonds with maturity $k - q$. It is easy to check that, in this case, the relevant first order condition is the following:

$$E_t(rms_{t,t+k}) + \frac{1}{2}V_t(rms_{t,t+k}) - E_t(\pi_{t,t+k}) + \frac{1}{2}V_t(\pi_{t,t+k}) + qi_{t,t+k}$$

$$+ (k-q)E_t(i_{t+q,t+k}) + \frac{(k-q)^2}{2}V_t(i_{t+q,t+k}) - \text{cov}_t(rms_{t,t+k}, \pi_{t,t+k})$$

$$+ (k-q)\text{cov}_t(rms_{t,t+k}, i_{t+q,t+k}) - (k-q)\text{cov}_t(\pi_{t,t+k}, i_{t+q,t+k}) = 0$$

$$(10A.3)$$

Subtracting (10A.3) from (10A.2), we arrive at equations (10.11) and (10.12) given in the text.

In addition, if $RR_{t,t+k}$ is used to represent the real rate of return per period of a zero-coupon bond issued at t, with a maturity term equal to k, it follows that, if this return is known in t, the corresponding first order condition takes the form

$$E_t(rms_{t,t+k}) + \frac{1}{2}V_t(rms_{t,t+k}) = -kr_{t,t+k} \qquad (10A.4)$$

where

$$r_{t,t+k} = \log(RR_{t,t+k})$$

Subtracting (10A.4) from (10A.2), we arrive at (10.13) and (10.14) given in the text. Particularising the first of these (10.13) for investments between $t+q$ and $t+k$ and taking conditional expectations in t on both sides of the equality, it is verified that

$$(k-q)E_t(i_{t+q,t+k}) = (k-q)E_t(r_{t+q,t+k}) + E_t(\pi_{t+q,t+k}) + E_t(PI_{t+q,t+k})$$

$$(10A.5)$$

Finally, substituting in (10A.5) the expectation about the future nominal interest rate in accordance with (10.12) in the text, we arrive at (10.15).

Notes

1 To simplify the algebra, interest rates are expressed here as percentages in annualised rates with continuous capitalisation.
2 The interest rate $i_{t,t+k}$ coincides with the rate of return of a k-period investment that consists of a purchase in t of an asset which matures in $t+k$ and which has no intermediate income flow between t and $t+k$.
3 This condition is necessary, because it is implausible that the true term structure will, for instance, take a wavy form. In other words, it would be difficult

to explain in economic terms, for example, that the 10-year interest rate (risk-free with respect to credit, tax, etc.) is much lower than the 11-year rate, or the latter much higher than the 12-year rate, in turn lower than the 13-year rate, etc.

4   Conventionally, the price of a bond price is expressed in terms of its yield to maturity. This yield is defined as the rate that, used to discount each of the payments of the bond, makes the present value of the future payment stream equal to the current market price of the bond. However, the yield to maturity of a coupon bond with m_v periods to maturity is not, in general, equal to $i_{t,t+mv}$, but rather a function of the coupon and of $i_{t,t+m}, i_{t,t+m_2}, \cdots i_{t,t+m_v}$, where $t + m_1, t + m_2, \cdots, t + m_v$ are the coupon payment dates. For this reason, yields to maturity are not useful for estimating the term structure (see, for example, Garbade, 1982).

5   This is the technique used to obtain the zero-coupon curve from interest rate swaps data.

6   The error term is justified by the fact that the observed prices are the mean between the bid and ask prices.

7   For a comparison of the different methods, see Núñez (1995).

8   The sum of the squared yield errors is minimised in the following way: given the functional form imposed, the price is estimated and the corresponding yield is calculated, and this is then compared with the observed one, where the criterion is to minimise the square of this error.

9   This is due to the fact that the relationship between yield error and price error is determined by:

$$(yield - yield_{obs}) = \frac{-(\hat{P} - P_{obs})}{\text{DURATION}} \frac{(1 + yield_{obs})}{P_{obs}}$$

10   As from January 1995 the series of term structures of interest rates estimated under Svensson's method is also available, using an intermediate criterion between the minimisation of the sum of the squared errors in price and that of the sum of the squared errors in yields, i.e. minimising the sum of the squared errors in price weighted by the inverse of the duration.

11   All between t and $t + k$.

12   From a formal standpoint, this premium includes both a risk premium in the strict sense (terms in covariances) and an additional component (the term in variance, produced by log-linearisation) that appears as a result of Jensen's inequality.

13   As in the case of term premia, this premium includes the term that measures Jensen's inequality.

14   See Shiller (1990). In Alcobendas (1995) a test is run for the Spanish case.

15   Note that (10.10) is an equilibrium condition and, therefore, a sufficient but not necessary condition of absence of arbitrage opportunities.

References

ALCOBENDAS, M.A. (1995) 'La teoría sobre las expectatives de tipos de interés para España. Evaluación de la prima de riesgo', CEMFI, mimeo.

AYUSO, J. (1996) 'Un análisis empírico de los tipos de interés reales *ex ante* en España', Investigations Economicas, xx(3).

AYUSO, J. and F. RESTOY (1996) 'Interest rate parity and foreign exchange risk premia in the ERM', *Journal of International Money and Finance*, June.

BACKUS, D. and S. ZIN (1994) 'Reverse engineering the yield curve', New York University Salomon Center, *Working Paper Series*, S–94–5.

BARR, D.G. and B. PESARAN (1995) 'An assessment of the relative importance of real interest rates, inflation and term premia in determining the prices of real and nominal UK bonds', Bank of England, *Working Paper Series*, 32.

GARBADE, K. (1982) *Securities markets*, New York: McGraw-Hill.

HUANG, C.F. and R. LITZENBERGER (1988) *Foundations for Financial Economics*, Amsterdam: North-Holland.

LEVIN, E.R. and L.S. COPELAND (1993) 'Reading the message from the UK indexed bond market: real interest rates, expected inflation and the risk premium', *The Manchester School*, 61, Supplement.

MCCULLOCH, J.H. (1971) 'Measuring the term structure of interest rates', *Journal of Business*, 44, January, 19–31.

MCCULLOCH, J.H. (1975) 'The tax-adjusted yield curve', *Journal of Finance*, 30, June, 811–30.

MISHKIN, F.S. (1992) 'Is the Fisher effect for real?', *Journal of Monetary Economics*, 30.

NELSON, C.R. and A.F. SIEGEL (1987) 'Parsimonious modeling of yield curves for US Treasury Bills', *Journal of Business*, 60 (4), 473–89.

NÚÑEZ, S. (1995) 'Estimación de la estructura temporal de los tipos de interés en España: elección entre métodos alternativos', Banco de España, *Documento de Trabajo*, 9522.

RESTOY, F. (1995) 'Determinantes de la curva de rendimientos: hipótesis expectacional y primas de riesgo', Banco de España, *Documento de Trabajo*, 9530.

SHILLER R. and J.H. MCCULLOCH (1990) 'The Term structure of Interest Rates' in B.M. Friedman and Hahn F.H. (editors) *Handbook of Monetary Economics*, 1, ch. 13, Amsterdam, North-Holland.

SVENSSON, L.E.O. (1994) 'Estimating and interpreting forward interest rates: Sweden 1992–1994', CEPR, *Discussion Paper*, 1051.

11 A BVAR Forecasting Model for the Spanish Economy

Luis Julián Álvarez, Fernando C. Ballabriga and Javier Jareño

INTRODUCTION

Prediction is often a high-risk exercise. It certainly is in the social sciences, for 3 reasons at least: (1) the relationship between the determinants of the phenomena to be predicted tend to be complex and, as a result, only partially known; (2) these determinants tend to be numerous; and (3) perhaps most importantly, the changes in most of these factors are driven largely by random components.

Naturally, economics is not impervious to these factors. However, any economic decision-making process requires weighing, to a greater or lesser extent, the trend of given future variables, so that even with all the attendant risks, economic predictions are perceived as necessary and are thus called for. In particular, forecasts concerning the main macroeconomic variables are of vital interest to any policy-maker responsible for macroeconomic stabilization as they can indicate how the economy will behave if economic policies remain unchanged and can thus serve as a warning that alternative policies should be implemented.

Whether explicitly or implicitly, economic forecasts are always based on a model. Predictions based on econometric models often have a more transparent, explicit basis than predictions made by experts, owing to the element of subjectivity usually present in the latter.

It is important that the assumptions on which projections are based be made explicit from a statistical standpoint, to facilitate the probabilistic characterization of future economic developments, something that is often not properly appreciated. As mentioned above, economic forecasts are inherently difficult, and this difficulty is visibly reflected in the high degree of uncertainty usually surrounding predictions. The logical approach in this situation is to attempt a meaningful characterization of this uncertainty. However, although it can be paradoxical, it is more common to encounter discussions about the decimal differences of various mean projections than about the probability that an economic variable will follow a given future path. Econometric models that incorporate a statistical specification of all their variables in fact make possible an assessment of the uncertainty of projections. This is a basic advantage over alternative procedures, and, in particular, over projections based on subjective perceptions.

For the Spanish economy, most macroeconomic forecasts made with a higher frequency than a year are based either on univariate time series models or on expert predictions,[1] producing a void in terms of forecasts based on econometric models that capture the interrelationships between economic variables and provide both objective measurements of the uncertainty surrounding forecasts as well as reliable quantifications of the probability of occurrence of given events. This void can be filled by building multivariate econometric models.

Following the change in monetary policy strategy brought about by the approval of the Law of Autonomy of the Banco de España and the consequent definition of future inflation[2] objectives, the analysis and prediction of prices have become even more important from the standpoint of the central bank. Consequently, the need for meaningful inflation forecasts has increased sharply, and so has the motivation for developing tools to make them. Because the work is as difficult as it is essential, the range of instruments developed to accomplish it must necessarily be wide. This being so, the multivariate econometric model discussed in this chapter supplements the existing methods of predicting inflation.

This chapter presents a small macroeconometric model for the Spanish economy. The model provides forecasts of the most relevant economic variables and can serve as an aid in making economic policy decisions. Following this introduction, we describe the basic aspects – both theoretical and practical – of the Bayesian Vector Autoregression (BVAR) methodology, which is the methodology chosen for the construction of the model. We describes the variables included in the forecasting model and the reasons for their selection. We then deal with the practical application of the methodology and highlight how it differs from customary uses of the BVAR methodology,[3] and present evidence of the forecasting performance of the model, with special emphasis on predicting inflation and using uncertainty intervals for forecast growth rates. A few final comments, complete the chapter.

BRIEF DESCRIPTION OF THE BVAR METHODOLOGY

VAR Models as a General Frame of Reference

According to Todd (1984), it is useful to think of the construction of an econometric model as a process which, in accordance with certain criteria, combines the historical information contained in the sample data with the prior statistical and economic information provided by the econometrician. The various modeling techniques can then be compared in terms of the type of prior information used and the weight assigned to it.

Of course, every modeling technique requires a minimum of prior information if it is to be usable, i.e. at least the information needed to select a group of relevant variables for purposes of the analysis and to establish an algebraic relationship among them. In fact, the selection of a vector Y of n components under the assumption that each of these components depends linearly on its own past values, the past values of the remaining components, and a vector Z with d deterministic variables (for example, an intercept or seasonal dummy variables), yields a model that in recent years has become a part of the empirical economist's tool kit:

$$Y(t) = B_1 Y(t-1) + B_2 Y(t-2) + \ldots + B_m Y(t-m) + DZ(t) + \epsilon(t) \quad (11.1)$$

where t is a temporal index, B_i represents matrices of order $n \times n$, D is $n \times d$, and ϵ is a vector of random disturbances of order n. Since (11.1) relates a vector of variables to its own past values, it is given the name Vector Autoregression (VAR). Moreover, because it includes only a minimum set of prior restrictions, it is often called the Unrestricted Vector Autoregression (UVAR) model.

As a theoretical framework, the UVAR model is quite general. Granger and Newbold (1986) assert that if the number of lags is not restricted and the matrices of coefficients are time-dependent, any random process can be expressed as a UVAR model. This general aspect of the model makes it an attractive point of departure for econometric modeling and a frame of reference indicative of the type of restrictions actually incorporated into alternative models, since representations of type (11.1) encompass any econometric simultaneous equations or time-series model.

Philosophy of the BVAR Methodology

While a source of theoretical appeal, the generality of the UVAR representation, because it is based on a generous parameterization of the model, also contains the seed of its chief practical deficiency. In fact, the number of coefficients to be estimated in a model such as (11.1) is $n(nm + d)$, which number increases quadratically with the size of the vector Y and multiplicatively with the number of lags included in each of its components. Thus, for example, a model with five endogenous variables, four lags per variable, and an intercept in each equation, would require the estimation of a total of 105 coefficients.

This is a serious problem in the adverse context in which empirical economic research is conducted, characterized as it is by the existence of sample information that tends to be both scarce and highly contaminated by random variability. What this actually means is that the econometrician cannot estimate UVAR models consisting of more than a relatively small number of variables without running the risk of overfitting, i.e. without running the risk that his estimates will be excessively influenced by accidental sample variability (*noise*), in contrast to systematic relationships (*signal*). The phenomenon of overfitting is very likely to occur when 3 elements converge in empirical analysis: a large number of parameters to be estimated, relatively scarce sample information, and a method of estimation designed to explain (fit) the sample data as fully as possible (e.g. least squares methods). These 3 elements definitely converge in UVAR models when the objectives of the analysis require the inclusion of a fairly large number of variables, as is usually the case, for example, when the variables that shape an economy's macroeconomic environment are to be modeled. Consequently, UVAR models are generally not recommended for forecasting.

The BVAR methodology was originally developed by Litterman (1980) and Doan, Litterman and Sims (1984) to propose a solution to the problem of overfitting UVAR models other than that which relies strictly on economic theory as a source of exclusion restrictions, as is the case of structural simultaneous equation models. In other words, an attempt was made to find a way of avoiding the influence in the estimates of accidental sample variability without having to choose whether to include or exclude lags from the different variables. In most cases, this dilemma prevents a realistic expression of the prior information normally available to the analyst, since there is generally no absolute certainty that the value of a coefficient is zero nor complete ignorance as to the value of the coefficients included in the model.

Stating the problem thus, the adoption of a Bayesian approach seems to be the natural solution. In other words, an information source expressed as a probability distribution for the coefficients of the model can be used, which – without putting all the weight on a single value and without being absolutely non-informative – represents a reasonable range of uncertainty and may therefore be modified by sample information if the two information sources differ substantially. If prior information is not excessively slack (minimally informative), only the systematic sample variability (*signal*) will be able to modify it, but not the accidental variability (*noise*), thereby reducing the risk of overfitting.

This concept is put into practice by combining (11.1) with a prior probability distribution for its coefficients. This combination results in what is known as a Bayesian vector autoregression (BVAR).

Specification of a BVAR Model

Undoubtedly, the distinguishing and most important feature of the process of specifying a BVAR model is the selection of the prior information. In principle, this information can come from many sources and take very different forms. The information described in this section originated in the empirical analysis of macroeconomic data and became known as the 'Minnesota prior' because of the professional relationship of its proponents with the Federal Reserve Bank of Minneapolis. The prior information used in more recent applications of the methodology tends to be more elaborate but has the same objective and retains many of the basic characteristics of the Minnesota prior information.

As indicated on p. 371, it is used to reduce the risk of overfitting, and this is the first aspect that should be stressed: the information is purely instrumental, and, as such, is not expected to be necessarily correct in average terms, but rather to contain a realistic range of possible data-generating mechanisms, the most appropriate of which can be selected to explain the variability of sample data.

The second notable aspect of the prior information used in the specification of a BVAR model is its empirical/statistical origin and the resultant lack of economic content. Specifically, the information incorporates 3 empirical regularities derived from the statistical analysis of time series:

1   The hypothesis that the best prediction of the future value of a series is its current value (the so-called random walk representation) is a good approximation of the behavior of many economic series
2   Lagged values that are closer together in time usually have more informative content concerning the current value of a given variable than lagged values that are farther apart in time
3   A variable's own lagged values usually have more informative content *vis-à-vis* its current value than the lagged values of other variables.

The most direct method of formalizing these regularities is to define independent normal distributions in accordance with statements 1–3 for each of the coefficients of (11.1). Attempting an individualized specification of each of the distributions, however, brings us back to the problem of overfitting, which is precisely what we wish to avoid. The best way, then, of rendering the concept operational is to establish functional dependency between all of the distributions and a small set of parameters (known as 'hyperparameters' in the methodological jargon) which can be used to control their basic dimensions in line with regularities 1–3.

Figure 11.1 shows, in terms of probability density functions, the type of prior distribution being described for the coefficients of a representative

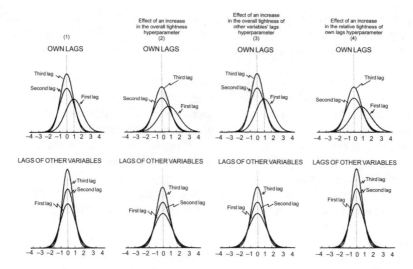

Figure 11.1   Prior distribution of the coefficients

equation of the system (11.1), where, for the sake of simplicity, it will be assumed that there are 3 lags. Column (1) shows how empirical regularities 1–3 are taken into account:

- 1 is represented by specifying the distribution of the coefficient of the first own lag with unit mean and the rest of the distributions with zero mean
- 2 is represented by reducing the variance of the distribution of the coefficients as the lag distance increases; thus, the more distant the lag, the more certain it is that its coefficient is zero
- the incorporation of 3 can be verified by comparing the upper part of the first column with the lower part and noting that the coefficients of the own lag have greater variance than the coefficients of other variables, showing that there is greater certainty as to the zero value of the latter.

These representations provide an idea of the nature of the small set of control parameters (or hyperparameters). Thus, one parameter will control the value of the distribution mean of the coefficient of the first own lag, another will control the variance of the own lag distributions, and a third will control the variance of the distributions of the lags of other variables. To avoid specifying parameters that control the variance for each lag, consideration is usually given to a functional form that inversely relates variance to the number of the lag, thereby introducing a fourth parameter to control the speed of variance reduction as lags increase.

Another frequently specified parameter controls the degree of overall uncertainty (*overall tightness*) of all the coefficients. It is also a determinant of the weight that sample information receives when the model is estimated.

Returning to Figure 11.1, column (2) shows the effect of an increase in this last parameter, which, as can be seen, causes a general rise in the variance of all the distributions. This implies reducing the weight of prior information relative to the weight of sample information. Column (3) shows the effect of an increase in the parameter that controls the uncertainty of the lags of other variables, which causes the variance of the distributions of the coefficients of these lags to increase without affecting own lags. This suggests greater interrelationship among variables. The opposite happens when the parameter that controls the variance of own lags (column (4)) is increased.

Perhaps the complete lack of economic content in the prior information of BVAR analysis may seem surprising. Recalling its instrumental nature can help in understanding it. In other words, while it is true that having an instrumental nature and incorporating economic content is not incompatible, it is no less so that the instrumental nature is purer if it is not mixed with possibly controversial economic assumptions. It is in this connection that it seems more appropriate to opt for economic neutrality *a priori*, so that a single specification can be accepted by economists with very different views of the true structure of the economy.

The specification of a BVAR model is completed when prior information is combined with sample information, which is done using Bayes' rule to obtain the posterior distribution of the coefficients of the model. The mean and the variance of this posterior distribution provide, respectively, the point estimators and the variances of the various coefficients of 11.1.

Advantages and Disadvantages of the BVAR Methodology

The main concepts described so far in this section can be properly summarized by saying that the attraction of the BVAR methodology is the flexibility and objectivity it brings to the process of specifying an econometric model. This is perhaps the main asset of the methodology.

The flexibility referred to means the flexibility to incorporate various types and forms of information into the specification process, to make possible a realistic and systematic expression of the uncertainty surrounding the working interrelationships in the economy under analysis. Intuition suggests that a flexible and systematic method of imposing restrictions can lead to greater accuracy in extracting the empirical regularities underlying sample variability. This being so, the estimators obtained will have to be more accurate (although they may be biased) than those derived using least squares methods. The result is that the final model will theoretically be of a better quality in terms of forecasting, and this will have been achieved through an objective process, i.e. a process based on the use of explicit statistical mechanisms that are perfectly reproducible and capable of probabilistically characterizing the future course of the modeled variables.

Regarding the reference in the preceding paragraph to the term 'forecasting', it should be briefly explained that it is being used in a broad sense, i.e. it refers both to what in the methodological jargon is known as unconditional forecasting and to conditional forecasting. The latter is conditional upon the set of sample data and a given restriction on the future course of the variables in the model. Unconditional forecasting, on the other hand, is conditional only upon the set of sample data and is, undoubtedly, the one most widely used in applications of the methodology, including the application described in this article.

The reason for this clarification is, in any case, twofold: (1) to emphasize the multivariate function of the BVAR methodology and its crucial importance in extracting stable interrelationships, and (2) to highlight the fact that one of the aims of the methodology is to overcome being a 'black box' by attempting to extract stable interrelationships that may be capable of a certain economic interpretation and thus may be useful, for example, in projecting the impact of given economic policy actions. Its purpose, therefore, is to be a substitute for or a complement to structural multivariate methods.

The question immediately arises, then, of how a plausible economic interpretation is to be obtained from a model that has been described thus far as lacking in economic content. The answer is that extracting an economic interpretation from the analysis requires that the BVAR model be supplemented with an additional set of economic restrictions. This is the identification stage of the model, which, in the BVAR methodology in particular and in the VAR methodology in general, follows the specification stage and is characterized by the use of the smallest and least controversial set of restrictions possible.[4]

Because the process of identifying the model is the final stage, a clear distinction can be made between the restrictions used in specifying the probabilistic mechanism of the model from those intended to give it economic content. On the other hand, the fact that the identification is based on a minimum number of restrictions renders the mechanism of economic interrelationships much less clear than it would be in an empirical model derived from a set of explicit theoretical assumptions. This lack of interpretative transparency is probably the most obvious disadvantage of the VAR methodology (UVAR or BVAR), but it is accepted because of the possibility of conforming the model more closely to the stable regularities of sample data.

Forecasting Performance of BVAR Models Compared to Other Procedures

Flexibility, objectivity, and the consequent possibility of a more accurate model constitute the logical framework highlighted in the preceding section as the main advantage of the BVAR methodology. That is certainly the theoretical logic, and one way of verifying whether this logic has a practical application is to examine the predictive record of BVAR models compared to other models.

Most of the literature on the comparative evaluation of unconditional forecasts of BVAR models in macroeconomic contexts take the 1980s as a reference period.[5] Their main conclusions are the following:

1 BVAR models are, on the whole, competitive with large-scale structural models and with univariate time series models, such as ARIMA models for example
2 BVAR models tend to be superior to large-scale structural models and univariate models in medium-and long-term predictive horizons
3 Their informative content usually differs from that of structural models; consequently, their predictions may be substantially different
4 BVAR models are clearly superior to UVAR models.

This set of conclusions, although pertaining to a specific sample period, shows that BVAR models are comparably accurate predictive instruments with certain additional advantages that other econometric models lack. This is especially reassuring since, as mentioned in the preceding section, VAR models – and BVAR models in particular – tend to be the only ones designed to associate objective probabilities with future economic events and a good predictive record is a good guarantee that such probabilities are reliable.

In summary, this section has described BVAR models as an alternative to simultaneous-equation models for making practical use of the general theoretical frame of reference provided by unrestricted VAR (UVAR) models, whose generous parameterization leads to overfitting when attempting to model more than a relatively small number of variables. BVAR models result from combining UVAR models with an *a priori* distribution for their coefficients. This distribution is empirical in origin and strictly instrumental in nature, as it does not attempt to give the model economic content, but rather to make its specification more flexible and more objective, which aspects ensure good predictive properties and are perhaps the main advantage of the BVAR methodology. These considerations suggest that the BVAR methodology may be useful in constructing a forecasting model. The following sections present the details and results of a specific application of this methodology to the Spanish economy.

SELECTION OF THE PRINCIPAL VARIABLES OF THE SPANISH ECONOMY

In most cases, the first decision to be made in building general econometric models is the selection of variables. In fact, the constraint imposed by data availability restricts the size of the model, so that despite the fact that the set of potentially relevant economic variables is large, a selection must be made. In Spain, this problem is complicated by the short time span of official statistics. The quarterly National Accounts time series start in 1970, whereas most monetary series begin in 1974. Models including both types of variables should therefore be used only for the analysis of sample periods beginning in 1974.

In short, the problem is one of obtaining as general a picture of the Spanish economy as possible, as the number of variables used in such a characterization cannot be very large, given the available sample period. With these premises, the first question should not be which are the most relevant variables in the Spanish economy, but in which sectors can this economy be structured? Once this sectorization has been accomplished, the next step is to determine which minimum set of variables characterizes each sector. The aim of this approach is to ensure that the set of variables chosen is both restricted and capable of characterizing the economy as a whole. The last step in this process consists of selecting the available statistical series that best approximate the selected variables. In keeping with this approach, the method of economic sectorization used in this study is based on the distinction between the external, monetary-financial, public and private (non-monetary) sectors, thus providing a complete, structured description of the Spanish economy. The variables and series selected for each sector are explained below. Table 11.1 shows the variables grouped by sector, the series used, and their sources.

External Sector

This sector represents the behavior of economic agents operating in the international environment, which is becoming increasingly important for the Spanish economy. In fact, the opening up of the Spanish economy to external markets (markedly so in the last decade) has led to a sharp increase in the relationships between the international and the domestic variables.

It therefore seems relevant to include in this model some variable(s) explicitly reflecting the external environment in which the Spanish economy has evolved. Given that one of the primary links between economies is the trade balance, it seems appropriate to base the selection on its determinants. Buisán and Gordo (1993) identify two determinants of Spanish exports and imports: competitiveness and world trade, respectively. In the

Table 11.1 Selection of variables

Sector	Variable (abbreviation)	Series	Source
EXTERNAL	WORLD ACTIVITY (GDP*)	GDP at constant prices of the OECD countries, base 1990. Seasonally adjusted series	OECD
	EXCHANGE RATE (E)	Nominal effective exchange rate vis-à-vis industrial countries. Index 1990 = 100, average of monthly data.	Banco de España
PUBLIC	PUBLIC DEFICIT (D)	Net government financing (revenue less expenditure), cumulative total of monthly data Series converted with non-centred moving averages of four terms, expressed as a percentage of nominal GDP	Banco de España
MONETARY	INTEREST RATE (I)	1-month interest rate in the interbank market, average of monthly data	Banco de España
	MONEY STOCK (M)	Liquid assets held by the public, average of monthly data, million pesetas.	Banco de España
PRIVATE	PRICES (CPI)	Consumer Price Index, index 1992 = 100, average of monthly data.	Instituto Nacional de Estadística; Matea and Regil (1993)
	WAGES (W)	Compensation per wage earner in national accounting terms, thousand pesetas.	Banco de España
	LEVEL OF ACTIVITY (GDP)	GDP at constant prices, base 1986, billion pesetas	Instituto Nacional de Estadística
	EMPLOYMENT (L)	Employed population according to the Labor Force Survey, thousand individuals	Instituto Nacional de Estadística; García Perea and Gómez (1994)

model, the exchange rate and the level of world activity will be used to approximate these concepts.

Generally speaking, the selection of the exchange rate has a dual purpose: (1) as a variable that conditions monetary policy, and (2) as the transmitter of external effects on the economy's purchasing power. Thus, the exchange rate will be indicative of the competitiveness of the national economy. To incorporate the exchange rate as a determinant of monetary policy, a good approximation of this variable for recent years would be the peseta/ D-Mark exchange rate series. However, if a perspective based on competitiveness is adopted, as is the case in this study, a more appropriate series is the nominal effective exchange rate (E) *vis-à-vis* industrial countries.

The key issue in selecting the series that approximates world activity is its geographical coverage. The existing empirical results for the Spanish economy (see Buisán and Gordo, 1994) suggest that the OECD environment is the most appropriate; consequently, the series selected was real gross domestic product at market prices for the OECD countries (GDP^*).

Monetary Sector

This sector represents the action of the monetary authority and the financial institutions. Two variables are considered: the interest rate and the money stock.

The interest rate is not only the preferred instrument for implementing monetary policy; it is also a determinant of the consumption, savings, and investment decisions of economic agents. Although numerous interest rates may be employed – both real and nominal, short- and long-term – a single interest rate is used for simplicity. It therefore seems appropriate that the selection of this interest rate be determined by the dual role of representing the effectiveness of monetary policy and its influence on the spending decisions of economic agents. The available evidence suggests that interbank market interest rates can adequately fulfil this dual role. Accordingly, the series selected is the '1-month interbank market interest rate' (I).

Consideration of the money stock variable is prompted by the fact that despite the loss of stability and predictability of the demand for money equations estimated in recent years, the money stock has been the intermediate objective of monetary policy until 1994 and is currently used as a preferred indicator in monetary programming. Consequently, the series selected to approximate the money stock is 'liquid assets held by the public' (M).

Public Sector

The purpose of this sector is to capture public sector economic activity. The complexity and diversity of public sector activity can be summed up by focusing on the budgetary aspect, which can in turn be characterized by the public deficit. Despite the limitations involved in reducing this sector to a single variable, this decision has the advantage of helping to keep the size of the model within manageable limits.

The series selected was Net Government Financing (D), for the following reasons: (1) because it accurately represents the net financial position of the government, as it records payments, collections, and financial operations on a daily basis, regardless of how the government keeps track of its operations; (2) because it is a deficit concept in a broad sense, which not only includes current expenditure and revenue, but also reflects the government's financial position; and (3) because it represents a compromise between fiscal shocks through the components of aggregate demand and through their effects on monetary variables.

Since much of the variability of this series is administrative in origin, it should not have economic effects.[6] The series was therefore smoothed using moving averages. In addition, the series is used in terms of nominal GDP, which is how it is usually presented.

Private Sector (Non-monetary)

The purpose of this sector is to represent the decisions of domestic agents with regard to production, investment, labor, and consumption. Price, wage, employment, and output levels were selected as variables characterizing the actions of domestic agents.

The inclusion of the price variable is justified for at least two reasons: (1) it is an important reference variable in the decision-making of economic agents, and (2) it directly reflects the national economy's inflationary situation, control of which is one of the monetary authority's highest priorities. The series chosen to represent prices was the consumer price index (*CPI*), as it is the series to which private economic agents usually refer.

The wage variable indicates the labor market situation and, no less importantly, the existence of nominal pressures on the economy that affect inflation. The series chosen to approximate this variable was compensation per wage earner (W). This variable is preferable to those derived from the official Wage Survey as it includes all wage costs relevant to production decisions.

Lastly, employment and output were the variables selected to reflect the level of real activity in the economy. The specific series chosen were the employed population (L) and gross domestic product (*GDP*).

A FORECASTING MODEL FOR THE SPANISH ECONOMY

Description of the Structure of the Model[7]

As mentioned above, the specification of prior information is not limited to the use of the Minnesota prior, although it can be viewed as a point of departure for more specific prior information, which will depend on the data used and the problem under study. Thus, in an effort to accommodate the existing characteristics, the prior information used in the model specified for the Spanish economy has the following characteristics:[8]

1   Unlike the Minnesota prior, in which the prior mean of the coefficient of the first own lag takes the value of one for all variables, two groups of variables with different means,[9] τ_0 and τ_1, are distinguished in the model. Deterministic variables have a zero prior mean.

2   As usual, it is assumed that the matrix of prior variances and covariances is diagonal; therefore, the coefficients of the model are independent.

3   All of the prior variances of the system depend on a global hyperparameter τ_2, which determines the relative weight of prior information. Thus, a zero value means that sample information is not taken into account, while an infinite value means that prior information is ignored.

4   The prior variance of own lags depends on hyperparameter τ_4, while the variance of the lags of the remaining variables depends on hyperparameters τ_3 and τ_4. The effect of these hyperparameters is the following: hyperparameter τ_3 controls the significance of the lags of the other variables. A small value means that there is little interaction between variables, while a large value means that the interactions are stronger. Hyperparameter τ_4 indicates to what extent lags closer together in time will have more informative content than lags more distant in time. Thus, if the value of this parameter is large, the distant coefficients are, *a priori*, less important, while their importance will be greater if the value is small.

5   The prior variance of the intercept term depends on hyperparameter τ_5. A large τ_5 value means that there is scarcely any prior information about the possible value of the constant, and a zero value means that the intercept is not included in the model.

6   Since the model includes variables that exhibit seasonal behavior (i.e. the consumer price index, liquid assets held by the public, and employment), seasonal dummies are included in the equations. Their prior variance depends on hyperparameter τ_6. A large τ_6 value indicates a high degree of uncertainty about the possible value of the coefficients associated with these seasonal variables, while a zero value means that they are not included.

7   In this study, it is assumed that coefficients vary over time. Specifically, each coefficient follows a random walk, the variance of which is given by hyperparameter τ_7. Obviously, if τ_7 is zero, the model does not vary over time.

8   The prior information under consideration implicitly assumes that all of the variables are endogenous. However, in small economies such as

that of Spain, is it more appropriate to consider world activity as exogenous, i.e. that it is not affected by domestic variables. To attain this objective, additional hyperparameters are introduced. The first of these, τ_8, captures the relative uncertainty of domestic variables in the equation for world activity. Exogeneity is obtained if τ_8 is zero. Hyperparameter τ_9, on the other hand, can be used to control the relative uncertainty of world activity in the rest of the system.

9   Although the VAR methodology tends to ignore the prior existence of exogenous variables, it is assumed in this model that the interest rate follows an AR(1) process exogenous to the rest of the system variables.[10]

10   The GDP and employment equations contain two broken trends as deterministic variables, with a break point at 1985:I. It should be noted that the use of deterministic trends in other cases (especially at the end of the sample period) usually creates serious problems when it comes to forecasting, as the resulting predictions are fairly inflexible in terms of taking into account new information. However, this is not necessarily true of models (such as the one under consideration) which time-varying coefficients as this variation allows for adapting the forecasts in light of the new information.

Estimation of Reduced Forms

Most of the series referred to in this analysis can be characterized as nonstationary processes. To take account of this fact, one possibility would be to estimate the model in differences. However, this method of proceeding would involve disregarding information on the presumable long-term relationships among these series. The unrestricted estimation of VAR models in levels gives consistent estimators that are asymptotically equivalent to those obtained using maximum likelihood.[11] On the other hand, the consistency of the estimators is unaffected by the introduction of prior information.[12] Consequently, the model was estimated without differencing the series.

In the model, the logarithmic transformation of all the series is considered, except for the interest rate and the public deficit, which are used in levels. The sample period used begins in 1974: I and ends in of 1993: II. The number of lags is 4.[13]

Efficiency gains occur in BVAR models if the system is jointly estimated instead of equation by equation, as is usually the case in the literature.[14] However, in this model, there were two reasons for preferring an equation by equation estimation procedure: (1) the high computational costs involved in a model of this size,[15] and (2) the preliminary results of joint estimation did not reveal any major differences relative to equation by equation estimation.

Reduced form estimation[16] requires specifying an objective function in terms of the set of parameters τ. Although it is common practice to maximize[17] the likelihood of the system, an alternative criterion, given that this is a forecasting model, is minimization of the mean square forecasting error.[18] The forecasting horizon selected was 1 year.[19]

The vector of hyperparameters (τ) that optimizes the criterion adopted[20] and coincides with the optimal vectors of the 2- and 3-year mean square errors is shown in Table 11.2.

The Forecasting Performance of the Model

Once the quarterly macroeconometric model has been specified and estimated, it must be evaluated in terms of its forecasting performance. An

Table 11.2 Hyperparameters associated with the reduced form

Hyperparameters	Estimated values
τ_0	0.921
τ_1	0.632
τ_2	0.58×10^{-2}
τ_3	0.0476
τ_4	1.688
τ_5	9×10^6
τ_6	81×10^9
τ_7	0.103×10^{-5}
τ_8	0.00
τ_9	1.00

Notes:
1. τ_0 Prior mean of the first lag of the dependent variable for the first group of variables $\{GDP^*, M, W, CPI, GDP, L\}$.
2. τ_1 Prior mean of the first lag of the dependent variable for the second group of variables $\{E, I, D\}$.
3. τ_2 Overall tightness.
4. τ_3 Relative tightness of other variables' lags.
5. τ_4 Relative tightness of own lags.
6. τ_5 Relative tightness of the constant term.
7. τ_6 Relative tightness of seasonal dummies.
8. τ_7 Variation of the coefficients over time.
9. τ_8 Relative tightness of the domestic variables in the world activity equation.
10. τ_9 Relative tightness of world activity in the rest of the system.
11. The set of seasonal variables consists of $\{M, CPI, L\}$. The set of non-seasonal variables consists of $\{GDP^*, E, I, D, W, GDP\}$.
Source: Authors' calculations.

initial evaluation can be based on the criterion used to estimate the model, i.e. the use of the 1-year mean square error as an optimizing criterion makes it a certainty that, within sample, this model is the one with the minimum forecasting error within this horizon.

Moreover, there are at least 3 other aspects of interest:[21] (1) how the model performs with horizons other than one year; (2) how well the model forecasts inflation, as the above-mentioned statistic is global. If it is especially important to obtain accurate forecasts for inflation, which is the case for the monetary authority, this global statistic is not necessarily relevant and it becomes necessary to perform a more detailed analysis of inflation forecasts; and, (3) the significance of the interrelationships between the different variables in the model. The estimate of the hyper-parameter that controls the uncertainty associated with other variables (see Table 11.2) is low which, together with the low value of the estimate for the hyperparameter associated with overall uncertainty, suggests that there is little interaction in the model, and, therefore, that this model is not very different from a model consisting of nine equations, in which each variable depends exclusively on its past values, which is what would happen if the hyperparameter that controls the uncertainty of other variables were zero.

To answer these questions, two alternative models[22] were considered. The results of these models will be compared with those obtained with the BVAR model. The first model considered was obtained by setting to zero the relative weight of the prior information, i.e. an unrestricted VAR (UVAR) model. In the second model, the prior information used in the BVAR model is restricted in order to block any interaction among variables, so that a set of equations is obtained in which each variable is determined exclusively by its own lags (referred to as a BAR model in the following, as it contains Bayesian prior information and an AR specification). Both models provide interesting benchmarks as, on the one hand, they allow for an assessment of the advantages of using a Bayesian approximation as opposed to an unrestricted estimate (when the BVAR model is compared with the UVAR model), and, on the other, they facilitate weighing the benefits of adopting a multivariate as opposed to a univariate model (when the BVAR model is compared with the BAR model).

As shown in Table 11.3, an initial approach to comparing these models can be based on their goodness of fit, approximated by the mean square forecasting error (MSFE). This table reveals the superiority of the BVAR model over the other models in all of the statistics used, showing that the BVAR model generally possesses better predictive qualities than the BAR and UVAR models, not only for one year, but for more extended periods as well.

Table 11.3 Overall fit of the models

	Models		
	BVAR	BAR	UVAR
Probability	4248.00	4006.00	685.00
1-year MSFE[1]	62.55	75.62	119.51
2-year MSFE	227.65	278.37	550.24
3-year MSFE	516.65	628.83	1599.66

Notes:
1. MSFE: mean square forecast error.
2. The larger the probability value, the better the fit of the model.
3. The larger the MSFE value, the worse the predictive performance of the model.
Source: Authors' calculations.

Although these statistics are global in nature and consequently make no distinction between variables, the main reason for using this model – as explained throughout this chapter – is to obtain accurate predictions of inflation, as well as those associated with the other private sector variables. Each variable must therefore be analyzed separately. One way of performing this analysis is to observe the mean absolute forecasting error of the different variables and models.

The results (see Table 11.4) leave no room for doubt. The BVAR model, analyzing each variable individually and for different forecasting horizons, represents, with few exceptions, a marked improvement over the other models. The improvements are especially remarkable in the case of the price variable, where the significant differences in the more distant horizons stand out. As for the other private sector variables, the BVAR model again proves superior in respect of wages, GDP, and employment, although at less distance from the BAR model for the last two variables.

Given the relevance of inflation analysis for the purposes of this book, and despite the global nature of the model, a closer examination of the characteristics of inflation forecasts generated by the BVAR model is necessary. Thus, from the standpoint of analyzing the economic environment, both the profile of the forecasts as well as their change (as new information is included) are key elements in defining the behavior of inflation. Accordingly (see Figures 11.2 and 11.3), forecasts were made for 1993–1995, using 1993: III as the initial forecasting origin and rolling this forecasting origin to the following quarters.[23]

One of the most striking details revealed by comparing the BVAR and UVAR models (see Figure 11.2) is the extreme instability of the UVAR-model, which leads to significant variations in the forecasts, with inflation

Table 11.4   Mean absolute error of forecast, 1990–4

	PRICES			GDP			EMPLOYMENT			WAGES		
	BVAR	BAR	UVAR	BVAR	BAR	UVAR	BVAR	BAR	UVAR	BVAR	BAR	UVAR
1 quarter	0.26	0.50	1.27	0.18	0.19	0.31	0.57	0.67	0.61	0.45	0.61	0.87
1 year	0.45	1.67	4.46	1.54	1.54	3.82	2.80	2.89	2.38	1.16	2.63	2.47
2 years	0.97	3.87	6.14	4.12	4.21	14.67	7.00	7.14	10.51	1.96	6.85	7.77
3 years	1.09	6.66	20.16	7.76	8.16	27.38	14.80	15.04	18.04	1.66	12.25	26.44

	Money stock			Exchange rate			Interest rate			Public Deficit		
	BVAR	BAR	UVAR	BVAR	BAR	UVAR	BVAR	BAR	UVAR	BVAR	BAR	UVAR
1 quarter	0.55	0.87	0.96	1.81	2.18	2.82	0.81	0.81	3.20	0.54	0.56	0.72
1 year	1.59	2.65	3.09	5.26	6.63	6.67	2.28	2.28	4.41	1.07	1.12	1.39
2 years	4.13	4.74	8.16	9.60	11.67	16.89	2.79	2.79	11.51	2.15	1.95	4.20
3 years	7.41	7.29	14.61	12.93	15.26	43.00	3.75	3.75	32.97	3.52	2.71	7.22

Notes:
1. Values in per cent of series level.
2. The shaded boxes correspond to the model with least absolute error.
Source: Authors' calculations

forecasts running as high as 12 percent. This instability is caused by the fact that the model overfits and, therefore, extrapolates as a signal non-systematic relationships among variables. In contrast, the BVAR model is distinguished both by the stability of predictions as new information is included and by the closeness of its forecasts to actual values, including those for extended forecasting horizons. The comparison of the BVAR and BAR models (see Figure 11.3) also puts the latter in a negative light. Despite its lack of stability problems, the BAR model predicts inflation rates very different from the actual rates, while at the same time appearing to be overly optimistic.[24]

In conclusion, the results obtained provide answers to the above questions:

1 The forecasting superiority of the BVAR model is not limited to 4 quarters, but encompasses shorter as well as longer horizons, both jointly (see Table 11.3) and for individual variables (see Table 11.4)

2 It is in forecasting the price variable that the superiority of the BVAR model over the other models becomes clear, and the differences are quite important (see Table 11.3 and Figures 11.2 and 11.3).

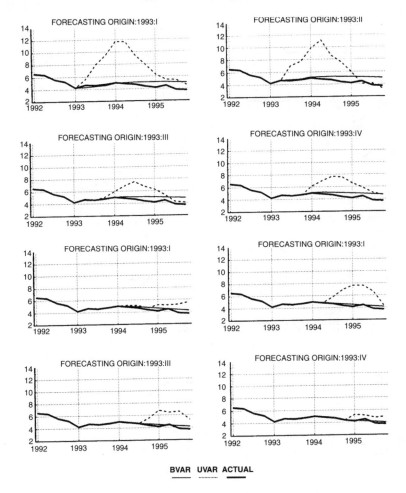

Figure 11.2 Comparison of BVAR and UVAR model forecasts, 1992–5, year-on-year inflation rate[1]

Note: 1 The inflation data for 1995 are adjusted for the effect of changes in indirect taxation.
Sources: Authors' calculations and INE.

3   Although the estimated hyperparameters and the resulting scant inter-relationship among variables might suggest that the BVAR model does not differ significantly from a model consisting of a set of nine univariate models, comparing the price forecasting performances of the BVAR and BAR models (see Figure 11.3) clearly shows that the differences between them are important and that the influence of the model's other variables is considerable when the BVAR model is used to forecast inflation.

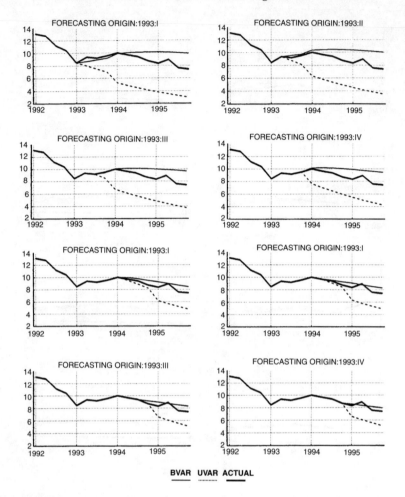

Figure 11.3 Comparison of BVAR and BAR model forecasts, 1992–5, year-on-year inflation rate[1]

Note: 1   The inflation data for 1995 are adjusted for the effect of changes in indirect taxation.
Sources: Authors' calculations and INE.

Forecasting and Uncertainty

Thus far, all references to forecasts, predictive qualities, and forecasting performance have been based on *point* estimates of the future values of the variables of the model. However this should not obscure the fact that when forecasts are based on econometric models, there is considerable interest in obtaining measurements of the uncertainty associated with these forecasts.

Knowledge of the uncertainty associated with forecasts is highly informative, as it allows not only for assessing with what accuracy the prediction was made (the greater the uncertainty, the less relevant the point forecast), but also how different forecasts are from actual values. In short, when attention is focused solely on point predictions, very important information is disregarded that could help the user of these forecasts assess their accuracy and arrive at an informed opinion.

Despite these considerations, economic authorities, international organizations, and private institutions rarely present forecasts accompanied by uncertainty measures, which may be due in part to a theoretical void. In fact, while numerous results are available for establishing confidence intervals in terms of forecasting the level of a series, this is not the case when interest is focused on its growth rate, which is what usually happens in macroeconomic forecasting, where, for example, GDP and CPI data are not usually expressed in terms of level values but in terms of growth rates. In this connection, and to ensure that the information extracted with the BVAR model described in this chapter is as complete as possible, Álvarez, Ballabriga and Jareño (1996b) analytically derive the probability distribution of the aforesaid growth rates when a VAR model has been used.

By way of example, Figure 11.4 illustrates uncertainty bands for inflation.[25] Specifically, the chart defines the values between which – according to the model – the projected inflation rate for 1994 and 1995 should be with a probability of 25 per cent (dark area), 50 per cent (including the medium and dark areas), and 75 per cent (including all 3 areas of the figure). As can be seen, although the point forecast (thick line) showed a gradual decline in inflation from 5 per cent to approximately 4 per cent, the model projected a probable band wider than one percentage point during most of the forecasting horizon.

The usefulness of this tool is not limited to gauging the reliability of forecasts; it can also be used for other purposes such as assessing the probability that a certain variable will be located below a given value, which can be relevant in the present situation.

One of the basic concerns in the current monetary policy strategy of the Banco de España, which is based on the establishment of direct inflation objectives, is assessing the probability that such objectives will be attained.[26] Once the probability density function of the projected inflation rate is known, the problem is estimating the cumulative probability within the target range. Figure 11.5 illustrates the nature of the problem. If an inflation rate below a given value is defined as a monetary policy objective (represented in the figure as 'objective'), the probability that this objective is attained is expressed quantitatively by the value of the area below the probability density function for values less than the target value.

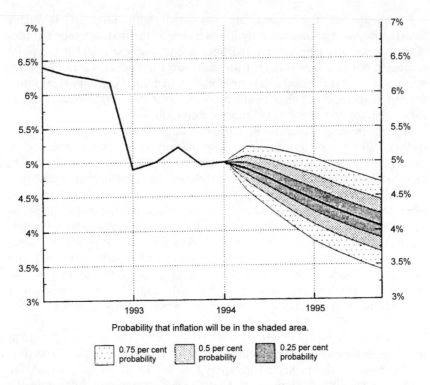

Figure 11.4   Uncertainty of forecast, 1992–5, year-on-year inflation rate

Notes: 1   Projections based on information up to 1994: 1.
2   The inflation data for 1995 are adjusted for the effect of changes in indirect taxation.
3   The shaded areasdelineate the region of uncertainty for the forecast associated with their corresponding probability level.
Sources: Authors' calculations and INE.

Figure 11.6 shows the variation in 1995 of the probability of attaining the intermediate inflation objective defined by the Banco de España[27] for the first few months of 1996. As shown in the figure, with information from the first quarter of the year, the probability was about 45 per cent. With information from the second quarter, probability decreased slightly to 40 per cent, at which point the outlook began to improve, with the result that probability climbed to 65 per cent with third quarter information and to 95 per cent with year-end information.

CONCLUDING REMARKS

This chapter has described a multivariate macroeconometric forecasting model that has recently been prepared for the Spanish economy. The model,

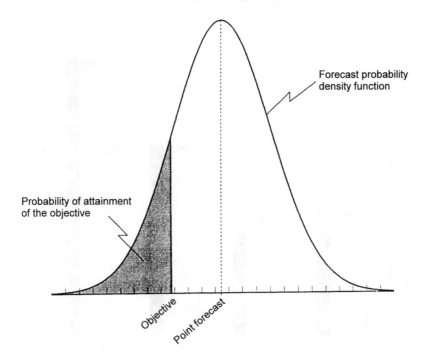

Forecast probability
density function

Probability of attainment
of the objective

Objective

Point forecast

Figure 11.5 Probability distribution and attainment of objectives
Sources: Authors' calculations.

which is quarterly and includes a small number of variables, was built to advance the empirical characterization of the Spanish macroeconomy using Bayesian techniques and elements typical of time series analysis.

While any advance in the empirical characterization of the Spanish economy is important in and of itself, the framework established by the recent Law on the Autonomy of the Banco de España sparked interest in the use of instruments that can aid in monetary policy-making. Specifically, the monetary policy strategy based on inflation objectives clearly highlights the importance of progressing in the identification of the determinants of inflation in Spain, as well as projecting its future trend.

As explained in the chapter, forecasting is a risky business. Therefore, measures of the uncertainty associated with projections become essential, as they make possible a complete description of the model's predictive implications and provide a more comprehensive means of responding to questions of interest to economic policy-makers.

The exercises presented concerning the model suggest that the interaction among different variables aids in forecasting the future behavior of inflation with greater accuracy than if the past of prices alone were consid-

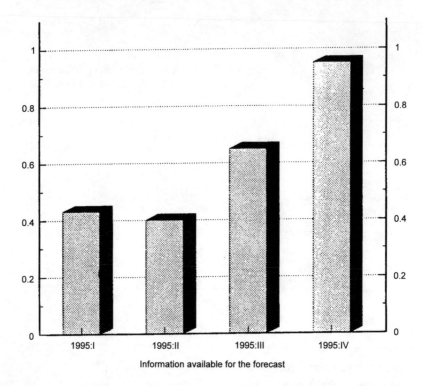

Figure 11.6   Probability of attainment of the intermediate inflation objective[1]
Note: 1   Objective defined as inflation below 4 per cent in 1994:1.

ered. Also of note is the stability of forecasts when new information is
received, especially when these projections are compared with others
obtained using methods that impose no restrictions on the data. These
results confirm that the BVAR model presented in this chapter, in addition
to being able to provide a general characterization of Spain's present and
future economic situation, can serve as a useful supplementary tool for
analyzing and forecasting inflation in Spain.

Appendix: The Prior Distribution Used in the BVAR Model

The purpose of this Appendix is to present the functional forms used in the BVAR model to relate the prior distribution of the model's coefficients to the set of hyperparameters.

It is assumed that the model's coefficients follow a Gaussian multivariate prior distribution. Defining the column vector that captures all of the model's coefficients as β yields:

$$\beta \sim N_{nm+d}(\mu, \Sigma) \tag{11A.1}$$

where n is the number of variables in the system, m is the number of lags in the VAR, and d the number of deterministic variables.

Thus, to characterize this distribution completely, it is necessary to specify the vector of means (μ) and the matrix of variances and covariances (Σ). Now, as it is assumed that the matrix of variances and covariances is diagonal, the coefficients of the model are independent. In other words, the following is obtained for each coefficient:

$$\beta_{ij}(s) \sim N(\mu_{ij}(s), \sigma_{ij}^2(s)) \quad \begin{matrix} i = 1, \ldots, n \\ j = 1, \ldots, n, \ldots, n+d \\ s = 1, \ldots, m \end{matrix} \tag{11A.2}$$

where i is the number of the equation, j is the number of the explanatory variable (both for the stochastic variables n of the system and for the deterministic variables d) and s is the lag number. Therefore, to characterize the distribution of each coefficient completely, it is only necessary to specify its prior mean and variance.

PRIOR MEAN OF THE STOCHASTIC VARIABLES[28]

$$\mu_{ij}(s) = \begin{cases} \tau_0 & i = j, i \in C_1 \\ & s = 1 \\ 0 & \text{otherwise} \end{cases} \tag{11A.3}$$

393

where C_1 refers to the set of world activity, money stock, compensation per wage earner, price, output, and employment variables. C_2 refers to the set of exchange rate, interest rate, and public deficit variables.

$$\mu_{ij}(s) = \begin{cases} \tau_1 & i = j, i \in C_2 \\ & s = 1 \\ 0 & \text{otherwise}; \end{cases} \qquad (11A.4)$$

PRIOR MEAN OF THE DETERMINISTIC VARIABLES

$$\mu_{ij}(s) = 0 \quad \begin{matrix} i = 1, \dots, n \\ j = n + 1, \dots, n + d \\ s = 0 \end{matrix} \qquad (11A.5)$$

$s = 0$, as it is assumed that the deterministic variables only have a contemporaneous effect.

PRIOR VARIANCE OF OWN LAGS[29]

$$\sigma_{ij}^2(s) = \frac{\tau_2}{s^{\tau_4}} \sigma_i^2 \quad i = j \quad \begin{matrix} i = 1, \dots, n \\ s = 1, \dots, m \end{matrix} \qquad (11A.6)$$

PRIOR VARIANCE OF THE LAGS OF THE OTHER VARIABLES

$$\sigma_{ij}^2(s) = \frac{\tau_2 \tau_3}{s^{\tau_4}} \frac{\sigma_i^2}{\sigma_j^2} \quad i \neq j \quad \begin{matrix} i = 1, \dots, n \\ j = 1, \dots, n \\ s = 1, \dots, m \end{matrix} \qquad (11A.7)$$

PRIOR VARIANCE OF THE CONSTANT TERM

$$\sigma_{ij}^2(s) = \tau_2 \tau_5 \sigma_i^2 \quad \begin{matrix} i = 1, \dots, n \\ j = n + 1 \\ s = 0 \end{matrix} \qquad (11A.8)$$

PRIOR VARIANCE OF THE BROKEN TREND

$$\sigma_{ij}^2(s) = \tau_2 \tau_5 \sigma_i^2 \quad \begin{array}{l} i = 8,9 \\ j = n+2 \\ s = 0 \end{array} \tag{11A.9}$$

where the eighth equation represents GDP and the ninth employment.

PRIOR VARIANCE OF THE SEASONAL DUMMIES

$$\sigma_{ij}(s)^2 = \tau_2 \tau_6 \sigma_i^2 . I_i \quad \begin{array}{l} i = 1,\ldots,n \\ j = n+3, n+4, n+5 \\ s = 0 \end{array} \tag{11A.10}$$

where I_i is 1 when the i variable is seasonal (as is true of the money stock, price, and employment variables) and 0 otherwise.

PRIOR VARIANCE OF THE LAGS OF THE REST OF THE SYSTEM IN THE WORLD ACTIVITY EQUATION

$$\sigma_{ij}^2(s) = \frac{\tau_2 \tau_3 \tau_8}{s^{\tau_4}} \frac{\sigma_i^2}{\sigma_j^2} \quad \begin{array}{l} i = 1 \\ j = 2,\ldots,n \\ s = 1,\ldots,m \end{array} \tag{11A.11}$$

PRIOR VARIANCE OF WORLD ACTIVITY IN THE REST OF THE SYSTEM

$$\sigma_{ij}^2(s) = \frac{\tau_2 \tau_3 \tau_9}{s^{\tau_4}} \frac{\sigma_i^2}{\sigma_j^2} \quad \begin{array}{l} i = 2,\ldots,n \\ j = 1 \\ s = 1,\ldots,m \end{array} \tag{11A.12}$$

where the world activity equation is the first in the system.

PRIOR VARIANCE OF THE LAGS OF THE REST OF THE SYSTEM
IN THE INTEREST RATE EQUATION

$$\sigma_{ij}^2(s) = \begin{cases} \tau_2 \sigma_i^2 I & i = j = 4 \\ & s = 1 \\ 0 \end{cases} \qquad (11A.13)$$

where the interest rate equation is the fourth in the system.

Notes

1   There are quarterly, single equation models for some variables, however.
2   See Banco de España (1995).
3   The very nature of this section requires a technical discussion. Readers unin-
     terested in these technical details can skip this section without jeopardizing
     their understanding of the rest of the chapter.
4   Bernanke (1986), Blanchard and Watson (1986), Sims (1986b), and Blanchard
     and Quah (1989) are seminal references in the literature on identification in
     the VAR analytical framework. Several applications to the Spanish economy
     can be found in Álvarez, Jareño and Sebastián (1993), Ballabriga and Sebas-
     tián (1993), and Álvarez and Sebastián (1995).
5   Notable references are Litterman (1986), McNees (1986), Runkle (1987), and
     Artis and Zhang (1990). Canova (1995) provides a fairly exhaustive review of
     the literature on the predictive capacity of the VAR methods.
6   For example, the fact that a surplus attributable to the tax schedule is gener-
     ated in one quarter does not mean that economic agents perceive it as an
     improvement in the government's accounts.
7   Readers not interested in the technical aspects can skip pp. 380–3 without
     risking not understanding the rest of the chapter.
8   Note that the specification used is broader than the one used in Álvarez, Bal-
     labriga and Jareño (1995). The updated specification can be found in Álvarez,
     Ballabriga and Jareño (1996a).
9   The functional relationship between the prior means and variances and the
     set of hyperparameters used is discussed in the Appendix.
10   The reason for this modeling is purely statistical, as it allows for improving
     both fit and predictive capacity. Taking this approach, tests performed with
     the exchange rate variable and the fiscal variable yielded no improvements, so
     that they were not finally modeled as AR(1) processes.
11   See Sims, Stock and Watson (1990) and Park and Phillips (1989).
12   See Sims (1991) and Álvarez and Ballabriga (1994).
13   Unrestricted models with five lags revealed a marked predictive decline.
14   See, for example, Sims (1989).
15   In this case, the ratio in terms of computing time for single equation versus
     multi equation estimation is 1:14,000.
16   Ballabriga (1991) describes the details of the estimation process.
17   For maximization purposes, once the objective function has been established,
     the Kalman filter and the nonstandard maximization routine described in
     Sims (1986a) are used.

18 The model is re-estimated with information up to t and is used to predict $t + s, s = 1, \ldots, k$. The range of t is the available sample.
19 The statistic averages the mean square errors of the different variables for the various predictive horizons. To prevent the criterion from excessively penalizing equations with high variability, the mean square error of each equation is divided by the residual variance of the $AR(m)$ model.
20 The likelihood of the system as an estimation criterion was also used. However, the results in terms of forecasting are somewhat inferior to those presented here.
21 The focus of this section is the model's capacity to forecast inflation, given the considerable relevance of this variable, as noted throughout this chapter. Consequently, other possible uses of the model, such as analysis of the overall consistency of its projections or the performance of simulation exercises, are not addressed.
22 Four lags are considered in both models.
23 The model was re-estimated with each new observation. However, the prior information did not vary.
24 The purpose of this exercise is obviously not to compare the BVAR model with a set of individual univariate specifications. Specifically, its interest lies in assessing the contribution to forecasting of the relationships between the model's several variables.
25 These forecasts are the result of a retrospective exercise taking into account information available up to 1994:I.
26 Another no less important concern would be the establishment of a reference path for inflation that leads to attainment of the stated objective. An analytical method based on the forecasts of ARIMA models, which can be used to estimate these paths, is found in Álvarez, Delrieu and Jareño (1997).
27 Although this intermediate objective is defined in terms of keeping the inflation rate, based on monthly data, between 3.5 per cent and 4 per cent, the definition used for this exercise considers the objective attained when the inflation rate is below 4 per cent, based on quarterly data.
28 It must be remembered that both prior means and prior variances are defined for the coefficients associated with the different variables of the model, and not for the variables themselves.
29 The σ_i^2 and σ_j^2 parameters measure the variability of the i and j variables, computed on the basis of the residual variance of $AR(m)$ univariate models, where m is the number of lags in the VAR.

References

ÁLVAREZ, L.J. and F.C. BALLABRIGA (1994) 'BVAR models in the context of cointegration: a Monte Carlo experiment', *Documento de Trabajo*, 9405, Servicio de Estudios, Banco de España.

ÁLVAREZ, L.J., F.C. BALLABRIGA and J. JAREÑO (1995) 'Un modelo macroeconométrico trimestral para la economía española', *Documento de Trabajo*, 9524, Servicio de Estudios, Banco de España.

ÁLVAREZ, L.J., F.C. BALLABRIGA and J. JAREÑO (1996a) 'Algunas características actuales del modelo BVAR para la economía española', *Documento Interno*, EC/1996/9, Servicio de Estudios, Banco de España.

ÁLVAREZ, L.J., F.C. BALLABRIGA and J. JAREÑO (1996b) 'Intervalos de confianza para tasas de crecimiento: una nota sobre modelos VAR', Servicio de Estudios, Banco de España, mimeo.

ÁLVAREZ, L.J., J.C. DELRIEU and J. JAREÑO (1997) 'Restricted forecasts and economic target monitoring: an application to the Spanish consumer price index', *Journal of Policy Modeling*, 19(3), June, 333–49.

ÁLVAREZ, L.J., J. JAREÑO and M. SEBASTIÁN (1993) 'Salarios privados, salarios públicos e inflación dual', *Papeles de Economía Española*, 56, 58–77.

ÁLVAREZ, L.J. and M. SEBASTIÁN (1995) 'La inflación latente en España: una perspectiva macroeconómica', *Documento de Trabajo*, 9521, Servicio de Estudios, Banco de España.

ARTIS, M. and W. ZHANG (1990) 'BVAR forecasts for the G-7', *International Journal of Forecasting*, 6, 349–62.

BALLABRIGA, F.C. (1991) 'Instrumentación de la metodología VAR', *Cuadernos Económicos de ICE*, 48, 85–104.

BALLABRIGA, F.C. and M. SEBASTIÁN (1993) 'Déficit público y tipos de interés en la economía española: ¿existe evidencia de causalidad?', *Revista Española de Economía*, 10, 283–306.

BANCO DE ESPAÑA (1995) 'Monetary policy objectives and implementation in 1995', *Economic Bulletin*, January.

BERNANKE, B. (1986) 'Alternative explanations of the money income correlation', *Carnegie–Rochester Conference Series in Public Policy*, 25, 49–100.

BLANCHARD, O. and D. QUAH (1989) 'The dynamic effects of aggregate demand and supply disturbances', *American Economic Review*, 79, 655–73.

BLANCHARD, O. and M. WATSON (1986) 'Are business cycles all alike?', R. Gordon (ed.), *The American Business Cycle*, Chicago: University of Chicago Press, 123–179.

BUISÁN, A. and E. GORDO (1994) 'Functiones de importación y exportación de la economía española', *Investigaciones Económicas*, 18, 165–192.

CANOVA, F. (1995) 'Vector autoregressive models: specification, estimation, inference and forecasting', in *Handbook of Applied Econometrics*, Pesaran, M.H. and M.R. Wickens, Oxford: Blackwell.

DOAN, T., R. LITTERMAN and C. SIMS (1984) 'Forecasting and conditional projections using realist prior distributions', *Econometric Reviews* 3(1), 1–100.

GARCÍA PEREA, P. and R. GÓMEZ (1994) 'Elaboración de series históricas de empleo a partir de la Encuesta de Población Activa (1964–1992)', *Documento de Trabajo*, 9409, Servicio de Estudios, Banco de España.

GRANGER, C.W.J. and P. NEWBOLD (1986) *Forecasting economic time series*, New York: Academic Press.

LITTERMAN, R. (1980) 'Techniques for forecasting with vector autoregressions', Ph.D. dissertation, University of Minnesota.

LITTERMAN, R. (1986) 'Forecasting with Bayesian vector autoregressions – five years of experience', *Journal of Business and Economic Statistics*, 4(1), 25–38.

MATEA, M. Ll. and A.V. REGIL (1993) 'El cambio de base del IPC. Construcción de series históricas homogéneas con base 1992', *Documento Interno*, C/1993/73, Servicio de Estudios, Banco de España.

MCNEES, S.K. (1986) 'Forecasting accuracy of alternatives techniques: a comparison of US macroeconomic forecasts', *Journal of Business and Economic Statistics*, 4(1), 5–15.

PARK, J.Y. and P.C.B. PHILLIPS (1989) 'Statistical inference in regressions with integrated processes. Part 2', *Econometric Theory*, 5, 95–131.

RUNKLE, D. (1987) 'Vector autoregression and reality', *Journal of Business and Economic Statistics*, 5, 437–54.

SIMS, C. (1986a) 'Bayesmth: a programme for multivariate Bayesian interpolation', *Discussion Paper*, 234, Center for Economic Research, University of Minnesota.

SIMS, C. (1986b) 'Are forecasting models usable for policy analysis', *Quarterly Review*, Federal Reserve Bank of Minneapolis, 10, 2–16.

SIMS, C. (1989) 'A nine variable probabilistic model of the US economy', *Discussion Paper* 14, Institute for Empirical Macroeconomics, Federal Reserve of Minneapolis.

SIMS, C. (1991) Comment on 'To criticize the critics' by Peter C.B. Phillips, *Journal of Applied Econometrics*, 6, 423–34.

SIMS, C., J. STOCK and M. WATSON (1990) 'Inference in linear time series models with some unit roots', *Econometrica*, 58, 113–44.

TODD, R. (1984) 'Improving economic forecasting with Bayesian vector autoregression', *Quarterly Review*, Federal Reserve Bank of Minneapolis, (Fall) 18–29.

12 Monetary Policy Instrumentation: Current Situation and Outlook

Eloísa Ortega and Gabriel Quirós

INTRODUCTION

Instrumentation encompasses all of the procedures, techniques and instruments that a central bank uses to achieve the degree of monetary tightness considered appropriate for attaining the final objective of monetary policy: price stability. Instrumentation is therefore a component of the general monetary control arrangements defined by the actions and interventions that the central bank must carry out in the financial markets to achieve this end.

Four separate instrumentation functions can be distinguished. First and foremost is attainment of the aforementioned degree of monetary tightness. The second function, signaling, relates both to how the central bank's monetary stance is communicated and the procedures used to influence economic agents' expectations and behavior. The third function consists of providing funds to the banking system to adjust its net, short-term liquidity position (deficit or surplus). Fourth, there is a close relationship between instrumentation and the steps taken to ensure the orderly functioning of the payments system, so that transactions in the financial markets (including those by the central bank) are carried out as securely and efficiently as possible.

In terms of its relationship to the rest of the book, this chapter bridges the description of the monetary control strategy and that of the monetary policy transmission mechanisms. Throughout the chapter, references to both these subjects are necessary, especially the former; otherwise, neither the design nor the logic of instrumentation would be comprehensible.

The chapter is organized as follows. We discuss the basic characteristics of monetary policy instrumentation and attempt to provide a general view of how the objectives or functions of instrumentation are fulfilled using the various procedures, techniques and instruments.

We then describe and discuss monetary policy instrumentation in Spain, opening with a discussion of its most important general characteristics, which in turn serves as the basis for an explanation of how the above-mentioned functions are fulfilled and what techniques and instruments the Banco de España uses for this purpose.

The description of monetary policy instrumentation in the European Union serves two purposes: (1) establishing a framework for comparative analysis of some of the most important aspects of monetary policy instrumentation in Spain, and (2) providing a basis for understanding the design of the instrumentation of the single monetary policy currently under discussion in the EMI. We begin by highlighting some of the differences in the configuration of the EU countries' monetary policies and then focus on the differences in their instrumentation, which is the central and most extensive part of this section and close with an analysis – based on the information obtained previously – of two specific aspects of monetary policy instrumentation in Spain: the Banco de España's procedures for signaling the monetary policy stance and the guarantees used in providing liquidity.

The final section outlines the major criteria for the design of single monetary policy instrumentation in the Monetary Union, with comments on the changes that will have to be made in Spanish monetary policy instrumentation to make it consistent with the monetary policy of the future ESCB.

BASIC ASPECTS OF INSTRUMENTATION: FUNCTIONS, PRINCIPLES AND ALTERNATIVE MODELS

It is a well known fact that central banks use different strategies to achieve their final monetary policy objective. These strategies differ essentially with respect to the indicators used to make monetary policy decisions and to the setting or not of intermediate objectives (monetary aggregates or exchange rate). Nevertheless, regardless of the strategy used, monetary policy decisions are implemented by modifying the terms on which central banks provide liquidity to banking institutions, which can be done by affecting the volume or the cost of the financing provided. The preference of central banks for one or another formula will determine the choice of the instrumental variable, which may be the supply of bank reserves, or, alternatively, short-term interest rates.

In the past, the choice of the operational variable was usually determined by the type of monetary strategy pursued. For example, the instrumentation of strategies in which intermediate objectives were defined in terms of monetary aggregates usually consisted of placing very strict controls on the supply of bank reserves, while the definition of intermediate exchange rate objectives involved a greater adjustment of short-term interest rates. In recent years, however, the argument over the operational variable has been settled in favor of controlling short-term interest rates, regardless of the type of monetary policy strategy pursued. The emergence of financial money markets, their growing integration at both the national and international levels, and, in Europe, the strategic importance of the exchange rate, have advised of reducing the volatility of interest rates and formulating economic policies that promote orderly interest rate movements. Monetary policy has contributed to this process via the generalization of short-term interest rates as an operational variable. This does not mean, however, that central banks accommodate every liquidity shock regardless of its origin or scale. On the contrary, basic liquidity management remains an important aspect of monetary instrumentation, especially for those central banks where the role of the monetary aggregates in monetary policy strategies is significant.[1]

In these circumstances, the degree of monetary tightness appropriate for attaining the final objective will be determined by the transmission of changes in short-term interbank interest rates (the only ones that central banks can influence) to the long-term funds markets, which is where the interest rates that ultimately affect the spending decisions of economic agents are negotiated.

The above considerations help define the *functions* that the set of monetary policy instruments and procedures used by central banks should fulfill. First, the instruments available to central banks should make it possible to guide movements in short-term interbank deposit market interest rates. Second, and given that interest rate expectations play a very important role as a catalyst in the transmission of interest rate movements from the short to the medium and long terms, the instruments selected should help signal the degree of monetary tightness considered optimal, and, if necessary, influence the formation of economic agents' expectations. This function can also be important in situations where central banks may be interested in distinguishing between interest rate movements aimed at modifying the general monetary policy stance from movements possibly geared toward combating temporary market strains.

The growing importance of interest rates as an operational variable should not, however, obscure other functions of monetary policy instruments, particularly with respect to liquidity management by central banks and the orderly functioning of payments systems. The two functions are closely interrelated, but a distinction should be maintained between them for explanatory purposes. From this perspective, the instruments available to central banks should facilitate their actions to act as a counterpart the banking system's net demand for or supply of liquidity. It may therefore be advisable to develop tools to stabilize institutions' demand for bank reserves, as this smooths forecasting of the system's liquidity requirements (and, in appropriate cases, the need for central bank intervention), and, depending on the circumstances, limits the presence of central banks in the money markets. Lastly, the operational framework should provide credit institutions with access to central bank liquidity – as a last resort – and facilitate the orderly functioning of payments systems.

The design of instruments, and decisions concerning how best to combine them (which may vary, depending on the characteristics of the existing financial structures), should be guided by a series of *criteria or principles*.

First, monetary policy instruments should make for efficient control of the operational variable (i.e. in the context described above, short-term interest rates), for purposes of both maintaining the desired levels and effecting changes in them. Second, monetary policy instrumentation should be based on – as well as promote – market mechanisms and free price formation. Accordingly, and insofar as possible, actions involving implicit subsidies or taxes should be avoided, as they distort unrestricted resource allocation. Third, simplicity is advisable: economy of techniques and instruments facilitates clear expression of the degree of monetary restrictiveness; therefore, any additional procedures proposed should be justified in a detailed cost-benefit analysis. Fourth, flexibility and symmetry should be sought: the control strategy must allow for both upward and downward interest rate movements, and must be capable of producing large or small changes in these rates with equal facility.

Central banks have a wide range of instruments at their disposal to fulfill instrumentation functions. The choice of instruments is influenced by the principles referred to above, and, when applicable, by the trade-off or substitution of one for another which is deemed appropriate. In defining them, a distinction should be made between the reserve requirement and all of the other instruments, techniques and procedures. The predominantly structural nature of the former and the functions it fulfils (chiefly related to liquidity management) warrant this distinction.

The reserve requirement, as is well known, is an instrument that requires credit institutions to maintain a cash balance (bank reserves) with the central bank, equal to a certain percentage of their liabilities. It should be pointed out that the current configuration of the reserve requirement in countries where it is used is the result of a profound transformation both in the functions that central banks assign to this instrument and in its specification. The reasons for this transformation are numerous and diverse: the liberalization of national financial systems and greater competition among them, the lesser importance attached to controlling monetary aggregates in monetary policy strategies, the shift toward the stricter monitoring of short-term interest rates, etc.[2]

As a result of this transformation, the reserve requirement today fulfills two basic functions. First, it helps stabilize the demand for bank reserves among institutions and indirectly eases the pressures on short-term interest rates. Second, it helps increase the system's dependence on the liquidity offered by the central bank. The first of these functions enables banks to use the bank reserves they maintain with the central bank as a liquidity buffer in the event of unexpected shocks.[3] To achieve this, the level of the reserve requirement must be sufficiently above that of the working balances (the balance of bank reserves that each institution needs to settle its interbank transactions) and it must be complied with in terms of the average for the maintenance period, the so-called averaging provisions. In this way, non-attainment of the average level on some days can be offset by surpluses on others. It is also advisable for the lag between the computation and maintenance periods to be long enough to allow banks sufficient time to adjust their reserves to the reserve requirements and consider the possibility of using surplus assets in the immediately following period. Lastly, efficient fulfilment of this function has nothing to do with the remuneration – full or partial – of required reserves.

The reserve requirement's function of increasing the banking system's dependence on the liquidity provided by the central bank is largely determined by the sign of the autonomous factors' contribution to the liquidity generation process. Its imposition may be advisable in countries where the combined effects of these factors create a constant liquidity overhang in the banking system and/or in which it is decided that the central bank's influence over money market conditions will be more effective if there is a net demand for liquidity in the banking system. The demands of a reserve requirement designed for complying with this function are few: the existence of a sufficiently high reserve ratio defined on a given base of bank liabilities.

Apart from the functions described above, it has been argued that the reserve requirement helps tighten central bank control over the money supply as it introduces a wedge between returns on monetary and non-monetary assets. It thus becomes possible to increase the elasticity of the demand for money to variations in the interest rates of alternative instruments and to reduce funds shifts between the two types of financial wealth. A more traditional justification of the usefulness of the reserve requirement for monetary control focused on the supply of bank reserves through the money multiplier, the stability of which over time made it possible to establish a relatively automatic relationship between the supply of bank reserves and the money stock. The disappearance of a sharp dividing line between monetary and non-monetary assets, the development of financial innovations, and the processes of disintermediation – which were in part initiated by high reserve requirements and a broad base of eligible liabilities – cast doubt on the effectiveness of the reserve requirement for this purpose. It should be noted that for the reserve requirement to fulfil this function, it must be high and it must be remunerated at below-market rates, which could entail a significant tax burden for the banking system. Lastly, in addition to functions more properly related to monetary policy, the reserve requirement has in the past played a clearer role in generating monetary income, normally associated with compensation for the services provided by central banks to banking institutions.

The remaining monetary policy instruments can be divided into two categories: (1) open market operations and (2) credit and deposit facilities, the so-called standing facilities. With these instruments, central banks endeavor to fulfill the various functions involved in executing monetary policy: stearing interest rates in the interbank deposit market, sending signals to the markets about the monetary policy stance, providing basic liquidity to the system, and facilitating the orderly functioning of the payments system.

The two basic characteristics differentiating both categories of instruments are the procedure for determining interest rates and the discretionarity the institutions have of gaining access to central bank financing. Thus, in the case of open market operations, transactions are always carried out at the initiative of the corresponding central bank, which determines the timing of the intervention, its sign, etc. The transactions are also executed at market prices, which is ensured because such operations take the form of tenders, in which institutions state amounts of liquidity and/or interest rates. In the case of credit or deposit facilities, on the other hand, transactions are executed at prices predetermined by the central bank, which normally differ upward or downward from market prices by a variable amount. Moreover, in this latter case, commercial banks decide when to use instruments of this type (although their use is sometimes conditional upon the application of specific quotas).

Central banks' open market operations to inject liquidity comprise various types of transactions: outright purchases of negotiable securities or purchases of such securities with resale agreements, asset purchases with resale agreements denominated in foreign currency (currency swaps), and collateralized loans.

Liquidity absorbing operations consist of sales of securities (outright or with repurchase agreements) from central banks' portfolios, the placement with credit institutions of paper issued by central banks themselves, or, in some cases, the taking of the institutions' deposits.

Within the category of open market operations there is an additional distinction between regular and fine-tuning operations. The former follow a predetermined schedule and are normally the centerpiece of monetary intervention, in terms of both the volume of funds involved and the signaling function of interest rate movements. Fine-tuning operations, on the other hand, allow for more precise or tighter control of monetary conditions, owing to their greater frequency and/or shorter term. As indicated above, open market operations usually take the form of tenders; in some cases, however, they may involve simpler procedures, wherein the central bank defines the terms of a transaction and communicates them to a small group of institutions. These operations, which are reserved for situations necessitating very rapid intervention, are known as bilateral operations.

The most common type of credit facility consists of granting collateralized credit at above-or below-market rates; deposit facilities, on the other hand, are usually remunerated at below-market rates. Each of these instruments fulfills a number of functions, the relative importance of which has also changed over time. Credit facilities offered at penal interest rates fulfill the basic function of last-resort lending, but they also make it possible to place a cap on interest rate movements in the money markets: banks, reacting to a liquidity squeeze or an upward interest rate adjustment, can turn to the central bank and obtain a known rate, thus limiting further increases in money market interest rates. Credit facilities at below-market interest rates, which were fairly common in the past, are used primarily to provide subsidized financing to the banking system, and because they normally involve longer terms, they are subject to predetermined quotas. Lastly, deposit facilities offer banks the possibility – in cases of excess liquidity and downward pressure on interest rates – of depositing their surpluses in a central bank account, which is remunerated at below-market rates, thereby establishing an interest rate floor.

The combination of open market operations and credit and deposit facilities allows central banks the possibility of designing fairly complex operational frameworks for signaling purposes and for influencing money market conditions. However, as will be seen hereafter, there are substantial differences in the selection of instruments. These differences are sometimes due to central banks' divergent opinions about the optimal degree of activism. Thus, at one end of the spectrum are central banks that build stabilizing elements into the demand for bank reserves and, through the design of credit and deposit facilities, limit their presence in the market. At the other end are central banks that choose other mechanisms and intervene more frequently, generally by making more intensive use of fine-tuning operations. In many cases, though, the differences are chiefly historical in origin. Viewed at this way, the strategic factors are of relatively minor importance.

MONETARY POLICY INSTRUMENTATION IN SPAIN

General Characteristics

Considerable efforts have had to be made in recent years to adapt Spanish monetary policy – and, specifically, its instrumentation – to the gradual liberalization and international integration of Spain's money and financial markets. Of particular relevance in this regard is the Banco de España's loss of room for manoeuvre in setting interest rates, owing to the participation of the peseta in the EMS exchange rate mechanism (ERM). In a surprising paradox, this has in turn necessitated greater control over short-term interest rates, given the sensitivity of the exchange rate to the interest rate spread *vis-à-vis* the external financial markets. Moreover, since February 1992, this control has been exercised against a background of completely unrestricted capital movements, which has considerably increased the importance of the external constraint in Spanish monetary policy.

The widening in August 1993 of the fluctuation bands of the currencies participating in the ERM reduced the weight of these external determinants, but, set against this positive development, there were subsequent episodes of instability in the international exchange and financial markets. A brief description of the instrumentation of Spanish monetary policy follows, which will serve as an introduction to this part of the Chapter.

Unrestricted capital movements and the participation of the peseta in the ERM have greatly influenced two aspects of instrumentation in recent years: to achieve a very strict control on short-term interest rates and the sizable reduction of the reserve requirement. The first aspect has already been explained. The second was prompted by the need to prevent the competitiveness of credit institutions from being adversely affected – in an open market increasingly integrated with the EU countries – by the increase in intermediation costs invariably associated with the existence of a reserve requirement (especially if the legal reserves are not remunerated or are remunerated at below-market rates).

A third general characteristic of Spanish instrumentation is that it is based essentially on open market operations (repo operations in particular). This is particularly striking in the European environment, where it is not uncommon to find permanent credit facilities for institutions and/or facilities for the deposit of excess banking system liquidity with the central bank. Moreover, the lack of facilities of this type, outside the context of market mechanisms, largely explains the fact that there is no public or official interest rate band in Spain. This ultimately has a bearing on the formulation of interest rate policy, which is implemented exclusively through the marginal 10-day repurchase rate.

Fourth, there are basically two maturities for the Banco de España's repo operations: 10 days or daily. This means that money market interventions are concentrated in the very short term (less than 2 weeks), which, again, is remarkable in the European context, where most central banks regulate market conditions for longer periods.

Fifth, in recent years, Spanish monetary policy has invariably been managed in a situation where the banking system is heavily dependent on

Banco de España liquidity. This has determined the sign of the central bank's interventions in the money market, which have traditionally involved supplying the system with basic liquidity. As described on p. 414, this situation has necessitated the mobilization of an equally large volume of securities eligible as collateral in liquidity injection operations, which has sometimes made it difficult to supply liquidity.

Sixth, the instrumentation of Spanish monetary policy is characterized by very frequent interventions in the money market by the Banco de España, compared to the norm in the European Union. It should be pointed out, however, that this greater frequency of intervention (or *degree of activism*) in the market is closely related to the especially short term of the operations.

The Instruments

Reserve Requirement

Following is a brief definition of the current reserve requirement: a legal requirement that 2 per cent of a broad range of credit institutions' balance sheet liabilities (known as *eligible liabilities*) be kept in an unremunerated account at the Banco de España. Compliance with the reserve requirement is based on a 10-day average: i.e. computing the average of eligible liabilities and the corresponding average of the balance of bank reserves kept in that account, 3 times a month. The calculation of the reserve requirement in average terms means that institutions could theoretically keep their accounts at zero for most of the 10-day period and limit the setting up of the required balance to a few days or to only 1.[4] Another important factor in the definition of the requirement is that the lag between the computation period for eligible liabilities and the maintenance period for bank reserves is only 2 days, which tends to increase the demand for liquidity on the last day of the maintenance period.

Successive reductions of the legal reserve requirement ratio to a level close to the *working balances* that institutions need to clear and settle their transactions have gradually reduced the liquidity buffer that higher ratios provided in the past. Thus, further hypothetical reductions of the ratio might increase the volatility of the daily demand for institutions' bank reserves and, consequently, the erratic nature of daily interest rates, given the current frequency of Banco de España interventions in the money markets.

Consequently, the closer the levels of the legal reserve requirement and the working balances, and the shorter the period for calculating and covering the former, the more often it will be necessary for the Banco de España to inject or drain liquidity. Therefore, the low level of the reserve ratio and the existence of so short a period (compared with the usual period of one month in other countries) require the Banco de España to maintain a more constant presence in the market.

Current Techniques, Instruments and Procedures

In implementing monetary policy, the Banco de España prefers to use open market operations, and to rely as little as possible on techniques involving bilateral relations between the Bank and its counterparties outside the market. Consequently, the involvement of the latter in operations regulating liquidity in the interbank market is marginal.

The basic features of the current system of monetary management which emerged in March 1990 were at the root of the reduction (from 17 per cent to 5 per cent) and modification of the reserve requirement ratio. In fact, the replacement of bank reserves in excess of 5 per cent (the level at which the new ratio was set) with Banco de España certificates led to the instantaneous creation of a portfolio of central bank liabilities held by institutions of just over 3 trillion pesetas, which the latter could use to obtain liquidity. Moreover, the system's book-entry configuration enable the creation of a secondary market for the settlement of operations through the Central Book-Entry System and the Money Market On-Line Service (STMD in its Spanish abbreviation).

Thus, the reduction of the reserve requirement and the issuance of certificates of deposit fulfilled all of the conditions for basing the liquidity injection and absorbing processes almost entirely on open market operations; specifically on repo operations. It can therefore be stated that the management of Spanish monetary policy in recent years has been underpinned and at the same time promoted by the unrestricted functioning of market and price formation mechanisms.

It seems important that this basic characteristic be preserved and reinforced, as it is a guarantee of efficiency. Moreover, as experience has shown, repo operations are a flexible and powerful tool for controlling short-term interest rates. Their ability to influence the structure of short-term rates, however, is less clear; the reason is that in repo operations, two prices are agreed upon simultaneously for the same instrument: the spot transaction price and the forward transaction price. In outright spot or forward transactions, on the other hand, only one price is agreed to and only one point on the yield curve is affected; consequently, it seems that these operations have a greater capacity to influence the shape of the curve. It can be stated, therefore, that the use of repo operations is consistent with the strategy of influencing only the shortest-dated segment of the curve, where it makes no sense to influence its shape. Moreover, the extensive use of outright operations would cause the central bank's outright securities portfolio to fluctuate enormously as a result of monetary intervention operations, and, finally, the operations carried out would be *long-term* liquidity injection or absorbing operations, this term being determined by the residual life of the instruments used. Lastly, it should be pointed out that a repo operation assumes that two guarantees would be obtained for the lender: the counterpart's personal guarantee and the guarantee of the issuer of the financial instrument involved. Conversely, in outright transactions, the former disappears and only the latter remains, thus increasing the credit risk for the central bank in liquidity injection operations.

There are basically two types of open market operations (see Figure 12.1): first, a 10-day repurchase tender for certificates of deposit and book-entry public securities, in which all credit institutions subject to the reserve requirement and which comply with it within every 10-day period are eligible to participate.[5] The purpose of this mechanism is to offer institutions a permanent facility, consistent both with the reserve requirement calculation period and with a time frame in which the central bank and the institutions can forecast liquidity requirements as accurately as possible.

Second, the central bank maintains a daily presence in the market by carrying out liquidity injection and absorbing operations (maturing the next business day) with a small group of institutions: market makers. As in the 10-day tender, these are repo operations in which the collateral used consists of the same instruments as in the former.[6]

Thus, a significant characteristic of the instrumentation of Spanish monetary policy is that the central bank's regular interventions in the money market occur are very short-dated: between 1 and 10 days, approximately. An important consequence of this strategy is that the interbank market yield curve as from the 10-day date, is not directly determined by the Banco de España, but rather by agents' expectations concerning movements of its interest rates. Two objectives are thus attained. The first is a general one: keeping interference in the free formation of prices to a minimum. The second objective is more specific: obtaining the most accurate information possible concerning agents' expectations about interest rate policy.

As a complement to open market operations, and only in exceptional situations, the *Bank* makes individual loans to credit institutions (known as *public securities-backed loans*). These operations are the counterpart of the Bank's function as lender of last resort. Institutions use these loans to settle their final debtor position when the markets close. The rates applied by the Bank are higher than those applicable to open market operations, to discourage their use.[7] There is an upper limit on the amount of this type of loan, set at 80 per cent of the applicant institution's own resources; moreover, certain assets are required to guarantee the loan, including those used in open market operations and other public sector instruments not included in the Book-Entry System (for instance, investment bonds), which are tending to be gradually phased out. In addition, since April 1997

411

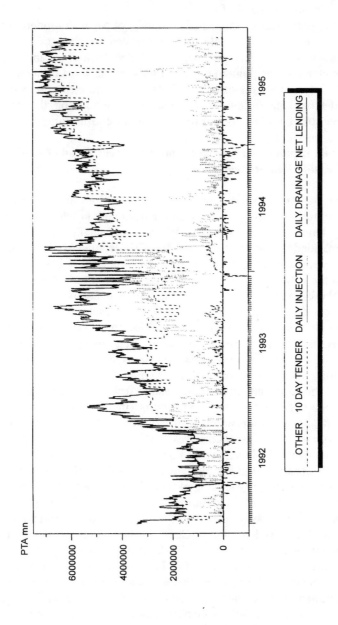

PTA mn

OTHER   10 DAY TENDER   DAILY INJECTION   DAILY DRAINAGE NET LENDING

Figure 12.1 Banco de España lending to the banking system, 1992–5
Source: Banco de España.

a marginal lending facility has been established, this being granted automatically to institutions in need of it.

As the foregoing infers, the instrumentation of Spanish monetary policy has been – and still is – significantly influenced by changes in and the characteristics of the reserve requirement. One of the most important of these characteristics, as pointed out previously, is the short calculation period, which determines, for example, the term of the basic financing provided to the banking system. It also has repercussions on the necessary degree of central bank activism in the interbank deposit market.

The Banco de España Balance Sheet and the Recent Trend of Banking System Liquidity Requirements

Most of the Banco de España's open market operations have been liquidity injection operations, carried out in an environment in which the Spanish banking system, as indicated on p. 408, has traditionally relied heavily on liquidity provided by the Banco de España. This dependence has been especially pronounced since the last quarter of 1992, which has required an increase in the volume of the Bank's injection operations in the money markets, and, therefore, a sizable upturn in the Banco de España's assets *vis-à-vis* the banking system. These rose from 1754 billion pesetas in September 1992 to a balance close to 6000 billion pesetas in December 1995 (see Figure 12.2).

The reasons for this increase are clearly demonstrated by aggregating the Banco de España's asset and liability items so as to ascertain the system's liquidity needs on the basis of its two main sources: one that captures the general monetary conditions and results from the combined effect of the autonomous liquidity generation factors (in the absence of a reserve requirement), and another, which is structural and discretionary, consisting of the reserve requirements themselves.[8]

This breakdown, which is given in Figure 12.2a, shows how, over the last 3 years, the increase in the liquidity needs of banks and savings banks has occurred as a result of the widening of their deficit liquidity position, caused by the restrictive nature of the autonomous factors. This has not been offset by the lesser demands associated with the reduction of the reserve requirement and the partial redemption of CEBES (Banco de España certificates). This combination of factors is radically different from that prevailing prior to 1992, in which the banking system's liquidity needs were largely determined by the central bank itself through the imposition of the reserve requirement in a context where the combined effect of the liquidity generation factors (demand for cash, net external assets, and net credit to the public sector) caused a surplus liquidity position in the banking system. In that setting, compliance with the reserve requirement increased the demand for funds to cover it and reversed the sign of the system's net liquidity needs.[9]

Figure 12.2b, on the other hand, shows changes in the various liquidity generation factors over the period in question, making it possible to

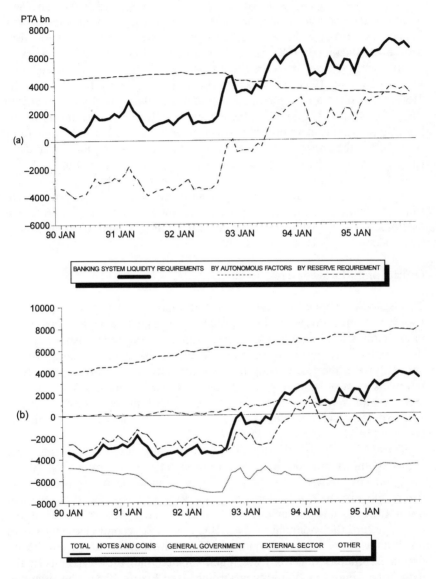

Figure 12.2 Banking system liquidity requirements and effect of autonomous factors, 1990–5

a Banking system liquidity requirements
b Effect of autonomous factors in determining liquidity requirements
Source: Banco de España.

pinpoint the reasons for the change in the sign of institutions' liquidity position as from 1992.

As shown in Figure 12.2b, since the final months of 1992 the expansive nature of the external sector has decreased as a result of Banco de España interventions to support the peseta exchange rate during the ERM crisis. Moreover, starting in 1993, the improvement and adjustment necessary to comply with Article 104A of the Maastricht Treaty, which entered into force in January 1994 and which prohibits the monetary financing of the Treasury, implied a permanent reduction in net Banco de España credit to the public sector. The break in the expansive nature recorded until then by both factors made it impossible to compensate, as had occurred in prior periods, for the contractive effect of the growth of the public demand for cash, which, at end-1995, accounted for just over 10.7 per cent of GDP.

This combination of factors meant that the Banco de España had to deal with a growing demand for liquidity from institutions and, on certain occasions in recent years, led to tensions in the money markets, caused by the lack of suitable securities in institutions' portfolios to guarantee the liquidity provided by the Banco de España.

Official and Market Interest Rates

The Banco de España's intervention in the money markets via the above-mentioned procedures enables an accurate adjustment of intervention interest rates to be made. This section examines the relationship between the various intervention rates available to the Banco de España (10-day and daily) and the relationship between the latter and interest rates in the interbank deposit market. Knowing to what extent movements of the former are transmitted along the yield curve makes it possible to pinpoint certain aspects of the monetary policy transmission mechanism, which is discussed in detail elsewhere in this book.

Figure 12.3, in which the 10-day and daily intervention rates are depicted, shows how the daily intervention rates pivot around the 10-day rate, and how, only in exceptional periods generally involving pressure on the peseta exchange rate, the Banco de España has made differentiated use of the daily and 10-day rates. This is particularly evident in 1993, in the period before the widening of the ERM bands. A second characteristic of this framework is that the deviations of the daily lending rates from the 10-day rate (liquidity injection) are much smaller than the deviations of the daily borrowing rates (liquidity absorbing) (see Figure 12.4). This asymmetry, which is only broken in the above-mentioned exceptional periods, exists in a context in which, as seen in the preceding paragraph, the intervention framework is dominated by the injection of liquidity (see Figure 12.5 and 12.6) and in which absorbing operations, relatively few in number,

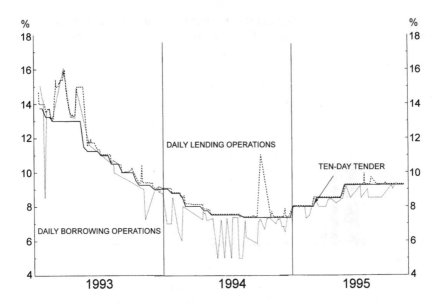

Figure 12.3 Banco de España intervention rates, 1993–5
Source: Banco de España.

are carried out at punitive rates (considerably *lower* than market rates). The reason for this asymmetry is that the injection rates generally indicate the degree of monetary tightness desired by the authorities, while the absorbing rates are basically associated with more technical aspects related to adjustments of institutions' liquidity in the final moments before the market closes and, more especially, on the last day of the 10-day mainten-ance period for bank reserves.

As indicated in Figures 12.7 and 12.8, the intervention rates guide interest rate movements in the shorter terms of the interbank deposit market (over-night and 1 month). The Banco de España's relatively frequent presence in the money markets has resulted in lower and decreasing volatility in both interest rates in the interbank deposit market throughout the sample period. In the case of the overnight rate, however, this decrease in volatility has been more pronounced (Table 12.1), reflecting not only more orderly devel-opments in the foreign exchange markets during most of the period, but also greater willingness on the part of the Banco de España to consider using the scope afforded by the ERM bands. These changes necessarily result in less frequent movements in the intervention interest rates in response to specific pressures on the peseta exchange rate. Nevertheless, the volatility of the interbank deposit market during this period is affected by the greater erraticism in the final days of the ten-day period applicable to bank reserves. The volatility in this segment of the interbank deposit market decreases when the last day of the ten-day period is excluded from the

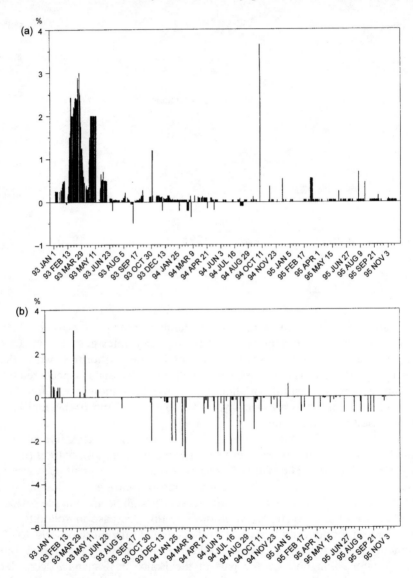

Figure 12.4 Spread between rate on daily lending and borrowing operations and 10-day intervention rate, 1993–5

a   Spread between rate on daily lending operations and 10-day intervention rate
b   Spread between rate on daily borrowing operations and 10-day intervention rate
Source: Banco de España.

calculation (see Table 12.2), which is consistent with the discussion on p. 408 concerning the conditioning factors that the definition of the reserve requirement brings to bear on institutions' liquidity adjustments.

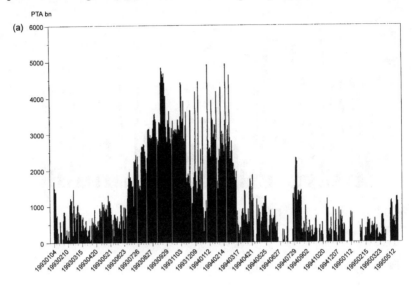

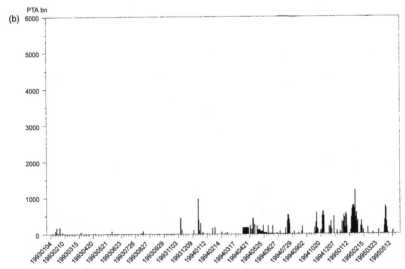

Figure 12.5 Volume of daily intervention lending and borrowing operations of the Banco de España, 1993–5

a   Lending operations
b   Borrowing operations
Source: Banco de España.

Moreover, the impact of movements in the Bank's intervention rates on rates in the interbank deposit market is generally felt very quickly, although the intensity of the response diminishes commensurately with the

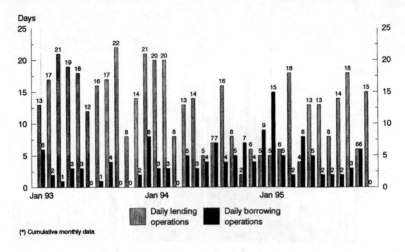

Figure 12.6   Banco de España, number of days of intervention, 1993–5
Source: Banco de España.

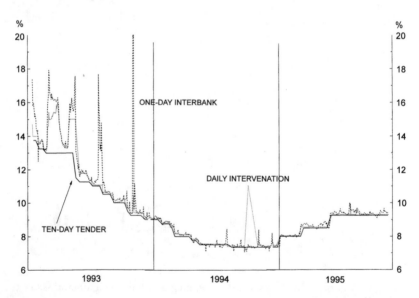

Figure 12.7   Banco de España and one-day interbank deposit market interest rates, 1993–5
Source: Banco de España.

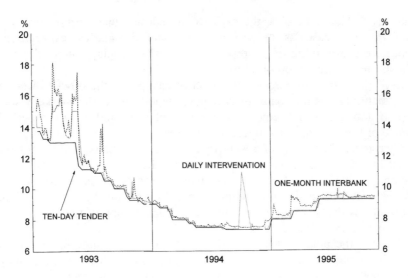

Figure 12.8 Banco de España and one-month interbank deposit market interest rates, 1993–5

Source: Banco de España.

Table 12.1 Interest rate volatility[1], 1993–5

Year	Overnight interbank/daily intervention rate	1-month interbank/daily intervention rate
1993	1.378	0.621
1994	0.349	0.348
1995	0.127	0.229

Note:
1 Calculated as the standard deviation of the spread between the overnight interbank and the daily intervention rate.

Table 12.2 Volatility of overnight interbank market interest rate[1], 1993–5

Year	Observed series	Adjusted series[2]
1993	2.590	2.389
1994	0.568	0.556
1995	0.558	0.550

Notes:
1 Calculated as the standard deviation.
2 Excludes data for the closing of the 10-day accounting period for bank reserves.

maturity.[10] This is because the capacity of central banks to influence forward rates decreases as the term increases, and also because expectations about the future trend of interest rates and inflation play a more decisive role in the determination of interest rates.

In Spain in the last 3 years, the effect of changes in the official rates on movements in the interbank market have depended on the market's success in anticipating movements in the official rates and on the expected course of future changes in intervention rates.

Therefore, the strongest response from the interbank market for all terms in 1993 could reflect, on the one hand, the capacity of the Banco de España in that period to transmit to markets the sequence and/or size of interest rate cuts made in the summer months, and, on the other, the firm expectations that it would persist in the instrumentation of that policy in a given period (see Figure 12.9).

In 1994, the possible lesser incidence of official rate movements would have been consistent with the mixed signals that seemed to be coming from short-and long-term rates. In the first half of the year, short-term rates fell steadily (as did the Banco de España's official rate), while interest rates on medium-and long-term debt began to increase as from February.

Lastly, in 1995, weaker responses in maturities as from 3 months could indicate agents' anticipation of interest rate changes that the Banco de España would later make. Thus, increases in the 10-day intervention rate in the first half of the year were preceded by a fairly significant increase in the positive slope of the yield curve. These movements were corrected in the second half of the year, against a background of improved inflationary prospects and expectations of an easing of monetary tightness, which, at year's end, would be confirmed by an initial cut in the Banco de España's interest rates. This process continued throughout 1996.

Monetary Instrumentation and Payments System

This section addresses the relationship between monetary policy instrumentation and the payments system. The discussion therefore focuses on what in the first two sections was described as the fourth function of monetary policy instrumentation. Specifically, 3 aspects will be discussed. First, a brief explanation is given of the organization of Spain's payments system, which will facilitate understanding its connection to monetary policy instrumentation and the functioning of the interbank markets. The second consists of identifying the area where day-to-day monetary management tends to merge with the central bank's efforts to deal with problems associated with the settlement of operations. To avoid excessive complexity, the explanation will be limited to situations foreseen by institutions or by the Banco de España while the interbank market is open. The third concerns

421

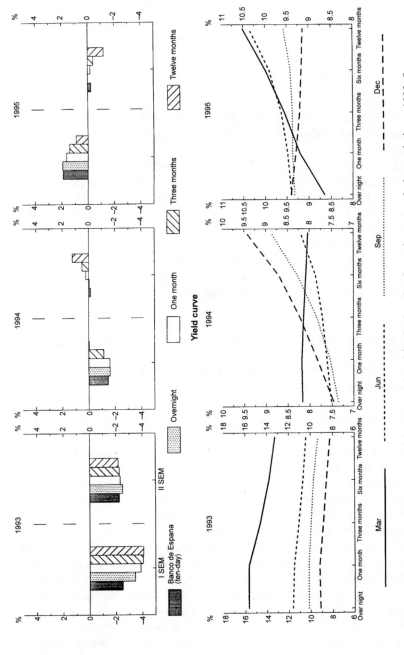

Figure 12.9 Intervention interest rate and rates negotiated in the interbank market, cumulative variations, 1993–5

Source: Banco de España.

the implications for monetary policy instrumentation of converting Spain's largest payments system (the Money Market On-Line Service, STMD) into a real-time gross (or continuous gross settlement) system, which is necessary for access to the third phase of Monetary Union.

The Current Payments System and Instrumentation

One of the characteristics of the Spanish payments system (see Gil and Nuñez, 1995) is that institutions' *cash* accounts with the Banco de España are used to settle all *major* transactions carried out by institutions which are members of the interbank deposits, government debt, Banco de España Certificates of Deposit, and FRA markets. These accounts are also used to settle net positions (debtor or creditor) resulting from their trades in the other organized Spanish financial markets (stock market, AIAF private fixed-income market and derivatives markets) and, owing to their transit through the Madrid Clearing House, in the foreign exchange markets.

The use of institutions' accounts with the Banco de España to settle major interbank payments thus indicates an initial connection between the functioning of the payments system and liquidity management. This centralization helps the Bank closely monitor institutions' individual positions in some of the larger markets at any given time of the day, and, therefore, that of the banking system as a whole.

In Spain, most large interbank payments are channeled through a gross settlement system at the end of the day (the STMD). The Banco de España, aided by the financial institutions, played a major role in the establishment and development of this system. The STMD is organized so as to record each operation matched in the interbank deposit market and in the government debt market, which enhances the quality and quantity of information available to the Banco de España concerning the functioning of these markets and the activities and positions of the participating institutions. The involvement of the Spanish central bank in the payments system is amplified by the fact that it is responsible for the *infrastructure* of the country's largest financial market – the government debt market – through the Government Debt Book-Entry System, which also represents a significant departure from some European countries.

Therefore, taking into account the fact that the basic aspect of monetary policy instrumentation consists of managing banks' cash balances in their accounts with the Banco de España through the reverse mobilization of public securities registered in such institutions' name in their securities accounts with the Book-Entry System, the close relationship between liquidity management and the payments system becomes evident.

A distinction should be made at this point between the clearing and settlement systems of the book-entry government debt market and the organized private fixed-income and stock markets, as this subject will be addressed later in relation to the possible extension of the collateral accepted by the Banco de España to include securities traded in these markets.

Both the stock market and the AIAF market have securities registration, clearing and settlement systems which are completely separate from those managed by the Banco de España (STMD and Government Debt Book-Entry System). This means that the Banco de España has no information on the securities accounts of the members of these markets and, therefore, no information on the activity in these accounts. As indicated above, the Banco de España *only* receives daily orders to transfer funds (cash) between the cash accounts of the members of these markets, owing to their net creditor or debtor (cash) positions in said markets.

In contrast, through the STMD and the Book-Entry System, the Banco de España has access to and control over securities accounts and transactions carried out in the book-entry government debt market by its members. Consequently, it is possible to track in full detail changes in the cash and securities balances recorded in the Book-Entry System for the market's members, these being, essentially, the Banco de España's counterparties.

The above suggests how easy it is for the Banco de España to execute repo operations with securities included in the Book-Entry System, and also how difficult it is, in the present circumstances, to expand them to include securities not registered with the System.

Difficulties in Obtaining Liquidity

As for the relationship between the procedures established to deal with problems anticipated in the settlement of operations (while the market is open) and day-to-day monetary management, the crucial distinction is that areas are involved which are actually different in nature but closely related through the central bank's daily operations. The former involve strategies aimed at the orderly functioning of the payments system, and the latter a set of procedures designed to achieve the desired degree of monetary tightness. Given the obvious priority that payments system considerations should have at all times and the exceptional nature of the situations involved, the conflicts that can arise between the two functions – such as the provision of a larger volume of liquidity or rates that are higher (depending on the control variable used) than those defined as objectives consistent with attainment of the targeted degree of monetary tightness – are resolved by accepting the transitory deviations from the targeted values, whether in the monetary base or in average intervention and market rates.

Difficulties anticipated while the market is open should be overcome – in principle, obviously – by the taking of funds in the interbank market. However, the possibility that the institution in question may have difficulty doing so should be weighed.

The basic distinction is that the institution may or may not have collateral for the taking of liquidity. If it does, the solution via the market or the Banco de España is easy. If it does not, however, the situation is actually one in which interbank deposit market participants have lost confidence in the institution concerned. In this case, obviously, the situation arising for the central bank is very complicated and its banking supervision staff will be involved in solving it.

In situations where an institution experiences immediate difficulties (limited to 1 day) in settling transactions, procedures will be decided upon which are an extension of day-to-day monetary management. In principle, these procedures will employ the same type of operations and collateral as are used in the latter, which, at the risk of repetition, would be the following. First, the Banco de España could consider a reverse repo, even if market a makers – which are the only counterparties of the Banco de España in day-to-day monetary management – are not involved, the instruments transacted being those usually encountered in these operations. Second, it may be that the institution does not have the usual collateral (book-entry public securities or Banco de España certificates of deposit), but does have public assets of another kind, which are not book-entry instruments but which are relatively residual and very illiquid. The Bank could consider accepting them as collateral for an overnight loan, as explained on p. 410. Third, and absolutely by way of exception, the Bank could grant an unsecured overnight loan if the institution does not have any of the kinds of collateral referred to in the above cases. It should be pointed out, however, that in all of these cases potential liquidity injection operations are involved, in which the institutions take the initiative and the authorities have to decide, based on more general considerations, whether or not to proceed.

The Bank only opens these financing channels as the closing of the market approaches, which also forces the institution to exhaust all other financing possibilities in the market. This is ensured because individual access to Banco de España financing is penalized both as a result of the higher cost of the financing and the fact that the institution must submit to a subsequent administrative procedure, which, because of its complexity, also serves as a deterrent. This procedure includes an official warning that the institution must endeavor to make use of the usual financing sources. Finally, in the process of adapting its operational framework to that of the ESCB, the Banco de España has established a marginal lending facility.

Towards a Real-time Gross Settlement System

This section deals with the possible influence that alternative definitions of the payments system (gross, net, continuous, or end-of-day) may have on instrumentation. In Spain, the focus will be the conversion from the current STMD to a real-time gross settlement system, as defined in the context of the European Union (see Nuñez, 1994).[11]

The STMD settlement system provides for the clearance of operations and, therefore, the settlement of participating agents' net balances, once the markets have closed. The debit and credit orders received are posted provisionally and will only become firm at the end of the day, if the institution making payment – in net terms – has a positive net balance at the close of the day, resulting from all of its operations in all markets (this disregards the normal fact that institutions usually have a cash balance or bank reserves when the market opens).

However, in November 1993, the Council of Governors of the EMI resolved that large-value interbank payments settled in the central banks of the European Union must be made through *gross, continuous systems*, in which a prior balance will foreseeably be required. This means that transactions communicated by market participants can only be settled if the counterparty paying in cash has a large enough balance in its central bank account when the central bank receives the order. Otherwise, the transaction will be placed on hold until the institution in question receives a cash payment of sufficient size.

Thus, under the new system, institutions may find that liquidity management is more complicated than at present. The principle of firm and immediate posting of transactions communicated will require the instantaneous and continuous availability of a sufficient balance in institutions' accounts, if the transaction generates a debtor position. If the balance is insufficient, institutions will find that such transactions are not settled, unlike the present procedure in which the debit in question can be offset by a subsequent credit, with the sole condition that it be communicated before the close of the STMD register. Therefore, it is to be expected that certain bottlenecks may occur, with transactions for settlement piling up in 'waiting lists'. Very close attention and follow-up will thus be required, both by institutions and by the central bank. The result will be what is known as the intraday *liquidity market*, which will force central banks to respond, one way or another, by providing the amounts necessary to keep such bottlenecks to a minimum.[12]

In short, this conversion will tend to drive up settlement costs and, therefore, deprive some markets of part of their operational flexibility. But it is to be hoped that it will also increase security and reduce the potential difficulties that the current system of settlement at market close can involve.

Lastly, it should be pointed out that the unification of large-value inter-bank payments systems in the European Union can be considered a necessity born of two factors. The first of these is the growing integration of European financial markets and the consequent, irreversible, increase in cross-border payments. This means that systemic risk transcends the national framework in an increasingly obvious way and thus becomes more difficult for national central banks to monitor. Hence the measures aimed at reinforcing the security of the payments system. The second factor is the need to equip the future ESCB with an integrated settlement system (see Sánchez Soliño, 1996). The linkage of real-time gross payments systems will result in the so-called TARGET system (Trans-European automated real-time gross settlement express transfer system), which will facilitate the settlement of monetary policy operations carried out by the ESCB.

INSTRUMENTATION IN THE EUROPEAN UNION COMPARED WITH THAT IN SPAIN

Some Differences in National Monetary Control Frameworks

To introduce the instrumentation of monetary policy in EU countries, it may be helpful to outline the guiding principles of their monetary control frameworks. Differences in these frameworks reflect widely differing factors, including macroeconomic concerns, the degree of openness of national economies, the level of financial market development and, perhaps no less importantly, the tradition and historical inertia of central bank practices. The combination of these factors results in individual monetary control frameworks with varying degrees of difference. In recent years, however, a shift toward unification has occurred, with a distinct increase in the importance of open market operations and a clear decrease in the level of the reserve requirement and the functions assigned to it.[13]

Major differences stem from the asymmetrical functioning of the ERM and from consideration of the D-Mark as its nominal anchor. This allows Germany to pursue a monetary control framework based on the strict control of liquidity held by the public, while the rest of the ERM countries are forced, to some extent, to adapt their monetary conditions to those of Germany.

In the latter countries this situation complicates the instrumentation of monetary policy. In an environment without exchange rate restrictions, the ideal situation was normally viewed as one in which variations in the degree of monetary tightness were transmitted rapidly and in their entirety to the capital and credit markets, or, what amounts to the same thing, were capable of causing parallel shifts in the term structure of interest rates in the economy. This remains true for countries such as Germany, but for countries such as Spain, the situation can give rise to more complex requirements. In some cases, changes in the degree of short-term monetary tightness, aimed exclusively at upholding exchange commitments in the immediate circumstances, should be confined to the money markets. Conversely, changes intended to influence the volume of private expenditure in the economy should be channeled through the capital and credit markets. However, this differentiation has evident limitations in cases where the various areas of financial markets are highly integrated.

Instrumentation in Other Countries

Reserve Requirements

Reserve requirements are still used by most European central banks. There are now only 3 European Union countries without any type of reserve requirement ratio: Belgium, Denmark, and Sweden. The United Kingdom could be included in this group were it not for a singular ratio of 0.35 per cent, which, at times, resembles a reserve requirement. However, the importance of this instrument in the operational framework has decreased in recent years, against a background in which the growth of financial markets and the move towards the full liberalization of capital movements between countries have encouraged financial innovations and cross-border shifts of bank deposits.

Still, there are significant differences in the role of the reserve requirement. Data for 1994 show that it was higher in Greece, Italy, and Portugal,[14] where the ratio was used by central banks to drain large quantities of liquidity from the system (see Table 12.3). In the other countries (except Austria and the Netherlands) the percentages of liquidity removed by the reserve requirement in 1994 were less than 2 per cent of GDP. In France, the figure was a minimal 0.1 per cent.

The differences in technical characteristics are also significant and affect the level of the reserve ratio – which ranges from a minimum of 0.35 per cent (considering the ratio applied in the United Kingdom) to 1 per cent in Finland and 15 per cent in Italy –, its remuneration (market, substantially below market, or zero), the definition of bank liabilities to which the ratio applies, the relative duration of the computation and maintenance periods for bank liabilities and reserves, the lag between the two, the possibility of complying with the compulsory ratio in terms of an average for the coverage period, etc. (see Table 12.3).

These differences are due in part to historical developments, but to a large extent, they also reflect discrepancies in the monetary policy function assigned to the reserve requirement by each central bank: reducing

Table 12.3 Characteristics of the reserve requirement in EU Countries*

	Spain	Germany	Austria	Belgium	Denmark	Finland	France	Greece	Netherlands	Italy	Ireland	Portugal	United Kingdom	Sweden
Level of the reserve requirement ratio	2%	1.5%–2% (depending on the deposit rate)	3%–5% (depending on the deposit rate)	Not applicable	Not applicable	1%–2% (depending on the deposit rate)	0.5%–1% (depending on the deposit rate)	9%[a]	variable[b]	15%	3%	2%	0.35%[c]	Not applicable
Remuneration	No	No	No	–	–	No	No	Yes (below-market)	Yes	Yes (below-market)	Yes	Yes (below-market)	No	–
Required reserves (% GDP) ++	1.4	1.3	2.8	–	–	1.3	0.1	4.3	3.7	6.7	1.3	16.5	0.2	–
Computation period	10 days	1 month	1 month	–	–	1 day	1 day	1 month	Not relevant	1 month	1 day	7 days	6 months	–
Maintenance period	10 days	1 month	1 month	–	–	1 month	1 month	1 month	Variable	1 month	1 month	7 days	6 months	–
Lag between the two	2 days	15 days	15 days	–	–	60 days	15 days	1 month	Not relevant	45 days	50 days	3 days	6 months	–
Averaging provisions	Yes	Yes	Yes	–	–	No	Yes	No	No	Yes	No	Yes	No	–

Notes:
a The maximum ratio applied to foreign currency deposits is 70%.
b The monetary ratio is applied in the Netherlands.
c In the United Kingdom, this ratio is calculated twice a year for the sole purpose of guaranteeing monetary income.
(*) With information to December 1995.
(+) According to central bank balance sheets for 1994.
Source: EMI (1995).

fluctuations in short-term interest rates, increasing the system's dependence on liquidity provided by the central bank, or tightening the central bank's control of the money supply.

At present, most central banks use reserve requirements primarily to stabilize short-term interest rates or to increase the reliance of banks on central bank financing. In some countries (Germany, Austria, Greece, and Italy), the reserve ratio is relatively high and its remuneration is low, which could also indicate that it is used to control the money stock. Yet, the existence of systems permitting compliance with the ratio in terms of period averages and fairly long lags between the computation and maintenance periods (Germany, Austria, and Italy) evidences its use primarily to stabilize the demand for reserves.[15] In France and in Spain, the extraordinary reduction in reserve requirements in recent years may have interfered at some point with their effectiveness in stabilizing interest rates.

Lastly, in Ireland, the Netherlands and Finland, the reserve requirement is used to increase reliance on central bank liquidity in a context of structural liquidity surplus, and in the United Kingdom solely to obtain a share of the monetary income which is considered compensation for the central bank's services to the banking system.

Current Techniques, Instruments and Procedures

Open Market Operations   In recent years, central banks have increasingly used open market operations as a liquidity injection technique.[16] Thus, in 1993 and 1994, the use of open market operations to supply liquidity in most countries averaged over 95 per cent of the overall total[17] (see Table 12.4). Only in Austria, Greece, Germany and the Netherlands were credit or deposit facilities still being used to supply a significant quantity of funds (100 per cent in Austria and 102 per cent in the Netherlands). This process has evolved in an environment where – as indicated above – orderly, short-term interest rate movements have become increasingly important in the various countries' monetary policy strategies and where open market operations have gained growing significance.

As Table 12.4 illustrates, one of the open market operations most widely used by most central banks to inject liquidity into the system is the execution of repo transactions with national securities. This is true for regular operations and, in most cases, for fine-tuning operations as well (Spain, Germany, Belgium, Denmark, France, Italy, Ireland, Portugal and the United Kingdom). Other operations, however, are gaining importance in some countries: outright operations in the United Kingdom, Belgium, Denmark, France and Sweden; currency swaps in Belgium, Sweden and Greece; and the issuance of central bank paper in Finland, the Netherlands, Denmark and the United Kingdom. In most cases, these are fine-tuning operations.

Table 12.4 Relative importance of open market operations and credit and deposit facilities in various central banks[1]

	Spain	Germany	Austria	Belgium	Denmark	Finland	France	Greece	Netherlands	Italy	Ireland	Portugal	United Kingdom	Sweden
Open market operations	**94.7**	**67.3**	**0.0**	**95.2**	**104.4**	**100.0**	**99.9**	**34.8**	**-2.7**	**97.5**	**97.0**	**117.2**	**95.6**	**101.6**
– Repos	120.3	76.7	0.0	117.6	98.1	-6.0	83.5	10.3	75.0	56.8	158.6	119.0	127.0	-77.5
– Outright purchases	11.4	2.2	0.0	28.2	52.1	0.0	16.4	0.0	0.0	0.0	0.0	0.0	51.2	72.0
– Other[2]	-37.0	-11.6	0.0	-50.6	-45.8	106.0	0.0	245.0	-77.7	40.7	-61.6	-1.8	-82.6	107.0
Credit and deposit facilities	**5.3**	**32.6**	**100.0**	**4.9**	**-4.4**	**0.0**	**0.1**	**65.2**	**102.7**	**2.6**	**3.0**	**-17.2**	**4.3**	**-1.6**
– Financing at below-market rates	0.0	31.8	100.0	3.9	0.0	0.0	0.0	90.1	102.7	2.4	0.0	0.0	0.0	0.0
– Financing at above-market rates	5.3[3]	0.8	0.0	3.1	0.0	0.0	0.1	5.9	0.0	0.2	8.3	0.0	4.3	0.5
– Deposit facility remunerated at below-market rates	0.0	0.0	0.0	-2.1	-4.4	0.0	0.0	-30.8	0.0	0.0	-5.3	-17.2	0.0	-2.1

Notes:
1 Average percentages calculated on the basis of the net supply of liquidity of various central banks for 1993 and 1994.
2 Including: currency swaps, currency repos, and issuance of paper by the respective central banks.
3 Including second-window loans.
Source: Escrivá J.L. and Fagán (1995).

The growing use of repos in central bank interventions is due to their greater flexibility in terms of frequency and, above all, their maturity. In addition, their effect on the conditions of markets in which the securities used as collateral are traded is practically nil, which is not always true for outright operations carried out in insufficiently liquid markets.

Operations of this type fulfill a wide variety of similar functions in all of the countries considered. In Spain, they are used to supply a growing share of liquidity. They can also be used to influence the trend of money market interest rates, signal their level, guide their day-to-day movements and, where applicable, reduce their volatility.

As for the specification of repos (both regular and fine-tuning), the differences in the basic characteristics (maturity, relative frequency, method of determining amounts, etc.) between countries are relatively few (see Table 12.5). Evidently, fine-tuning operations occur more frequently (daily or whenever daily changes in market conditions so dictate) than regular operations (which, in most cases, are weekly or fortnightly) and their maturity is shorter (between 1 day and one week in fine-tuning operations, except in Greece, and between one week and one month in regular operations, except in the Netherlands). As for counterparties, in most countries credit institutions are the reference group with which central banks conduct their regular intervention operations, while fine-tuning operations normally involve a smaller number of institutions, namely market-makers.

In this regard, the most important differences between the European countries are related to the greater or lesser involvement of central banks in the money markets via fine-tuning operations, and to collateral. Although in most countries negotiable public securities make up most of the collateral used by banks in intervention operations, private paper–normally non-negotiable–is also used to a large extent in some countries: Germany, Austria and the United Kingdom.

Credit and Deposit Facilities   Credit and deposit facilities exist in one form or another in all EU countries except Spain, although their use differs substantially from country to country. Credit facilities with non-market rates (above or below) and a deposit facility remunerated at below-market rates are the most common forms.

All EU countries except Denmark, the Netherlands and Spain have credit facilities with higher-than-market rates. In some of these countries, the role of the credit facility in signaling interest rate movements is more distinct (Lombard rate in Germany, 5–10 day pensions in France, special advances in Italy, etc.)

Only in Germany, Austria, the Netherlands and Greece are credit facilities with below-market rates used for this purpose (which is sometimes justified from the standpoint of offsetting the costs associated with the

Table 12.5 Open market operations

	Spain	Germany	Austria	Belgium	Denmark	Finland	France	Greece	Netherland	Italy	Ireland	Portugal	United Kingdom	Sweden
Regular														
Frequency	Every 10 days	Every week	–	Every week*	Every week	–	Twice a week	–	Every 4 days*	Every 4 days	–	Every week	Twice a month*	Every week
Maturity	10 days	14 days		7 days	14 days	–	1 week	–	2–8 days	Up to 1 month	–	7 days	2–5 weeks	15 days
Collateral	Govt paper CB paper	Govt and priv. paper	–	Govt and priv. paper	Govt paper	–	Govt and priv. paper*	–	Govt paper. priv. paper and CB paper	Govt paper	–	Govt paper and CB paper	Govt paper	Govt paper. priv. paper and CB paper MM
Counterparties	Cr Inst.	Cr Inst.	–	Cr Inst.	Cr Inst	–	Cr Inst.	–	Cr Inst.	–	–	Cr. Inst.+	Cr Inst	–
'Fine tuning'														
Frequency	Daily	Variable	Variable	Daily	Variable	Variable	Variable***	Variable	–	–	Daily	Variable	Variable	–
Maturity	1.2 days	1 or more days	1 week	3 days	>14 days	1 month	1 day	1–6 months	–	–	1 day; 1 month	> 7 days	2–3 weeks	–
Collateral	Govt paper and CB paper	Govt and priv. paper	Govt and priv. paper	Govt paper	CB paper	Govt paper, priv. paper CB paper MM	Govt and priv. paper**	Govt paper	–	–	Govt paper	Govt paper. CB paper	Govt paper. Treasury notes and bank notes	–
Counterparties	MM	Cr Inst.	Cr Inst.	MM	Cr Inst.	–	Cr Inst.	Cr Inst.	–	–	Cr Inst.	Cr Inst.	MM	–

Notes: * Regular operations are also carried out using collateralized loans. ** Includes mobilized bank credits. *** Fine-tuning operations are also carried out using collateralized loans. **CB paper:** Paper issued by the central bank. **CR Inst.:** Credit institutions, approximate **Cr Inst.+:** Larger group of institutions. **MM:** Market-makers. *Source:* Aspetsberber (1995) and EMI (1995) reserve requirement, although it should also be considered simply a result of historical inertia). Other central banks (Belgium and Italy) use this facility to broaden the spectrum of instruments capable of signaling monetary policy decisions. Lastly, Germany and Austria believe that the rediscount rate limits downward movements in market interest rates.

Five central banks in the European Union have a deposit facility remunerated at below-market rates: Denmark, Sweden, Finland, Ireland and Belgium. This facility is used to establish an interest rate floor.

In some countries of the Union (see Table 12.6), these facilities are combined to create a system to limit market interest rate movements (Belgium, Germany, Greece, Ireland, Italy, Portugal, Austria, Finland and Sweden) and to determine an official rate band or corridor, the width of which varies from country to country. In many cases, this system is combined with open market operations to guide interest rate movements more precisely within this corridor.

Table 12.6   Representative intervention interest rates[1]

	Upper limit	*Lower limit*	*Market rate*
Germany	Lombard (4.50%)	Discount rate (2.50%)	Repo tender (3.30%)
Austria	Lombard (4.75%)	Discount rate (2.50%)	Marginal repos (3.20%)
Belgium	Emergency rate (6.00%)	Discount rate (2.50%)	Marginal repos (3.20%)
Denmark		Discount rate (3.25%)	Certificate tender (3.80%)
Spain			10-days tender (7.75%)
France	5–10 day loans (5.50%)		Loan tender (3.70%)
Finland			Tender rate (3.75%)
Ireland	Short-term facility (6.25%)	1-day deposits (3.00%)	
Netherlands	Special advances (2.70%)	Regular advances (2.00%)	
Portugal	Emergency rate (9.00%)	Liquidity absorption rate (6.80%)	
United Kingdom	Base rate (6%%)		
Sweden	Loan rate (7.50%)	Deposit rate (6%)	Repo operations (6.90%)

Note:
1 Level at end-April 1996.
Source: Compiled by authors.

The Signaling Function: Comparative Analysis

Implementation of the set of credit and deposit facilities described in the preceding section has enabled many European countries to develop relatively complex signaling strategies, whereunder movements in credit facility interest rates tend to be more permanent (and longer-term) than movements in the interest rates of open market operations. This differs significantly from the instrumentation strategy currently pursued by the Banco de España. This section addresses this topic.

The situation in terms of signaling and providing information about the degree of monetary tightness is especially simple in Spain. There is only one official interest rate: the marginal 10-day repurchase rate. There is no public maximum rate such as the German *Lombard rate*, nor, consequently, is there an official band of maximum and minimum rates. The rates set by the Bank in its daily operations with market-makers to inject or drain liquidity are not official either. This simplicity in signaling and providing information on the degree of monetary tightness, which is a unique aspect of Spanish monetary policy instrumentation, merits a closer look.

Although it is somewhat elementary, perhaps it will be best to begin the discussion with the observation that if the authorities are to attain the desired level of short-term interest rates with any degree of efficiency, it is essential that economic agents should know what it is. Obviously, then, the level must be clearly stated. At the same time, however, sufficient room for discretionarity should be maintained so that the degree of monetary tightness can be adjusted without compromising the *credibility* of the channels through which interest rates are signaled.

Indeed, in the past at least, the need to allow room for manoeuvre was especially important when the prospective rate adjustment was prompted by the difficulty of maintaining a specific parity for the peseta, or by the need to have it appreciate or depreciate. One important consideration is that it is impossible to predict with any degree of accuracy how the rates should be adjusted to achieve the desired result. In responding to a movement in interest rates, the exchange rate will normally tend either to exceed or to fall below the targeted level, so that any change in the reference rates for this purpose should be made with extreme caution. Thus, European central banks have frequently *tested* the reaction of the exchange rate by giving a series of signals that a change in the degree of monetary tightness was imminent, so as to observe the effects on the exchange rate and ultimately be able to determine the most appropriate interest rate adjustment.

Moreover, the explicit announcement of daily intervention rates by the central bank can give them an *official* character, so that they are perceived as reflecting the degree of monetary tightness desired by the authorities, in response to the performance of the economy's fundamentals. This can lead to confusion if the daily rates respond solely to foreign exchange considerations or to mere liquidity or reserve requirement management. These concerns led the Banco de España to cease announcing daily intervention rates in February 1993 and to point to the marginal 10-day repurchase rate as the only official rate reflecting the degree of monetary tightness considered consistent with non-inflationary economic growth.

The wisdom of establishing an official fluctuation band for market interest rates has also been raised quite frequently. This proposal is made because many European central banks (with a few exceptions such as the Bank of England) have such a band. The precise definition of a band for market interest rates requires the use of two instruments: one for injecting or draining liquidity (which determines the lower limit of the band) and a punitive-type mechanism used to supply the liquidity requested by banks (which determines the upper limit).

The paradigmatic case is Germany, where the lower limit is determined by the rediscount rate of the commercial paper presented by institutions and the upper limit by the Lombard lending rate. In addition, the Bundesbank holds weekly tenders for the purchase of public and private securities with resale agreements, through which it supplies most of the liquidity. Market rates tend to hover around the tender rate and move away from it when upward (toward the Lombard rate) or downward (toward the rediscount rate) expectations prevail.

In Spain's case there is no lower limit similar to the rediscount rate. But this floor can be readily set in place via the offering to market-makers of repurchase transactions, on the following trading day, at times when downward pressure on market rates is detected. The upper limit is set by the rates demanded for last-resort loans. In both cases, however, the limits are *not* announced, which accords a considerable degree of discretionarity to the authorities.

Therefore, the apparent flexibility that moving the weekly repo rate within the band defined by the Lombard and discount rates provides to the German monetary authorities is not easily adaptable to Spain's situation. Moreover, the value of releasing the rate is debatable, as the authorities may feel compelled to advocate raising or lowering daily interest rates beyond the upper or lower limit of the band under intense positive or negative pressure on their currency. They would thus be forced to shift the position of the band or to broaden it, leading the market to alter its long-term expectations in a manner contrary to the requirements arising from domestic objectives. Obviously, to avoid these problems, a very wide band could be publicised, far removed from market interest rates. But it would then lose its value as a signal of the degree of monetary tightness and credit institutions using it to adjust their cash position would be unduly penalized.

On the other hand, the argument in favor of adopting an official band is that it would more closely align the formal instrumentation strategy with common practice in the rest of Europe and would thus allow for a more fluid transmission of interest rate movements in the European countries to the Banco de España's rates. In this same connection, in some European countries with equally significant foreign exchange constraints, the Lombard rate is suspended temporarily when a decision is made to support the local currency by raising daily interest rates above the Lombard rate.

Liquidity Loan Guarantees

There is broad consensus on the need for the liquidity lent to the banking system by central banks to be sufficiently guaranteed. In this way, two objectives are achieved: first, virtual elimination of credit risk in the operations of public institutions such as central banks; and second, greater stringency in the execution of monetary policy. However, in this area of instrumentation there are differences between the European countries, with respect to both the public or private nature of the paper used in liquidity injection operations and the financial characteristics of such instruments (negotiability, whether paperless or not, liquidity).

On the one hand, two countries – Germany and Austria – guarantee a majority portion of the liquidity granted to the banking system with private paper. Another, France, accepts banking institutions' private sector credit portfolio as collateral for the liquidity it lends them. In the remaining countries – except for some variations in the Netherlands and the United Kingdom – the paper of public issuers is used almost exclusively.

In this context, and as part of the preparatory third-stage monetary policy tasks being conducted in the EMI, the idea that collateral may be either public or private has gained ground. This position is further reinforced by the Maastricht Treaty's explicit prohibition of any type of preferential access to credit institutions by government administrations or agencies (Article 104A). However, the application of this rule is conditional upon the existence of private securities markets sufficiently liquid to allow for trading large amounts without thereby distorting price formation.

In Spain, this matter is compounded by the difficulties sometimes encountered as a result of the scarcity of eligible collateral. The persistence of these difficulties after successive reductions of the reserve requirement and the issuance of certificates of deposit has constituted the greatest hindrance to monetary policy instrumentation in Spain in recent years.[16]

In order to overcome these difficulties, the Banco de España has broadened recently the range of securities which may be pledged to secure operations, extending it to private fixed-income securities and equity. When specifying this set of securities, the Banco de España has taken into account the state of the preparatory work for determining the eligible assets for monetary policy operations in EMU. In this respect, the assets currently accepted constitute a good approximation to the securities traded in Spain which will appear in the lists to be published in 1998 specifying the assets which will be acceptedby the ESCB as collateral for its monetary policy lending operations. To date, the new assets are basically being used to secure overnight credit operations and so facilitate the smooth operation of the new real-time settlement system. Their use as collateral in monetary policy lending operations, which has already commenced in the daily lending operations, will become generalized during 1998.

OUTLOOK

This final section discusses the outlook for monetary policy instrumentation in the European countries and, more specifically, in Spain. This requires attempting to outline the most salient characteristics of the set of instruments expected to be available to the ESCB. Comparison of this operational framework with the current status of monetary instrumentation in the European countries (described on pp. 427–35) gives a rough idea of the adaptation that each EU country will have to make. The last section deals specifically with Spain.

Instrumentation of the Single Monetary Policy

As of its establishment (in July 1998), the ECB should make final decisions concerning the monetary policy strategy and the instrumentation model to be adopted by the European System of central banks (ESCB) in the third stage of Monetary Union. The Treaty stipulates, however, that the EMI should complete the preparatory tasks (essentially involving monetary policy instruments and operating procedures) prior to that date, to facilitate the decision-making process. This should make it possible to pinpoint sufficiently in advance where the greatest harmonization efforts are needed and to advance the discussion of optimum strategy and instrumentation models. The guidelines provided by the Treaty on these two aspects are imprecise. It establishes the attainment of price stability as a primary objective of the ESCB but says nothing about the best way of accomplishing it. References to the operational framework are also scant.

In the EMI, the discussion of monetary policy strategy is not closed (see EMI 1997b). So far, the decision has been to rule out the establishment of an exchange rate objective, as a strategy of this type is considered appropriate only for small, very open economies in which inflation is strongly influenced by the currency's exchange rate.

In addition, strategies establishing targets in terms of nominal income have been discorded, since data on changes in this variable become available with a delay and are subject to considerable revision. And so too have those anchored on interest rates, in view of the complexity of their application.

Moreover the decision on whether the ESCB would apply a monetary targeting or an inflation targeting strategy is still open. The persistence of numerous doubts about the economic and financial environment in which the ESCB will operate at the start of stage 3 argues against choosing one or the other of these two options at the current stage of the discussion. These uncertainties relate primarily to the degree of stability of the demand for money in the Union as a whole and to the changes that the monetary policy transmission mechanism could undergo, both in the Union as a whole and in each of the member countries. The preparatory tasks currently occupying the EMI include delving into both issues.

Much greater progress has been made with the operational framework. First, it is believed that the proper functioning of the single monetary policy should result in the leveling of interest rates in the euro interbank deposit market, in response to movements in official interest rates and/or the appearance of autonomous shocks affecting liquidity generation in some part of the Union.[20] This condition should hold, regardless of the degree of decentralization of monetary policy. It is further required that the ESCB should have sufficiently harmonized instruments to work with and the payments systems and interbank markets must be fully integrated.

Second, agreement has been reached concerning the functions and principles of the optimum operational framework.[21] As far as the functions are concerned, the set of instruments selected should make it possible to guide market interest rates, control their volatility, signal monetary policy intentions, provide financing to the banking system, drain liquidity, and influence the degree of banking system reliance on central bank liquidity. A second group of functions would include helping control the monetary aggregates and ensuring the proper functioning of payments systems.

The principles agreed upon are those of efficiency in attaining the proposed objectives, compliance with market rules, non-discrimination between institutions and issuers, decentralization, harmonization, simplicity and transparency, continuity, and conformity with the ESCB's decision-making structure. Only with respect to the principles of decentralization and harmonization could full implementation be made conditional upon non-interference with other principles and, in particular, with operating efficiency and costs. The principle of harmonization should apply both to the monetary policy instruments available to national central banks and to the collateral accepted in intervention operations. The difficulties involved in attaining this latter objective are not insignificant, given the current differences.

Lastly, agreement has been reached concerning the basic instrumentation model to be used in stage 3. This model was selected for two reasons: (1) it gives the ESCB a sufficient degree of flexibility, which is important as its decision-making bodies will be responsible from the outset of stage 3 for defining and executing monetary policy; and (2) it is consistent with the decentralized management of monetary policy, an option preferred by the various central banks as the discussion of this subject has progressed.

The basic instrumentation model in stage 3 would consist (see EMI, 1995 and 1997a;c), first, of both regular and fine-tuning open market operations. These would be carried out primarily with repos, although other options are available (outright purchases, currency swaps, issuance of central bank paper, etc). The main function of operations of this type would be to guide market interest rates, although they will normally be used to supply liquidity to the banking system and may also fulfill signaling functions.

Second, the ESCB will have at least two facilities: a credit facility with above-market interest rates and a deposit facility with below-market rates. Both facilities, which will be established without limits, will define a corridor for interest rate movements. In addition, the rates associated with both instruments could be used by the ESCB to signal changes in monetary policy stance. Lastly, it has been decided that, once in place, the ESCB should have the option of imposing a reserve requirement on credit institutions. Accordingly, it will be necessary to undertake the preparatory work sufficiently in advance, given that at present, significant differences remain between countries in terms of regulating this instrument. In principle, the reserve requirement should be defined in such a way that it fulfills the functions of stabilizing the bank reserves markets and facilitating monetary control.

It has also been agreed that the ESCB should operate with a broad set of counterparties.[22] To seek to overcome the difficulty of harmonizing the collateral used in intervention operations, two lists have been created. The first lists the securities issued by the various countries which are approved by the ECB and which must be accepted by all central banks. The second, a national list, is designed to preserve *individual* operating practices established in various countries at the request of national central banks, in accordance with ECB guidelines. Care must nevertheless be taken to ensure that public and private securities are treated equally. In general, the specific characteristics of the various instruments have yet to be determined, although, as indicated above, the instruments should be fully operational by early 1999.[23]

In view of the discussion in this and in previous sections, the instrument-ation strategies currently being pursued in most European central banks will have to undergo some changes in the near future to adapt them to the model that will prevail once the Monetary Union is formed. The changes to be made in Spain are outlined in the following section.

The Adaptation of Spanish Monetary Policy

Technically speaking, the Banco de España's current instrumentation strat-egy differs from the proposal for monetary policy implementation in the third stage of Monetary Union. But the differences are more apparent than real, with the sole exception of the collateral accepted as security for loans to the banking system.

In fact, for the most part, both approaches are based on repurchase ten-ders, both 10-day (regular) and daily (fine-tuning). In this respect, then, instrumentation in the third stage would be a continuation of Banco de España's current practice.

As far as the official limits on intervention rates are concerned, the pro-posal approved by the EMI consists of setting an upper rate through a Lombard-type loan, and a lower rate through the remuneration of daily deposits made by banking institutions and accepted automatically by the ESCB. Neither of these instruments is currently used by the Banco de España, but both can be easily set in place. The first would use the system currently supporting monetary regulation loans. The change would have greater implications for strategy than for operations: the upper interven-tion rates would be fixed publicly. The second instrument, which involves reverse repurchase transactions with market-makers, can be implemented immediately. Again, the implications are more general than technical. The current system is more market-oriented, insofar as market-makers are responsible for taking up or intermediating in the drainage of excess liquid-ity, which steps up trading in the interbank market. Under the automatic deposit system open to all institutions, however, this would cease to be the case.

Therefore, what has been called the *basic framework* for instrumentation of the single monetary policy could easily be applied by the Banco de España. This is also true in many other respects.

The issues posing most difficulties in terms of adapting Spanish monet-ary policy implementation are the changes needed to payment systems and the use, as collateral, of private paper, since Spanish implementation focuses on government paper.

In the payment system area, the reform to adapt the Spanish system to the requirements of the future European system for the settlement of large-value payments, known as 'TARGET', is under way. TARGET will be a basic element in the operation of the euro money market and in the implementation of the single monetary policy from 1999. As a consequence of this reform, the various interbank operations channelled through the Money Market On-Line Service are gradually being incorporated into a new settlement system which grants them finality at the time they are made. The first step was to introduce in the real-time process pure fund transfers, which are the simplest ones as no prior clearing process is involved. The next step involved the introduction of real-time settlement for the clearing systems of specific markets (i.e. fixed-income private markets, stock exchange market, derivatives markets). The next step closing the system has been the introduction of real-time into large-value payment systems. The aforementioned mechanisms support payment flows for the entire financial system, both domestically and in its relations with other national systems. This process will continue during 1998.

In relation to eligible assets for loans to eligible counterparties, the Banco de España has, under a gradualist approach, initiated the use of private paper as collateral, subject to certain restrictions. As a result, private bonds and equities traded on official markets have been admitterd as collateral since May 1997. On specifying this set of securities, the Banco de España has taken into account the state of the preparatory work for determining the eligible assets for monetary policy operations in EMU. In this respect, the assets currently admitted are a good approximation to the securities traded in Spain which will feature in the lists to be published in 1998 specifying the assets which will be accepted by the ESCB as collateral for its monetary policy lending operations.

Due to the non-existence of repo transactions in the official organized markets other than the market for book-entry debt, securities are at present only being mobilised via pledging. The necessary involvement of a notary public in this pocedure entails considerable cost and administrative delay, whereby institutions' use of this mechanism would at this intial stage probably be limited.

The inclusion of private securities traded on the stock and AIAF markets in regular open market operations via repos poses more difficulties. But these are in the process of being ironed out. The main problems are of a legal nature: the lack of regulations in these markets for transacting repo operations and the Banco de España's lack of legal capacity to operate in them. In all likelihood, the Banco de España will be able to mobilize these securities via repos by the first quarter of 1998, once the technical difficulties have been overcome and after having reformed the legal underpinnings of the workings of the aforementioned official markets.

At present, these securities are used both as collateral for intra-day credit operations – related, as earlier stated, to the TARGET system

– and for monetary policy lending operations in daily interventions. In 1998, once the above- mentioned reform is complete, their use will be extended to the monetary policy operations implemented via the ten-day repurchase tender.

There are admittedly difficulties in fully incorporating repo operations with private paper into the general implementation framework. But it seems clear that the inclusion of private securities in the Banco de España's open market operations increases the range of guarantees and allows not only for a larger volume of collateral, but also greater balance in the use of public and private securities for implementaion purposes. Moreover, and as was true of public securities in the past, the Banco de España's acceptance of private paper in its intervention operations may promote the growth of private markets.

Notes

1   Monetary control in Spain, the development of which in recent years is described in Ayuso and Escrivá (1996), Chapter 3 in this volume and, previously, in Escrivá and Malo de Molina (1991) and in Ayuso and Escrivá (1993), has largely followed this pattern. The liberalization of the Spanish economy in the latter part of the 1980s and the entry into exchange rate agreements in the context of the EU have determined the selection of overnight interest rates as the instrumental variable. Escrivá and Santos (1991) give a detailed account of the theoretical and empirical reasons for this change in the instrumental variable.

2   For more information on how this relates to Spain, see: Banco de España (1990); Sanz and Val de Lara (1993), and Santos (1993).

3   A discussion of the stabilizing function of the reserve requirement can be found in Santos (1993) and Ayuso, Haldane and Restoy (1994).

4   It should be pointed out that this situation is useful more for explanatory purposes than as a description of reality since, in practice, and given the fact that institutions' current accounts with the Banco de España are subject both to compliance with the reserve requirement and to settlement of their operations in the interbank markets, they will always tend to have sufficient balances to settle their net debtor positions.

5   Certain institutions, such as credit cooperatives, can comply on a monthly basis, in which case they do not participate in the 10-day tender.

6   Moreover, the Banco de España does not use margins or any other type of measure to prevent a hypothetical movement (downward) in the market price of the collateral from leaving a marginal portion of the liquidity provided without *effective* guarantees. The very short term of the operations and the high quality of the paper accepted make it unnecessary.

7   It should be pointed out, however, that individual loans are not an automatic means of gaining access to central bank liquidity by the institutions. On the contrary, the authorities decide whether to grant such requests on the basis of the conditions they wish to create in the money market.

8   A grouping of these characteristics can be found in Escrivá and Fagán (1995). According to the latter, central bank Credit to the Banking System (ACSB) results from:

$$ACSB = E - ANE - CNSP + OPN + AC$$

where:
E   = cash held by the public
ANE = net external assets
CNSP = net credit to the public sector
OPN = other net liabilities
AC   = bank reserves and balance of CEBES

9   A more detailed analysis of the autonomous liquidity factors in the period prior to the reform of the reserve requirement can be found in Sanz and Val de Lara (1993).

10 Ayuso Hardane and Restoy (1994), based on the estimation of equations for the mean and conditional variance of interbank market interest rates in various periods between January 1988 and January 1993, find that the adjustment of overnight rates to movements in official rates is complete within the space of two days, and that the degree of adjustment decreases as the maturity of the operation increases. By means of a correlation analysis, Estrada, Sastre and Vega (1994) also show how quickly official interest rate movements are transmitted to the various tranches of the yield curve in the period January 1988–September 1993. A new estimate of said correlations for 1993–5 confirms these results and yields values ranging from 74 per cent for the 4-month term and 65 per cent for the 4-year term.

11 For purposes of monetary policy management, the other funds-transfer systems and the specific details of the conversion in progress can be ignored.

12 It remains to be seen what actual difficulties the new system will pose. In any case, it is likely that some institutions will have intra-day cash balances large enough to lend, while most of them may have an hour-to-hour profile of debits and credits in their accounts that will require them to borrow funds throughout most of the session, since it is only toward the end of the session that cash payments are received. If the banking system as a whole, i.e. its net position, were subject to such *profiles*, it would have to turn to the central bank – especially in the event of a net liquidity shortage during the day – to smooth the settlement of operations. Hence, the so-called *intra-day liquidity market*.

13 For an overview and general discussion of the organization of national monetary control frameworks, see Goodhart and Viñals (1994).

14 In Portugal in 1995, the reserve requirement was reduced very substantially, which, of course, reduced the volume of funds drained with this instrument.

15 An overview of the role of the reserve requirement in Germany can be found in Deutsche Bundesbank (1994).

16 A comparative analysis of open market operations can be found in Aspetsberger (1995).

17 As this information suggests, all EU central banks provide financing on net terms to the corresponding credit institutions. This does not mean, however, that in all of the countries in question the effect of the autonomous liquidity generation factors systematically results in debtor positions with the central

bank. In fact, in the Netherlands and Finland, the resulting net position is a creditor position. However, the imposition of a reserve requirement in the former and the issuance of central bank paper in the latter ultimately led to bank dependency on liquidity provided by the central bank.

18   For this reason, currency swaps have been used also to control liquidity: purchases of foreign currency with resale agreements, using pesetas.

19   The main references are contained in Articles 19 (reserve requirement) and 20 (other monetary control instruments) of the Statutes of the ESCB and the European central bank.

20   This does not mean complete uniformity in the degree of monetary tightness in the various countries. Differences will persist in economic and financial structures, which will prevent monetary policy decisions from having the same effect in the various countries.

21   The principles to be adhered to in the selected operational framework are described in the EMI Convergence Report, published in the autumn of 1995. The functions are explained in the EMI Annual Report for 1995.

22   The EMI is currently working on defining this set of counterparties. In principle, it could be even broader than that made up by credit institutions. Thus, the possibility of including the mutual funds operating in the money markets is under consideration, although this decision will ultimately be determined by risk control considerations.

23   Accordingly, it may be necessary for the preparatory work to be completed by end-1997, which would allow a margin of approximately six months to evaluate their performance.

References

ASPETSBERBER, A. (1995) 'Open market operations in EU countries', *Staff Paper*, 3, European Monetary Institute.

AYUSO, J. and J.L. ESCRIVÁ (1993) 'La evolución del control monetario en España', *Working Document*, 9325, Research Department, Banco de España.

AYUSO, J. and J.L. ESCRIVÁ (1996) 'Trends in the monetary policy strategy in Spain', in this volume.

AYUSO, J.A.G. HALDANE and F. RESTOY (1994) 'Volatility transmission along the money market yield curve', *Working Document*, 9403, Research Department, Banco de España.

BANCO DE ESPAÑA (1990) 'Cambios recientes en la instrumentación de la política monetaria', *Boletin Económico*, Banco de España, May.

DEUTSCHE BUNDESBANK (1994) 'Money market management by the Deutsche Bundesbank', *Deutsche Bundesbank Monthly Report*, May.

ESCRIVÁ J.L. and G.P. FAGÁN (1995) 'Empirical assessment of monetary policy and procedures in EU countries', *Staff Paper*, 2, European Monetary Institute.

ESCRIVÁ, J.L. and J.L. MALO DE MOLINA (1991) 'La instrumentación de la política monetaria española en el marco de la integración europea', *Working Document*, 9104, Research Department, Banco de España.

ESCRIVÁ, J.L. and R. SANTOS (1991) 'Un estudio del cambio de régimen en la variable instrumental del control monetario en España', *Working Document*, 9111, Research Department, Banco de España.

ESTRADA, A.M.T. SASTRE and J.L. VEGA (1994) 'El mecanismo de transmisión de los tipos de interés: el caso español', *Working Document*, 9408, Research Department, Banco de España.

EUROPEAN MONETARY INSTITUTE (EMI) (1995a) *Progress towards convergence*, November.
EUROPEAN MONETARY INSTITUTE (EMI) (1995b), *Annual report*, 1994.
EUROPEAN MONETARY INSTITUTE (EMI) (1996), *Annual report*, 1995.
EUROPEAN MONETARY INSTITUTE (EMI) (1997a), *The single monetary policy in stage Three. Specification of the operational framework.*
EUROPEAN MONETARY INSTITUTE (EMI 1997b), *The single monetary policy in stage Three. Elements of the monetary policy strategy of the ESCB.*
EUROPEAN MONETARY INSTITUTE (EMI 1997c), *The single monetary policy in stage Three. General Documentation on ESCB monetary policy instruments and procedures*
GIL, G. and S. NÚÑEZ (1995) 'Sistema de pagos en España: presente y futuro', *XXII Jornadas de Mercado Monetario*, Intermoney.
GOODHART, C.A.E. and J.M. VIÑALS (1994) 'Strategy and tactics of monetary policy: examples from Europe and the antipodes', *Working Document*, 9425, Research Department, Banco de España.
NÚÑEZ, S. (1994) 'Perspectivas de los sistemas de pagos. Una reflexión crítica', *Working Document*, 9429, Research Department, Banco de España.
QUIRÓS, G. (1995) 'Mercados financieros alemanes', *Working Document*, 9528, Research Department, Banco de España.
SÁNCHEZ SOLIÑO, A. (1996) 'La Union Monetaria y la liquidación de las operaciones de mercado monetario', *Perspectivas del Sistema Financiero*, 53, FIES.
SANTOS, R. (1993), 'On the reserve requirement and the process of Monetary Union', *Economic Bulletin*, Banco de España, October.
SANZ, B. and M. VAL DE LARA (1993), 'Monetary implementation techniques in Spain', *Economic Bulletin*, Banco de España, October.

Part IV
The Monetary Policy
Transmission Mechanism

13 The Role of the Banking System in the Monetary Transmission Mechanism

María Teresa Sastre de Miguel

INTRODUCTION

Economic theory has always attached particular importance to the role played by banking intermediaries in the monetary policy transmission mechanism. Their ability to issue highly liquid assets and thereby contribute to the money creation process makes them key agents in determining the growth of the money supply in an economy. Nevertheless, in the 1970s neither the academic world nor the economic authorities paid much attention to banking behavior, since they considered that changes in the stock of money were basically determined, and with considerable precision, by central bank control of the monetary base and changes in the cash reserve requirement. For that reason, the money supply was considered exogenous.

The process of financial liberalization and innovation in the 1980s rendered this approach to monetary analysis unsustainable. Renewed attention was paid to the theories of some economists who, in the 1950s had underscored the importance of financial intermediation in the execution of monetary policy.[1] In the 1980s recognition of the existence of market imperfections derived from a lack of perfect information, led to numerous articles stressing, once again, the importance of financial markets and intermediaries in the allocation of capital in an economy, given their particular ability to cope with such imperfections. The type of financial institutions and instruments that constitute the financial structure of an economy, together with the criteria that guide their decisions, have, in this view, a major influence on the savings and investment plans of non financial agents and hence on the economy's real activity.[2]

More recently, this school of thought has opted for the analysis of several mechanisms – other than the traditional money and interest rate channels – through which various aspects of the financial structure of an economy eventually affect the level of activity. One of these channels is what is now known as the *credit channel*, which underscores the importance

of bank loans in the monetary transmission process, due to imperfect substitutability among the several items of bank balance sheets and among the
different sources of funding of some non financial agents. According to
this approach, the decisions taken by banking institutions regarding the
availability of credit after shifts in the degree of monetary restriction affect
the expenditure plans of other economic agents, thereby heightening the
impact of monetary policy on the level of economic activity. A study of the
credit channel in the Spanish case is to be found in an article by Hernando
(1997).

In recent years, attention has also focused on the importance of another
type of financial mechanism operating via changes in the present value of
the net wealth of economic agents and which differs from the wealth effect
– the impact of interest rates on the market value of this wealth. These
changes necessarily affect the value of the collateral available to back the
demand for funding and may therefore lead to fluctuations in the level of
expenditure of agents. However, the shifts in the present value of the assets
and liabilities making up the net wealth of economic agents also influence
the cost of borrowed funds by affecting the availability of funds and the
interest rates charged by lenders.

Even more recently, some authors have considered both channels – the
bank credit channel and that wrought by changes in the value of the net
wealth of economic agents – as part of a credit channel in the broad sense,
which operates when the *supply of credit* diminishes, either because of
imperfect substitution of diverse bank assets or because of changes in the
net wealth value, and which tends to reinforce, through several ways, the
traditional transmission mechanism via the interest rate.[3]

Thus, a broad consensus appears to have been reached regarding the
importance of financial conditions in explaining the fluctuations in the level
of economic activity. In that sense, the financial institutions and markets
that play an important role in channeling the flow of savings and funds are
those with the greatest potential capacity to influence the expenditure decisions of economic agents. As providers of borrowed funds and of instruments in which private sector savings can be invested, banking institutions
are key factors in financial transmission mechanisms.

In the traditional interest rate mechanism, the decisions taken by banking institutions regarding their deposit and lending rates have a direct
impact on the cost of borrowed funds and incentives to save. This affects
consumption, because it alters the relative attractiveness of saving *vis-à-vis*
expenditure (substitution effect), modifies the disposable income derived
from the net revenue provided by the various assets and liabilities that constitute wealth (income effect), and changes the market value of wealth
(wealth effect). Likewise, investment is affected by the cost of borrowing,
which alters the user cost of capital (substitution effect) and companies'

net interest payments (income effect). In this way, various components of aggregate demand are affected by the interest rate levels set by banking institutions. Estrada, Hernands and Valles (1996) provide some evidence of this impact, although it only makes reference to the interest rate substitution effect.

According to the bank credit channel, banks can exert considerable influence on the availability of borrowed funds, given the scant extent to which banks financing can be substituted by alternative sources of funding for certain groups of economic agents. Thus the ability of consumers and companies to undertake new expenditure plans can change.

Finally, within the risk assessment process associated with lending, banks review borrowers' collateral and, on this basis, determine how much to lend and at what rate. Similarly, the decisions they take on the interest they are prepared to pay on savings instruments affect the level and distribution of the net wealth of economic agents and hence the value of the collateral put up by borrowers.

In the case of Spain, the share of banking intermediaries in the overall assets and liabilities that make up the financial wealth of the private sector is relatively large. Credit institutions handle around 55 per cent of the financial liabilities of households and a similar proportion of their assets – more than 65 per cent if investment funds are included. In the case of firms, the proportions are somewhat lower (30 per cent of liabilities and 25 per cent of assets), given the greater importance of inter-company loans and self-financing.

In recent years, however, banks have become much less important as channelers of financial flows in various countries. More and more economic agents are taking advantage of the development of non intermediated financial markets and of the notably stronger competition among credit and savings institutions as a result of the emergence of new financial intermediaries.

Nevertheless, banks continue to play a key role in financing most borrowers, particularly those for whom bank loans are the only source of funds. This is true of households and small firms, although the latter also have acces to the trade credit provided by suppliers. Informational asymmetries characterizing this group of borrowers are much stronger than that of other groups and exacerbates the difficulty of tapping nonbank financial markets which usually entails a high level of fixed costs. Banks are specially equipped to deal with such market imperfections derived from asymmetric information in credit markets, since they enjoy cost advantages in monitoring and assessing risks and can obtain information through customer relationships.[4]

In the same vein, the development of nonintermediated financial markets and new instruments, as well as of non-bank intermediaries, has not stopped banking institutions from being the main depositories of the savings of a large group of savers who maintain their preference for traditional institutions of proven solvency.

For that reason it is worth to analyze the decisions that guide banking behavior as a way to improve our understanding of the process of transmission of monetary impulses to the real economy.

This chapter analyzes banks' interest rate decisions. Thus it focuses on one of the phases in the traditional mechanism of the monetary transmission via interest rates. Hernando (1997) reviews the evidence of a credit channel in the Spanish case, its impact on the composition of the borrowed funds of firms, and the differential between bank lending rates and market rates. In addition, Chapter 15 examines the impact of agents' balance sheet in determining the sign and dimensions of the income and wealth effects, and at the same time, the degree to which such effects are influenced by banking activities.

The aim of this chapter is to describe the factors that have influenced interest rates in the Spanish banking system since the interest rate liberalization process was completed in the second half of the 1980s and to analyze the effect they have had on the monetary transmission process in practice. To that end, we first outline some of the typical features of the historical behavior of interest rates, and then analyze the major factors in more recent interest rate trends.

BASIC FEATURES OF THE BEHAVIOUR OF BANK INTEREST RATES

An initial insight into some of the main characteristics of the interest rates in the Spanish banking system can be derived from an analysis of the relationship between the deposit and lending rates of banks and savings banks and those in money and government debt markets. The latter are usually considered the 'market rates', in the sense that they reflect the relevant opportunity cost of the deposit and lending interest rate decisions taken by banking institutions. In addition, these market rates reflect in a different way shifts in the Banco de España's intervention rate and, consequently, variations in the tone of monetary policy.[5] Thus, an adequate description of the main characteristics of the relationship between these market rates and the interest rates set by banks is indeed relevant when it comes to analyzing the transmission of monetary impulses to bank interest rates.

There are numerous interesting aspects of this relationship, but perhaps the most important ones from the point of view of the monetary transmission mechanism can be summarized in the following questions:

- To what extent, and how swiftly, do bank interest rates respond to variations in market rates?
- Do bank deposit and lending rates react in the same way?
- Have the liberalization of financial markets, the internationalization of the Spanish economy, and the hightening of competition in the banking sector noticeably altered the relationship between bank rates and market rates?
- Do interest rates for different kinds of banking operations react in a homogeneous fashion? Do different institutions react in different ways?

To answer these questions, we have used data on interest rates for new operations carried out each month that deposit money institutions regularly report to the Banco de España. To simplify the analysis, we use composite rates with different degrees of aggregation (by term and/or instrument), which are weighted averages of the interest rates of the borrowing and lending transactions of Spanish banking institutions.[6]

The financial institutions studied in this chapter comprises private banks and savings banks. Although credit cooperatives are also deposit-money institutions, they have not been included in the analysis because information on their interest rates is only available for a short period.

Using these data on the composite deposit and lending rates of the banks and savings banks in question, we calculated several correlations with market rates considered to be sufficiently representative. Specifically,we used the interest rate for 3-month interbank operations and the internal rate of return on government debt with an over-2-year maturity. Table 13.1 presents those correlations obtained using the quarterly data of the corresponding stationary series from the time when bank lending rates and most deposit rates were liberalized, i.e. for the period between the second quarter of 1981 and the fourth quarter of 1995. Likewise, figures are given for the period since the creation of the Central Book-Entry Office for government debt trading, for which homogeneous data are available for the internal rate of return on government debt.

The behavior of the differentials between lending and deposit rates and market rates is indicative of the intensity and speed with which the former respond to changes in the latter. If that response were of the same magnitude as the changes, and if it were instantaneous, the differentials would be constant and the correlation between them and market rates would be zero. However, as Figure 13.1 shows, the differential between the interest rates of banking institutions increases when money market rates fall, and decreases in periods in which the latter increase, thereby giving rise to a correlation of a negative sign (see Table 13.1), reflecting a contemporary – within the same quarter – response of less than unity. This finding holds

Table 13.1 Bank rates and market rates, banks and savings banks, Pearson's correlation coefficient[1]

	Interbank rate[2] (*1st diff.*)	Debt rate[3] (*1st diff.*)
Period: 1981: III–1995: IV		
Lending rate (1st diff.)	0.69	n.a.
Deposit rate (1st diff.)	0.39	n.a.
Lending rate – Deposit rate (1st diff.)	0.77	n.a.
Lending rate – Interbank rate	−0.48	n.a.
Deposit rate – Interbank rate	−0.34	n.a.
Period: 1987: IV–1995: IV		
Lending rate (1st diff.)	0.82	0.60
Deposit rate (1st diff.)	0.60	0.47
Lending rate – Deposit rate (1st diff.)	0.84	0.58
Lending rate – Interbank rate	−0.52	−0.48
Deposit rate – Interbank rate	–	–
Lending rate – Debt rate	−0.42	−0.56
Deposit rate – Debt rate	−0.40	−0.54

Notes:
1 Dashes indicate non-significant correlations.
2 Average rate for 3-month interbank operations.
3 Internal rate of return on government debt securities maturing at more than 2 years.

when we calculate correlations with the interest rates on the secondary government debt market.

On the other hand, the lack of correlation between the deposit rate differential and variations in the 3-month interbank rate in the final part of the sample (see Table 13.1) is related to the tendency for this differential to diminish, in absolute terms, since price competition in bank deposits began.[7]

Although both the composite lending rate and the corresponding composite deposit rate reacted less strongly than the changes recorded in market rates, the former have in the past responded more than the latter. This is reflected in the higher correlations in Table 13.1 for lending rates.[8] As a result, the spread between deposit and lending rates has, on average, remained in line with market rates (see the positive correlation in Table 13.1) and, basically, with money market interest rates (see Figure 13.2), which are, in the first instance, the ones that reflect steps taken by the monetary authorities.

The extent of the connection between bank interest rates and money market rates has increased notably in the 1990s, with much swifter responses and an increase in the overall long-term impact, for both lending

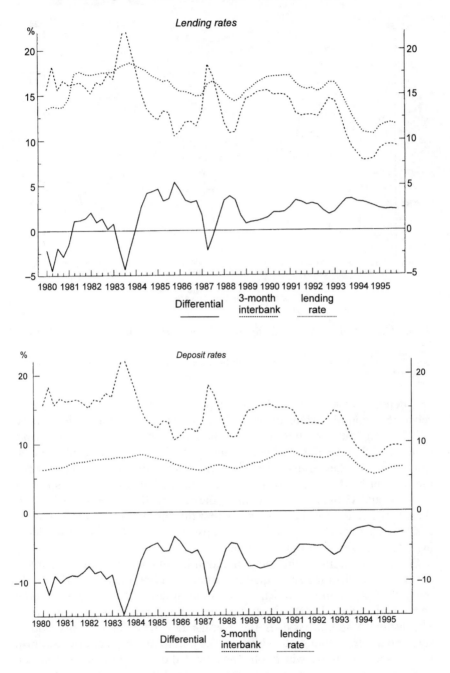

Figure 13.1 Bank interest rates and market interest rates

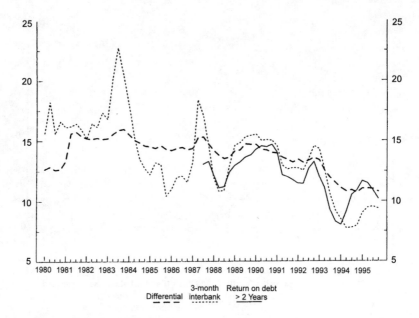

Figure 13.2 Market rates and differential[1] between lending and deposit rates, 1980–95

Note: 1 We have made the average value of the differential coincide with the sample average of the interbank rate

and deposit rates. This can be observed in Figures 13.3 and 13.4, which relate the monthly values of banks' and savings banks' composite deposit and lending rates to the official Banco de España rate for the same months, while revealing, through a unitary sloping line, what could be considered a complete transmission.[9] In the 1980s, the connection between the rate set by the monetary authorities and the lending rate was still very tenuous, and virtually non existent in the case of the deposit rate. Nevertheless, the charts for the 1990s show that this link has gradually increased, and is currently on the complete transmission line in the case of the lending rate and close to it in the case of the deposit rate.

Evidence pointing in the same direction is obtained when a comparison is made of the lending rate equations in Sastre (1991) and Sáez (1996). In the first of these studies, which analyzes the situation in the 1980s, for both banks and savings banks, the composite lending rate was determined by establishing a spread *vis-à-vis* the average rate paid for deposits, with a very moderate response to shifts in the interbank market. By contrast, in the second study, which observes how the transmission mechanism works in a more recent period – end of the 1980s and the 1990s – the response of bank lending rates to movements in the overnight interbank

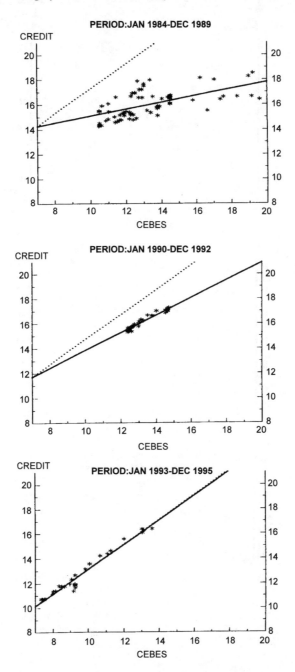

Figure 13.3 Relation between lending rate and the Banco de España intervention rate

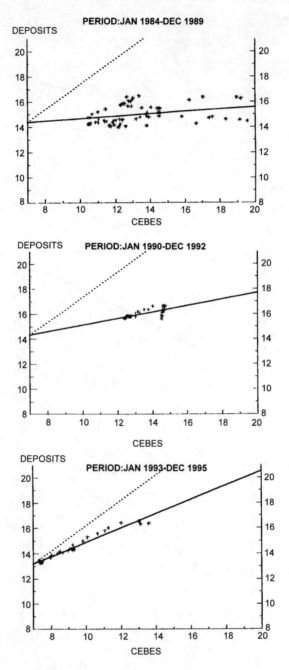

Figure 13.4 Relation between deposit interest rate and Banco de España intervention rate, 1984–95

rate is close to unity, and is swifter than that reflected in the first study's specifications.

In the following section of this chapter, we examine the factors underlying this greater speed and intensity in the process of transmission of monetary policy to the cost of bank financing and the yield on deposits.

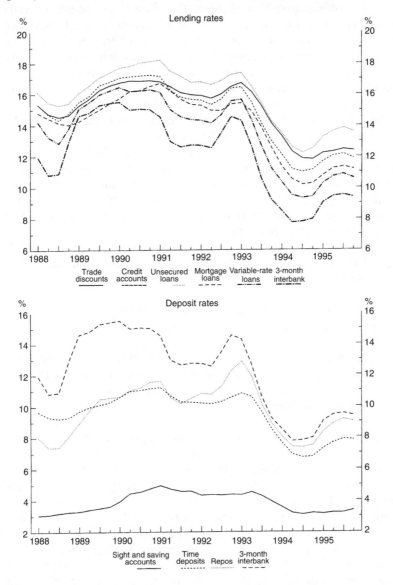

Figure 13.5   Composite rates by instrument

So far, information has been provided for composite interest rates, which incorporate a high level of aggregation. However, when disaggregated by instrument (see Figure 13.5),[10] considerable differences emerge in both the level and behavior over time of the respective interest rates. Thus the interest rate for unsecured loans, for instance, is consistently higher than that for mortgage-backed loans. The same is true of interest rates on fixed term deposits and repos *vis-à-vis* current accounts and savings accounts. Similarly, Sáez, Sánchez and Sastre (1994) show major differences in the degree of transmission of monetary impulses in the case of more novel instruments available on the Spanish banking market at the end of the 1980s – variable interest rate loans and repos – compared with more traditional instruments – fixed-rate loans and deposits.

The same paper also shows how different terms, for the same instrument, produce only very slight differences in degree of response to changes in market rates, mainly because most lending and deposit operations are for a typical term (trade discounting tends to be for 3 months, mortgages for periods of over 5 years, while current accounts and savings deposits are usually at sight. Only in the case of fixed-term deposits is there a clearly different degree of sensitivity between those with maturities of 1 year or less and those with longer terms.

Table 13.2 shows the dynamic response of interest rates for various kinds of lending and deposit operations to shifts in the 3-month interbank rate. The main findings are:

- In almost all lending transactions, the overall long-term effect is close to unity; in contrast, deposit rates respond more slowly, and the total effect is less
- The kinds of credit that react most swiftly to shifts in interbank rates are credit accounts and, especially, variable interest rate loans without mortgage backing. On the deposit side, government debt repos are the quickest to react and show the greatest overall impact.

These differences in the level and sensitivity of bank rates to changes in one of the short-term markets may partly be due to differences in the management costs of the various transactions under consideration. However, the most obvious reason for these differences is the fact that the instruments – on the lending or deposit side – are not perfect substitutes, either because each has a different purpose or because the kind of client differs.

One example of instruments that appear to be used for different purposes is the case of current accounts as opposed to time deposits. Although – during the period known as the 'super accounts war' – they had a high degree of substitutability, they have now become clearly differentiated. Thus both savings accounts and current accounts today appear to serve

Table 13.2 Dynamic response of bank interest rates, classification by instrument
(Effective period: 1988: IV–1995: IV)

| | Banks and savings banks | | | |
	Contemp.	Half-year	1 year	Total
Loans				
● Fixed-rate credit				
● Trade discount	0.33	0.52	0.71	0.85
● Credit accounts	0.57	0.72	0.86	0.94
● Unsecured loans	0.44	0.65	0.79	0.82
● Mortgage loans	0.34	0.60	0.87	0.93
● Variable-rate credit	0.71	0.89	0.98	1.01
Deposits				
Current and savings accounts	0.05	0.14	0.22	0.26
Time deposits	0.28	0.49	0.68	0.66
Repos	0.59	0.81	0.84	0.81

Note: Responses obtained by estimating equations with an error correction
mechanism to capture the relationship between the interest rate on each kind of
loan and deposit and the 3-month interbank rate.

mainly as means of payment, while time deposits are one means of invest-
ing savings in order to obtain a market rate return; accordingly, their interest rates tend to move more in line with money market and government
debt market rates.

An alternative to a breakdown by instrument is to disaggregate according to groups of banking institutions that supposedly adopt similar pricing
policies. One criterion that could serve to make this kind of classification
is product specialization, which is defined by the market segment or segments that each institution targets. Sánchez and Sastre (1995) test the
validity of this criterion for obtaining groups of institutions which are relatively homogeneous, but at the same time sufficiently differentiated. Their
findings indicate that the type of customer or market segment that an institution targets significantly affects its price policy, profitability, and solvency. Manzano and Galmés (1996) also confirm the validity of this
classification when they estimate differing impacts of interbank interest
rates on intermediaries' price policies, depending on their product specialization.

Taking this criterion and using statistical techniques known as clustering,
Sánchez and Sastre (1995) arrive at four groups of institutions:

– *Group 1* Includes mainly national commercial banks, covering, according to average 1995 data, 46 per cent of bank loans and the same proportion of private sector deposits at banks and savings banks.

– *Group 2* Comprises almost all savings banks. Its market share of the sector's total loans is also 46 per cent. In private sector creditor funds, the figure is 50 per cent.
– *Group 3* Consisting mostly of foreign banks and a small number of national banks. It absorbs 13 per cent of the market of personal documented loans and 11 per cent of variable rate financing.
– *Group 4* Merchant banks and others devoted to activities other than commercial banking. This group plays only a minor role in traditional banking sector transactions with the private sector.

Figure 13.6 shows the composite lending and deposit rates for these four groups.[11] Considerable differences in behavior can be observed, especially as regards the composite rate for deposits. Group 4 offers the highest return on savings, while the remaining groups also differ significantly among themselves, although such differences have become less marked in recent years.

The composite lending rates in Groups 1 and 2 show roughly similar behavior and are generally higher than those set by non-commercial and foreign banks – Groups 3 and 4. These charts also show that the differences in interest rate levels of the four groups considered are greater on the deposit side than in respect of loans.

In concluding this section, the following points summarize the main features of the relationship between bank interest rates and money market and debt market rates:

1 Historically, bank interest rates have been moderately sensitive to changes in market rates, as shown by long-term responses of less than unity and by relatively prolonged responses.
2 The extent to which variations in money market interest rates are transmitted to lending rates is greater, on average, than for deposit transactions. As a result, the differential between lending and deposit rates tends to evolve in line with the situation on short-term markets, which are the markets most influenced by monetary policy stance.
3 Since the late 1980s, bank lending and deposit rates have become notably more sensitive to changes in the Banco de España's intervention rate, a development that has also been accompanied, by greater speed in the transmission of monetary impulses.
4 The dynamics and magnitude of the response of bank rates to changes in money markets vary greatly from one group of institutions to another, depending on the market segments they deal with. They also vary according to the different loan and deposit instruments in question.

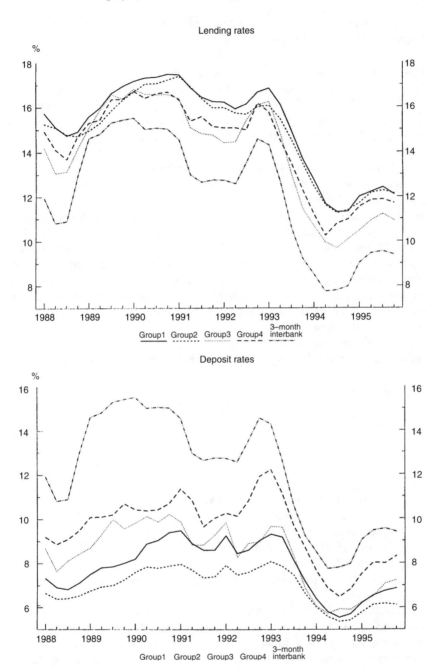

Figure 13.6   Composite interest rates, by group of product specialization, 1988–95

EXPLANATORY FACTORS IN THE RECENT BEHAVIOUR OF BANK INTEREST RATES

Having drawn attention to the main empirical regularities observed in Spanish interest rates since the start of the liberalization process, it is worth inquiring into the underlying explanatory factors of their behavior. To that end, a simple theoretical model will help us, generalizing somewhat, to elucidate the determining factors in lending and deposit rates.

This approach results from combining the Klein–Monti model[12] habitually found in studies of bank behaviour and a simple model of imperfect competition with product differentiation usually found in industrial economics textbooks. Both models assume that bank intermediaries maximize benefits in the current period without adopting an inter-temporal perspective, and that they are price setters, on both loan and deposit markets. The Klein–Monti model establishes the existence of a third, competitive market – which may be the interbank market – where the intermediaries are not able to influence prices, and which they resort to in order to earn a return on excess liquidity or else to borrow from, if the demand for credit requires so. This is, in other words, a buffer market which allows for adjustments between the lending and deposit markets.

According to this model, the decisions taken by a bank intermediary i are defined by the following first-order conditions:

$$r_L^i = (1 + \frac{1}{\varepsilon_L^i})^{-1}[r_I + c_L^i] \tag{13.1}$$

$$r_D^i = (1 + \frac{1}{\varepsilon_D^i})^{-1}[r_I - c_D^i] \tag{13.2}$$

where:

r_L^i: interest rate on loans granted by i;

r_D^i: interest rate that i pays for deposits

r_I: representative interbank rate; identical for all intermediaries

$\varepsilon_L^i, \varepsilon_D^i$: elasticities of credit demand and deposit supply, respectively, for each intermediary i;

c_L^i, c_D^i: marginal operating costs of loans and deposits.

According to (13.1), the banking firm sets the lending rate r_L in such a way as to make the marginal income and marginal cost of the loan equal. The marginal cost is a function of the opportunity cost as reflected by a market rate, such as the interbank rate, and the increase in operating costs derived from raising the volume of loans instead of borrowing on the interbank market. Similarly, (13.2) indicates that a banking intermediary establishes the interest rate on deposits r_D in such a way that there is no difference between raising additional funds in the interbank market or in the deposits market. In the latter case, the marginal cost is the sum of two components: the increase in costs due to the fact that the supply of deposits is not perfectly elastic and the increase in operating expenses produced by increasing the level of deposits.

With both loans and deposits, the response of interest rates to variations in the marginal – financial and operating – cost is a function of the price elasticity for each of those markets, which, in principle, may vary at any point on the credit demand and deposit supply curves.

The Klein–Monti model assumes that banking intermediaries have market power in both the lending and deposit markets, but it does not envisage the possibility of a strategic interaction among them. Thus market structure is not fully reflected in this model. To incorporate the possibility that an institution's decisions on prices and volumes depend on actions undertaken by competitors, plus the existence of product differentiation (derived in the case of banking from the fact that the market each entity serves differs from others), the most adequate models are those which assume imperfect competition with product differentiation.

In this new context, two further variables appear in the equilibrium conditions that determine lending and deposit rates:

$\varepsilon_L^{ij}, \varepsilon_D^{ij}$: substitution elasticities between products of intermediaries i and j in loan and deposit markets

e_L^{ij}, e_D^{ij}: changes in the prices of competitor j when i decides to change its prices, in other words, conjectural variations between (i, j) in loan and deposit markets.

In an imperfect competition model with product differentiation in the loan and deposit markets, the factors conditioning the interest rates fixed by banking intermediaries are as follows:

$$r_L^i = \left[1 + \frac{1}{\varepsilon_L^i + \sum_{j \neq i} \varepsilon_L^{ij} e_L^{ij}} \right]^{-1} [r_I + c_L^i] \tag{13.3}$$

$$r_i^D = \left[1 + \frac{1}{\varepsilon_D^i + \sum_{j \neq i} \varepsilon_D^{ij} e_D^{ij}} \right]^{-1} [r_I - c_D^i] \tag{13.4}$$

These equations indicate that the sensitivity of bank interest rates no longer depends solely on the price elasticity of each banking institution's own market as in (13.1) and (13.2) but also on the type of strategic interaction among participants in the same market and the degree to which their products – or different client segments – can be substituted for one another.

Nevertheless, this framework is still insufficient to explain how banks behave, because it fails to take into account the risk inherent in granting a loan because of uncertainty as to whether the interest will be paid and the principal repaid.[13] If this is borne in mind, (13.3) allows us to calculate the expected return on the loan portfolio R_L^i, which is a function of:

$$R_L^i = g[\underline{r_L^i}, p(\cdot)]$$

where:

r_L^i: interest rate vector of $(k \times 1)$ dimension established by the ith bank for k types of credit in its market;

$p^i(\cdot)$: Non-performing loan probability function, which depends, in turn, on the interest rate on loan $(r_L^i(k))$ for the class k customer and on the overall state of the economy (y)

Consequently, the condition determining the interest rate for the class k customer can be expressed as an implicit function that depends on the following variables:

$$H_k^i\left[r_L^i(k), p^i(r_L^i(k), y), \varepsilon_L^i, \varepsilon_L^{ij}, e_L^{ij}, r_I, c_L^i\right] = 0 \qquad (13.5)$$

According to (13.5) and (13.4), banks fix lending and deposit rates in terms of: the marginal – financial and operating – cost, the price-elasticity of demand, the type of strategic interaction among the institutions operating in the loan and deposits market, the degree of substitution with competing products or markets, and, lastly, the probability distribution of non-perfoming loans.

Within this set of factors, this chapter focuses on the following: the marginal financial cost, the market structure shaping the type of strategic interaction among deposit money institutions in Spain, certain aspects of different market segments that give rise to differing values of elasticity in the demand for credit and supply of deposits, the influence of the economic cycle on the risk premium that intermediaries possibly incorporate in their interest rates, and, finally, the level of operating costs. Although, for analytical purposes, we take a separate look at each of these, it is worth pointing out that most of them are closely interrelated.

Marginal Financial Cost and the Behaviour of Money Markets and Public Debt Markets

The charts tracking the behaviour over time of money market interest rates and bank lending and deposit rates, together with the correlation values in Table 13.1, reveal the existence of a close relationship between them. This is consistent with the hypothesis that banking institutions consider money market interest rates a relevant gauge of the opportunity cost of their decisions on lending and deposit rates, and, in this respect, these interest rates could be considered approximations to the marginal financial cost shown in (13.4) and (13.5).

This evidence is confirmed in the estimations of this relationship carried out in several of the above-mentioned papers. Thus Sáez (1996) presents two cointegrating relations between interest rates for fixed-rate financing and floating-rate financing, on the one hand, and the overnight interbank rate, on the other, with a long-run response close to unity. Likewise, Manzano and Galmés (1996) have estimated relationships between composite lending and deposit rates and the 3-month interbank rate using a quarterly average panel data for the 1991–4 period, considering a breakdown of banks in the four product specialized groups mentioned above. The results of these estimations, listed in Table 13.3, confirm the existence of important differences between the four groups of institutions with respect to the degree of transmission of monetary impulses. The savings bank group – Group 2 – shows the slowest and least intense response, in both lending and deposit transactions, while Group 1 stands in an intermediate position between the savings banks and Groups 3 and 4, which respond with the greatest speed and intensity to movements in the interbank market, for both lending and deposit operations.

As noted at the start of the section, in Spain both the public debt market and the interbank market constitute alternative markets to which banking intermediaries can resort for borrowing or lending, although the average

Table 13.3   Response of bank rates to the 3-month interbank rate, classification by groups of product specialization

	Contemp.	Lending Rate 1 quarter	Half-year	Total effect
Group 1	0.42	0.83	–	1.25
Group 2	0.25	0.24	0.16	0.66
Group 3	0.74	0.40	–	1.15
Group 4	0.75	0.43	–	1.18
	Contemp.	Deposit Rate 1 quarter	Total effect	
Group 1	0.21	0.46	0.67	
Group 2	0.20	0.42	0.63	
Group 3	0.24	0.45	0.69	
Group 4	0.46	0.34	0.81	

Source: Manzano and Galmés (1996).

term for the assets traded in the former is longer than that for interbank operations, which are mostly very short-term. Although the Klein–Monti model eschews consideration of the terms of bank loans and deposits, it seems logical to suppose that their marginal financial cost is determined by the interest rate for an alternative asset/liability on a competitive market and for the same term.[14] Thus, we could hypothesize that the interbank rate is the market of reference for shorter-term bank loans and deposits and that public debt interest rates are the market of reference for longer-term loans (mortgages, for instance). An alternative empirical version of this hypothesis would be to consider that the reference rate representing the opportunity cost of the different bank loans and deposits – basically, the former, which have a longer average maturity – is a combination of money market interest rates and expectations as to their future behavior, which are reflected, along with other factors, by debt market rates.

Recent analysis, to be found in Sáez (1996), on the lending rates of bank and savings banks, presents empirical evidence apparently backing this hypothesis. Both the composite rate for variable interest rate transactions and fixed rate financing depend, according to this study, on the overnight interbank rate and on the differential between the rates for 1-year and 1-day operations, which would, under certain assumptions, reflect expectations for that term regarding interest rate levels. The incorporation of this last variable substantially improves the adjustment *vis-à-vis* previous models for lending rates.

In an attempt to confirm the hypothesis that the reference rate to estimate the marginal financial cost of bank loans and deposits depends on their terms, we have broken down the interest rate for fixed-rate operations into composite rates for the short and long term, respectively, and have also distinguished between two groups of institutions: banks and savings banks.[15] Using quarterly data, several equations were estimated for these interest rates as well as for the rate for variable rate non-mortgage financing. They show the behavior of these rates in terms of a short-term interbank market rate – for 3-month operations – and the interest rate differential between the internal rate of return on government debt with an over-2-year maturity and the aforementioned short tranche of the interbank market.[16] Likewise, equations were estimated in which the only explanatory variable is the interbank market interest rate, or, alternatively, the debt market rate, in an attempt to discern the importance of each in explaining short- and long-term rates.

Table 13.4 lists the main statistics to emerge from these estimations.[17] In every instance, it is confirmed that the best results are obtained when both the interbank rate and the differential between it and the debt market rate are incorporated as explanatory variables. However, when, instead of this formula, only one interest rate is used, the results deteriorate in various ways.

Table 13.4   Reference markets for lending rates[1,2]

	Banks			Savings Banks		
	Interb. and differ.	Interbank	Debt	Interb. and differ.	Interbank	Debt
			Long-term operations			
α	−0.35(6.6)	−0.30(4.7)	−0.30(9.1)	−0.27(19.6)	−0.20(4.2)	−0.28(23.1)
σ	0.18	0.25	0.24	0.09	0.16	0.09
$\Delta\sigma(\%)$	–	39	33	–	78	0
BPL (4)	2.17	3.14	6.54	1.52	5.40	0.55
Residuals	–	↑ var (94–95)	↑ var (94)	–	↑ var (93–95)	–
			Short-term operations			
α	−0.19(5.6)	−0.41(4.3)	−0.18(3.0)	−0.18(8.1)	−0.19(2.8)	−0.21(10.2)
σ	0.21	0.21	0.26	0.19	0.21	0.19
$\Delta\sigma(\%)$	–	2	24	–	11	0
BPL (4)	1.50	2.55	0.47	3.65	1.68	1.67
Residuals	–	–	–	–	–	–
			Variable-rate operations			
α	−0.40(8.8)	−0.51(6.5)	−0.15(2.0)	−0.33(18.0)	−0.20(2.7)	−0.14(2.4)
σ	0.10	0.11	0.31	0.07	0.11	0.21
$\Delta\sigma(\%)$	–	10	210	–	57	200
BPL (4)	0.59	2.02	4.46	0.79	5.06	0.12
Residuals	–	–	↑ var (93–94)	–	–	–

Notes: 1. Data used: the 3-month interbank rate, the internal rate of return on state debt maturing at more than 2-years and the differential between these interest rates; the short-term rate is an average of the interest rates on operations maturing at 1 year or less, and the long-term rate refers to operations with maturity of more than 1 year (for further details, see tables 13 A. 1–3 in the Appendix).
2. A selection of the statistics from each of the estimated equations is presented: α is the coefficient of the error correction term (its t-ratio is given in brackets); σ is the equation's standard error; $\Delta\sigma$ (per cent) is the percentage increase this represents *vis-à-vis* the equation with a lower standard error; BPL (4) is the Box–Pierce–Ljung statistic for 4th order serial correlation; also indicated are the periods in which a notable increase in the variance of the residuals occurs.

Explaining the long-term rates in terms of what occurs in short tranches in the interbank market worsened the adjustment, especially around the years 1994 and 1995. On the other hand, using just the public debt interest rate yields, for savings banks, virtually identical results as those of the equation which includes both the interbank rate and the differential. In respect of short-term rates, the worst results are obtained, for banks, with the public debt market interest rate, and for savings banks with the interbank rate. In both models, the existence of cointegration was rejected. Explaining the banks' variable rate solely in terms of the interbank market yields findings similar to those of the formula which also incorporates the differential. Nevertheless, in the case of savings banks, neither the interbank rate nor the debt market rate alone satisfactorily explains their variable rate.

These results confirm the hypothesis already put forward regarding the importance of the future outlook for interest rates in banking intermediaries' price decisions. In the specific case of banks, expectations are especially relevant in determining long-term lending rates, and less important in explaining short-term rates and the interest rate for variable-rate financing. For their part, savings banks behave as if they take the expectations implied by the debt market into account when setting both their short-term rates and those for longer-term loans, as well as the rates for variable rate financing. This kind of behavior by savings banks may be due to the low proportion – around 20 per cent – of short-term loans in their portfolios, which may lead them to simplify somewhat when calculating the rates that serve as references for their marginal financial cost.

The influence of the public debt market on banks' price policies has been notable with regard to deposit rates since the mid-1980s, when the public sector increasingly resorted to the market to raise funds, thereby giving savers the opportunity to invest in assets other than bank deposits.[18] This impact has increased in recent years with the emergence of investment funds, whose portfolios mostly consist of government debt securities, which are also a substitute for deposits and repos. Nevertheless, the impact of the government securities on bank lending rates was not perceived until more recently, when a distinct pattern arose between the behavior of this market and that of money markets (see Figure 13.2). The role that public debt market appears to play in the decision-making processes of Spanish banking intermediaries is to provide information regarding the persistence over time of the interest rate levels on money markets. This makes it a key market for decisions regarding the price of longer-term loans.

Changes in the Market Structure of the Banking Industry

Since the late 1980s, a large number of Spanish banking intermediaries have been undergoing major changes in competitive strategy, one of the main changes being the start of widespread price competition. The chief factors at play include: the liberalization of the financial system, the development of new markets and intermediaries, and the prospect of a single Europe-wide financial services market. These factors have gradually altered the nature of strategic interaction among Spanish banks, which used to compete almost exclusively in terms of customer services (basically, branch proximity to customers), but now compete much more via interest rates. This development has been gradual and slightly perceptible, although there have occasionally been more notorious instances, well-known to the general public. As a result of this process, the structure of bank markets has been transformed, on both the loan and the deposits side, giving rise to greater competition in the sector.

Several studies have analyzed this progressive transformation of the Spanish banking system. Here we should mention Caminal, Gual and Vives (1990), Gual (1992), and Vives (1996), which furnish empirical evidence on the degree of concentration, margins, interest rates, and other features that, in principle, denote the degree of competition in a market, and at the same time analyze the impact of the 3 aforementioned factors propelling this process.

The main consequences of the increased competition in prices in the Spanish banking system have been:

1 A significant reduction in the dispersion of deposit rates, which does not appear to have occurred in lending rates (see Table 13.5). One of the possible reasons for this difference is the apparently different level of competition in the two markets up to 1993.[19] Thus, until that year, lending rates were generally less dispersed than bank deposit rates. However, in recent years, bank deposit rates have gradually become more homogeneous, in such a way that the degree of dispersion of the returns on deposits has become similar or lower to the degree of dispersion of lending rates in most of the product groups mentioned earlier.

2 A significant narrowing in the differential between the deposit rate and money market rates (see Table 13.6a). Composite lending rates, on the other hand, have shown no defined trend in recent years, although the increase in the average differential *vis-à-vis* money market interest rates in the 1993–5 period might have suggested otherwise. That increase was actually due to the characteristic inertia of the response of bank rates to changes in market rates, which leads to increases in the differential when interest rates fall and vice versa (see p. 453). The strong declines

Table 13.5 Degree of dispersion of bank interest rates, 1988–95
(Percentile 90–Percentile 10)

Year	Group 1		Group 2		Group 3		Group 4	
	Loans	Deposits	Loans	Deposits	Loans	Deposits	Loans	Deposits
1988	2.6	2.6	2.6	2.7	3.9	5.3	5.1	3.4
1989	2.1	3.2	2.8	3.5	2.6	7.0	2.7	5.1
1990	2.0	3.2	3.4	3.5	2.5	7.6	2.8	7.2
1991	2.6	3.0	2.7	2.8	3.9	6.7	4.7	5.3
1992	2.6	2.5	2.3	2.6	3.5	7.3	5.1	3.7
1993	3.2	2.0	2.4	2.7	2.9	5.7	5.9	3.1
1994	4.2	1.9	2.4	2.1	3.3	3.8	3.9	1.9
1995	2.1	2.2	2.3	2.3	2.2	3.3	3.6	2.3
1988–92	2.4	2.9	2.8	3.0	3.3	6.8	4.1	4.9
1993–5	3.2	2.0	2.4	2.4	2.8	4.3	4.5	2.4

Table 13.6	Bank interest rates, 1988–95, classification by groups of product
specialization
(a) Differential *vis-à-vis* the 3-month interbank rate

(Percentage points)

| Year | Group 1 | | Group 2 | | Group 3 | | Group 4 | |
	Loans	Deposits	Loans	Deposits	Loans	Deposits	Loans	Deposits
1988	3.5	−4.6	3.3	−5.2	1.9	−3.4	2.7	−2.6
1989	1.2	−7.3	0.6	−8.1	0.9	−5.7	0.9	−5.0
1990	2.2	−6.3	1.9	−7.4	1.4	−5.3	1.5	−4.7
1991	3.5	−4.4	3.4	−5.6	2.0	−4.0	2.4	−2.8
1992	2.9	−4.5	2.5	−5.6	1.7	−4.4	2.0	−2.6
1993	3.7	−3.2	3.2	−4.3	2.1	−3.1	2.4	−1.4
1994	3.9	−2.1	3.7	−2.4	2.0	−2.2	2.8	−1.1
1995	2.9	−2.9	2.7	−3.3	1.6	−2.8	2.4	−1.6
1988–92	2,0	−5.4	2.3	−6.4	1.6	−4.6	1.9	−3.5
1993–5	3.5	−2.7	3.2	−3.3	1.9	−2.7	2.5	−1.4

(b) *Differential between lending and deposit rates*

(Percentage points)

Year	Group 1	Group 2	Group 3	Group 4
1988	8.1	8.5	5.4	5.4
1989	8.5	8.6	6.7	6.0
1990	8.5	9.3	6.9	6.2
1991	7.9	9.0	5.9	5.0
1992	7.4	8.1	6.2	4.6
1993	7.0	7.4	5.1	3.8
1994	6.0	6.1	4.2	3.8
1995	5.5	5.9	4.1	3.9

in interbank market rates in 1993 and part of 1994 thus probably
explain the widening in the differential, in a way similar to what happened in 1988 and 1991.

3	A continuous reduction in the spread between lending and deposit
rates, and thus in bank margins (see Table 13.6b), largely as a result of
the narrowing of the differential between interest rates on deposits and
repos *vis-à-vis* market rates.

The narrowing of the differential between deposit rates and market rates
and the convergence towards more homogeneous bank interest rates have
led to a swifter and more effective transmission of money market movements to rates paid for bank deposits. Greater competition in the banking
sector throughout the 1990s has therefore helped spur the transmission of

measures taken by the monetary authorities to final savers, who take decisions regarding the components of aggregate demand.

On the lending side, however, interest rate differentials and the degree of dispersion in lending rates have remained relatively stable in the 1990s, which indicates that there have not been any major changes in the speed with which movements in market rates are transmitted – with the exception of some types of credit, such as mortgages.[20] Nevertheless, the overall long-term response of lending rates has indeed tended to increase in the 1990s (see Figure 13.3 and the comments on p. 456 of this chapter), thereby enhancing the impact of monetary policy on the cost of borrowing.

Structural Features in the Price Elasticity of Different Market Segments

Analysis of at least partly disaggregated bank rates (for instance, by institutional group according to product specialisation or by type of loan and deposit transaction) reveals that they vary greatly in their levels and also in their dynamic response to shifts in interbank market rates, and hence to modifications in the Banco de España's intervention rate.

One of the main reasons for these differences is undoubtedly the type of customer targeted and the relative predominance of a given customer type in the demand for each loan or deposit instrument. The defining features of a given customer type or market segment not only affect the price elasticity of the demand for credit and supply of savings. They also influence other variables, such as operating costs, type of strategic interaction, and the extent to which customers of different banking institutions are substitutable. These, in turn, are additional factors at play in their lending and deposit rates policy.

The range of customer types is very broad. Nevertheless, for the purposes of this study, it suffices to distinguish between the following groups:

– households
– small-sized firms
– medium and large-sized firms.

Only partial statistics exist on the distribution of these 3 types of customer among Spanish banking institutions. According to the supplementary data sent to the Banco de España by these institutions along with their balance sheets, banks concentrate on corporate financing, while savings banks have traditionally focused more on households.[21] With this information and the data on the average size of loans of the different banking groups (see Table 13.7), we can assume the following distribution:

– Savings banks – Group 2 institutions – practice retail banking, mainly with households and small firms.

Table 13.7 Average size of credit operations, 1989–95, classification by group of product specialization

(Millions)

| Year | Group 1 | | | Group 2 | | |
	Discount	Credit acts	Unsecured loans	Discount	Credit acts	Unsecured loans
1989	0.4	8.9	8.3	0.6	4.9	0.7
1990	3.6	8.9	3.4	0.3	4.8	0.7
1991	1.1	15.0	3.6	0.3	4.6	1.2
1992	0.6	12.4	3.8	0.5	5.1	0.7
1993	0.4	10.2	3.7	0.4	5.5	0.7
1994	0.4	9.0	2.2	0.4	6.0	0.8
1995	0.4	8.4	1.5	0.5	6.5	0.8
	Group 3			Group 4		
1989	1.0	103.1	146.9	0.4	133.1	61.1
1990	2.6	108.4	169.2	1.8	98.3	45.5
1991	9.4	102.1	137.9	0.4	97.7	34.9
1992	9.8	104.1	122.3	3.4	70.5	29.7
1993	7.3	107.1	200.0	1.7	33.6	63.6
1994	20.1	92.6	159.9	4.2	48.9	50.6
1995	11.0	66.5	248.7	7.5	52.3	12.3

Source: Banco de España.

- Most Spanish commercial banks – Group 1 – deal mainly with the corporate sector. Despite the fact that this group's business with households has increased in recent years, especially with the upper-income bracket, this business is minor, except in the case of the big banks.
- Part of the foreign bank group – Group 3 – is geared to financing large corporations, the sector most easily accessible for intermediaries with few branches.
- Non-commercial banks – Group 4 – provide services, such as advice on all kinds of investments, asset management, underwriting of securities issues, etc., to large corporations and high-income households.

In the following section, we outline some of the structural features of the 3 market segments and their impact on the interest rates of their financial transactions with banking institutions.

Households

Households usually resort to the banking system to finance the purchase of housing and consumer durables, and they bank their savings, mainly in the form of deposits, although recently also in the form of repos.

Informational asymmetries characterizing this group of economic agents are very strong – the lender (the bank) knows little about the borrower's future capacity to pay – which either limits the availability of credit or tends to increase the risk premium, particularly in the purchase of consumer durables, for which the main instrument is unsecured loans. In housing loans, on the other hand, this problem is offset by physical collateral and the low probability of non-payment in this kind of credit. For that reason the interest charged on mortgage loans is lower than for unsecured loans.

Households tend to distinguish firmly between instruments used for operational purposes (current accounts and savings accounts) and those used for investment purposes (time deposits), because of the means of payment functions associated with the former. This explains, to a large extent, the difference between current account and savings account interest rates compared with others, as well as their relative insensitivity to money market conditions.

The costs involved in substituting or transferring loans and deposits to another institution are not negligible (commissions charged for opening and closing accounts, changes in billing addresses, and so on), and, in the case of mortgages, may be quite onerous. Households also attach great importance to ready access to a bank branch, so that the cost of transferring to a more distant branch may offset the advantages of a higher return on their savings.

These preferences and the existence of none too negligible switching costs help explain the scant importance that households have traditionally attached to returns on their deposits,[22] thus creating a market with very low price elasticity.[23] Although this situation is gradually changing, in effect it has clearly caused a very limited and slow transmission of monetary impulses to the deposit rates offered by savings banks, which are the institutions serving most of this market segment.

Small Firms

These companies contact the banking system mainly as a source of financing and for liquidity management purposes. The credit they obtain is mainly via trade discounts and unsecured loans. Secured loans may also have become a habitual way of obtaining financing, given the much wider informational asymmetries that they present to the lending institutions' as compared with larger firms.

Small enterprises are a market segment with some structural features resembling those of households. Thus the information gap or asymmetry for the banks financing them is also considerable. However, banking institutions differ in the methods they apply to reduce the costs derived from that lack of information. The client's credit record becomes a key factor lessening the degree of uncertainty and hence the risk premium implicit in the interest rate. Sometimes a steady relationship between bank and client makes it possible for a small firm to obtain a loan that it probably would not obtain from an institution approached for the first time.[24] Such circumstances enhance customer loyalty, because of the substantial increase in the costs of transferring to another banking intermediary. This translates into a reduction in the price elasticity of credit demand.

In this scenario, it is also much more likely that banks and their long-standing clients reach implicit agreements to hedge against future shifts in market interest rates, in such a way that banks exercise moderation in passing on the changes in their marginal financial costs.[25]

These factors explain why interest rates on trade discounts and unsecured loans granted by Spanish commercial banks and savings banks do not fully reflect measures taken by the monetary authority, or do so only after a certain time lag.

Medium- and Large-sized Firms

These companies receive loans from the banking system and, in some cases, have direct access to securities markets. Probably the most common form of financing they use are loans with variable interest rates, subject to frequent revision, and credit accounts. As depositors, presumably they use the banking system for cash management and to obtain a return on cash surpluses, which they invest in time deposits and repos.

The structural features of large firms differ markedly from those of the two aforementioned market segments. First, for such companies, the cost of switching banks or resorting directly to capital and securities markets is much lower, thus increasing the price elasticity of the demand for bank loans. Second, companies in this group are usually better known – if listed on the stock exchange, they even have to publish their accounts – so that notably more information is available for these companies than for smaller enterprises. Thus the risk premium implicit in the interest rates they pay for loans tends to be lower. The upshot of all this is that this group obtains both cheaper loans and a better return on its cash surpluses. This is consistent with the level and degree of response reflected in the composite lending and deposit rates of foreign banks.

The fact that the managers of these corporations are relatively familiar with general economic conditions and with financial markets may explain their greater propensity to resort to variable interest rate loans, as one way to hedge against future swings in market interest rates. The demand for this kind of financing by large corporations probably explains the swift and virtually total transmission shown by non-mortgage variable interest loans in most banking institutions.

In short, banking institutions' price policies and, hence, the degree to which their interest rates respond to measures taken by the monetary authorities, depend, to a significant extent, on the structural features – such as those discussed here – of the markets they face.

Impact of the Economic Cycle on Bank Lending Rates

In principle, it is difficult to estimate the impact of the economic cycle on bank lending rates. Nevertheless, it can be assumed that the overall state of the economy has some kind of effect on the average risk of bank loan portfolios and therefore on the probability of non-performing loans. According to (13.5), banking institutions will reflect any increase in this probability in their interest rates in an attemp to limit the drop in their expected average return. However, an increase in bank lending rates could make adverse selection problems more severe, thus raising the number of overdue and non-performing loans and lowering the average return on bank loan portfolios. This is why banking intermediaries react in a recession by restricting credit for higher-risk borrowers[26] or by demanding additional guarantees.

A third option is for banks to redirect their credit policy toward activities that involve more collateral and at the same time have a lower incidence of non-payment, such as housing loans.

It is not easy to ascertain the strategies pursued by Spanish banks during the last recession, which caused a considerably higher default ratio (see Figure 13.7), because of the problems associated with estimating the risk premium implicit in lending rates and because of the difficulty in distinguishing empirically between a restriction in the supply of credit and a fall in the credit demand. Furthermore, offsetting the tendency for interest rates to increase because of the greater credit risk is there a tendency for them to decline due to the lower demand for financing in periods of recession.

Despite these difficulties, Table 13.8 attempts to present some evidence, which should, however, be interpreted with caution. This table shows the correlation between one measure of the risk premium incorporated into lending rates and the default ratio (non-performing loans as a percentage of total loans), distinguishing among several groups with different product specialization. In addition, the table shows the coefficient of correlation between defaults, on the one hand, and the growth of total credit and of mortgage loans, on the other.

To estimate the risk premium, we used the differential between the composite lending rate and the prime rate of each institution, the latter being the rate for the best clients. In principle, this variable ought to be a better approximation to the risk premium than a differential with respect to a

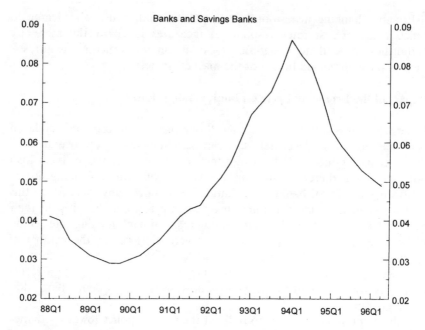

Figure 13.7   Default ratio

risk-free asset, such as government debt securities. Given that they are traded in different markets, a number of factors affect bank rates – operating costs, degree of price competition, market segment – but do not influence money market and debt market interest rates. They are, however, incorporated into the prime rate of each institution.

The results in Table 13.8 suggest that there was an increase in the default ratio of the various groups parallel to a slowdown in the growth rate of bank credit. However, it is not possible to discern to what extent this was due to demand factors or to a more limited supply of credit. In

Table 13.8   Default ratio, credit and risk premium, Spearman's correlation coefficient (Period: 1988–95, individual data)

| | Default ratio | | | |
	Group 1	Group 2	Group 3	Group 4
Lending rate – Prime rate	0.10	–	0.41	0.32
Growth of credit	−0.49	−0.39	−0.39	−0.44
% Mortgages/Credit	0.29	–	0.37	–

Note: – = non-significant correlations.

some groups, – i.e. private banks specialized in commercial banking (Groups 1 and 3) – a positive relation is detected between the proportion of mortgage loans as a percentage of total loans and the default ratio, which would appear to indicate a certain reorientation in the lending policies of these institutions.[27] Bearing in mind that the core activity of these two groups is the provision of loans to firms – hard hit by the recession in the early 1990s – it would appear reasonable to suppose that it was in these groups that a shift towards lower-risk activities took place. In contrast, in the savings bank group, which focuses on loans to households, there is no sign of a reorganization of loan portfolios in favour of mortgage-backed loans as a result of the increase in bad loans. This supports the hypothesis that the aforementioned relationships between interest rates and credit growth were not the outcome of a demand phenomenon widespread with generally among all the institutions.

The greater probability of non-performing loans reflected in the rise in the default ratio in the early 1990s translated only in some cases into an increase in the risk premium included in lending rates. Foreign banks specialized in large corporations were the group that most reflected this greater probability in their interest rates, most likely because this market segment is less affected by adverse selection and asymmetric information problems. In contrast, Group 1 banks, which serve a higher proportion of small corporate clients, appear to have responded with more moderate increases in the risk premium. Finally, savings banks, which are much less informed about their customers, apparently did not reflect the greater probability of non-performing loans in their lending rates.

In short, the recession in Spain in 1992 and 1993, which brought with it an increase in the proportion of non-performing loans and defaults, induced varying responses by banking institutions, although it is worth remembering the difficulty of identifying these responses as solely a supply phenomenon. Thus, whereas Spanish commercial banks and savings banks barely reflected the higher risk level in their lending rates, foreign banks increased the cost of funds for large corporations.

Influence of Operating Costs

According to (13.4) and (13.5), the marginal operating cost of increasing the loan portfolio or the level of deposits influences bank interest rates and therefore has an impact on the relationship between these rates and the market rates that reflect the marginal financial cost. As mentioned earlier, this relationship has undergone significant changes since the interest rate liberalization process ended in the latter half of the 1980s. A major factor in that respect was the increasing widespread price competition among banking intermediaries, a development that was softened somewhat by the recession in 1992 and 1993. The impact of operating costs on this process is a topic still to be analyzed and one for which hardly any empirical evidence exists.

In principle, it is to be expected that the narrowing of the spread between lending and deposit rates in the Spanish banking system, in all market segments, had been accompanied by a parallel drop in the growth of operating costs, as banks sought to maintain their profitability and solvency. However, a merely descriptive analysis of some information available on the trends in operating costs in each of the Spanish banking institutions raises doubts whether this process actually took place on such a wide scale.

An analysis of average non-financial costs, estimated as the percentage of operating costs *vis-à-vis* the total balance sheet, signals significant differences between some of the groups of institutions with different product specialization (see the different values for each group's distribution in Figure 13.8). The institutions specialized in traditional retail banking – Groups 1 and 2 – show higher operating costs per unit of asset than Groups 3 and 4, which focus on large corporations and non-commercial banking. Both these activities require far less in terms of size and branch infrastructure than is needed to serve small-and medium-sized firms or households. As pointed out earlier, this type of customer attaches great importance, even today, to having a branch nearby. At the same time, banking institutions themselves have an additional interest in staying close, because it facilitates the follow-up and monitoring of the loans they grant and narrows the information asymmetry regarding the risk of each customer.

Thus, it is possible to confirm the widespread view that the level of operating costs is closely linked to the structural features of the different market segments served by banking institutions in Spain.

Additionally, Figure 13.8 shows unequal developments over time in operating costs per unit of asset for each group of institutions. Thus, whereas intermediaries in Group 3 and a large number of those in Group 4 partly offset the deterioration in their marginal net revenue by gradually reducing their operating costs, those institutions specialized in retail banking showed either stagnation – Group 2 – or even an increase in operating costs, as in the case of Group 1. Figure 13.8 reveals an upward shift of the whole distribution of this Group. It also shows that although the savings banks with a higher level of operating expenses per unit of asset (i.e. higher than the median) have managed to moderate this variable in recent years, such costs were higher in 1994 than in 1988. Consequently, the behavior of retail banks' operating costs has barely helped offset the deterioration in the spread between lending and deposit rates in recent years.

Microeconomic theory suggests that the truly relevant costs in determining bank interest rates are the marginal costs of obtaining deposits and

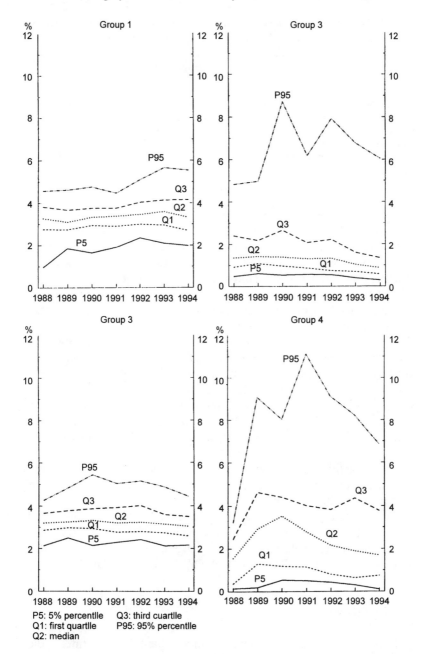

Figure 13.8 Average total operating expenses, by group of product specialization, 1988–94

Table 13.9   Operating expenses and interest rates, Spearman's correlation
coefficient (Period: 1988–95, individual data)

| | Operating expenses/Average total assets | | | |
	Group 1	Group 2	Group 3	Group 4
(Lending rate – 3-month interbank)	0.35	0.22	0.40	0.24
(Lending rate – Debt > 2 year)	0.35	0.32	0.45	0.26
(Deposit rate – 3-month interbank)	–	−0.19	–	−0.23
(Deposit rate – Debt > 2 year)	–	−0.13	–	−0.19

Note: – = non-significant correlations.

granting loans, which may differ. However, the accounting data available
(operating expenses per unit of asset, for example) are a mere approximation to the average costs of lending and deposit transactions as a whole,
which makes it very difficult to estimate the precise costs of each of these
two activities. Given this difficulty in obtaining adequate estimates of the
marginal costs of loans and deposits, in this section we use operating costs
per unit of asset in order to analyze the relationship between operating
costs and the price policies pursued by banks and savings banks.

Some insights into this relationship can be obtained from the correlations shown in Table 13.9 for the different groups of institutions classified
according to their product specialization. The differentials between lending
rates and the rates on money and government debt markets correlate positively, for all groups, with the level of operating expenses per unit of asset.
However, only in Groups 2 and 4 are such expenses negatively correlated
to the differentials between deposit rates and interbank and debt market
rates.

The sign of these correlations and the behavior of operating costs over
time appear to indicate that the moderation in these costs was only a
minor factor in the acceleration and greater intensity of the transmission
of interest rates in the 1990s, except in the case of wholesale and merchant
banks – Groups 3 and 4. These two already had lower differentials with
money and debt markets than the other groups and also responded more
swiftly to changes in the Banco de España's intervention rate.

CONCLUSIONS

This chapter's analysis of the determinants in bank interest rates indicates
that a number of structural factors, specific to each market segment, play
an important role in shaping, the response of these rates to changes in
market rates and therefore affect the transmission of movements in the

Banco de España's intervention rate to some of the interest rates that are key to agents' expenditure decisions. For this reason, an analysis distinguishing between groups of institutions serving different customers and showing sufficiently distinct patterns of behavior clearly improves our understanding of the process of transmission of monetary impulses and the impact of monetary policy decisions on the components of aggregate demand.

The liberalization of financial markets, both domestically and in the context of international capital movements, and the resulting increase in competition have greatly enhanced the sensitivity of banking intermediaries' lending and deposit rates to shifts in market interest rates, as well as the speed with which they react. The impact of these changes on the strategic rivalry among Spanish banks has been particularly marked in the deposits market, initially the least competitive market.

This increase, since the end of the 1980s, in the sensitivity of bank rates to movements in the Banco de España's intervention rate has enhanced the ability of monetary policy to affect agents' savings and investment decisions swiftly.

This chapter also examined other factors that may have had a bearing on the process of transmission of monetary policy to interest rates – such as the economic cycle and operating costs per unit of product. The findings indicate that these factors only played a significant role in some institutions specialized in wholesale banking or non-commercial bank activities. In retail banking, by contrast, the behavior of operating costs contributed vey little in reducing the differential *vis-á-vis* market rates, while the increase in the average risk of this sector's loan portfolio in the last recession had scant impact on the average level of lending rates.

Presumably, as technological progress and banks' commercial strategies gradually induce changes in customers preferences, the economic value of having an extensive branch network will tend to decline and will encourage retail banks to reduce the number of branches, thereby substantially lowering operating costs. These developments will be reinforced by the gains in productivity that are likely to be derived from more extensive computerization, and from the transformation of the organizational structures, and the job skills of employees in Spain's banking industry.

APPENDIX: COMPOSITE LENDING RATE EQUATIONS, BY TERM

Definition of Variables

A   The lending rates are the simple arithmetic mean of each institution's interest rates calculated as follows:

- Short-term rate. Covers interest rates of the following types of fixed-rate credit weighted by their respective balance:

  - Trade discount ($\leqslant 3$ months)
  - Unsecured loans < 1 year)
  - Credit accounts (< 1 year)

- Long-term rate. Covers interest rates of the following fixed-rate operations:

  - Unsecured loans ($\geqslant 1$ year)
  - Mortgage-backed loans ($\geqslant 1$ year)

- Variable rate. Simple average of the interest rates of variable-rate operations without a mortgage guarantee, which are revised:

  - every month
  - every quarter
  - at intervals longer than a quarter

B The interbank rate ($r3m$) refers to the 3-month interbank rate.
C The debt rate ($rdeu$) is the internal rate of return in the secondary market on government securities maturing in 2 years or more.

Table 13A.1 Lending rates of banks and savings banks, relation to the interbank and debt markets

$$\Delta Y_t = k + \alpha[y - \beta_1 r3m - \beta_2(rdeu - r3m)]_{t-1}$$
$$+\gamma(L)\Delta r3m_t + \omega(L)\Delta(rdeu - r3m)_t + \phi(L)\Delta y_{t-1} + \epsilon_t$$

	Banks			Savings Banks		
y	Long	Short	Variable	Long[1]	Short	Variable
k						
α	−0.35 (6.6)	−0.19 (5.6)	−0.40 (8.8)	−0.27 (19.6)	−0.18 (8.1)	−0.33 (18.0)
β_1	1.23 (150.5)	1.10 (66.0)	1.11 (267.8)	1.19 (209.1)	1.22 (73.5)	1.11 (304.0)
β_2	0.88 (7.4)	0.91 (3.8)	0.26 (4.4)	1.20 (14.7)	1.22 (5.1)	0.49 (9.4)
γ_0	0.42 (9.5)	0.43 (8.9)	0.79 (31.6)	0.19 (8.3)	0.16 (3.5)	0.55 (30.4)
ω_0				0.14 (3.2)		
ϕ_1	−0.24 (2.0)					
R^2	0.90	0.86	0.98	0.96	0.81	0.98
σ	0.18	0.21	0.10	0.09	0.19	0.07
D–W	1.90	1.90	1.98	2.00	1.60	1.65
BPL (4)	2.17	1.50	0.59	1.52	3.65	0.79
Period	1988: I– 1995: IV	1988: II– 1995: IV	1988: II– 1995: IV	1988: II– 1995: IV	1988: II– 1995: IV	1988: II– 1995: IV

Note: 1 This equation also incorporates a dummy variable to reflect an impulse in 1992: I.

Table 13A.2   Lending rates of banks and savings banks, relation to the interbank market

$$\Delta y_t = k + \alpha[y - \beta_1 r3m]_{t-1} + \gamma(L)\Delta r3m_t + \phi(L)\Delta y_{t-1} + \epsilon_t$$

	Banks			Savings Banks		
y	Long	Short	Variable	Long[1]	Short	Variable
k	0.85 (2.0)	1.83 (3.0)	0.54 (2.9)	1.03 (3.2)	1.08 (1.9)	0.31 (1.5)
α	−0.30 (4.7)	−0.41 (4.3)	−0.51 (6.5)	−0.20 (4.2)	−0.19 (2.8)	−0.20 (2.7)
β_1	1.00 (13.3)	0.74 (16.0)	1.02 (52.3)	0.76 (10.3)	0.75 (6.3)	0.97 (19.2)
γ_0	0.46 (8.6)	0.44 (9.2)	0.81 (31.0)	0.22 (6.3)	0.20 (3.8)	0.55 (20.2)
ϕ_1				0.47 (4.7)	0.27 (1.9)	0.22 (3.1)
R^2	0.81	0.86	0.98	0.89	0.78	0.97
σ	0.25	0.21	0.11	0.16	0.21	0.11
$\Delta\sigma(\%)$	39	2	10	78	11	57
D–W	1.70	1.66	1.64	1.58	1.90	1.42
BPL (4)	3.14	2.55	2.02	5.40	1.68	5.06
Period	1988: II– 1995: IV	1988: II– 1995: IV	1988: II– 1995: IV	1988: I– 1995: IV	1988: I– 1995: IV	1988: I– 1995: IV

Note: 1. This equation also incorporates a dummy variable to reflect an impulse in 1992: I.

Table 13A.3   Lending rates of banks and savings banks, relation to the debt market

$$\Delta y_t = k + \alpha[y - \beta_2 rdeu]_{t-1} + \omega(L)\Delta rdeu_t + \phi(L)\Delta y_{t-1} + \epsilon_t$$

	Banks			Savings Banks		
y	Long	Short	Variable	Long[1]	Short	Variable
k						
α	−0.30 (9.1)	−0.18 (3.0)	−0.15 (2.0)	−0.28 (23.1)	−0.21 (10.2)	−0.14 (2.4)
β_2	1.24 (101.4)	1.11 (50.7)	1.12 (36.3)	1.19 (224.2)	1.22 (88.4)	1.12 (50.7)
ω_0	0.32 (6.3)	0.34 (6.0)	0.59 (8.6)	0.18 (8.9)	0.16 (4.1)	0.43 (9.4)
ϕ_1		0.26 (1.9)	0.37 (4.4)			0.43 (4.4)
R^2	0.82	0.77	0.86	0.96	0.83	0.89
σ	0.24	0.26	0.31	0.09	0.19	0.21
$\Delta\sigma(\%)$	33	24	210	0	0	200
D–W	1.86	2.07	1.90	1.81	1.83	2.03
BPL (4)	6.54	0.47	4.46	0.55	1.67	0.12
Period	1988: II– 1995: IV	1988: I– 1995: IV	1988: 1– 1995: 7	1988: II– 1995: IV	1988: II– 1995: IV	1988: I– 1995: IV

Note: 1. This equation also incorporates a dummy variable to reflect an impulse in 1992: I.

Notes

1   See, *inter alia*, Gurley and Shaw (1960).
2   See Gertler (1988), which reviews the literature on the relationship between financial structure and macroeconomic variables.
3   See, for example, Hubbard (1994), Bernanke, Gertler and Gilchrist (1994) and Mishkin (1996).
4   See Diamond (1984) and Fama (1985) on some of the advantages banks have in dealing with the problems derived from the existence of asymmetric information in the credit market.
5   In the case of the interbank market, findings by Ayuso, Haldane and Restoy (1994) indicate that the different terms in this market, especially the shortest, rapidly incorporate changes in the Banco de España's intervention rate with an elasticity of one.
6   On how these data are constructed, see Cuenca (1994) and Manzano and Galmés (1996)
7   In first half 1996 this tendency for the differential between the deposit rate and interbank interest rates to decline became more marked, indicating that the successive drops in the Banco de España's intervention rate were transmitted with unusual alacrity to bank deposit rates.
8   See also the findings reported in Estrada *et al.* (1994) and Manzano and Galmés (1996).
9   The regression slope of the variables in levels is an estimator of the long-term effect, which may differ, as in this case, from the contemporary response.
10   The composite rates for each instrument were calculated as the simple average of the rates of each institution.
11   The composite rates for each group were calculated as the simple average of the composite rates of each institution.
12   See Klein (1971) and Monti (1973).
13   The findings of Slovin and Sushka (1984) indicate that the most appropriate theoretical framework for presenting empirical evidence on banking firms' performance should combine portfolio theory and price-setting in an imperfect competition market.
14   See, for instance, the suggestion made in this regard by Borio and Fritz (1995).
15   Short-term interest rates are taken to be those of fixed-rate loans for under *1 year*, while long-term rates include the rates on transactions of more than 1 year. The Appendix (pp. 483–4) lists the information included in each of these composite rates.
16   In principle, this differential reflects expectations regarding the future behavior of interest rates for terms other than that considered in Sáez (1996). Nevertheless, the charts of both variables and several estimations carried out indicate that they essentially contain the same basic information.
17   Details of the estimations are given in tables 13A.1–3 in the Appendix.
18   See Sastre (1991) on the influence of the government debt market on the deposit rates of banks and savings banks.
19   Manzano and Galmés (1996) and Vives (1996) also supply evidence that could be similarly interpreted.
20   The main changes in this regard occurred towards the end of the 1980s.
21   See Fuentes (1996).
22   Coello (1996) contains a more detailed analysis of the part played by both variables – proximity to a bank branch and interest rate – in the supply of deposits.

23 Some empirical evidence for a relatively rigid supply of deposits is found in Manzano and Sastre (1995).
24 On the influence of the habitual bank-customer relationship on the availability of credit, see Petersen and Rajan (1994).
25 On this aspect, see Fried and Howitt (1980).
26 See Stiglitz and Weiss (1981).
27 Fuentes (1995) provides evidence along the same lines.

References

AYUSO, J., A.G. HALDANE and F. RESTOY (1994) 'Volatility transmission along the money market yield curve', Banco de España *Working Paper*, 9403.
BERNANKE, B., M. GERTLER and S. GILCHRIST (1994) 'The financial accelerator and the flight to quality', NBER, *Working Paper*, 4789.
BORIO, C., and W. FRITZ (1995) 'The response of short-term bank lending rates to policy rates: a cross-country perspective', BIS, May.
CAMINAL, R., J. GUAL and X. VIVES (1990) 'Competition in Spanish Banking', in J. Dermine (ed.) *European banking after 1992*, Oxford: Basil Blackwell.
COELLO, J. (1996) 'El mercado de depósitos español (1985–1994): Bancos versus Cajas de Ahorros', Resumen 96–01, FEDEA.
CUENCA, J.A. (1994) 'Variables para el estudio del sector monetario. Agregados monetarios y crediticios, y tipos de interés sintéticos', Banco de España, Working Paper, 9416.
DIAMOND, D.W. (1984) 'Financial intermediation and delegated monitoring', *Review of Economic Studies*, 51, 393–414.
ESTRADA, A. I. HERNANDO and J. VALLÉS, J. (1996) 'El impacto de los tipos de interés sobre el gasto privado', Chapter 14 in this volume.
ESTRADA, A., T. SASTRE and J.L. VEGA (1994) 'El mecanismo de transmisión de los tipos de interés: el caso español', Banco de España, *Working Paper*, 9408.
FAMA, E.F. (1985) 'What's different about banks?', *Journal of Monetary Economics*, 15, 29–39.
FRIED, J. and HOWITT, P. (1980) 'Credit rationing and implicit contract theory', *Journal of Money, Credit and Banking*, 12, August, 471–87.
FUENTES, I. (1995) 'Evolución reciente del crédito bancario: efectos sobre la financiación de las familias y de las empresas', Banco de España, *Boletín Económico*, November.
FUENTES, I. (1996) 'La traslación de los movimientos en los tipos de interés de los mercados monetarios a las operaciones de las cajas de ahorros', *Cuadernos de Información Económica*, 107, 84–91.
GUAL, J. (1992) 'La competencia en el sector bancario español', BBV Foundation, *Colección Documenta*.
GERTLER, M. (1988) 'Financial structure and aggregate economic activity: an overview', *Journal of Money, Credit and Banking*, August, 20, 559–88.
GURLEY, J. and E. SHAW (1960) *Money in a theory of finance*, Washington, DC: Brookings Institution.
HERNANDO, I. (1997) 'El canal crediticio en la transmisión de la política monetaria', in *La política monetaria y la inflación en España*, Servicio de Estudios del Banco de España, Madno: Alianza Editorial.

488   María Teresa Sastre de Miguel

HUBBARD, R.G. (1994) 'Is there a "credit channel" for monetary policy?', NBER, Working Paper, 4977.

KLEIN (1971) 'A theory of the banking firm', *Journal of Money, Credit and Banking*, May, 205–18.

MANZANO, M.C. and S. GALMÉS (1996) 'Credit institutions' price policies and type of customer: impact on the monetary transmission mechanism', Banco de España, Working Paper, 9605.

MANZANO, M.C. and T. SASTRE (1995) 'Factores relevantes en la determinación del margen de explotación de bancos y cajas de ahorros', Banco de España, Working Paper, 9514.

MISHKIN, F. (1996) 'The channels of monetary transmission: lessons for monetary policy', paper presented at the working sessions on *Financial cycles and growth* sponsored by the Bank of France, January 1996.

MONTI (1973) 'A theoretical model of bank behavior and its implications for monetary policy', *Société Universitaire Européenne de Recherches Financiéres*, reprint of *L'Industria*, 2, 1971.

PEÑALOSA, J. (1996) 'The financial position of agents and monetary policy', Chapter 15 in this volume.

PETERSEN, M.A. and R.G. RAJAN (1994) 'The benefits of lending relationships: evidence from small business data', *Journal of Finance*, 59(1), 3–37.

SÁEZ, F.J. (1996) 'La relación entre los tipos de interés del crédito bancario y los del mercado interbancario', Banco de España, *Boletín Económico*, May.

SÁEZ, F.J., J.M. SÁNCHEZ, J.M. and M.T. SASTRE (1994) 'Los mercados de operaciones bancarias en España: especialización productiva y competencia', Banco de España, Working Paper, 9410.

SÁNCHEZ, J.M. and M.T. SASTRE (1995) '¿Es el tamaño un factor explicativo de las diferencias entre entidades bancarias?', Banco de España, Working Paper, 9512.

SASTRE, M.T. (1991) 'La determinación de los tipos de interés activos y pasivos de bancos y cajas de ahorros', Banco de España, *Estudios Económicos*, 45.

SLOVIN, M.B. and M.E. SUSHKA (1984) 'A note on the evidence on alternative models of the banking firm', *Journal of Banking and Finance*, 8, 99–108.

STIGLITZ, J. E. A. and WEISS (1981) 'Credit rationing in markets with imperfect information', *American Economic Review*, 71, June, 393–410.

VIVES, X. (1996) 'La competencia en la banca española', meeting on *La banca mañana [Banking Tomorrow]*, El Escorial, 15–16 April.

14 The Impact of Interest Rates on Private Spending in Spain

Ángel Estrada, Ignacio Hernando and
Javier Vallés

INTERODUCTION

INTRODUCTION

Most macroeconomic policies attempt either to encourage saving and investment, to attain long-term growth, or to adjust expenditure in the different phases of the business cycle to make changes smoother. Both objectives assume that fiscal and monetary policy are able temporarily to affect the real interest rate and therefore that policy measures will have some impact on spending behaviour. This chapter leaves aside the first phase of the transmission of monetary policy – i.e. the impact of shifts in official rates on rates relevant for economic agents – and, assuming that variations in nominal rates are transferred to real rates, focuses specifically on the assessment of the impact of changes in an interest rate considered representative for economic agents on their spending.

The empirical analysis is based on observations for the 1972–94 period of the Spanish economy and uses quarterly data. Two distinct methodologies are employed. The first involves estimating the demand for consumption and demand for investment, differentiating both by types of good and by agents. These estimations take into account restrictions among the relevant variables of neoclassical investment and consumption models, and use an error correction mechanism in the specification. The second approach reviews the possible endogeneity nature of interest rates and the other determinants of agents' decisions, and estimates different Vector Autoregressive (VAR) models for the components of private spending.

The first approach attempts to measure how far real interest rates directly help explain variations in consumption and investment and compares their significance with that of other factors, using estimations of structural equations which model consumers' and companies' expenditure decisions. On the basis of these estimations, we analyze the effects that variations in the interest rate have on each expenditure decision, assuming that other variables remain unchanged. This exercise is designed to discern both the magnitude and timing of such changes. It is, nevertheless, a partial equilibrium exercise which only captures a direct effect caused by the change in the valuation of goods in different periods induced by a change in the interest rate; that is to say, we are considering one specific piece in the transmission mechanism and ignoring the other channels.

The findings of that exercise are conditioned by the assumption that the explanatory variables in spending decisions are exogenous. To offset that limitation, we also employ an alternative methodology: estimation of a reduced form equation, a VAR. Using this approach, which contemplates the possibility of interest rates being endogenous, we analyze the impact of changes in the interest rate not anticipated by economic agents. This exercise yields an assessment of the overall impact of the measures studied without distinguishing between the relative significance of the different channels.

The rest of the chapter is structured as follows. We summarize the theoretical arguments relating interest rates to spending decisions. We then present the theoretical household and corporate demand models, along with the econometric results for Spain. We perform a simulation of changes in the nominal interest rate and compare the results for the various different components of private spending. We then set out the findings obtained by applying the VAR methodology and finally draw the conclusions of this study.

THEORETICAL ASPECTS

Economic analysis acknowledges that consumers and corporations plan their consumption and investment decisions in an intertemporal context. The value that agents place on goods in different periods corresponds to the interest rate in the economy. Thus, for consumers, an increase in the real interest rate diminishes the present value of future consumption; in other words, future consumption becomes cheaper and, for that reason, part of present consumption is postponed. This is what is known as *intertemporal substitution effect*. For corporations, the interest rate is a component of the *user cost of capital* which is also determined by capital depreciation and the relative price of capital goods net of depreciation allowances. The user cost represents the value of a unit of investment for the company, which it expects to equal the market value of an already installed unit of capital. In the event of an increase in the interest rate, companies will reduce their demand for investment goods as the cost of capital rises and the present value of their future profits diminishes.

Along with those effects, which imply an alteration in the relative value attached to goods in different periods, variations in interest rates will generate a *wealth effect* on the expenditure demands of consumers and companies. Specifically, increases in the interest rate diminish the present value of assets and consequently reduce agents' borrowing capacity because of the lower value of the collateral they can provide.

The final effect of changes in the real interest rate on spending decisions should consider an additional channel: the *income effect* (changes induced in interest payments and earnings), which will depend on how the population is distributed between lenders and borrowers. Firstly, given the net creditor position of consumers in Spain as a whole, this effect on consumption will be positive (see Peñalosa, 1998), although its magnitude will vary according to the distribution of wealth in the population. In that regard, the major increase in public debt in countries such as Spain in recent years has created an additional vehicle for a positive income effect on savers, who are essentially the consumers, as a result of increases in the real interest rate. If these agents are Ricardian, the income effect will be partly offset by the effect of an expected upcoming increase in taxes. Secondly, in the case of companies, which on the whole are in a net debtor position, the income effect will reinforce the substitution effect.

The above analysis assumes that agents correctly predict their future income and the evolution of relative factor prices. *Expectations* about these variables and the real interest rate will affect the dynamics of the components of private spending, as well as the intensity of responses to changes in their explanatory variables. In addition, one important factor to consider and which is generally ignored in traditional analysis is *credit market imperfections*.

The existence of asymmetrical information in the credit market means, first, that the various financial assets are not perfect substitutes; and second, that a differential or premium is established between the cost of borrowed funds and the cost of agents' internal funds. Thus, changes in interest rates induced, for instance, by monetary policy measures will have an additional impact via two channels. Firstly, a contraction of the supply of bank credit will particularly affect those agents that depend on it most, and, secondly, it will increase the premium on external financing (see Hernando, 1997). The traditional way to reflect these effects is to incorporate into investment demand some variable measuring the flow of own funds or the stock of assets capable of being used as collateral.

As mentioned above, this study forgoes analysis of the transmission from the nominal interest rate that the monetary authorities attempt to control to the interest rates relevant for agent's expenditure decisions. In the estimations that follow, we have taken the average weighted lending rate as an approximation for the latter. The process of transmission from the intervention rate to the average lending rate is difficult to quantify and to distribute over time. In this mechanism, the role of the banking system is crucial (see Sastre, 1998), since it is the main source of financing in Spain. In any case, transmission will depend on the degree of competition, on the price expectations generated by changes in monetary policy, and on the economy's cyclical position. The type of instruments habitually used for financing – generally short-term and fixed-term loans – should also be considered.

Finally, it should be borne in mind that there is a different relevant interest rate for each component of private demand. In that sense, it is likely that assets with a longer maturity (i.e. infrastructure or housing), which also have longer-term financing, are less affected than other assets - especially consumer durables – by changes in short-term nominal interest rates which are more closely linked to monetary policy measures. The reason lies in the term structure of interest rates which relates short-and long-term financial assets. Nevertheless, the analysis put forward in this chapter commits a simplification in the sense of analyzing the response of the various components of private demand to a single interest rate.

QUARTERLY DEMAND EQUATIONS FOR THE COMPONENTS OF HOUSEHOLD AND CORPORATE SPENDING

The aim of this section is to present the equations estimated for some household and corporate spending components, using quarterly data. The equations will subsequently be used to simulate the impact of changes in interest rates. Three expenditure groups are considered for households: non-durable goods and services, durable goods, and domestic residential investment (housing purchases), and one group for companies: private productive investment.

An initial subsection thus analyzes the decisions of households and states the basic theoretical model used for the subsequent estimations. A second subsection similarly studies corporate decisions. The econometric methodology employed is identical in each case: in the long run, the restrictions derived from a theoretical model rationalizing spending decisions are imposed. In contrast, in the short run, other variables are added and the sample is allowed to determine the dynamics with which each of them appears. This procedure is due, on the one hand, to the considerable complexity associated with short-term adjustments (liquidity constraints, adjustment costs, etc.) and, on the other, to the fact that the quarterly data used are not from Quarterly National Accounts but from Annual National Accounts converted to a quarterly basis. For that reason, annual data are used to select the variables forming part of the long-term relationships.

Table 14.1 summarizes the results of the estimations of the equations for the various components of private spending for the 1972:3–1994:4 period,

Table 14.1 Explanatory variables for the components of private spending

Explanatory variables	Consumption Non-durable (C^{nd})		Consumption durable (C^d)		Investment domestic residential (I^{dr})		Investment private productive (I^{pp})	
	Short-run[1] (1)	Long-run (2)	Short-run[1] (3)	Long-run (4)	Short-run[1] (5)	Long-run (6)	Short-run[1] (7)	Long-run (8)
Income[2]	0.22	0.81	0.36	0.90	0.77	0.39	0.97	1.00
Financial wealth	–	0.07	–	–	–	–	–	–
Housing wealth	0.01	–	0.02	–	0.02	–	–	–
Interest rate[3]	−0.44	–	−0.33	−0.20	0	−0.48	−0.12	−1.49
Inflation[4]	−0.27	–	−0.61	–	–	–	–	–
Relative prices[5]	−0.52	–	–	–	–	−0.84	–	–
Other factors								
Real wage[6]	–	–	–	–	–	–	−0.05	0.43
Relative price of consumption–energy	–	–	0	−0.13	–	–	–	–
Relative price of intermediate imports– production	–	–	–	–	–	–	−0.08	−0.23
Other[7]	−0.03	–	−0.18	–	–	–	0.08	1.71

Notes:
1 Sum of the coefficients in first differences.
2 Disposable income for C^{nd}, C^d and I^{dr}, production for I^{pp}
3 User cost for C^d and I^{pp} and real interest rate for C^{nd} and I^{dr}. All of them are semi-elasticities.
4 Inflation measured as the difference of the corresponding deflator.
5 Relative price between non durables and total consumption for C^{nd}, deflator for I^{dr} and total consumption for I^{dr}.
6 Nominal wage divided by the production deflator.
7 Unemployment rate for C^{nd} and C^d and utilization rate for I^{pp}.

differentiating between the short and long-term effects of each of the explanatory variables. In addition, the tables in the Appendixes contain the econometric estimations for each component of private expenditure.

Household Decisions

The theoretical framework used to model consumer spending decisions assumes that consumers have identical preferences, live a finite number of periods, and derive utility from consuming goods and services that can be classified as: directly consumed goods and services (non-durable consumption, C^{nd}); durable consumption (C^d), and energy (E) combined by agents to generate services (S^d); and investment goods (domestic residential, I^{dr}), the use of which also generates consumption services (S^h).

According to the theoretical model, presented in Appendix 1, consumers solve an intertemporal optimization problem in order to distribute their expenditure among different goods in different periods. Under certain assumptions regarding consumer preferences, it is given that spending on non-durable consumer goods and the stocks of durable goods and housing are a function of their respective relative prices and of agents' permanent income. The limitations of the statistics available are crucial when it comes to moving from the theoretical to the empirical model (see Appendix 1). Concretely, the specifications chosen to represent stationary relationships in levels determine the demands for the 3 types of good as functions of variables that approximate agents' permanent income – disposable income, non-human wealth, and real interest rate (user cost in the case of durable goods) – and of the prices of goods:

$$c^{nd*} = \alpha'_{nd} + \beta_{nd}yd^* + \theta_{1nd}\frac{WF}{YD} + \theta_{2nd}\frac{WH}{YD} + \theta_{3nd}\frac{WD}{YD} + \gamma_{1nd}p^{nd*} + \gamma_{2nd}RR^*$$

$$(14.1)$$

$$c^{d*} = \alpha'_{d} + \beta_{d}yd^* + \theta_{1d}\frac{WF}{YD} + \theta_{2d}\frac{WH}{YD} + \theta_{3d}\frac{WD}{YD} + \gamma_{1d}cud^* + \gamma_{2d}p^{e*} \quad (14.2)$$

$$i^{dr*} = \alpha'_{h} + \beta_{h}yd^* + \theta_{1h}\frac{WF}{YD} + \theta_{2h}\frac{WH}{YD} + \theta_{3h}\frac{WD}{YD} + \gamma_{1h}p^{h*} + \gamma_{2h}RRH^* \quad (14.3)$$

where YD is disposable income, WF financial wealth, WD wealth in durable goods, WH wealth in housing, P^{nd*} the relative price of non-durable goods, RR^* the real interest rate, CUD^* the user cost of durable goods, P^{e*} the relative price of energy, P^{h*} the relative price of housing, and RRH^* the real interest rate associated with housing. The lower case letters denote logarithms and the asterisks real-terms variables.

As stated earlier, the econometric methodology used is that of cointegration, testing whether all the variables specified in (14.1)–(14.3) or only a subset of them were necessary to obtain some stationary residuals in levels. In the short run, the specifications are much more flexible, since other possible explanatory variables are added.[1]

Table 14.1 summarizes the results of the estimations of the equations for the various components of private spending, distinguishing between short[2] and long-run effects. Columns (1) and (2) of the table show the coefficients of the explanatory variables in the estimation of expenditure on non-durable consumption goods. They can be seen in greater detail in Table 14A.1 of Appendix 1 (p. 512). In the long run, disposable income and the

financial wealth-disposable income ratio were sufficient to obtain a cointegration vector with elasticities of 0.81 and 0.07[3], respectively. The stationarity of this vector is reflected in the high t-ratio estimated for the coefficient
of the error correction mechanism[4]. These elasticities appear to be somewhat low compared with those obtained using annual data (0.94 and 0.17),
which are much more in line with those estimated for other countries (see,
for instance, Muellbauer and Lattimore, 1994). The remaining wealth variables are not significant (in fact, they also fail to appear in the other long-
term relationships, due probably to their very low liquidity). Nor is the
relative price of non-durable goods significant (it is almost a constant variable). And nor is the real interest rate significant. This latter result shows
how difficult it is to obtain an intertemporal substitution effect using aggregate consumption data.

In the short run, a complicated set of lags emerges. Changes in income
have a positive *net* effect on the change in non-durable consumption, this
being the most relevant variable for an explanation of its short-term behaviour. Shifts in the housing wealth–income ratio work in the same direction
and this impact helps to explain the marked increase in consumption
towards the end of the 1980s and the slowdown in the early 1990s. By contrast, in none of the equations is the variation of the durable goods or
financial wealth – disposable income ratio significant in the short run. In
the first of these cases, the results are hardly surprising, given that second-
hand markets for these types of good are still under-developed in Spain.
For their part, changes in real interest rates have a negative impact. It
should be pointed out here that, using annual data, changes in real interest
rates have much less effect and have a one-year lag. On the other hand, a
negative impact is estimated for changes in the rate of inflation which may
reflect the wealth effect – via capital losses – on spending on non-durable
consumption. Finally, changes in the relative price of non-durable consumption have a negative impact and the same is true of the unemployment rate. This is consistent with an interpretation to be found in recent
studies, whereby this latter variable is considered a proxy for individuals'
uncertainty about their future income.

In the long run, then, income determines the behaviour of non-durable
consumption, while, in the short run, the impact of changes in income
(which is the biggest impact) can be seen to be accompanied by the effect
associated with the non-financial wealth of economic agents, by a certain
degree of inter- and intra-temporal substitution (between nondurable consumption goods and other goods) and by the uncertainty about income.
Although over the long term this model is observationally equivalent to a
Keynesian framework according to which individuals consume a constant
proportion of their disposable income, the inclusion of the short run
makes it similar to a model in which there are agents who make decisions

based on their permanent income and others who act on the basis of their disposable income.

Columns (3) and (4) of Table 14.1 present the results of the estimation of the equation for expenditure on consumer durables, detailed in Table 14A.2 of Appendix 1. The long-term relationship includes household disposable income, the user cost and the relative price of energy, with elasticity estimations of 0.90 and 0.13 for disposable income and the relative price of energy, respectively, and a semi-elasticity of 0.20 for the user cost. As in the previous case, the stationarity of the cointegration vector is reflected in its high t-ratio. Compared with the annual results, once again we note that the income elasticity is much lower (annual data yield 1.40). This makes it impossible to obtain a unit average elasticity (0.82 with quarterly data) for household private consumption as an aggregate, whereas this is obtained with annual data. That elasticity continues to be low when compared with that obtained using the MOISEES model (0.93) based on the aggregate consumption equation (see Molinas *et al.*, 1990). The inclusion of the user cost in the durable goods equation allows interest rates to have some – albeit slight (−0.03 on average) – negative impact on long-term aggregate consumption.

In the short run, changes in disposable income are once again the main determinant of change in spending on durables (the impact is stronger than that found on non-durable goods spending). Changes in the housing wealth – disposable income ratio also have a positive and contemporaneous impact, which says something about the complementarity links between home purchases and part of expenditure on durables (an aspect not considered in the theoretical model). The user cost has a negative impact on this type of good. The relative price of energy has a negative impact on changes in durables. As with non-durable goods, changes in the unemployment rate are significant (and larger in terms of size), thereby reinforcing its interpretation as an indicator of future uncertainty, and, changes in the inflation rate have a negative impact.

Finally, as regards household decisions, columns (5) and (6) of Table 14.1 contain the equation estimated for domestic residential investment (detailed in Table 14A.3 in Appendix 1), whose long term seems more similar to that of durable goods spending as the financial wealth – disposable income ratio does not appear. Disposable income has a positive, but very low (0.39) elasticity, which is repeated when annual data are used in the estimation. The relative price and real interest rate have, as expected, a negative impact and in the case of the latter, its semi-elasticity (-0.48) is higher in absolute terms than that of the user cost in the case of durable goods. The income elasticity estimated appears too low, using both quarterly and annual data; for example, it was 1.24 in the equation included in the MOISEES model, although the real interest rate did not appear in this specification. This low income elasticity could be due to the way in which the dependent variable is accounted for.[5]

In the short term, disposable income is again the main determinant of domestic residential investment (and the impact is higher than that of the two previously analyzed cases); the housing wealth – disposable income ratio is also significant and, surprisingly, only accelerations in real interest rates appear marginally, which is difficult to explain theoretically.

Although the tables do not show it, the 3 equations analyzed include a series of dummy variables in 1993, which assume a shift to a lower level in the non-durable and durable expenditure statistics. All the equations have a high R^2, with the domestic residential investment equation showing the worst fit. The tests for stationarity, normality, and absence of autocorrelation and heteroscedasticity are accepted at the standard significance levels.

Corporate Decisions

The corporate investment decision model used in this section is based on the consideration that the demand for productive capital depends on the return it is expected to yield. How to measure that return directly is a difficult task, especially when working with aggregate data. An alternative approach is to specify an investment function which depends on determinants of the expected return on capital without having to measure it. This approach, which is quite common in the literature, is also adopted here.

The theoretical model, summarized in Appendix 2, is based on the hypothesis that companies produce by combining 3 factors: capital (K), labour (L) and imported intermediate goods (M). Firms decide the optimum level of the inputs they demand with a view to maximizing profits, depending on the technology at their disposal and on the equation determining capital accumulation. The solution of firms optimization problem gives rise to a long-term neo-classical-style relationship in which the demand for capital depends on output and relative factor prices.

The specification of the long-term relationship includes the degree of capacity utilization. This variable is a proxy for deviations of output with respect to expected demand (which is the real determinant of the desired stock of capital) or for the intensity with which the productive factors are used. Finally, by assuming the existence of adjustment costs in adapting the stock of capital, it is possible to derive an investment function based on the determinants of the demand for capital. In this way, the equation finally estimated as a long-term relationship for private productive investment (I^{pp}) is expressed as follows:

$$i^{pp*} = \Psi_0' + pb^* + \Psi_2'w^* + \Psi_3'p^{m*} + \Psi_4 cu^* + \Psi_5'ut \qquad (14.4)$$

where the lower case letters denote logarithms and the asterisks real-terms variables. *PB* is gross output, *W* is wages per employee, P^M is the price of imported intermediate goods, *CU* the user cost of capital, and *UT* the degree of capacity utilization. As noted in Appendix 2, in the case of constant returns to scale, the output coefficient should be equal to 1; the real wages coefficient and the coefficient for the relative price of imported intermediate goods should be positive – in such a way that the factor substitution effect predominates – and the user cost coefficient should be negative. Furthermore, the coefficient for the degree of capacity utilization is expected to be positive, since it may be reflecting both unexpected changes in demand when planning output and the degree of intensity with which productive factors are used.

The most satisfactory results for the private productive investment function are shown in columns (7) and (8) of Table 14.1 and, in greater detail, in Table 14B.1 of Appendix 2. As can be seen, in this component long-term relationship, all the variables included in expression (14.4) were significant, although the cointegration relationship passes the tests at a lower level of significance than was obtained in the consumer goods equations. In the case of gross output, it was demonstrated that its coefficient was equal to unity, while the other variables had the expected signs, except for the relative price of imported intermediate goods. The reason for this finding may be that it reflects supply shocks given that these imports are mostly energy products. Wages have a positive impact, i.e. for a given level of output a wage increase leads to labor being replaced by capital. The user cost has a negative effect, representing a semi-elasticity of 1.49 (the highest of all the components analyzed). The degree of capacity utilization has a positive sign, but much higher than unity. If this is compared with findings using annual data, the results are similar. When compared with other studies, these results are similar to the investment equation in the MOISEES model in the unit value of elasticity *vis-à-vis* the output variable and in the parameter obtained for degree of capacity utilization; on the other hand, the elasticity of the user cost in absolute terms is much lower in this case (-0.20 compared to -0.60) and inflation, which could be what increases the effect of the user cost, does not appear. Apparently, it is the relative price of energy which plays such a role here. Another study in which the price of energy is included multiplicatively with output is that carried out by Espasa and Senra (1993). It shows an output elasticity higher than unity, while the user cost has a markedly lower elasticity in absolute terms (-0.09).

In the short run, changes in private productive investment are basically determined by changes in output, while the remaining relative prices have a negative impact. In this respect, it is worth noting how, in the short run, capital and labour are complementary factors (unlike what we saw for the long run), possibly because of the undoubted incidence that a change in the price of a quasi-fixed factor such as labour has on available resources in the short run. As with the equations for household decisions, tests validating the model are accepted at standard significance levels.

SIMULATION OF THE EFFECTS OF CHANGES IN INTEREST RATES

This section attempts to assess the effects of a one-point increase in the long-term nominal interest rate on the various components of private spending.[6] To that end we have carried out simulations considering temporary increases (over 1 year) in the interest rate, based on the aggregate demand equations estimated for Spain in the previous section. Before discussing on the findings, it is worth defining the scope of the exercises.

Firstly, the simulations presented here look only at *direct effects*, in the sense of effects produced by changes in the user cost (in the durable consumption and private productive investment equations) or by changes in the real interest rate (in the non-durable consumption or domestic residential investment equations), assuming that all the other variables remain constant. These simulations thus reflect the intertemporal substitution channel and ignore the income and wealth channels, which may operate with a longer time lag. We do not consider either the possible endogeneity of the user cost and the real interest rate. In a more general model, these variables are determined by the interaction of savers and investors. In equilibrium, the expected return on assets should equal the utility of postponing a unit of consumption and saving it for future consumption, and the level of the real interest rate would be linked to both technological and preference factors. This relationship is taken into account in a later section, in which we posit a reduced form simultaneous model. This section also avoids the effects induced by changes in income, wages, the wealth of economic agents or the exchange rate.

Secondly, changes in expenditure components as a result of variations in the interest rate are not necessarily to be interpreted as agents' response to changes in monetary policy variables, since we are ignoring the initial stage of the process of transmission of monetary policy measures; in other words, the impact of variations in the Banco de España intervention rate on the interest rates relevant for household and corporate spending decisions.

Thirdly, the simulations assume that the temporary increases in nominal interest rates affects also temporarily to real interest rates. To the extent that this pass-through derives from monetary disturbances and is accompanied by a lowering of inflationary expectations, the simulated effects would underestimate the real *direct effects*.

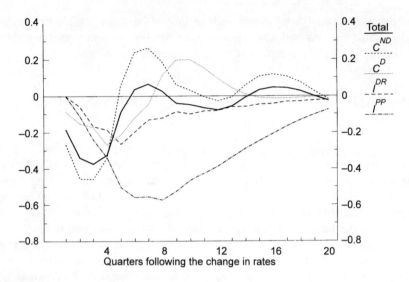

Figure 14.1   Simulation of interest rates, responses of the demand components[1]

Note: 1. Estimated responses of each demand component to a 1-year increase of 1 percentage point in the nominal interest rate. Deviation from the reference path.

The effects of the changes in interest rates analyzed in this section were obtained by using the equations estimated in the previous section, simulating dynamically[7] the 1990–4 period. The results presented for each component of private spending are the percentages by which the simulated values deviate from the simulation with the observed data.

Figure 14.1 shows the simulated responses of the different components of private spending to a *temporary* (over 1 year) increase of 1 point in the nominal interest rate considered. Table 14.2 reflects both the maximum impact of these responses and the average impacts during the first and second year after the change in the interest rate.

The pattern over time of the impact on each of the components of private spending varies considerably. The effect of interest rates on *non-durable consumption* is concentrated in the first year and is the most significant among all the private expenditure components, although it slows rapidly from the fourth quarter onwards and produces positive responses. Using annual data, the response is less marked and takes longer, due to the short-term dynamics of real interest rates. For that reason, confidence in the simulated effect is not excessive.

As regards the demand for *durable consumption goods*, the simulated measure – as in the case of domestic residential investment – affects the user cost only via a decline in the real interest rate, since we have not taken into account the taxation affecting consumers. The highest intensity

Table 14.2   Effects of an increase in the nominal long-term interest rate of 1 percentage point during 1 year[1]

	Maximum effect	Quarter in which is produced	First year average effect	Second year average effect
Domestic private demand	−0.37	3rd	−0.31	0.00
Consumption	−0.42	3rd	−0.35	0.15
Non-durable goods	−0.46	3rd	−0.38	0.19
Durable goods	−0.27	4th	−0.17	−0.07
Investment	−0.48	6th	−0.16	−0.46
Domestic residential	−0.26	5th	−0.10	−0.18
Private productive	−0.57	8th	−0.17	−0.55

Note: 1. Dynamic simulations realized with the estimated equations. Percentage deviations with respect to the reference level (i.e. without change in the interest rate).

is reached around the fourth quarter, declining markedly thereafter and even reaching positive levels in year 3.

In the case of domestic residential investment, the biggest effect is around the fifth quarter, after which it diminishes, though less so than in the case of durable consumption, with no positive effects emerging in any year.

With regard to *private productive investment*, the response is most intense in the eighth quarter, gradually subsiding thereafter and disappearing at the end of year 5. The measure simulated has a dual effect on the user cost: first an immediate impact caused by the increase in the real interest rate and, second, an effect of the same sign as a result of the decline in the present value of the future investment tax relief associated with the increase in the real interest rate. We should stress that both the magnitude and profile of the simulations may be biased because of non-inclusion of financial variables (e.g. cash flow) in the specification.

Comparing the accumulated effects of the interest rate with those reflected in the simulation presented in Estrada, Sastre and Vega (1994), a first major difference is the much more marked effects obtained in that study, despite the fact that it evaluated the impact of one percentage point changes in the intervention rate (which, according to that study's own estimations, are not passed on in their entirety to rates relevant for agents). The reason for such differences in the simulated effects lies in the fact that the exercise by Estrada, Sastre and Vega considered a wider portion of the transmission mechanism, including effects induced through agents' disposable income and wealth.[8] The magnitude of the differences underscores the relevance of the induced effects that have not been considered in this section. In the following section, the methodology adopted allows for a joint consideration of the various transmission channels.

THE ENDOGENEITY OF CHANGES IN INTEREST RATES

There is a problem with simulating the effects of changes in the interest rate on spending decisions. Although the weak exogeneity of the contemporaneous regressors has been statistically accepted in the estimations, it is quite likely that the strong exogeneity condition is not met (see Engle, Hendry and Richard, 1983), this being necessary to perform a dynamic simulation. In economic terms, this would suggest that these variables are jointly determined and also influenced by third variables not expressly considered, such as technological, fiscal, or labour market disturbances. To take them properly into account, it would be best to perform a joint estimation allowing us to review the effects of all the transmission channels on the demand for consumer and investment goods.

One simple way to avoid the possible problem of endogeneity without specifying a structural model, that would have to define the channels through which monetary policy exerts influence, is to use a Vector Autoregressive model (VAR). A VAR is a system of equations in which all the variables are considered endogenous. The econometric estimation consists of regressing the present values of each variable in the system on its own lags and on those of the other variables in the system. This methodology is designed, first, to depict the responses of each of the demand components to an interest rate disturbance and to assess its relative importance vis-à-vis other disturbances; and second, to study the consistency of these findings with those obtained in simulations based on the estimations of demand equations.

Nevertheless, it has to be remembered that, even using this methodology, changes in long-term nominal interest rates should not be considered as indicative of the change in tone of monetary policy, because the interest rates may be responding to a fiscal shock or to a supply disruption. With that limitation it is fair to consider that, whatever the instrumentation of monetary policy to fulfil its intermediate objectives (whether quantities- or interest rates-based), it will affect long-term interest rates. At the same time, the formation of expectations by agents or the degree of substitutability between different financial assets will affect the term structure of interest rates and, hence, the magnitude and propagation of the impact of monetary policy decisions on the variables most likely to affect agents' spending decisions.

A VAR model has been estimated for each of the demand components considered: non-durable consumption goods (C^{nd}), durable consumption goods (C^d), domestic residential investment (I^{dr}), and private productive investment (I^{pp}). The macroeconomic variables considered were similar to those used in the estimations of the demand equations (p. 494 and 497). The two VAR models with consumption goods include five variables. In each case (durable and non-durable consumption goods), in addition to spending on the respective type of good, the same four variables are considered: national income, as a scale variable; the relative price of energy, as a way of reflecting possible supply shocks; and, as nominal variables, the long-term nominal interest rate and the logarithmic differences of the GDP deflator. The two VAR models for investment goods contain six variables. In each, in addition to the respective investment demand, there are four variables in common and one specific variable. The latter is the scale variable, which is final demand in the case of private productive investment and, in the case of domestic residential investment, disposable income. The four common variables included are two relative prices -for imported intermediate goods (which behave rather like the relative price of energy) and wages per employee-and two nominal variables: the long-term nominal interest rate and the logarithmic differences of the GDP deflator.

Although this methodology avoids imposing a priori restrictions on the relationship between variables when it comes to identifying disturbances in each variable that are not correlated with the others, it is necessary to impose some contemporaneous restrictions. The identification was made following the order of the variables in the system, and it can be justified in accordance with information lags in agents' decisions. Disposable income or final demand comes first, indicating that disturbances in these real variables are the original source of variability, as in a classical approach. The interest rate is the last variable in the system, suggesting that it may respond contemporaneously to changes in one or other of the remaining variables.[9] Investment or consumption can only respond contemporaneously to changes in aggregate demand and only with a lag to changes in nominal variables.

The model was estimated with all the variables in levels,[10] to make it as comparable as possible with previous simulation exercises. The sample period, which also coincides with that used in the estimations of the demand equations, is 1972:3–1994:4. At this stage, it is worth recalling the two basic differences between the simulation exercises performed with this methodology and those presented in the previous section. Firstly, the simulations carried out using the VAR approach focus on the impact of unexpected disturbances, while the simulations based on the demand equations serve to analyze the effect of changes – both anticipated and unexpected – on the interest rate. Secondly, the simulations carried out using the VAR approach consider the effects of various transmission channels on the private spending components, unlike the simulations performed on the basis of structural equations, which basically incorporate the intertemporal substitution channel.

The findings of the simulations with VAR models indicate that, in general, the four types of goods have a similar sign response to the different disturbances. The various components of real expenditure respond

positively to a temporary disturbance in income or in the level of activity.
An innovation in the variation of aggregate prices contracts consumption

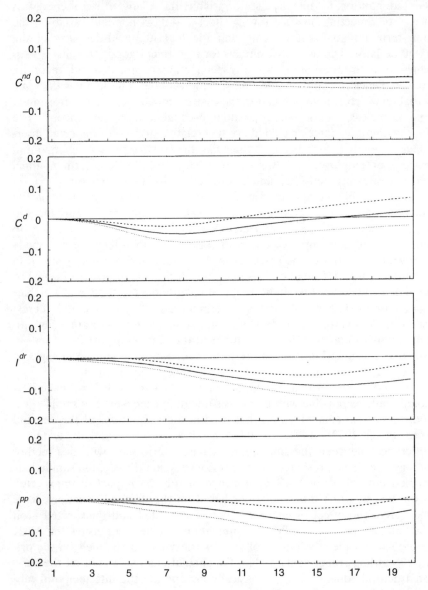

Figure 14.2   A shock in the interest rate, responses of the demand components[1]

Note: 1.   Estimated responses of each demand component to a 4-quarter shock of 1 standard deviation. Each response includes the average value and 1 standard deviation band calculated from a Monte Carlo experiment.

and investment, although in the case of private productive investment this effect only appears in the long run and with consumption goods it is of a temporary nature. A positive innovation in the relative prices of energy or of imported intermediate goods also reduces expenditure immediately and temporarily. An increase in real wages contracts investment; however, this complementary goods effect is of a more permanent nature than in the case of energy sector inputs.

Figure 14.2 shows the response in the level of each of the demand components to a temporary innovation in the interest rate. Figure 14.2 includes the average value and one standard deviation band of the response. Table 14.3 shows the maximum effect achieved and the average effect on each expenditure component during the first and second year after the innovation. That innovation represents the effect on expenditure of an increase in the unexplained component in the interest rate equation which is orthogonal to the other residuals in the VAR system. As mentioned earlier, unlike this exercise, the effects on the demand equations in the previous section derived from an increase in the interest rate that includes both the expected and the unexpected components and reflected only the direct impact.

Although in all four cases the contractive effects are temporary, their pattern over time varies considerably. Consumption respond earlier, but to a lesser extent, than investment. The *consumption of non-durable goods*, the weightiest component in overall demand, reacts least in terms of magnitude but with the greatest persistence, a result countering that found with the estimated demand equation. With durable consumption, the greatest effect is reached earlier, but it is less intense than the effect found with investment goods.

Table 14.3 Anticipated change in the nominal long-term interest rate during 1 year[1]

	Maximum effect	*Quarter in which is produced*	*First year average effect*	*Second year average effect*
Domestic private demand	−1.65	15th	−0.25	−1.04
Consumption	−1.52	15th	−0.30	−1.12
Non-durable goods	−1.78	18th	−0.24	−0.74
Durable goods	−5.04	8th	−0.75	−4.30
Investment	−7.09	15th	−0.01	−1.58
Domestic residential	−8.97	16th	−0.35	−2.39
Private productive	−6.54	15th	−0.03	−1.34

Note: 1. Response to a shock in the interest rate. Changes in percentage points with respect to level of the reference level (i.e. without change in the interest rate).

The effect on *investment* is greatest around the fourth year and it is bigger than the effect on consumption. Once one adds the responses of consumption and investment, the results are in line with those obtained in Escrivá and Haldane (1994), which suggest that monetary measures have a greater impact on private investment than on private consumption. The differences between the two types of investment are the longer lag in the response of residential investment and the lesser contraction of private productive investment.

In the long run, the findings are consistent with the better fit shown by accelerator-type investment models compared to neoclassical models (see, for instance, Gordon and Veitch, 1986, for the United States) and with Hall's random walk model for aggregate consumption (1981). In the short run (during the first year following a disturbance), innovations in the interest rate explain less than 10 per cent of the variance in consumption and investment.

Comparison with the interest rate elasticities of the consumer goods estimated on pp. 512–13 also reveals differences in their size. Although non-durable goods, comparatively speaking, respond least to interest rates (their average effect is −0.7 per cent in year 2), in the estimated demand for *non-durable consumption*, the responses are highly significant in the first quarters. The greatest discrepancy appears in the comparison of simulations with *durable goods*. The effect is a 0.7 per cent drop in the first year and 4.3 per cent in year two. The greater sensitivity encountered in VAR analysis may reflect 3 additional channels: first, the wealth effect, which lowers the present value of the net wealth of consumers; next, complementarity with the demand for domestic residential investment goods; and finally, the importance of the credit channel for consumers, because they are agents who are highly dependent on bank financing and for whom, probably, the cost of borrowed funds depends significantly on the collateral they provide.

The significance and time lag in the response of *private productive investment* is consistent with the existence of a credit channel reinforcing the impact of monetary policies for non-financial enterprises (see, for instance, Bernanke and Gertler, 1995). Faced with an interest rate hike, firms perceive an increase in their financial costs; and for that reason, their cash flow, and later their sales and profits, will drop. Large companies may try to alleviate the temporary drop in cash flow by increasing their short-term borrowing, but small firms will have to reduce costs and output, using up stocks and cutting back on investment. In Spain, at a desegregated level, there is evidence of the importance of this channel for investment decisions, as well as of differences in the way companies behave depending on their size (see, for example, Hernando and Vallés, 1992).

The size of the effect of an innovation in the interest rate for *private productive investment* estimated in the VAR model is greater – from the first year on – than that found in the investment demand simulation. On average, during the first year, the effect of a 1-point increase in the interest rate is −0.03 per cent, while in investment demand the effect is −0.17 per cent. In year two, the effect is bigger in the VAR simulation, with an average drop of 1.34 per cent compared with the demand equation's 0.55 per cent. As regards *domestic residential investment*, the differences are even more significant, above all 1 year after the innovation.

Finally, it is worth pointing out that the simulations conducted, both with the structural equations of the different components of private demand and with the VAR models, are very much conditioned by the period analyzed. In the first part of the sample, interest rates varied much less, mainly because financial markets in Spain were still incipient. Thus, an estimation of VAR models in the 1982–94 period reveals a swifter and less persistent response of the various different components of expenditure to unexpected shifts in interest rates than in the period as a whole, a finding that is consistent with the existence of more efficient financial markets.

CONCLUSIONS

This study has gathered evidence on the influence of interest rates on household and corporate spending decisions. It chose an extensive sample period (1972–94), during which both financial markets and goods and factor markets in Spain underwent considerable structural changes. Consequently, the quantitative results constitute an average for a very heterogeneous period.

The results of the estimations of the equations for the various components of private demand imply that, in the long run, non-durable consumption is basically determined by disposable income. This variable is also the main determinant in the cases of durable consumption and domestic residential investment, although, in both components, the real interest rate also plays an important part. For its part, the long-term behaviour of private productive investment is conditioned by demand and by the user cost of capital.

The estimated size of the direct effect of a temporary (1-year) 1-point increase in interest rates on national private demand is – on average for the first year – slightly over −0.3 per cent. That effect takes other determinants of expenditure decisions as given, so that what is involved is a direct effect. Transmission of the change in interest rates is concentrated in the early quarters (reaching a maximum impact of −0.4 per cent), with the private productive investment component being the slowest to respond.

Using VAR methodology, we also analyzed the effects of changes in interest rates on each of the components of private expenditure. This exercise takes the possible endogeneity of interest rates into account and thereby combines the effects of all transmission channels on consumption and investment. In addition, these simulations consider only the impact of unexpected disturbances on the interest rate. These two features of simulations using VAR models explain why greater effects result than with simulations based on structural equations. Thus, the average effect in the first year of a 1-point increase in interest rates (for 1 year) for total private demand is around −0.2 per cent. However, the transmission of the effect is much slower than when only direct effects were considered, with the maximum effect (−1.6 per cent) occurring at the end of the fourth year. If the same analysis is carried out in a more recent period, the aggregate effect is less marked and transmission somewhat swifter. Even so, transmission is still slower than with the direct-effects simulations, because in that case other channels presumably operating with a longer time lag were not included. Thus, while the average effect in the first year of a 1-point increase in the interest rate for a year for total private demand is greater in absolute terms in simulations based on structural equations than in simulations using VAR models (−0.31 as opposed to −0.25, respectively), the average impact in the second year is greater in the latter (−1.04).

Further, it is noteworthy that in both simulation exercises a greater average effect is obtained in the first year (and a lower average effect in the second year) on consumption than on investment, revealing a slower but more intense and persistent response in the case of investment goods.

Finally, in the simulations based on structural equations, the private expenditure component responding with the greatest intensity during the first year is non-durable consumption, while in year two private productive investment has the greatest incidence. By contrast, in the simulations using VAR models, the biggest effect during the first 2 years of increases in interest rates is in durable consumption; yet for longer terms it is private productive investment that shows the greatest impact.

These results offer an assessment of the influence of real interest rates on the spending decisions of private agents. Nevertheless, it is worth pointing out that the association of disturbances in real interest rates with monetary policy measures is not immediate. Yet given that those measures could have a short-term effect on real interest rates, monetary policy measures should bear in mind both the time lag in their effect on aggregate real expenditure and the different impact they have on the various components of expenditure.

Appendix 1: Consumer Expenditure Functions

The theoretical model underlying the analysis contained on pp. 493–7 regarding consumers' expenditure decisions is a model with no uncertainty and no financial restrictions.[11] Consumers have identical preferences, live a finite number of periods, and derive profit from consuming goods and services. These can be classified as: directly consumed goods and services (non-durable consumption, C^{nd}); durable consumer goods (C^d), and energy (E) combined by agents to generate services (S^d); and investment goods (domestic residential, I^{dr}), the use of which also generates consumption services (S^h).

Given that in each period consumers will derive profit from C^{nd}, S^d and S^h, the intertemporal problem they face is the following:

$$\text{Max } V(U(C_1^{nd}, S_1^d, S_1^h), \ldots, U(C_T^{nd}, S_T^d, S_T^h))$$

subject to

$$A_t = (1+r)A_{t-1} + Y_t - P_t^{nd}C_t^{nd} - P_t^d C_t^d - P_t^e E_t - P_H^h I_t^{dr} \tag{14A.1}$$

$$C_t^d = KD_t - KD_{t-1} + \delta^d KD_{t-1} \tag{14A.2}$$

$$I_t^{dr} = KH_t - KH_{t-1} + \delta^h KH_{t-1} \tag{14A.3}$$

$$S_t^d = \alpha_1 KD_t + \alpha_2 E_t \tag{14A.4}$$

$$E_t = \alpha_3 KD_t \tag{14A.5}$$

$$S_t^h = KH_t \tag{14A.6}$$

$$A_T \geq 0 \tag{14A.7}$$

where A is non-human wealth, r the nominal interest rate, Y labour income, P^{nd}, P^d, P^e, and P^h the prices of each of the goods and services considered, KD and KH the stocks of durable goods and housing, respectively, and δ^d, δ^h their depreciation rates that are assumed to be constant.

The first restriction shows how the financial wealth of agents evolves over time (the interest rate is assumed to be constant); (14A.2) and (14A.3) determine the accumulation of stocks of durable goods and housing. The 3 following equations are simple production functions for the services of these same goods and, finally, (14A.7) is the condition that prevents agents of being with a positive terminal indebtedness.

Given that the utility function is intertemporally separable and that interest rates are assumed to be constant, this problem can be solved in two stages: in the first, economic agents allocate their income to each period and, in the second, they assign each period's expenditure to each good. Assuming isoelastic profit functions that are separable among goods:

$$U(C_t^{nd}, KD_t, KH_t) = \frac{\alpha_{nd}}{a}\left(\frac{C_t^{nd}}{\alpha_{nd}}\right)^a + \frac{\alpha_d}{a}\left(\frac{KD_t}{\alpha_d}\right)^a + \frac{\alpha}{a}\left(\frac{KH_t}{\alpha}\right)^a \qquad (14A.8)$$

where α_{nd}, α_d, α_h and a are parameters associated with the utility function, the solution would be of the following type (lower case letters denote logarithms):

$$c_t^{nd*} = \alpha_{nd} + \frac{1}{a-1}p_t^{nd*} + yp_t^* \qquad (14A.9)$$

$$kd_t^* = \alpha_d + \frac{1}{a-1}cud_t^* + yp_t^* \qquad (14A.10)$$

$$kh_t^* = \alpha_v + \frac{1}{a-1}cuh_t^* + yp_t^* \qquad (14A.11)$$

where:

$$P^{nd*} = \frac{P^{nd}}{P} \qquad (14A.12)$$

$$CUD^* = \frac{\alpha_3 P^e + P^d - \frac{P_{+1}^d(1-\delta^d)}{1+r}}{P} \qquad (14A.13)$$

$$CUH^* = \frac{P^h - \frac{P_{+1}^h(1-\delta^h)}{1+r}}{P} \qquad (14A.14)$$

$$YP^* = \frac{A_{-1} + \sum^T \frac{Y}{1+r} + P^d(1-\delta^d)KD_{-1} + P^h(1-\delta^h)KH_{-1}}{P} \qquad (14A.15)$$

$$P = \left\{(P^{nd})^{\frac{a}{a-1}}\alpha_{nd} + (CUD)^{\frac{a}{a-1}}\alpha_d + (CUH)^{\frac{a}{a-1}}\alpha\right\}^{\frac{a-1}{a}} \qquad (14A.16)$$

These expressions are quite simple to interpret: spending on each of the goods is going to be a proportion of economic agents' permanent income (14A.15), corrected to take into account the relative prices effect. In the case of goods with some degree of durability, the price takes the well-known form of a user cost.[12]

Moving from the theoretical to the empirical model is always the most complicated step, due to the existing limitations in terms of statistical sources. As regards the variables to be explained, the basic source is the

National Accounts; this means that expenditure on nondurable consumer goods is going to include expenditure on energy and the spending imputed to home ownership, since it is impossible to omit these two components (mainly during the first years of the sample). We do not model the evolution of stocks, KD or KH. Instead it considers the expenditure on durables (C^d) and domestic residential investment (I^{dr}).[13]

As for the explanatory variables, an approximation to the aggregate price index (P) is obtained with the aggregate consumption deflator, which does not exactly match expression (14A.16), because it does not consider the durability of the goods. The other prices are the National Accounts deflators, while for the price of energy we have used the deflator for energy sector imports. In calculating user cost, we have relaxed the hypothesis that the nominal interest rate is constant and assume perfect prediction of prices. In the particular case of durable consumption, we have separated the traditional user cost component (CUD^*) and the price of energy on its own (P^{e*}), because the value of parameter α_3 is unknown; and, in the case of housing, we have desegregated the relative price (P^{h^*}) of the real interest rate (RRH^*), since the latter does not always have positive values.

The most difficult variable to approximate is permanent income (YP^*). Like Muellbauer and Lattimore (1994), we use disposable income (as defined in the National Accounts) and a ratio of wealth to that same variable.[14] In addition, wealth is broken down into financial (WF), durables (WD), and housing (WH), in an attempt to take into account the different degree of liquidity of each type of asset.

Thus, as pointed out in the main text of the chapter, the specifications chosen to represent long-term relationships in the demands for each of the components of expenditure are the following:

$$c^{nd^*} = \alpha'_{nd} + \beta_{nd}yd^* + \theta_{1nd}\frac{WF}{YD} + \theta_{2nd}\frac{WH}{YD} + \theta_{3nd}\frac{WD}{YD} + \gamma_{1nd}p^{nd^*} + \gamma_{2nd}RR^*$$

$$(14A.17)$$

$$c^{d^*} = \alpha'_d + \beta_d yd^* + \theta_{1d}\frac{WF}{YD} + \theta_{2d}\frac{WH}{YD} + \theta_{3d}\frac{WD}{YD} + \gamma_{1d}cud^* + \gamma_{2d}p^{e^*}$$

$$(14A.18)$$

$$i^{dr^*} = \alpha'_h + \beta_h yd^* + \theta_{1h}\frac{WF}{YD} + \theta_{2h}\frac{WH}{YD} + \theta_{3h}\frac{WD}{YD} + \gamma_{1h}p^{h^*} + \gamma_{2h}RRH^*$$

$$(14A.19)$$

Tables 14A.1–14A.3 contain the estimations of the equations of the different components of household expenditure. They include as long-term explanatory variables those that turned out to be statistically significant.

Table 14A.1 Expenditure on non-durable consumer goods, OLS estimation

$$\Delta c^{nd^*} = \underset{(12.66)}{0.80} \; \Delta c^{nd^*}_{-1} - \underset{(-7.42)}{0.39} \; \Delta c^{nd^*}_{-2} - \underset{(-4.90)}{0.31} \; \Delta c^{nd^*}_{-5} + \underset{(8.05)}{0.11} \; (\Delta yd^* + \Delta yd^*_{-2})$$

$$-3\Delta^2 yd^*_{-3} + \underset{(8.27)}{0.01} \; \left(\Delta \left(\frac{WH}{YD}\right)_{-1} - 2\Delta^2 \left(\frac{WH}{YD}\right)_{-3} \right) - \underset{(-4.82)}{0.27} \; (\Delta RR + \Delta^2 p^{nd})$$

$$- \underset{(-5.10)}{0.17} \; (\Delta RR_{-5} - \Delta^2 p^{nd}_{-2} + \Delta^2 p^{nd}_{-4}) - \underset{(-3.39)}{0.52} \; \Delta p^{nd^*}_{-4} - \underset{(-4.33)}{0.03} \; (\Delta u_{-1} - 3\Delta^2 u_{-4})$$

$$- \underset{(-5.53)}{0.10} \; (c^{nd^*}_{-1} - \underset{(-3.11)}{1.29} - \underset{(-17.00)}{0.81} \; yd^*_{-1} - \underset{(-6.88)}{0.07} \; \left(\frac{WF}{YD}\right)_{-1} + \text{seasonals}$$

$R^2 = 0.91, \sigma^* 100 = 0.23, D\text{-}W = 2.06$
Corr (6) = 1.12, Corr (4) = 1.31, Corr (2) = 2.16,
Arch (6) = 0.43, Norm = 0.06

Notes: Estimation period: 1972: 3–1994:4. The statistic t appears in brackets. u, rate of unemployment; seasonal variables are only included for the period 1981–4, Corr(*) is the value of statistic F which tests for the existence of order * serial correlation in the residuals; Arch(*) is a statistic of the same type as the previous one, for testing order * heteroscedasticity in the residuals; Norm. is the traditional Bera–Jarque residual normality test.

Table 14A.2 Expenditure on durable consumer goods, OLS estimation

$$\Delta c^{d*} = \underset{(9.36)}{0.71} \; \Delta c^{d*}_{-1} - \underset{(-2.04)}{0.16} \; \Delta c^{d*}_{-2} + \underset{(3.21)}{0.36} \; \Delta yd^* + \underset{(3.03)}{0.02} \; \Delta \left(\frac{WH}{YD}\right)$$

$$- \underset{(-4.93)}{0.03} \; \Delta cud^* - \underset{(-4.78)}{0.03} \; \Delta cud^*_{-3} - \underset{(-3.38)}{0.19} \; (\Delta^2 p^d + \Delta^2 p^d_{-2}) - \underset{(-2.44)}{0.23} \; \Delta^2 p^d_{-3}$$

$$- \underset{(-2.91)}{0.02} \; \Delta p^{e*} + \underset{(1.97)}{0.02} \; \Delta p^{e*}_{-2} - \underset{(-4.00)}{0.38} \; \Delta u + \underset{(2.79)}{0.43} \; \Delta u_{-1} - \underset{(-2.19)}{0.23} \; \Delta u_{-2}$$

$$- \underset{(-6.45)}{0.16} \; (c^{d*}_{-1} + \underset{(1.39)}{1.28} - \underset{(-10.02)}{0.90} \; yd^*_{-1} + \underset{(1.89)}{0.03} \; cud^*_{-1} + \underset{(6.14)}{0.13} \; p^{e*}_{-1}) + \text{seasonals}$$

$R^2 = 0.90, \sigma^* 100 = 0.78, D\text{-}W = 1.86$
Corr (6) = 0.54, Corr (4) = 0.73, Corr (2) = 0.59,
Arch (6) = 0.86, Norm = 1.18

Notes: Estimation period: 1972:3–1994:4. Statistic t appears in brackets. See also notes to Table 14A.1.

Table 14A.3 Domestic residential investment, OLS estimation

$$\Delta i^{dr*} = \underset{(3.23)}{0.22} \ \Delta i^{dr*}_{-1} - \underset{(-2.94)}{0.19} \ \Delta i^{dr*}_{-3} + \underset{(4.03)}{0.27} \ \Delta i^{dr*}_{-4} - \underset{(-2.09)}{0.13} \ \Delta i^{dr*}_{5} + \underset{(2.05)}{0.40} \ \Delta yd^{*}$$

$$+ \underset{(1.82)}{0.37} \ \Delta yd^{*}_{-2} + \underset{(2.05)}{0.02} \ \Delta\left(\frac{WH}{YD}\right)_{-5} - \underset{(-1.35)}{0.04} \ \Delta^{2}RRV^{*}_{-2} - \underset{(-1.43)}{0.05} \ \Delta^{2}RRH^{*}_{-4}$$

$$- \underset{(-3.83)}{0.13} \ (i^{dr*}_{-1} - \underset{(-1.80)}{2.70} - \underset{(-2.21)}{0.39} \ yd^{*}_{-1} + \underset{(2.36)}{0.48} \ RRH^{*}_{-1} + \underset{(3.66)}{0.84} \ p^{h*}_{-1})$$

$R^2 = 0.74, \sigma * 100 = 1.84, D\text{–}W = 1.84$
Corr (6) = 0.43, Corr (4) = 0.48, Corr (2) = 0.17,
Arch (6) = 0.48, Norm = 1.23

Notes: Estimation period: 1972:3–1994:4. Statistic t appears in brackets. See also notes to Table 14A.1.

Appendix 2: The Private Productive Investment Function

The theoretical model underpinning the analysis on p. 497–9 is based on the hypothesis that firms produce by combining 3 factors: capital (K), labour (L), and imported intermediary goods (M), which makes it necessary to distinguish between value added (VA) and gross output (PB). The technology at the company's disposal could be represented as follows:

$$VA = VA(K,L) \quad \text{and} \quad PB = PB(VA,M) \qquad (14B.1)$$

Entrepreneurs decide the optimum level of the inputs they require to maximize profits subject on the technology and the equation which determines the accumulation of capital; in this way, they solve the following optimization problem:

$$\text{Max} \sum_{i=t}^{\infty} \frac{1}{(1+r)^t} (P_t PB_t - W_t L_t - P_t^I I_t - P_t^M M_t)$$

subject to:

$$I_t = K_t - K_{t-1} + \delta K_{t-1} \qquad (14B.2)$$

$$PB_t = PB(K_t, L_t, M_t) \qquad (14B.3)$$

where P is the price of gross output, W wages per employee, P^I the price of investment goods, I investment, P^M the price of imported intermediate goods, r the real interest rate and δ the rate of depreciation of capital, which is assumed to be constant.

Based on the first order conditions (and using logarithmic approximations), the following optimal demand for capital can be derived:

$$k^* = \Psi_0 + \Psi_1 pb^* + \Psi_2 w^* + \Psi_3 p^{m*} + \Psi_4 cu^* \qquad (14B.4)$$

where the variables with asterisks indicate that they have been divided by the price of the goods produced and the expression of the user cost is:

$$CU^* = \frac{P^I - \dfrac{P^I_{+1}(1-\delta)}{1+r}}{P} \qquad (14B.5)$$

The value of the parameters in (14B.4) depends on the specification of the production function. In the case of constant returns to scale Ψ_1 must be equal to 1, Ψ_2 and Ψ_3 must be positive, and Ψ_4 negative. In the Cobb–Douglas case, the equivalent expression would be:

$$k^* = \Psi_0 + pb^* + \beta(1-\alpha)w^* + (1-\beta)p^{m*} + (\alpha\beta - 1)cu^* \qquad (14B.6)$$

where α, β are the parameters of that production function, which, assuming constant returns to scale and perfect competition, would correspond to the weights of the surplus in the value added and of the value added over output respectively.

As with durable consumer goods and housing, the stock is not incorporated into the model, but rather the corresponding flow. Assuming the existence of adjustments costs, it is possible to derive an investment function on the basis of the determinants of the demand for capital.[15] The econometric specification adds linearly the degree of utilization of installed capacity (ut). This variable can approximate both, changes in demand not considered when output was planned, and the degree of intensity with which productive factors are utilized. The equation finally estimated is:

$$i^{pp*} = \Psi'_0 + pb^* + \Psi'_2 w^* + \Psi'_3 p^{m*} + \Psi'_4 cu^* + \Psi'_5 ut \qquad (14B.7)$$

in which output has been made to appear with a coefficient of 1,[16] as this was statistically accepted in the estimation.

The investment variable in the model is private productive investment, defined as total gross fixed capital formation, less public investment and domestic residential investment. Gross output is calculated as the sum of the value added of the private sector, without either taxes or intermediate goods imports (based on customs data reconciled with the National Accounts figures). Wages correspond to private sector wages per employee, the price of intermediate goods imports is that of their deflator, and the user cost utilizes data for the deflator of private productive investment and the nominal interest rate. Expected inflation is approximated by its current level. In addition, in the specification presented, the user cost has been corrected for fiscal factors.[17]

Table 14B.1 contains the estimation of the private productive investment function.

Table 14B.1   Private productive investment, OLS estimation

$$\Delta i^{pp*} = \begin{array}{c} 0.74 \\ (13.04) \end{array} \Delta i^{pp*'}_{-1} - \begin{array}{c} 0.34 \\ (-4.37) \end{array} \Delta^2 i^{pp*'}_{-2} + \begin{array}{c} 1.88 \\ (9.49) \end{array} \Delta pb^* - \begin{array}{c} 1.55 \\ (-5.88) \end{array} \Delta pb^*_{-3}$$

$$+ \begin{array}{c} 0.64 \\ (2.30) \end{array} \Delta pb^*_{-4} + \begin{array}{c} 0.18 \\ (3.39) \end{array} \Delta \Delta_4 w^* - \begin{array}{c} 0.23 \\ (-3.42) \end{array} \Delta w^*_{-2} - \begin{array}{c} 0.08 \\ (-2.85) \end{array} \Delta p^{m*}_{-4}$$

$$- \begin{array}{c} 0.06 \\ (-2.93) \end{array} (\Delta CUCF^*_{-1} + \Delta CUCF^*_{-4}) + \begin{array}{c} 0.08 \\ (-3.38) \end{array} \Delta ut$$

$$- \begin{array}{c} 0.03 \\ (-3.26) \end{array} (i^{pp*'}_{-1} + \begin{array}{c} 15.02 \\ (3.35) \end{array} - pb^*_{-1} - \begin{array}{c} 0.43 \\ (-2.48) \end{array} w^*_{-1} + \begin{array}{c} 0.23 \\ (2.31) \end{array} p^{m*}_{-1}$$

$$+ \begin{array}{c} 1.49 \\ (1.99) \end{array} CUCF^*_{-1} - \begin{array}{c} 1.71 \\ (-2.10) \end{array} ut_{-2})$$

$R^2 = 0.93, \sigma^*100 = 0.73, D\text{–}W = 1.86$
Corr (6) = 0.29, Corr (4) = 0.17, Corr (2) = 0.36,
Arch (6) = 0.94, Norm = 2.15

Notes: Estimation period: 1972:3–1994:4. Statistic t appears in brackets.
CUCF is the tax-adjusted user cost.

Notes

1   All the estimations presented are ordinary least square estimations, since the instrumental variable estimations produced similar results, which makes it possible to accept the hypothesis that theoretically endogenous variables could be considered weakly exogenous at this level of aggregation.

2   The short-term effects are obtained by adding the different lags with which the explanatory variables appear in differences.

3   Actually it is a semielasticity *vis-à-vis* the wealth-income ratio.

4   Despite that, the unit root tests for residuals of the cointegration vectors or those obtained with Johanssen's methodology are only exceeded at 10 per cent significance level.

5   This variable includes both the private and government sponsored housing segments. Moreover, each period records only the value of what was built in that period.

6   We use a synthetic interest rate which mainly includes long-term government securities and long-term private company bonds. See Cuenca (1994).

7   In other words, the values simulated for each component of private demand in a given period are taken into account in the simulation for the following period.

8   In addition, neither the variables converted to a quarterly basis nor the sample period coincide completely.

9   Changes in the order of identification only affect the contemporaneous effects of the interest rate on the other variables, not the pattern over time.
10   The model is estimated in levels in order to reflect the possible cointegration relationships found on p. 492–9. The non-stationarity of the variables is not expected to distort short-term impulse-response findings, that are subsequently analyzed.
11   This is a fairly conventional model in the literature (see, for instance, Spinnewyn, 1981, Estrada, 1993).
12   In the case of durable consumption, the traditional user cost is broadened to include the price of energy, which recovers its *intermediate goods* property.
13   This is not a serious problem for the specification because, if a stock grows at a constant rate, the flow feeding it does so at the same rate. For that reason, the expressions would be identical to (14A.10) and (14A.11), except for their constant terms.
14   In fact, these authors advocate using labour income instead of disposable income, because if wealth is also included, some double accounting is incurred; moreover, inflation may alter its behaviour. Leaving aside possible conceptual problems in measuring labour income, some tests carried out using a variable that approximated labour incomes produced worse results than those of disposable income.
15   See Andrés *et al.* (1988, 1989) for a detailed analysis of the relationship between demand for capital and the investment function. In particular, they demonstrate how investment will depend on the same variables as those determining the demand for capital and, moreover, on the rates of change of those same variables. Nevertheless, as they point out, 'the exclusion of these rates from the long-term relationship does not introduce any misspecification bias, because all of them are stationary (I(O)) variables whose contribution to the error component is dominated by the relationship between the first order integrated variables.'
16   Capital utilization was not given the same treatment because it is a variable derived from surveys and refers, exclusively, to utilization of just one of the factors: capital.
17   The user cost adopts negative values in certain quarters; for that reason it is not included in logarithms.

References

ANDRÉS, J., A. ESCRIBANO, C. MOLINAS and D. TAGUAS (1988) 'Una función agregada de inversión productiva privada para la economía española', *Working Paper*, SGPE-D-88006, DG de Planificación. Ministerio de Economía y Hacienda.
ANDRÉS, J., A. ESCRIBANO, C. MOLINAS and D. TAGUAS (1989) *La inversión en España. Econometría con restricciones de equilibrio*, (ed.) Antoni Bosch, Instituto de Estudios Fiscales.
BERNANKE, B. and M. GERTLER (1995) 'Inside the black box: the credit channel of monetary policy transmission', *Journal of Economic Perspectives*, 9, 27–48.
CUENCA, J.A. (1994) 'Variables para el estudio del sector monetario: agregados monetarios y crediticios, y tipos de interés sintéticos', Banco de España, *Working Paper*, 9416.
ENGLE, R.F., D.F. HENDRY and J.F. RICHARD (1983) 'Exogeneity', *Econometrica*, 51, 277–304.

ESCRIVÁ, J.L. and A. HALDANE (1994) 'El mecanismo de transmisión de los tipos de interés en España: estimación basada en desagregaciones sectoriales', Banco de España, *Working Paper*, 9414.

ESPASA, A. and E. SENRA (1993) 'Consideraciones sobre la función de inversión en España', Universidad Carlos III de Madrid, *Working Paper*, 9302.

ESTRADA, A. (1993) 'Una función de bienes de consumo duradero para España', *Revista Española de Economía*, 10.

ESTRADA, A., T. SASTRE and J.L. VEGA (1994) 'El mecanismo de transmisión de los tipos de interés: el caso español', Banco de España, *Working Paper*, 9408.

GORDON, R. and J.M. VEITCH (1986) 'Fixed investment in the American business cycle, 1919–83', in R. Gordon (ed.) *The American business cycle: continuity and change*, Chicago: University of Chicago Press.

HALL, R. (1981) 'Intertemporal substitution in consumption', NBER, *Working Paper*, 720.

HERNANDO, I. (1997) 'El canal crediticio en la transmisión de la política monetaria', in *La política monetaria y la inflación en España*, Servicio de Estudios del Banco de España, Madrid: Alianza Editorial.

HERNANDO, I. and VALLÉS, J. (1992) 'Inversión y restricciones financieras: evidencia en las empresas manufactureras españolas', *Moneda y Crédito*, 195, 185–222.

MOLINAS, C. *et al.* (1990) 'MOISEES. Un modelo de investigación y simulación de la economía española', ed. Antoni Bosch, Instituto de Estudios Fiscales.

MUELLBAUER, J. and L. LATTIMORE (1994) 'The consumption function: a theoretical and empirical overview', mimeo.

PEÑALOSA, J. (1998) 'The financial position of economic agents and monetary policy', Chapter 15 in this volume.

SASTRE, T. (1998) 'The role of the banking system in the monetary transmission', Chapter 13 in this volume.

SPINNEWYN, F. (1981) 'Rational habit formation', *European Economic Review*, 15, 91–109.

15 The Financial Position of Economic Agents and Monetary Policy

Juan María Peñalosa

(Spain)

E52

INTRODUCTION[1]

Monetary policy tries to achieve price stability by modifying the financial conditions of the economy, which affect the rate of growth of nominal income, the behaviour of the exchange rate and agents' inflationary expectations. The influence of central bank decisions on agents' behaviour and, hence, on the way income and prices behave, is exerted through various channels (see King, 1994). The aim of this study is to analyse how the financial position of agents influences the transmission of monetary impulses.[2]

Firstly, the transmission of shifts in interest rates controlled by the central bank – normally very short-term rates – to other terms and markets affects the various agents' incentives to save and borrow. The response of economic agents to these changes in interest rates depends on the magnitude of substitution effects (because of changes in the relative attractiveness of saving as opposed to expending), income effects (changes in net financial income received), and wealth effects (changes induced in the market value of the net balance of real and financial assets). The financial position of agents, i.e. the structure of their financial assets and liabilities, is the main determinant of the magnitude of the income and wealth effects.

Secondly, changes in the degree of relative tightness of monetary policy affect the behaviour of the exchange rate of the local currency and this produces an income effect and a wealth effect for agents with a foreign currency-denominated financial position, thereby potentially influencing their expenditure decisions.

Thirdly, monetary policy affects the availability and terms of bank credit, which, in the absence of perfect substitution by other sources of funding, may influence agents' spending decisions, especially those most dependent on that credit, such as households and smaller firms.

The magnitude of the income effect and wealth effect in the traditional monetary channel, the impact of exchange rate movements and the availability and terms of access to bank credit, which constitute a major part of

519

the monetary transmission mechanism, ultimately depend on the financial position of agents.[3] This position occupies an intermediate place in what could be termed the conventional monetary policy transmission framework, being located between the different market interest rates and the exchange rate connection, addressed in Chapter 13 of this book and in Gordo and Sánchez (1997), and the determination of the effect entailed by agents' reaction on nominal expenditure in the economy, analyzed in Chapter 14.[4]

Hence, a study of the financial structure of the various sectors is a prerequisite for an assessment of the monetary policy transmission mechanism. The nature of that structure may delay or accelerate the propagation of monetary impulses.[5] Here it should be stressed that the financial position of economic sectors cannot itself define the power of monetary policy. On the one hand, it is just one more 'cog' in the transmission mechanism; and on the other, because there are other transmission channels that bypass that particular 'cog' (the process operating via the exchange rate or agents' inflation expectations, for instance).[6]

The financial position of agents has been considered in a broad sense, in such a way that it includes both quantifiable aspects, such as the level of each sector's financial assets and liabilities, their composition, and the conditions governing their remuneration, and also aspects more difficult to measure, such as the ability of different agents to accede to borrowed funds or their sensitivity to changes in interest rates. This approach also allows us to analyse the relative impact of monetary policy on each sector, a task that has yet to be undertaken in any exhaustive way.

Specifically, the aspects of the financial structure of agents analysed in this chapter are:

(a) *Net financial wealth.* Changes in interest rates generate an *income effect*, which, depending on the initial outstanding balance of financial assets and liabilities and the extent to which the return thereon is sensitive to changes in interest rates, may either enhance or hamper the transmission of monetary policy.

(b) *The maturities of financial balances.* Given that central bank decisions have a greater impact on short-term interest rates, the bigger the net short-term debtor position at this maturity, and the greater the frequency of short-term borrowing, the more powerful transmission will be.

(c) *The frequency with which interest rates on financial instruments are revised and their reference.* If agents' financial liabilities are contractually long-term, but their remuneration is periodically revised, such remuneration can be adapted to the monetary conditions prevailing in the market, thereby enhancing the transmission of monetary policy via the aforementioned income effect. In the case of financial assets, the income effect will interfere less in monetary policy transmission if the remuneration thereon is not revised frequently.

(d) *The composition of financial wealth.* If it is accepted that changes in interest rates are passed on to the rate at which future income flows on some financial investments are discounted, and hence to their market prices, greater monetary tightness would tend to reduce the present value of agents' financial wealth, and vice-versa, so that this effect would reinforce the monetary policy transmission mechanism. In this regard, the financial assets considered likely to undergo changes in their market value as a result of changes in interest rates are negotiable fixed-income and variable yield securities.

(e) *The degree of bank intermediation.* Monetary policy decisions are usually considered to be transmitted with special intensity through decisions taken by national credit institutions, which depend, to a large extent, on how money markets behave (see Manzano and Galmés, 1995). In response to movements in short-term rates, institutions change the interest rates on their assets and liabilities and, sometimes, also the volume of credit they make available. Moreover, in recent years, *heightened competition among banks* has accelerated transmission from short-term interest rates to the rates on bank instruments. In contrast, the impact of monetary policy on the financial terms negotiated with other non-bank lenders (such as other companies or non-resident entities) is generally less marked. In principle, therefore, it could be thought that the larger the proportion of financial claims on and liabilities to the credit system, the more powerful the transmission mechanism. Likewise, if we assume the existence of a credit channel in which changes in the supply of bank credit reinforce monetary policy decisions, the more agents depend on that source of finance, the greater the effectiveness of monetary policy (on this aspect, see Hernando, 1997). Finally, the transmission of monetary impulses to the various agents is closely related to the type of banking institution they deal with. In this regard, those institutions that specialize in larger clients, such as companies, can be seen to respond more swiftly and intensely to variations in monetary conditions, whereas those whose clientele is mainly composed of households and small firms appear to be less flexible to such changes.[7]

(f) *Non-bank financing options: foreign currency loans, intercompany loans, and securities markets.* Not all agents have equal access to these alternative sources of financing. In general, the bigger the size of the agent, the greater its ability to tap funds outside banking channels. Using these alternative sources allows agents to devise more flexible financing strategies that are less tied to changes in monetary policy and less expensive. Diversification of the sources of funds also ensures that

financing will be available even at times of credit rationing. Nevertheless, in the medium term, insofar as monetary impulses are transmitted
to all tranches and markets and the exchange rate moves in line with
the uncovered interest rate differential, the cost advantages of these
alternatives could diminish or even be completely erased.

(g) *Sensitivity to changes in interest rates.* Monetary policy alters the relative
    attractiveness of saving or spending, so that there is always a *substitu-
    tion effect* which works in the direction set by monetary policy.
    Although, in principle, this effect is relatively independent of agents'
    financial position, in certain circumstances the capacity to embark on
    new expenditure using borrowed funds may be affected by the initial
    financial position. Agents with a greater volume of net financial assets,
    which are bigger and which dominate financial markets, or else are in
    a better negotiating position will generally have fewer liquidity con-
    straints and therefore be able to maintain their expenditure decisions
    and borrowing plans, even in times of greater monetary tightness. The
    use of *hedging instruments* or derivatives also means that the financial
    conditions for these agents are less vulnerable to changes in monetary
    policy. In contrast, such changes could have a significant impact on
    smaller-sized agents, especially households and small firms, whose
    access to bank credit is heavily dependent on the relationship between
    their disposable income and the financial burden their debt repres-
    ents.

This chapter is structured as follows. We analyse the general features of
non-financial agents' financial position and underscore the main differences among them. We then examine the part played by the financial position of households and firms within the monetary transmission process,
and address general government. The last section sets out the main conclusions of this study.

GENERAL FEATURES OF THE FINANCIAL POSITIONS OF NON-FINANCIAL SECTORS

In the non-financial resident sectors, households provide net financial
resources to fund companies' debtor positions and, above all, those of general government. Figures 15.1 and 15.2 show how the financial wealth and
the level of financial assets and liabilities of these sectors have behaved in
the past. Noteworthy in this period is the improvement in the financial
position of the private – and especially the corporate[8] – sector, and the
marked expansion of government indebtedness, which has ultimately dominated the overall debt profile.

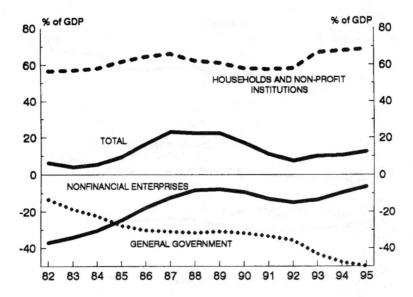

Figure 15.1   Net financial wealth[1] 1982–95

Note: 1   Financial assets *less* financial liabilities; equities are not included in corporate liabilities.

Source: Banco de España.

To make an initial overall assessment of the degree of influence that monetary policy could have on the financial situation of the various sectors, we calculated the proportion of financial assets and liabilities to which market interest rates apply, or could apply[9], for each of the sectors (see Figure 15.3). According to these ratios, on the assets side households show the greatest sensitivity to changes in monetary policy. Over 60 per cent of their financial assets are in that category, compared to around one-third in the case of companies and general government. On the liabilities side, the general government sector has most debt at market rates: 90 per cent of the total in 1995, compared with one-quarter at the beginning of the 1980s. Households are in an intermediate position, with a little over 60 per cent of their liabilities in instruments subject to incur market rates, while companies are the agents best able to tap funds at a cost less related to monetary policy instruments (mainly by resorting to own funds and intercompany loans).

Table 15.1 calculates the income effect that would occur if changes in the official Banco de España rate were transferred in their entirety to the interest rates on the financial assets and liabilities of the economic sectors susceptible to receive market-rate returns. All figures are for 1995.

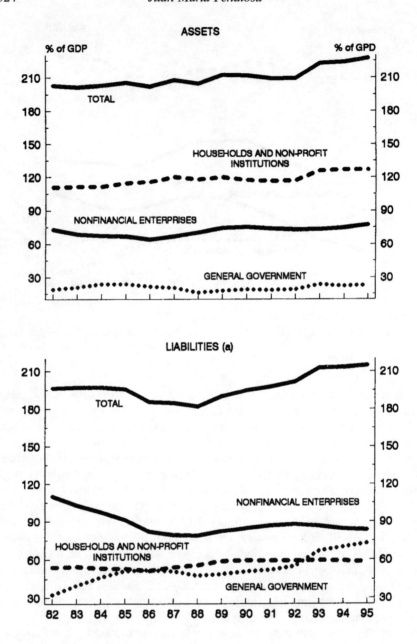

Figure 15.2   Financial assets and liabilities, 1982–95

Note: 1   In the case of non-financial enterprises, equities are not included.
Source: Banco de España.

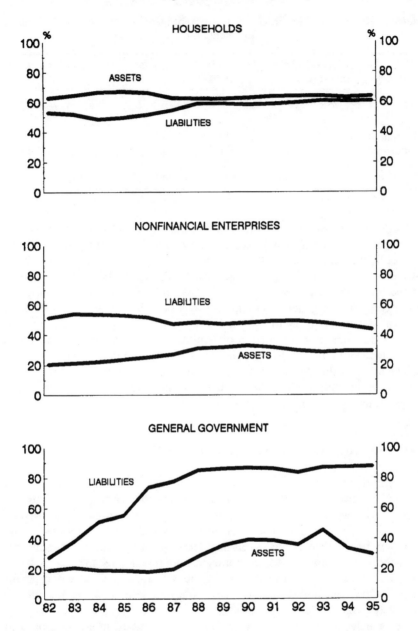

Figure 15.3 Financial assets and liabilities susceptible to be remunerated at market rates, 1982–95, share of the total

Source: Banco de España.

Table 15.1 Income effect produced by a 1-point increase in the Banco de España intervention rate

	Assets subject to market rates		Liabilities subject to market rates		Net financial income	
	% of total	% of GDP	% of total	% of GDP	% of GDP	% dispos. income
Households	64	81	61	35	0,46	0.7
Companies	29	23	44	51	−0, 28	−2.2
Gen.gvt	30	7	88	64	−0, 57	−4.0
Total		111		150	−0, 39	

Under these assumptions, the total net income effect would be negative, i.e. monetary tightness would reduce the disposable income of non-financial resident sectors as a whole. The most significant negative impact would be felt by companies and general government: the 1-point increase in the intervention rate would reduce disposable income for companies by 2 per cent and for general government by 4 per cent. In terms of GDP, the general government sector would be most sensitive to monetary policy, since it has a greater proportion of liabilities subject to market rates as a percentage of GDP and because it hardly has any financial assets to offset the changes in the degree of monetary tightness. As for households, their disposable income would react positively to an increase in the intervention rate because of their high net creditor position.

THE FINANCIAL POSITION OF HOUSEHOLDS

Household expenditure decisions (consumption and investment in housing) account for two-thirds of GDP and this sector provides the main source of savings with which to finance corporate and general government borrowing. The behaviour of households also helps ease cyclical swings in the economy because household spending decisions are generally less sensitive than those of companies to temporary economic circumstances. Insofar as their decisions are based more on structural factors, such as a permanent income flow, the ability of monetary policy to influence them could be relatively weaker.

Nevertheless, some factors do preserve the ability of monetary policy to make an impact. Firstly, the occurrence of disturbances of various kinds, such as liquidity squeezes, may interfere with the relationship between spending decisions and permanent income. Secondly, agents may find it difficult to evaluate their permanent income and, as a result, tend to go by the recent behaviour of their disposable income, in accordance with an adaptive expectations model. Lastly, demand policies may be assumed to have a certain power to influence agents' medium-term expectations. If so, they would be altering the expected level of permanent income and thereby exerting influence on the short-term behaviour of households. Thus, in all these cases, some room would be left for monetary policy to influence household expenditure decisions (see Mauskopf, 1990).

Specifically, the existence of *financial* constraints on household indebtedness is one of the main channels through which monetary policy affects these agents' expenditure decisions. Households have a *limited capacity to accommodate increases in interest rate levels*, since credit institutions refuse to finance households for which the repayment installments on a loan exceed a certain percentage of their disposable income (or what they consider to be their permanent income). This means that for households whose disposable income is close to the minimum required for financial institutions to grant them a loan, an increase in interest rates will mean that they fail to qualify. As a result they will not receive financing and will not be able to increase their expenditure, which in turn means that monetary policy will have effectively achieved its goal of moderating expenditure. In these circumstances, lower-income families will only be able to resort to bank loans if they can provide secured or financial guarantees. In this sense, the ability of families to accommodate tougher monetary conditions thus depends on their level of income and of their accumulated financial and real wealth.

The most notable feature of households' financial position is their traditional *positive net financial wealth* which, over the past decade, has ranged between 55 per cent and 70 per cent of GDP (see Figure 15.4). Changes in financial wealth are mostly explained by the behaviour of financial assets, in such a way that households' expenditure and saving decisions appear to manifest themselves more in a reduction and increase, respectively, of financial assets than in oscillations of the opposite sign in their borrowing, which emerges as much more stable as a percentage of GDP. This could indicate both a certain reluctance of households to borrow beyond their expectations of income, approximated by the behaviour of GDP, and prudence on the part of credit institutions with regard to financing households, in order not to increase their levels of credit risk.

In terms of instruments, and on the financial assets side, the most important item is liquid assets, which account for over half the total, even though in recent years their share has diminished as a result of the rise of investment funds and insurance transactions[10] (Figure 15.5). On the liability side, loans granted by the credit system which likewise account for over half of total liabilities, have increased in relative importance over the past decade, while intercompany financing has diminished in relative terms,

528   *Juan María Peñalosa*

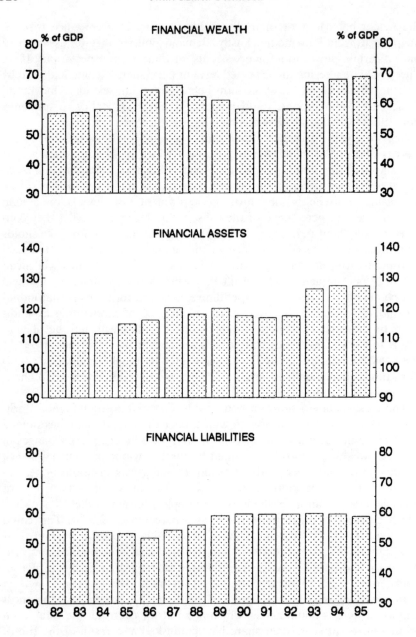

Figure 15.4 Financial position of households, 1982–95
Source: Banco de España.

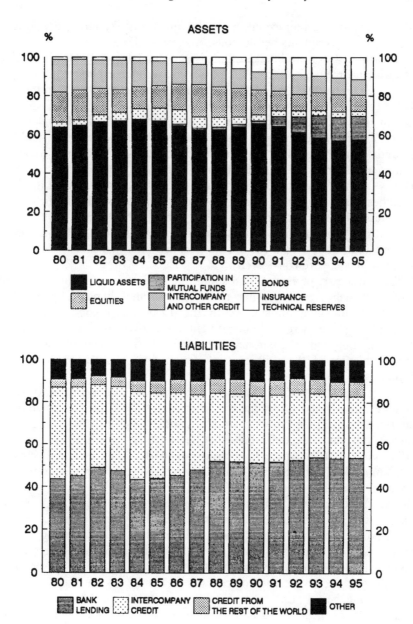

Figure 15.5 Financial structure of households, 1980–95
Source: Banco de España.

which may, to a certain extent, be a consequence of the reduced weight of individual entrepreneurs within households as a whole.

Households' net creditor position is the main factor determining that financial income derived from the possession of financial assets (over 7 per cent of GDP in 1995) exceeds the financial expenses deriving from the sector's borrowing (3 per cent of GDP). However, despite the considerable size of that net creditor position (almost 70 per cent of GDP), the net financial income received by households, which has remained stable at around 4 per cent of GDP (see Figure 15.6), makes only a minor contribution to households' disposable income (around 6 per cent on average). This is due not so much to a very high level of interest rates on financial liabilities, but rather to a relatively low return on assets. The implicit interest rate on households' financial assets, although higher in 1995 than the implicit cost of borrowing, is around 5.5 per cent, which implies a slightly positive real interest rate (or even a negative one, if the taxes associated with that income are considered).

The lower part of Figure 15.6 shows the rate of interest for household assets and liabilities susceptible to be remunerated at market rates. The process of deregulation starting in the 1980s, heightened competition among banks, the increase in investment alternatives and the improvement in information and transparency of financial markets have all contributed to a reduction of the differential between interest rates on loans and deposits.

In net terms in 1995, households had a net creditor position to which market rates applied equivalent to 45 per cent of GDP, placing Spain in an intermediate position between countries with a high private savings rate, such as Italy and Belgium, where that net position exceeds 100 per cent of GDP, and countries where households are fairly highly indebted, such as the United Kingdom, Sweden, and Denmark, where the remunerated net financial position is a debtor one.

The existence of a high net creditor position in households would suggest that changes in the level of interest rates lead to variations of the same sign in households' disposable income, thereby giving rise to an *income effect* that could partly offset the impact of changes in monetary policy on those agents' expenditure decisions. As analyzed in the previous section, in the extreme case of changes in the Banco de España's intervention rate being passed on in their entirety to the interest rates for households' financial assets and liabilities subject to remuneration, a one-point increase in that intervention rate would generate an increase in net financial income equivalent to 0.45 per cent of GDP (0.7 per cent of households' disposable income), resulting from increases in financial income and expenditure of 0.8 per cent and 0.35 per cent of GDP, respectively.

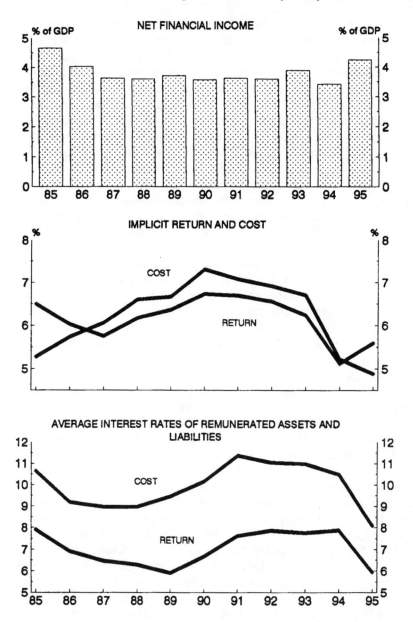

Figure 15.6 Financial income and expenses of households, 1985–95
Source: Banco de España.

However, the impact of monetary policy on households' expenditure decisions via this income effect may be less than these figures indicate. Given that there is probably an asymmetrical distribution of households' financial income and expenditure depending on income levels, the ultimate impact of monetary policy on this sector's expenditure decisions might not be the same as that deduced from changes in net financial income for households as a whole. On the one hand, if the households obtaining most net financial income were to be the higher-income households – which have a lower marginal propensity to consume and fewer financial constraints on consumption – the changes in their disposable income caused by changes in interest rates would affect these households' savings more than their consumption. By contrast, lower-income households would probably register net financial expenses and liquidity constraints, so that changes in the Banco de España intervention rate would affect their disposable income and their consumption in the direction intended by monetary policy.

Compared with companies, households place a larger proportion of their financial investments in liquid assets, while the *maturity* of their financial liabilities is longer. As can be seen in Figure 15.5, 57 per cent of the financial assets of households are liquid (almost 70 per cent, if participations in mutual funds are considered liquid), as opposed to less than 30 per cent in the case of companies. The main financing obtained by households is in the form of mortgage loans, which are normally long-term (10 to 20 years).[11] These characteristics suggest that monetary policy has less of an impact on households than on companies: on the one hand, financial income would appear to adapt swiftly to the level of interest rates, generating an income effect opposed to monetary policy intentions; and on the other, the financial costs of borrowing would appear to be determined, in principle, by the pattern of medium- and long-term financing (see Escrivá and Haldane, 1994).

The capacity of monetary policy to influence household disposable income is considerably strengthened when one analyzes the percentage of loan transactions whose costs are revised periodically in order to bring them into line with market conditions. The proportion of *floating interest loans* in total credit granted by deposit money institutions to households and firms has been increasing rapidly in the past decade and currently accounts for more than one third of the total (see Figure 15.7). Since these loans are normally geared to money market interest rates, or at least bear some relation to them, the fact that they make up a high proportion increases the part played by short-term rates in determining the financial costs of economic agents, their disposable income, and their readiness to borrow. In addition, the increase in floating-rate borrowing may make it easier to contain inflationary expectations because, in this case, unlike fixed-rate loans, borrowers cannot diminish the financial burden of the debt by resorting to higher inflation. Indeed, the financial cost in real

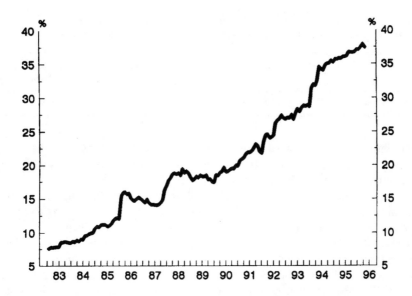

Figure 15.7 Floating-interest credit from deposit money institutions to households and companies,[1] 1983–96

Note: 1 Share of total credit.
Source: Banco de España.

terms could even increase with ever greater rates of inflation. Consequently, extensive use of floating-rate loans may help increase households' and companies' aversion to inflation.

The expansion of *floating-rate loans* has been especially important in the case of mortgages. The reference interest rate used to update these loans is of great importance for assessing to what extent that updating brings the cost of long-term credit in line with interest rates negotiated in the money markets. The Banco de España recommended in 1993 that institutions use some specific references when setting their floating-rate mortgage loans: some average of the institutions' lending rates, government debt rates, or one-year interbank rates (see Banco de España, 1993).[12]

Although the references used for mortgages were traditionally relatively rigid when there were changes in the level of short-term interest rates, in recent years the two have come closer together. Currently most banks gear their floating- rate mortgage loans to the one-year interbank deposit rate (MIBOR), while savings banks tend to employ the CECA (the national confederation of savings banks) lending rate as a reference. In order to evaluate the capacity of monetary policy to influence the costs of mortgage loans, we have analysed the correlation between the references used for floating-rate mortgage loans and the Banco de España intervention rate

Table 15.2 Correlation between changes in the Banco de España intervention rate and changes in the mortgage market reference rates, January 1991–May 1996

1-year MIBOR	CECA indicator	Mortgage loan index banks	Mortgage loan index savings banks	Government debt index
0.73	0.51	0.53	0.43	0.59

(see Table 15.2). It shows how the reference rate most commonly used by private banks – the 1-year MIBOR – is that which most correlates with the Banco de España intervention rate.

There are no data on the proportion of floating-rate mortgages as a percentage of total mortgage loans, although this type of loan seems to have become the norm in recent years. During this period, moreover, the volume of loans for home purchases has grown enormously. Given that mortgages account for two-thirds of loans by deposit money institutions to households and that households hardly receive any other long-term credit, the proliferation of floating rate loans implies that the monetary conditions set by the Banco de España are increasingly more influential in determining the financial costs borne by households.

Nevertheless, the impact of monetary policy on households' financial expenditure, via its effect on mortgage rates, does not appear to be very great, since mortgage loans outstanding only account for 20 per cent of households' disposable income. Thus, if for example all outstanding mortgages were of the floating-rate type and reflected in their entirety changes in short-term interest rates, a 1-point increase in short-term interest rates would mean PTA 110bn more in annual interest payments, or 0.2 per cent of household disposable income in 1995. However, as mentioned earlier, the income allocated to home purchases is very unevenly distributed among households, so that it is likely that changes in the level of interest rates will abruptly affect the capacity to consume and save of households saddled with mortgage payments.

The increase in investment in housing (two-thirds of the increase in the volume of secured loans since 1990 probably corresponds to home purchase loans) and banking institutions' conservative lending policies have led to a sharp increase in the proportion of *secured loans* in the past decade. In 1995 it exceeded 40 per cent of the total (see Figure 15.8). In this regard, some credit institutions opted to administer the supply of credit not by raising interest rates but by demanding that the borrower provide security.[13] The share in total bank credit of secured loans to households and firms is similar to that found in the main European countries; only in Anglo-Saxon countries is the proportion larger (around 60 per cent) (see Borio, 1995).

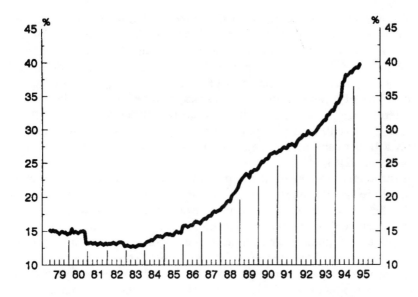

Figure 15.8 Secured credit granted by deposit institutions to households and companies,[1] 1979–95

Note: 1.   Share of total credit.
Source: Banco de España.

Changes in interest rates also generate a *wealth effect* in households that
may have repercussions on expenditure. Assuming that the interest rate
affects the discounted cash flow from future income and services generated
by the wealth held by households in the form of (fixed-and floating-rate)
financial and real estate (housing) assets, a reduction in interest rates
implies an increase in the value of that wealth at market prices (and vice
versa). Insofar as this increase encourages household spending, the wealth
effect will function in the sense intended by monetary policy.

The change in the value of real assets caused by variations in interest
rates may induce changes in the borrowing capacity of households and
encourage them to spend. This appears to occur in countries where it is
customary to ask for mortgage loans for purposes other than house purchases.[14] In the Spanish case, there is no evidence to suggest that changes
in the values of household dwellings induces changes in their expenditure
decisions. A decline in interest rates entails an increase in the demand for
housing in that it reduces the financial costs implicit in the financing of
such purchases and because the relative price of real as opposed to financial assets diminishes. Nevertheless, this does not appear to constitute in
itself an incentive for home-owners to increase their demand for consumer
goods.

The impact of interest rates on the market value of fixed- income and variable-yield assets is more marked, although the wealth held in such assets by households is not very substantial. In 1995, these securities amounted to a little over 13 per cent of household financial assets and were the equivalent of 17 per cent of GDP. Considering a relatively pro- longed flow of income from such securities, a 10 per cent drop in the level of interest rates and, hence, of the discount rate (from, for instance, 10 per cent to 9 per cent, or from 5 per cent to 4.5 per cent) would, theoretically, imply a 10 per cent increase in the value of those assets (almost 2 per cent in terms of GDP).

It is difficult to estimate the impact of changes in wealth on household expenditure. As the paper written for this volume by Estrada, Hernando and Vallés (1998) shows, there is no evidence that financial wealth signific- antly affects any component of expenditure in the short term. Only over the long term is there a weak transmission of financial wealth to demand for consumer durables (see also Estrada, 1992). This weak link between financial wealth and expenditure may to a certain extent be explained by the fact that families with a higher level of income and fewer liquidity con- straints are those that possess a higher percentage of that wealth. In any case, to a greater or lesser extent, the wealth effect tends to enhance the transmission of monetary policy.

The *degree of intermediation* of households' financial assets and liabilities has not changed much in recent years. Notable on the assets side is the surge in mutual funds in the early 1990s, which entailed a certain weaken- ing of the previous growth trend in bank deposits and repos. Insofar as these funds mainly invest in short-term assets,[15] the income effect, contrary to the transmission of monetary policy mentioned earlier on, may be re- inforced. However, the fact that these funds enjoy considerable tax benefits when held for a relatively long period implies that those participat- ing in them have a fiscal cost to pay when liquidating, which suggests that the revaluation they accumulate may be considered more as an increase in the financial wealth of households than as an increase in disposable income.[16]

Investment in pension and retirement schemes has also increased nota- bly in recent years and looks set to continue growing, attenuating the sens- itivity of households' financial income and expenditure to changes in interest rates. Indeed, on the one hand – given that the idea of such schemes is to attain an adequate return in the fairly distant future – the securities chosen are usually medium-and long-term assets, which are less vulnerable to changes in monetary policy; and on the other, there are restrictions on the liquidation of participations in such schemes, so that changes in the values of those assets have less of an impact on investors' expenditure decisions in the short run.

On the liabilities side, households have few *other financing alternatives* apart from bank loans in pesetas. Recourse to intercompany credit is only possible for financing purchases of normally not too expensive consumer goods and to postpone for a short period repayment of debt assumed for certain purchases (made, for instance with credit cards issued by large retail outlets). In addition, access to bank credit has become easier and the terms more flexible (instant bank loans, the possibility of obtaining floating interest rates and flexible terms, increasingly widespread use of credit cards, etc.). It is necessary to resort to bank credit for most expenditure decisions requiring borrowed funds and especially for the decision to incur a major household debt, such as that needed to purchase a home. Thus

Table 15.3   Summary of the financial position of households

1. Positive and high net financial wealth	70 per cent of GDP in 1995	−
Positive net financial income	Around 4 per cent of GDP (6 per cent of disposable income)	
About 60 per cent of assets and liabilities are subject to market		
interest rates	Proviso: asymmetric distribution of financial income and expenditure	
2. Fairly liquid assets	ALP + mutual funds account for 70 per cent of the total	−
Medium- and long-term liabilities	Mortgage loans account for 2/3 of bank credit to households	
3. Expansion of floating-rate loans	More than one-third of all credit for companies and households is with a floating rate of interest (10 per cent 10 years ago) Diversity of reference rates	++
4. Low amount of financial wealth in the form of bonds and equities (sensitive to changes in interest rates)	These instruments only account for 13 per cent of total financial assets	+
5. Bank lending predominates	Over half total liabilities	++
6. Few financing alternatives	Doubts about the magnitude and flexibility of intercompany credit	++
7. Limited ability to accommodate increases in interest rates	Major financial restrictions based on disposable income and wealth	++

Note: The plus and minus signs in the last column seek to indicate the extent to which the particular features of the financial position moderately (+) or considerably (++) enhance the transmission of monetary policy or hamper it to a greater (−−) or lesser (−) degree.

there is *very little leeway for households to obtain financing outside channels escaping the influence of monetary policy*.

Finally, Table 15.3 summarises the main features of the financial position of households and how they relate to monetary policy transmission.

THE FINANCIAL POSITION OF COMPANIES

Most of the output and employment in the Spanish economy is concentrated in nonfinancial companies. Hence, the importance of discussing to what extent restrictive monetary policy would aim to influence the behaviour of the financial conditions governing business activities. On the one hand, companies provide the supply of goods and services, so that the more extensive and flexible that supply can be, the fewer the inflationary pressures in the economy. This suggests that monetary policy geared to curbing inflation should try to interfere as little as possible in corporate expenditure decisions. On the other hand, companies take numerous decisions that bear significantly on the equilibrium between output and prices in the economy. Wage agreements with workers, the demand for intermediate and capital goods, and mark-up and pricing policies are some of the decisions taken in the corporate sphere which have a significant effect on inflation. For that reason, monetary policy is also concerned that such decisions should be compatible with price stability.

Monetary policy mainly affects companies via changes in the *cost of capital*, which is a measure of the return needed to cover a company's financial, tax and depreciation costs. When interest rates change, they alter existing borrowing costs and the incentives to take on new liabilities, at the same time as altering the possibilities of resorting to share issues as a way of expanding the company's own funds. Consequently, the relative demand for capital will also change: if the cost of capital increases because of higher interest rates, some investment plans with a return close to that cost will not be pursued, whereas other companies will try to maintain profitability by cutting internal costs as much as they can. Thus an increase in interest rates tends to depress economic activity in the short run (via both supply and demand) and to dampen inflationary pressures.

An increase in interest rates also implies a lowering of the relative price of financial as opposed to real assets, an effect which will tend to depress investment and increase saving. Figure 15.9 shows, in broad outline, how the differential between the after-tax return on companies' own funds and the interest rate on an alternative financial asset, such as Treasury bills, bears some direct relation to companies' investment in fixed capital.

Monetary policy also has a more direct influence on companies, by altering their *expectations* regarding the future behaviour of economic activity

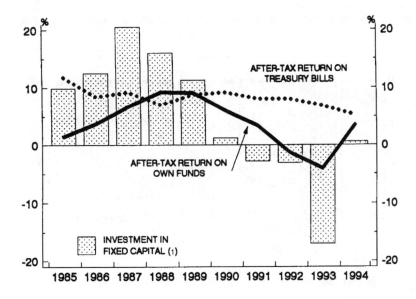

Figure 15.9 Return on own funds of companies reporting to the Central Balance Sheet Office and return on alternative financial investment, 1985–94

Note: 1. Rate of change.
Source: Banco de España.

and inflation. A tight monetary policy geared to reducing demand pressures in the economy can have a rapid impact on corporate decisions regarding their best expansion strategy, how much to pay for productive factors, and pricing. In this sense, changes in monetary policy may affect company decisions, without there necessarily having to be any change in their financial costs.

From a theoretical point of view, Modigliani and Miller (1958) maintained that, under certain circumstances, the value of a company is independent of its financial position: according to these authors, given perfect capital and credit markets, the proportion of own or borrowed funds in a company's liabilities is irrelevant for analysis of corporate performance. That being so, the capacity of monetary policy to influence corporate decisions by altering their financing costs will be much reduced. In practice, however, the markets tapped for corporate funding are far from matching the theoretical conditions underlying such an assumption. They suffer from numerous imperfections: fiscal distortions, asymmetrical information, meaning that various costs are incurred in order to select clients and ration credit using nonprice mechanisms, etc. As a result, numerous companies depend on credit to finance their expenditure decisions, so that the interest rate on such credit is, generally, the relevant marginal cost that companies have to bear in mind when designing their expansion strategy (see Friedman, 1989).

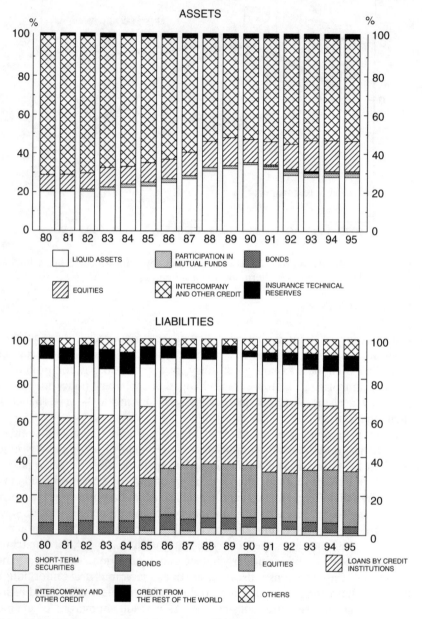

Figure 15.10   Corporate financial structure, 1980–95
Source: Banco de España.

In the corporate financial balance sheet, shown in Figure 15.10, the most significant asset item is client financing (or intercompany credit). It accounts for almost half of total assets and yields an unknown amount of interest, although there are signs that it is relatively less dependent on changes in the overall financial conditions in the economy than other sources of financing, which makes it difficult to talk of transmission of monetary impulses to the costs of such financing. Companies' liquid assets account for less than 30 per cent of financial assets, with the same percentage of financial assets earning market rates (compared with around 60 per cent, in both cases, for households). On the liabilities side, the 3 principal sources of corporate financing are bank credit, self-financing and intercompany credit, in that order. Commercial paper and bond issues and foreign loans do not play a significant part in company financing as a whole. The difference between interest-bearing financial assets and liabilities for Spanish companies in 1995 amounted to a debtor position of under 30 per cent of GDP, which is lower than in most European countries.

The influence of monetary policy on corporate expenditure decisions is strengthened as a result of companies' net debtor position (see Figure 15.11). This, together with the higher level of interest rates on financial liabilities than on financial assets, generates an income effect, which lowers the disposable income of companies when interest rates increase. Net corporate financial expenses rose to over 4 per cent of GDP in 1995, equivalent to almost half the sector's disposable income.

The average return on total liabilities in 1995 was 6.5 per cent, while assets yielded only a little over 2 per cent on average, which meant a net cost of four points: 3 points less than in 1985. This relative reduction in corporate net borrowing costs is not due to the changes in the lending and deposit rates negotiated at market rates, where the spread has remained around six points (see the lower part of Figure 15.12), but rather to greater recourse to other sources of financing that were either free or bore interest rates below market levels, such as self-financing or intercompany credit. The income effect favoring monetary policy has declined in the past decade, as a result of the marked drop in companies' debtor position: the effect of changes in interest rates on corporate liabilities has been partly offset by the drop in their volume.

In the extreme event, contemplated earlier, of changes in the Banco de España's intervention rate being transmitted in their entirety to the rates for companies' interest-bearing financial assets and liabilities, a one-point increase in that rate would increase net corporate financial expenses by 0.3 per cent of GDP, equal to 2 per cent of corporate disposable income.

The relatively short-dated maturity negotiated for a large part of companies' financial liabilities favours monetary policy transmission. On one hand, there is very little issuance of long-term securities, given the

small size of the capital market in Spain: outstanding corporate bonds
accounted for only 3 per cent of total corporate liabilities in 1995. On the

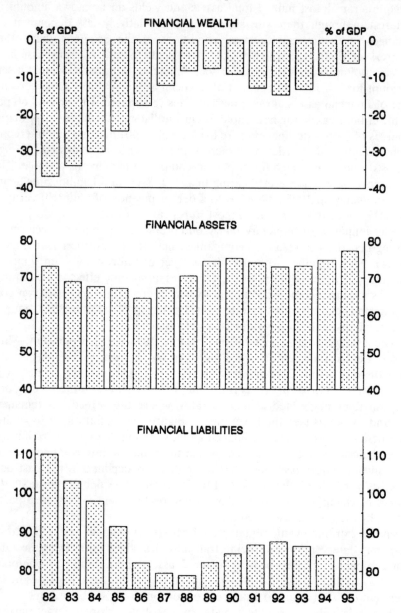

Figure 15.11   Financial position of companies, 1982–95
Source: Banco de España.

other, although there are no detailed data on the maturities of banking transactions with nonfinancial companies, bank lending to companies

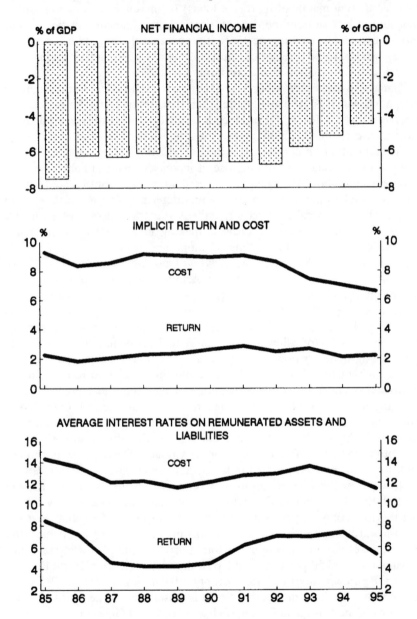

Figure 15.12   Corporate financial income and expenses, 1985–95
Source: Banco de España.

must, on average, be for terms considerably shorter than the (four-year) maturity calculated for total credit to the private sector, because household debt (consisting mainly of mortgage loans) is for relatively long maturities. Despite the lack of itemised data on floating-rate financing for households and for companies (see Figure 15.7), it seems that the bulk of it is for companies, which would strengthen the transmission of monetary impulses to price and cost formation in the corporate sector.

Changes in monetary policy also generate a *wealth effect* in nonfinancial companies which is probably greater than that observed for households. A drop in interest rates would produce a positive wealth effect in companies through two channels. Firstly, it increases the value of shares in other companies appearing under assets, while revaluation of a company's own shares – even though, accountingwise, it increases financial liabilities – is a positive signal about the company's possibilities of expansion and affects the way it tackles investment decisions and determines costs, mark-ups and prices. Thus this wealth effect strengthens the transmission of monetary policy, disciplining corporate decision-making in periods of tight money and encouraging expansion in times of monetary easing.[17]

The extent to which companies depend on bank loans and the possibility of accommodating changes in national monetary policy by resorting to alternative sources of funding is, very largely, a function of the *size* of the company. The bigger the company, the greater its bargaining power *vis-à-vis* national and foreign credit institutions, as well as other companies. Accordingly, size is a factor allowing companies to isolate themselves from the influence of monetary policy.[18] In general, small- and medium-size companies are highly dependent on bank credit and their ability to resort to alternative sources of funds is relatively limited. Given that the average Spanish company is small, or at any rate smaller than the average European company, one could, broadly speaking, conclude that Spanish companies are relatively highly dependent on bank lending, and therefore also fairly highly susceptible to being influenced by monetary policy. Thus, the proportion of bank loans in total borrowed funds for companies rose to 50 per cent in 1994, while in the case of companies reporting to the Banco de España Central Balance Sheet Office, which on average are considerably larger, that ratio was only 35 per cent. Moreover, the available data show that the trend towards bank disintermediation was mainly in larger companies; the percentage of bank financing in the total borrowed funds of companies has remained around 50 per cent in the past decade, while for Central Balance Sheet Office companies that ratio dropped from 48 per cent in 1985 to 35 per cent in 1994. This means that Spain is closer now to the ratios of other countries in the European Union, such as France and Germany.

Differences in the capacity to substitute sources of financing and to provide sufficient collateral have also rendered the size of a company a

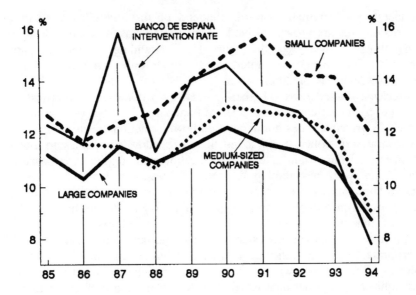

Figure 15.13   Implicit financial cost of remunerated borrowed funds, 1985–94
Source: Banco de España.

relevant factor in explaining the *cost of borrowed funds*. Central Balance
Sheet data clearly show that the smaller the company, the greater the cost
of borrowed funds (see Figure 15.13). The differential in financial costs of
small and large enterprises was around 3 points in 1994. A partial link can
also be perceived between the behaviour of those costs and the Banco de
España's intervention rate. Estrada and Vallés (1995) also find that the
risk premium increases with a company's *level of indebtedness*; in addition,
the *younger* the company, the more intense the connection.

As regards *alternatives to bank financing*, the fact that they have not
markedly increased their share of the total should not lead us to underestimate the complementary part they can play in certain restrictive phases.
Disintermediation has taken place, to some extent, through four channels:
the issuance of commercial paper, foreign loans, intercompany credit and
the expansion of own funds. These sources of funding accounted in 1995
for 55 per cent of all nonfinancial company liabilities, as opposed to 51 per
cent in 1985.

Possibly the least significant alternative option is commercial paper as it
is issued only by large and sufficiently solvent companies, features that
would also facilitate their access to bank credit. Issuing commercial paper
allows companies to absorb part of the banking net interest margin and
thereby reduce the cost of borrowing. Commercial paper in circulation

accelerated substantially towards the end of the 1980s, as a result of restrictions on the growth of bank credit to the private sector. However, once those curbs ended, the figure for outstanding commercial paper began to decline and accounted, in 1995, for only 2 per cent of total corporate financial liabilities.

Foreign currency loans, whether granted by a domestic or non-resident institution, permit companies access to financing at a lower rate of interest which, in principle, does not depend on how the national central bank pursues monetary policy. Such loans therefore allow companies to isolate themselves, to a certain extent, from the financial conditions imposed on the economy by monetary policy. Nevertheless, this kind of borrowing makes companies more vulnerable to the exchange rate of the local currency, which introduces a note of uncertainty regarding the final effective cost of this financing in local currency terms and may make it more difficult for a company to establish a medium-and long-term strategy.[19] Corporate foreign currency-denominated liabilities amounted to 10.8 per cent of GDP in 1995, whereas foreign currency-denominated assets were the equivalent of 6 per cent of GDP. Although the share of such liabilities in total liabilities was not high, in certain specific periods major flows have been recorded: thus, in the 1991–3 period, over one-quarter of all the finds raised by companies came in the form of foreign currency loans.

Intercompany credit is one short-term financial alternative to bank lending. At root, it is usually temporary in nature, tied to commercial transactions and dependent on the financial situation of other companies, so that not all businesses can resort to this source of financing at the same time. Under certain circumstances, however, this type of funding may help attenuate the impact of a recession or of financial restrictions on some group of companies, by allowing them to postpone payment of their trade debts (see, in this connection, García-Vaquero and Maza, 1996).

The *expansion of own funds*, through both share issues and building up of reserves, charged against profits generated, is the fund-raising method that is least dependent on monetary policy, and it has in fact been increasingly used by Spanish companies. The volume of companies' equity, the sum of capital and reserves, which used to account for 20 per cent of total corporate financial liabilities in 1985, accounted for 26 per cent in 1995, while in terms of GDP the increase was from 22 per cent in 1985 to 31 per cent in 1995. This source of financing is obviously limited by the financial and cyclical conditions of the economy and by shareholder pressure for *dividends*. That pressure does not appear, in general, to be very intense: as shown in a study by Chuliá (1993), which analyzes the dividend policy between 1983 and 1991 of the companies co-operating with the Central Balance Sheet Office that reported profits, only one-third of the companies in the sample paid dividends to their shareholders. It would thus appear that, when profits were sufficient, a large portion went into the companies' own funds, helping to finance the business and reducing borrowing costs.

The *proportion of own funds* in companies' total financial liabilities also provides an idea of the degree of influence of monetary policy because the bigger that ratio or the capacity to increase it, the greater a company's independence from monetary and financial conditions. In general, the view that own funds are a constraint on monetary policy implies that there is an *expansionary bias* in its effects. Indeed, in upswings, when monetary conditions tend to be tight in order to contain inflation, companies make more profits and hence can tap them more frequently rather than resorting to borrowed funds. Conversely, in periods of recession, companies depend more on borrowed funds and are more sensitive to the – under such circumstances normally more lax–monetary conditions set by the central bank.

Figure 15.14 shows the relative significance of own funds in corporate financial structure. It shows how for Spanish companies – especially those in the Central Balance Sheet Office's statistics – the behaviour of own funds is in line with developments in the business cycle, which suggests a certain decline in the capacity of monetary policy to rein in the increase in nominal expenditure in upswings. This ratio can also be seen to be higher in Central Balance Sheet companies, which suggests that in larger companies, which are a majority in that sample, there is a greater tendency to resort to share issues and self-financing. Finally, it is worth pointing out

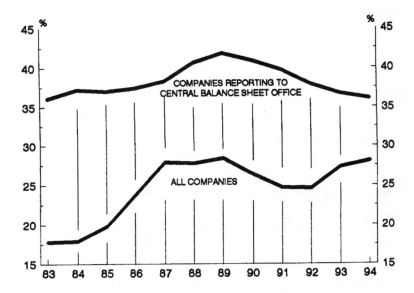

Figure 15.14   Share of own funds in total financial liabilities, 1983–94
Source: Banco de España.

that, according to the BACH project data, the share of own funds in Spanish manufacturers' financial liabilities is similar to that reported in other European countries, such as France, the United Kingdom or Belgium.

If the interest rates for bank credit to companies respond more than money market rates to changes in monetary policy, that policy will exert a certain amount of influence on corporate decisions via the so-called *credit channel* analyzed by Hernando (1997). This channel operates via restrictions on the supply of credit from lending institutions, so that its impact is greatest on those economic agents that cannot find a perfect alternative financing substitute for bank credit, which is particularly the case of smaller enterprises. The relative importance of this credit channel in business decision-making is not too clear although, as Dale and Haldane (1993)

Table 15.4 Summary of the financial position of companies

1. Negative net financial wealth, but improving Negative net financial income	−6% of GDP in 1995 (−30% 10 years earlier) About 4% of GDP (50% of disposable income)	++
2. Relatively illiquid assets Liabilities with a variety of maturities	ALP + mutual funds account for 30% of the total Although short-term bank financing is important	+
3. Expansion of floating-rate loans	No disaggregated information exists, although the increase in mortgage loans for households would only explain half the expansion of floating-rate credit in recent years	+
4. Wealth effect on value of own shares	The behaviour of the price of company shares affects the chances of expanding own funds	++
5. Bank lending predominant	30% of total liabilities (greater weight in small enterprises)	+
6. Alternative financing options (depends on the size of the company)	Commercial paper, foreign loans, intercompany credit, own funds	−
7. Some capacity of companies to accommodate interest rate increases	Less liquidity restrictions than households; although limited use of hedging instruments and narrow securities markets	0

Note: The plus and minus signs in the last column are meant to indicate whether those particular features of the financial position moderately (+) or considerably (++) enhance the transmission of monetary policy or hamper it to a greater (−−) or lesser (−) extent or turn out to be neutral (0).

argue, this channel probably affects companies applying for financing for the first time more than existing borrowers.

Table 15.4 summarizes the main characteristics of the relationship between the financial position of companies and the transmission of monetary policy.

THE FINANCIAL POSITION OF GENERAL GOVERNMENT

The economic significance of general government (hereafter GG) is quite considerable. Although they only directly affect 21 per cent of total domestic output (the sum of government consumption and investment), they perform a very important income redistribution role, which sustains a sizeable part of total private sector consumer good and investment demand. Thus, a quarter of households' disposable income derives from government transfers, while over one-third of corporate disposable income corresponds to current and capital subsidies. As regards financial activities, it should be pointed out that in 1995 one-third of the total financial liabilities of resident sectors corresponded to GG.

Monetary policy influences general government financial variables through various channels. Firstly, to the extent that monetary policy affects the pace of economic activity, government income and expenditures are altered and so, also, is the public deficit. Secondly, the central bank's intervention rate affects the cost of government borrowing, when changes in money market interest rates are passed through to the maturities relevant for the financing of the deficit. The ultimate effect of those changes on general government financial expenditure will depend, on the one hand, on the maturity of the debt accumulated and, on the other, on the degree of consistency perceived between monetary and budgetary policy (on this see Marín and Peñalosa, 1997).

The financial restrictions applied in recent years – particularly the prohibition on resorting to Banco de España loans or on obliging lending institutions to meet investment coefficients for financing the public deficit – mean that GG financing requirements over the last few years have been covered by the market, mainly by recourse to the short-term securities markets (until 1989) and to the medium- and long-term securities markets (since 1990). In 1995, 70 per cent of GG liabilities were in the form of securities, as compared with a little over 10 per cent in the 1980s (see Figure 15.15). Also noteworthy is the increasing share of foreign currency loans: in 1995, over 8 per cent of GG liabilities was foreign currency-denominated, an amount equivalent to almost 6 per cent of GDP. For their part, Banco de España loans have progressively become less important. On the assets side, the increase in the volume of deposits since 1993 largely corresponds to a

deposit made by the State in the Banco de España in order to meet potential liquidity needs following the prohibition on running overdrafts.

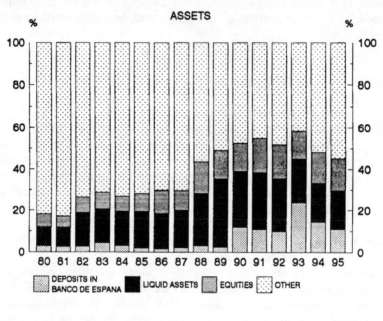

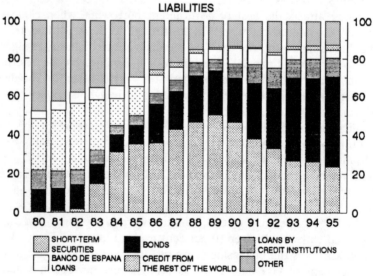

Figure 15.15   Financial structure of general government, 1980–95
Source: Banco de España.

The GG net financial position has deteriorated sharply in the past decade (see Figure 15.16), as a result of the accumulation of heavy public

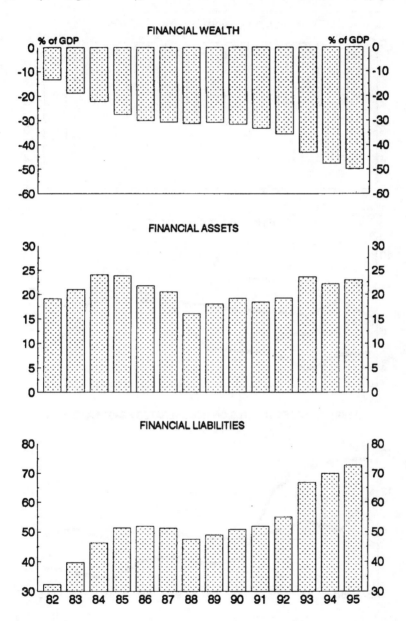

Figure 15.16   Financial position of general government, 1982–95
Source: Banco de España.

deficits. Net financial expenses increased, as a percentage of GDP, from 2
per cent in 1985 to over 4 per cent in 1995. The interest rates implicit in

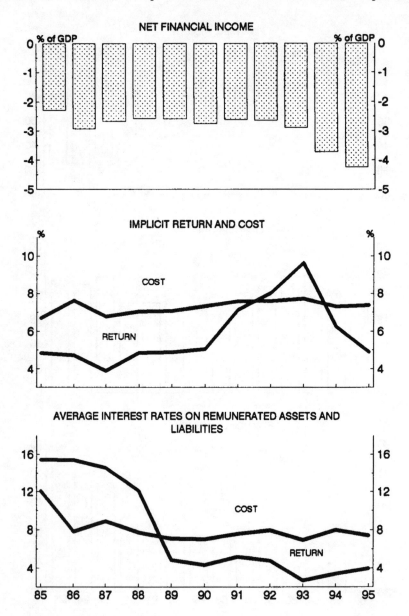

Figure 15.17   Financial income and expenses of general government, 1985–95
Source: Banco de España.

the sector's financial income and expenditure are shown in Figure 15.17: although the average cost of remunerated liabilities appears to be relatively stable, it has to be borne in mind that it has moved much closer towards market rate levels and, given the decline in the rate of inflation, that it disguises an increase in the real interest rate on the debt. In any event, this structure demonstrates that changes in interest rates give rise to a negative *income effect*: if the change in short-term interest rates were to be passed on in its entirety to the interest rates on potentially remunerated financial assets and liabilities, a one-point increase in the intervention rate would, other things being equal, generate an increase in net financial expenses of PTA 400bn at 1995 prices, the equivalent, approximately, of 0.6 per cent of GDP.

The impact of monetary policy on the cost of government borrowing declines as the maturity of the liability instruments lengthens. Thus Table 15.5 shows how the correlation between the intervention rate and the rates of interest on government securities diminishes with the maturity, both contemporaneously and with a lag of a few months.

Until a few years ago, the average *maturity* of GG debt was very short: in 1990, the average life of negotiable government debt, which accounted for 64 per cent of total GG liabilities, was barely 1 year, whereas in 1995 it was over 3 years (see Figure 15.18). Nevertheless, the considerable relative weight even today of short-term securities in total debt means that the weight of short-term interest rates in the financial cost of the debt is relatively high: the short-term securities, which accounted in 1995 for 24 per cent of total GG financial liabilities and amounted to one-third of government securities, had at that time an average life span of only 6 months.

A significant portion of GG financial assets are variable-yield securities, i.e. shares in State companies, some of which yield high income, both in the form of dividends (Telefónica, REPSOL, etc.) and in capital gains (privatization proceeds). Changes in interest rates may affect the value of this *wealth*, in such a way as to reinforce the monetary policy transmission

Table 15.5 Correlation between changes in the Banco de España intervention rate and interest rates on government securities (January 1990–April 1996[a])

	1–year bills	3–year bonds	10–year bonds
Contemporaneous	0.74	0.52	0.36
With a lag of:			
1 month	0.43	0.19	0.10
2 months	0.14	0.06	0.06
3 months	0.14	–	–

Note: a Except for the 10-year bonds, for which the period considered was December 1991–April 1996.

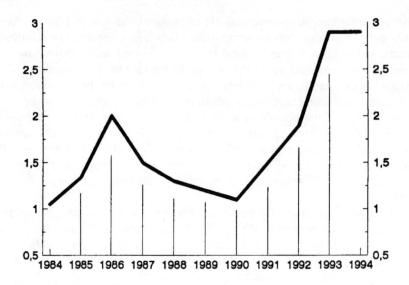

Figure 15.18   Average life of negotiable government debt,[1] 1984–94

Note: 1   Measured in years.
Source: Banco de España.

channel. Indeed, greater monetary tightness could lead to low state profits and a less favorable outlook regarding the proceeds expected from the possible privatization of some of those companies, which in turn would lead to changes in other parts of the Budget in order to meet the public deficit target. All in all, this effect cannot be considered to be particularly intense.

The *degree of dependence on banks* for the financing of government debt has declined significantly over the past decade as a result of the development of the government debt book-entry market and of greater private sector demand for government securities, especially from mutual funds and non-residents. There are numerous *alternative financing options* open to GG. In particular since 1993, when recourse to Banco de España loans was prohibited, the Treasury has widened its sources of financing and diversified in term of instruments, maturities and the currencies in which they are denominated (see Muñoz de la Peña, 1995).

Although changes in the Banco de España intervention rate affect the cost of GG funding, it cannot be deduced that the central bank is able to use this rate *systematically* as an instrument with which to help reduce that cost. An easing of monetary policy will help reduce interest rates for all maturities, if economic agents consider that policy consistent with the inflation outlook. Conversely, if the central bank were to implement an expansive monetary policy with a view to reducing the financial burden of the debt and without taking the phase of the business cycle into account, the attendant loss of credibility would generate greater expectations of future inflation, increases in medium- and long-term interest rates, and greater difficulty in obtaining financing, so that the gains in terms of a decline in short-term interest rates would be very short-lived. In this respect, the process of liberalization, financial deregulation and the elimination of GG financial privileges have led markets to exert a *disciplining effect* on the economy by making financial conditions tighter when they sense that the economic policy pursued is not compatible with price stability (see Alejano and Peñalosa, 1995). Thus, although the financial cost of GG liabilities is not completely unrelated to the monetary policy stance, the best way to reduce inflationary expectations, the average level of long-term interest rates and, ultimately, the cost of government borrowing is to implement a monetary policy geared exclusively to achieving price stability (see Table 15.6)

Table 15.6   Summary of the general government financial position

1. Negative and rapidly deteriorating financial wealth Negative net financial income 90 per cent of liabilities remunerated at market rates	−50% of GDP in 1995 (−25% 10 years earlier) More than 4% of GDP	++
2. Average maturity of negotiable debt: 3 years (in 1990: 1 year)	Although one-quarter of the financing comes from money markets	+
3. Very little floating-rate financing		0
4. Modest wealth effect	Although the potential capital gains arising from selling shares in companies may be considerable.	+
5. Limited significance of bank credit	Mainly used by territorial governments	0
6. Alternative financing options: numerous and extended after the financial restrictions of the Maastricht Treaty	Active presence in various markets, maturities and currencies	−
7. Limited ability to accommodate increases in interest rates	Previously high; now: financial restrictions + deficit and debt targets	+

Note: The plus and minus signs in the last column are meant to indicate whether those particular features of the financial position moderately (+) or considerably (++) enhance the transmission of monetary policy or hamper it to a greater (−−) or lesser (−) extent or turn out to be neutral (0).

CONCLUSIONS

Analysis of the financial position of economic sectors proves crucial for assessing the effectiveness and speed of the monetary policy transmission mechanism, because the changes wrought by such policy in the monetary and financial conditions prevailing in the economy have different effects on economic agents' expenditure decisions, depending on the financial structure of each sector, the nature of its assets and liabilities, and the financial restrictions that each economic agent faces. This study has examined the financial position of households, companies and general government in the Spanish economy in the past decade, along with the outlook for each. To that end, we established a set of criteria for defining the financial position in question and helping to assess to what extent it enhances or hampers the transmission of monetary policy.

Table 15.7 attempts to summarize the main conclusions of the study, assigning a value to each of these basic criteria. These assessments are not meant to provide comparisons with other countries but simply to list the greater or lesser estimated impact of the criteria described on the transmission of monetary policy in Spain[20]. Moreover, the fact that some of the criteria mentioned may be substitutable makes it necessary to treat with caution the conclusions that may be drawn from this table:

(a) The financial position of the Spanish non-financial sector generally *favors* the transmission of monetary policy. Traditional *uncertainty* over the degree of financial stability in the medium term – which leads to a greater demand for short-term financing, a rise in floating-rate lending, and under-developed private capital markets – and the relative importance of the *banking system* – which is more intensely influenced by monetary policy – are two of the principal reasons for this.

(b) Despite this overall assessment, there are important *sectoral differences*:

In the case of *households*, the feature that most favors transmission of monetary policy is the heavy dependence on bank lending to finance major expenditure decisions (housing and durable consumer goods). Although the maturity for such loans is relatively long, and therefore the conditions governing them possibly less dependent on monetary policy, the proliferation of floating-rate loans to households has allowed monetary policy to have a significant impact in determining the financial costs of these economic agents. In addition, the income effect, which runs counter to transmission of monetary policy in this sector, does not appear to be very important, despite households' strong creditor position. Also, the uneven distribution of

Table 15.7 Summary of the part played by economic agents' financial position in the transmission of monetary policy

	Households	Companies	GG
(a) Income effect	−	++	++
(b) Length of maturity	−	+	+
(c) Frequency of revision of interest rates and reference rates	++	+	0
(d) Wealth effect	+	++	+
(e) Degree of banking intermediation	++	+	0
(f) Alternative sources of finance: * foreign currency financing * intercompany credit * securities markets	++	−	−
(g) Sensitivity to changes in interest rates	++	0	+

Notes:
−− Considerably hampers transmission of monetary policy.
− Hampers it to a moderate degree.
0 Does not affect transmission of monetary policy.
+ Favours transmission to a moderate degree.
++ Considerably enhances it.

financial income and expenses between different income groups could give rise to divergence between households' net financial income and demand.

The influence of monetary policy on *corporate* decisions is mainly explained by the sector's net debtor position and the relatively short maturity of a large part of its liabilities. On the other hand, companies enjoy greater leeway to diversify their sources of funding and isolate themselves from changes in short-term interest rates. In any case, it is important to stress that the size of a company is a key to its responsiveness to changes in monetary policy: the larger the company, the greater its apparent capacity to shield itself from the effects of monetary policy.

As regards general government the effects of monetary policy have become more intense following the obligation on this sector to resort to market financing (financial discipline), while the increased importance attached to public deficit targets (fiscal discipline) has meant that those effects may not be accommodated. The direct impact of monetary policy on the cost of government borrowing is largely explained by the relatively high level of short-term debt, the interest on which moves in line with changes in money market interest rates.

(c) As for the *outlook* on the future role of the financial position of economic agents in the transmission of monetary policy, there are no

clear signs of it being either strengthened or weakened. Intense financial deregulation and liberalization, which will encourage swifter and
closer links between interest rates in all markets, together with the
high and growing volume of floating-rate credit could help reinforce
such transmission. In addition, the proliferation of floating-rate loans
could reduce debtors' incentives to generate inflation as a way of
reducing the financial burden on fixed-rate loans. These factors could
be offset by the fact that for some agents that process of integration
in turn facilitates the search for alternative sources of financing,
allows participation by new financial intermediaries and increases the
number of factors unrelated to national monetary policy but which
play a part in determining the interest rates on financial instruments.
Moreover, the achievement of greater nominal stability in the Spanish
economy could lead to greater development of long-term markets,
which are relatively unaffected by monetary policy implementation.

Appendix: Ranges of Values Used to Classify the Criteria Defining the Role of the Financial Position of Sectors in the Monetary Policy Transmission Mechanism (see Table 15.7, p. 557)

(a) Income effect	Measure	Changes in net financial income as a percentage of disposable income when the intervention rate rises 1 percentage point.
		$--\quad-\quad0\quad+\quad++$
	Interval	$> 1; (0; 1); (0); (-1; 0); < -1$
(b) Length of maturity	Measure	Percentage of borrowed funds with a maturity of 4 year or less.
		$--\quad-\quad0\quad+\quad++$
	Interval	$< 5; (5, 15); (15, 25); (25, 35); > 35$
(c) Frequency of revision of interest rates	Measure	Percentage of floating-rate liabilities.
		$0\quad+\quad++$
	Interval	$< 5; (5; 20); > 20$
(d) Wealth effect	Measure	Change in financial wealth as a percentage of disposable income when the intervention rate rises 1 percentage point.
		$0\quad+\quad++$
	Interval	$> -1; (-1; -4); < -4$
(e) Degree of banking intermediation	Measure	Percentage of liabilities to credit institutions.
		$0\quad+\quad++$
	Interval	$< 25; (25; 50); > 50$

559

(f) Alternative sources of financing	Qualitative assessment based on the considerations presented in this chapter
(g) Sensitivity to changes in interest rates	

Notes

1   The statistical data for this study were prepared by Luis Ángel Maza.
2   Pursuing a similar objective, Borio (1995) and Kneeshaw (1995) make an international comparison of the part played by the financial position of companies and households in the transmission of monetary policy.
3   This study considers the financial position on which monetary policy acts as a given factor, and as a result it does not take into account possible restructuring of financial assets and liabilities induced by monetary impulses. However, insofar as the financial structure as a whole generally responds slowly to changes in monetary policy, the approach adopted in this chapter could still be valid.
4   This chapter does not address the final impact of monetary policy on economic agents' expenditure decisions. Rather, it assesses the extent to which movements in short-term interest rates, in conjunction with agents' financial position, affect some of the determinants of those expenditure decisions, such as disposable income, financial wealth, or economic agents' borrowing capacity.
5   The financial position of economic agents is considered to affect, above all, the *speed* at which monetary impulses are transmitted. Even though the *intensity* of that transmission process will also undoubtedly be affected, in some cases it proves harder to demonstrate because it is more difficult to evaluate the ultimate effects of transmission after a lengthy period.
6   See the outline in Peñalosa (1996, p.9).
7   In this connection, see Manzano and Galmés (1996) and Sastre (1998), Chapter 13 in this volume.
8   Variable-yield securities were not taken into account in corporate liabilities when calculating either the financial wealth of this sector or total financial liabilities. The increase in such securities not only does not indicate a deterioration in the financial position of companies; on the contrary, it implies an improvement in their expansion possibilities.
9   On the financial assets side, the instruments susceptible to be paid market rates are bank deposits, short-term securities, bonds and participations in mutual funds. On the financial liabilities side, the instruments considered were short-term securities, bonds, loans granted by the credit system, and credit from the rest of the world.
10 Although a sizable portion of the participations in mutual funds is invested in liquid assets (Treasury bills and asset repos), and as such is computed under ALP, in this classification we have preferred to segregate these participations,

in order to analyze their behaviour and particular characteristics in greater detail.

11   There are no data breaking down the maturities at which credit institutions grant loans to households, only data on the maturities for both corporations and households together. Thus, on average, loans to the private sector have an approximately 4- year maturity. In the case of households, this maturity is probably considerably longer, since at least two-thirds of the financing received is for home purchases and such loans are usually for longer terms.

12   Specifically, the recommended reference rates were: (a) an average rate of new over-3-year mortgage loans to finance private housing purchases; (b) an average rate for medium-and long-term loans by savings banks, based on the CECA formula; (c) the rate of return in the secondary market for book-entry government debt, maturing within 2 to 6 years; and (d) the monthly 4-year MIBOR average.

13   Thus the marked increase in secured loans in recent years could be interpreted as an indicator of greater rationing in bank lending, which probably will have meant that economic agents lacking sufficient goods to put up as collateral have suffered considerable financial restrictions (see Fuentes, 1995).

14   Thus, in the United States, the frequent use of secured loans to finance consumer expenditure or some other type of expenditure (*home equities*) reinforces the relationship between, on the one hand, households' borrowing capacity and their demand for consumer durables and, on the other, changes in the level of interest rates and in the market value of housing. See Canner and Luckett (1994) and Mauskopf (1990).

15   Treasury bills and securities repos account for about 75 per cent of the total net asset value of mutual funds.

16   All these considerations regarding the tax incentives to maintain mutual funds have been modified following the recent reform. This places a ceiling of 20 per cent on the tax rate applicable to capital gains arising from the funds.

17   The impact of changes in interest rates on wealth kept in the form of fixed income or real estate is less important in the case of nonfinancial companies. As regards the former, not much fixed income is in the hands of nonfinancial companies: less than 2 per cent of their financial assets is invested in fixed income. As regards the latter, although changes in real estate prices may affect decisions as to where companies are located and can lead to extraordinary results, such outcomes are complementary to companies' main activities and their influence on expenditure decisions is generally not a major determining factor.

18   According to estimations by Hernando (1995), the companies best able to replace bank credit with other sources of finance are also those which, all other things being equal, have the highest levels of investment.

19   Sometimes this kind of borrowing is a response to a tightening of national monetary policy and it benefits from the stability or even appreciation of the local currency that may result from the greater restrictiveness of monetary policy. However, this type of advantage is usually short-lived and cannot serve as a basis for companies' medium-term borrowing strategy.

20   The Appendix (p.559) lists the ranges of values used to make this classification.

562   *Juan María Peñalosa*

References

ALEJANO, A. and J.M. PEÑALOSA (1995) 'La integración financiera de la economía española: efectos sobre los mercados financieros y la política monetaria', Banco de España, Servicio de Estudios, *Documento de Trabajo*, 9525.

BANCO DE ESPAÑA (1993) 'Tipos de referencia recomendados para las operaciones de crédito hipotecario a tipo de interés variable', *Boletín Económico*, Banco de España, December.

BANCO DE ESPAÑA (1995) *Resultados anuales de las empresas no financieras de la Central de Balances, 1994.*

BORIO, C. (1995) 'The structure of credit to the non-government sector and the transmission mechanism of monetary policy', Bank for International Settlements, *Working Paper*, 24.

BORIO, C. and W. FRITZ (1995) 'The response of short-term bank lending rates to policy rates: a cross-country perspective', Bank for International Settlements, *Working Paper*, 27.

CANNER, G.B. and C.A. LUCKETT (1994) 'Home equity lending: evidence from recent surveys', *Federal Reserve Bulletin*, July.

COTTARELLI C. and A. KOURELIS (1994) 'Financial structure, bank lending rates and the transmission mechanism of monetary policy', *IMF Staff Papers*, 41, 4.

CHULIÁ, C. (1993) 'Política de dividendos en la empresa española no financiera', *Boletín Económico*, Banco de España, February.

CHULIÁ, C. and I. FUENTES (1993) 'La financiación y el endeudamiento de las empresas no financieras y las familias', *Boletín Económico*, Banco de España, February.

DALE, S. and A.G. HALDANE (1993) 'Bank behaviour and the monetary transmission mechanism', *Bank of England Quarterly Bulletin*, November.

ESCRIVÁ, J.L. and A.G. HALDANE (1994), 'The interest rate transmission mechanism: sectorial estimates for Spain', Banco de España, Servicio de Estudios, *Documento de Trabajo*, 9414.

ESTRADA, A. (1992) 'Una función de consumo de bienes duraderos', Banco de España, Servicio de Estudios, *Documento de Trabajo*, 9228.

ESTRADA, A. and J. VALLÉS (1995): 'Inversión y costes financieros: evidencia en España con datos de panel', Banco de España, Servicio de Estudios, *Documento de Trabajo*, 9506.

ESTRADA, A., I. HERNANDO and J. VALLÉS (1998) 'The impact of interest rates on private spending', Chapter 14 in this volume.

ESTRADA, A., T. SASTRE and J.L. VEGA (1994) 'El mecanismo de transmisión de los tipos de interés: el caso español', Banco de España, Servicio de Estudios, *Documento de Trabajo*, 9408.

FRIEDMAN, B. (1989) 'Capital, credit and money markets', in John Eatwell, Murray Milgate, Peter Newman (eds.) *The New Palgrave–Money*, London: Macmillan, 72–87.

FUENTES, I. (1993) 'El crédito bancario en España, 1988–1993', *Boletín Económico*, Banco de España, December.

FUENTES, I. (1995) 'Evolución reciente del crédito bancario: efectos sobre la financiación de las familias y las empresas', *Boletín Económico*, Banco de España, November.

GARCÍA-VAQUERO, V. and L.A. MAZA (1996) 'Crédito interempresarial: evolución reciente y efectos sobre el sistema económico', *Boletín Económico*, Banco de España, March.

GORDO, E. and C. SÁNCHEZ (1997) 'El papel del tipo de cambio en el mecanismo de transmisión de la política monetaria', in *La política monetaria y la inflación en España*, Servicio de Estudios del Banco de España, Madrid: Alianza Editorial.

HERNANDO, I. (1995) 'Política monetaria y estructura financiera de las empresas', Banco de España, Servicio de Estudios, *Documento de Trabajo*, 9520.

HERNANDO, I. (1997) 'El canal crediticio en la transmisión de la política monetaria', in *La política monetaria y la inflación en España*, Servicio de Estudios del Banco de España, Madrid: Alianza Editorial.

KING, M. (1994) 'The transmission mechanism of monetary policy', *Bank of England Quarterly Bulletin*, August.

KNEESHAW, J. T. (1995) 'A survey of non-financial sector balance sheets in industrialised countries: implications for the monetary policy transmission mechanism', Bank for International Settlements, *Working Paper*, 25.

MANZANO, M.C. and S. GALMÉS (1995) 'El mercado interbancario de depósitos y las entidades de crédito', *Boletín Económico* Banco de España, February.

MANZANO, M.C. and S. GALMÉS (1996) 'Políticas de precios de las entidades de crédito y tipo de clientela: efectos sobre el mecanismo de transmisión', Banco de España, Servicio de Estudios, *Documento de Trabajo*, 9605.

MARÍN, J. and J.M. PEÑALOSA (1997) 'Implicaciones del marco institucional y de la política presupuestaria para la política monetaria en España', in *La política monetaria y la inflación en España*, Servicio de Estudios del Banco de España, Madrid: Alianza Editorial.

MAUSKOPF, E. (1990) 'The transmission channels of monetary policy: how have they changed?', *Federal Reserve Bulletin*, December.

MESTRE, R. (1995) 'A macroeconomic evaluation of the Spanish monetary policy transmission mechanism', Banco de España, Servicio de Estudios, *Documento de Trabajo*, 9504.

MODIGLIANI, F. and M.H. MILLER (1958) 'The cost of capital, corporation finance and the theory of investment', *American Economic Review* 48, June.

MUÑOZ DE LA PEÑA, E. (1995) 'Nuevos instrumentos del Tesoro para la captación de recursos', *Boletín Económico*, Banco de España, September.

PEÑALOSA, J.M. (1994) 'Determinantes financieros de la recuperación del consumo privado', *Boletín Económico*, Banco de España, June.

PEÑALOSA, J.M. (1996) 'El papel de la posición financiera de los agentes económicos en la transmisión de la política monetaria', Banco de España, Estudios Económicos, 54.

SASTRE, T. (1991) 'La determinación de los tipos de interés activos y pasivos de bancos y cajas de ahorros', Banco de España, Estudios Económicos, 45.

SASTRE, T. (1998) 'The role of the banking system in the monetary transmission mechanism', Chapter 13 in this volume.

16 A Structural Model for the Analysis of the Monetary Policy Transmission Mechanism

Javier Andrés, Ricardo Mestre and
Javier Vallés

E58   E52   E17
E44

INTRODUCTION

Monetary policy plays an important role in stabilizing economic fluctuations and, especially, in controlling the rate of inflation in an economy. This chapter analyzes the monetary transmission mechanism in Spain by carrying out a series of simulation exercises using a macroeconomic model with a high degree of aggregation. These exercises serve to compare the behaviour of the rate of inflation and the rate of growth of GDP in the base scenario with their behaviour in various alternative monetary policy settings.

Using these simulation exercises, this study evaluates the response of inflation and the rate of growth, once all other endogenous variables (exchange rate, real long-term interest rate, demand for real balances, etc.) have been appropriately adjusted. In the macroeconomic model used, no explicit distinction is drawn between the various components of expenditure or income. The more disaggregated expenditure side analysis is carried out by Estrada, Hernando, and Vallés in Chapter 14 in this book. A high degree of aggregation makes it difficult to perform a detailed analysis of monetary transmission channels, but it does offer answers to some major questions that are less sensitive to alterations in the model's specifications. Such issues are, in particular, the response of demand to variations in the interest rate, the importance of competitiveness in monetary transmission, or the speed with which expectations are adjusted.

The simulation model's specifications take into account the new Spanish monetary policy regime adopted in the setting of European economic integration. Institutionally, that change is manifest in a stronger gearing of monetary policy towards price stability. In this context, monetary policy is understood to mean the determination of a short-term nominal interest rate consistent with the central bank's inflation target. As for the way financial markets operate, the gradual opening up of the Spanish economy and its incorporation into international markets mean that economic agents expectations play an important part in determining nominal and real variables in the economy.

The rest of the chapter is structured as follows. We first summarize the most salient aspects of the monetary transmission mechanism and the development of the concrete model described in this chapter, and second we present the results of the simulations of various disinflationary strategies. The final section summarizes the main conclusions of the chapter.

MONETARY POLICY TRANSMISSION: AN AGGREGATE SUPPLY AND DEMAND MODEL

Monetary policy affects inflation, the unemployment rate or the rate of growth of an economy by altering aggregate supply and demand. The set of channels influencing supply and demand is what is known as the monetary transmission mechanism. Before describing its main features, it is worth making two specific points. First, it is necessary to specify the environment in which monetary policy operates. Generally speaking, monetary policy has no major real impact in an economy in which all markets are in equilibrium and economic agents act rationally, given the immediate response of prices to excess demand. For that reason, we shall focus on the effects of monetary policy in the first instance on nominal variables. If, additionally, some kind of nominal rigidity exists, monetary policy will, at least temporarily, affect real magnitudes in the economy.[1]

Second, the relative speed with which monetary measures have an impact on prices and quantities determines the cost associated with each monetary policy strategy and hence its viability. Nevertheless in this chapter we will not study the determinants of the speed of responses to monetary impulses. The main point of reference in this regard is built into the dynamic structure of the empirical model, which conditions the results of the simulations.

The nature of the transmission channels depends on the way monetary policy is formulated. Thus, a central bank may employ strategies based on targets for a particular monetary aggregate or else it may choose to determine a path for short-term interest rates consistent with its goal of price stability or stability for any other nominal variable (the exchange rate, for instance).[2] As is generally recognized, the type of uncertainty prevailing in an economy affects optimal selection of one or other monetary strategy (see Poole, 1970). Nevertheless, the instability of many estimations of the demand for monetary aggregates weakened their reputation as a reliable guide to monetary policy stance in many countries and relegated these to the role of being important indicators only. Two reasons have been put forward in the literature to explain the short-term instability of the demand for money (Taylor, 1995). One is the development of financial markets and their deregulation. The other is the gradual opening up of economies and the consequent impact of new variables on the relationship between monetary aggregates and the expenditure decisions taken by economic agents. The following sections deal with the transmission mechanism under each of these monetary strategies.

The Transmission Mechanism Based on a Monetary Aggregate

Figure 16.1 depicts the main effects of monetary policy on the (cyclical component of) GDP and on inflation, via the various markets in an economy. Most of these effects are independent of whether monetary policy is defined in terms of a monetary aggregate or a specific interest rate, but let us assume, for the time being, that the monetary measure is understood to be the establishment of a monetary aggregate target $\{M_t\}$.[3] In an economy in which the existence of some market imperfection generates insufficient demand, the effectiveness of monetary policy depends, fundamentally, on its impact on relative prices: the interest rate, the exchange rate, and real wages. Changes in the real interest rate allow alterations in the structure of demand over time, causing, in the event of a monetary contraction, a "delay" in certain consumption and investment decisions. Apart from this intertemporal substitution effect, interest rates can also have an impact on demand via their income and wealth effects. Likewise, the fact that domestically produced goods become relatively more expensive leads companies to reduce market share by reducing external demand. Aggregate supply (prices and wages) will also be affected by the cheapening of imported goods and by economic agents' expectations.

The most conventional monetary policy channel is the one that operates via the interest rate (*liquidity effect*). Restrictive monetary policy produces

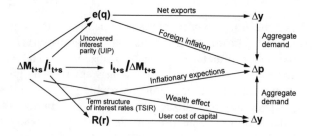

Figure 16.1   Money supply, output and inflation

a temporary increase in the short-term nominal interest rate (usually its impact in the interbank market is immediate). In their calculations of the user cost of capital for long-term expenditure decisions, companies and consumers use some long-term interest rate or the bank lending rate as a benchmark. The mechanism by which short-term rate signals affect the long-term rate is complex, since it is conditioned by the nature and degree of competitiveness of the financial system, the structure of short and long-term loans in corporate liabilities, and by financial markets' own perception of how temporary the change in the interest rate is likely to be. Furthermore, monetary policy can alter the relative risk premia attached to certain assets. However, monetary impulse transmission through the whole structure of assets takes time, even when the various interest rates tend to move together, and does not always proceed in a linear way.

Changes in the money supply also affect the exchange rate. How this effect operates depends notably on the degree of openness of the economy and, in particular, on the degree of international financial integration. If capital mobility is very high, the only sustainable exchange rate will be that which, risk premia aside, guarantees equality in the returns expected on domestic and similar foreign assets, when compared using the same currency. "Uncovered interest parity" is one way to represent this condition, so that the nominal interest rate differs from the expected rate depending on expectations as to the future behaviour of the interest rate differential and risk premium. Variations in a monetary aggregate affect nominal parity via 3 channels. First, the relative level of domestic money supply affects exchange rate projections. Second, the interest rate differential caused by temporary changes in the supply of real balances determines the rate of depreciation. Finally, the way monetary policy is conducted is one of the factors influencing the risk premium that investors require as an incentive to invest in domestic assets.

Generally speaking, restrictive monetary policy temporarily increases the interest rate differential, which contributes to an appreciation of the currency to an extent that creates expectations of an upcoming depreciation.[4] In addition, such a policy may lead to a reduction in the exchange rate risk for foreign investors that helps capital inflows. Appreciation sets in motion two types of effects that help control inflation. On the one hand, the loss of competitiveness leads to a decline in net exports, and to a drop in demand pressure. On the other, the relative cheapening of imported goods reduces imported inflation and tempers wage demands.

Changes in the money supply also have an effect on aggregate supply and demand that does not operate exclusively via relative prices. Monetary policy affects the net wealth of the private sector because of its impact on the level of net assets held by that sector and on their market value via the relative price structure of financial and real assets. This *wealth effect* is the main channel through which monetary policy affects monetarist models (Metzler, 1995). There is also a direct relationship between the volume of credit to the private sector and the level of expenditure of companies and consumers. In the event of some kind of market imperfection derived from asymmetric information, the marginal cost of the different forms of corporate (and consumer) financing is not equal. Specifically, a monetary policy that causes increases in the interest rate also raises the relative cost of external financing for less financially solvent firms. The *credit channel* is manifest in the restriction on the supply of bank loans associated with monetary contraction, and in the difficulty in gaining access to other external funds, both of which possibly reduce private expenditure.[5]

Finally, monetary policy may have a direct impact on inflation if the central bank is capable of influencing economic agents expectations. In the case of restrictive monetary policy, this *expectations effect* is manifest in an impact on aggregate supply, through a dampening of wage demands and of the growth in nominal costs, while, on the demand side, it reinforces the increase in real interest rates associated with monetary contraction. How long this increase lasts depends on how stable the drop in inflation is. As inflation falls real balances recover with the nominal interest rate dropping in line with the new rate of inflation.

The Transmission Mechanism Based on Interest Rates

The above section describes the main channels through which monetary impulses are transmitted to the real economy and affect inflation. Monetary policy in Spain is more geared to a framework in which the central bank steers the current nominal interest rate in accordance with its inflation target, making use of the various instruments at its disposal to make sure that the rate stays within the desired bounds.[6] In this case, *i* becomes the exogenous monetary policy variable and *M* endogenous. For a given interest rate value, the monetary transmission channels operate more or less as described in the previous section, as Figure 16.1 shows. Nevertheless, this definition of monetary policy gives rise to at least 3 particularities in the way monetary transmission functions and which are worth noting.

The first refers to the type of policies that can be applied to lower inflation in an economy with higher initial levels of inflation and nominal interest rates than the countries in its immediate environment (with which it is financially integrated). Transmission of a permanent reduction in the rate of growth of the money supply operates via an increase in interest rates that may ultimately fall when inflation declines and the supply of real balances recovers. For that reason, the equivalent of a *permanent reduction* in the rate of growth of the money supply is a *temporary*, not a permanent, increase in interest rates.

This observation leads us to a second particularity in the interest rate transmission mechanism. In financially integrated economies, capital mobility tends, in the medium and long term, to make real interest rates homogeneous. Thus, in that time frame, the reduction in the inflation differential is associated with a corresponding decline in the nominal interest rate differential.[7] When the central bank uses the money supply, this is achieved "automatically" if monetary contraction succeeds in lowering inflation. When the monetary authorities use the interest rate as an instrument, they can apply a policy emulating the effect of a permanent drop in the money supply by temporarily increasing the interest rate (*vis-à-vis* a starting point) and then reducing it later in line with the international rate. However, in theory, the possibility of an immediate and permanent reduction in the nominal interest rate, as an anti-inflationary strategy, cannot be discarded although in practice, as we argue in the following section, it turns out to be inviable.

The third main characteristic associated with a framework in which the monetary authorities control the interest rate is the difficulty of correctly determining the value of the nominal variables. When the money supply is exogenously determined, it constitutes the nominal anchor for the economy. Nominal indeterminacy with an interest rates rule appears in a wide range of models. In a closed economy with fixed prices, the price level will be determined by past history. However, when prices are fixed rationally, Sargent and Wallace (1975) demonstrated that the price level is indeterminate.

In an open economy, in which the exchange rate is determined according to rational expectations, the nonexistence of a nominal anchor gives rise to a basic lack of determination of the exchange rate and of the other nominal variables in the economy. The main effect of this lack of determination, both theoretically and empirically, is the difficulty of correctly evaluating the cost of alternative anti-inflationary strategies. The following sections will address this point in greater detail, once the economic model has been specified.

A Macroeconomic Aggregate Supply and Demand Model

We consider an open economy model, with a given level of external output and international trade.[8] The government determines fiscal policy exogenously.[9] There are four financial assets: money, short-term domestic bonds, long-term domestic bonds, and foreign assets, which means that 3 financial market equilibrium conditions are required to determine the relative prices of those assets. The short-term interest rate is established by the monetary authorities. The model can be expressed as a function of the following set of equations showing the behaviour of aggregate demand[10] and supply:

$$y_t - y_t^p = \alpha_{10} + \alpha_{11}r_t + \alpha_{12}q_t + \alpha_{13}g_t + \alpha_{14}a_t + \alpha_{15}y_t^* + \epsilon_{yt} \qquad IS \quad (16.1)$$

$$m_t - p_t = \alpha_{20} + \alpha_{21}R_t + \alpha_{22}i_t + \alpha_{23}y_t + \epsilon_{mt} \qquad LM \quad (16.2)$$

$$r_t \equiv R_t - E[\Delta p_{t+1/t}] \qquad RIR \quad (16.3)$$

$$R_t = (1-b)i_t + bE[R_{t+1/t}] + \epsilon_{it} \qquad TSIR \quad (16.4)$$

$$i_t = i_t^* + E(e_{t+1/t}) - e_t + \epsilon_{et} \qquad UIP \quad (16.5)$$

$$\Delta P_t^d = \alpha_{60} + \alpha_{61}E[\Delta P_t^d] + \alpha_{62}E[\Delta e_t + \Delta P_t^*] + \alpha_{63}(Y_t - Y_t^p) + \epsilon_{pt} \qquad AS \quad (16.6)$$

$$\Delta p_t = \alpha_{70} + \alpha_{71}\mu_t + \alpha_{72}\Delta p_t^d + \alpha_{73}(\Delta p_t^* + \Delta e_t) + \epsilon_{pt} \qquad CPI \quad (16.7)$$

The endogenous variables are: cyclical output[11] $(y_t - y_t^p)$, the change in domestic prices measured by the GDP deflator (Δp_t^d), the money stock in real terms $(m_t - p_t)$, the long-term nominal interest rate (R_t), the real interest rate (r_t), the exchange rate (e_t), and inflation (Δp_t) as measured by the CPI. The exogenous variables are: potential output (y_t^p), the fiscal policy indicator (g_t), world income (y_t^*), the short-term interest rate (i_t), external inflation (Δp_t^*) and the share of imports in income (μ_t). The exchange rate is defined as the value of the foreign currency in local currency terms, and q_t is the real exchange rate. The definition of wealth (a_t) only includes real balances for lack of other quarterly asset figures. All the variables are expressed as logarithms, except the interest rates. We assume that the expectations in the financial equations ((16.3), (16.4) and (16.5)) are fully anticipated by economic agents. Conversely, the supply-side rigidities (16.6) imply that expectations are formed by past values of the explanatory variables. Before describing the estimations of the equations in the model, we shall briefly explain the specifications chosen for each of them.

(16.1) represents aggregate demand as a function of the long-term real interest rate, the real exchange rate, a fiscal indicator, the level of wealth, and world income. Thus, changes in relative prices operate through 3 channels in aggregate demand: the substitution effect between consumption and saving and between domestic and foreign goods; the positive income effect for economic agents who are net creditors; and, finally, a wealth effect which increases the value of residents' assets in the event of declines in the interest rate or depreciations of the local currency.

The econometric evidence for Spain reveals a negative effect of real interest rates on the components of final demand for goods and services. That is the finding of estimations made using annual investment functions (Andrés, Escribano, Molinas and Taguas, 1989) and consumption functions (Estrada, 1993). Similar evidence is obtained using quarterly data on the demand for durable and nondurable consumer goods and on the demand for domestic housing and private sector productive investment (see Chapter 14 by Estrada, Hernando and Vallés in this book). The results of these calculations reveal a moderate impact of the real interest rate (compared to the effect of other variables) appearing after a certain time lag. This significant impact of the real interest rate on consumption and investment is not to be found in the same degree of intensity on the more aggregate magnitudes: output and inflation. The available evidence suggests that short-term interest rates are much less of a guide to the level of economic activity and price behaviour than changes in the money stock (Alvarez, Ballabriga and Jareno, 1995). Our model reflects the direct impact of the money stock by including the stock of liquid assets held by the public (ALP) in the determinants of aggregate demand.[12]

The real exchange rate is an important variable in analyzing the monetary transmission mechanism. The gradual opening up of the Spanish economy has increased the possibilities of substituting external demand for domestic demand depending on how our prices behave *vis-à-vis* those abroad.[13] Moreover, in an economy that is fully integrated with the outside world, the possibilities of influencing aggregate demand in the short term are not just limited to the real (after-tax) interest rate: they include the exchange rate as well. In the long term, nevertheless, the real interest rate will be determined by that prevailing abroad and the real exchange rate will be determined by structural parameters in the economy.

The other two variables determining aggregate demand are external output and the government's fiscal position. The variations in external output may be reflected in domestic demand via declines or increases in exports. At the same time, it is to be expected that the public deficit has a direct impact on aggregate demand, quite apart from indirect effects via the interest rate[14] and competitiveness.

As for the other equations, the demand for real balances (16.2) depends on the level of income and the two types of nominal interest rates: short and long-term. (16.3) defines the real interest rate. (16.4) and (16.5) complete the financial structure of the model and relate the interest rate controlled by the monetary authorities to those interest rates variables and exchange rates that influence economic agents' expenditure decisions.

Variations in the intervention interest rate are initially transmitted to the money market and from there to the equilibrium rate in the lending and deposit markets. According to Ayuso Haldane and Restoy (1994), in Spain the interbank rate responds fully and relatively swiftly to shifts in the intervention rate. That finding justifies using a short-term interbank rate as an exogenous rate.[15] The transmission of monetary policy signals to the rates that determine spending by economic agents will depend on the structure of the financial sector. Among other determining factors, of particular importance are the liquidity and degree of maturity of the different assets and the degree of competition among financial institutions. The fact that much of the spending by economic agents in Spain depends on external funding and that the composition of bank assets is sensitive to monetary policy could lead one to consider the lending rate of financial institutions as a relevant interest rate in expenditure equations. Nevertheless, in this paper we have opted to take the long-term debt rate as an indicator of the cost of capital in consumption and investment decisions, owing to the similar influence that both variables exert in the demand equation. The term structure of interest rates-equation (4)-is represented in the model as an arbitrage condition between short and long-term nominal interest rates: the long-term interest rate being the present value of expected short-term interest rates.

Our model uses the uncovered parity of interest rates – (16.5) – to reflect the way monetary policy affects the exchange rate. This implies that perfect capital mobility is the best way to represent the degree of financial integration of our economy with the outside world. The error term in this relationship allows for possible temporary shifts in the exchange rate due to the emergence of risk premia or speculative runs in exchange markets that are unrelated to macroeconomic variables.

We shall assume that the financial sector makes rational predictions of future changes in monetary policy. The developments expected in short-term interest rates determine both the long-term interest rate – through the term structure of interest rates – and the behaviour of the exchange rate through uncovered interest rate parity. The inclusion of this arbitrage condition has some additional advantages. First, it allows us to attribute a predominant role in monetary transmission to economic agents expectations regarding future monetary policy. The second advantage is that this obviates the need for a more complex model, which would have to incorporate other assets and a study of the productive structure of the financial sector.

Aggregate supply in the economy is represented by (16.6) and (16.7). (16.6) is a Phillips curve which relates domestic inflation to inflationary expectations and demand pressure. Inflationary expectations are represented in the model as a function of price variations in the past, for both domestic and foreign goods. Inclusion in the equation of a variable reflecting the business cycle situation of the economy makes it possible to measure the response of prices to excess supply or demand in goods markets. (16.7) is a dynamic version of the consumer price index definition. In the long-term solution of (16.6) and (16.7), nominal homogeneity is assumed[16]. The current version of the model does include possible supply shifts, such as variations in raw materials prices, changes in indirect taxation, or deviations in the relationship between wages and productivity. For the sake of simplicity, we have also eschewed incorporating a set of price and wage equations, even though this means sacrificing data regarding determinants of the degree of nominal rigidity influencing monetary transmission.

MONETARY POLICY SIMULATIONS

The Estimated Model

The estimated long-term version of the model is presented in Table 16.1, and the short-term estimations are to be found in the Appendix (p. 588). The explanatory variables were selected on the basis of lags in those same variables and of contemporary and past values of the other endogenous and exogenous variables. The maximum number of lags considered was

Table 16.1 The estimated model: long-run solution

$$\Delta y_t = \underset{(4.4)}{1.89} \ \Delta^2 g_t - \underset{(1.2)}{0.08} \ \Delta r_t + \underset{(3.3)}{0.11} \ \Delta q_t + \underset{(4.8)}{0.33} \ \Delta (m_t - p_t) + \underset{(2.5)}{0.47} \ \Delta y_t^* + \epsilon_{yt} \qquad \text{IS (16.1)}$$

$$m_t - p_t = -5.5 - \underset{(0.8)}{0.03} \ \Delta R_t - \underset{(1.7)}{0.15} \ \Delta i_t + \underset{(23.5)}{1.25} \ y_t + \epsilon_{mt} \qquad \text{LM (16.2)}$$

$$r_t \equiv R_t - E[\Delta p_{t+1/t}] \qquad \text{RIR (16.3)}$$

$$R_t = \underset{(*)}{(1 - 0.91)} i_t + \underset{(13.4)}{0.91} \ E[R_{t+1/t}] + \epsilon_{it} \qquad \text{TSIR (16.4)}$$

$$i_t = i_t^* + E(e_{t+1/t}) - e_t + \epsilon_{et} \qquad \text{UIP (16.5)}$$

$$\Delta p_t^d = \underset{(1.5)}{0.98} \ E[\Delta p_t^d] + \underset{(*)}{0.02} \ E[\Delta e_t + \Delta p_t^*] + \underset{(3.7)}{0.25} \ \Delta y_t + \epsilon_{pt} \qquad \text{AS (16.6)}$$

$$\Delta p_t = - \underset{(3.4)}{0.57} \ \Delta^2 p_t^d + \underset{(3.7)}{0.14} \ (\Delta^2 p_t^* + \Delta^2 e_t) + \underset{(*)}{\Delta} \ p_t^d + \epsilon_{pt} \qquad \text{CPI (16.7)}$$

Note: Definition of endogenous variables:
*: restricted.
$-\Delta y_t$, rate of growth of GDP
$-\Delta p_t^d$, GDP deflator inflation
$-\Delta p_t$, CPI inflation
$-e_t$, nominal exchange rate (q_t real exchange rate)
$-R_t$, nominal long-term interest rate
$-r_t$, real interest rate
$-m_t - p_t$, supply of real balances.

Definition of exogenous variables:
$-g_t$, government consumption
$-y_t^*$, world income
$-i_t$, short-term interest rate
$-i_t^*$, external short-term interest rate
$-\Delta p_t^*$, external inflation.

eight, the idea being to register correlations within and between annual periods. The selection criteria were the significance of each variable, on its own and as part of the set, and its stability. Each equation was estimated using instrumental variables for the sample period 1970:1–1994:4. Past values of all the endogenous and exogenous variables of the model were taken as instruments.[17]

When estimated, (16.1), corresponding to *IS*, shows a persistent rate of growth of output over 4 periods. The external output cycle (y^*) affects Spanish output after a 2-quarter lag. While the real rate of exchange (q) has an impact on aggregate output in the same period, an increase in the long-term real interest rate (r) only contracts demand after a 7-quarter lag. The wealth effect is reflected here in the rate of growth of real monetary balances (m/p). This wealth effect is represented in the model by excluding assets abroad and making a separate estimation of demand for ALP.

The fiscal impulse variable in the *IS* equation is measured according to the second differences in public consumption (g).[18] The econometric specifications chosen limited the dynamics of variable g in such a way as to restrict its long-term elasticity in the model to zero.[19] There are various reasons for restricting this estimate in order to ensure that the fiscal variable has only a transitory impact. On the one hand, the sample period was characterized by a steady increase in the ratio of government consumption to GDP that is unlikely to be repeated in future. Moreover, we know that shifts in government consumption are not the only relevant variable for measuring all the effects of the government's budgetary restrictions. Finally, the fiscal policy exercises carried out in the unrestricted model generate a very high and implausible value[20] for the fiscal multiplier.

In the demand for real balances (16.2), ($m - p$) corresponds to a broad monetary aggregate, ALP2, which includes commercial paper as well as short-term public debt. This is the aggregate used as a relevant indicator by the Banco de España for monetary planning purposes. A long-term relationship is estimated between income and real balances, which implies an elasticity somewhat greater than one. The short-term variables are, apart from a lag in the variable itself, lags in the long-term nominal interest rate (R) – which measures the return on assets other than money – and accelerations in the inflation rate ($\Delta^2 p$). The 3-month interbank rate (i) figures weakly in this relationship, also with a minus sign. This may measure the effect on demand of a change in the money supply that is not reflected in longer-term rates. Such demand for money, for reasons of simplicity, does not reflect the interaction between the return on assets included in ALPs and the return on alternative assets that in earlier estimations proved to be important for the Spanish economy (Cabrero, Escrivá and Sastre (1993) and Vega (1998), chapter 4 in this book).

A linear approximation has been estimated for the arbitrage condition between the interbank interest rate and the long-term debt rate (16.4). The parameter estimated compares the return on two assets with different maturities, assuming risk neutrality and rational expectations by economic agents.[21] The existence of a relationship of cointegration between short and long-term interest rates was tested and accepted, and parameter b of (16.4) was subsequently estimated. This estimated value implies a very similar steady state value for the long-term interest rate to that obtained for other countries (Taylor, 1993). (16.5), which assumes interest rate parity, incorporates a risk premium.

(16.6) on domestic prices (Δp^d), as estimated in this version of the model, proxies inflationary expectations by lag values of foreign and domestic prices, and proxies demand pressure by the lagged coefficient of GDP growth. Price accelerations appear as additional regressors. This calculation yields a figure for the impact of external prices of 0.03, for a sample period in which the Spanish economy opened up considerably, so that a much higher figure is likely in the future with a more integrated economy. For the simulation, we took a higher figure (0.13), which, in our opinion, is closer to the current weight of imports in the national economy. This greater responsiveness of economic agents to expected changes in external prices accelerates the convergence between domestic and foreign variables.

The last equation estimated in Table 16.1 deals with the consumer price index (Δp), a variable for which a relationship of cointegration with domestic prices has been found. The equation was therefore estimated taking ($\Delta p - \Delta p^d$) as the explanatory variable. External prices have only a transitory effect on the consumer price index and their permanent impact on inflation will be via domestic prices' expectations. The long-term restrictions contained in this equation (coefficient of 1 for domestic prices and 0 for external prices) are accepted statistically.

The Determination of Nominal Magnitudes and of the Monetary Policy Strategy

The financial structure of the model described in the previous section allows us to analyze the behaviour of the central bank in its goal of controlling inflation by establishing an interest rate path. Despite its simplicity, this framework underscores certain basic issues that the central bank faces in designing monetary policy and which affect use of the model for simulation purposes.

The long-term solution of (16.1)–(16.7) can be represented as follows:

$$i = i^* + \Delta e \qquad (16.8)$$

$$\Delta p = \Delta p^* + \Delta e \qquad (16.9)$$

this last condition being derived from the fact that the economy cannot systematically gain or lose competitiveness.[22] (16.8) and (16.9) determine the level of the long-term real interest rate, which should be at the international level. In this case, reducing domestic inflation to the international level requires setting the domestic interest rate (i) at the international level (i^*).

$$i - \Delta p = i^* - \Delta p^* \qquad (16.10)$$

In light of this long-term condition, one query concerns the path that the domestic interest rate must follow from a starting-point in which the economy has a positive inflation differential *vis-à-vis* external inflation. As earlier pointed out, an immediate and permanent reduction of the nominal interest rate cannot be dismissed out of hand. A Central Bank move in this direction gives rise to an immediate expansion, which in turn produces a generalized loss of competitiveness via an initial increase in inflation. If the central bank were able to maintain this policy indefinitely, sooner or later the deterioration in the trade balance would end up producing a recession, and along with it a decline in inflation. Now, in practice, a temporary increase in inflation may erode the credibility of the ultimate objective, which makes this strategy completely inviable. This suggests the need for a more suitable, in the end equivalent, monetary strategy (that is: $\Delta p = \Delta p^*$), which involves temporarily increasing the domestic interest rate – thereby encouraging a contraction – in order then gradually to reduce it to its long-term level as inflation goals are attained. Unlike the previous case, the goal of controlling inflation is attained more rapidly, although the costs in terms of output and employment are brought forward in time.

The existence of two quite opposite interest rate paths that lead, nevertheless, to the same long-term objective, indicates that there are indeed numerous intermediate alternatives, the relative advantages of which have to be assessed. In order to make that assessment of these or other economic policy strategies, it is necessary to know how the nominal exchange rate reacts to shifts in the economic environment. The greater the sensitivity of the nominal exchange rate to interest rate movements, the more intensely inflation will respond in the short term to changes in the nominal interest rate. What does the model represented in (16.1)–(16.7) tell us about the behaviour of the exchange rate when confronted with a change in the pre-announced interest rate path? Unfortunately, not enough. Fulfillment of the uncovered interest rate parity condition indicates that the current exchange rate value differs from the expected value by an amount equal to the interest rates differential, but that tells us nothing about the expected value itself. This value is determined by, among other factors, the level of the domestic money supply in relation to the supply of foreign currency. When the Central Bank fixes the interest rate, the money supply is endogenous and how it moves depends on the behaviour of the price level, which in turn depends on the behaviour of the exchange rate. In this way, the level of the nominal variables remains undetermined and it is not possible to predict the response of the exchange rate to a specific monetary policy measure.[23] Thus, while it is possible to calculate the exact level that real variables will reach, the existence of multiple solutions for the nominal variables implies that the transition path between two long-term equilibria is not unique.

Nominal indeterminacy is a feature of a wide range of models. A solution to this problem involves incorporating another equation into the model which, in one form or another, fixes the value of some nominal value. The generic form of such an equation is that of a feedback rule, according to which the monetary authorities react by varying the interest rate when some variable (X) deviates by more than a desired margin from its target value.[24] This way of constructing the model nevertheless poses some problems, particularly in respect of the choice of target variable.[25] If X stands for the *price level* or *parity of the peseta*, the feedback rule could be understood as an equation fixing a target of the monetary authority in terms of these variables (in either direction). However, this would be an inappropriate representation of monetary policy in Spain.[26] For the simulation exercises we discuss below, a further condition has been added to the model. Specifically, it is assumed that an immediate reduction in interest rates leads to a depreciation of the peseta. Conversely, the peseta appreciates when the Central Bank raises interest rates. This assumption does not, however, solve the issue of how large is the magnitude of the exchange rate response. We will return to this point in our description of the simulation exercises.

Simulations

This section will assess the relative importance of the channels through which monetary policy operates by simulating, with the help of the model described in the previous section, the impact associated with alternative interest rate (and exchange rate) paths. These exercises have not been carried out in order to lay down how the Banco de España's monetary policy should be implemented; our goal is more modest and restricted to analyzing within a given framework the importance of certain monetary policy transmission mechanisms. Consequently, no attempt has been made to establish optimum inflation targets or plausible ranges of fluctuation around them.[27] All the simulations are compared with a hypothetical scenario, independent of the model itself, in which it is assumed that domestic and foreign economic activity grows by 2 per cent a year, domestic prices by 5 per cent per annum, and external prices by 3 per cent annually. The simulations reflect the transition between an equilibrium with 5 per cent inflation to another with 3 per cent inflation. The object of the exercise is to establish the procedures and costs of eliminating the inflation differential *vis-à-vis* the rest of the world. The linearity of the model, at least with regard to the variables expressed as logarithms, makes it possible to isolate these responses from the baseline, which thus becomes of secondary importance. The simulations were carried out by solving forward the financial variables, which means that the values for those variables anticipated by economic agents coincide with what was actually simulated. All the equations employ residuals, in such a way that each equation reproduces, for each period, the datum given in the scenario.

Given the structure of the model, the 2-point reduction in domestic inflation requires an equivalent, long-term, reduction in the domestic interest rate. First, we shall simulate the effects of an *immediate and permanent reduction of interest rates of 2 points* (simulation 1). As discussed in the previous section, the instantaneous response of the exchange rate has to be imposed on the basis of criteria independent of the model. A reasonable hypothesis is that the 2-point lowering of interest rates goes together with an initial nominal exchange rate depreciation of 5 per cent.[28] Figures 16.2 and 16.3 show the behaviour of inflation and GDP growth after application of this policy. The most notable feature of this simulation emerges in the inflation rate profile for the time period under consideration. Although this monetary policy measure ultimately leads to the targeted level of inflation, the reduction in interest rates and the nominal depreciation produce a temporary increase in inflation. Such a resurgence of inflation may endanger the deflation process itself, as we discuss later. Despite the modest exchange rate depreciation, its short-term impact on inflation is considerable: for over a year, inflation remains higher than 6 per cent and only starts declining after 3 years.[29] This effect is due to the increase in external prices, which swiftly and strongly raises inflationary expectations and affects demand pressure, albeit not to the same extent.

The initial depreciation of the currency is, therefore, inflationary. How does a decline in inflation take place later? The elimination of the interest rates differential overtime leads the nominal exchange rate to stabilize around the new value obtained after the 5 per cent drop in impact. Thereafter, on the supply side, imported inflation drops immediately from the 5 per cent envisaged in the base scenario[30] to 3 per cent (the pace at which external prices increase), thereby helping to dampen inflationary expectations and, thus, domestic inflation. Moreover, with domestic prices still

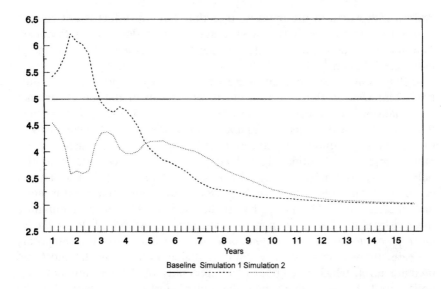

Figure 16.2 Alternative interest rate strategies, inflation (CPI) rate, annualized

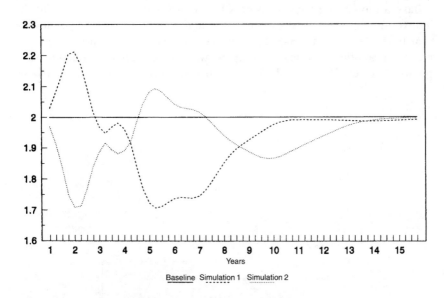

Figure 16.3 Alternative interest rate strategies, GDP growth, annualized

rising faster than those of our competitors, our products become more expensive, which reduces external demand and sparks off a temporary recession, which also moderates inflation. Reduction of the nominal interest rate works in the opposite direction, but this effect is not enough to offset the loss in competitiveness. Later on, the reduction in inflationary expectations allows the real interest rate to recover and this, too, helps moderate inflation.[31]

A reduction in the nominal interest rate ensures, in principle, a reduction of inflation in the long run, but if, as a result of the initial currency depreciation, the process of transition requires a higher inflation than that prevailing at the outset, a *legitimate doubt* arises as to the *credibility* of this policy for economic agents. If they are sceptical about achievement of the objective of ultimately reducing inflation and consider that this policy is not sustainable, it may take time for inflation to fall or it may not do so at all, and this in turn would prevent the planned reduction in nominal interest rates. The policy has to be credible. One way to minimize these risks is to effect a *temporary increase in interest rates, before reducing them permanently to the international level.* Thanks to this temporary increase, there is less risk of generating higher inflation in the short and medium term, which strengthens the credibility of the anti-inflationary - policy itself. Let us observe how this policy works in the context of the model.

Take a monetary policy measure which consists of raising by 1 point the intervention interest rate for one year and then returning the following year to the level of the base scenario; the interest rate is then reduced by 1 point for another 3 years, ending up with a permanent reduction of 2 points. Figures 16.4 and 16.5, respectively, show the behaviour of the

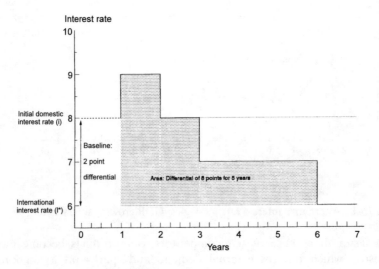

Figure 16.4 Simulation of monetary policy: behaviour of interest rate

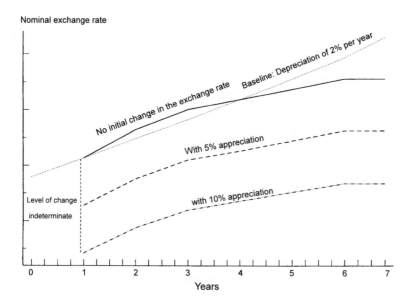

Figure 16.5   Exchange rate consistent with interest rate differential

nominal interest rate and nominal exchange rate, making 3 alternative assumptions regarding the appreciation in impact.

In accordance with uncovered interest parity, this exercise unequivocally determines the behaviour of the nominal exchange rate. This is consistent with an 8-point depreciation in the years of the transition (equal to the sum of the interest rates differentials during the first five years of the simulation), stabilizing when the domestic interest rate is at the international level. However, given nominal indeterminacy, it is not known at what level this exchange rate behaviour is established. To solve this indeterminacy, an *instantaneous appreciation of 5 per cent* is assumed to accompany the increase in the interest rate (simulation 2).[32] The findings of simulation 2 are also shown in Figures 16.2 and 16.3 to facilitate comparison. Figures 16.6 and 16.7 show the behaviour of the real interest rate and the real exchange rate in both simulations. Inflation declines in the first year by a little more than 1 point, stabilizing at around 4 per cent for the following 5 years, and beginning thereafter a gradual decline to its new long-term level of 3 per cent. GDP grows, the first year, by 0.25 per cent less than in the base scenario, gradually recovering thereafter to reach its long-term growth level in 4 years, followed by a small cycle.

The initial drop in inflation is mainly due to the (expected) cheapening of imported goods: a supply effect that dampens inflationary expectations. The minor contraction thereby induced serves to keep inflation below its

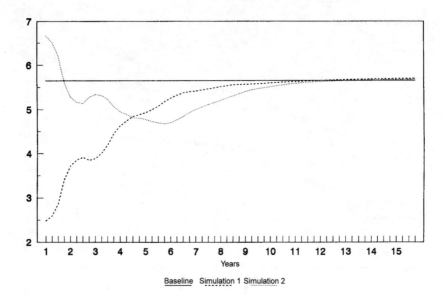

Figure 16.6 Real interest rate

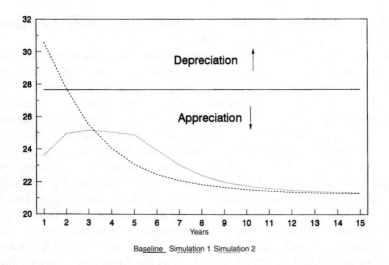

Figure 16.7 Real exchange rate

initial level in the following periods in which parity no longer helps moderate inflation. This contraction is basically caused by the demand inertia following upon the initial appreciation (Figure 16.7), not via interest rates (Figure 16.6), since economic agents very quickly anticipate that they will fall in long-term nominal values. The comparison with simulation 1 clearly shows that inflation responds more quickly to a temporary increase in interest rates, although the convergence towards the long-term inflation rate target of 3 per cent is faster if the reduction in interest rates is immediate. This apparent asymmetry is explained almost completely by the different pattern of response of the nominal exchange rate and it confirms the predominance of the competitiveness channel in the monetary transmission mechanism in the case of Spain.

In the exercise shown in simulation 1, the initial depreciation had an inflationary impact; later on, as the nominal exchange rate stabilizes, a swift drop in competitiveness occurs[33] which helps dampen inflation. When, on the contrary, the temporary increase in interest rates causes the exchange rate to over-react (simulation 2), the strong initial appreciation has an immediate deflationary impact. However, after the initial phase, and while the interest rates differential with the outside world continues to be positive (and even higher than at the baseline), the national currency depreciates and part of the competitiveness lost is recovered. This helps cushion the impact of recession and induces a slight rise in inflation.

Even when the monetary authorities opt for a temporary increase in interest rates to induce a rapid drop in inflation, it definitely seems that the best thing is to reduce to the maximum the period in which an interest rate differential causes a temporary depreciation (see Figure 16.7). The more credible the monetary authorities' efforts to reduce inflation are, the quicker they will be able to proceed to lower interest rates in a manner compatible with that objective. One way of increasing credibility is to carry out supply-side structural reforms.[34] Another way would be to obtain fiscal policy backing. This chapter does not, however, go into such coordinated strategies.

Given that the assumption in the simulations regarding the initial depreciation of the currency remains arbitrary, two further simulations were carried out in order to compare the sensitivity of the findings to the behaviour of the exchange rate. On the assumption that there is an initial variation in the nominal interest rate analogous to that in simulation 2, the nominal exchange rate is allowed *to appreciate immediately by 0 per cent* (simulation 3) and *10 per cent* (simulation 4), respectively. Following this initial reaction, there is a subsequent depreciation of 8 points derived from the accumulated interest rates differential. The behaviour of the rate of inflation and the rate of growth of GDP are also shown in Figures 16.8 and 16.9, along with the results of simulation 2 (appreciation of 5 per cent). With an effective 10 per cent appreciation of the peseta, we note that

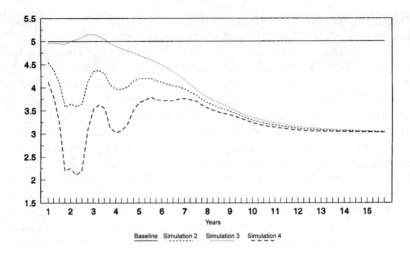

Figure 16.8   Inflation (CPI) rate, annualized

inflation declines by more than two points in the first year, in part due to a slight 0.3 per cent recession compared to growth at the outset, but mainly due to the rapid decline in external inflation and its favourable impact on domestic price formation. On the other hand, if we assume no appreciation,

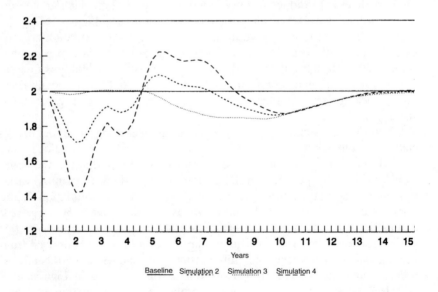

Figure 16.9   Growth of GDP

monetary policy induces a path in which inflation declines, but more slowly.

The short and long-term output costs of the various monetary policy strategies are summarized in Table 16.2. The long-term costs are obtained by adding the GDP losses incurred each year. Having constructed the model with GDP growth rates, our measure for assessing costs is given by the GDP level itself, which does not necessarily have to return to the original level.[35] By this criterion, the long-term cost of the permanent 2-point drop in inflation is the same in all the simulations: a little under 1 per cent of the original GDP[36] per year. The results in the table also show, in each simulation, the importance of short-term behaviour as the key factor to be borne in mind in assessing the relative advantages of each kind of monetary policy. The sacrifice ratio (growth in output divided by the increase in inflation) in the first two years of simulations 2, 3, and 4 indicates that the lower the exchange rate appreciation associated with the temporary increase in interest rates, the lower the cost of the policies in those years.

Table 16.2   Impact and real cost of the simulations

Simulation	Initial change in the exchange rate[1]	Inflation differential				Growth of output differential				
		Year 1	Year 2	Year 3	Year 4	Year 1	Year 2	Year 3	Year 4	Long term[2] %
Monetary policies										
1 Immediate reduction of interest rates with initial depreciation	5%	1.24	0.29	−0.16	−0.77	0.20	0.01	−0.01	−0.22	−0.92
2 Temporary increase in interest rates and initial appreciation	−5%	−1.41	−0.87	−0.90	−0.86	−0.25	−0.15	−0.13	0.04	−0.92
3 Temporary increase in interest rates	0%	−0.07	0.15	−0.02	−0.24	−0.01	0.00	0.00	−0.01	−0.92
4 Temporary increase in interest rates and initial appreciation	−10%	−2.79	−1.93	−1.82	−1.51	−1.51	−0.31	−0.27	0.08	−0.92

Notes:
1 A positive figure denotes a depreciation.
2 Accumulated sum of the growth in output once the model reaches the steady state solution.

CONCLUSIONS

This chapter has focused on the description of an aggregate model of the monetary transmission mechanism in the Spanish economy, designed with a view to evaluating, through simulation methods, alternative monetary policy strategies. The model incorporates the main channels through which central bank policy can affect the inflation rate. The parameters for the model were based on data for the 1973–94 period. Nonetheless, the model was specifically construed to reflect the main features of monetary transmission today. Thus, monetary policy is defined as a short- term interest rate path geared to achieving an inflation target. At the same time, the increasing openness of the economy reinforces the role of competitiveness in the transmission of monetary impulses. Finally, the efficiency of financial markets means that the impact of economic agents' expectations regarding the future behaviour of asset prices must be taken explicitly into account.

Solving the model has drawn attention to a few consequences of abandoning the establishment of an intermediate objective in terms of some monetary aggregate. Automatic adjustment of the money supply, aimed at keeping the interest rate within established values, leads to the indeterminacy of nominal magnitudes, particularly the price level and interest rate. Although it is true that this indeterminacy has no impact on the value of real variables, the short-term responses of inflation and competitiveness are indeed affected. To sidestep this problem, the model has been given a terminal exchange rate value, which has a considerable effect on the short-term cost of the different disinflationary policies. Taking the necessary precautions that derive from this limitation, the simulations do show a series of regularities, which are summarized very briefly in Table 16.2.

The achievement of a permanent reduction of the Spanish rate of inflation to the average level of inflation prevailing in Spain's trading partners presupposes, sooner or later, reducing nominal interest rates by at least as much as the current inflation differential. A policy in which that reduction in nominal interest rates is carried out immediately runs the risk of generating a short-term resurgence of inflation, unless it is accompanied by tougher fiscal policy or appropriate supply-side policies. If these policies are not promptly and forfully applied, the currency depreciates and this leads to a period of temporarily higher inflation. That, in turn, could seriously erode the anti-inflationary credibility of the monetary policy strategy being pursued, making the ultimate objective harder to attain.

Judging by the simulations carried out, the most credible way to reduce inflation is by temporarily increasing interest rates, which leads to a temporary slowing down of the rate of output growth. In this case, inflation converges towards its long-term value, remaining below the initial figure, while the magnitude of the initial response depends on the degree of appreciation of the nominal exchange rate. The simulations also show that the degree of competitiveness plays a very important part in monetary transmission. Moreover, this effect acts powerfully on the supply side, lowering expectations of imported inflation and, with them, wage demands.

Although the long-term effects of all the anti-inflationary strategies analyzed are similar, the structure over time of the response of inflation and GDP depends crucially on how competitiveness develops. Indeed, variations in the real exchange rate appear to be the most important of the channels making up monetary transmission mechanism in our country. The fact that tradable goods become relatively more expensive as a result of a more restrictive monetary policy induces a fall in aggregate demand and dampens inflationary expectations. The magnitude of this expectations effect or supply effect is one of the key determinants of the strength of the transmission mechanism and more empirical evidence has to be gathered concerning it. Likewise, it is necessary to broaden our knowledge of the response of the nominal exchange rate to variations in the expected path of interest rates in order to overcome one of the main limitations in the study of the monetary transmission mechanism within a framework of direct inflation targets.

Appendix: The Estimated Model

The sample period is 1970:1–1994:4. All the equations have been estimated using instrumental variables such as the lags of the variables up to the eighth period as well as deterministic variables. The figures in brackets indicate the t-statistical for regressions and, for autocorrelation tests, the degree of marginal significance.

Equation *IS* (16.1):

$$\Delta y_t = 0.0001 + 1.1489\,\Delta y_{t-1} - 0.2610\,\Delta y_{t-2} + 0.1498\,\Delta y_{t-3}$$
$$\quad\;\; (0.50) \quad\;\; (16.77) \qquad\qquad (2.49) \qquad\qquad\quad (1.80)$$

$$- 0.2502\,\Delta y_{t-4} + 0.0706\,\Delta\left(\tfrac{m}{p}\right)_{t-1} + 0.0521\,\Delta^2\left(\tfrac{m}{p}\right)_{t-6} + 0.0506\,\Delta y^*_{t-2}$$
$$\quad (3.79) \qquad\qquad (4.83) \qquad\qquad\;\; (3.31) \qquad\qquad\quad\; (1.69)$$

$$+ 0.0887\,\Delta y^*_{t-4} - 0.0390\,\Delta y^*_{t-8} + 0.0232\,\Delta q_t - 0.0134\,\Delta^2 q_{t-6}$$
$$\quad (3.41) \qquad\qquad\; (1.82) \qquad\qquad (4.09) \qquad\quad\; (3.87)$$

$$+ 0.0462\,\Delta r_{t-1} - 0.0631\,\Delta r_{t-7} + 0.2441\,\Delta^2 g_t - 0.1089\,\Delta^2 g_{t-1}$$
$$\quad (2.76) \qquad\qquad (3.58) \qquad\qquad (6.87) \qquad\qquad (3.11)$$

$$+ 0.1076\,\Delta^2 g_{t-2} + 0.1076\,\Delta^2 g_{t-7} + 0.0042\ \text{Dummy } 80:1$$
$$\quad (3.57) \qquad\qquad\;\; (3.57) \qquad\qquad\;\;\; (3.65)$$

$$- 0.0165\ \text{Dummy } 80:2 - 0.0025\ \text{Dummy } 92:3$$
$$\quad (13.04) \qquad\qquad\qquad\;\; (2.20)$$

$\bar{R}^2 = 0.95$; standard error $= 0.0010$; First order autocorrelation test: $X^2(1) = 2.7099$; First to fourth order autocorrelation test: $X^2(4) = 3.927$
$$\qquad\qquad (0.09) \qquad\qquad\qquad\qquad\qquad\qquad\qquad\qquad\qquad\quad (0.41)$$

Equation *LM* (16.2):

$$\Delta\left(\tfrac{m}{p}\right)_t = - 2.2652 + 0.5519\,\Delta\left(\tfrac{m}{p}\right)_{t-1} - 0.1953\,\Delta R_t + 0.2746\,\Delta R_{t-1}$$
$$\qquad\qquad (4.66) \qquad (6.66) \qquad\qquad\quad\; (1.60) \qquad\quad\;\; (2.54)$$

$$- 0.2265\,\Delta R_{t-2} - 0.0551\,\Delta i_{t-3} - 0.4256\,\Delta^2 p_t - 0.406\left(\tfrac{m}{p}\right)_{t-1}$$
$$\quad (2.29) \qquad\qquad (1.62) \qquad\qquad (3.11) \qquad\;\; (5.33)$$

$$+ 0.5105\,y_{t-1} + 0.0016\ \text{trend} - 0.0136\ \text{seasonal } T1$$
$$\quad (5.06) \qquad\quad (5.13) \qquad\qquad\;\; (5.16)$$

$$- 0.0067 \text{ seasonal } T2 - 0.0117 \text{ step } 92:1 + 0.0111 \text{ step } 93:4$$
$$(2.34) \qquad\qquad\qquad (2.30) \qquad\qquad\qquad (2.06)$$

$\bar{R}^2 = 0.72$; standard error $= 0.0047$; First order autocorrelation test: $X^2(1) = 2.3647$; First to fourth order autocorrelation test: $X^2(4) =$
     (0.12)
15.02
(0.004)

    Equation for the term structure of interest rates, TSIR (16.4):

$$(R_t - i_t) = \underset{(13.3)}{0.91} \ (R_{t+1} - i_t)$$

$\bar{R}^2 = 0.72$; standard error $= 0.8731$; First order autocorrelation test: $X^2(1) = \underset{(0.8 \times 10^{-3})}{0.91}$; First to fourth order autocorrelation test: $X^2(4) =$
14.41
(0.006)

Aggregate supply equation, AS (16.6):

$$\Delta p_t^d = \underset{(14.85)}{0.8061} \ \Delta p_{t-1}^d + \underset{(3.05)}{0.1563} \ \Delta p_{T-7}^d - \underset{(1.96)}{0.2003} \ \Delta^2 p_{t-1}^d$$

$$+ \underset{(1.56)}{0.0241} \ (\Delta p_{t-1}^* + \Delta e_{t-1}) + \underset{(1.52)}{0.0185} \ (\Delta^2 p_{t-5}^* + \Delta^2 e_{t-5}) + \underset{(3.73)}{0.2607} \ \Delta y_{t-1}$$

$$- \underset{(1.65)}{0.0021} \ \text{Seasonal } T1 - \underset{(1.19)}{0.0014} \ \text{Seasonal } T2 - \underset{(1.72)}{0.0021} \ \text{Seasonal } T3$$

$\bar{R}^2 = 0.87$; standard error $= 0.0045$; First order autocorrelation test: $X^2(1) = -0.09396$; First to fourth order autocorrelation test: $X^2(4) =$ 2.6964
(0.60)

CPI equation (16.7):

$$(\Delta p_t - \Delta p_t^d) = - \underset{(1.85)}{0.1453} \ \Delta^2 p_{t-2} - \underset{(2.16)}{0.1598} \ \Delta^2 p_{t-3} + \underset{(2.30)}{0.1481} \ \Delta^2 p_{t-6}$$

$$+ \underset{(2.85)}{0.1823} \ \Delta^2 p_{t-8} - \underset{(2.62)}{0.6957} \ \Delta^2 p_t^d + \underset{(1.30)}{0.0497} \ \Delta^2 p_t^* + \underset{(1.70)}{0.9458} \ \Delta^2 p_{t-1}^*$$

$\bar{R}^2 = 0.29$; standard error $= 0.045$; First order autocorrelation test: $X^2(1) = 3.4001$; First to fourth order autocorrelation test: $X^2(4) = 6.09$
     (0.06)   (0.19)

Notes

1   It is assumed that productive capacity is fixed and that it does not respond to changes in the interest rate. This being so, monetary policy has no impact on its potential growth level. The presence of hysteresis could generate long-term effects that are not dealt with in this chapter.

2   None of these frameworks should be ascribed to a specific set of monetary policy instruments.

3   Economic agents take this value as the basis for their expectations of the future behavior of the monetary authorities. This objective could also be defined in terms of rates of growth of the money stock.

4   As a result of which the exchange rate should overreact and thereby attain a higher level than that pertaining after a period of depreciation.

5   Bernanke and Gertler (1995) offer empirical evidence and theoretical arguments in support of the existence of this effect. Hernando (1997) analyzes the importance of the credit channel in monetary policy transmission in Spain.

6   See Bank of Spain (1994)

7   The real interest rate is determined at the international level. In a closed economy, it also depends on preferences and technology, but it is possible to alter it in the short term.

8   See Dornbusch (1976), Duguay (1994), Buiter and Miller (1981) and Taylor (1995).

9   To simplify the model, one fiscal policy indicator is defined and the public sector budget restriction is not explicitly included. The interaction between monetary policy and fiscal policy is discussed in Canzoneri and Diba (1997), chapter 5 in this book or Marín and Peñalosa (1997).

10   The variables in (16.1) should be understood as deviations from their long-term level or trend.

11   For which the rate of growth of GDP would be another approximation. In this case, however, the model is not neutral in the traditional sense because monetary policy affects the *level* of GDP in the long term as well as its composition. Nevertheless, after the adjustments in the nominal variables, the economy recovers the rate of growth considered to be that pertaining to a steady state.

12   However, this inclusion can be interpreted in two different, albeit not mutually exclusive, ways. We might be dealing with a credit channel in monetary transmission or else with a wealth effect reflecting the influence of changes in monetary policy on the relative prices of assets.

13   This appears to be an important variable in the Spanish economy, since the effective exchange rate is one of the main determinants of net exports (see, for instance, Buisán and Gordo, 1994, and Bajo and Montero, 1995).

14   In Spain, the evidence in this regard is not conclusive. Thus, whereas Ballabriga and Sebastián (1993) do not find a causal relationship between interest rates and the deficit, Raymond and Palet (1990) do report a direct effect.

15   For the purposes of this paper, we prefer this to the alternative of endogenizing the interest rate as a function of the reaction of the monetary authorities (see, for instance, the estimations by Escrivá and Santos, 1991).

16   So that an increase in domestic inflation and in imported inflation gives rise to an equivalent increase in the CPI inflation rate.

17   These estimations would have been more efficient if the residual correlation between equations had been taken into account (estimating 3SLS, for instance). We will leave that task for future research.

18 This is the only variable available in *Quarterly National Accounts*.
19 This differs from the elasticity estimated for the sample period (0.6), which coincided with a period in which the growth of government consumption far exceeded that of GDP.
20 Compared to the values generated by other models, such as the NIGEM, for the Spanish economy and economies similar to ours.
21 See Ayuso and Núñez (1996), chapter 10 in this book to obtain a tern structure with zero coupon assets.
22 In addition, the output gap has to close in the long run.
23 For a more detailed discussion of this point, see Andrés, Mestre and Vallés (1996).
24 This type of rule takes up McCallum's (1981) proposed solution to the non-uniqueness problem. Application of monetary policy by fixing an intermediate objective in quantitative terms would indeed be a specific instance of such rules, in which X is the money supply.
25 At the same time, inclusion of a feedback rule appears to be logical in a model representing, from the outside, the behavior of the monetary authorities, but not as an element to be taken into account in monetary policy decisions. Moreover, choice of an optimal rule implies first tackling the ever-complex question of the definition of a target function of the monetary authorities.
26 Nominal stability targets are generally expressed in terms of the inflation rate, which is compatible with very different price level values. Establishing a target in *inflation rate* terms does not solve the indeterminacy problem (Dhar *et al.*, 1995).
27 See, for example, Haldane and Salmon (1995).
28 All these figures exclude the risk premium (which is exogenous) and are, moreover, approximate, given that the original movements are expressed as logarithms.
29 While generating a small expansion of GDP for two years (Figure 16.3).
30 Resulting from 3 per cent external price inflation, plus 2 per cent permanent depreciation of the domestic currency.
31 The behavior of the real interest rate and the real exchange rate are reflected in Figures 16.6 and 16.7, which we comment on below.
32 The history of the variable itself can give us an idea of the jump: only very occasionally has the currency appreciated or depreciated by more than 5 per cent in nominal terms (on 6 occasions in our sample period). In fact, this jump is almost twice the standard deviation in the nominal exchange rate. Almost the same is true of the real exchange rate which has only occasionally registered variations of that magnitude within a single quarter.
33 Figure 16.7 shows an appreciation of the real exchange rate from the first period onwards.
34 Which the model could take into account by altering the constant term in (16.6), for instance, or via an autonomous reduction in inflationary expectations.
35 As was argued earlier on, a transitory response of the rate of growth to deflationary policy assumes that there is a permanent effect on the level of output. In that sense, the model is not strictly neutral, even though it returns to the initial rate of growth of GDP.
36 This drop in GDP is the result of a corresponding 5 per cent loss of competitiveness.

References

ALVAREZ, L.J., F.C. BALLABRIGA and J. JAREÑO (1995) 'Un modelo macro-econométrico trimestral para la economía española', Banco de España, *Working Paper*, 9524.

ANDRÉS, J., R. MESTRE and J. VALLÉS (1996) 'Un modelo estructural para el anólisis del mecunísmo de transmision monetaria', Banco de España, *Working Paper*, 9629.

ANDRÉS, J., A. ESCRIBANO, C. MOLINAS and D. TAGUAS (1989) 'La inversión en España', *Moneda y Crédito*, 188, 67–95.

AYUSO, J. and S. NÚÑEZ (1997) 'The yield curve as an indicator for monetary policy', chapter 10 in this volume.

AYUSO, J., A. HALDANE and F. RESTOY (1994) 'Volatility transmission along the money market yield curve', Banco de España, *Working Paper*, 9403.

BAJO, O. and M. MONTERO (1995) 'Un modelo ampliado del comercio exterior español', *Moneda y Crédito*, 201, 153–82.

BALLABRIGA, F.C. and M. SEBASTIÁN (1993) 'Déficit Público y tipos de interés en la economía española: ¿existe evidencia de causalidad?, *Revista Española de Economía*, 16, 283–306.

BANCO DE ESPAÑA (1996) 'Objectivos c instrumentalización de la politica monetaria en 1995 1, *Boletin Económico*, December.

BERNANKE, B. and M. GERTLER (1995) 'Inside the black box: the credit channel of monetary policy transmission', *Journal of Economic Perspectives*, 4, 27–48.

BUISÁN, A. and E. GORDO (1994) 'Funciones de importación y exportación de la economía española', *Investigaciones Económicas*, 18, 165–92.

BUITER, W. and M. MILLER (1981) 'Monetary policy and international competitiveness: the problems of adjustment', *Oxford Economic Papers*, vol 33, 143–175.

CABRERO, A., J.L. ESCRIVÁ and T. SASTRE (1993) 'Demand equations on the new monetary aggregates', *Serie de Estudios Económicos*, 52, Banco de España.

CANZONERI, M. and B. DIBA (1997) 'Fiscal restrictions on central banks independence and on price stability', chapter 5 in this volume.

DHAR, J.K., P.G. FISHER, A.M. HOLLAND and D.L. PAIN (1995) 'Interest rate effects in the Bank of England medium-term forecasting model', Bank of International Settlements.

DORNBUSCH, R. (1976) 'Expectations and exchange rate dynamics', *Journal of Political Economy*, 84, 1161–76.

DUGUAY, P. (1994) 'Empirical evidence on the strength of the monetary transmission mechanism in Canada', *Journal of Monetary Economics*, 33, 39–61.

ESCRIVÁ, J.L. and R. SANTOS (1991) 'Un estudio del cambio de régimen en la variable instrumental del control monetario en España', Banco de España, *Documento de Trabajo*, 9111.

ESTRADA, A., I. HERNANDO and J. VALLÉS (1997) 'The impact of interest rates on private spending', chapter 14 in this volume.

ESTRADA, A., T. SASTRE and J.L. VEGA (1994) 'El mecanismo de transmisión de los tipos de interés: el caso español', Banco de España, *Documento de Trabajo*, 9408.

ESTRADA, A. (1993) 'Una función de consumo de bienes duraderos', *Revista Española de Economía*, 10, 135–62.

HALDANE, A. and C.K. SALMON (1995) 'Three issues on inflation targets', in A.L. Haldane (ed.), *Targeting Inflation*, London: Bank of England.

HERNANDO, I. (1997) 'El canal crediticio en la transmisión de la política monetaria', in *La política monetaria y la inflación en España*, Servicio de Estudios del Banco de España, Madrid: Alianza Editorial.

MARÍN, J. and J.M. PEÑALOSA (1997) chapter 15 'Implicaciones del marco Institucional y de la politica presprestavia para la politica monetaria en España', in *La Politica monetaria, la inflación en España*, Servico de Estudios, Madrid: Alianza Editorial.

McCALLUM, B. (1981) 'Price level determinancy with interest rate policy rule and rational expectations', *Journal of Monetary Economics*, 8, 319–29.

METZLER, A. (1995) 'Monetary, credit and (other) transmission processes: a monetarist perspective', *Journal of Economic Perspectives*, 4, 49–72.

POOLE, W. (1970) 'Optimal choice of monetary policy instruments in a simple stochastic macro model', *Quarterly Journal of Economics*, 84, 197–216.

RAYMOND, J.L. and J. PALET (1990) 'Factores determinantes de los tipos de interés reales en España', *Papeles de Economía Española*, 43, 144–60.

ROUBINI, A and S. KIM (1995) 'Monetary policy and exchange rates in Europe', Yale University, mimeo.

SARGENT, T. and N. WALLACE (1975) 'Rational expectations, the optimal monetary instrument and the optimal money supply rule', *Journal of Political Economy*, 83, 241–54.

TAYLOR, J. (1993) *Macroeconomic Policy in a world economy*, New York: W.W. Norton.

TAYLOR, J.B. (1995) 'The monetary transmission mechanism: an empirical framework', *Journal of Economics Perspectives*, 4, 11–26.

VEGA, J.L. (1998) 'The long-run broad money demand function', Chapter 4 in this volume.

Index